The Official

Precious Moments

Collector's Guide

to
FIGURINES

John & Malinda Bomm

COLLECTOR BOOKS
A Division of Schroeder Publishing Co., Inc.

COLLECTOR BOOKS
P.O. Box 3009
Paducah, Kentucky 42002-3009

www.collectorbooks.com

The current values in this book should be used only as a guide. They are not
intended to set prices, which vary from one section of the country to another.
Auction prices as well as dealer prices vary greatly and are affected by condition
as well as demand. Neither the authors nor the publisher assume responsibility for
any losses that might be incurred as a result of consulting this guide.

Searching For A Publisher?

We are always looking for people knowledgeable within their fields. If you
feel that there is a real need for a book on your collectible subject and have a large
comprehensive collection, contact Collector Books.

Contents

A Note from The Authors

Prices listed in this publication are guidelines only. Pricing is determined by location, condition of item, coloring, with or without box, and of course, demand. The authors of this book take no responsibility for variations in pricing. Pricing should be used only as a generalization, not an actual.

Acknowledgments

Malinda and I wish to thank our mother for all the input, information collecting, and phone calling she had to do to make this book possible. She spent many, many hours of work helping put this book together.

An extra special thank you goes to Janet Cox and Karen Bardwell from Enesco, Inc. Without their help this book would not have been completed. They have backed us up by sending us all the information they could find, beg, steal, or borrow from their vast library. We send a super thank you to both of them.

Thank you to Robert Marchant and Tracey Wardell, members of Sharing The Magic Precious Moments Club in Orlando, Florida, and Brenda Miller for lending us pictures of some of the pieces we could not find.

If anyone has any information not found in this book, please contact John and Malinda Bomm at pmguides@hotmail.com.

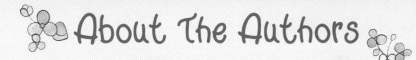

About The Authors

John and Malinda Bomm are residents of Orlando, Florida. John was born in Amityville, New York in 1962. He, his younger brother, and parents stayed in New York until 1972 when his father was transferred to Pennsylvania. They lived in the beautiful Amish country there for three years until John's father was transferred again, this time to New Jersey. John completed his education in New Jersey and at the age of 16 started working for Pathmark Supermarkets as a cart boy and cashier. When John turned 18 he started building a race car, one of his passions through his growing years. Because of his race car building, John became a top mechanic and worked with his parents in the service station they owned. John is now an assistant parts manager for Rolling Hills Ford in Clermont, Florida.

Malinda was born in 1962 on Naha Air Force Base in Okinawa, Japan. Her father was an Air Force Master Sergeant at the time. Her mother was a native of Okinawa. Malinda and her parents lived in Okinawa for nine years until they moved to Langley Air Force Base in Virginia. Malinda completed her education at Tabb High School in Virginia. She moved to New Jersey in 1987 where she met future husband John. When John's parents moved to Florida, John and Malinda made the move with them. They were married on Valentine's Day, 1991, and several years later adopted four children: Eric, 12; Gerard, 10; Ramey, 7; and Sirjesim, 6. Malinda is now a health claims examiner for a large city agency.

Through Malinda, John developed a love of Precious Moments collectibles. Malinda and John's collection has expanded from five Precious Moments figurines to approximately 900 pieces, including bisque figurines, dolls, plates, water globes, and much more. Several rooms in their house showcase their collection. This is their second Precious Moments book. They authored *The Official Precious Moments Collector's Guide to Company Dolls*, also published by Collector Books, in 2003.

The Story Of Precious Moments

Sam Butcher

Samuel John Butcher was born on January 1, 1939. He was the third of five children who grew up in a very poor family. As a child, he spent hours underneath the dining room table writing stories and illustrating them. Even in kindergarten, his dream of becoming an artist was evident, when he illustrated *Little Black Sambo* and made a box with a movie crank that worked like a movie screen — the whole school admired it. At this young age his talent was recognized by both family and friends.

When Sam was in high school in the fall of 1957, he met Katie Cushman, who he married on December 27, 1959. They had five children: Jon, Philip, Tammy, Debbie, and Timmy. Though life was very busy, Sam continued following his dream of becoming an artist.

Over the years Sam found the Lord and devoted his life to him. His strong spiritual commitment led him to employment at the International Child Evangelism Fellowship in Grand Rapids, Michigan. It was there that he learned how to study the Bible, and his desire to spread God's love to others grew. It was also there that he met Bill Biel, who later became his dear friend and business partner. In 1971 Sam and Bill decided to leave their jobs and go out on their own as commercial artists. With no money, a bit of poster paint, and the talents God gave them, they formed their own company, "Jonathan & David," with Sam as illustrator and Bill, designer.

In 1975 Sam and Bill were invited to attend the Christian Booksellers Convention in Anaheim, California. It was then that they began preparing greeting cards featuring tear-drop-eyed children, and Bill came up with the name "Precious Moments." This idea was a huge success at the convention, and their tiny booth was overrun with customers — $10,000 worth of orders were placed. All the men needed was the money to produce the cards and fill the orders. They went to the bank with orders in hand, but were turned down. They decided to try the Christian Businessmen's Association, who told them to put their trust in the Lord. And eventually, Sam met a wealthy man who offered to loan him $25,000 to start up his business.

That first year (1975) Sam's and Bill's first major projects were Christmas cards and Bicentennial cards. To offset their costs and help pay bills, they also painted Christmas scenes on store windows and garages. During the second CBA convention in Atlantic City, Sam and Bill introduced four posters: *"Jesus Loves Me," "Praise the Lord Anyhow," "Prayer Changes Things,"* and *"God Is Love."* At the same time, their Precious Moments greeting card ministry continued to grow in acceptance and blessings to those associated with the growing company of Jonathan & David.

Through all the struggles, Sam and Bill kept their senses of humor, and asked the Lord to guide and direct them in sharing the Gospel through the ministry of the Precious Moments greeting cards.

Early in 1978, Sam and Bill were both in the studio when a man by the name of Eugene Freedman called. He was the president and chief executive officer of Enesco Imports Corporation, a company heavily involved in the giftware industry, headquartered in the Chicago suburb of Elk Grove Village. Freedman had seen some of the Precious Moments cards, including *I Will Make You Fishers Of Men*. Freedman wanted to know if Sam and Bill would be interested in making Precious Moments into three-dimensional art through porcelain figurines.

Sam and Bill had a special relationship. Sam was an artist, not a businessman. The two decided to part ways in March of 1984. Sam sold his interest in Jonathan and David, Inc., the greeting card company, to Bill. They remained friends for many years.

The Enesco Beginning

Eugene Freedman

By 1978, when Eugene ("Gene") Freedman approached Sam Butcher and Bill Biel about making Precious Moments into porcelain figurines, Enesco Imports Corporation had been involved in the giftware industry for many years. Freedman had served in the U.S. Navy in the South Pacific during World War II, and when he returned from the service, he was not sure just what he wanted to do with his life. He worked in Milwaukee for a while in a dismantling defense production plant.

In the late 1940s, Freedman took a job as a salesman for a Milwaukee firm that manufactured miniatures. He became familiar with many companies that are still customers of Enesco today. In the early 1950s he started his own company which produced injection molded plastics as well as decorative figurines. The company grew to a point where he needed a partner to help run the business.

In 1958, Freedman left this firm and embarked upon another new venture. He and six employees purchased the N. Shure Company, a large wholesale merchandising catalog operation. This later evolved into Enesco Imports Corp., a natural phonetic progression from the initials of the original company, N. S. Co.

On a trip to the Orient, Freedman made a stopover in Los Angeles for their spring gift show. There, a friend brought him some greeting cards and posters that featured illustrations of children with soulful, teardop eyes, the Precious Moments cards. He was so taken by these drawings that he immediately thought of someone who could capture in clay the warmth and expressions of these special little children — Yasuhei Fujioka-San of Nagoya, Japan.

Freedman called Sam Butcher and Bill Biel, and pleaded with them to come to Enesco in Chicago. Coincidentally, both men were in the process of finding someone to make their prints into porcelain figurines. Freedman traveled to Japan and returned with a porcelain figurine of a girl and boy sitting on a tree stump (*Love One Another*). He brought it to Sam and Bill at their office. Sam fell to his knees and cradled the little figurine in his hands, whispering "Look Bill, look." It was a great thrill to see his artwork transformed.

Sam and Bill did not commit themselves that day, but they did take the figurine home with them and told Freedman they would give him their decision at a later date. Freedman was back in the Orient when he received word that Sam and Bill loved the figurine but wanted to work directly with the sculptor. The arrangements were made. Even though Sam and Fujioka-San did not speak the same language, their love of art became a common factor, and they quickly became friends.

Sam's first trip to the Orient to meet the artist that would be transforming his drawings into figurines was an experience that made a deep impact on his life. Sam and Fujioka-San worked on the Precious Moments sculptures for hours and hours, day after day. Though they could not communicate verbally, the two artists had an apparent "heart to heart" connection.

The next step for Freedman, now that the artist and sculptor were together, was to find a factory to produce the figurines. Although the models were being sculpted in

Japan, the cost of production there was rising due to the increase in the standard of living. Freedman turned to a long-time friend, Paul Chang, who had worked for Enesco Imports at one time. Chang struck an agreement with Fujioka-San to establish a ceramic factory, Pearl Taiwan, in Miaoli, Taiwan. This became the home of many skilled ceramists and the place where Precious Moments figurines were first manufactured.

Yasuhei Fujioka-San

There were 21 original Precious Moments figurines painstakingly and endearingly produced at the Pearl Taiwan factory. They were shipped to Chicago, where they were introduced to the giftware trade in the fall of 1978. In addition to *Love One Another* (E-1376), the figurines in the first presentation were: *Love Lifted Me* (E-1375A), *Prayer Changes Things* (E-1375B), *Jesus Loves Me* (E-1372G and E-1372B, both girl and boy figurines), *Jesus Is The Light* (E-1373G), *Smile, God Loves You* (E-1373B), *He Leadeth Me* (E-1377A), *God Loveth A Cheerful Giver* (E-1378), *Love Is Kind* (E-1379A), *God Understands* (E-1379B), *O, How I Love Jesus* (E-1380B), *His Burden Is Light* (E-1380G), *Jesus Is The Answer* (E-1381R), *We Have Seen His Star* (E-2010), *Come Let Us Adore Him* (E-2011), *Praise The Lord Anyhow* (E-1374B), *He Careth For You* (E-1377B), *Make A Joyful Noise* (E-1374G), *Jesus Is Born* (E-2809), and *Unto Us A Child Is Born* (E-2013). The little Precious Moments children, with their messages of hope, love, faith, and trust, were very well received.

Enesco Imports Corporation pays very close attention to detail, especially with their Precious Moments pieces. The company had been a reputable giftware manufacturer until that point, but because of the strong public response and quick popularity of Precious Moments figurines, Enesco soon became known as a producer of collectibles as well. Consumers were instantly drawn to Precious Moments figurines, whose messages of loving, caring, and sharing are cherished by collectors today. Annual releases are always eagerly anticipated by consumers.

Errors And Variations

Item #	Name and Valuable Information

12238   *Mini Clown Figurines* (A-B-C-D)
On many of these clowns the inscription was written as CROWN.

12262   *I Get A Bang Out Of You*
This figurine has been found with *Lord Keep Me On The Ball* understamp.

12416   *Have A Heavenly Christmas* (Ornament)
On some of the 1987 wreaths the words "Heaven Bound" are upside-down.

102229   *O Worship The Lord*
Many collectors have found this piece missing the "O."

111155   *Faith Takes The Plunge*
Some of the figurines that debuted in 1988 and 1989 had smiles and some had frowns.

115231   *You Are My Main Event*
The strings on the balloons are sometimes pink instead of white.

128708   *Owl Be Home For Christmas* (Ornament)
This 1996 ornament has been found with the date missing.

136204   *It's A Girl*
Pieces have been found with one shoe not painted.

136255   *Age 6*
On some pieces, the heart with the age number is missing. Most pieces with decals have missing decals but this piece has the entire heart missing.

183873   *Age 10*
Some pieces are missing the bowling pins.

192368   *Give Ability A Chance*
Has been found without the Easter Seals Lily symbol.

260940   *From The Time I Spotted You I Knew We'd Be Friends*
The word "Know" has been found on some pieces instead of "Knew." The monkeys on some pieces are very dark brown instead of light brown.

261130   *Have You Any Room For Jesus*
The word "Bowling" has been found misspelled on the calendar.

306843   *20 Years And The Vision's Still The Same*
On a small amount of the commemorative figurines, the Sword and Eyeglasses marks both appear.

306916   *Friendship Hits The Spot*
Many pieces have been found with the table missing. Inspiration decals were incorrectly spelled "Freindship."

Item #   Name and Valuable Information

520748   *Friendship Hits The Spot*
          Variation one has a misspelling: *Freindship Hits The Spot*. On variation two,
          the table between the two girls is missing.

520756   *Jesus Is The Only Way*
          Dates have been omitted on some and have been placed incorrectly on others.

520772   *Many Moons In The Same Canoe, Blessum You*
          Over the years, the Indians' hair has been darkened.

520802   *My Days Are Blue Without You*
          Some pieces have a frown or puckered mouth instead of a smile.

522279   *A Reflection Of His Love*
          Pieces have been found with a white or blue water reflection in the fountain.

522317   *Merry Christmas Deer*
          All figurines with the Bow and Arrow mark had no Precious Moments logo.

523011   *There's A Christian Welcome Here*
          On some of the Chapel Exclusive pieces, the angel's hair hides his right
          eyebrow.

523704   *May Your Christmas Be A Happy Home* (Ornament)
          This ornament shows a boy wearing either a yellow or blue shirt. The yel-
          low shirt is considered the variation.

524352   *What The World Needs Now*
          Pieces have been found with the Bible missing from the table.

524425   *May Only Good Things Come Your Way*
          Some pieces have the butterfly on top of the net while others have the butter-
          fly on the right side of the net, upside-down.

526053   *Pretty As A Princess*
          On some pieces one point on the princess's crown is not painted gold.

527106   *He Is Not Here For He Is Risen As He Said*
          On the sign outside the tomb some exclusives pieces read "Math" instead
          of "Matt."

528609   *Sending My Love Your Way*
          Variation one, the kite held by the girl is missing its stripes. Variation two,
          the kitten is sometimes missing completely.

529540   *Park Bench*
          Pieces were found glazed over and unpainted.

531634   *Who's Gonna Fill Your Shoes?*
          Some pieces have been found with no bows on the girl's shoes.

Errors And Variations

Item #	Name and Valuable Information

531952 *Dropping In For The Holidays*
Pieces have been found with the "Egg Nog" and the decal upside-down. The cup of this piece came in either pink or blue.

730068 *The Future Is In Our Hands*
On some pieces, the girl is holding a cardinal instead of a bluebird.

B-0102 *A Smile's The Cymbal Of Joy*
The word "Cymbal" was misspelled "Symbol" on some Charter Member Figurines.

E-0202 *But Love Goes On Forever*
Some of these pieces were reproduced after production was ended. Those pieces were sent to Canada and are identified with the Dove mark.

E-0535 *Love Is Patient — Boy* (Ornament)
Some pieces have been found with the "Merry Christmas" upside-down.

E-1373B *Smile, God Loves You*
The boy sometimes has a black eye and sometimes a brown eye.

E-1374B *Praise The Lord Anyhow*
On some pieces the puppy has a brown nose and on some it has a black nose.

E-1377B *He Careth For You*
The inspirations on E-1377A (*He Leadeth Me*) and this piece were sometimes swapped.

E-2013 *Unto Us A Child Is Born*
Pieces have been reported with the words placed on the pages incorrectly.

E-2362 *Baby's First Christmas* (Ornament)
In variation one, the girl's straight hair appears curly. In variation two, the girl has curly hair, but the decal on the bottom of the piece is missing.

E-2372 *Baby's First Christmas* (Ornament)
The inspiration did not come with the first pieces that were produced. Right before the piece was Suspended, an inspiration was included.

E-2395 *Come Let Us Adore Him* (set of 11)
The original set included a boy holding a lamb. Later he was replaced by a shepherd wearing a turban.

E-2805 *Wishing You A Season Filled With Joy*
The figurine with the dove year mark shows a dog with both eyes painted black instead of one single painted eye.

E-2837 *Groom*
Two different molds were used for this piece; on one, the boy's hands are hidden by his sleeves, and on the other, the boy's hands can be seen.

12   ♥ Loving ♥ Caring ♥ Sharing ♥

Item # Name and Valuable Information

E-2854 *God Blessed Our Year Together With So Much Love And Happiness*
God Blessed Our Years (plural) is the error on some of the decals of these first anniversary pieces.

E-3110B *Loving Is Sharing — Boy*
Pieces have been found with the dog missing or with the boy's lollipop unpainted.

E-3111 *Be Not Weary In Well Doing*
Some pieces had the inspiration printed as *Be Not Weary And Well Doing*.

E-4724 *Rejoicing With You*
Sometimes the "e" in Bible is covered by the girl's hand.

E-5200 *Bear Ye One Another's Burdens*
The original figurine shows the boy with a smile yet others have been found with a little circle mouth.

E-5214 *Prayer Changes Things*
In some cases, the words "Holy Bible" were put on the back of the book. Some were found with "Holy Bible" on the figurine upside-down.

E-5379 *Isn't He Precious*
This piece has been seen completely without paint.

E-5624 *They Followed The Star* (set of three)
It has been noted that the camels originally came without blankets.

E-5679 *Let The Heavens Rejoice*
The Precious Moments decal is missing on some of the pieces.

E-7156R *I Believe In Miracles*
The variation is the lack of the inscribed "Sam B" on the bottom of the pieces. The boy's head is also smaller on some.

E-9266 & *Our Love Is Heaven-scent*
E-9266B *I'm Falling For Somebunny*
Both pieces were made with the incorrect inspiration *Somebunny Cares*.

E-9268 *Nobody's Perfect!*
On this figurine, the boy has either a smile or a frown on his face.

PM-831 *Dawn's Early Light*
A Dove mark has been found on the bottom of some of these pieces.

PM-961 *Teach Us To Love One Another*
Pieces have been found with decals upside-down.

PM-971 *You Will Always Be A Treasure To Me*
Has been found with a heart mark.

The Original "21"

The original 21 figurines were introduced in 1979.

Jesus Loves Me (boy), E-1372B

Jesus Loves Me (girl), E-1372G

Smile, God Loves You, E-1373B

Jesus Is The Light, E-1373G

Praise The Lord Anyhow, E-1374B

Make A Joyful Noise, E-1374G

Love Lifted Me, E-1375A

Prayer Changes Things, E-1375B

Love One Another, E-1376

He Leadeth Me, E-1377A

He Careth For You, E-1377B

God Loveth A Cheerful Giver, E-1378

Love Is Kind, E-1379A

God Understands, E-1379B

O, How I Love Jesus, E-1380B

His Burden Is Light, E-1380G

Jesus Is The Answer, E-1381

We Have Seen His Star, E-2010

Come Let Us Adore Him, E-2011

Jesus Is Born, E-2012

Unto Us A Child Is Born, E-2013

Precious Moments Figurines' Stories

☐ *Onward Christian Soldiers*, E-0523

Sam could hardly wait to paint this idea. This little soldier carried the message to Sam to keep going when things got tough.

☐ *His Eye Is On The Sparrow*, E-0530

This figurine was first made as a card for a man who Sam had met. It was later made into a figurine. The man's son had committed suicide after returning home from war. The family was sent many cards at the death of their son, but Sam's card really touched them. The painting helped the family know that God had it in his hands from the very beginning.

☐ *Praise The Lord Anyhow*, E-1374B

Philip, Sam's second son, was the inspiration for this figurine. Sam said you couldn't spend much time with Philip before you threw up your hands lovingly and said, "Praise The Lord Anyhow!"

☐ *Love One Another*, E-1376

This was the first Precious Moments drawing. Tammy, Sam's daughter, sat by "Uncle Bill" on a stool back-to-back and the love she portrayed for Uncle Bill was the inspiration for the first Precious Moments figurine. The original art was stolen from the Jonathan & David Company.

☐ *God Loveth A Cheerful Giver*, E-1378

Debbie, Sam's daughter, inspired this piece. Sam will probably never forget Debbie, with her box full of puppies, asking him if any of his friends needed a pet.

☐ *Love Is Kind*, E-1379A

Sam's son, Timmy, was the subject for this figurine. Timmy is the nature boy who liked to spend a lot of his time alone when he was small. He also enjoys painting and music.

☑ *Make A Joyful Noise*, E-1374G

This figurine is one of the "original 21" introduced in 1978. Sam and Bill were driving on a country road when they came across a woman with a bumper sticker on her car that read, "Honk If You Love Jesus." Sam honked the car horn; she looked up, forgetting the instruction on her bumper sticker, thinking they were very rude young men. She gave them a dirty look and mouthed some nasty words. He pointed to the sticker, honked again, and drove away. Sam was inspired by this and created the image of a little girl nose-to-nose with a goose. It was originally called *Honk If You Love Jesus*. The title was changed before production.

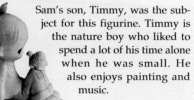

☑ *O, How I Love Jesus*, E-1380B

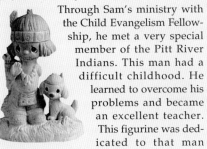

Through Sam's ministry with the Child Evangelism Fellowship, he met a very special member of the Pitt River Indians. This man had a difficult childhood. He learned to overcome his problems and became an excellent teacher. This figurine was dedicated to that man from the mountains of Northern California.

☑ *His Burden Is Light*, E-1380G

This little Indian girl figurine is another result of Sam's experience with the Pitt River Indians. Though life was not easy for them, the Indians kept their traditional ways and never gave their burdens to the Lord. As time went on they left their old traditions and embraced the Lord.

☐ *To God Be The Glory*, E-2823

Sam will never forget the day he saw Fujioka-San's sculpture of *To God Be The Glory*. He says it captures the story of his life. He feels that the Lord has been good to him and has blessed all his work.

☐ *God Sends the Gift Of His Love*, E-6613

Sam's grandniece inspired him to create this piece. She looked precious in her frilly Christmas dress her mom made for her. Sam felt the little child was God's special gift to her parents.

☐ *I Believe In Miracles*, E-7156

Sam's former partner, Bill, was given no hope for his eyesight, but through prayer Bill's sight was restored. This figurine also became the official gift of Child's Wish, an organization for terminally ill children.

☐ *Part of Me Wants To Be Good*, 12149

A very special young man, Albern Cuidad, who lived in the Philippines, was the inspiration for this figurine. He was always getting into trouble but he was so loveable you couldn't help but like him. He often said, "Please forgive me, I really meant to be good." The little boy in the figurine *Part of Me Wants To Be Good* is modeled after Albern.

☐ *I'm Sending You A White Christmas*, E-2829

Sam's mother was born in Michigan, but moved to Florida at an early age. After the death of her father, her mother moved the family back to Michigan. Sam's mother was only five years old and had never seen snow. The first time she saw snow, his mother was found packing snowballs in a box to mail to her relatives in Florida.

☐ *Lord, I'm Coming Home,* 100110

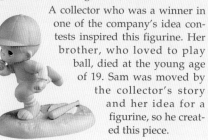

A collector who was a winner in one of the company's idea contests inspired this figurine. Her brother, who loved to play ball, died at the young age of 19. Sam was moved by the collector's story and her idea for a figurine, so he created this piece.

☐ *God Bless The Day We Found You,* 100145

Heather was the adopted daughter of the Butchers. She was five years old when she was adopted. They were struggling to make ends meet but knew they wanted her for a daughter. Because of his love for Heather, Sam created *God Bless The Day We Found You,* to celebrate the love that comes with an adopted child.

☐ *The Lord Giveth, And The Lord Taketh Away,* 100226

After a trip to the Philippines, Sam arrived home and found total chaos. He found his wife Kate standing beside the tipped-over birdcage looking at bird feathers all over the floor. The cat had eaten the canary. Though it was a sad experience, Sam envisioned this figurine, *The Lord Giveth And The Lord Taketh Away.*

☐ *Only One Life To Offer,* 325309

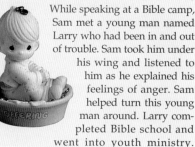

While speaking at a Bible camp, Sam met a young man named Larry who had been in and out of trouble. Sam took him under his wing and listened to him as he explained his feelings of anger. Sam helped turn this young man around. Larry completed Bible school and went into youth ministry. When Larry was less than 40 years old, he called Sam and asked for money for an operation; he had stomach cancer. The surgery was not successful. He died, leaving a wife and two children. This figurine was dedicated to him.

☐ *The Good Lord Will Always Uphold Us,* 325325

A special friend of Sam's was a missionary in South Africa. Even though she had had rheumatoid arthritis since childhood, she faithfully served the Lord. This figurine was designed to honor Sam's faithful friend, Lory Burg.

☐ *Heaven Must Have Sent You,* 521388

Nancy Laptad, an employee in Sam's office, was always there when he needed financial advice. Nancy, though she was seen on a daily basis, did not realize how important she was. The figurine was dedicated to Nancy because she was always there when she was needed.

☐ *No Tears Past The Gate,* 101826

No Tears Past The Gate was painted to comfort Sam's assistant in the Philippines, Levi, whose sister was dying. She was 18 when she died. The painting was presented to Levi just a few weeks afterwards. Levi became one of Sam's most devoted workers. He was promoted to manager, then vice-president and later president of the company.

☐ *Merry Christmas Deer*, 522317

A five-year-old girl adopted from an orphanage wanted all her Christmas gifts except one sent to her friends at the orphanage. All she wanted to keep was a stuffed reindeer. On the way home from delivering the toys, her reindeer got stuck in the door of a subway train and was lost forever. Several years ago, this lady wrote to Sam and asked him to help her find the Precious Moments ornament of a little reindeer with a teddy bear on his back. Sam sent the ornament from his private collection. The story inspired Sam to create this figurine of a little girl hanging ornaments on the antlers of a reindeer.

☐ *Count Your Many Blessings*, 879274

Sam designed this figurine for a collector named Penny who lived in Canada. She gave Sam Canadian pennies and bugged him for years to make a figurine of her. At the 2000 Collectors Christmas Weekend she was asked to come on stage. As she was helping Sam she picked up a cloth and found her figurine *Count Your Many Blessings*.

☐ *Hello, Lord, It's Me Again*, PM-811

Jon, Sam's oldest son, inspired this figurine after a romantic setback. Sam envisioned this little guy with a Dear Jon letter. He is on the phone and there is a tear running down his cheek. He's saying, *Hello Lord, It's Me Again*. Jon later found Patti and married her.

☐ *Smile, God Loves You*, PM-821

Sam believes that outward appearances don't matter and that "you can't judge a book by its cover."

☐ *Put On A Happy Face*, PM-822

This figurine was made to inspire collectors to show their happy side. Sam says it's really hard to take off your mask and show a "sunny side." This little clown figurine became an instant success and won the hearts of collectors.

☐ *Collecting Friends Along The Way*, PM-002

Sam has met many people that have been touched by the Precious Moments collection, and he says it brings him joy to see how much the figurines mean to them. This figurine was designed to honor all the special people in our lives, be they family, friends, or club members. There are 20 animals sculpted on the figurine in commemoration of the twentieth anniversary of the club.

Precious Moments figurines' Stories

☐ *Trust In The Lord To The Finish*, **PM-842**

Sam began the painting for this figurine on his way to the Philippines. His youngest brother, Hank, always loved driving race cars.

☐ *Grandma's Prayer*, **PM-861**

This figurine is a loving tribute to Sam's grand-mother, who remind-ed Sam often that she was praying for him.

☐ *The Lord Is My Shepherd*, **PM-851**

Sam's daughter, Debbie, was the inspiration for this figurine. She has a warm sensitive spirit and has contributed greatly to the Pre-cious Moments line. She could handle all the very difficult prob-lems in her life. This piece is a symbol of God's promise that, he, as the Good Shepherd, is always there to meet our every need.

☐ *I'm Following Jesus*, **PM-862**

After encountering a jobless Filipino friend, Carlito, Sam was inspired to create this fig-urine. Carlito and his family trusted the Lord to take care of their needs. Eventually, Carlito got his own cab, which has a sign in the window that reads, "I'm Following Jesus."

☐ *I Love To Tell The Story*, **PM-852**

Inspired by the old Christian song, this piece was dedicated to Pastor Royal Blue who led Sam to the Lord Jesus. The child is speaking to a lamb, which symbolizes a pastor feed-ing God's flock with the bread of life, the word of God.

☐ *Focusing In On Those Precious Moments*, **C-0018**

Sam attended a col-lectibles show in Edison, New Jersey, in the spring of 1999. He presented this special ver-sion of the 1998 club figurine to Rosemarie who belongs to the Happi-ness Is Belonging Club and the Precious Moments Collectible Treasures website. Sam states, "She is one of the most giving, kindest people and has a huge giving heart."

How To Clean Your Precious Moments

Here are some tips to help keep your collection clean and safe. The most important thing is to keep your pieces in a safe, smoke-free area, and out of direct sunlight. Enesco recommends hand washing your pieces using warm water, any mild soap, and to wipe them with a damp cloth. Place something soft underneath the area in which you are working just in case the piece gets dropped. When finished, wipe the item off with a soft towel and set it aside to dry completely. If you have intentions of reselling the pieces, try to keep all the original packaging. There is a higher resale value on the secondary market if everything is complete.

What Is Sam Butcher's Signature Worth?

No one can put a value on Sam Butcher's signature on a Precious Moments figurine. Appraisers have set a higher value on a signed piece since he is the artist. The system they seem to use averages out to approximately $30.00 on easily acquired pieces and approximately $50.00 on pieces that are harder to find. With certain special pieces the price could go up to an additional $100.00. Eugene Freedman's signature does not increase the value of a piece, yet Yasuhei Fujioka-San's signature could add $25.00 and Shuhei Fujioka's (his brother) could add $15.00.

Annual Production Marks

The annual production marks, located on the bottoms of the bases of Precious Moments figurines, reveal the year of the figurine's production and symbolize an inspirational message.

Unmarked: No Mark, before 1981

Triangle, Mid-1981
Symbol of the Holy Trinity — God the Father, God the Son, and God the Holy Ghost.

Hourglass, 1982
Represents the time we have on earth to serve the Lord.

Fish, 1983
Earliest symbol used by believers of the early apostolic church.

Cross, 1984
Symbol of Christianity recognized worldwide.

Dove, 1985
Symbol of love and peace.

Olive Branch, 1986
Symbol of peace and understanding.

Cedar Tree, 1987
Symbol of strength, beauty, and preservation.

Flower, 1988
Represents God's love for his children.

Bow & Arrow, 1989
Represents the power of the Bible.

Flame, 1990
For those who have gone through the fire of life and found comfort in believing.

Vessel, 1991
A reminder of God's love which flows through the vessel of life.

G-Clef, 1992
Symbolizes the harmony of God's love.

Trumpet, 1993
Represents loving, caring, and sharing; also signified a battle cry and a herald of victory.

Butterfly, 1994
Represents the rebirth of man who comes from darkness into the light.

Ship, 1995
Ships, which are mentioned many times in the Scriptures, symbolically portray a message of hope.

Heart, 1996
Symbol of love.

Sword, 1997
From Hebrews 4:12, *For the Word of God is quick and powerful, and sharper than any two edged sword.*

Eyeglasses, 1998
Symbolizes Precious Moments' twentieth year and "the vision's still the same."

Star, 1999
From Matthew 2:2, *Where is He who has been born King of the Jews? For we have seen His star in the east and have come to worship Him.*

Egg, 2000
From Sam Butcher: *I have chosen the egg because it symbolizes the new millennium and a new beginning. Just as we know little of what the twenty-first century will bring, no one knows what is taking place inside an egg. Nor will they completely understand until it is hatched and God's wonderful plan is revealed. The egg speaks of birth, of new things to come — things known only to God alone.*

Sandal, 2001
The sandal represents our journey with the Lord.

Cross in Heart, 2002
Keeping faith in your heart, Sam chose a cross surrounded by a heart to symbolize faith. It is representative of the importance of faith now and in the next century.

Crown, 2003
The crown represents glory, dignity, and sovereignty. This is what Sam Butcher feels Precious Moments is all about.

Three-Petal Flower, 2004
In the world of Precious Moments, each petal in this flower symbolizes part of the message "loving, caring, and sharing."

Special Production Marks

◇ Diamond
Appears on #10334, *We Belong To The Lord*.

🏴 Flag
Appears on 1991 editions of *Bless Those Who Serve Their Country* figurines.

 Rosebud
Appears on #525049, *Good Friends Are Forever*.

🏴 Flag
Appears on 1992 editions of *Bless Those Who Serve Their Country* figurines.

Easter Seals Lily
Appears on annual figurines that benefit Easter Seals.

🏴 Four-Star Flag
Appears on 2002 *America Forever* series.

Know The Secondary Market

How do you find out about the production of Precious Moments pieces? Where do you start searching for these items? Precious Moments figurines have been produced by Enesco since 1978. Finding outdated pieces can be difficult or easy, depending on the piece for which you are searching. The secondary market is the place to find these difficult Suspended, Retired, or Closed pieces.

The secondary market helps when a piece is no longer available at retail stores or at the retirement of the piece. When a piece is Retired, production is stopped on that piece. As the piece is sold out in the stores it becomes almost impossible to purchase. This same piece becomes more valuable on the secondary market and the collector is more willing to pay a higher price, thus increasing the value of the item. The collector today has more opportunity in the market because of the Internet. Most collectors have computers and can go to different websites that deal with the secondary market. The collector can check out these sites to purchase some of those difficult to find pieces. We have listed some of these on page 404.

Enesco has several ways to end the production of a piece. When a piece is Retired, the mold is broken and cannot be produced again. No notice is given to the collector when a piece is Retired. The collector is given only a small amount of time to purchase a piece that will be pulled out of production. Suspended pieces are temporarily taken out of production but can be brought back into production at a later date with a change of some sort to the piece. Dated figurines or pieces with a limited production time are called Closed pieces. They were produced for a limited time, possibly for one year, or in a limited quantity.

In addition to these pieces there are others produced for certain occasions or events. These are called Special Event, Limited Edition, and Club Member Exclusive figurines. Dated Annual means that the piece was issued for one year and includes a date on the figurine; Annuals were issued for one year only, but do not have dates on them. The ongoing, or "Open," pieces can be purchased at retail dealers or on Internet sites. Pieces produced before mid-1981 had no symbol on the understamp and are called "Unmarked." Precious Moments plates and ornaments were not marked until 1984.

Know the item you are purchasing on the secondary market and examine it for damage. Watch for dings, hairline cracks, paint discoloration, or other damage. Watch for fakes! There are some out there. Know your collection, read price guides, know what you are looking at. Only you can determine what you want in your collection — with or without boxes, damaged pieces bought at a good price, or pieces in mint condition. It's all up to you.

How To Use Your Precious Moments Price Guide

Many collectors confuse the copyright date with the date of issue. You must refer to the annual production symbol, not the date, to determine what year your pieces were manufactured. This price guide shows the suggested retail price for each piece. It lists when it was introduced and shows the changes in production symbols for the piece.

This guide lists items in the index at the back of the book in numerical order. The Enesco pieces manufactured from 1982 to the present are numbered on the understamp. If you do not know the number but do know the name of the piece, check the general index in the back of the book. The quickest and most accurate means of identification is the item number that appears on the understamp of most items manufactured from 1982 to the present. This number also appears in ads, brochures, and catalogs.

Remember: Errors are made all the time; unmarked pieces can sometimes be pieces that were just not marked.

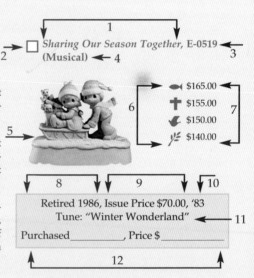

1. **Title** — Spiritual name given to the piece.

2. **Checkbox for Inventory** — Box making it possible to keep track of personal collection.

3. **Enesco Item Number** — The quickest and most accurate means of identification; appears on the understamp of most items.

4. **Object** — Tells whether item is something other than a figurine — ornament, musical, frame, plate, plaque, box, etc. (If nothing is listed in parentheses, it is a figurine.)

5. **Picture** — Photo of the item.

6. **Production Symbols** — Enesco's Annual Production Symbols; shows all symbols used for a particular figurine.

7. **Secondary Market Value** — The cost of the item when it is sold on the secondary market, according to production mark.

8. **Production Status** — States if the piece has been Suspended or Retired, is a Limited Edition, Annual or Dated Annual, Club Member Exclusive, Special Event, or Open (still available). Date is included if known.

9. **Issue Price** — The cost of the item at the time it was first introduced.

10. **Year Introduced** — Lists the year the piece was first issued.

11. **Collector Information** — Gives important facts about the piece: series, number in set, or name of tune played by musical pieces.

12. **Purchase Information** — Gives the collector space to record information on the purchase date and price for each piece.

General figurines

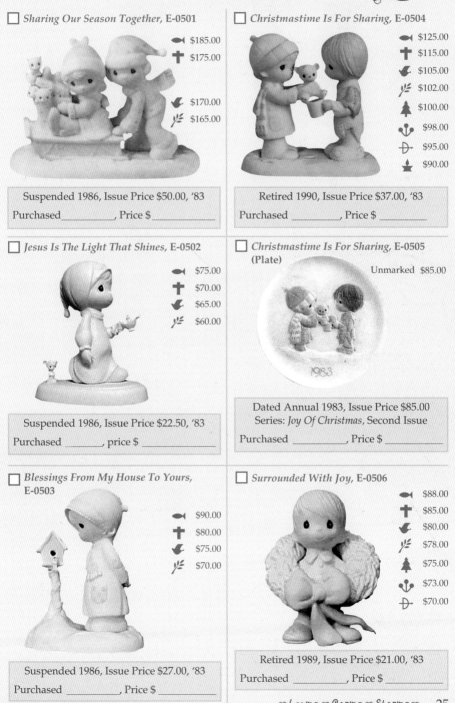

☐ *Sharing Our Season Together*, E-0501

- 🐟 $185.00
- ✝ $175.00
- 🕊 $170.00
- ⚘ $165.00

Suspended 1986, Issue Price $50.00, '83
Purchased_____, Price $ _____

☐ *Christmastime Is For Sharing*, E-0504

- 🐟 $125.00
- ✝ $115.00
- 🕊 $105.00
- ⚘ $102.00
- 🌲 $100.00
- ⚓ $98.00
- ☩ $95.00
- ☦ $90.00

Retired 1990, Issue Price $37.00, '83
Purchased _____, Price $ _____

☐ *Jesus Is The Light That Shines*, E-0502

- 🐟 $75.00
- ✝ $70.00
- 🕊 $65.00
- ⚘ $60.00

Suspended 1986, Issue Price $22.50, '83
Purchased _____, price $ _____

☐ *Christmastime Is For Sharing*, E-0505
(Plate)

Unmarked $85.00

Dated Annual 1983, Issue Price $85.00
Series: *Joy Of Christmas*, Second Issue
Purchased _____, Price $ _____

☐ *Blessings From My House To Yours*,
E-0503

- 🐟 $90.00
- ✝ $80.00
- 🕊 $75.00
- ⚘ $70.00

Suspended 1986, Issue Price $27.00, '83
Purchased _____, Price $ _____

☐ *Surrounded With Joy*, E-0506

- 🐟 $88.00
- ✝ $85.00
- 🕊 $80.00
- ⚘ $78.00
- 🌲 $75.00
- ⚓ $73.00
- ☦ $70.00

Retired 1989, Issue Price $21.00, '83
Purchased _____, Price $ _____

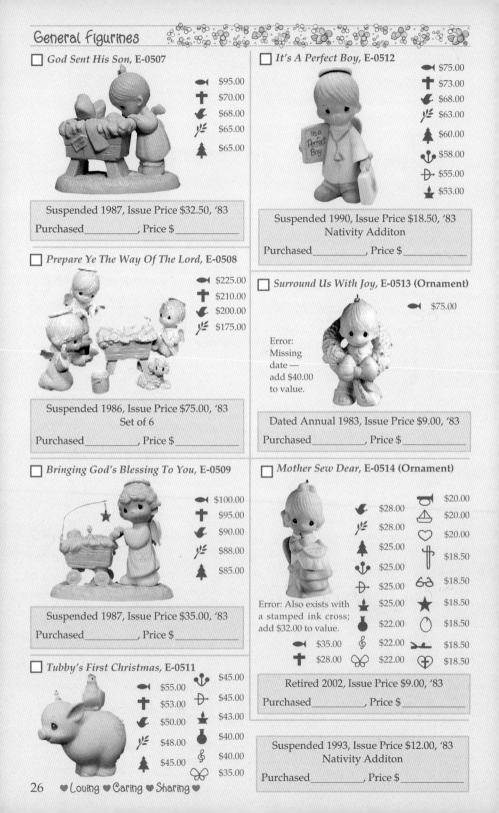

☐ **God Sent His Son**, E-0507

🐟 $95.00
✝ $70.00
🕊 $68.00
🌿 $65.00
🌲 $65.00

Suspended 1987, Issue Price $32.50, '83
Purchased_____, Price $_____

☐ **Prepare Ye The Way Of The Lord**, E-0508

🐟 $225.00
✝ $210.00
🕊 $200.00
🌿 $175.00

Suspended 1986, Issue Price $75.00, '83
Set of 6
Purchased_____, Price $_____

☐ **Bringing God's Blessing To You**, E-0509

🐟 $100.00
✝ $95.00
🕊 $90.00
🌿 $88.00
🌲 $85.00

Suspended 1987, Issue Price $35.00, '83
Purchased_____, Price $_____

☐ **Tubby's First Christmas**, E-0511

🐟 $55.00   ⚓ $45.00
✝ $53.00   ⅃ $45.00
🕊 $50.00   🕯 $43.00
🌿 $48.00   🔨 $40.00
🌲 $45.00   ✆ $40.00
           ∞ $35.00

☐ **It's A Perfect Boy**, E-0512

🐟 $75.00
✝ $73.00
🕊 $68.00
🌿 $63.00
🌲 $60.00
⚓ $58.00
⅃ $55.00
🔨 $53.00

Suspended 1990, Issue Price $18.50, '83
Nativity Additon
Purchased_____, Price $_____

☐ **Surround Us With Joy**, E-0513 (Ornament)

🐟 $75.00

Error:
Missing
date —
add $40.00
to value.

Dated Annual 1983, Issue Price $9.00, '83
Purchased_____, Price $_____

☐ **Mother Sew Dear**, E-0514 (Ornament)

🕊 $28.00   ⅃ $20.00
🌿 $28.00   △ $20.00
🌲 $25.00   ♡ $20.00
⚓ $25.00   ✝ $18.50
⅃ $25.00   68 $18.50
🔨 $25.00   ★ $18.50

Error: Also exists with
a stamped ink cross;
add $32.00 to value.
🔨 $22.00   ○ $18.50
🐟 $35.00   ✆ $22.00   🔆 $18.50
✝ $28.00   ∞ $22.00   ⊕ $18.50

Retired 2002, Issue Price $9.00, '83
Purchased_____, Price $_____

Suspended 1993, Issue Price $12.00, '83
Nativity Additon
Purchased_____, Price $_____

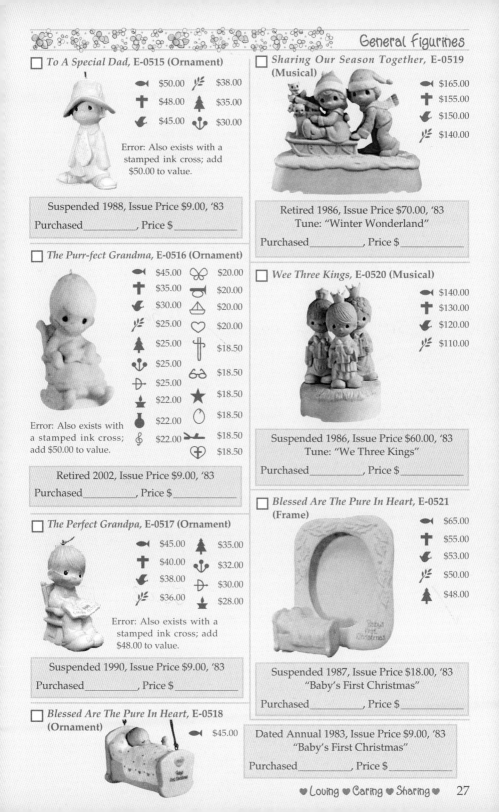

☐ *To A Special Dad,* E-0515 (Ornament)

🐟 $50.00   🌿 $38.00
✝ $48.00   🌲 $35.00
🕊 $45.00   ⚓ $30.00

Error: Also exists with a
stamped ink cross; add
$50.00 to value.

Suspended 1988, Issue Price $9.00, '83

Purchased_____, Price $_____

☐ *The Purr-fect Grandma,* E-0516 (Ornament)

🐟 $45.00   🦋 $20.00
✝ $35.00   🎺 $20.00
🕊 $30.00   ⛵ $20.00
🌿 $25.00   ♡ $20.00
🌲 $25.00   ✝ $18.50
⚓ $25.00   👓 $18.50
⊕ $25.00   ⭐ $18.50
🕯 $22.00   ◯ $18.50
🔔 $22.00
🎼 $22.00   ⤳ $18.50
            ⊕ $18.50

Error: Also exists with
a stamped ink cross;
add $50.00 to value.

Retired 2002, Issue Price $9.00, '83

Purchased_____, Price $_____

☐ *The Perfect Grandpa,* E-0517 (Ornament)

🐟 $45.00   🌲 $35.00
✝ $40.00   ⚓ $32.00
🕊 $38.00   ⊕ $30.00
🌿 $36.00   ⭐ $28.00

Error: Also exists with a
stamped ink cross; add
$48.00 to value.

Suspended 1990, Issue Price $9.00, '83

Purchased_____, Price $_____

☐ *Blessed Are The Pure In Heart,* E-0518
(Ornament)

🐟 $45.00

☐ *Sharing Our Season Together,* E-0519
(Musical)

🐟 $165.00
✝ $155.00
🕊 $150.00
🌿 $140.00

Retired 1986, Issue Price $70.00, '83
Tune: "Winter Wonderland"

Purchased_____, Price $_____

☐ *Wee Three Kings,* E-0520 (Musical)

🐟 $140.00
✝ $130.00
🕊 $120.00
🌿 $110.00

Suspended 1986, Issue Price $60.00, '83
Tune: "We Three Kings"

Purchased_____, Price $_____

☐ *Blessed Are The Pure In Heart,* E-0521
(Frame)

🐟 $65.00
✝ $55.00
🕊 $53.00
🌿 $50.00
🌲 $48.00

Suspended 1987, Issue Price $18.00, '83
"Baby's First Christmas"

Purchased_____, Price $_____

Dated Annual 1983, Issue Price $9.00, '83
"Baby's First Christmas"

Purchased_____, Price $_____

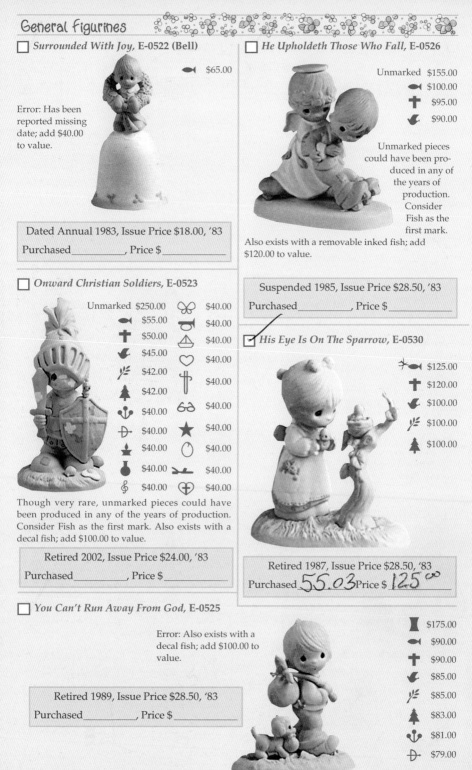

☐ **Surrounded With Joy, E-0522 (Bell)**

🐟 $65.00

Error: Has been reported missing date; add $40.00 to value.

Dated Annual 1983, Issue Price $18.00, '83
Purchased_____, Price $_____

☐ **Onward Christian Soldiers, E-0523**

Unmarked	$250.00	🦋	$40.00
🐟	$55.00	⌒	$40.00
✝	$50.00	△	$40.00
🕊	$45.00	♡	$40.00
🌿	$42.00	†	$40.00
🌲	$42.00		
⚓	$40.00	👓	$40.00
Ð	$40.00	★	$40.00
🔔	$40.00	◯	$40.00
🍶	$40.00	✈	$40.00
§	$40.00	⊕	$40.00

Though very rare, unmarked pieces could have been produced in any of the years of production. Consider Fish as the first mark. Also exists with a decal fish; add $100.00 to value.

Retired 2002, Issue Price $24.00, '83
Purchased_____, Price $_____

☐ **You Can't Run Away From God, E-0525**

Error: Also exists with a decal fish; add $100.00 to value.

Retired 1989, Issue Price $28.50, '83
Purchased_____, Price $_____

☐ **He Upholdeth Those Who Fall, E-0526**

Unmarked	$155.00
🐟	$100.00
✝	$95.00
🕊	$90.00

Unmarked pieces could have been produced in any of the years of production. Consider Fish as the first mark.

Also exists with a removable inked fish; add $120.00 to value.

Suspended 1985, Issue Price $28.50, '83
Purchased_____, Price $_____

☑ **His Eye Is On The Sparrow, E-0530**

🎣	$125.00
✝	$120.00
🕊	$100.00
🌿	$100.00
🌲	$100.00

Retired 1987, Issue Price $28.50, '83
Purchased 55.03 Price $ 125.00

🏺	$175.00
🐟	$90.00
✝	$90.00
🕊	$85.00
🌿	$85.00
🌲	$83.00
⚓	$81.00
Ð	$79.00

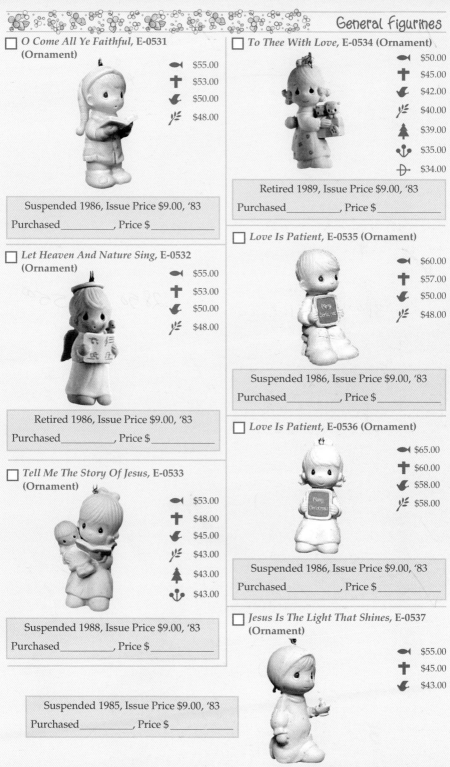

☐ *O Come All Ye Faithful*, E-0531
(Ornament)

🐟 $55.00
✝ $53.00
🕊 $50.00
🌿 $48.00

Suspended 1986, Issue Price $9.00, '83
Purchased_____, Price $_____

☐ *Let Heaven And Nature Sing*, E-0532
(Ornament)

🐟 $55.00
✝ $53.00
🕊 $50.00
🌿 $48.00

Retired 1986, Issue Price $9.00, '83
Purchased_____, Price $_____

☐ *Tell Me The Story Of Jesus*, E-0533
(Ornament)

🐟 $53.00
✝ $48.00
🕊 $45.00
🌿 $43.00
🌲 $43.00
⚓ $43.00

Suspended 1988, Issue Price $9.00, '83
Purchased_____, Price $_____

☐ *To Thee With Love*, E-0534 (Ornament)

🐟 $50.00
✝ $45.00
🕊 $42.00
🌿 $40.00
🌲 $39.00
⚓ $35.00
Ⅎ $34.00

Retired 1989, Issue Price $9.00, '83
Purchased_____, Price $_____

☐ *Love Is Patient*, E-0535 (Ornament)

🐟 $60.00
✝ $57.00
🕊 $50.00
🌿 $48.00

Suspended 1986, Issue Price $9.00, '83
Purchased_____, Price $_____

☐ *Love Is Patient*, E-0536 (Ornament)

🐟 $65.00
✝ $60.00
🕊 $58.00
🌿 $58.00

Suspended 1986, Issue Price $9.00, '83
Purchased_____, Price $_____

☐ *Jesus Is The Light That Shines*, E-0537
(Ornament)

🐟 $55.00
✝ $45.00
🕊 $43.00

Suspended 1985, Issue Price $9.00, '83
Purchased_____, Price $_____

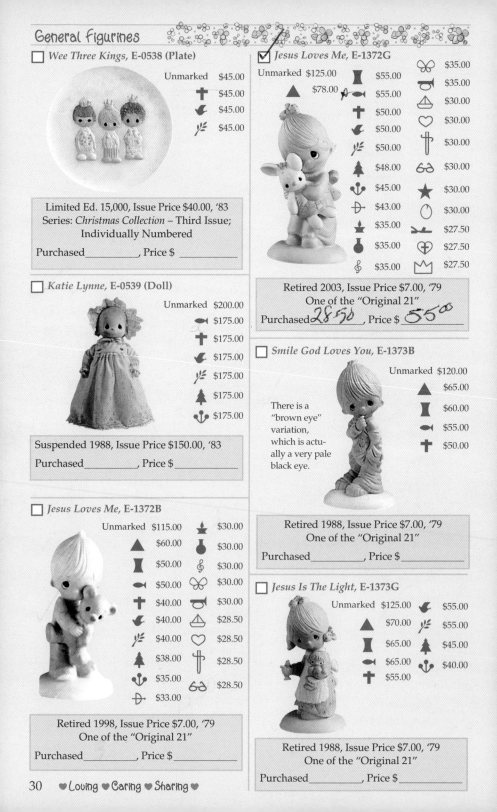

☐ *Wee Three Kings*, E-0538 (Plate)

Unmarked	$45.00
✝	$45.00
🕊	$45.00
🌿	$45.00

Limited Ed. 15,000, Issue Price $40.00, '83
Series: *Christmas Collection* – Third Issue;
Individually Numbered

Purchased_____, Price $ _____

☐ *Katie Lynne*, E-0539 (Doll)

Unmarked	$200.00
🐟	$175.00
✝	$175.00
🕊	$175.00
🌿	$175.00
🌲	$175.00
⚓	$175.00

Suspended 1988, Issue Price $150.00, '83

Purchased_____, Price $ _____

☐ *Jesus Loves Me*, E-1372B

Unmarked	$115.00	🔥	$30.00
▲	$60.00	🌶	$30.00
I	$50.00	𝄞	$30.00
🐟	$50.00	🦋	$30.00
✝	$40.00	📯	$30.00
🕊	$40.00	⛵	$28.50
🌿	$40.00	♡	$28.50
🌲	$38.00	⳨	$28.50
⚓	$35.00	👓	$28.50
⌐	$33.00		

Retired 1998, Issue Price $7.00, '79
One of the "Original 21"

Purchased_____, Price $ _____

☑ *Jesus Loves Me*, E-1372G

Unmarked	$125.00	🦋	$35.00
▲	$78.00	📯	$35.00
I	$55.00	⛵	$30.00
🐟	$55.00	♡	$30.00
✝	$50.00	⳨	$30.00
🕊	$50.00	👓	$30.00
🌿	$50.00	★	$30.00
🌲	$48.00	◯	$30.00
⚓	$45.00	⌐	$27.50
⳨	$43.00	🕆	$27.50
🔥	$35.00	👑	$27.50
🌶	$35.00		
𝄞	$35.00		

Retired 2003, Issue Price $7.00, '79
One of the "Original 21"

Purchased 28-50, Price $ 550

☐ *Smile God Loves You*, E-1373B

Unmarked	$120.00
▲	$65.00
I	$60.00
🐟	$55.00
✝	$50.00

There is a "brown eye" variation, which is actually a very pale black eye.

Retired 1988, Issue Price $7.00, '79
One of the "Original 21"

Purchased_____, Price $ _____

☐ *Jesus Is The Light*, E-1373G

Unmarked	$125.00	🕊	$55.00
▲	$70.00	🌿	$55.00
I	$65.00	🌲	$45.00
🐟	$65.00	⚓	$40.00
✝	$55.00		

Retired 1988, Issue Price $7.00, '79
One of the "Original 21"

Purchased_____, Price $ _____

Praise The Lord Anyhow, E-1374B

There are variations in the color of the dog's nose (brown or black) and variations in the color of ice cream.

Unmarked	$125.00	
▲	$110.00	
✗ I	$85.00	

Retired 1982, Issue Price $8.00, '79
One of the "Original 21"
Purchased _55 00_, Price $ _85 00_

Prayer Changes Things, E-1375B

Unmarked	$220.00
▲	$165.00
I	$165.00
⊷	$160.00
✝	$155.00

Suspended 1984, Issue Price $11.00, '79
One of the "Original 21"
Purchased _____, Price $ _____

Make A Joyful Noise, E-1374G

2

✗ Unmarked	$115.00	🔔	$32.50
▲	$55.00	𝄞	$32.50
I	$45.00	�	$32.50
⊷	$35.00	⊐	$32.50
✝	$35.00	△	$32.50
🕊	$35.00	♡	$32.50
⅏	$35.00	✝	$32.50
🌲	$32.50	👓	$32.50
⚓	$32.50	★	$32.50
Ð	$32.50	◯	$32.50
⚜	$32.50		

Figurine has experienced mold shrinkage problems; variations in the position of the goose are common.

Retired 2000, Issue Price $8.00, '79
One of the "Original 21"
Purchased _12 50_, Price $ _115 00_

Love Lifted Me, E-1375A

Unmarked	$155.00
▲	$95.00
I	$90.00
⊷	$90.00
✝	$88.00
◄	$88.00
⅏	$88.00

🌲	$85.00	🔔	$70.00
⚓	$75.00	𝄞	$70.00
Ð	$73.00	✤	$65.00
⚜	$70.00		

Retired 1993, Issue Price $11.00, '79
One of the "Original 21"
Purchased _____, Price $ _____

Love One Another, E-1376

Ebayer Lied about neck

Unmarked	$130.00	◄	$46.00
▲	$72.00	⅏	$45.00
I	$55.00	🌲	$45.00
⊷	$50.00	⚓	$45.00
✝	$48.00	Ð	$44.00
⚜	$42.00		
🔔	$40.00		
𝄞	$40.00		
✤	$40.00		
⊐	$40.00 ✗		
△	$40.00		
♡	$40.00		
✝	$40.00		
👓	$40.00		
★	$40.00		
◯	$40.00		
⤚	$40.00		
✛	$40.00		
♛	$40.00		

Open, Issue Price $10.00, '79
One of the "Original 21"
Purchased _42 00_, Price $ _40 00_

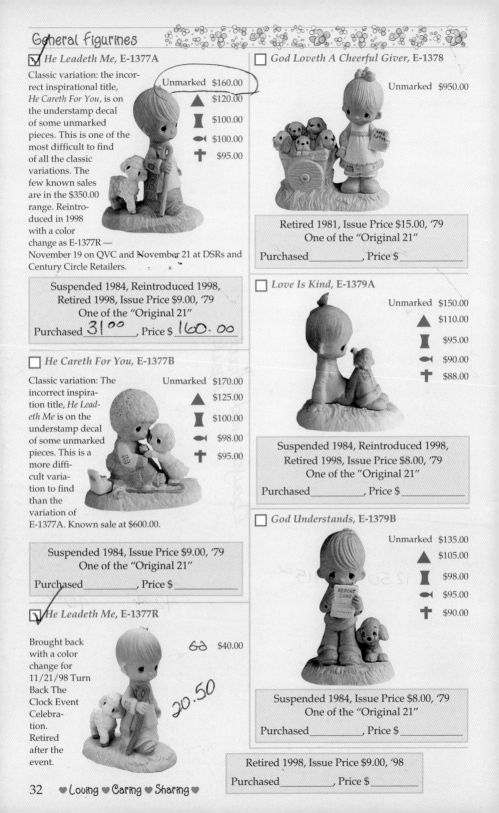

He Leadeth Me, E-1377A

Classic variation: the incorrect inspirational title, *He Careth For You*, is on the understamp decal of some unmarked pieces. This is one of the most difficult to find of all the classic variations. The few known sales are in the $350.00 range. Reintroduced in 1998 with a color change as E-1377R — November 19 on QVC and November 21 at DSRs and Century Circle Retailers.

Unmarked $160.00
▲ $120.00
I $100.00
🐟 $100.00
✝ $95.00

Suspended 1984, Reintroduced 1998,
Retired 1998, Issue Price $9.00, '79
One of the "Original 21"
Purchased **31 00**, Price $ **160. 00**

He Careth For You, E-1377B

Classic variation: The incorrect inspiration title, *He Leadeth Me* is on the understamp decal of some unmarked pieces. This is a more difficult variation to find than the variation of E-1377A. Known sale at $600.00.

Unmarked $170.00
▲ $125.00
I $100.00
🐟 $98.00
✝ $95.00

Suspended 1984, Issue Price $9.00, '79
One of the "Original 21"
Purchased_____, Price $_____

He Leadeth Me, E-1377R

Brought back with a color change for 11/21/98 Turn Back The Clock Event Celebration. Retired after the event.

👓 $40.00

20.50

God Loveth A Cheerful Giver, E-1378

Unmarked $950.00

Retired 1981, Issue Price $15.00, '79
One of the "Original 21"
Purchased_____, Price $_____

Love Is Kind, E-1379A

Unmarked $150.00
▲ $110.00
I $95.00
🐟 $90.00
✝ $88.00

Suspended 1984, Reintroduced 1998,
Retired 1998, Issue Price $8.00, '79
One of the "Original 21"
Purchased_____, Price $_____

God Understands, E-1379B

Unmarked $135.00
▲ $105.00
I $98.00
🐟 $95.00
✝ $90.00

Suspended 1984, Issue Price $8.00, '79
One of the "Original 21"
Purchased_____, Price $_____

Retired 1998, Issue Price $9.00, '98
Purchased_____, Price $_____

God Understands, E-1379BR

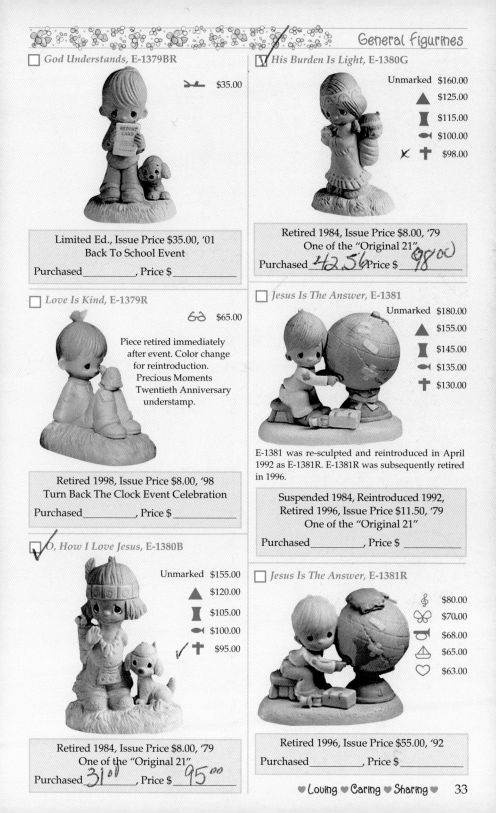

$35.00

Limited Ed., Issue Price $35.00, '01
Back To School Event

Purchased_____, Price $ _____

His Burden Is Light, E-1380G

Unmarked $160.00

▲ $125.00

Ⅰ $115.00

◀ $100.00

✗ ✝ $98.00

Retired 1984, Issue Price $8.00, '79
One of the "Original 21"

Purchased 42.56 Price $ 9800

Love Is Kind, E-1379R

$65.00

Piece retired immediately
after event. Color change
for reintroduction.
Precious Moments
Twentieth Anniversary
understamp.

Retired 1998, Issue Price $8.00, '98
Turn Back The Clock Event Celebration

Purchased_____, Price $ _____

Jesus Is The Answer, E-1381

Unmarked $180.00

▲ $155.00

Ⅰ $145.00

◀ $135.00

✝ $130.00

E-1381 was re-sculpted and reintroduced in April
1992 as E-1381R. E-1381R was subsequently retired
in 1996.

Suspended 1984, Reintroduced 1992,
Retired 1996, Issue Price $11.50, '79
One of the "Original 21"

Purchased_____, Price $ _____

O, How I Love Jesus, E-1380B

Unmarked $155.00

▲ $120.00

Ⅰ $105.00

◀ $100.00

✓ ✝ $95.00

Retired 1984, Issue Price $8.00, '79
One of the "Original 21"

Purchased 31.00, Price $ 95.00

Jesus Is The Answer, E-1381R

⅌ $80.00

⅋ $70.00

◖ $68.00

△ $65.00

♡ $63.00

Retired 1996, Issue Price $55.00, '92

Purchased_____, Price $ _____

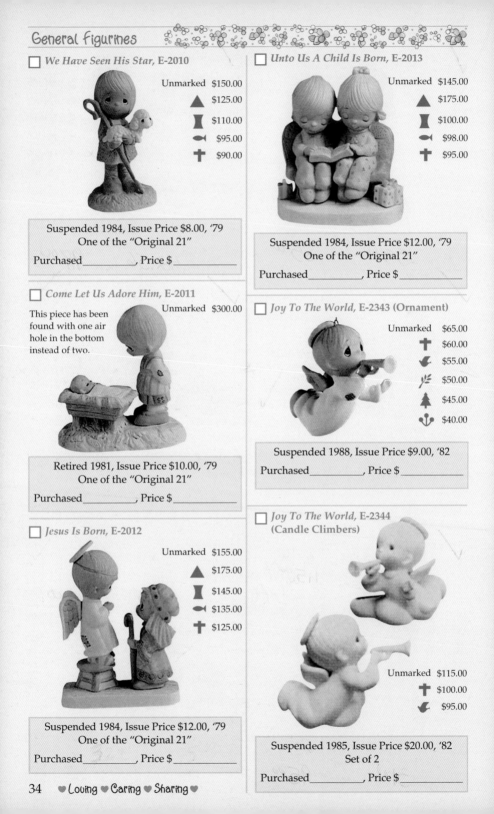

☐ *We Have Seen His Star*, E-2010

Unmarked	$150.00
▲	$125.00
❚	$110.00
🐟	$95.00
✝	$90.00

Suspended 1984, Issue Price $8.00, '79
One of the "Original 21"

Purchased_____, Price $ _____

☐ *Come Let Us Adore Him*, E-2011

This piece has been found with one air hole in the bottom instead of two.

Unmarked $300.00

Retired 1981, Issue Price $10.00, '79
One of the "Original 21"

Purchased_____, Price $ _____

☐ *Jesus Is Born*, E-2012

Unmarked	$155.00
▲	$175.00
❚	$145.00
🐟	$135.00
✝	$125.00

Suspended 1984, Issue Price $12.00, '79
One of the "Original 21"

Purchased_____, Price $ _____

☐ *Unto Us A Child Is Born*, E-2013

Unmarked	$145.00
▲	$175.00
❚	$100.00
🐟	$98.00
✝	$95.00

Suspended 1984, Issue Price $12.00, '79
One of the "Original 21"

Purchased_____, Price $ _____

☐ *Joy To The World*, E-2343 (Ornament)

Unmarked	$65.00
✝	$60.00
🕊	$55.00
🌿	$50.00
🌲	$45.00
⚓	$40.00

Suspended 1988, Issue Price $9.00, '82

Purchased_____, Price $ _____

☐ *Joy To The World*, E-2344
(Candle Climbers)

Unmarked	$115.00
✝	$100.00
🕊	$95.00

Suspended 1985, Issue Price $20.00, '82
Set of 2

Purchased_____, Price $ _____

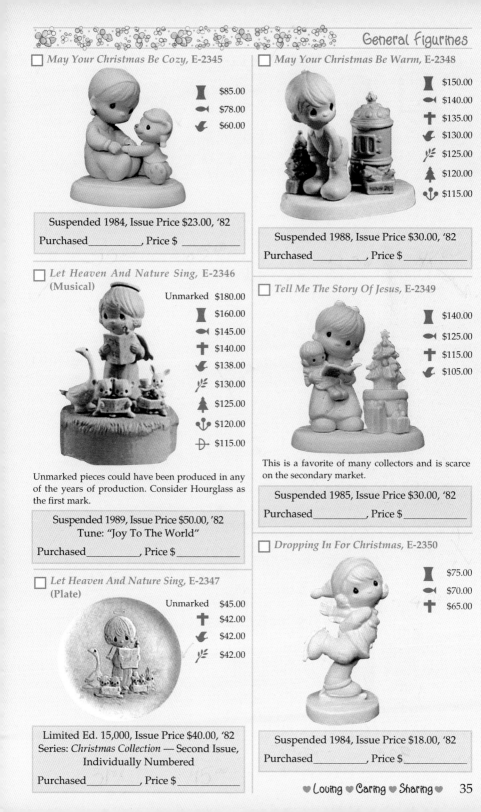

□ *May Your Christmas Be Cozy*, E-2345

▮ $85.00
🐟 $78.00
🕊 $60.00

Suspended 1984, Issue Price $23.00, '82
Purchased_____, Price $_____

□ *Let Heaven And Nature Sing*, E-2346
(Musical)

Unmarked $180.00
▮ $160.00
🐟 $145.00
✝ $140.00
🕊 $138.00
🌿 $130.00
🌲 $125.00
⚓ $120.00
⊅ $115.00

Unmarked pieces could have been produced in any of the years of production. Consider Hourglass as the first mark.

Suspended 1989, Issue Price $50.00, '82
Tune: "Joy To The World"
Purchased_____, Price $_____

□ *Let Heaven And Nature Sing*, E-2347
(Plate)

Unmarked $45.00
✝ $42.00
🕊 $42.00
🌿 $42.00

Limited Ed. 15,000, Issue Price $40.00, '82
Series: *Christmas Collection* — Second Issue, Individually Numbered
Purchased_____, Price $_____

□ *May Your Christmas Be Warm*, E-2348

▮ $150.00
🐟 $140.00
✝ $135.00
🕊 $130.00
🌿 $125.00
🌲 $120.00
⚓ $115.00

Suspended 1988, Issue Price $30.00, '82
Purchased_____, Price $_____

□ *Tell Me The Story Of Jesus*, E-2349

▮ $140.00
🐟 $125.00
✝ $115.00
🕊 $105.00

This is a favorite of many collectors and is scarce on the secondary market.

Suspended 1985, Issue Price $30.00, '82
Purchased_____, Price $_____

□ *Dropping In For Christmas*, E-2350

▮ $75.00
🐟 $70.00
✝ $65.00

Suspended 1984, Issue Price $18.00, '82
Purchased_____, Price $_____

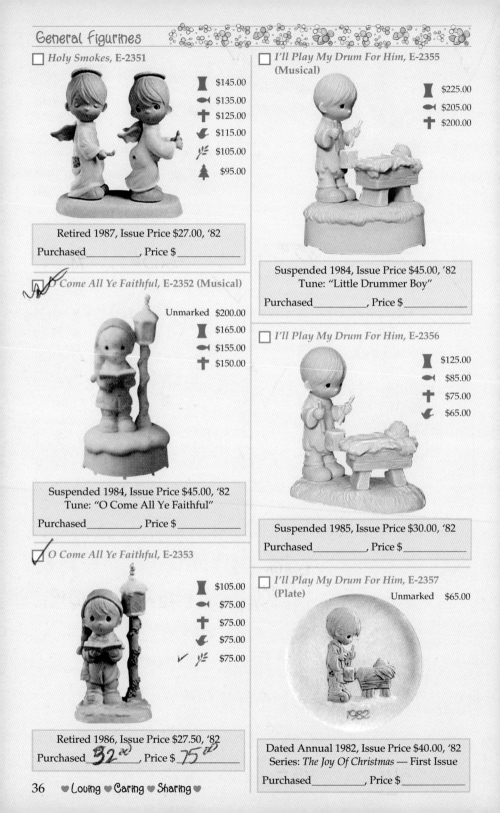

☐ *Holy Smokes*, E-2351

🕯	$145.00
🐟	$135.00
✝	$125.00
🕊	$115.00
🌿	$105.00
🌲	$95.00

Retired 1987, Issue Price $27.00, '82

Purchased_____, Price $_____

☑ *O Come All Ye Faithful*, E-2352 (Musical)

Unmarked	$200.00
🕯	$165.00
🐟	$155.00
✝	$150.00

Suspended 1984, Issue Price $45.00, '82
Tune: "O Come All Ye Faithful"

Purchased_____, Price $_____

☑ *O Come All Ye Faithful*, E-2353

🕯	$105.00
🐟	$75.00
✝	$75.00
🕊	$75.00
✓ 🌿	$75.00

Retired 1986, Issue Price $27.50, '82

Purchased _32ᵒᵒ_, Price $ _75ᵒᵒ_

36   ♥ Loving ♥ Caring ♥ Sharing ♥

☐ *I'll Play My Drum For Him*, E-2355
(Musical)

🕯	$225.00
🐟	$205.00
✝	$200.00

Suspended 1984, Issue Price $45.00, '82
Tune: "Little Drummer Boy"

Purchased_____, Price $_____

☐ *I'll Play My Drum For Him*, E-2356

🕯	$125.00
🐟	$85.00
✝	$75.00
🕊	$65.00

Suspended 1985, Issue Price $30.00, '82

Purchased_____, Price $_____

☐ *I'll Play My Drum For Him*, E-2357
(Plate)

Unmarked $65.00

Dated Annual 1982, Issue Price $40.00, '82
Series: *The Joy Of Christmas* — First Issue

Purchased_____, Price $_____

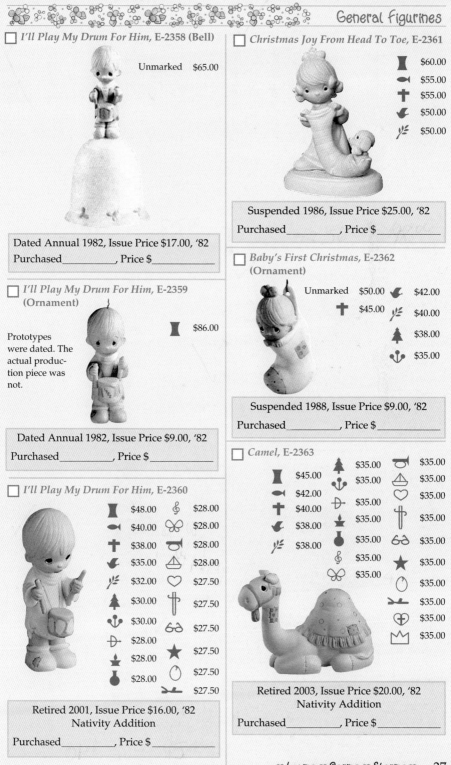

☐ *I'll Play My Drum For Him*, E-2358 (Bell)

Unmarked $65.00

Dated Annual 1982, Issue Price $17.00, '82
Purchased_____, Price $_____

☐ *I'll Play My Drum For Him*, E-2359
(Ornament)

Prototypes were dated. The actual production piece was not.

🛋 $86.00

Dated Annual 1982, Issue Price $9.00, '82
Purchased_____, Price $_____

☐ *I'll Play My Drum For Him*, E-2360

🛋 $48.00		🎵 $28.00
🐟 $40.00		🦋 $28.00
✝ $38.00		⬭ $28.00
🌿 $35.00		△ $28.00
🌿 $32.00		♡ $27.50
🌲 $30.00		🕇 $27.50
⚓ $30.00		👓 $27.50
⊶ $28.00		★ $27.50
☀ $28.00		◯ $27.50
● $28.00		⊱ $27.50

Retired 2001, Issue Price $16.00, '82
Nativity Addition
Purchased_____, Price $_____

☐ *Christmas Joy From Head To Toe*, E-2361

🛋	$60.00
🐟	$55.00
✝	$55.00
🌿	$50.00
🌿	$50.00

Suspended 1986, Issue Price $25.00, '82
Purchased_____, Price $_____

☐ *Baby's First Christmas*, E-2362
(Ornament)

Unmarked	$50.00	🐦	$42.00
	✝ $45.00	🌿	$40.00
		🌲	$38.00
		⚓	$35.00

Suspended 1988, Issue Price $9.00, '82
Purchased_____, Price $_____

☐ *Camel*, E-2363

🛋 $45.00	🌲 $35.00	⊶ $35.00
🐟 $42.00	⚓ $35.00	△ $35.00
✝ $40.00	⊶ $35.00	♡ $35.00
🌿 $38.00	☀ $35.00	🕇 $35.00
🌿 $38.00	● $35.00	👓 $35.00
🎵 $35.00		★ $35.00
🦋 $35.00		◯ $35.00
		⊱ $35.00
		⊕ $35.00
		♛ $35.00

Retired 2003, Issue Price $20.00, '82
Nativity Addition
Purchased_____, Price $_____

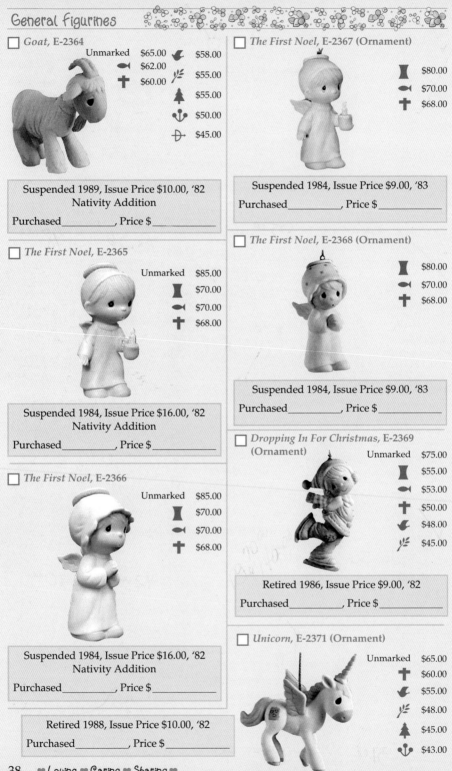

Goat, E-2364

Unmarked	$65.00
🕊	$58.00
✚	$62.00
✝	$60.00
🌿	$55.00
🌲	$55.00
⚓	$50.00
⊕	$45.00

Suspended 1989, Issue Price $10.00, '82
Nativity Addition

Purchased_____, Price $_____

The First Noel, E-2365

Unmarked	$85.00
■	$70.00
🐟	$70.00
✝	$68.00

Suspended 1984, Issue Price $16.00, '82
Nativity Addition

Purchased_____, Price $_____

The First Noel, E-2366

Unmarked	$85.00
■	$70.00
🐟	$70.00
✝	$68.00

Suspended 1984, Issue Price $16.00, '82
Nativity Addition

Purchased_____, Price $_____

Retired 1988, Issue Price $10.00, '82

Purchased_____, Price $_____

The First Noel, E-2367 (Ornament)

■	$80.00
🐟	$70.00
✝	$68.00

Suspended 1984, Issue Price $9.00, '83

Purchased_____, Price $_____

The First Noel, E-2368 (Ornament)

■	$80.00
🐟	$70.00
✝	$68.00

Suspended 1984, Issue Price $9.00, '83

Purchased_____, Price $_____

Dropping In For Christmas, E-2369 (Ornament)

Unmarked	$75.00
■	$55.00
🐟	$53.00
✝	$50.00
🍃	$48.00
🌿	$45.00

Retired 1986, Issue Price $9.00, '82

Purchased_____, Price $_____

Unicorn, E-2371 (Ornament)

Unmarked	$65.00
✝	$60.00
🕊	$55.00
🌿	$48.00
🌲	$45.00
⚓	$43.00

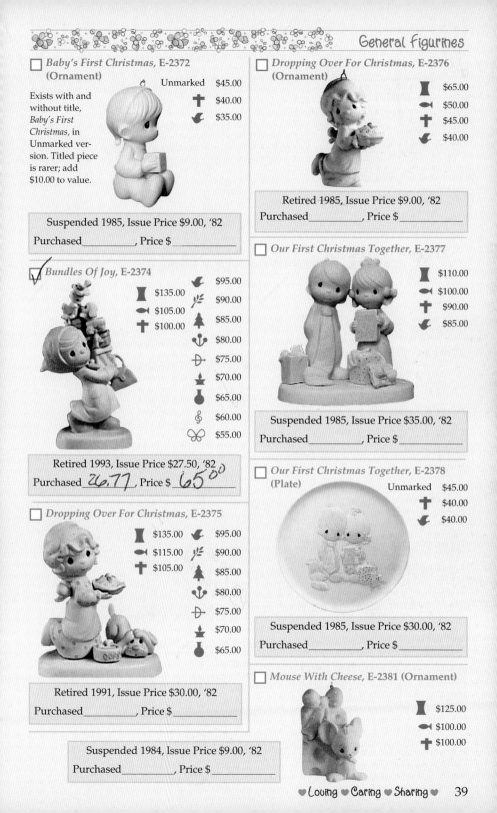

□ *Baby's First Christmas*, E-2372
(Ornament)

Exists with and without title, *Baby's First Christmas*, in Unmarked version. Titled piece is rarer; add $10.00 to value.

	Unmarked	$45.00
✝		$40.00
⚓		$35.00

Suspended 1985, Issue Price $9.00, '82

Purchased_____, Price $_____

☑ *Bundles Of Joy*, E-2374

❙	$135.00	⚓	$95.00
🐟	$105.00	🌿	$90.00
✝	$100.00	🌲	$85.00
		⚓	$80.00
		⊅	$75.00
		⚱	$70.00
		⬥	$65.00
		𝄞	$60.00
		🦋	$55.00

Retired 1993, Issue Price $27.50, '82

Purchased _26.77_, Price $ _65.00_

□ *Dropping Over For Christmas*, E-2375

❙	$135.00	⚓	$95.00
🐟	$115.00	🌿	$90.00
✝	$105.00	🌲	$85.00
		⚓	$80.00
		⊅	$75.00
		⚱	$70.00
		⬥	$65.00

Retired 1991, Issue Price $30.00, '82

Purchased_____, Price $_____

□ *Dropping Over For Christmas*, E-2376
(Ornament)

❙		$65.00
🐟		$50.00
✝		$45.00
⚓		$40.00

Retired 1985, Issue Price $9.00, '82

Purchased_____, Price $_____

□ *Our First Christmas Together*, E-2377

❙		$110.00
🐟		$100.00
✝		$90.00
⚓		$85.00

Suspended 1985, Issue Price $35.00, '82

Purchased_____, Price $_____

□ *Our First Christmas Together*, E-2378
(Plate)

	Unmarked	$45.00
✝		$40.00
⚓		$40.00

Suspended 1985, Issue Price $30.00, '82

Purchased_____, Price $_____

□ *Mouse With Cheese*, E-2381 (Ornament)

❙		$125.00
🐟		$100.00
✝		$100.00

Suspended 1984, Issue Price $9.00, '82

Purchased_____, Price $_____

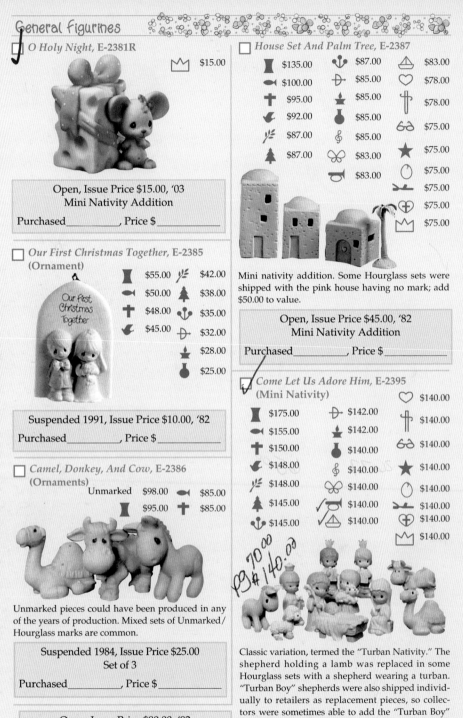

☑ O Holy Night, E-2381R

[crown] $15.00

> Open, Issue Price $15.00, '03
> Mini Nativity Addition
>
> Purchased_____, Price $_____

☐ Our First Christmas Together, E-2385 (Ornament)

Mark	Price	Mark	Price
[bar]	$55.00	[leaf]	$42.00
[fish]	$50.00	[tree]	$38.00
[cross]	$48.00	[anchor]	$35.00
[flower]	$45.00	[D]	$32.00
[flame]	$28.00		
[bulb]	$25.00		

> Suspended 1991, Issue Price $10.00, '82
>
> Purchased_____, Price $_____

☐ Camel, Donkey, And Cow, E-2386 (Ornaments)

Mark	Price	Mark	Price
Unmarked	$98.00	[fish]	$85.00
[bar]	$95.00	[cross]	$85.00

Unmarked pieces could have been produced in any of the years of production. Mixed sets of Unmarked/Hourglass marks are common.

> Suspended 1984, Issue Price $25.00
> Set of 3
>
> Purchased_____, Price $_____

> Open, Issue Price $80.00, '82
> Set of 11
>
> Purchased_____, Price $_____

☐ House Set And Palm Tree, E-2387

Mark	Price	Mark	Price	Mark	Price
[bar]	$135.00	[anchor]	$87.00	[sailboat]	$83.00
[fish]	$100.00	[D]	$85.00	[heart]	$78.00
[cross]	$95.00	[flame]	$85.00	[dagger]	$78.00
[flower]	$92.00	[bulb]	$85.00	[glasses]	$75.00
[leaf]	$87.00	[clef]	$85.00	[star]	$75.00
[tree]	$87.00	[butterfly]	$83.00	[oval]	$75.00
		[trumpet]	$83.00	[arrow]	$75.00
				[cross-circle]	$75.00
				[crown]	$75.00

Mini nativity addition. Some Hourglass sets were shipped with the pink house having no mark; add $50.00 to value.

> Open, Issue Price $45.00, '82
> Mini Nativity Addition
>
> Purchased_____, Price $_____

☑ Come Let Us Adore Him, E-2395 (Mini Nativity)

Mark	Price	Mark	Price	Mark	Price
[bar]	$175.00	[D]	$142.00	[heart]	$140.00
[fish]	$155.00	[flame]	$142.00	[cross]	$140.00
[cross]	$150.00	[bulb]	$140.00	[glasses]	$140.00
[flower]	$148.00	[clef]	$140.00	[star]	$140.00
[leaf]	$148.00	[butterfly]	$140.00	[oval]	$140.00
[tree]	$145.00	[trumpet]	$140.00	[arrow]	$140.00
[anchor]	$145.00	[triangle]	$140.00	[cross-circle]	$140.00
				[crown]	$140.00

[handwritten: $70.00 / $140.00]

Classic variation, termed the "Turban Nativity." The shepherd holding a lamb was replaced in some Hourglass sets with a shepherd wearing a turban. "Turban Boy" shepherds were also shipped individually to retailers as replacement pieces, so collectors were sometimes able to add the "Turban Boy" as a twelfth piece to this 11-piece mini nativity set. For the "Turban Nativity" the value is $225.00. The individual "Turban Boy" piece is valued at $95.00. Add $95.00 to the value of the mini nativity if the "Turban Boy" is added as a twelfth piece.

☐ *Come Let Us Adore Him*, E-2800 (Nativity)

Unmarked $200.00 ⚒ $170.00 ✝ $160.00
▲ $185.00 ◄ $165.00 🕊 $155.00

This set was re-sculpted; the new version is #104000.

Discontinued, Issue Price $60.00, '80
Set of 9

Purchased_____, Price $_____

☐ *Jesus Is Born*, E-2801

Unmarked $375.00
▲ $350.00
⚒ $325.00
◄ $300.00
✝ $300.00

Suspended 1984, Issue Price $37.50, '80
Purchased_____, Price $_____

☐ *Christmas Is A Time To Share*, E-2802

Unmarked $120.00
▲ $100.00
⚒ $85.00
◄ $80.00
✝ $75.00
🕊 $75.00

Piece was Suspended in 1984, yet exists with the 1985 Dove annual production symbol.

Suspended 1984, Issue Price $20.00, '80
Purchased_____, Price $_____

☐ *Crown Him Lord Of All*, E-2803

Unmarked $95.00
▲ $90.00
⚒ $85.00
◄ $85.00
✝ $80.00
🕊 $80.00

Piece was suspended in 1984, yet exists with the 1985 Dove annual production symbol.

Suspended 1984, Issue Price $20.00, '80
Purchased_____, Price $_____

☑ *Peace On Earth*, E-2804

Unmarked $155.00
▲ $135.00
⚒ $135.00
◄ $125.00
✝ $120.00

Suspended 1984, Reintroduced 1999,
Retired 1999, Issue Price $20.00, '80
Purchased_____, Price $ 135 00

☐ *Peace On Earth*, E-2804R

★ $50.00

This is a revision of E-2804 of the boy angel on globe with teddy bear, which was Suspended in 1984. This version features a girl angel with a cat. The globe also sits square on the base instead of being tilted.

Retired 1999, Issue Price $50.00, '99
Catalog Exclusive

Purchased_____, Price $_____

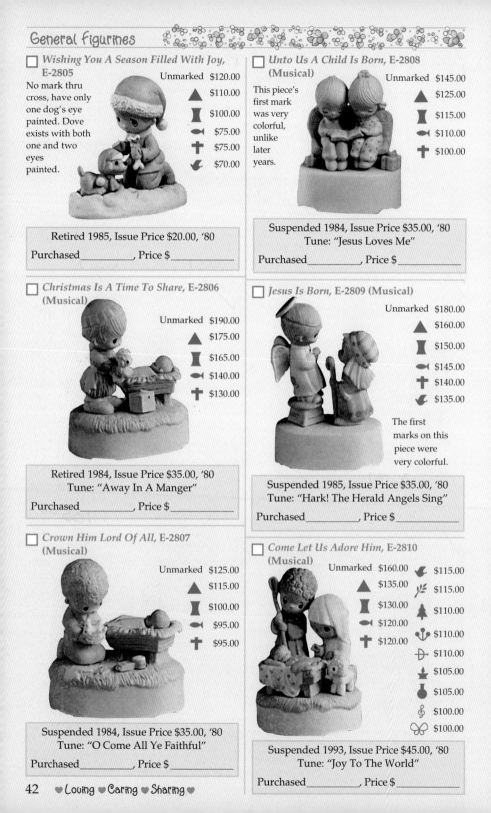

☐ *Wishing You A Season Filled With Joy,* E-2805

No mark thru cross, have only one dog's eye painted. Dove exists with both one and two eyes painted.

Unmarked	$120.00
▲	$110.00
▐	$100.00
◄	$75.00
✝	$75.00
◢	$70.00

Retired 1985, Issue Price $20.00, '80

Purchased_____, Price $_____

☐ *Christmas Is A Time To Share,* E-2806 (Musical)

Unmarked	$190.00
▲	$175.00
▐	$165.00
◄	$140.00
✝	$130.00

Retired 1984, Issue Price $35.00, '80
Tune: "Away In A Manger"

Purchased_____, Price $_____

☐ *Crown Him Lord Of All,* E-2807 (Musical)

Unmarked	$125.00
▲	$115.00
▐	$100.00
◄	$95.00
✝	$95.00

Suspended 1984, Issue Price $35.00, '80
Tune: "O Come All Ye Faithful"

Purchased_____, Price $_____

☐ *Unto Us A Child Is Born,* E-2808 (Musical)

This piece's first mark was very colorful, unlike later years.

Unmarked	$145.00
▲	$125.00
▐	$115.00
◄	$110.00
✝	$100.00

Suspended 1984, Issue Price $35.00, '80
Tune: "Jesus Loves Me"

Purchased_____, Price $_____

☐ *Jesus Is Born,* E-2809 (Musical)

Unmarked	$180.00
▲	$160.00
▐	$150.00
◄	$145.00
✝	$140.00
◢	$135.00

The first marks on this piece were very colorful.

Suspended 1985, Issue Price $35.00, '80
Tune: "Hark! The Herald Angels Sing"

Purchased_____, Price $_____

☐ *Come Let Us Adore Him,* E-2810 (Musical)

Unmarked	$160.00	◢	$115.00
▲	$135.00	⅍	$115.00
▐	$130.00	♠	$110.00
◄	$120.00	⚓	$110.00
✝	$120.00	Ð	$110.00
		⚜	$105.00
		♦	$105.00
		§	$100.00
		∞	$100.00

Suspended 1993, Issue Price $45.00, '80
Tune: "Joy To The World"

Purchased_____, Price $_____

☑ You Have Touched So Many Hearts, E-2821

🐟	$75.00	⚓	$43.00
✝	$68.00	⚓	$43.00
🕊	$45.00	⌐	$40.00
🌿	$45.00	🔔	$40.00
		🔔	$40.00
		ℰ	$40.00
		🦋	$40.00
		⊐	$40.00
		△	$40.00
		♡	$40.00

Suspended 1996, Issue Price $25.00, '84

Purchased _9.99_, Price $ _75 00_

☐ This Is Your Day To Shine, E-2822

🐟	$155.00
✝	$105.00
🕊	$95.00
🌿	$90.00
🌲	$80.00
⚓	$79.00

Retired 1988, Issue Price $37.50, '84

Purchased _____, Price $ _____

☐ To God Be The Glory, E-2823

🐟	$125.00
✝	$85.00
🕊	$85.00
🌿	$85.00
🌲	$80.00

Suspended 1987, Issue Price $40.00, '84

Purchased _____, Price $ _____

☐ To God Be The Glory, E-2823R

◯	$50.00

The frame was changed to gold and the flowers were changed to roses.

Limited To One Day Only, Issue Price $45.00, '00

Purchased _____, Price $ _____

☐ To A Very Special Mom, E-2824

✝	$53.00	⊐	$40.00
🕊	$49.00	△	$40.00
🌿	$47.00	♡	$40.00
🌲	$45.00	⍦	$40.00
⚓	$42.00	👓	$40.00
⌐	$42.00	★	$40.00
🔔	$42.00	◯	$40.00
🔔	$40.00	⟫	$40.00
ℰ	$40.00	⊕	$40.00
🦋	$40.00	👑	$40.00

This is a popular piece for Mother's Day.

Retired 2003, Issue Price $27.50, '84

Purchased _____, Price $ _____

☐ To A Very Special Sister, E-2825

✝	$75.00	🌲	$55.00	ℰ	$52.00
🕊	$60.00	⚓	$55.00	🦋	$50.00
🌿	$58.00	⌐	$52.00	⊐	$50.00
		🔔	$52.00	△	$50.00
		🔔	$52.00	♡	$50.00
				⍦	$50.00
				👓	$50.00
				★	$50.00
				◯	$50.00
				⟫	$50.00

Retired 2001, Issue Price $37.50, '84

Purchased _____, Price $ _____

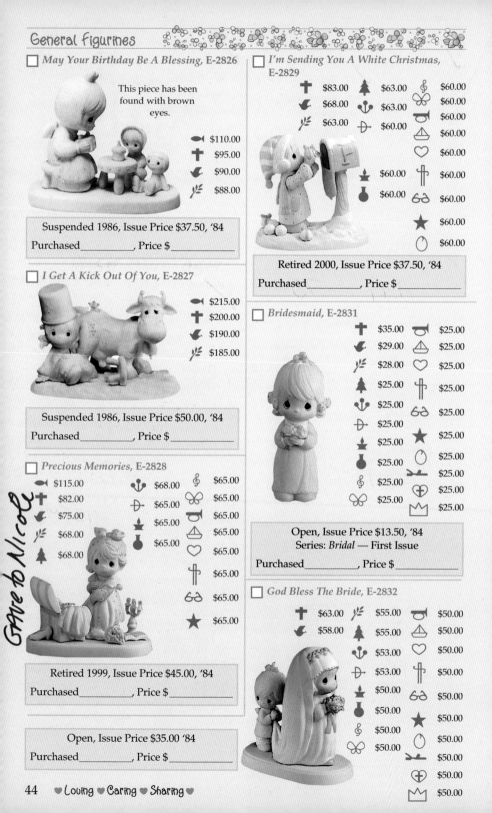

☐ *May Your Birthday Be A Blessing*, E-2826

This piece has been found with brown eyes.

🐟	$110.00
✝	$95.00
🕊	$90.00
🌿	$88.00

Suspended 1986, Issue Price $37.50, '84

Purchased_____, Price $_____

☐ *I Get A Kick Out Of You*, E-2827

🐟	$215.00
✝	$200.00
🕊	$190.00
🌿	$185.00

Suspended 1986, Issue Price $50.00, '84

Purchased_____, Price $_____

☐ *Precious Memories*, E-2828

🐟 $115.00	⚓ $68.00	🎵 $65.00	
✝ $82.00	D $65.00	🦋 $65.00	
🕊 $75.00	⚗ $65.00	🎺 $65.00	
🌿 $68.00	🍶 $65.00	△ $65.00	
❄ $68.00		♡ $65.00	
		✝ $65.00	
		👓 $65.00	
		★ $65.00	

Retired 1999, Issue Price $45.00, '84

Purchased_____, Price $_____

Open, Issue Price $35.00 '84

Purchased_____, Price $_____

(handwritten in left margin) Gave to Nicole

☐ *I'm Sending You A White Christmas*, E-2829

✝	$83.00	🌲	$63.00	🎵	$60.00
🕊	$68.00	⚓	$63.00	🦋	$60.00
🌿	$63.00	D	$60.00	🎺	$60.00
				△	$60.00
				♡	$60.00
⚗	$60.00			✝	$60.00
🍶	$60.00			👓	$60.00
				★	$60.00
				○	$60.00

Retired 2000, Issue Price $37.50, '84

Purchased_____, Price $_____

☐ *Bridesmaid*, E-2831

✝	$35.00	🎺	$25.00
🕊	$29.00	△	$25.00
🌿	$28.00	♡	$25.00
🌲	$25.00	✝	$25.00
⚓	$25.00	👓	$25.00
D	$25.00	★	$25.00
⚗	$25.00	○	$25.00
🍶	$25.00	🏹	$25.00
🎵	$25.00	⊕	$25.00
🦋	$25.00	👑	$25.00

Open, Issue Price $13.50, '84
Series: *Bridal* — First Issue

Purchased_____, Price $_____

☐ *God Bless The Bride*, E-2832

✝	$63.00	🌿	$55.00	🎺	$50.00
🕊	$58.00	🌲	$55.00	△	$50.00
		⚓	$53.00	♡	$50.00
		D	$53.00	✝	$50.00
		⚗	$50.00	👓	$50.00
		🍶	$50.00	★	$50.00
		🎵	$50.00	○	$50.00
		🦋	$50.00	🏹	$50.00
				⊕	$50.00
				👑	$50.00

Ring Bearer, E-2833

Symbol	Price	Symbol	Price	Symbol	Price
(dove)	$25.00	(leaf)	$19.00	(sailboat)	$18.50
		(tree)	$19.00	(heart)	$18.50
		(anchor)	$19.00	(cross)	$18.50
		(bow & arrow)	$18.50		
		(candle)	$18.50	(eyeglasses)	$18.50
		(flower)	$18.50	(star)	$18.50
		(clef)	$18.50	(egg)	$18.50
		(butterfly)	$18.50	(sword)	$18.50

Retired 2003, Issue Price $11.00, '85
Series: *Bridal* — Fourth Issue

Purchased_____, Price $_____

Sharing Our Joy Together, E-2834

Symbol	Price
(leaf)	$68.00
(tree)	$58.00
(anchor)	$55.00
(bow & arrow)	$52.00
(candle)	$47.00
(flower)	$43.00

Suspended 1991, Issue Price $31.00, '86

Purchased_____, Price $_____

Flower Girl, E-2835

Symbol	Price	Symbol	Price	Symbol	Price
(dove)	$25.00	(tree)	$19.00	(sailboat)	$18.50
(leaf)	$19.00	(anchor)	$19.00	(heart)	$18.50
		(bow & arrow)	$18.50	(cross)	$18.50
		(candle)	$18.50	(eyeglasses)	$18.50
		(flower)	$18.50	(star)	$18.50
		(clef)	$18.50	(egg)	$18.50
		(butterfly)	$18.50	(sword)	$18.50
		(trumpet)	$18.50	(cross+heart)	$18.00
				(crown)	$18.00

Open, Issue Price $11.00, '85
Series: *Bridal* — Third Issue

Purchased_____, Price $_____

Best Man, E-2836

Symbol	Price	Symbol	Price	Symbol	Price
(cross)	$30.00	(leaf)	$28.00	(sailboat)	$25.00
(dove)	$28.00	(tree)	$25.00	(heart)	$25.00
		(anchor)	$25.00	(cross)	$25.00
		(bow & arrow)	$25.00	(eyeglasses)	$25.00
		(candle)	$25.00	(star)	$25.00
		(flower)	$25.00	(egg)	$25.00
		(clef)	$25.00	(sword)	$25.00
		(butterfly)	$25.00	(cross+heart)	$25.00
		(trumpet)	$25.00	(crown)	$25.00

Open, Issue Price $13.50, '84
Series: *Bridal* — Third Issue

Purchased_____, Price $_____

Groom, E-2837

Symbol	Price	Symbol	Price
		(sailboat)	$27.50
(leaf)	$35.00	(heart)	$27.50
(tree)	$33.00	(cross)	$27.50
(anchor)	$30.00		
(bow & arrow)	$30.00	(eyeglasses)	$27.50
(candle)	$27.50	(star)	$27.50
(flower)	$27.50	(egg)	$27.50
(clef)	$27.50	(sword)	$27.50
(butterfly)	$27.50	(cross+heart)	$27.50
(trumpet)	$27.50	(crown)	$27.50

Termed the "No Hands Groom" during the first year of production (Olive Branch), this piece was first produced with no hands. The mold was changed for the subsequent years (Cedar Tree to present) to show the boy's hands.

Open, Issue Price $15.00, '86
Series: *Bridal* — Sixth Issue

Purchased_____, Price $_____

This Is the Day Which The Lord Hath Made, E-2838

Symbol	Price
(tree)	$235.00

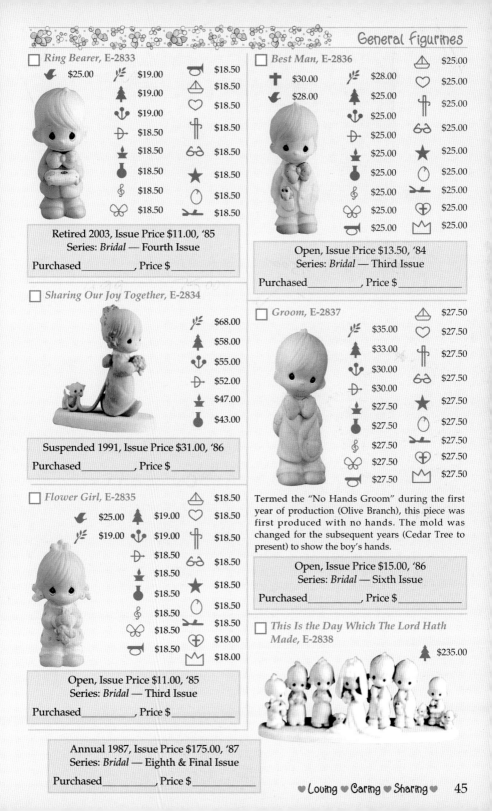

Annual 1987, Issue Price $175.00, '87
Series: *Bridal* — Eighth & Final Issue

Purchased_____, Price $_____

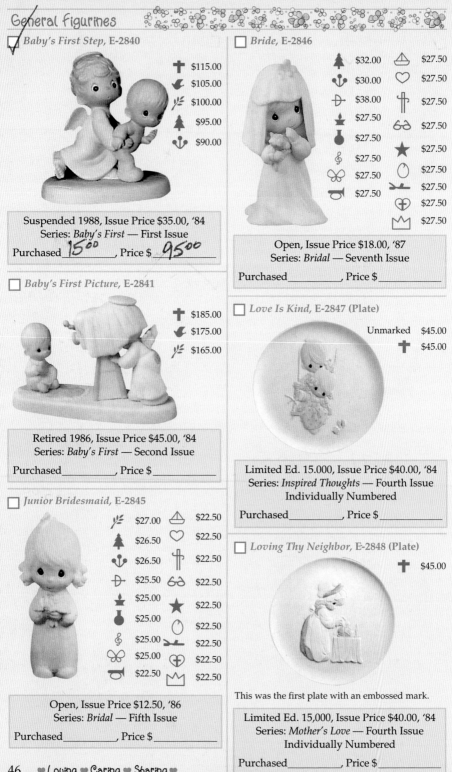

Baby's First Step, E-2840

✝	$115.00
🕊	$105.00
🌿	$100.00
🌲	$95.00
⚓	$90.00

Suspended 1988, Issue Price $35.00, '84
Series: *Baby's First* — First Issue
Purchased _15ºº_, Price $ _95ºº_

Baby's First Picture, E-2841

✝	$185.00
🕊	$175.00
🌿	$165.00

Retired 1986, Issue Price $45.00, '84
Series: *Baby's First* — Second Issue
Purchased _____, Price $ _____

Junior Bridesmaid, E-2845

🌿	$27.00	△	$22.50
🌲	$26.50	♡	$22.50
⚓	$26.50	✝	$22.50
⤵	$25.50	👓	$22.50
🕯	$25.00	★	$22.50
🔔	$25.00	○	$22.50
𝄞	$25.00	⤶	$22.50
🦋	$25.00	⊕	$22.50
⌒	$22.50	👑	$22.50

Open, Issue Price $12.50, '86
Series: *Bridal* — Fifth Issue
Purchased _____, Price $ _____

Bride, E-2846

🌲	$32.00	△	$27.50
⚓	$30.00	♡	$27.50
⤵	$38.00	✝	$27.50
🕯	$27.50	👓	$27.50
🔔	$27.50	★	$27.50
𝄞	$27.50	○	$27.50
🦋	$27.50	⤶	$27.50
⌒	$27.50	⊕	$27.50
		👑	$27.50

Open, Issue Price $18.00, '87
Series: *Bridal* — Seventh Issue
Purchased _____, Price $ _____

Love Is Kind, E-2847 (Plate)

Unmarked	$45.00
✝	$45.00

Limited Ed. 15,000, Issue Price $40.00, '84
Series: *Inspired Thoughts* — Fourth Issue
Individually Numbered
Purchased _____, Price $ _____

Loving Thy Neighbor, E-2848 (Plate)

✝	$45.00

This was the first plate with an embossed mark.

Limited Ed. 15,000, Issue Price $40.00, '84
Series: *Mother's Love* — Fourth Issue
Individually Numbered
Purchased _____, Price $ _____

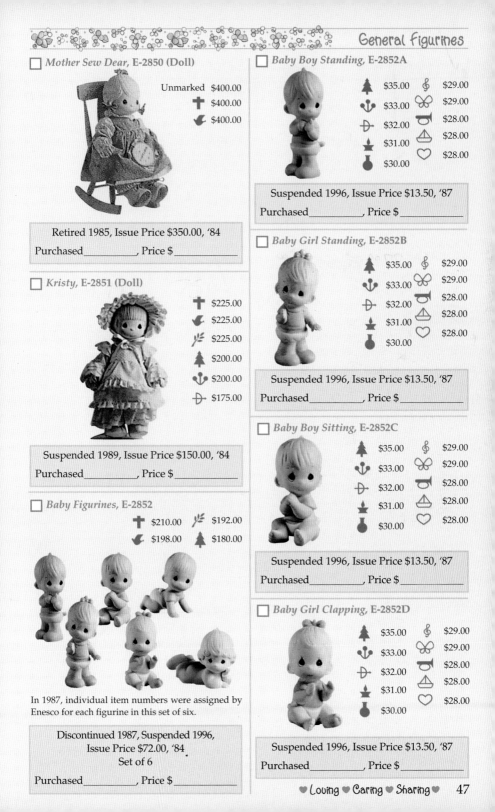

☐ *Mother Sew Dear*, E-2850 (Doll)

Unmarked $400.00
✝ $400.00
🕊 $400.00

Retired 1985, Issue Price $350.00, '84
Purchased_____, Price $_____

☐ *Kristy*, E-2851 (Doll)

✝ $225.00
🕊 $225.00
🌿 $225.00
🌲 $200.00
⚓ $200.00
🔔 $175.00

Suspended 1989, Issue Price $150.00, '84
Purchased_____, Price $_____

☐ *Baby Figurines*, E-2852

✝ $210.00   🌿 $192.00
🕊 $198.00   🌲 $180.00

In 1987, individual item numbers were assigned by Enesco for each figurine in this set of six.

Discontinued 1987, Suspended 1996,
Issue Price $72.00, '84
Set of 6
Purchased_____, Price $_____

☐ *Baby Boy Standing*, E-2852A

🌲 $35.00   𝄞 $29.00
⚓ $33.00   🦋 $29.00
🔱 $32.00   ⬧ $28.00
🏵 $31.00   △ $28.00
🔔 $30.00   ♡ $28.00

Suspended 1996, Issue Price $13.50, '87
Purchased_____, Price $_____

☐ *Baby Girl Standing*, E-2852B

🌲 $35.00   𝄞 $29.00
⚓ $33.00   🦋 $29.00
🔱 $32.00   ⬧ $28.00
🏵 $31.00   △ $28.00
🔔 $30.00   ♡ $28.00

Suspended 1996, Issue Price $13.50, '87
Purchased_____, Price $_____

☐ *Baby Boy Sitting*, E-2852C

🌲 $35.00   𝄞 $29.00
⚓ $33.00   🦋 $29.00
🔱 $32.00   ⬧ $28.00
🏵 $31.00   △ $28.00
🔔 $30.00   ♡ $28.00

Suspended 1996, Issue Price $13.50, '87
Purchased_____, Price $_____

☐ *Baby Girl Clapping*, E-2852D

🌲 $35.00   𝄞 $29.00
⚓ $33.00   🦋 $29.00
🔱 $32.00   ⬧ $28.00
🏵 $31.00   △ $28.00
🔔 $30.00   ♡ $28.00

Suspended 1996, Issue Price $13.50, '87
Purchased_____, Price $_____

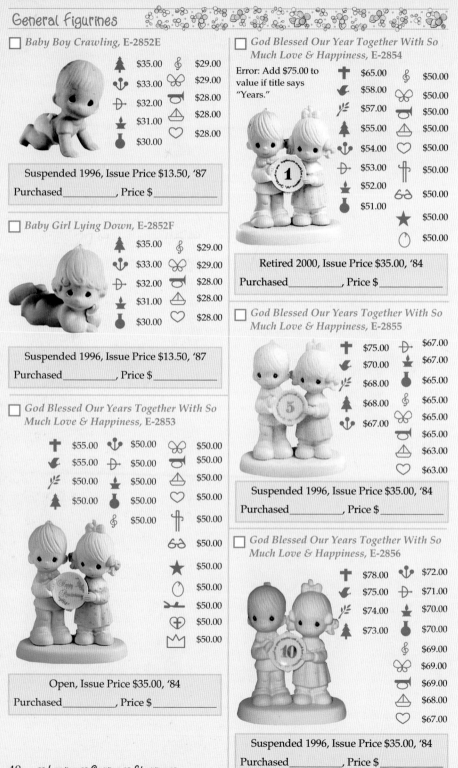

Baby Boy Crawling, E-2852E

♠	$35.00	♪	$29.00
⚓	$33.00	🦋	$29.00
⋺	$32.00	📯	$28.00
♠	$31.00	△	$28.00
♦	$30.00	♡	$28.00

Suspended 1996, Issue Price $13.50, '87

Purchased_____, Price $_____

Baby Girl Lying Down, E-2852F

♠	$35.00	♪	$29.00
⚓	$33.00	🦋	$29.00
⋺	$32.00	📯	$28.00
♠	$31.00	△	$28.00
♦	$30.00	♡	$28.00

Suspended 1996, Issue Price $13.50, '87

Purchased_____, Price $_____

God Blessed Our Years Together With So Much Love & Happiness, E-2853

✝	$55.00	⚓	$50.00
🕊	$55.00	⋺	$50.00
🌿	$50.00	♠	$50.00
♠	$50.00	♦	$50.00
♪	$50.00		
🦋	$50.00		
📯	$50.00		
△	$50.00		
♡	$50.00		
🕆	$50.00		
6ə	$50.00		
★	$50.00		
◯	$50.00		
⊁	$50.00		
⊕	$50.00		
♕	$50.00		

Open, Issue Price $35.00, '84

Purchased_____, Price $_____

God Blessed Our Year Together With So Much Love & Happiness, E-2854

Error: Add $75.00 to value if title says "Years."

✝	$65.00	♪	$50.00
🕊	$58.00	🦋	$50.00
🌿	$57.00	📯	$50.00
♠	$55.00	△	$50.00
⚓	$54.00	♡	$50.00
⋺	$53.00	🕆	$50.00
♠	$52.00	6ə	$50.00
♦	$51.00		
★	$50.00		
◯	$50.00		

Retired 2000, Issue Price $35.00, '84

Purchased_____, Price $_____

God Blessed Our Years Together With So Much Love & Happiness, E-2855

✝	$75.00	⋺	$67.00
🕊	$70.00	♠	$67.00
🌿	$68.00	♦	$65.00
♠	$68.00	♪	$65.00
⚓	$67.00	🦋	$65.00
		📯	$65.00
		△	$63.00
		♡	$63.00

Suspended 1996, Issue Price $35.00, '84

Purchased_____, Price $_____

God Blessed Our Years Together With So Much Love & Happiness, E-2856

✝	$78.00	⚓	$72.00
🕊	$75.00	⋺	$71.00
🌿	$74.00	♠	$70.00
♠	$73.00	♦	$70.00
		♪	$69.00
		🦋	$69.00
		📯	$69.00
		△	$68.00
		♡	$67.00

Suspended 1996, Issue Price $35.00, '84

Purchased_____, Price $_____

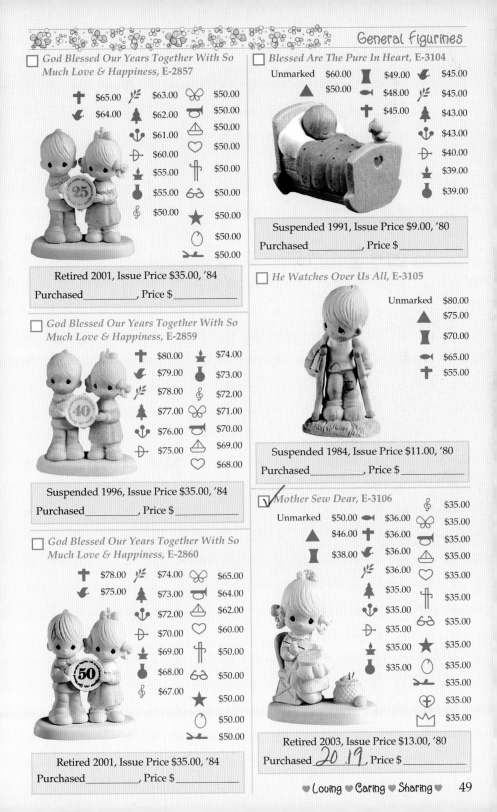

God Blessed Our Years Together With So Much Love & Happiness, E-2857

✝	$65.00	🌿	$63.00	🦋	$50.00
🕊	$64.00	🌲	$62.00	📯	$50.00
		⚓	$61.00	⛵	$50.00
		⋺	$60.00	♡	$50.00
		🕯	$55.00	✝	$50.00
		⚲	$55.00	👓	$50.00
		𝄞	$50.00	★	$50.00
				◯	$50.00
				✂	$50.00

Retired 2001, Issue Price $35.00, '84

Purchased_____, Price $_____

God Blessed Our Years Together With So Much Love & Happiness, E-2859

✝	$80.00	⚲	$74.00
🕊	$79.00	🕯	$73.00
🌿	$78.00	𝄞	$72.00
🌲	$77.00	🦋	$71.00
⚓	$76.00	📯	$70.00
⋺	$75.00	⛵	$69.00
		♡	$68.00

Suspended 1996, Issue Price $35.00, '84

Purchased_____, Price $_____

God Blessed Our Years Together With So Much Love & Happiness, E-2860

✝	$78.00	🌿	$74.00	👓	$65.00
🕊	$75.00	🌲	$73.00	📯	$64.00
		⚓	$72.00	⛵	$62.00
		⋺	$70.00	♡	$60.00
		🕯	$69.00	✝	$50.00
		⚲	$68.00	👓	$50.00
		𝄞	$67.00	★	$50.00
				◯	$50.00
				✂	$50.00

Retired 2001, Issue Price $35.00, '84

Purchased_____, Price $_____

Blessed Are The Pure In Heart, E-3104

Unmarked	$60.00	⚲	$49.00	🕊	$45.00
▲	$50.00	🐟	$48.00	🌿	$45.00
		✝	$45.00	🌲	$43.00
				⚓	$43.00
				⋺	$40.00
				🕯	$39.00
				⚲	$39.00

Suspended 1991, Issue Price $9.00, '80

Purchased_____, Price $_____

He Watches Over Us All, E-3105

Unmarked	$80.00
▲	$75.00
⚲	$70.00
🐟	$65.00
✝	$55.00

Suspended 1984, Issue Price $11.00, '80

Purchased_____, Price $_____

Mother Sew Dear, E-3106

				𝄞	$35.00
Unmarked	$50.00	🐟	$36.00	👓	$35.00
▲	$46.00	✝	$36.00	📯	$35.00
⚲	$38.00	🕊	$36.00	⛵	$35.00
		🌿	$36.00	♡	$35.00
		🌲	$35.00	✝	$35.00
		⚓	$35.00	👓	$35.00
		⋺	$35.00	★	$35.00
		🕯	$35.00	◯	$35.00
		⚲	$35.00	✂	$35.00
				⊕	$35.00
				👑	$35.00

Retired 2003, Issue Price $13.00, '80

Purchased _20_ _19_, Price $_____

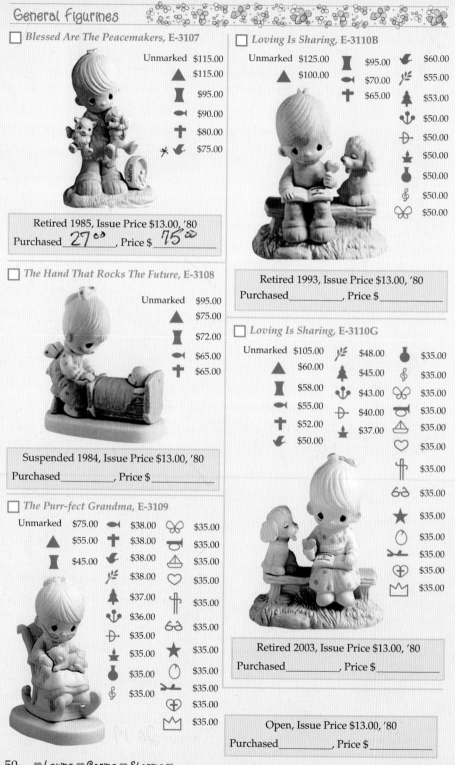

General Figurines

☐ *Blessed Are The Peacemakers*, E-3107

Unmarked	$115.00
▲	$115.00
工	$95.00
⊷	$90.00
✝	$80.00
✳ ⬌	$75.00

Retired 1985, Issue Price $13.00, '80

Purchased ___27°°___, Price $ ___75°°___

☐ *The Hand That Rocks The Future*, E-3108

Unmarked	$95.00
▲	$75.00
工	$72.00
⊷	$65.00
✝	$65.00

Suspended 1984, Issue Price $13.00, '80

Purchased _____, Price $ _____

☐ *The Purr-fect Grandma*, E-3109

Unmarked	$75.00	⊷	$38.00	✖	$35.00
▲	$55.00	✝	$38.00	⬯	$35.00
工	$45.00	⬌	$38.00	△	$35.00
		ℐ	$38.00	♡	$35.00
		♠	$37.00	⯗	$35.00
		⚓	$36.00	✖	$35.00
		⌀	$35.00	★	$35.00
		⬧	$35.00	○	$35.00
		⬮	$35.00	⤷	$35.00
		♪	$35.00	⊕	$35.00
				♛	$35.00

☐ *Loving Is Sharing*, E-3110B

Unmarked	$125.00	工	$95.00	⬌	$60.00
▲	$100.00	⊷	$70.00	ℐ	$55.00
		✝	$65.00	♠	$53.00
				⚓	$50.00
				⬧	$50.00
				⯗	$50.00
				⬮	$50.00
				♪	$50.00
				✖	$50.00

Retired 1993, Issue Price $13.00, '80

Purchased _____, Price $ _____

☐ *Loving Is Sharing*, E-3110G

Unmarked	$105.00	ℐ	$48.00	⬮	$35.00
▲	$60.00	♠	$45.00	♪	$35.00
工	$58.00	⚓	$43.00	✖	$35.00
⊷	$55.00	⬧	$40.00	△	$35.00
✝	$52.00	⯗	$37.00	♡	$35.00
⬌	$50.00			✝	$35.00
				⤷	$35.00
				★	$35.00
				○	$35.00
				⤷	$35.00
				⊕	$35.00
				♛	$35.00

Retired 2003, Issue Price $13.00, '80

Purchased _____, Price $ _____

Open, Issue Price $13.00, '80

Purchased _____, Price $ _____

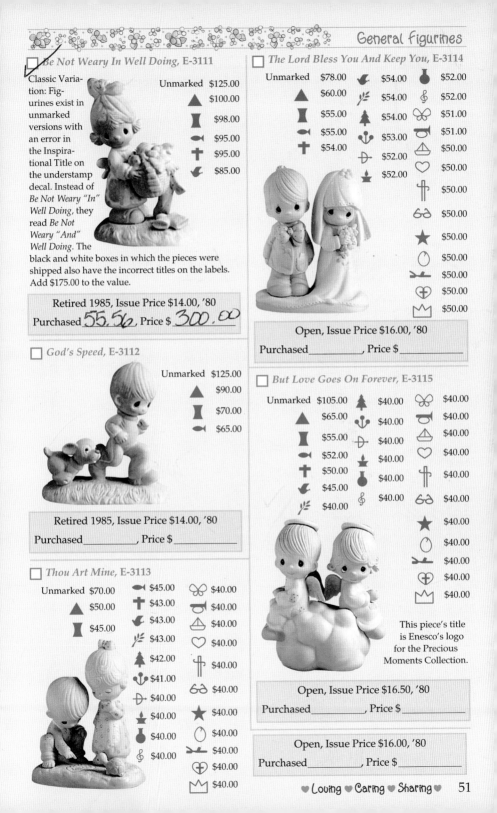

Be Not Weary In Well Doing, E-3111

Classic Variation: Figurines exist in unmarked versions with an error in the Inspirational Title on the understamp decal. Instead of *Be Not Weary "In" Well Doing*, they read *Be Not Weary "And" Well Doing*. The black and white boxes in which the pieces were shipped also have the incorrect titles on the labels. Add $175.00 to the value.

Unmarked	$125.00
▲	$100.00
I	$98.00
⤻	$95.00
†	$95.00
⌇	$85.00

Retired 1985, Issue Price $14.00, '80

Purchased 55.56, Price $ 300.00

God's Speed, E-3112

Unmarked	$125.00
▲	$90.00
I	$70.00
⤻	$65.00

Retired 1985, Issue Price $14.00, '80

Purchased_____, Price $_____

Thou Art Mine, E-3113

Unmarked	$70.00	⤻	$45.00	◇◇	$40.00
▲	$50.00	†	$43.00	⊐	$40.00
I	$45.00	⌇	$43.00	△	$40.00
		⁎⁄	$43.00	♡	$40.00
		🌲	$42.00	╫	$40.00
		⚓	$41.00	👓	$40.00
		⌀	$40.00	★	$40.00
		🕯	$40.00	◐	$40.00
		🔔	$40.00	⤛	$40.00
		𝄞	$40.00	✛	$40.00
				♛	$40.00

The Lord Bless You And Keep You, E-3114

Unmarked	$78.00	⌇	$54.00	🍶	$52.00
▲	$60.00	⁎⁄	$54.00	𝄞	$52.00
I	$55.00	🌲	$54.00	◇◇	$51.00
⤻	$55.00	⚓	$53.00	⊐	$51.00
†	$54.00	⌀	$52.00	△	$50.00
		🕯	$52.00	♡	$50.00
				╫	$50.00
				👓	$50.00
				★	$50.00
				◐	$50.00
				⤛	$50.00
				✛	$50.00
				♛	$50.00

Open, Issue Price $16.00, '80

Purchased_____, Price $_____

But Love Goes On Forever, E-3115

Unmarked	$105.00	🌲	$40.00	◇◇	$40.00
▲	$65.00	⚓	$40.00	⊐	$40.00
I	$55.00	⌀	$40.00	△	$40.00
⤻	$52.00	🕯	$40.00	♡	$40.00
†	$50.00	🔔	$40.00	╫	$40.00
⌇	$45.00	𝄞	$40.00	👓	$40.00
⁎⁄	$40.00			★	$40.00
				◐	$40.00
				⤛	$40.00
				✛	$40.00
				♛	$40.00

This piece's title is Enesco's logo for the Precious Moments Collection.

Open, Issue Price $16.50, '80

Purchased_____, Price $_____

Open, Issue Price $16.00, '80

Purchased_____, Price $_____

Thee I Love, E-3116

Unmarked $155.00	✶ $93.00	✝ $85.00
▲ $95.00	🐟 $90.00	⚓ $80.00
		❦ $78.00
		🌲 $75.00
		⚓ $73.00
		⊅ $70.00
		🕯 $68.00
		⚱ $68.00
		𝄞 $68.00
		❀ $65.00
		⌒ $65.00

This piece was dark and colorful during its first year of production.

Retired 1994, Issue Price $16.50, '80
Purchased_____, Price $_____

Walking By Faith, E-3117

Unmarked $125.00	✝ $100.00	⚱ $80.00
▲ $115.00	❦ $95.00	𝄞 $80.00
✶ $110.00	❦ $90.00	❀ $80.00
🐟 $105.00	🌲 $85.00	⌒ $80.00
	⚓ $80.00	⛵ $80.00
	⊅ $80.00	♡ $80.00
	🕯 $80.00	✝ $80.00
		👓 $80.00
		★ $80.00
		◯ $80.00

Retired 2000, Issue Price $35.00, '80
Purchased_____, Price $_____

Suspended 1986, Issue Price $13.00, '80
Purchased_____, Price $_____

Eggs Over Easy, E-3118

Unmarked	$135.00
▲	$105.00
✶	$85.00
🐟	$75.00

Some collectors have said the eggs are missing from their pieces.

Retired 1983, Issue Price $13.00, '80
Purchased_____, Price $_____

It's What's Inside That Counts, E-3119

Unmarked	$135.00
▲	$125.00
✶	$105.00
🐟	$100.00
✝	$95.00

Look for this piece with either the Triangle mark or Unmarked because of the darker colors.

Suspended 1984, Issue Price $13.00, '80
Purchased_____, Price $_____

To Thee With Love, E-3120

Unmarked	$90.00
▲	$65.00
✶	$63.00
🐟	$60.00
✝	$58.00
❦	$55.00
❦	$53.00
🌲	$50.00

Piece was Suspended in 1986, yet exists with the 1987 Cedar Tree annual production symbol.

☐ *The Lord Bless You And Keep You, E-4720*

	Unmarked	$42.50
▲		$40.00
⫞		$38.00
🐟		$35.00
✝		$34.00
🕊		$33.00
⸙		$32.00
🌲		$31.00

Suspended 1987, Issue Price $14.00, '81
Purchased_____, Price $_____

☐ *The Lord Bless You And Keep You, E-4721*

	Unmarked	$75.00			
▲		$50.00	✂		$35.00
⫞		$49.00	∞		$35.00
🐟		$48.00	⋈		$35.00
✝		$47.00	△		$35.00
🕊		$46.00	♡		$35.00
⸙		$45.00	⳨		$35.00
🌲		$44.00	👓		$35.00
⚓		$43.00	★		$35.00
⫟		$42.00	◯		$35.00
⚒		$41.00	⊶		$35.00
⚭		$40.00	⊕		$35.00
			♛		$35.00

Open, Issue Price $14.00, '81
Purchased_____, Price $_____

☐ *The Lord Bless You And Keep You, E-4721D*

◯	$35.00
⊶	$35.00
⊕	$35.00
♛	$35.00

Open, Issue Price $35.00, '00
Purchased_____, Price $_____

☑ *Love Cannot Break A True Friendship, E-4722*

	Unmarked	$140.00
▲		$130.00
⫞ ✗		$120.00
🐟		$105.00
✝		$98.00
🕊		$95.00

Suspended 1985, Issue Price $22.50, '81
Purchased _45.76_ Price $ _120.00_

☑ *Peace Amid The Storm, E-4723*

	Unmarked	$100.00
▲		$90.00
⫞		$75.00
🐟		$70.00
✝		$65.00

Suspended 1984, Issue Price $22.50, '81
Purchased _18.51_, Price $ _100.00_

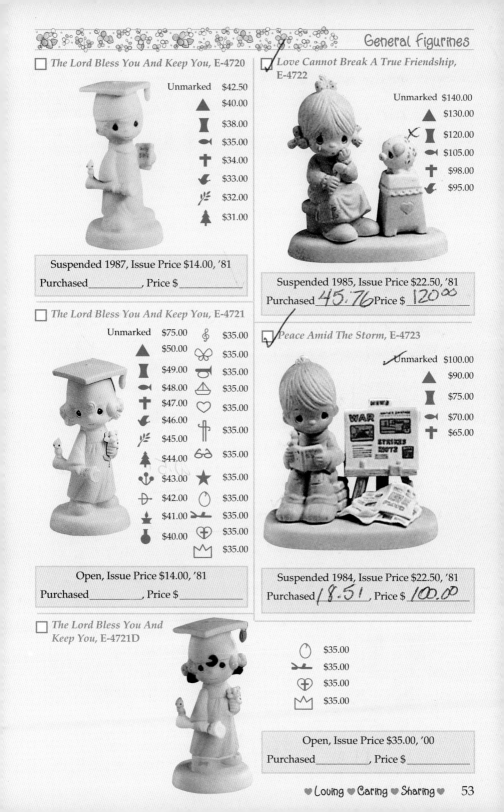

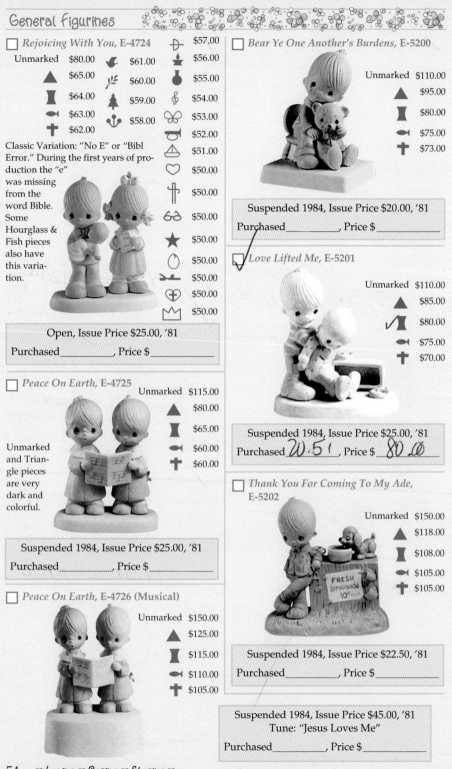

Rejoicing With You, E-4724

Unmarked	$80.00	🕯 $61.00	⚓	$57.00
▲	$65.00	🌿 $60.00		$56.00
I	$64.00	🌲 $59.00		$55.00
🐟	$63.00	⚓ $58.00		$54.00
✝	$62.00		🦋	$53.00
			📯	$52.00
			△	$51.00
			♡	$50.00
			✝	$50.00
			6∂	$50.00
			★	$50.00
			○	$50.00
			✂	$50.00
			⊕	$50.00
			👑	$50.00

Classic Variation: "No E" or "Bibl Error." During the first years of production the "e" was missing from the word Bible. Some Hourglass & Fish pieces also have this variation.

> Open, Issue Price $25.00, '81
> Purchased_____, Price $_____

Peace On Earth, E-4725

Unmarked	$115.00
▲	$80.00
I	$65.00
🐟	$60.00
✝	$60.00

Unmarked and Triangle pieces are very dark and colorful.

> Suspended 1984, Issue Price $25.00, '81
> Purchased_____, Price $_____

Peace On Earth, E-4726 (Musical)

Unmarked	$150.00
▲	$125.00
I	$115.00
🐟	$110.00
✝	$105.00

> Suspended 1984, Issue Price $45.00, '81
> Tune: "Jesus Loves Me"
> Purchased_____, Price $_____

Bear Ye One Another's Burdens, E-5200

Unmarked	$110.00
▲	$95.00
I	$80.00
🐟	$75.00
✝	$73.00

> Suspended 1984, Issue Price $20.00, '81
> Purchased_____, Price $_____

Love Lifted Me, E-5201

Unmarked	$110.00
▲	$85.00
✓ I	$80.00
🐟	$75.00
✝	$70.00

> Suspended 1984, Issue Price $25.00, '81
> Purchased _W.5 1_, Price $ _80.0_

Thank You For Coming To My Ade, E-5202

Unmarked	$150.00
▲	$118.00
I	$108.00
🐟	$105.00
✝	$105.00

> Suspended 1984, Issue Price $22.50, '81
> Purchased_____, Price $_____

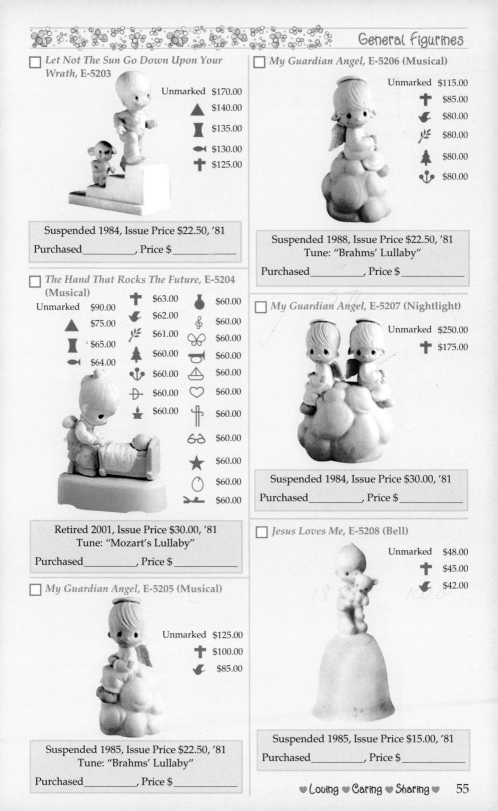

☐ *Let Not The Sun Go Down Upon Your Wrath*, E-5203

Unmarked	$170.00
▲	$140.00
◰	$135.00
🐟	$130.00
✝	$125.00

Suspended 1984, Issue Price $22.50, '81

Purchased_____, Price $_____

☐ *The Hand That Rocks The Future*, E-5204 (Musical)

Unmarked	$90.00	✝	$63.00	🎵	$60.00
▲	$75.00	✈	$62.00	🎼	$60.00
◰	$65.00	🌿	$61.00	🦋	$60.00
🐟	$64.00	🌲	$60.00	📯	$60.00
		⚓	$60.00	⛵	$60.00
		⊢	$60.00	♡	$60.00
		🔥	$60.00	✝	$60.00
				👓	$60.00
				★	$60.00
				◯	$60.00
				🐚	$60.00

Retired 2001, Issue Price $30.00, '81
Tune: "Mozart's Lullaby"

Purchased_____, Price $_____

☐ *My Guardian Angel*, E-5205 (Musical)

Unmarked	$125.00
✝	$100.00
✈	$85.00

Suspended 1985, Issue Price $22.50, '81
Tune: "Brahms' Lullaby"

Purchased_____, Price $_____

☐ *My Guardian Angel*, E-5206 (Musical)

Unmarked	$115.00
✝	$85.00
✈	$80.00
🌿	$80.00
🌲	$80.00
⚓	$80.00

Suspended 1988, Issue Price $22.50, '81
Tune: "Brahms' Lullaby"

Purchased_____, Price $_____

☐ *My Guardian Angel*, E-5207 (Nightlight)

Unmarked	$250.00
✝	$175.00

Suspended 1984, Issue Price $30.00, '81

Purchased_____, Price $_____

☐ *Jesus Loves Me*, E-5208 (Bell)

Unmarked	$48.00
✝	$45.00
✈	$42.00

Suspended 1985, Issue Price $15.00, '81

Purchased_____, Price $_____

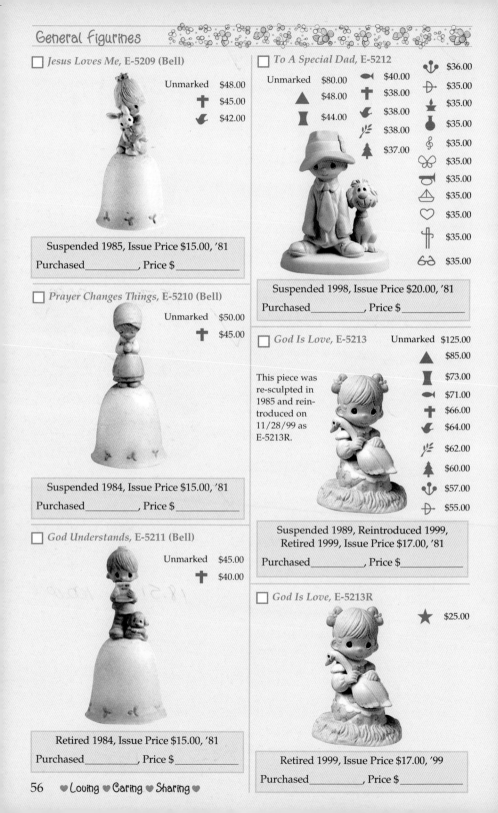

☐ *Jesus Loves Me*, E-5209 (Bell)

	Unmarked	$48.00
✝		$45.00
🕊		$42.00

Suspended 1985, Issue Price $15.00, '81

Purchased_____, Price $_____

☐ *Prayer Changes Things*, E-5210 (Bell)

| | Unmarked | $50.00 |
| ✝ | | $45.00 |

Suspended 1984, Issue Price $15.00, '81

Purchased_____, Price $_____

☐ *God Understands*, E-5211 (Bell)

| | Unmarked | $45.00 |
| ✝ | | $40.00 |

Retired 1984, Issue Price $15.00, '81

Purchased_____, Price $_____

☐ *To A Special Dad*, E-5212

	Unmarked	$80.00	🐟	$40.00	⚓	$36.00
▲		$48.00	✝	$38.00	⅁	$35.00
▮		$44.00	🕊	$38.00	🕯	$35.00
			⚘	$38.00	⚲	$35.00
			🌲	$37.00	♪	$35.00
					🦋	$35.00
					📯	$35.00
					△	$35.00
					♡	$35.00
					⳼	$35.00
					6ა	$35.00

Suspended 1998, Issue Price $20.00, '81

Purchased_____, Price $_____

☐ *God Is Love*, E-5213

	Unmarked	$125.00
▲		$85.00
▮		$73.00
🐟		$71.00
✝		$66.00
🕊		$64.00
⚘		$62.00
🌲		$60.00
⚓		$57.00
⅁		$55.00

This piece was re-sculpted in 1985 and reintroduced on 11/28/99 as E-5213R.

Suspended 1989, Reintroduced 1999, Retired 1999, Issue Price $17.00, '81

Purchased_____, Price $_____

☐ *God Is Love*, E-5213R

| ★ | $25.00 |

Retired 1999, Issue Price $17.00, '99

Purchased_____, Price $_____

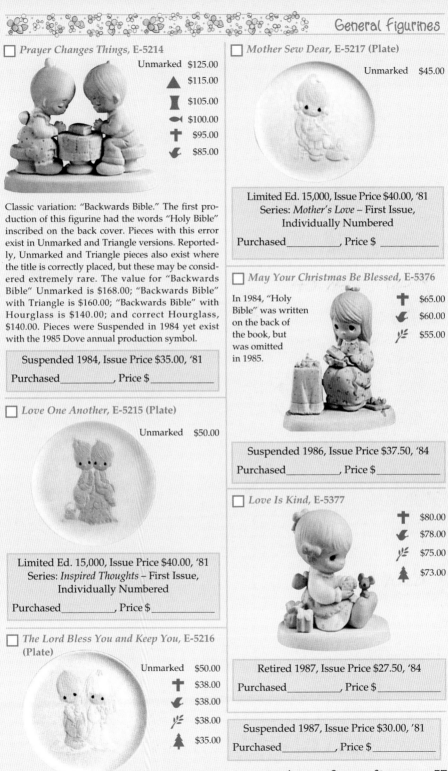

☐ *Prayer Changes Things*, E-5214

Unmarked $125.00

▲ $115.00

✖ $105.00

⬗ $100.00

✝ $95.00

➷ $85.00

Classic variation: "Backwards Bible." The first production of this figurine had the words "Holy Bible" inscribed on the back cover. Pieces with this error exist in Unmarked and Triangle versions. Reportedly, Unmarked and Triangle pieces also exist where the title is correctly placed, but these may be considered extremely rare. The value for "Backwards Bible" Unmarked is $168.00; "Backwards Bible" with Triangle is $160.00; "Backwards Bible" with Hourglass is $140.00; and correct Hourglass, $140.00. Pieces were Suspended in 1984 yet exist with the 1985 Dove annual production symbol.

Suspended 1984, Issue Price $35.00, '81

Purchased_____, Price $ _____

☐ *Love One Another*, E-5215 (Plate)

Unmarked $50.00

Limited Ed. 15,000, Issue Price $40.00, '81
Series: *Inspired Thoughts* – First Issue,
Individually Numbered

Purchased_____, Price $ _____

☐ *The Lord Bless You and Keep You*, E-5216
(Plate)

Unmarked $50.00

✝ $38.00

➷ $38.00

⅊ $38.00

🌲 $35.00

☐ *Mother Sew Dear*, E-5217 (Plate)

Unmarked $45.00

Limited Ed. 15,000, Issue Price $40.00, '81
Series: *Mother's Love* – First Issue,
Individually Numbered

Purchased_____, Price $ _____

☐ *May Your Christmas Be Blessed*, E-5376

In 1984, "Holy Bible" was written on the back of the book, but was omitted in 1985.

✝ $65.00

➷ $60.00

⅊ $55.00

Suspended 1986, Issue Price $37.50, '84

Purchased_____, Price $ _____

☐ *Love Is Kind*, E-5377

✝ $80.00

➷ $78.00

⅊ $75.00

🌲 $73.00

Retired 1987, Issue Price $27.50, '84

Purchased_____, Price $ _____

Suspended 1987, Issue Price $30.00, '81

Purchased_____, Price $ _____

☐ *Joy To The World*, E-5378

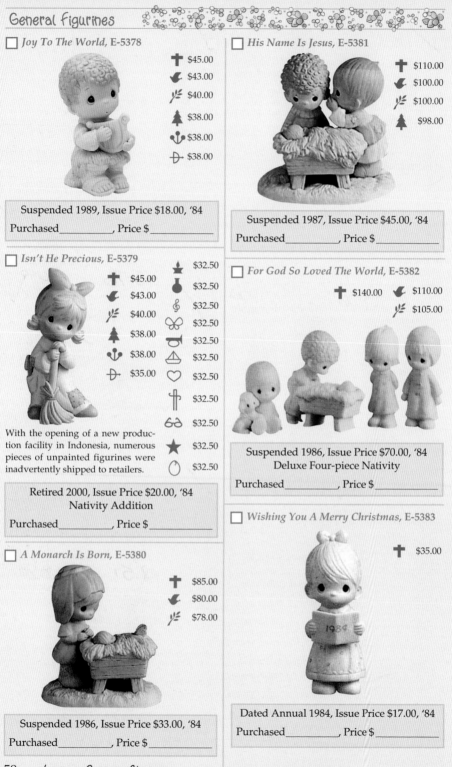

✝ $45.00
🕊 $43.00
🌿 $40.00
🌲 $38.00
⚓ $38.00
⊅ $38.00

Suspended 1989, Issue Price $18.00, '84

Purchased_____, Price $_____

☐ *Isn't He Precious*, E-5379

✝ $45.00
🕊 $43.00
🌿 $40.00
🌲 $38.00
⚓ $38.00
⊅ $35.00

△ $32.50
🜂 $32.50
🎼 $32.50
🦋 $32.50
⌒ $32.50
⛵ $32.50
♡ $32.50
✝ $32.50
👓 $32.50
★ $32.50
◯ $32.50

With the opening of a new production facility in Indonesia, numerous pieces of unpainted figurines were inadvertently shipped to retailers.

Retired 2000, Issue Price $20.00, '84
Nativity Addition

Purchased_____, Price $_____

☐ *A Monarch Is Born*, E-5380

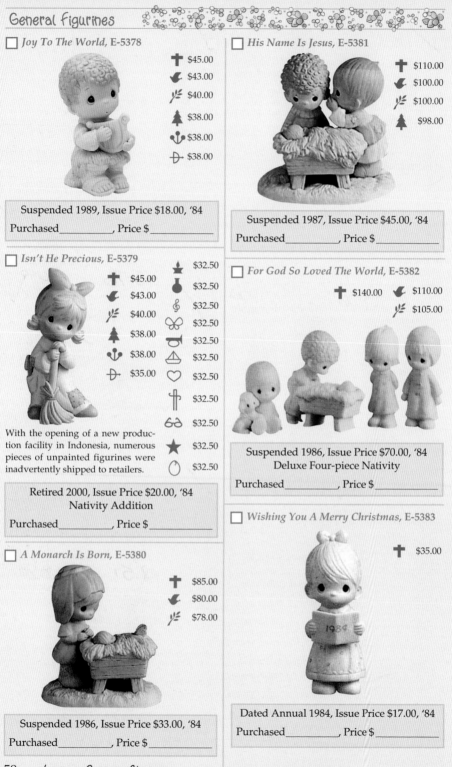

✝ $85.00
🕊 $80.00
🌿 $78.00

Suspended 1986, Issue Price $33.00, '84

Purchased_____, Price $_____

☐ *His Name Is Jesus*, E-5381

✝ $110.00
🕊 $100.00
🌿 $100.00
🌲 $98.00

Suspended 1987, Issue Price $45.00, '84

Purchased_____, Price $_____

☐ *For God So Loved The World*, E-5382

✝ $140.00   🕊 $110.00
🌿 $105.00

Suspended 1986, Issue Price $70.00, '84
Deluxe Four-piece Nativity

Purchased_____, Price $_____

☐ *Wishing You A Merry Christmas*, E-5383

✝ $35.00

Dated Annual 1984, Issue Price $17.00, '84

Purchased_____, Price $_____

☐ *I'll Play My Drum For Him*, E-5384

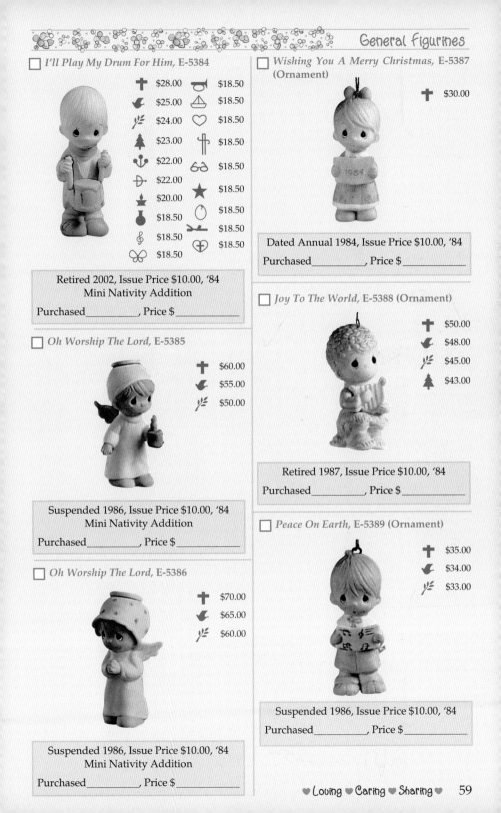

✝	$28.00	🎺	$18.50
🕊	$25.00	△	$18.50
〞	$24.00	♡	$18.50
🌲	$23.00	⚓	$18.50
⚓	$22.00	👓	$18.50
⌀	$22.00		
🕯	$20.00	★	$18.50
♪	$18.50	○	$18.50
§	$18.50	⤙	$18.50
∞	$18.50	⊕	$18.50

Retired 2002, Issue Price $10.00, '84
Mini Nativity Addition

Purchased_____, Price $_____

☐ *Oh Worship The Lord*, E-5385

✝ $60.00
🕊 $55.00
〞 $50.00

Suspended 1986, Issue Price $10.00, '84
Mini Nativity Addition

Purchased_____, Price $_____

☐ *Oh Worship The Lord*, E-5386

✝ $70.00
🕊 $65.00
〞 $60.00

Suspended 1986, Issue Price $10.00, '84
Mini Nativity Addition

Purchased_____, Price $_____

☐ *Wishing You A Merry Christmas*, E-5387
(Ornament)

✝ $30.00

Dated Annual 1984, Issue Price $10.00, '84

Purchased_____, Price $_____

☐ *Joy To The World*, E-5388 (Ornament)

✝ $50.00
🕊 $48.00
〞 $45.00
🌲 $43.00

Retired 1987, Issue Price $10.00, '84

Purchased_____, Price $_____

☐ *Peace On Earth*, E-5389 (Ornament)

✝ $35.00
🕊 $34.00
〞 $33.00

Suspended 1986, Issue Price $10.00, '84

Purchased_____, Price $_____

☐ *May God Bless You With A Perfect Holiday Season*, E-5390 (Ornament)

✝ $30.00
🕊 $28.00
🌿 $25.00
🌲 $24.00
⚓ $23.00
🎷 $22.00

Suspended 1989, Issue Price $10.00, '84

Purchased_____, Price $_____

☐ *Love Is Kind*, E-5391 (Ornament)

✝ $40.00
🕊 $30.00
🌿 $28.00
🌲 $27.00
⚓ $26.00
🎷 $25.00

Suspended 1989, Issue Price $10.00, '84

Purchased_____, Price $_____

☐ *Blessed Are The Pure In Heart*, E-5392 (Ornament)

✝ $35.00

Dated Annual 1984, Issue Price $10.00, '84
"Baby's First Christmas"

Purchased_____, Price $_____

☐ *Wishing You A Merry Christmas*, E-5393 (Bell)

✝ $45.00

Dated Annual 1984, Issue Price $19.00, '84

Purchased_____, Price $_____

☐ *Wishing You A Merry Christmas*, E-5394 (Musical)

✝ $125.00
🕊 $115.00
🌿 $105.00

Suspended 1986, Issue Price $55.00, '84
Tune: "We Wish You A Merry Christmas"

Purchased_____, Price $_____

☐ *Unto Us A Child Is Born*, E-5395 (Plate)

Unmarked $50.00
✝ $45.00

Limited Ed. 15,000, Issue Price $40.00, '84
Series: *Christmas Collection* – Fourth Issue,
Individually Numbered

Purchased_____, Price $_____

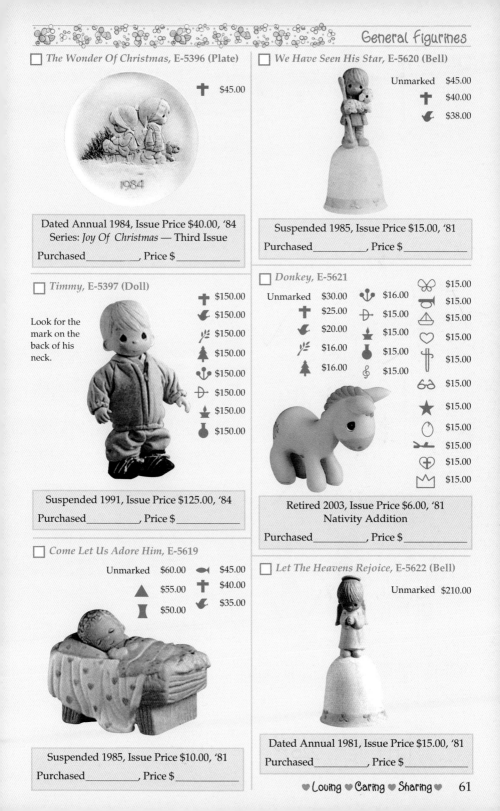

☐ *The Wonder Of Christmas*, E-5396 (Plate)

✝ $45.00

1984

Dated Annual 1984, Issue Price $40.00, '84
Series: *Joy Of Christmas* — Third Issue

Purchased_____, Price $_____

☐ *Timmy*, E-5397 (Doll)

Look for the
mark on the
back of his
neck.

✝ $150.00
🕊 $150.00
𝐽 $150.00
🌲 $150.00
⚓ $150.00
🕊 $150.00
🔥 $150.00
🔔 $150.00

Suspended 1991, Issue Price $125.00, '84

Purchased_____, Price $_____

☐ *Come Let Us Adore Him*, E-5619

Unmarked $60.00   🐟 $45.00
🔺 $55.00   ✝ $40.00
𝐈 $50.00   🕊 $35.00

Suspended 1985, Issue Price $10.00, '81

Purchased_____, Price $_____

☐ *We Have Seen His Star*, E-5620 (Bell)

Unmarked $45.00
✝ $40.00
🕊 $38.00

Suspended 1985, Issue Price $15.00, '81

Purchased_____, Price $_____

☐ *Donkey*, E-5621

Unmarked $30.00   ⚓ $16.00   🦋 $15.00
✝ $25.00   🌿 $15.00   🎺 $15.00
🕊 $20.00   🕯 $15.00   🔺 $15.00
𝐽 $16.00   🔔 $15.00   ♡ $15.00
🌲 $16.00   𝄞 $15.00   🕇 $15.00
                              6∂ $15.00
                              ★ $15.00
                              ◯ $15.00
                              ✂ $15.00
                              ⊕ $15.00
                              ♙ $15.00

Retired 2003, Issue Price $6.00, '81
Nativity Addition

Purchased_____, Price $_____

☐ *Let The Heavens Rejoice*, E-5622 (Bell)

Unmarked $210.00

Dated Annual 1981, Issue Price $15.00, '81

Purchased_____, Price $_____

♥ Loving ♥ Caring ♥ Sharing ♥   61

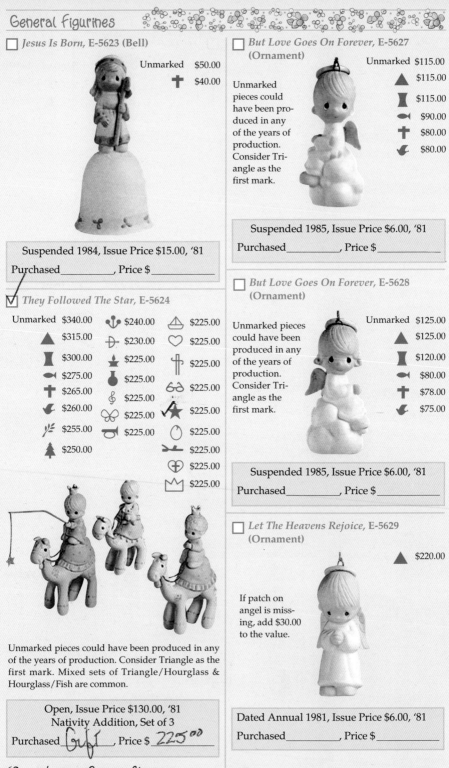

☐ *Jesus Is Born*, E-5623 (Bell)

Unmarked	$50.00
✝	$40.00

Suspended 1984, Issue Price $15.00, '81

Purchased_____, Price $_____

☑ *They Followed The Star*, E-5624

Unmarked	$340.00	⚓	$240.00	△	$225.00
▲	$315.00	⫯	$230.00	♡	$225.00
⌶	$300.00	☽	$225.00	⳨	$225.00
⬿	$275.00	●	$225.00	6ठ	$225.00
✝	$265.00	♪	$225.00	★	$225.00
↙	$260.00	∞	$225.00	◯	$225.00
⚘	$255.00	⤳	$225.00	⤳	$225.00
♠	$250.00			✠	$225.00
				♔	$225.00

Unmarked pieces could have been produced in any of the years of production. Consider Triangle as the first mark. Mixed sets of Triangle/Hourglass & Hourglass/Fish are common.

Open, Issue Price $130.00, '81
Nativity Addition, Set of 3
Purchased _Gift_, Price $ _225.00_

☐ *But Love Goes On Forever*, E-5627
(Ornament)

Unmarked	$115.00
▲	$115.00
⌶	$115.00
⬿	$90.00
✝	$80.00
↙	$80.00

Unmarked pieces could have been produced in any of the years of production. Consider Triangle as the first mark.

Suspended 1985, Issue Price $6.00, '81

Purchased_____, Price $_____

☐ *But Love Goes On Forever*, E-5628
(Ornament)

Unmarked	$125.00
▲	$125.00
⌶	$120.00
⬿	$80.00
✝	$78.00
↙	$75.00

Unmarked pieces could have been produced in any of the years of production. Consider Triangle as the first mark.

Suspended 1985, Issue Price $6.00, '81

Purchased_____, Price $_____

☐ *Let The Heavens Rejoice*, E-5629
(Ornament)

▲	$220.00

If patch on angel is missing, add $30.00 to the value.

Dated Annual 1981, Issue Price $6.00, '81

Purchased_____, Price $_____

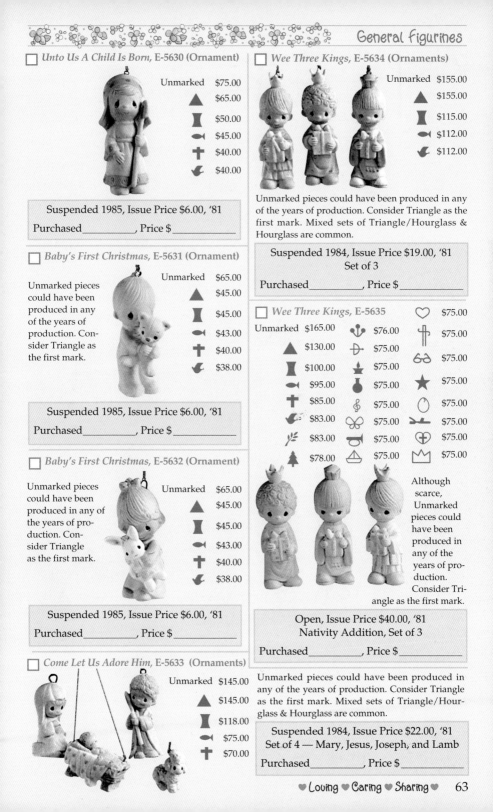

☐ *Unto Us A Child Is Born,* E-5630 (Ornament)

Mark	Price
Unmarked	$75.00
Triangle	$65.00
Hourglass	$50.00
Fish	$45.00
Cross	$40.00
Dove	$40.00

Suspended 1985, Issue Price $6.00, '81
Purchased__________, Price $____________

☐ *Baby's First Christmas,* E-5631 (Ornament)

Unmarked pieces could have been produced in any of the years of production. Consider Triangle as the first mark.

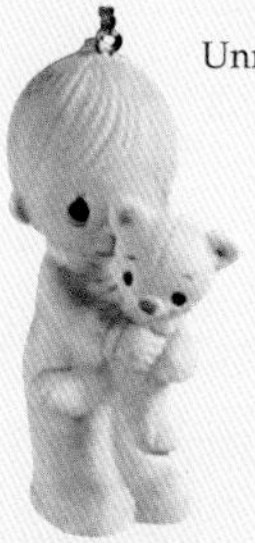

Mark	Price
Unmarked	$65.00
Triangle	$45.00
Hourglass	$45.00
Fish	$43.00
Cross	$40.00
Dove	$38.00

Suspended 1985, Issue Price $6.00, '81
Purchased__________, Price $____________

☐ *Baby's First Christmas,* E-5632 (Ornament)

Unmarked pieces could have been produced in any of the years of production. Consider Triangle as the first mark.

Mark	Price
Unmarked	$65.00
Triangle	$45.00
Hourglass	$45.00
Fish	$43.00
Cross	$40.00
Dove	$38.00

Suspended 1985, Issue Price $6.00, '81
Purchased__________, Price $____________

☐ *Come Let Us Adore Him,* E-5633 (Ornaments)

Mark	Price
Unmarked	$145.00
Triangle	$145.00
Hourglass	$118.00
Fish	$75.00
Cross	$70.00

Unmarked pieces could have been produced in any of the years of production. Consider Triangle as the first mark. Mixed sets of Triangle/Hourglass & Hourglass are common.

Suspended 1984, Issue Price $22.00, '81
Set of 4 — Mary, Jesus, Joseph, and Lamb
Purchased__________, Price $____________

☐ *Wee Three Kings,* E-5634 (Ornaments)

Mark	Price
Unmarked	$155.00
Triangle	$155.00
Hourglass	$115.00
Fish	$112.00
Dove	$112.00

Unmarked pieces could have been produced in any of the years of production. Consider Triangle as the first mark. Mixed sets of Triangle/Hourglass & Hourglass are common.

Suspended 1984, Issue Price $19.00, '81
Set of 3
Purchased__________, Price $____________

☐ *Wee Three Kings,* E-5635

Mark	Price	Mark	Price	Mark	Price
Unmarked	$165.00	Flower	$76.00	Heart	$75.00
Triangle	$130.00	Bow & Arrow	$75.00	Sword	$75.00
Hourglass	$100.00	Flame	$75.00	Eyeglasses	$75.00
Fish	$95.00	Vessel	$75.00	Star	$75.00
Cross	$85.00	G-Clef	$75.00	Egg	$75.00
Dove	$83.00	Butterfly	$75.00	Sandal	$75.00
Olive Branch	$83.00	Trumpet	$75.00	Cross in Heart	$75.00
Cedar Tree	$78.00	Ship	$75.00	Crown	$75.00

Although scarce, Unmarked pieces could have been produced in any of the years of production. Consider Triangle as the first mark.

Open, Issue Price $40.00, '81
Nativity Addition, Set of 3
Purchased__________, Price $____________

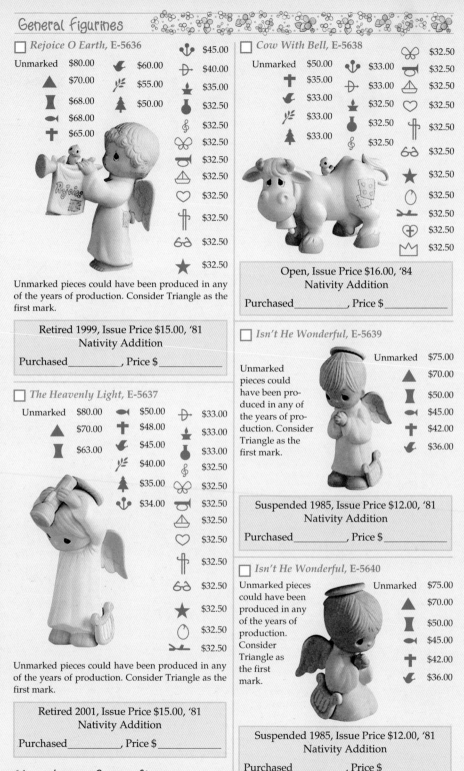

☐ *Rejoice O Earth*, E-5636

Unmarked	$80.00	♥	$60.00	⊅	$40.00
▲	$70.00	⅍	$55.00	⚚	$35.00
Ⅱ	$68.00	🌲	$50.00	⚱	$32.50
🐟	$68.00			♪	$32.50
✝	$65.00			✾	$32.50
				⊟	$32.50
				△	$32.50
				♡	$32.50
				✝	$32.50
				👓	$32.50
				★	$32.50

Unmarked pieces could have been produced in any of the years of production. Consider Triangle as the first mark.

Retired 1999, Issue Price $15.00, '81
Nativity Addition

Purchased_____, Price $_____

☐ *The Heavenly Light*, E-5637

Unmarked	$80.00	🐟	$50.00	⊅	$33.00
▲	$70.00	✝	$48.00	⚚	$33.00
Ⅱ	$63.00	♥	$45.00	⚱	$33.00
		⅍	$40.00	♪	$32.50
		🌲	$35.00	✾	$32.50
		⅍	$34.00	⊟	$32.50
				△	$32.50
				♡	$32.50
				✝	$32.50
				👓	$32.50
				★	$32.50
				◯	$32.50
				⊁	$32.50

Unmarked pieces could have been produced in any of the years of production. Consider Triangle as the first mark.

Retired 2001, Issue Price $15.00, '81
Nativity Addition

Purchased_____, Price $_____

☐ *Cow With Bell*, E-5638

Unmarked	$50.00	⅍	$33.00	🎺	$32.50
✝	$35.00	⊅	$33.00	△	$32.50
♥	$33.00	⚚	$32.50	♡	$32.50
⅍	$33.00	⚱	$32.50	✝	$32.50
🌲	$33.00	♪	$32.50	👓	$32.50
				★	$32.50
				◯	$32.50
				⊁	$32.50
				⊕	$32.50
				👑	$32.50
✾	$32.50				

Open, Issue Price $16.00, '84
Nativity Addition

Purchased_____, Price $_____

☐ *Isn't He Wonderful*, E-5639

Unmarked	$75.00
▲	$70.00
Ⅱ	$50.00
🐟	$45.00
✝	$42.00
♥	$36.00

Unmarked pieces could have been produced in any of the years of production. Consider Triangle as the first mark.

Suspended 1985, Issue Price $12.00, '81
Nativity Addition

Purchased_____, Price $_____

☐ *Isn't He Wonderful*, E-5640

Unmarked	$75.00
▲	$70.00
Ⅱ	$50.00
🐟	$45.00
✝	$42.00
♥	$36.00

Unmarked pieces could have been produced in any of the years of production. Consider Triangle as the first mark.

Suspended 1985, Issue Price $12.00, '81
Nativity Addition

Purchased_____, Price $_____

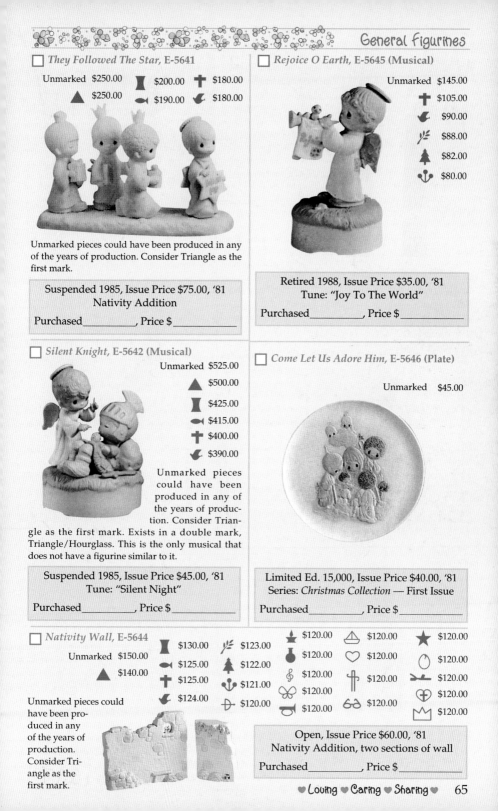

□ *They Followed The Star*, E-5641

Unmarked $250.00   𝕀 $200.00   ✝ $180.00
   ▲ $250.00   ⌖ $190.00   ⌑ $180.00

Unmarked pieces could have been produced in any of the years of production. Consider Triangle as the first mark.

Suspended 1985, Issue Price $75.00, '81
Nativity Addition
Purchased_____, Price $_____

□ *Rejoice O Earth*, E-5645 (Musical)

Unmarked $145.00
✝ $105.00
⌑ $90.00
𝄞 $88.00
▲ $82.00
⚓ $80.00

Retired 1988, Issue Price $35.00, '81
Tune: "Joy To The World"
Purchased_____, Price $_____

□ *Silent Knight*, E-5642 (Musical)

Unmarked $525.00
▲ $500.00
𝕀 $425.00
⌖ $415.00
✝ $400.00
⌑ $390.00

Unmarked pieces could have been produced in any of the years of production. Consider Triangle as the first mark. Exists in a double mark, Triangle/Hourglass. This is the only musical that does not have a figurine similar to it.

Suspended 1985, Issue Price $45.00, '81
Tune: "Silent Night"
Purchased_____, Price $_____

□ *Come Let Us Adore Him*, E-5646 (Plate)

Unmarked $45.00

Limited Ed. 15,000, Issue Price $40.00, '81
Series: *Christmas Collection* — First Issue
Purchased_____, Price $_____

□ *Nativity Wall*, E-5644

Unmarked $150.00
   ▲ $140.00

𝕀 $130.00	𝄞 $123.00	⚡ $120.00	△ $120.00	★ $120.00
⌖ $125.00	▲ $122.00	☗ $120.00	♡ $120.00	◯ $120.00
✝ $125.00	⚓ $121.00	𝄞 $120.00	⛨ $120.00	⤳ $120.00
⌑ $124.00	Ɖ $120.00	⚘ $120.00	𝌆 $120.00	⊕ $120.00
		⌇ $120.00	⚭ $120.00	♕ $120.00

Unmarked pieces could have been produced in any of the years of production. Consider Triangle as the first mark.

Open, Issue Price $60.00, '81
Nativity Addition, two sections of wall
Purchased_____, Price $_____

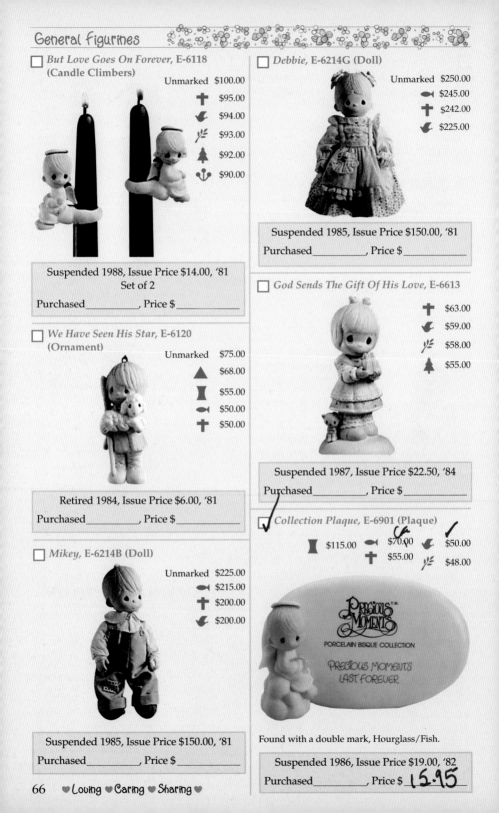

But Love Goes On Forever, E-6118
(Candle Climbers)

Unmarked	$100.00
✝	$95.00
🕊	$94.00
🌿	$93.00
🌲	$92.00
⚓	$90.00

Suspended 1988, Issue Price $14.00, '81
Set of 2

Purchased_____, Price $_____

We Have Seen His Star, E-6120
(Ornament)

Unmarked	$75.00
▲	$68.00
𝕀	$55.00
🐟	$50.00
✝	$50.00

Retired 1984, Issue Price $6.00, '81

Purchased_____, Price $_____

Mikey, E-6214B (Doll)

Unmarked	$225.00
🐟	$215.00
✝	$200.00
🕊	$200.00

Suspended 1985, Issue Price $150.00, '81

Purchased_____, Price $_____

Debbie, E-6214G (Doll)

Unmarked	$250.00
🐟	$245.00
✝	$242.00
🕊	$225.00

Suspended 1985, Issue Price $150.00, '81

Purchased_____, Price $_____

God Sends The Gift Of His Love, E-6613

✝	$63.00
🕊	$59.00
🌿	$58.00
🌲	$55.00

Suspended 1987, Issue Price $22.50, '84

Purchased_____, Price $_____

Collection Plaque, E-6901 (Plaque)

𝕀 $115.00	🐟 $70.00	🕊 $50.00
	✝ $55.00	🌿 $48.00

Found with a double mark, Hourglass/Fish.

Suspended 1986, Issue Price $19.00, '82

Purchased_____, Price $ 15.95

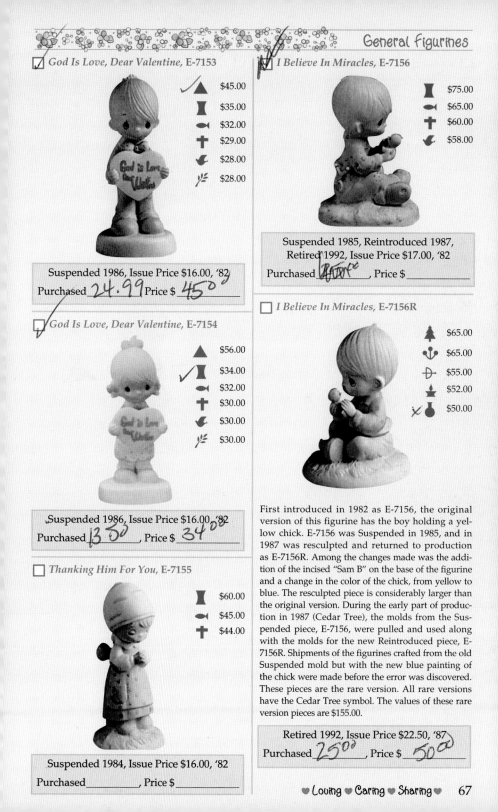

☑ *God Is Love, Dear Valentine*, E-7153

▲	$45.00
I	$35.00
⋈	$32.00
†	$29.00
✔	$28.00
⅓	$28.00

Suspended 1986, Issue Price $16.00, '82
Purchased *24.99* Price $ *45⁰⁰*

☑ *God Is Love, Dear Valentine*, E-7154

▲	$56.00
I	$34.00
⋈	$32.00
†	$30.00
✔	$30.00
⅓	$30.00

Suspended 1986, Issue Price $16.00, '82
Purchased *13 50*, Price $ *34⁰⁰*

☐ *Thanking Him For You*, E-7155

I	$60.00
⋈	$45.00
†	$44.00

Suspended 1984, Issue Price $16.00, '82
Purchased_____, Price $_____

☑ *I Believe In Miracles*, E-7156

I	$75.00
⋈	$65.00
†	$60.00
✔	$58.00

Suspended 1985, Reintroduced 1987,
Retired 1992, Issue Price $17.00, '82
Purchased *before*, Price $_____

☐ *I Believe In Miracles*, E-7156R

🌲	$65.00
⚓	$65.00
‑Ð‑	$55.00
⚒	$52.00
✗	$50.00

First introduced in 1982 as E-7156, the original version of this figurine has the boy holding a yellow chick. E-7156 was Suspended in 1985, and in 1987 was resculpted and returned to production as E-7156R. Among the changes made was the addition of the incised "Sam B" on the base of the figurine and a change in the color of the chick, from yellow to blue. The resculpted piece is considerably larger than the original version. During the early part of production in 1987 (Cedar Tree), the molds from the Suspended piece, E-7156, were pulled and used along with the molds for the new Reintroduced piece, E-7156R. Shipments of the figurines crafted from the old Suspended mold but with the new blue painting of the chick were made before the error was discovered. These pieces are the rare version. All rare versions have the Cedar Tree symbol. The values of these rare version pieces are $155.00.

Retired 1992, Issue Price $22.50, '87
Purchased *25⁰⁰*, Price $ *50⁰⁰*

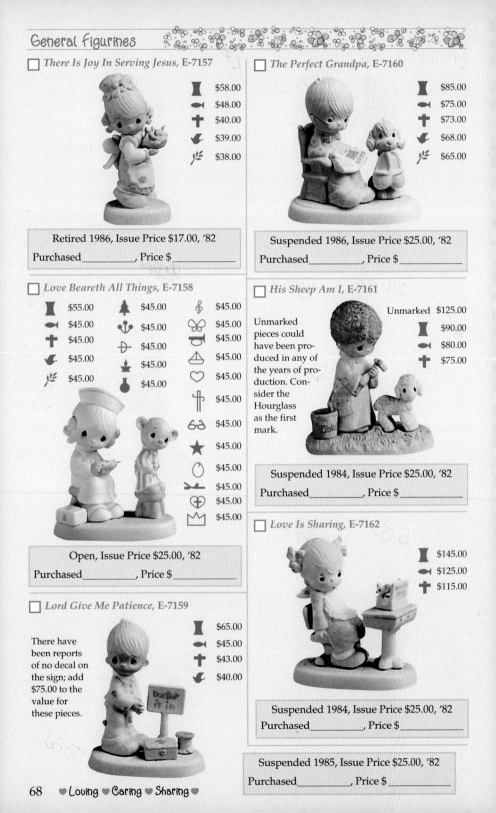

☐ *There Is Joy In Serving Jesus*, E-7157

🗡 $58.00
🐟 $48.00
✝ $40.00
🕊 $39.00
🌿 $38.00

Retired 1986, Issue Price $17.00, '82
Purchased_____, Price $_____

☐ *The Perfect Grandpa*, E-7160

🗡 $85.00
🐟 $75.00
✝ $73.00
🕊 $68.00
🌿 $65.00

Suspended 1986, Issue Price $25.00, '82
Purchased_____, Price $_____

☐ *Love Beareth All Things*, E-7158

🗡 $55.00 🌲 $45.00 ♪ $45.00
🐟 $45.00 ⚓ $45.00 🦋 $45.00
✝ $45.00 ⌐ $45.00 ⊓ $45.00
🕊 $45.00 🔥 $45.00 ⛵ $45.00
🌿 $45.00 🌡 $45.00 ♡ $45.00
🕆 $45.00
👓 $45.00
★ $45.00
○ $45.00
⊁ $45.00
⊕ $45.00
♔ $45.00

Open, Issue Price $25.00, '82
Purchased_____, Price $_____

☐ *His Sheep Am I*, E-7161

Unmarked $125.00

Unmarked pieces could have been produced in any of the years of production. Consider the Hourglass as the first mark.

🗡 $90.00
🐟 $80.00
✝ $75.00

Suspended 1984, Issue Price $25.00, '82
Purchased_____, Price $_____

☐ *Lord Give Me Patience*, E-7159

There have been reports of no decal on the sign; add $75.00 to the value for these pieces.

🗡 $65.00
🐟 $45.00
✝ $43.00
🕊 $40.00

☐ *Love Is Sharing*, E-7162

🗡 $145.00
🐟 $125.00
✝ $115.00

Suspended 1984, Issue Price $25.00, '82
Purchased_____, Price $_____

Suspended 1985, Issue Price $25.00, '82
Purchased_____, Price $_____

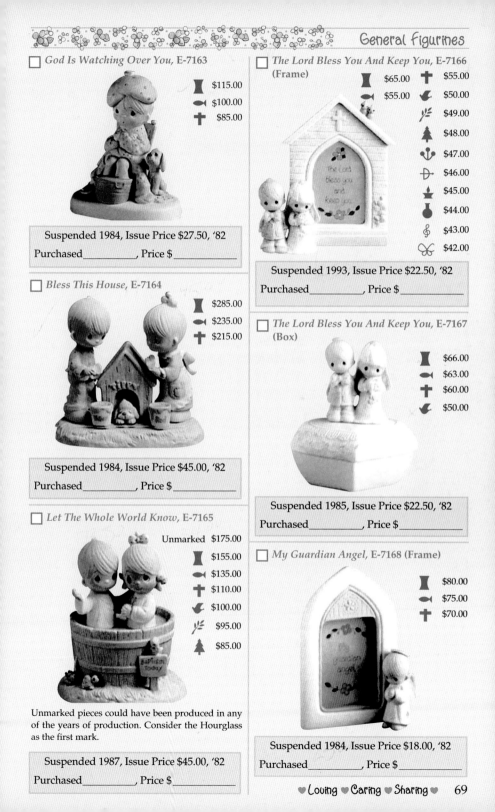

☐ *God Is Watching Over You*, E-7163

🕯 $115.00
🐟 $100.00
✝ $85.00

Suspended 1984, Issue Price $27.50, '82

Purchased_____, Price $_____

☐ *Bless This House*, E-7164

🕯 $285.00
🐟 $235.00
✝ $215.00

Suspended 1984, Issue Price $45.00, '82

Purchased_____, Price $_____

☐ *Let The Whole World Know*, E-7165

Unmarked $175.00
🕯 $155.00
🐟 $135.00
✝ $110.00
🕊 $100.00
🌿 $95.00
🌲 $85.00

Unmarked pieces could have been produced in any of the years of production. Consider the Hourglass as the first mark.

Suspended 1987, Issue Price $45.00, '82

Purchased_____, Price $_____

☐ *The Lord Bless You And Keep You*, E-7166 (Frame)

🕯 $65.00   ✝ $55.00
🐟 $55.00   🕊 $50.00
🌿 $49.00
🌲 $48.00
⚓ $47.00
🔔 $46.00
🕯 $45.00
🍶 $44.00
🎼 $43.00
✂ $42.00

Suspended 1993, Issue Price $22.50, '82

Purchased_____, Price $_____

☐ *The Lord Bless You And Keep You*, E-7167 (Box)

🕯 $66.00
🐟 $63.00
✝ $60.00
🕊 $50.00

Suspended 1985, Issue Price $22.50, '82

Purchased_____, Price $_____

☐ *My Guardian Angel*, E-7168 (Frame)

🕯 $80.00
🐟 $75.00
✝ $70.00

Suspended 1984, Issue Price $18.00, '82

Purchased_____, Price $_____

☐ *My Guardian Angel*, E-7169 (Frame)

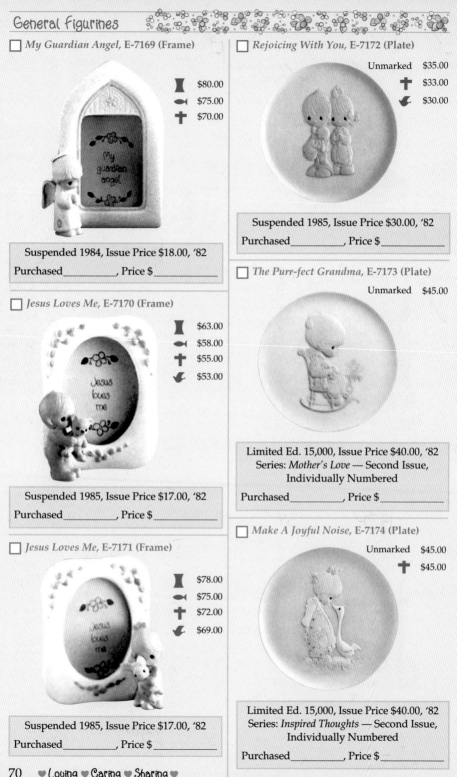

🏆 $80.00
🐟 $75.00
✝ $70.00

Suspended 1984, Issue Price $18.00, '82

Purchased_____, Price $_____

☐ *Jesus Loves Me*, E-7170 (Frame)

🏆 $63.00
🐟 $58.00
✝ $55.00
🕊 $53.00

Suspended 1985, Issue Price $17.00, '82

Purchased_____, Price $_____

☐ *Jesus Loves Me*, E-7171 (Frame)

🏆 $78.00
🐟 $75.00
✝ $72.00
🕊 $69.00

Suspended 1985, Issue Price $17.00, '82

Purchased_____, Price $_____

☐ *Rejoicing With You*, E-7172 (Plate)

Unmarked $35.00
✝ $33.00
🕊 $30.00

Suspended 1985, Issue Price $30.00, '82

Purchased_____, Price $_____

☐ *The Purr-fect Grandma*, E-7173 (Plate)

Unmarked $45.00

Limited Ed. 15,000, Issue Price $40.00, '82
Series: *Mother's Love* — Second Issue,
Individually Numbered

Purchased_____, Price $_____

☐ *Make A Joyful Noise*, E-7174 (Plate)

Unmarked $45.00
✝ $45.00

Limited Ed. 15,000, Issue Price $40.00, '82
Series: *Inspired Thoughts* — Second Issue,
Individually Numbered

Purchased_____, Price $_____

☐ *The Lord Bless You And Keep You*, E-7175
(Bell)

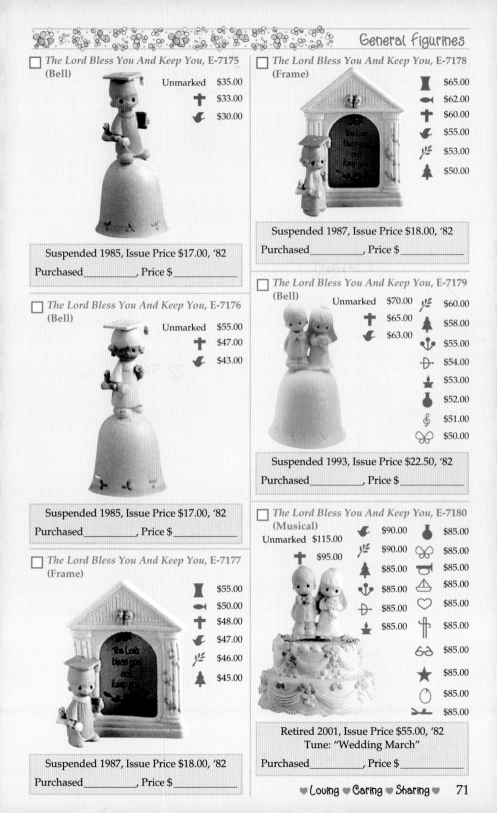

Unmarked	$35.00
✝	$33.00
🕊	$30.00

Suspended 1985, Issue Price $17.00, '82

Purchased_____, Price $_____

☐ *The Lord Bless You And Keep You*, E-7176
(Bell)

Unmarked	$55.00
✝	$47.00
🕊	$43.00

Suspended 1985, Issue Price $17.00, '82

Purchased_____, Price $_____

☐ *The Lord Bless You And Keep You*, E-7177
(Frame)

▮	$55.00
🐟	$50.00
✝	$48.00
🕊	$47.00
🌿	$46.00
🌲	$45.00

Suspended 1987, Issue Price $18.00, '82

Purchased_____, Price $_____

☐ *The Lord Bless You And Keep You*, E-7178
(Frame)

▮	$65.00
🐟	$62.00
✝	$60.00
🕊	$55.00
🌿	$53.00
🌲	$50.00

Suspended 1987, Issue Price $18.00, '82

Purchased_____, Price $_____

☐ *The Lord Bless You And Keep You*, E-7179
(Bell)

Unmarked	$70.00	🌿	$60.00
✝	$65.00	🌲	$58.00
🕊	$63.00	⚓	$55.00
		⌓	$54.00
		🕯	$53.00
		🏺	$52.00
		🎵	$51.00
		🦋	$50.00

Suspended 1993, Issue Price $22.50, '82

Purchased_____, Price $_____

☐ *The Lord Bless You And Keep You*, E-7180
(Musical)

Unmarked	$115.00	🕊	$90.00	🏺	$85.00
✝	$95.00	🌿	$90.00	🦋	$85.00
		🌲	$85.00	🎺	$85.00
		⚓	$85.00	△	$85.00
		⌓	$85.00	♡	$85.00
		🕯	$85.00	🕆	$85.00
				👓	$85.00
				★	$85.00
				◯	$85.00
				⊱	$85.00

Retired 2001, Issue Price $55.00, '82
Tune: "Wedding March"

Purchased_____, Price $_____

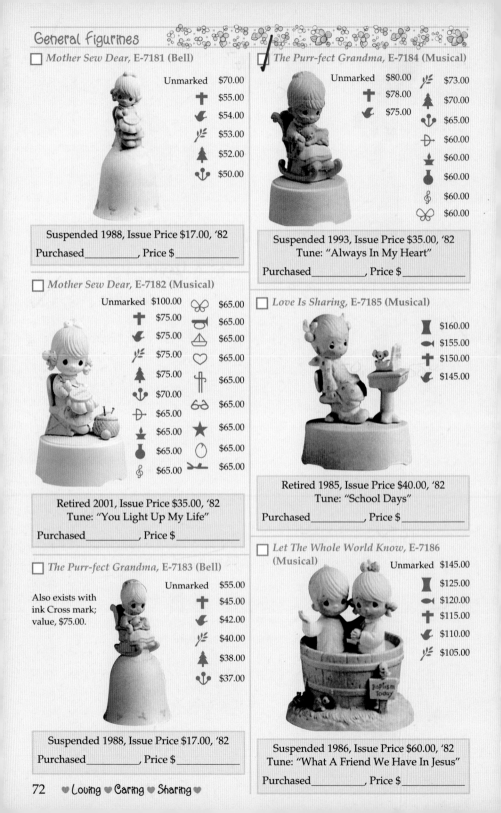

Mother Sew Dear, E-7181 (Bell)

Unmarked	$70.00
✝	$55.00
🕊	$54.00
🌿	$53.00
🌲	$52.00
⚓	$50.00

Suspended 1988, Issue Price $17.00, '82

Purchased_____, Price $_____

Mother Sew Dear, E-7182 (Musical)

Unmarked	$100.00	🦋	$65.00
✝	$75.00	📯	$65.00
🕊	$75.00	△	$65.00
🌿	$75.00	♡	$65.00
🌲	$75.00	✝	$65.00
⚓	$70.00	👓	$65.00
⬡	$65.00	★	$65.00
⚑	$65.00	◯	$65.00
🔔	$65.00	✂	$65.00

Retired 2001, Issue Price $35.00, '82
Tune: "You Light Up My Life"

Purchased_____, Price $_____

The Purr-fect Grandma, E-7183 (Bell)

Also exists with
ink Cross mark;
value, $75.00.

Unmarked	$55.00
✝	$45.00
🕊	$42.00
🌿	$40.00
🌲	$38.00
⚓	$37.00

Suspended 1988, Issue Price $17.00, '82

Purchased_____, Price $_____

The Purr-fect Grandma, E-7184 (Musical)

Unmarked	$80.00	🌿	$73.00
✝	$78.00	🌲	$70.00
🕊	$75.00	⚓	$65.00
		⬡	$60.00
		⚑	$60.00
		🔔	$60.00
		𝄞	$60.00
		🦋	$60.00

Suspended 1993, Issue Price $35.00, '82
Tune: "Always In My Heart"

Purchased_____, Price $_____

Love Is Sharing, E-7185 (Musical)

⌛	$160.00
🐟	$155.00
✝	$150.00
🕊	$145.00

Retired 1985, Issue Price $40.00, '82
Tune: "School Days"

Purchased_____, Price $_____

Let The Whole World Know, E-7186 (Musical)

Unmarked	$145.00
⌛	$125.00
🐟	$120.00
✝	$115.00
🕊	$110.00
🌿	$105.00

Suspended 1986, Issue Price $60.00, '82
Tune: "What A Friend We Have In Jesus"

Purchased_____, Price $_____

☐ *Mother Sew Dear*, E-7241 (Frame)

$58.00
$55.00
$45.00
$40.00
$38.00

Suspended 1986, Issue Price $18.00, '82

Purchased_____, Price $_____

☐ *The Purr-fect Grandma*, E-7242 (Frame)

$55.00
$50.00
$48.00
$46.00
$45.00
$44.00
$42.00

Suspended 1988, Issue Price $18.00, '82

Purchased_____, Price $_____

☐ *Cubby*, E-7267B (Doll)

Unmarked $475.00

Individually numbered on foot. Comes with certificate of authenticity.

Limited Ed. 5,000, Issue Price $200.00, '82

Purchased_____, Price $_____

☐ *Tammy*, E-7267G (Doll)

Unmarked $600.00

Individually numbered on foot. Comes with certificate of authenticity.

Limited Ed. 5,000, Issue Price $300.00, '82

Purchased_____, Price $_____

☐ *But Love Goes On Forever*, E-7350 (Retailer's Dome)

Unmarked $750.00
$855.00

Without dome, $675.00.

Special Gift, '84

Purchased_____, Price $_____

☐ *Love Is Patient*, E-9251

$93.00
$63.00
$60.00

Also exists with Cross decal; value $86.00.

Suspended 1985, Issue Price $35.00, '83

Purchased_____, Price $_____

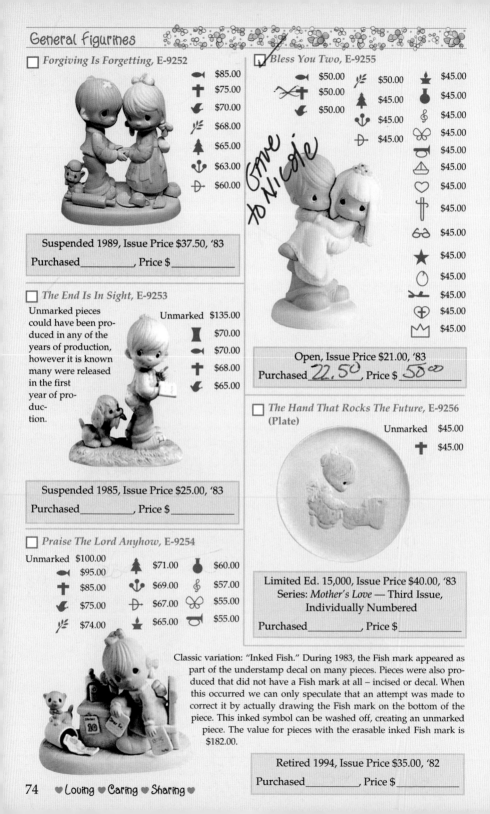

Forgiving Is Forgetting, E-9252

🐟	$85.00
✝	$75.00
🐟	$70.00
🌿	$68.00
🌲	$65.00
⚓	$63.00
ꝺ	$60.00

Suspended 1989, Issue Price $37.50, '83
Purchased_____, Price $_____

The End Is In Sight, E-9253

Unmarked pieces could have been produced in any of the years of production, however it is known many were released in the first year of production.

Unmarked	$135.00
ꓮ	$70.00
🐟	$70.00
✝	$68.00
🐟	$65.00

Suspended 1985, Issue Price $25.00, '83
Purchased_____, Price $_____

Praise The Lord Anyhow, E-9254

Unmarked	$100.00				
🐟	$95.00	🌲	$71.00	🏺	$60.00
✝	$85.00	⚓	$69.00	♪	$57.00
🐟	$75.00	ꝺ	$67.00	🦋	$55.00
🌿	$74.00	★	$65.00	⌒	$55.00

Bless You Two, E-9255

🐟	$50.00	🌿	$50.00	🕯	$45.00
✝	$50.00	🌲	$45.00	🏺	$45.00
🐟	$50.00	⚓	$45.00	♪	$45.00
		ꝺ	$45.00	🦋	$45.00
				⌒	$45.00
				△	$45.00
				♡	$45.00
				♱	$45.00
				6∂	$45.00
				★	$45.00
				○	$45.00
				⊱	$45.00
				⊕	$45.00
				♛	$45.00

Gave to Nicole

Open, Issue Price $21.00, '83
Purchased 22.50, Price $ 50.00

The Hand That Rocks The Future, E-9256 (Plate)

Unmarked	$45.00
✝	$45.00

Limited Ed. 15,000, Issue Price $40.00, '83
Series: *Mother's Love* — Third Issue,
Individually Numbered
Purchased_____, Price $_____

Classic variation: "Inked Fish." During 1983, the Fish mark appeared as part of the understamp decal on many pieces. Pieces were also produced that did not have a Fish mark at all – incised or decal. When this occurred we can only speculate that an attempt was made to correct it by actually drawing the Fish mark on the bottom of the piece. This inked symbol can be washed off, creating an unmarked piece. The value for pieces with the erasable inked Fish mark is $182.00.

Retired 1994, Issue Price $35.00, '82
Purchased_____, Price $_____

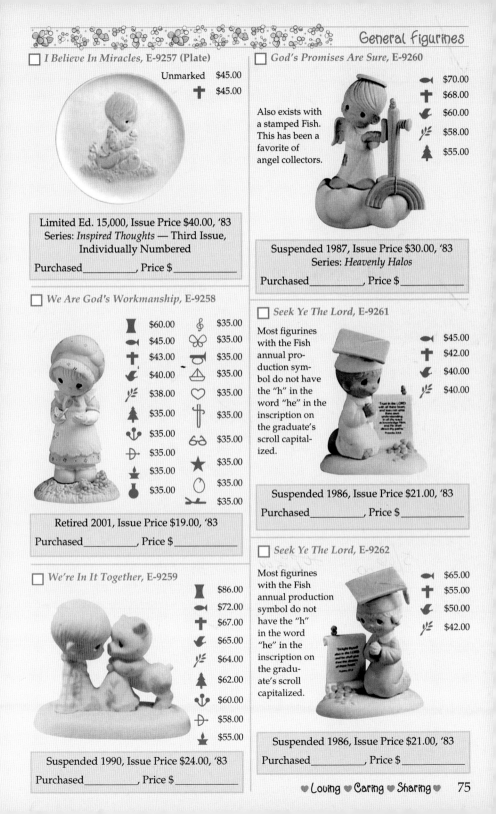

☐ *I Believe In Miracles, E-9257 (Plate)*

Unmarked	$45.00
✝	$45.00

Limited Ed. 15,000, Issue Price $40.00, '83
Series: *Inspired Thoughts* — Third Issue,
Individually Numbered

Purchased_____, Price $_____

☐ *We Are God's Workmanship, E-9258*

‖	$60.00	ᗦ	$35.00
➤	$45.00	✿	$35.00
✝	$43.00	▽	$35.00
✔	$40.00	△	$35.00
⅊	$38.00	♡	$35.00
▲	$35.00	✝	$35.00
⚓	$35.00	6∂	$35.00
Ð	$35.00	★	$35.00
▲	$35.00	○	$35.00
●	$35.00	⤸	$35.00

Retired 2001, Issue Price $19.00, '83

Purchased_____, Price $_____

☐ *We're In It Together, E-9259*

‖	$86.00
➤	$72.00
✝	$67.00
✔	$65.00
⅊	$64.00
▲	$62.00
⚓	$60.00
Ð	$58.00
▲	$55.00

Suspended 1990, Issue Price $24.00, '83

Purchased_____, Price $_____

☐ *God's Promises Are Sure, E-9260*

Also exists with
a stamped Fish.
This has been a
favorite of
angel collectors.

➤	$70.00
✝	$68.00
✔	$60.00
⅊	$58.00
▲	$55.00

Suspended 1987, Issue Price $30.00, '83
Series: *Heavenly Halos*

Purchased_____, Price $_____

☐ *Seek Ye The Lord, E-9261*

Most figurines
with the Fish
annual pro-
duction sym-
bol do not have
the "h" in the
word "he" in the
inscription on
the graduate's
scroll capital-
ized.

➤	$45.00
✝	$42.00
✔	$40.00
⅊	$40.00

Suspended 1986, Issue Price $21.00, '83

Purchased_____, Price $_____

☐ *Seek Ye The Lord, E-9262*

Most figurines
with the Fish
annual production
symbol do not
have the "h"
in the word
"he" in the
inscription on
the gradu-
ate's scroll
capitalized.

➤	$65.00
✝	$55.00
✔	$50.00
⅊	$42.00

Suspended 1986, Issue Price $21.00, '83

Purchased_____, Price $_____

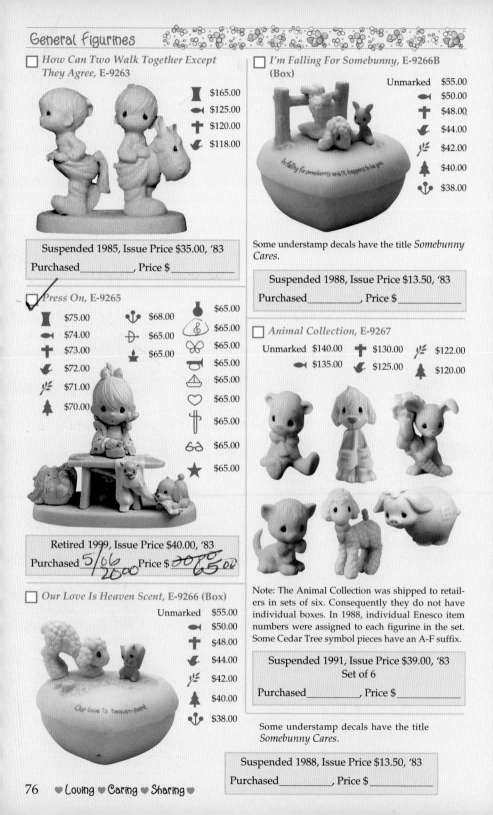

□ *How Can Two Walk Together Except They Agree*, E-9263

⚮	$165.00
⟾	$125.00
✝	$120.00
✈	$118.00

Suspended 1985, Issue Price $35.00, '83

Purchased_____, Price $_____

☑ *Press On*, E-9265

⚮ $75.00	⚓ $68.00		⚱ $65.00
⟾ $74.00	⇥ $65.00		ⓢ $65.00
✝ $73.00	✦ $65.00		✺ $65.00
✈ $72.00			⌐ $65.00
⁂ $71.00			△ $65.00
🌲 $70.00			♡ $65.00
			⸶ $65.00
			👓 $65.00
			★ $65.00

Retired 1999, Issue Price $40.00, '83

Purchased 5/06 Price $ 2000 6500

□ *Our Love Is Heaven Scent*, E-9266 (Box)

Unmarked	$55.00
⟾	$50.00
✝	$48.00
✈	$44.00
⁂	$42.00
🌲	$40.00
⚓	$38.00

□ *I'm Falling For Somebunny*, E-9266B (Box)

Unmarked	$55.00
⟾	$50.00
✝	$48.00
✈	$44.00
⁂	$42.00
🌲	$40.00
⚓	$38.00

Some understamp decals have the title *Somebunny Cares*.

Suspended 1988, Issue Price $13.50, '83

Purchased_____, Price $_____

□ *Animal Collection*, E-9267

Unmarked $140.00	✝ $130.00	⁂ $122.00
⟾ $135.00	✈ $125.00	🌲 $120.00

Note: The Animal Collection was shipped to retailers in sets of six. Consequently they do not have individual boxes. In 1988, individual Enesco item numbers were assigned to each figurine in the set. Some Cedar Tree symbol pieces have an A-F suffix.

Suspended 1991, Issue Price $39.00, '83
Set of 6

Purchased_____, Price $_____

Some understamp decals have the title *Somebunny Cares.*

Suspended 1988, Issue Price $13.50, '83

Purchased_____, Price $_____

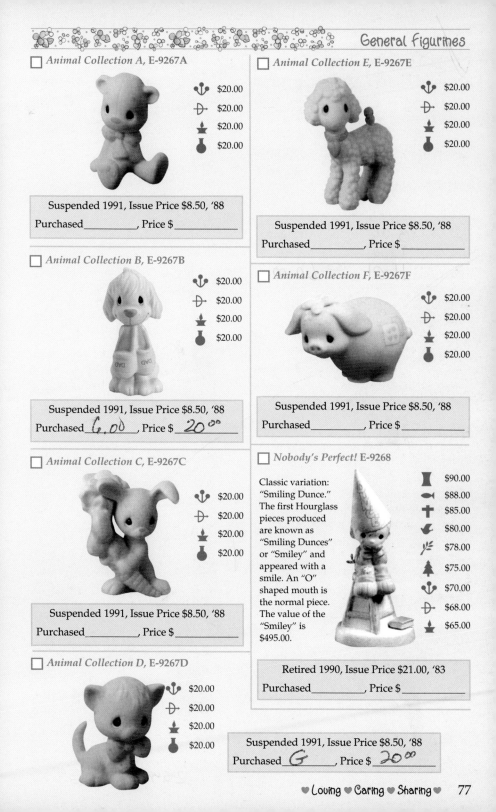

☐ *Animal Collection A*, E-9267A

⚓ $20.00
🦋 $20.00
🕯 $20.00
🍶 $20.00

Suspended 1991, Issue Price $8.50, '88
Purchased_____, Price $_____

☐ *Animal Collection B*, E-9267B

⚓ $20.00
🦋 $20.00
🕯 $20.00
🍶 $20.00

Suspended 1991, Issue Price $8.50, '88
Purchased _6.00_ , Price $ _20⁰⁰_

☐ *Animal Collection C*, E-9267C

⚓ $20.00
🦋 $20.00
🕯 $20.00
🍶 $20.00

Suspended 1991, Issue Price $8.50, '88
Purchased_____, Price $_____

☐ *Animal Collection D*, E-9267D

⚓ $20.00
🦋 $20.00
🕯 $20.00
🍶 $20.00

☐ *Animal Collection E*, E-9267E

⚓ $20.00
🦋 $20.00
🕯 $20.00
🍶 $20.00

Suspended 1991, Issue Price $8.50, '88
Purchased_____, Price $_____

☐ *Animal Collection F*, E-9267F

⚓ $20.00
🦋 $20.00
🕯 $20.00
🍶 $20.00

Suspended 1991, Issue Price $8.50, '88
Purchased_____, Price $_____

☐ *Nobody's Perfect!* E-9268

Classic variation: "Smiling Dunce." The first Hourglass pieces produced are known as "Smiling Dunces" or "Smiley" and appeared with a smile. An "O" shaped mouth is the normal piece. The value of the "Smiley" is $495.00.

🗡 $90.00
🐟 $88.00
✝ $85.00
🐚 $80.00
🌿 $78.00
🌲 $75.00
⚓ $70.00
🦋 $68.00
🕯 $65.00

Retired 1990, Issue Price $21.00, '83
Purchased_____, Price $_____

Suspended 1991, Issue Price $8.50, '88
Purchased _G_ , Price $ _20⁰⁰_

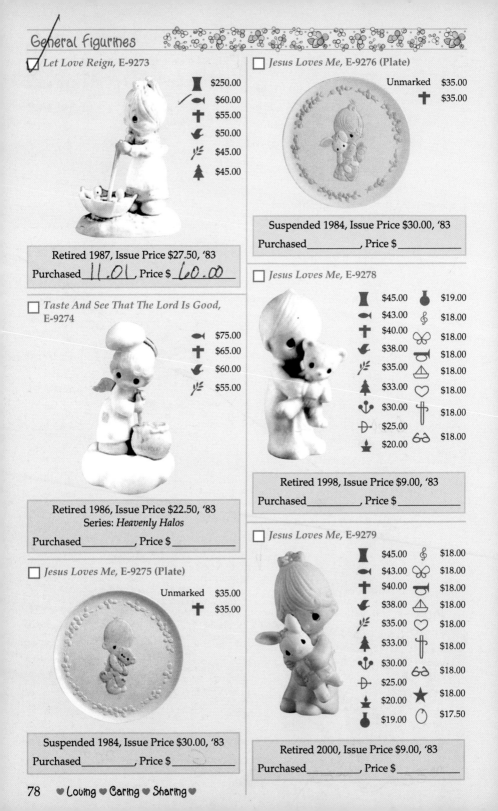

Let Love Reign, E-9273

🏺	$250.00
🐟	$60.00
✝	$55.00
🕊	$50.00
🌿	$45.00
🌲	$45.00

Retired 1987, Issue Price $27.50, '83

Purchased __11.01__, Price $ __60.00__

Taste And See That The Lord Is Good, E-9274

🐟	$75.00
✝	$65.00
🕊	$60.00
🌿	$55.00

Retired 1986, Issue Price $22.50, '83
Series: *Heavenly Halos*

Purchased _____, Price $ _____

Jesus Loves Me, E-9275 (Plate)

Unmarked	$35.00
✝	$35.00

Suspended 1984, Issue Price $30.00, '83

Purchased _____, Price $ _____

Jesus Loves Me, E-9276 (Plate)

Unmarked	$35.00
✝	$35.00

Suspended 1984, Issue Price $30.00, '83

Purchased _____, Price $ _____

Jesus Loves Me, E-9278

🏺	$45.00	🏺	$19.00
🐟	$43.00	🎼	$18.00
✝	$40.00	🦋	$18.00
🕊	$38.00	📯	$18.00
🌿	$35.00	⛵	$18.00
🌲	$33.00	♡	$18.00
⚓	$30.00	✝	$18.00
⌥	$25.00	👓	$18.00
🔥	$20.00		

Retired 1998, Issue Price $9.00, '83

Purchased _____, Price $ _____

Jesus Loves Me, E-9279

🏺	$45.00	🎼	$18.00
🐟	$43.00	🦋	$18.00
✝	$40.00	📯	$18.00
🕊	$38.00	⛵	$18.00
🌿	$35.00	♡	$18.00
🌲	$33.00	✝	$18.00
⚓	$30.00	👓	$18.00
⌥	$25.00	⭐	$18.00
🔥	$20.00	◯	$17.50
🍶	$19.00		

Retired 2000, Issue Price $9.00, '83

Purchased _____, Price $ _____

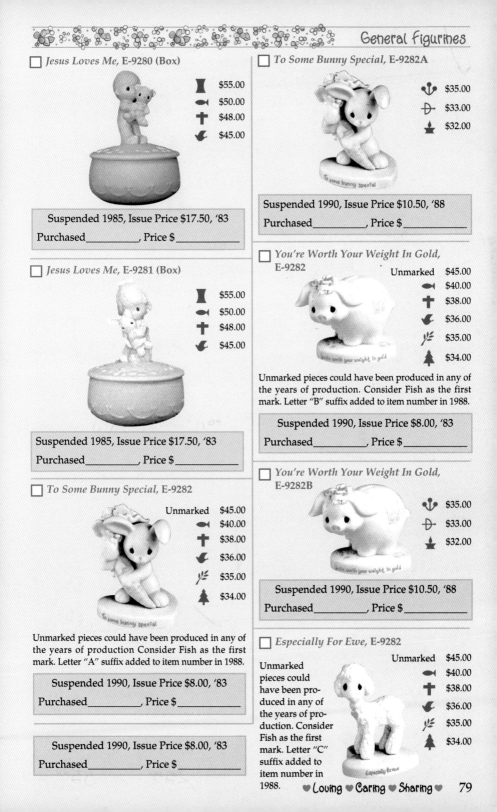

☐ *Jesus Loves Me*, E-9280 (Box)

🎗 $55.00
🐟 $50.00
✝ $48.00
🌿 $45.00

Suspended 1985, Issue Price $17.50, '83
Purchased_____, Price $_____

☐ *Jesus Loves Me*, E-9281 (Box)

🎗 $55.00
🐟 $50.00
✝ $48.00
🌿 $45.00

Suspended 1985, Issue Price $17.50, '83
Purchased_____, Price $_____

☐ *To Some Bunny Special*, E-9282

Unmarked $45.00
🐟 $40.00
✝ $38.00
🌿 $36.00
🌿 $35.00
🌲 $34.00

Unmarked pieces could have been produced in any of the years of production Consider Fish as the first mark. Letter "A" suffix added to item number in 1988.

Suspended 1990, Issue Price $8.00, '83
Purchased_____, Price $_____

Suspended 1990, Issue Price $8.00, '83
Purchased_____, Price $_____

☐ *To Some Bunny Special*, E-9282A

⚓ $35.00
🔔 $33.00
🔨 $32.00

Suspended 1990, Issue Price $10.50, '88
Purchased_____, Price $_____

☐ *You're Worth Your Weight In Gold*, E-9282

Unmarked $45.00
🐟 $40.00
✝ $38.00
🌿 $36.00
🌿 $35.00
🌲 $34.00

Unmarked pieces could have been produced in any of the years of production. Consider Fish as the first mark. Letter "B" suffix added to item number in 1988.

Suspended 1990, Issue Price $8.00, '83
Purchased_____, Price $_____

☐ *You're Worth Your Weight In Gold*, E-9282B

⚓ $35.00
🔔 $33.00
🔨 $32.00

Suspended 1990, Issue Price $10.50, '88
Purchased_____, Price $_____

☐ *Especially For Ewe*, E-9282

Unmarked $45.00
🐟 $40.00
✝ $38.00
🌿 $36.00
🌿 $35.00
🌲 $34.00

Unmarked pieces could have been produced in any of the years of production. Consider Fish as the first mark. Letter "C" suffix added to item number in 1988.

General Figurines

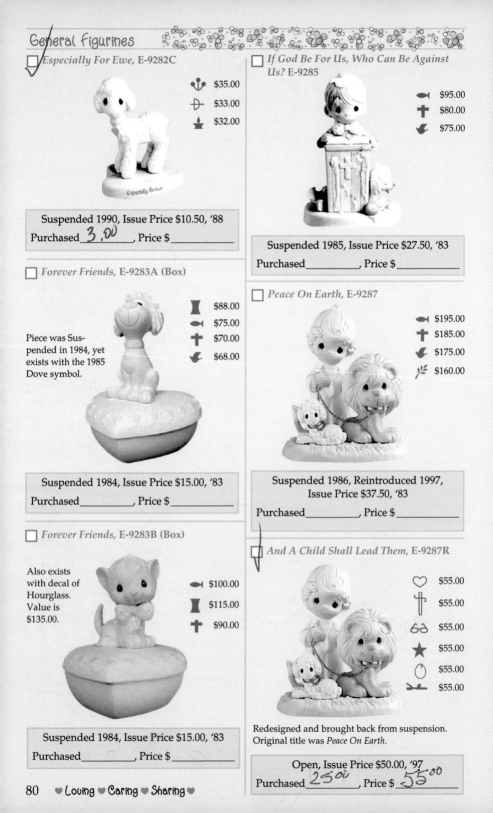

☐ *Especially For Ewe*, E-9282C

⚓ $35.00
🔱 $33.00
⚜ $32.00

Suspended 1990, Issue Price $10.50, '88

Purchased _3.00_ , Price $ _____

☐ *Forever Friends*, E-9283A (Box)

Piece was Suspended in 1984, yet exists with the 1985 Dove symbol.

🏺 $88.00
🐟 $75.00
✝ $70.00
🕊 $68.00

Suspended 1984, Issue Price $15.00, '83

Purchased _____ , Price $ _____

☐ *Forever Friends*, E-9283B (Box)

Also exists with decal of Hourglass. Value is $135.00.

🐟 $100.00
🏺 $115.00
✝ $90.00

Suspended 1984, Issue Price $15.00, '83

Purchased _____ , Price $ _____

☐ *If God Be For Us, Who Can Be Against Us?* E-9285

🐟 $95.00
✝ $80.00
🕊 $75.00

Suspended 1985, Issue Price $27.50, '83

Purchased _____ , Price $ _____

☐ *Peace On Earth*, E-9287

🐟 $195.00
✝ $185.00
🕊 $175.00
🌿 $160.00

Suspended 1986, Reintroduced 1997, Issue Price $37.50, '83

Purchased _____ , Price $ _____

☐ *And A Child Shall Lead Them*, E-9287R

♡ $55.00
† $55.00
👓 $55.00
★ $55.00
◯ $55.00
⤛ $55.00

Redesigned and brought back from suspension. Original title was *Peace On Earth*.

Open, Issue Price $50.00, '97

Purchased _2500_ , Price $ _5500_

80 ♥ Loving ♥ Caring ♥ Sharing ♥

☐ *Sending You A Rainbow*, E-9288

🐟 $95.00
✝ $90.00
🕊 $85.00
🎋 $80.00

Suspended 1986, Issue Price $22.50, '83
Series: *Heavenly Halos*

Purchased_____, Price $_____

☑ *Love Covers All*, 12009

✝ $70.00   ⚓ $60.00
🕊 $68.00   Ð $58.00
✓🎋 $65.00   🕯 $55.00
🌲 $62.00   ● $52.00

Suspended 1991, Issue Price $27.50, '85

Purchased _27.50_ Price $ _65.00_

☐ *Trust In The Lord*, E-9289

🐟 $78.00
✝ $73.00
🕊 $68.00
🎋 $63.00
🌲 $60.00

Suspended 1987, Issue Price $20.00, '83
Series: *Heavenly Halos*

Purchased_____, Price $_____

☐ *Loving You*, 12017 (Frame)

✝ $60.00
🕊 $56.00
🎋 $55.00
🌲 $53.00

Suspended 1987, Issue Price $19.00, '85

Purchased_____, Price $_____

☐ *Collecting Life's Most Precious Moments*,
11547 (Medallion)

👑 $35.00

Available only at the Donald E. Stephens Convention Center through Krause Publications.

Limited Ed. 3,500, Issue Price $33.00, '03

Purchased_____, Price $_____

☐ *Loving You*, 12025 (Frame)

✝ $60.00
🕊 $56.00
🎋 $55.00
🌲 $53.00

Suspended 1987, Issue Price $19.00, '85

Purchased_____, Price $_____

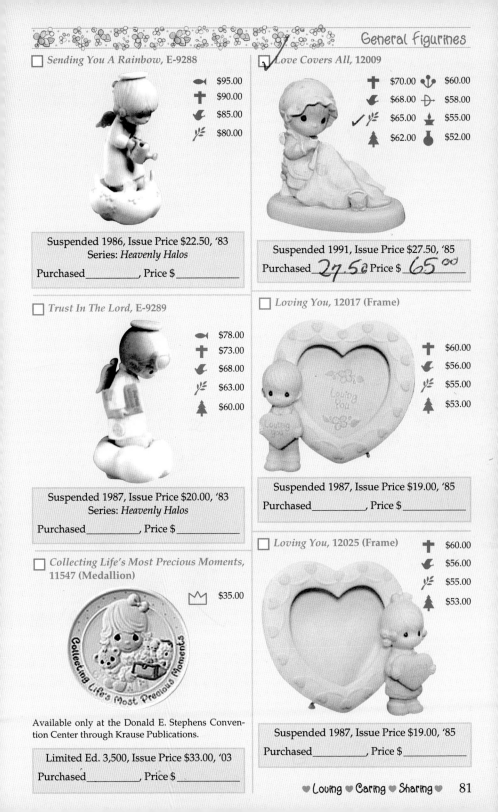

☐ *God's Precious Gift*, 12033 (Frame)

🕊 $110.00

🌿 $95.00

🌲 $90.00

Suspended 1987, Issue Price $19.00, '85

Purchased_____, Price $_____

☐ *God's Precious Gift*, 12041 (Frame)

🕊 $55.00

🌿 $50.00

🌲 $48.00

⚓ $45.00

Ð $43.00

🕯 $40.00

🍶 $38.00

𝄞 $35.00

Suspended 1992, Issue Price $19.00, '85

Purchased_____, Price $_____

☐ *The Voice Of Spring*, 12068

✝ $250.00

🕊 $250.00

Annual 1985, Issue Price $30.00, '85

Series: *The Four Seasons* — First Issue

Purchased_____, Price $_____

☐ *Summer's Joy*, 12076

✝ $125.00

🕊 $115.00

Annual 1985, Issue Price $30.00, '85

Series: *The Four Seasons* — Second Issue

Purchased_____, Price $_____

☐ *Autumn's Praise*, 12084

🕊 $55.00

🌿 $55.00

Annual 1986, Issue Price $30.00, '86

Series: *The Four Seasons* — Third Issue

Purchased_____, Price $_____

☐ *Winter's Song*, 12092

🕊 $135.00

🌿 $115.00

Annual 1986, Issue Price $30.00, '86

Series: *The Four Seasons* — Fourth Issue

Purchased_____, Price $_____

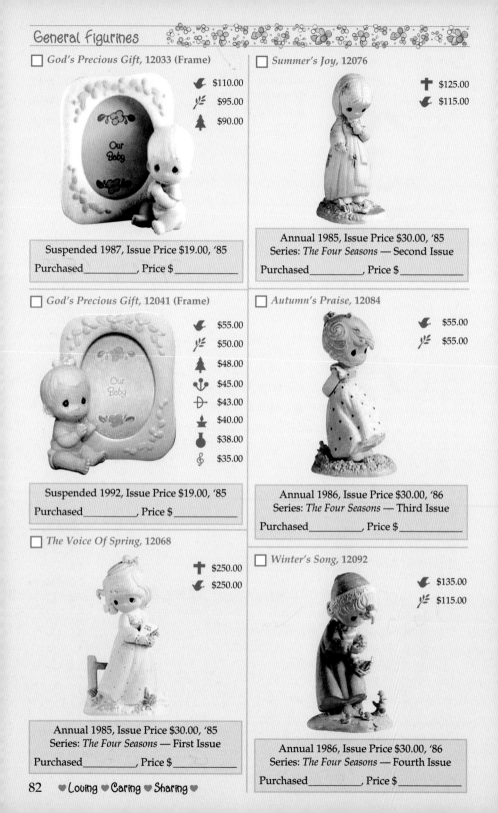

☐ *The Voice Of Spring,* 12106 (Plate)

✝ $65.00

🕊 $55.00

Annual 1985, Issue Price $40.00, '85
Series: *The Four Seasons* — First Issue

Purchased_____, Price $_____

☐ *Summer's Joy,* 12114 (Plate)

✝ $55.00

🕊 $45.00

Annual 1985, Issue Price $40.00, '85
Series: *The Four Seasons* — Second Issue

Purchased_____, Price $_____

☐ *Autumn's Praise,* 12122 (Plate)

🌿 $45.00

Annual 1986, Issue Price $40.00, '86
Series: *The Four Seasons* — Third Issue

Purchased_____, Price $_____

☐ *Winter's Song,* 12130 (Plate)

🍂 $50.00

🌿 $45.00

Annual 1986, Issue Price $40.00, '86
Series: *The Four Seasons* — Fourth Issue

Purchased_____, Price $_____

☐ *Part Of Me Wants To Be Good,* 12149

✝ $90.00

🍂 $85.00

🌿 $80.00

🌲 $79.00

⚓ $78.00

🕊 $77.00

Suspended 1989, Issue Price $19.00, '85

Purchased_____, Price $_____

☐ *This Is The Day (Which) The Lord Has Made,* 12157

Error: The first pieces were produced with the error *This Is The Day Which The Lord Has Made.* The inscription was changed to omit the "which."

🌿 $80.00

🌲 $45.00

⚓ $42.00

🕊 $40.00

🔔 $39.00

Suspended 1990, Issue Price $20.00, '87

Purchased_____, Price $_____

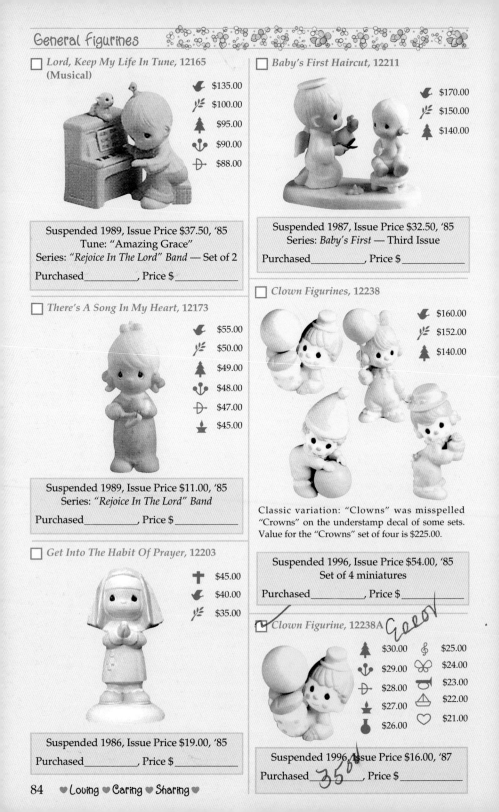

Lord, Keep My Life In Tune, 12165
(Musical)

- 🕊 $135.00
- 🌿 $100.00
- 🌲 $95.00
- ⚓ $90.00
- ⌇ $88.00

Suspended 1989, Issue Price $37.50, '85
Tune: "Amazing Grace"
Series: *"Rejoice In The Lord" Band* — Set of 2
Purchased_____, Price $_____

There's A Song In My Heart, 12173

- 🕊 $55.00
- 🌿 $50.00
- 🌲 $49.00
- ⚓ $48.00
- ⌇ $47.00
- ✴ $45.00

Suspended 1989, Issue Price $11.00, '85
Series: *"Rejoice In The Lord" Band*
Purchased_____, Price $_____

Get Into The Habit Of Prayer, 12203

- ✝ $45.00
- 🕊 $40.00
- 🌿 $35.00

Suspended 1986, Issue Price $19.00, '85
Purchased_____, Price $_____

Baby's First Haircut, 12211

- 🕊 $170.00
- 🌿 $150.00
- 🌲 $140.00

Suspended 1987, Issue Price $32.50, '85
Series: *Baby's First* — Third Issue
Purchased_____, Price $_____

Clown Figurines, 12238

- 🕊 $160.00
- 🌿 $152.00
- 🌲 $140.00

Classic variation: "Clowns" was misspelled
"Crowns" on the understamp decal of some sets.
Value for the "Crowns" set of four is $225.00.

Suspended 1996, Issue Price $54.00, '85
Set of 4 miniatures
Purchased_____, Price $_____

Clown Figurine, 12238A

- 🌲 $30.00
- ⚓ $29.00
- ⌇ $28.00
- ✴ $27.00
- ⚗ $26.00
- ♪ $25.00
- 🦋 $24.00
- 📯 $23.00
- △ $22.00
- ♡ $21.00

Suspended 1996, Issue Price $16.00, '87
Purchased _35⁰⁰_, Price $_____

☑ *Clown Figurine*, 12238B

🎄	$30.00	🎼	$25.00
⚓	$29.00	🦋	$24.00
⅁	$28.00	📯	$23.00
✦	$27.00	⛵	$22.00
🍶	$26.00	♡	$21.00

error

Suspended 1996, Issue Price $16.00, '87
Purchased **35⁰⁰**, Price $_____

☐ *Clown Figurine*, 12238C

🎄	$30.00	🎼	$25.00
⚓	$29.00	🦋	$24.00
⅁	$28.00	📯	$23.00
✦	$27.00	⛵	$22.00
🍶	$26.00	♡	$21.00

Suspended 1996, Issue Price $16.00, '87
Purchased **22⁰⁰**, Price $_____

☐ *Clown Figurine*, 12238D

🎄	$30.00	🎼	$25.00
⚓	$29.00	🦋	$24.00
⅁	$28.00	⛵	$22.00
✦	$27.00	♡	$21.00
🍶	$26.00		

error

Suspended 1996, Issue Price $16.00, '87
Purchased **35⁰⁰**, Price $_____

☐ *Precious Moments Last Forever*, 12246
(Plaque)

This is the first medallion introduced in the Precious Moments collection. It was a gift to new club members.

✝ $100.00

Annual 1984, Issue Price $10.00, '84
Sharing Season Gift
Purchased_____, Price $_____

☐ *Love Covers All*, 12254 (Thimble)

🦜	$20.00
⅄	$18.00
🎄	$17.00
⚓	$16.00
⅁	$15.00
✦	$14.00

Suspended 1990, Issue Price $5.50, '85
Purchased_____, Price $_____

☐ *I Get A Bang Out Of You*, 12262

🦜	$75.00	✦	$65.00
⅄	$70.00	🍶	$64.00
🎄	$68.00	🎼	$62.00
⚓	$67.00	🦋	$61.00
⅁	$66.00	📯	$60.00
		⛵	$59.00
		♡	$58.00
		✝	$57.00

Retired 1997, Issue Price $30.00, '85
Series: *Clown* — First Issue
Purchased_____, Price $_____

☑ *Lord Keep Me On The Ball*, 12270

✗ ⅄	$70.00	🍶	$55.00
🎄	$65.00	🎼	$53.00
⚓	$62.00	🦋	$48.00
⅁	$60.00	📯	$45.00
✦	$58.00	⛵	$45.00
		♡	$45.00
		✝	$45.00
		6d	$45.00

Suspended 1998, Issue Price $30.00, '86
Series: *Clown* — Fourth Issue
Purchased_____, Price $ **70⁰⁰**

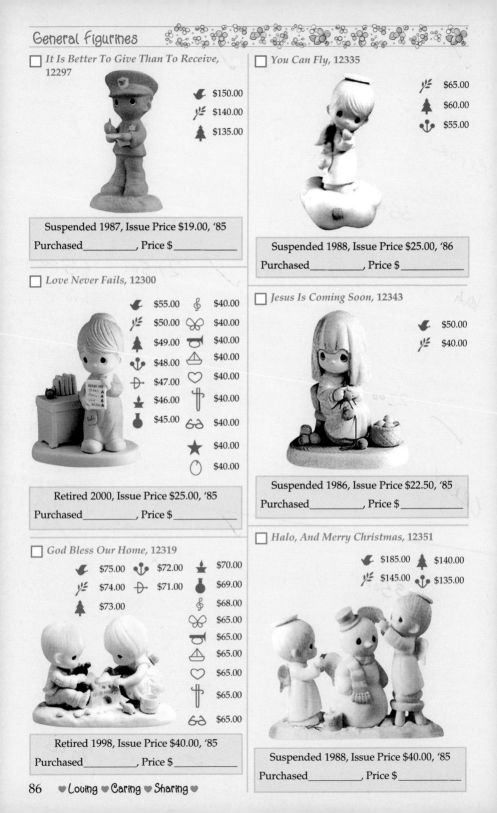

☐ *It Is Better To Give Than To Receive,* 12297

🕊 $150.00
🌿 $140.00
🌲 $135.00

Suspended 1987, Issue Price $19.00, '85
Purchased_____, Price $_____

☐ *Love Never Fails,* 12300

🕊 $55.00   𝄞 $40.00
🌿 $50.00   🦋 $40.00
🌲 $49.00   📯 $40.00
⚓ $48.00   ⛵ $40.00
🔱 $47.00   ❤ $40.00
🕯 $46.00   ✝ $40.00
🔔 $45.00   👓 $40.00
             ★ $40.00
             ○ $40.00

Retired 2000, Issue Price $25.00, '85
Purchased_____, Price $_____

☐ *God Bless Our Home,* 12319

🕊 $75.00   ⚓ $72.00   ★ $70.00
🌿 $74.00   🔱 $71.00   🔔 $69.00
🌲 $73.00   𝄞 $68.00
                          🦋 $65.00
                          📯 $65.00
                          ⛵ $65.00
                          ❤ $65.00
                          ✝ $65.00
                          👓 $65.00

Retired 1998, Issue Price $40.00, '85
Purchased_____, Price $_____

☐ *You Can Fly,* 12335

🌿 $65.00
🌲 $60.00
⚓ $55.00

Suspended 1988, Issue Price $25.00, '86
Purchased_____, Price $_____

☐ *Jesus Is Coming Soon,* 12343

🕊 $50.00
🌿 $40.00

Suspended 1986, Issue Price $22.50, '85
Purchased_____, Price $_____

☐ *Halo, And Merry Christmas,* 12351

🕊 $185.00   🌲 $140.00
🌿 $145.00   🔱 $135.00

Suspended 1988, Issue Price $40.00, '85
Purchased_____, Price $_____

☐ *Happiness Is The Lord*, 12378

🕊 $45.00
🌿 $40.00
🌲 $37.00
⚓ $36.00
🔔 $35.00
🔥 $34.00

Suspended 1990, Issue Price $15.00, '85
Series: *"Rejoice In The Lord"* Band

Purchased_____, Price $_____

☐ *Lord Give Me A Song*, 12386

🕊 $45.00
🌿 $40.00
🌲 $37.00
⚓ $36.00
🔔 $35.00
🔥 $34.00

Suspended 1990, Issue Price $15.00, '85
Series: *"Rejoice In The Lord"* Band

Purchased_____, Price $_____

☐ *He Is My Song*, 12394

🕊 $55.00
🌿 $53.00
🌲 $53.00
⚓ $50.00
🔔 $48.00
🔥 $45.00

Suspended 1990, Issue Price $17.50, '85
Set of 2

Purchased_____, Price $_____

☐ *We Saw A Star*, 12408 (Musical)

🕊 $125.00   🌿 $115.00
🌲 $105.00

Suspended 1987, Issue Price $50.00, '85
Tune: "Joy To The World" — Set of 3

Purchased_____, Price $_____

☐ *Have A Heavenly Christmas*, 12416
(Ornament)

🕊 $25.00   🌿 $24.00   🏺 $20.00
🌲 $23.00   🎼 $20.00
⚓ $22.00   ✖ $20.00
🔔 $21.00   🎺 $20.00
🔥 $20.00   ⛵ $20.00
♡ $20.00
✝ $20.00

There are Cedar Tree pieces with two hooks from
the Retailer's Wreath, #11465 (see page 141). There
are also some ornaments, again from the Retailer's
Wreath, that have the inscription "Heaven Bound"
upside-down.

Suspended 1998, Reintroduced 1998,
Retired 1998, Issue Price $12.00, '85

Purchased_____, Price $_____

☐ *Have A Heavenly Journey*, 12416R

👓 $25.00

Dated Annual 1998, Issue Price $25.00, '98
Care-A-Van Exclusive

Purchased_____, Price $_____

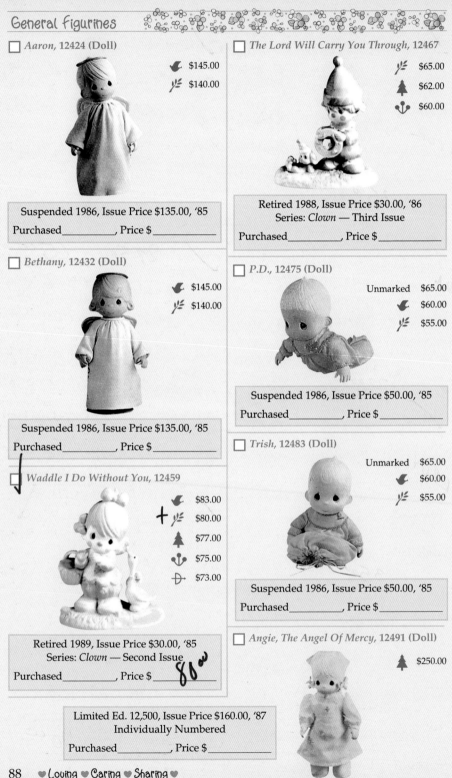

☐ *Aaron*, 12424 (Doll)

🕊 $145.00
🌿 $140.00

Suspended 1986, Issue Price $135.00, '85
Purchased_____, Price $_____

☐ *The Lord Will Carry You Through*, 12467

🌿 $65.00
🌲 $62.00
⚓ $60.00

Retired 1988, Issue Price $30.00, '86
Series: *Clown* — Third Issue
Purchased_____, Price $_____

☐ *Bethany*, 12432 (Doll)

🕊 $145.00
🌿 $140.00

Suspended 1986, Issue Price $135.00, '85
Purchased_____, Price $_____

☐ *P.D.*, 12475 (Doll)

Unmarked $65.00
🕊 $60.00
🌿 $55.00

Suspended 1986, Issue Price $50.00, '85
Purchased_____, Price $_____

☐ *Waddle I Do Without You*, 12459

🕊 $83.00
🌿 $80.00
🌲 $77.00
⚓ $75.00
↱ $73.00

Retired 1989, Issue Price $30.00, '85
Series: *Clown* — Second Issue
Purchased_____, Price $_____80.00__

☐ *Trish*, 12483 (Doll)

Unmarked $65.00
🕊 $60.00
🌿 $55.00

Suspended 1986, Issue Price $50.00, '85
Purchased_____, Price $_____

☐ *Angie, The Angel Of Mercy*, 12491 (Doll)

🌲 $250.00

Limited Ed. 12,500, Issue Price $160.00, '87
Individually Numbered
Purchased_____, Price $_____

Lord Keep My Life In Tune, 12580 (Musical)

💮	$250.00
🌲	$245.00
⚓	$240.00
⊕	$235.00
🕯	$230.00

Suspended 1990, Issue Price $37.50, '87
Tune: "I'd Like To Teach The World To Sing"
Series: *"Rejoice In The Lord" Band* — Set of 2

Purchased_____, Price $_____

Mother Sew Dear, 13293 (Thimble)

🐦	$15.00	✂	$8.00
💮	$14.00	🎺	$8.00
🌲	$13.00	⛵	$8.00
⚓	$12.00	♡	$8.00
⊕	$11.00	✝	$8.00
🕯	$10.00	👓	$8.00
🏺	$9.00	★	$8.00
𝄞	$8.00		

Retired 1999, Issue Price $5.50, '85

Purchased_____, Price $_____

The Purr-fect Grandma, 13307 (Thimble)

🐦	$20.00	✂	$10.00
💮	$19.00	🎺	$9.00
🌲	$18.00	⛵	$8.00
⚓	$17.00	♡	$8.00
⊕	$15.00	✝	$8.00
🕯	$13.00	👓	$8.00
🏺	$12.00	★	$8.00
𝄞	$11.00		

Retired 1999, Issue Price $5.50, '85

Purchased_____, Price $_____

Tell Me The Story Of Jesus, 15237 (Plate)

🐦 $95.00

Dated Annual 1985, Issue Price $40.00, '85
Series: *Joy Of Christmas* — Fourth Issue

Purchased_____, Price $_____

May Your Christmas Be Delightful, 15482

🐦	$55.00	⚓	$48.00
💮	$53.00	⊕	$45.00
🌲	$50.00	🕯	$44.00
		🏺	$43.00
		𝄞	$42.00
		✂	$41.00
		🎺	$40.00

Suspended 1994, Issue Price $25.00, '85

Purchased_____, Price $_____

Honk If You Love Jesus, 15490

		𝄞	$20.00
🐦	$30.00	✂	$20.00
💮	$28.00	🎺	$20.00
🌲	$25.00	⛵	$20.00
⚓	$24.00	♡	$20.00
⊕	$23.00	✝	$20.00
🕯	$22.00	👓	$20.00
🏺	$21.00	★	$20.00
		○	$20.00
		🍀	$20.00

Retired 2001, Issue Price $13.00, '85
Nativity Addition — Set of 2

Purchased_____, Price $_____

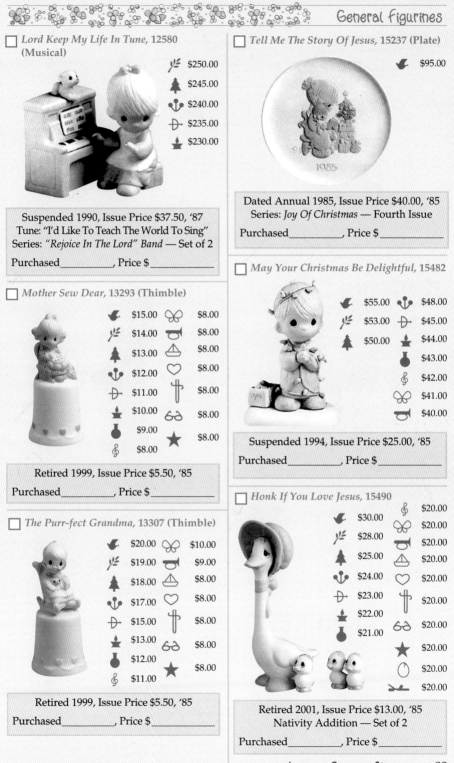

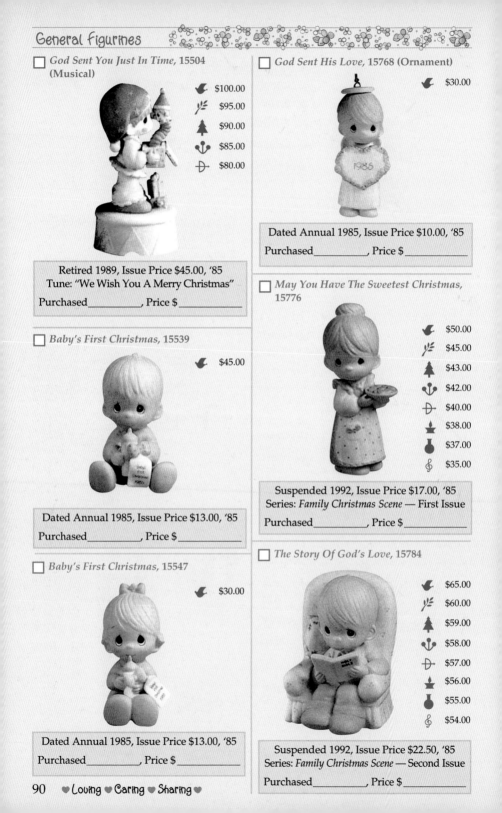

☐ *God Sent You Just In Time*, 15504
(Musical)

🕊 $100.00
🌿 $95.00
🌲 $90.00
⚓ $85.00
🏹 $80.00

Retired 1989, Issue Price $45.00, '85
Tune: "We Wish You A Merry Christmas"
Purchased_____, Price $_____

☐ *Baby's First Christmas*, 15539

🕊 $45.00

Dated Annual 1985, Issue Price $13.00, '85
Purchased_____, Price $_____

☐ *Baby's First Christmas*, 15547

🕊 $30.00

Dated Annual 1985, Issue Price $13.00, '85
Purchased_____, Price $_____

☐ *God Sent His Love*, 15768 (Ornament)

🕊 $30.00

Dated Annual 1985, Issue Price $10.00, '85
Purchased_____, Price $_____

☐ *May You Have The Sweetest Christmas*,
15776

🕊 $50.00
🌿 $45.00
🌲 $43.00
⚓ $42.00
🏹 $40.00
🕯 $38.00
🍶 $37.00
🎼 $35.00

Suspended 1992, Issue Price $17.00, '85
Series: *Family Christmas Scene* — First Issue
Purchased_____, Price $_____

☐ *The Story Of God's Love*, 15784

🕊 $65.00
🌿 $60.00
🌲 $59.00
⚓ $58.00
🏹 $57.00
🕯 $56.00
🍶 $55.00
🎼 $54.00

Suspended 1992, Issue Price $22.50, '85
Series: *Family Christmas Scene* — Second Issue
Purchased_____, Price $_____

☐ *Tell Me A Story*, 15792

Unmarked
pieces are
known to
exist.

🕊 $30.00
🌿 $29.00
🎄 $28.00
⚓ $27.00
⅁ $26.00
✦ $25.00
◖ $24.00
𝄞 $23.00

Suspended 1992, Issue Price $10.00, '85
Series: *Family Christmas Scene* — Third Issue
Purchased_____, Price $_____

☐ *God Gave His Best*, 15806

🕊 $55.00
🌿 $38.00
🎄 $35.00
⚓ $33.00
⅁ $31.00
✦ $30.00
◖ $29.00
𝄞 $28.00

Suspended 1992, Issue Price $13.00, '85
Series: *Family Christmas Scene* — Fourth Issue
Purchased_____, Price $_____

☐ *Silent Night*, 15814 (Musical)

🕊 $110.00
🌿 $105.00
🎄 $100.00
⚓ $98.00
⅁ $95.00
✦ $90.00
◖ $87.00
𝄞 $86.00

Suspended 1992, Issue Price $37.50, '85
Tune: "Silent Night"
Series: *Family Christmas Scene* — Fifth Issue
Purchased_____, Price $_____

☐ *May Your Christmas Be Happy*, 15822
(Ornament)

🕊 $48.00
🌿 $45.00
🎄 $43.00
⚓ $42.00
⅁ $40.00

Suspended 1989, Issue Price $10.00, '85
Purchased_____, Price $_____

☐ *Happiness Is The Lord*, 15830
(Ornament)

🕊 $35.00
🌿 $33.00
🎄 $32.00
⚓ $31.00
⅁ $30.00

Suspended 1989, Issue Price $10.00, '85
Purchased_____, Price $_____

☐ *May Your Christmas Be Delightful*, 15849
(Ornament)

🕊 $32.00
🌿 $28.00
🎄 $27.00
⚓ $26.00
⅁ $25.00
✦ $24.00
◖ $23.00
𝄞 $22.00
🦋 $21.00

Suspended 1993, Reintroduced 1999,
Issue Price $10.00, '85
Purchased_____, Price $_____

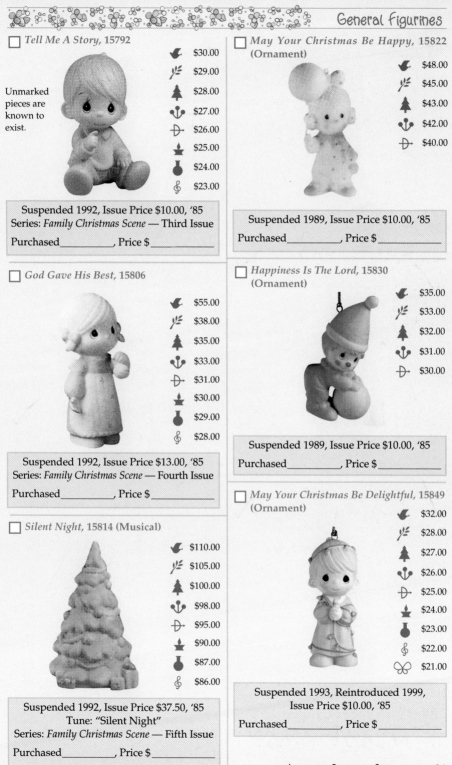

☐ *May Your Christmas Be Delightful,* 15849R (Ornament)

👓 $20.00
⭐ $20.00
◯ $20.00
🛷 $20.00

Open, Issue Price $20.00, '99

Purchased_____, Price $_____

☐ *Honk If You Love Jesus,* 15857 (Ornament)

🕊 $35.00   🌲 $33.00
🌿 $34.00   ⚓ $32.00
         ⊅ $31.00
         ♦ $30.00
         🏺 $29.00
         𝄞 $28.00
         🦋 $27.00

Suspended 1993, Issue Price $10.00, '85

Purchased_____, Price $_____

☐ *God Sent His Love,* 15865 (Thimble)

🕊 $36.00

Dated Annual 1985, Issue Price $5.50, '85

Purchased_____, Price $_____

☐ *God Sent His Love,* 15873 (Bell)

🕊 $28.00

Dated Annual 1985, Issue Price $19.00, '85

Purchased_____, Price $_____

☐ *God Sent His Love,* 15881

🕊 $35.00

God Sent
His Love
1985

Dated Annual 1985, Issue Price $17.00, '85

Purchased_____, Price $_____

☐ *Baby's First Christmas,* 15903 (Ornament)

🕊 $25.00

Dated Annual 1985, Issue Price $10.00, '85

Purchased_____, Price $_____

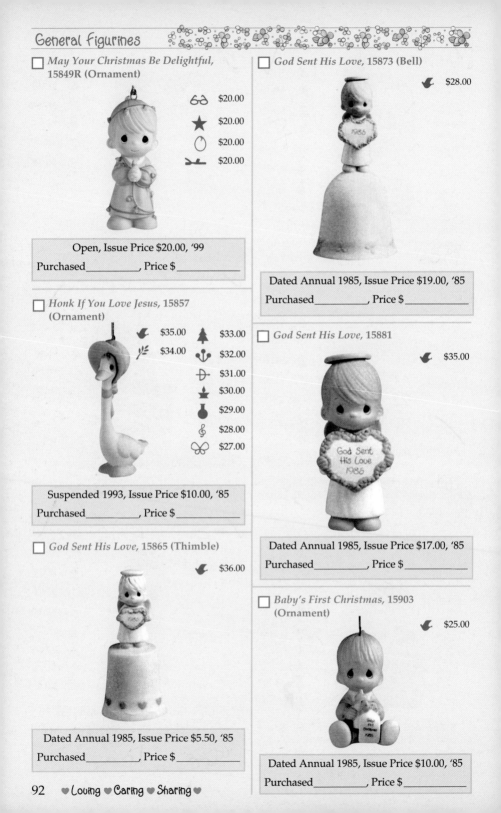

☐ *Baby's First Christmas*, 15911
(Ornament)

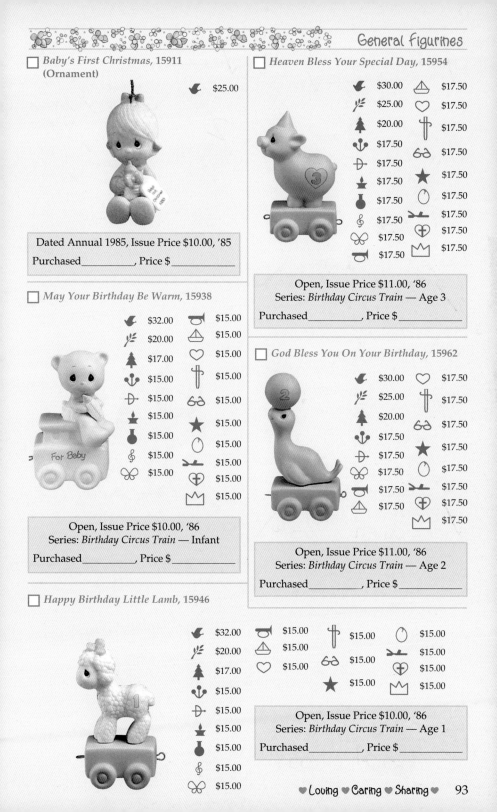

🕊 $25.00

Dated Annual 1985, Issue Price $10.00, '85
Purchased_____, Price $ _____

☐ *May Your Birthday Be Warm*, 15938

🕊 $32.00		📯 $15.00
🌿 $20.00		⛵ $15.00
🎄 $17.00		♡ $15.00
⚓ $15.00		✝ $15.00
⅁ $15.00		👓 $15.00
🔔 $15.00		★ $15.00
🧪 $15.00		◯ $15.00
𝄞 $15.00		✈ $15.00
🦋 $15.00		✚ $15.00
		👑 $15.00

Open, Issue Price $10.00, '86
Series: *Birthday Circus Train — Infant*
Purchased_____, Price $ _____

☐ *Happy Birthday Little Lamb*, 15946

🕊 $32.00	
🌿 $20.00	
🎄 $17.00	
⚓ $15.00	
⅁ $15.00	
🔔 $15.00	
🧪 $15.00	
𝄞 $15.00	
🦋 $15.00	

📯 $15.00	✝ $15.00	◯ $15.00
⛵ $15.00	👓 $15.00	✈ $15.00
♡ $15.00	★ $15.00	✚ $15.00
		👑 $15.00

Open, Issue Price $10.00, '86
Series: *Birthday Circus Train — Age 1*
Purchased_____, Price $ _____

☐ *Heaven Bless Your Special Day*, 15954

🕊 $30.00	⛵ $17.50
🌿 $25.00	♡ $17.50
🎄 $20.00	✝ $17.50
⚓ $17.50	👓 $17.50
⅁ $17.50	★ $17.50
🔔 $17.50	◯ $17.50
🧪 $17.50	✈ $17.50
𝄞 $17.50	✚ $17.50
🦋 $17.50	👑 $17.50
📯 $17.50	

Open, Issue Price $11.00, '86
Series: *Birthday Circus Train — Age 3*
Purchased_____, Price $ _____

☐ *God Bless You On Your Birthday*, 15962

🕊 $30.00	♡ $17.50
🌿 $25.00	✝ $17.50
🎄 $20.00	👓 $17.50
⚓ $17.50	★ $17.50
⅁ $17.50	◯ $17.50
🦋 $17.50	✈ $17.50
🔔 $17.50	✚ $17.50
⛵ $17.50	👑 $17.50

Open, Issue Price $11.00, '86
Series: *Birthday Circus Train — Age 2*
Purchased_____, Price $ _____

May Your Birthday Be Gigantic, 15970

$26.00 $20.00
$24.00 $20.00
$21.00 $20.00
$20.00 $20.00
$20.00 $20.00
$20.00 $20.00
$20.00 $20.00
$20.00 $20.00
$20.00 $20.00
$20.00

Open, Issue Price $12.50, '86
Series: *Birthday Circus Train* — Age 4
Purchased_____, Price $ _____

Bless The Days Of Our Youth, 16004

$30.00 $22.50
$25.00 $22.50
$24.00 $22.50
$23.00 $22.50
$23.00
$23.00 $22.50
$22.50 $22.50
$22.50 $22.50
$22.50 $22.50
$22.50

Open, Issue Price $15.00, '86
Series: *Birthday Circus Train*
Purchased_____, Price $ _____

This Day Is Something To Roar About, 15989

$30.00 $22.50
$25.00 $22.50
$24.00 $22.50
$23.00 $22.50
$23.00
$23.00 $22.50
$22.50 $22.50
$22.50 $22.50
$22.50 $22.50
$22.50

Open, Issue Price $13.50, '86
Series: *Birthday Circus Train* — Age 5
Purchased_____, Price $ _____

Baby's First Trip, 16012

$285.00
$265.00
$260.00
$255.00

Suspended 1989, Issue Price $32.50, '86
Series: *Baby's First* — Fourth Issue
Purchased_____, Price $ _____

Keep Looking Up, 15997

$30.00 $22.50 $22.50 $22.50
$25.00 $22.50 $22.50 $22.50
$24.00 $22.50 $22.50 $22.50
$23.00 $22.50
$23.00
$23.00
$22.50
$22.50

Open, Issue Price $13.50, '86
Series: *Birthday Circus Train* — Age 6
Purchased_____, Price $ _____

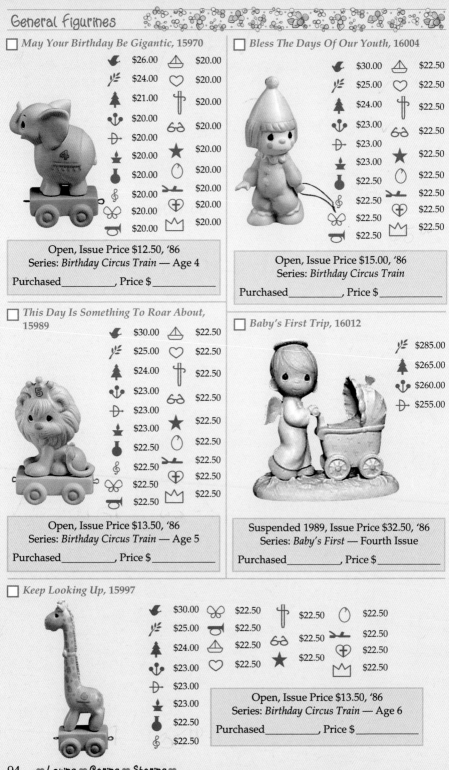

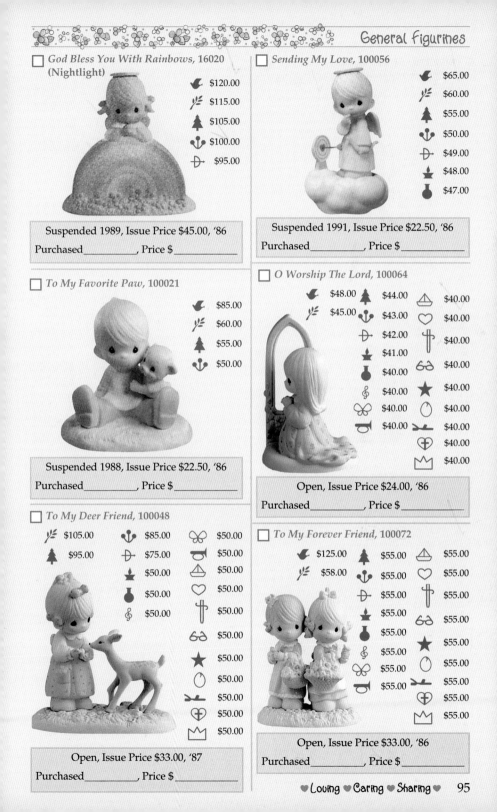

☐ *God Bless You With Rainbows*, 16020
(Nightlight)

🕊 $120.00
🌿 $115.00
🌲 $105.00
⚓ $100.00
🔔 $95.00

Suspended 1989, Issue Price $45.00, '86
Purchased_____, Price $_____

☐ *Sending My Love*, 100056

🕊 $65.00
🌿 $60.00
🌲 $55.00
⚓ $50.00
🔔 $49.00
🕯 $48.00
🥚 $47.00

Suspended 1991, Issue Price $22.50, '86
Purchased_____, Price $_____

☐ *To My Favorite Paw*, 100021

🕊 $85.00
🌿 $60.00
🌲 $55.00
⚓ $50.00

Suspended 1988, Issue Price $22.50, '86
Purchased_____, Price $_____

☐ *O Worship The Lord*, 100064

🕊 $48.00	🌲 $44.00	⛵ $40.00
🌿 $45.00	⚓ $43.00	♡ $40.00
	🔔 $42.00	🕇 $40.00
	🕯 $41.00	
	🥚 $40.00	👓 $40.00
	🎵 $40.00	★ $40.00
	🦋 $40.00	◯ $40.00
	🎺 $40.00	⤙ $40.00
		✝ $40.00
		👑 $40.00

Open, Issue Price $24.00, '86
Purchased_____, Price $_____

☐ *To My Deer Friend*, 100048

🌿 $105.00	⚓ $85.00	🦋 $50.00
🌲 $95.00	🔔 $75.00	🎺 $50.00
	🕯 $50.00	⛵ $50.00
	🥚 $50.00	♡ $50.00
	🎵 $50.00	🕇 $50.00
		👓 $50.00
		★ $50.00
		◯ $50.00
		⤙ $50.00
		✝ $50.00
		👑 $50.00

Open, Issue Price $33.00, '87
Purchased_____, Price $_____

☐ *To My Forever Friend*, 100072

🕊 $125.00	🌲 $55.00	⛵ $55.00
🌿 $58.00	⚓ $55.00	♡ $55.00
	🔔 $55.00	🕇 $55.00
	🕯 $55.00	👓 $55.00
	🥚 $55.00	★ $55.00
	🎵 $55.00	◯ $55.00
	🦋 $55.00	⤙ $55.00
	🎺 $55.00	✝ $55.00
		👑 $55.00

Open, Issue Price $33.00, '86
Purchased_____, Price $_____

☐ He's The Healer Of Broken Hearts, 100080

🌿 $55.00	⚓ $50.00	🔔 $50.00
🌲 $50.00	⌓ $50.00	🔥 $50.00
	✉ $50.00	🦋 $50.00
		📯 $50.00
		△ $50.00
		♡ $50.00
		✝ $50.00
		👓 $50.00
		★ $50.00

Retired 1999, Issue Price $33.00, '87

Purchased_____, Price $_____

☐ Make Me A Blessing, 100102

🌿	$105.00
🌲	$70.00
⚓	$69.00
⌓	$67.00
🔥	$65.00

Retired 1990, Issue Price $35.00, '87

Purchased_____, Price $_____

☑ Lord, I'm Coming Home, 100110

🐦 $90.00	🌲 $44.00	📯 $35.00
🌿 $45.00	⚓ $43.00	△ $35.00
	⌓ $42.00	♡ $35.00
	🔥 $41.00	✝ $35.00
	🔔 $40.00	👓 $35.00
	⌓ $35.00	★ $35.00
	🦋 $35.00	○ $35.00
		✂ $35.00
		⊕ $35.00
		♛ $35.00

Retired 2003, Issue Price $22.50, '86

Purchased _25.31_, Price $_35.00_

☑ Lord Keep Me On My Toes, 100129

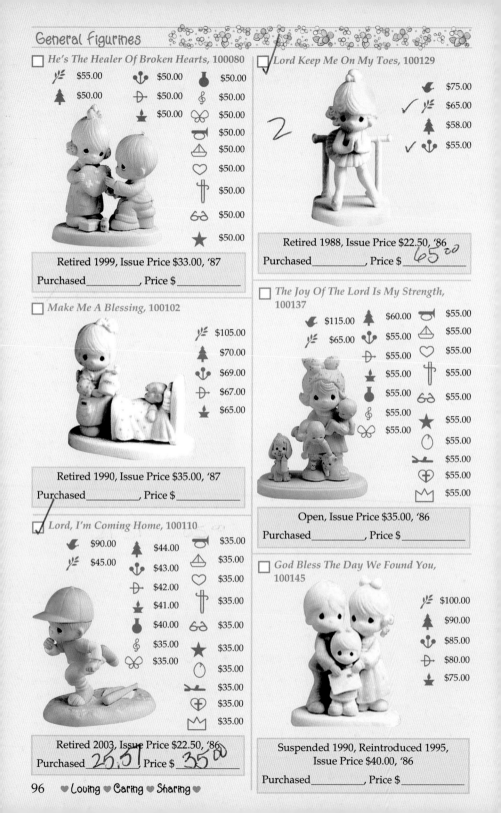

2

🐦	$75.00
✓ 🌿	$65.00
🌲	$58.00
✓ ⚓	$55.00

Retired 1988, Issue Price $22.50, '86

Purchased_____, Price $_65.00_

☐ The Joy Of The Lord Is My Strength, 100137

🐦 $115.00	🌲 $60.00	📯 $55.00
🌿 $65.00	⚓ $55.00	△ $55.00
	⌓ $55.00	♡ $55.00
	🔥 $55.00	✝ $55.00
	🔔 $55.00	👓 $55.00
	⌓ $55.00	★ $55.00
	🦋 $55.00	○ $55.00
		✂ $55.00
		⊕ $55.00
		♛ $55.00

Open, Issue Price $35.00, '86

Purchased_____, Price $_____

☐ God Bless The Day We Found You, 100145

🌿	$100.00
🌲	$90.00
⚓	$85.00
⌓	$80.00
🔥	$75.00

Suspended 1990, Reintroduced 1995, Issue Price $40.00, '86

Purchased_____, Price $_____

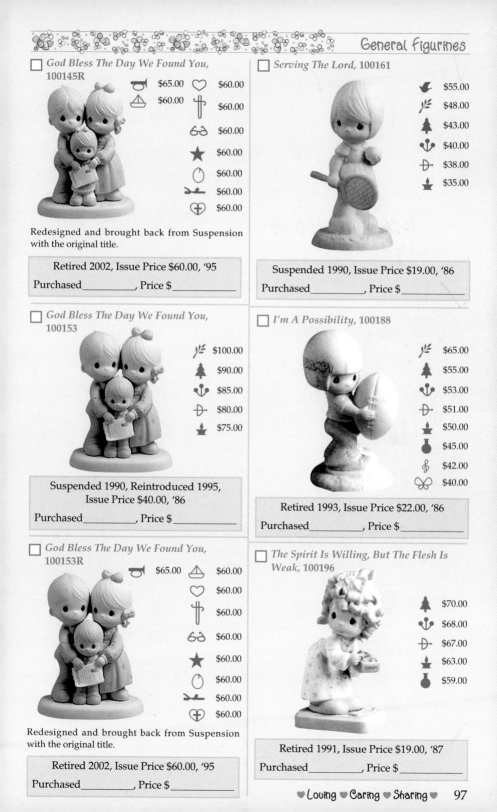

God Bless The Day We Found You, 100145R

♡ $65.00   ♡ $60.00
△ $60.00   ✝ $60.00
           👓 $60.00
           ★ $60.00
           ◯ $60.00
           ⌐ $60.00
           ✚ $60.00

Redesigned and brought back from Suspension with the original title.

Retired 2002, Issue Price $60.00, '95

Purchased_____, Price $_____

God Bless The Day We Found You, 100153

✿ $100.00
🌲 $90.00
⚓ $85.00
Ð $80.00
✦ $75.00

Suspended 1990, Reintroduced 1995, Issue Price $40.00, '86

Purchased_____, Price $_____

God Bless The Day We Found You, 100153R

🎺 $65.00   △ $60.00
           ♡ $60.00
           ✝ $60.00
           👓 $60.00
           ★ $60.00
           ◯ $60.00
           ⌐ $60.00
           ✚ $60.00

Redesigned and brought back from Suspension with the original title.

Retired 2002, Issue Price $60.00, '95

Purchased_____, Price $_____

Serving The Lord, 100161

🕊 $55.00
🌿 $48.00
🌲 $43.00
⚓ $40.00
Ð $38.00
✦ $35.00

Suspended 1990, Issue Price $19.00, '86

Purchased_____, Price $_____

I'm A Possibility, 100188

🌿 $65.00
🌲 $55.00
⚓ $53.00
Ð $51.00
✦ $50.00
◉ $45.00
𝄞 $42.00
∞ $40.00

Retired 1993, Issue Price $22.00, '86

Purchased_____, Price $_____

The Spirit Is Willing, But The Flesh Is Weak, 100196

🌲 $70.00
⚓ $68.00
Ð $67.00
✦ $63.00
◉ $59.00

Retired 1991, Issue Price $19.00, '87

Purchased_____, Price $_____

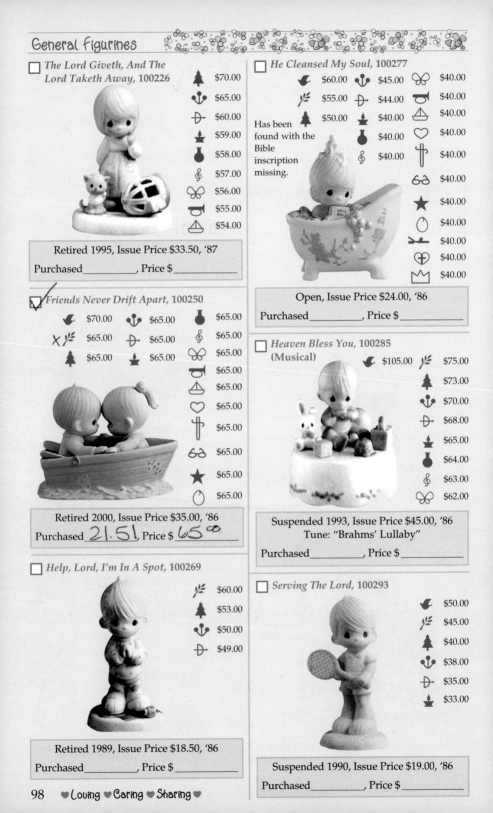

The Lord Giveth, And The Lord Taketh Away, 100226

🌲 $70.00
⚓ $65.00
⊅ $60.00
🕯 $59.00
🍶 $58.00
𝄞 $57.00
🦋 $56.00
📯 $55.00
⛵ $54.00

Retired 1995, Issue Price $33.50, '87

Purchased_____, Price $_____

✓ Friends Never Drift Apart, 100250

🐦 $70.00   ⚓ $65.00   🍶 $65.00
✗ 🌿 $65.00   ⊅ $65.00   𝄞 $65.00
🌲 $65.00   🕯 $65.00   🦋 $65.00
📯 $65.00
⛵ $65.00
♡ $65.00
✝ $65.00
👓 $65.00
★ $65.00
◯ $65.00

Retired 2000, Issue Price $35.00, '86

Purchased _21.51_, Price $ _65.00_

Help, Lord, I'm In A Spot, 100269

🌿 $60.00
🌲 $53.00
⚓ $50.00
⊅ $49.00

Retired 1989, Issue Price $18.50, '86

Purchased_____, Price $_____

He Cleansed My Soul, 100277

🐦 $60.00   ⚓ $45.00   🦋 $40.00
🌿 $55.00   ⊅ $44.00   📯 $40.00

Has been found with the Bible inscription missing.

🌲 $50.00   🕯 $40.00   △ $40.00
🍶 $40.00   ♡ $40.00
𝄞 $40.00   ✝ $40.00
👓 $40.00
★ $40.00
◯ $40.00
✂ $40.00
✛ $40.00
👑 $40.00

Open, Issue Price $24.00, '86

Purchased_____, Price $_____

Heaven Bless You, 100285 (Musical)

🐦 $105.00   🌿 $75.00
🌲 $73.00
⚓ $70.00
⊅ $68.00
🕯 $65.00
🍶 $64.00
𝄞 $63.00
🦋 $62.00

Suspended 1993, Issue Price $45.00, '86
Tune: "Brahms' Lullaby"

Purchased_____, Price $_____

Serving The Lord, 100293

🐦 $50.00
🌿 $45.00
🌲 $40.00
⚓ $38.00
⊅ $35.00
🕯 $33.00

Suspended 1990, Issue Price $19.00, '86

Purchased_____, Price $_____

☐ *Bong Bong*, 100455 (Doll)

🌿 $300.00

Individually numbered on foot. Includes certificate of authenticity.

Limited Ed. 12,000, Issue Price $150.00, '86

Purchased_____, Price $_____

☐ *Candy*, 100463 (Doll)

🌿 $300.00

Individually numbered on foot. Includes certificate of authenticity.

Limited Ed. 12,000, Issue Price $150.00, '86

Purchased_____, Price $_____

☐ *God Bless Our Family*, 100498

🌲 $63.00   ⊅ $58.00   ⚗ $54.00
⚓ $60.00   ⚖ $55.00   𝄞 $53.00
                                  ∞ $52.00
                                  🎺 $51.00
                                  ⛵ $50.00
                                  ♡ $50.00
                                  ✝ $50.00
                                  👓 $50.00
                                  ★ $50.00

Retired 1999, Issue Price $35.00, '87

Purchased_____, Price $_____

☐ *God Bless Our Family*, 100501

🌲 $63.00   ⊅ $58.00   ⚗ $54.00
⚓ $60.00   ⚖ $55.00   𝄞 $53.00
                                  ∞ $52.00
                                  🎺 $51.00
                                  ⛵ $50.00
                                  ♡ $50.00
                                  ✝ $50.00
                                  👓 $50.00
                                  ★ $50.00

Retired 1999, Issue Price $35.00, '87

Purchased_____, Price $_____

☐ *Scent From Above*, 100528

🌿 $70.00
🌲 $69.00
⚓ $68.00
⊅ $67.00
⚖ $66.00
⚗ $65.00

Retired 1991, Issue Price $19.00, '87

Purchased_____, Price $_____

☐ *I Picked A Very Special Mom*, 100536

🌿 $75.00
🌲 $65.00

Annual 1987, Issue Price $37.50, '87

Purchased_____, Price $_____

General figurines

☑ *Brotherly Love*, 100544

✓ 🌿 $100.00
🌲 $85.00
⚓ $83.00
⌀ $80.00

Suspended 1989, Issue Price $37.00, '86
Purchased *16.56*, Price $ *100.00*

☐ *God Is Love, Dear Valentine*, 100625 (Thimble)

🕊 $20.00
🌿 $15.00
🌲 $13.00
⚓ $11.00
⌀ $10.00

Suspended 1989, Issue Price $5.50, '86
Purchased_____, Price $_____

☐ *The Lord Bless You And Keep You*, 100633 (Thimble)

🕊 $20.00
🌿 $18.00
🌲 $15.00
⚓ $14.00
⌀ $13.00
🕯 $12.00
🏺 $11.00

Suspended 1991, Issue Price $5.50, '86
Purchased_____, Price $_____

☐ *Four Seasons*, 100641 (Thimbles)

🕊 $150.00
🌿 $95.00

Annual 1986, Issue Price $20.00, '86
Four Seasons Thimbles, Set of 4
Purchased_____, Price $_____

☐ *Clowns*, 100668 (Thimbles)

🌿 $40.00
🌲 $35.00
⚓ $30.00

Suspended 1988, Issue Price $11.00, '86
Set of 2
Purchased_____, Price $_____

☐ *Cherishing Each Special Moment*, 101233

☩ $50.00
♛ $50.00

Open, Issue Price $50.00, '02
Series: *Motherhood* — Third Issue
Purchased_____, Price $_____

☐ *A Penny A Kiss, A Penny A Hug*, 101234

✈ $35.00

Limited Ed., Issue Price $35.00, '01
Authorized Retailer Event, 3/2/01
Purchased_____, Price $_____

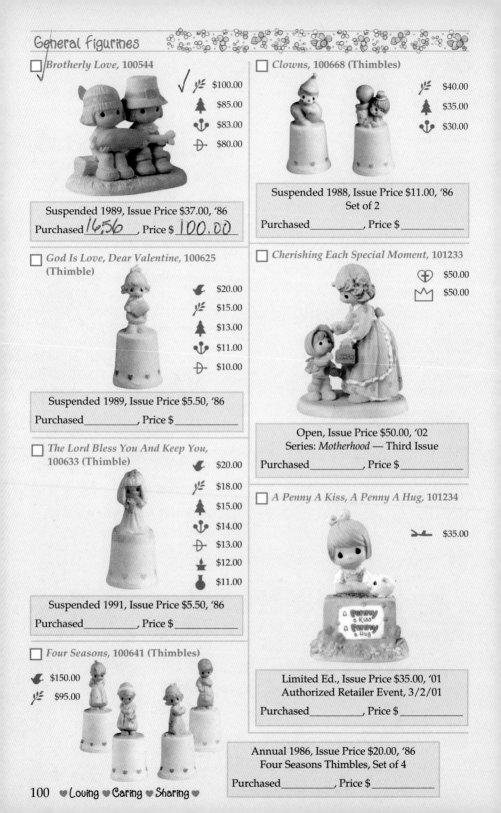

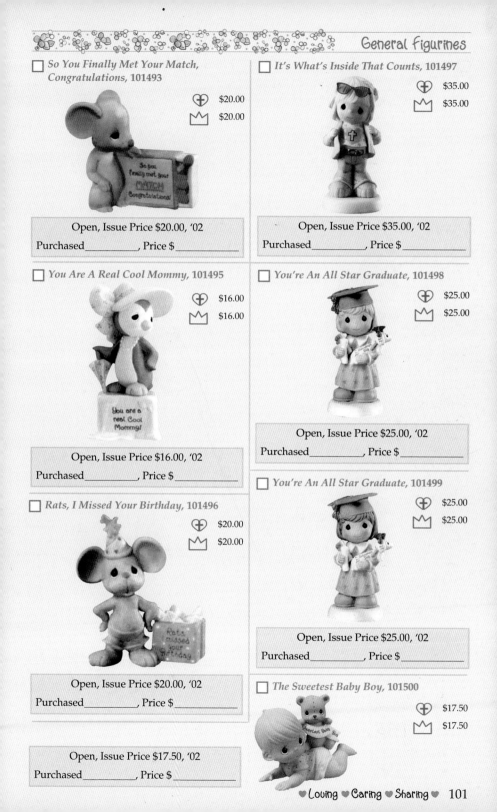

☐ *So You Finally Met Your Match, Congratulations*, 101493

✝ $20.00
♛ $20.00

Open, Issue Price $20.00, '02
Purchased_____, Price $_____

☐ *You Are A Real Cool Mommy*, 101495

✝ $16.00
♛ $16.00

Open, Issue Price $16.00, '02
Purchased_____, Price $_____

☐ *Rats, I Missed Your Birthday*, 101496

✝ $20.00
♛ $20.00

Open, Issue Price $20.00, '02
Purchased_____, Price $_____

☐ *It's What's Inside That Counts*, 101497

✝ $35.00
♛ $35.00

Open, Issue Price $35.00, '02
Purchased_____, Price $_____

☐ *You're An All Star Graduate*, 101498

✝ $25.00
♛ $25.00

Open, Issue Price $25.00, '02
Purchased_____, Price $_____

☐ *You're An All Star Graduate*, 101499

✝ $25.00
♛ $25.00

Open, Issue Price $25.00, '02
Purchased_____, Price $_____

☐ *The Sweetest Baby Boy*, 101500

✝ $17.50
♛ $17.50

Open, Issue Price $17.50, '02
Purchased_____, Price $_____

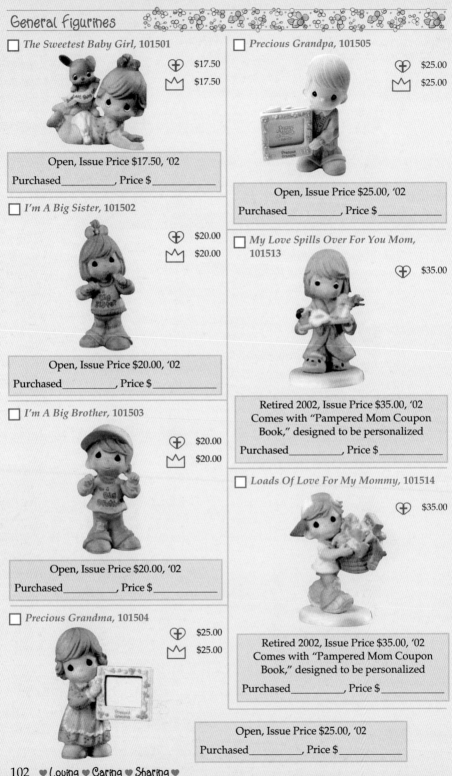

☐ *The Sweetest Baby Girl,* 101501

✛ $17.50
♔ $17.50

Open, Issue Price $17.50, '02

Purchased_____, Price $_____

☐ *I'm A Big Sister,* 101502

✛ $20.00
♔ $20.00

Open, Issue Price $20.00, '02

Purchased_____, Price $_____

☐ *I'm A Big Brother,* 101503

✛ $20.00
♔ $20.00

Open, Issue Price $20.00, '02

Purchased_____, Price $_____

☐ *Precious Grandma,* 101504

✛ $25.00
♔ $25.00

☐ *Precious Grandpa,* 101505

✛ $25.00
♔ $25.00

Open, Issue Price $25.00, '02

Purchased_____, Price $_____

☐ *My Love Spills Over For You Mom,* 101513

✛ $35.00

Retired 2002, Issue Price $35.00, '02
Comes with "Pampered Mom Coupon Book," designed to be personalized

Purchased_____, Price $_____

☐ *Loads Of Love For My Mommy,* 101514

✛ $35.00

Retired 2002, Issue Price $35.00, '02
Comes with "Pampered Mom Coupon Book," designed to be personalized

Purchased_____, Price $_____

Open, Issue Price $25.00, '02

Purchased_____, Price $_____

☐ *January — Snowdrop, "Pure And Gentle,"* **101515**

✝ $40.00
♔ $40.00

Open, Issue Price $40.00, '02
Series: *Calendar Girls*

Purchased_____, Price $_____

☐ *April — Lily, "Virtuous,"* **101519**

✝ $40.00
♔ $40.00

Open, Issue Price $40.00, '02
Series: *Calendar Girls*

Purchased_____, Price $_____

☐ *February — Carnation, "Bold And Brave,"* **101517**

✝ $40.00
♔ $40.00

Open, Issue Price $40.00, '02
Series: *Calendar Girls*

Purchased_____, Price $_____

☐ *May — Hawthorn, "Bright And Hopeful,"* **101520**

✝ $40.00
♔ $40.00

Open, Issue Price $40.00, '02
Series: *Calendar Girls*

Purchased_____, Price $_____

☐ *March — Violet, "Modest,"* **101518**

✝ $40.00
♔ $40.00

Open, Issue Price $40.00, '02
Series: *Calendar Girls*

Purchased_____, Price $_____

☐ *June — Rose, "Beautiful,"* **101521**

✝ $40.00
♔ $40.00

Open, Issue Price $40.00, '02
Series: *Calendar Girls*

Purchased_____, Price $_____

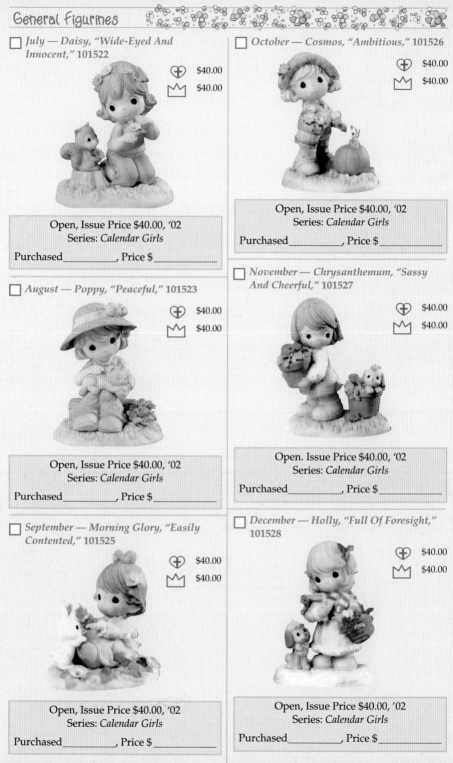

☐ *July — Daisy, "Wide-Eyed And Innocent,"* 101522

✤ $40.00
♔ $40.00

Open, Issue Price $40.00, '02
Series: *Calendar Girls*
Purchased_____, Price $_____

☐ *August — Poppy, "Peaceful,"* 101523

✤ $40.00
♔ $40.00

Open, Issue Price $40.00, '02
Series: *Calendar Girls*
Purchased_____, Price $_____

☐ *September — Morning Glory, "Easily Contented,"* 101525

✤ $40.00
♔ $40.00

Open, Issue Price $40.00, '02
Series: *Calendar Girls*
Purchased_____, Price $_____

☐ *October — Cosmos, "Ambitious,"* 101526

✤ $40.00
♔ $40.00

Open, Issue Price $40.00, '02
Series: *Calendar Girls*
Purchased_____, Price $_____

☐ *November — Chrysanthemum, "Sassy And Cheerful,"* 101527

✤ $40.00
♔ $40.00

Open. Issue Price $40.00, '02
Series: *Calendar Girls*
Purchased_____, Price $_____

☐ *December — Holly, "Full Of Foresight,"* 101528

✤ $40.00
♔ $40.00

Open, Issue Price $40.00, '02
Series: *Calendar Girls*
Purchased_____, Price $_____

☐ *Friends Are Never Far Behind*, 101543

✚ $45.00

Limited Ed. 5,000, Issue Price $45.00, '02
Series: *Smiles Forever* — Fifth Issue

Purchased_____, Price $_____

☐ *Our Love Is Heaven Scent*, 101546

✚ $30.00

Limited Ed. 5,000, Issue Price $30.00, '02
Series: *Smiles Forever* — Fourth Issue

Purchased_____, Price $_____

☐ *Love Is On Its Way*, 101544

✚ $30.00

Limited Ed. 5,000, Issue Price $30.00, '02
Series: *Smiles Forever* — First Issue

Purchased_____, Price $_____

☐ *Life Never Smelled So Sweet*, 101547

✚ $30.00

Limited Ed. 5,000, Issue Price $30.00, '02
Series: *Smiles Forever* — Third Issue

Purchased_____, Price $_____

☐ *Planting The Seeds Of Love*, 101548

✚ $99.50

Limited Ed. 7,500, Issue Price $99.50, '02
CCR Exclusive

Purchased_____, Price $_____

☐ *Lord, Help Me Clean Up My Act*, 101545

✚ $30.00

Limited Ed. 5,000, Issue Price $30.00, '02
Series: *Smiles Forever* — Second Issue

Purchased_____, Price $_____

☐ *Precious Moments In Paradise,* **101549**

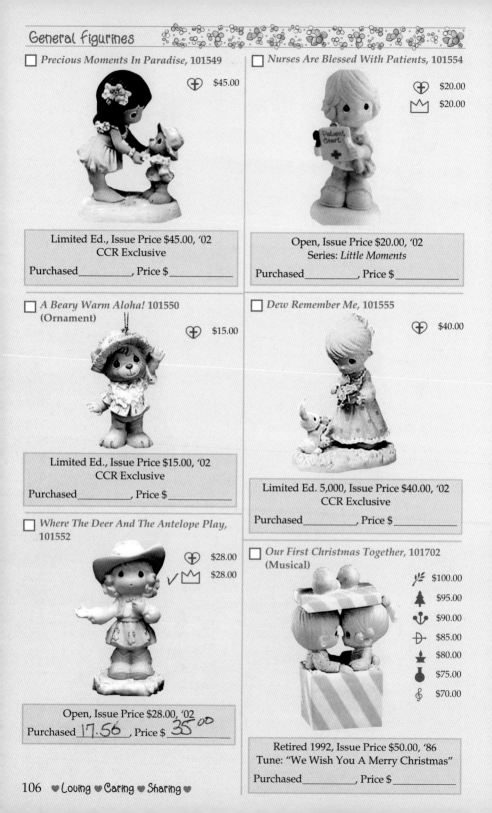

⊕ $45.00

Limited Ed., Issue Price $45.00, '02
CCR Exclusive

Purchased_____, Price $_____

☐ *Nurses Are Blessed With Patients,* **101554**

⊕ $20.00
♛ $20.00

Open, Issue Price $20.00, '02
Series: *Little Moments*

Purchased_____, Price $_____

☐ *A Beary Warm Aloha!* **101550**
  (Ornament)

⊕ $15.00

Limited Ed., Issue Price $15.00, '02
CCR Exclusive

Purchased_____, Price $_____

☐ *Dew Remember Me,* **101555**

⊕ $40.00

Limited Ed. 5,000, Issue Price $40.00, '02
CCR Exclusive

Purchased_____, Price $_____

☐ *Where The Deer And The Antelope Play,*
  101552

⊕ $28.00
✓ ♛ $28.00

Open, Issue Price $28.00, '02

Purchased 17.56 , Price $ 35 ⁰⁰

☐ *Our First Christmas Together,* **101702**
  (Musical)

⚘ $100.00
🌲 $95.00
⚓ $90.00
⊢ $85.00
✹ $80.00
⬥ $75.00
𝄞 $70.00

Retired 1992, Issue Price $50.00, '86
Tune: "We Wish You A Merry Christmas"

Purchased_____, Price $_____

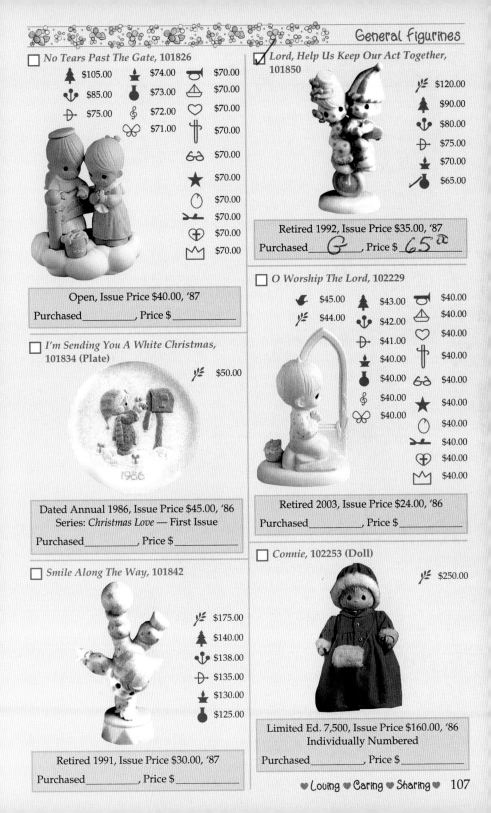

☐ *No Tears Past The Gate, 101826*

🌲	$105.00	⬥	$74.00	⌒	$70.00
⚓	$85.00	⬦	$73.00	⛵	$70.00
➥	$75.00	⚘	$72.00	♡	$70.00
		✿	$71.00	✝	$70.00
				👓	$70.00
				★	$70.00
				◯	$70.00
				✂	$70.00
				✠	$70.00
				♔	$70.00

Open, Issue Price $40.00, '87

Purchased_____, Price $_____

☐ *I'm Sending You A White Christmas, 101834 (Plate)*

🌿 $50.00

Dated Annual 1986, Issue Price $45.00, '86
Series: *Christmas Love* — First Issue

Purchased_____, Price $_____

☐ *Smile Along The Way, 101842*

🌿	$175.00
🌲	$140.00
⚓	$138.00
➥	$135.00
✠	$130.00
⬦	$125.00

Retired 1991, Issue Price $30.00, '87

Purchased_____, Price $_____

☑ *Lord, Help Us Keep Our Act Together, 101850*

🌿	$120.00
🌲	$90.00
⚓	$80.00
➥	$75.00
✠	$70.00
✦	$65.00

Retired 1992, Issue Price $35.00, '87

Purchased_____*G*_____, Price $ _65ⓐ_

☐ *O Worship The Lord, 102229*

🐦	$45.00	🌲	$43.00	⌒	$40.00
🌿	$44.00	⚓	$42.00	⛵	$40.00
		➥	$41.00	♡	$40.00
		✠	$40.00	✝	$40.00
		⬦	$40.00	👓	$40.00
		⚘	$40.00	★	$40.00
		✿	$40.00	◯	$40.00
				✂	$40.00
				✠	$40.00
				♔	$40.00

Retired 2003, Issue Price $24.00, '86

Purchased_____, Price $_____

☐ *Connie, 102253 (Doll)*

🌿 $250.00

Limited Ed. 7,500, Issue Price $160.00, '86
Individually Numbered

Purchased_____, Price $_____

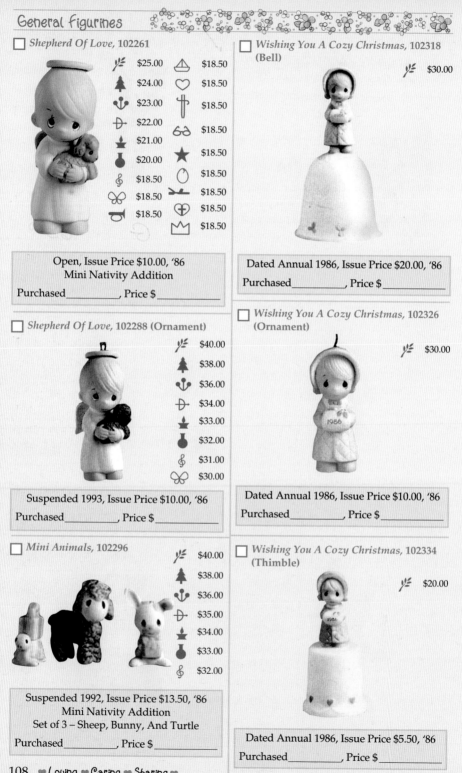

☐ *Shepherd Of Love*, 102261

🌿	$25.00	⛵	$18.50
🌲	$24.00	♡	$18.50
⚓	$23.00	✝	$18.50
⊕	$22.00	👓	$18.50
🕯	$21.00		
🕯	$20.00	★	$18.50
𝄞	$18.50	◯	$18.50
🦋	$18.50	✂	$18.50
♫	$18.50	✛	$18.50
		👑	$18.50

Open, Issue Price $10.00, '86
Mini Nativity Addition

Purchased_____, Price $_____

☐ *Shepherd Of Love*, 102288 (Ornament)

🌿	$40.00
🌲	$38.00
⚓	$36.00
⊕	$34.00
🕯	$33.00
🕯	$32.00
𝄞	$31.00
🦋	$30.00

Suspended 1993, Issue Price $10.00, '86

Purchased_____, Price $_____

☐ *Mini Animals*, 102296

🌿	$40.00
🌲	$38.00
⚓	$36.00
⊕	$35.00
🕯	$34.00
🕯	$33.00
𝄞	$32.00

Suspended 1992, Issue Price $13.50, '86
Mini Nativity Addition
Set of 3 – Sheep, Bunny, And Turtle

Purchased_____, Price $_____

☐ *Wishing You A Cozy Christmas*, 102318
(Bell)

🌿 $30.00

Dated Annual 1986, Issue Price $20.00, '86

Purchased_____, Price $_____

☐ *Wishing You A Cozy Christmas*, 102326
(Ornament)

🌿 $30.00

Dated Annual 1986, Issue Price $10.00, '86

Purchased_____, Price $_____

☐ *Wishing You A Cozy Christmas*, 102334
(Thimble)

🌿 $20.00

Dated Annual 1986, Issue Price $5.50, '86

Purchased_____, Price $_____

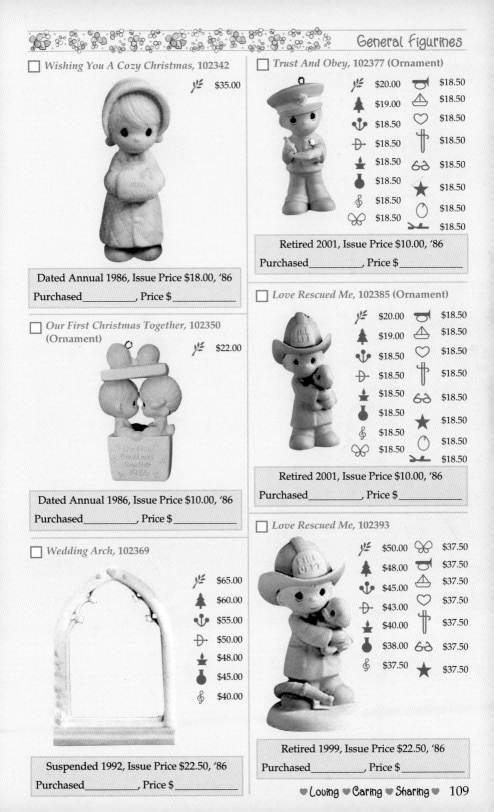

☐ *Wishing You A Cozy Christmas*, 102342

🌿 $35.00

Dated Annual 1986, Issue Price $18.00, '86
Purchased_____, Price $_____

☐ *Our First Christmas Together*, 102350
(Ornament)

🌿 $22.00

Dated Annual 1986, Issue Price $10.00, '86
Purchased_____, Price $_____

☐ *Wedding Arch*, 102369

🌿 $65.00
🌲 $60.00
⚓ $55.00
🕊 $50.00
🕯 $48.00
🔔 $45.00
𝄞 $40.00

Suspended 1992, Issue Price $22.50, '86
Purchased_____, Price $_____

☐ *Trust And Obey*, 102377 (Ornament)

🌿 $20.00   🐚 $18.50
🌲 $19.00   ⛵ $18.50
⚓ $18.50   ♡ $18.50
🕊 $18.50   ✝ $18.50
🕯 $18.50   👓 $18.50
🔔 $18.50   ★ $18.50
𝄞 $18.50   ◯ $18.50
🦋 $18.50   ✈ $18.50

Retired 2001, Issue Price $10.00, '86
Purchased_____, Price $_____

☐ *Love Rescued Me*, 102385 (Ornament)

🌿 $20.00   🐚 $18.50
🌲 $19.00   ⛵ $18.50
⚓ $18.50   ♡ $18.50
🕊 $18.50   ✝ $18.50
🕯 $18.50   👓 $18.50
🔔 $18.50   ★ $18.50
𝄞 $18.50   ◯ $18.50
🦋 $18.50   ✈ $18.50

Retired 2001, Issue Price $10.00, '86
Purchased_____, Price $_____

☐ *Love Rescued Me*, 102393

🌿 $50.00   🦋 $37.50
🌲 $48.00   🐚 $37.50
⚓ $45.00   ⛵ $37.50
🕊 $43.00   ♡ $37.50
🕯 $40.00   ✝ $37.50
🔔 $38.00   👓 $37.50
𝄞 $37.50   ★ $37.50

Retired 1999, Issue Price $22.50, '86
Purchased_____, Price $_____

General Figurines

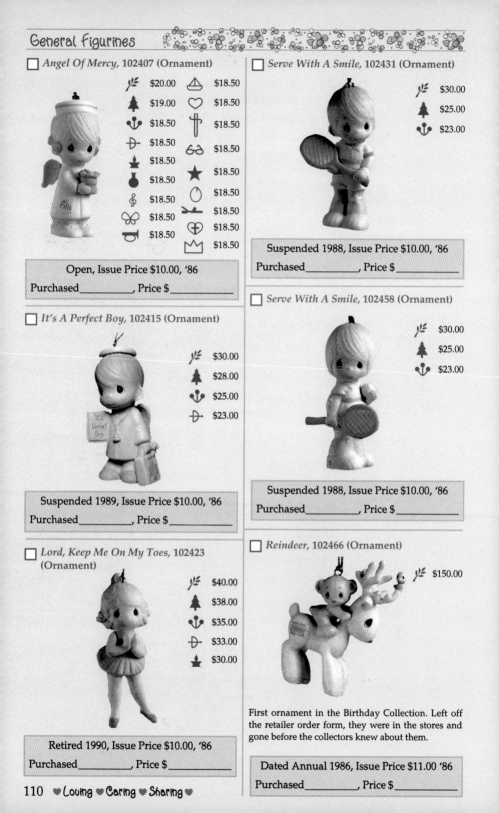

☐ *Angel Of Mercy*, 102407 (Ornament)

🌿	$20.00	⛵	$18.50
🌲	$19.00	♡	$18.50
⚓	$18.50	✝	$18.50
⌐	$18.50	👓	$18.50
☀	$18.50	★	$18.50
◈	$18.50		
🎵	$18.50	○	$18.50
🦋	$18.50	↣	$18.50
📯	$18.50	✠	$18.50
		👑	$18.50

Open, Issue Price $10.00, '86

Purchased_____, Price $_____

☐ *It's A Perfect Boy*, 102415 (Ornament)

🌿	$30.00
🌲	$28.00
⚓	$25.00
⌐	$23.00

Suspended 1989, Issue Price $10.00, '86

Purchased_____, Price $_____

☐ *Lord, Keep Me On My Toes*, 102423 (Ornament)

🌿	$40.00
🌲	$38.00
⚓	$35.00
⌐	$33.00
☀	$30.00

Retired 1990, Issue Price $10.00, '86

Purchased_____, Price $_____

☐ *Serve With A Smile*, 102431 (Ornament)

🌿	$30.00
🌲	$25.00
⚓	$23.00

Suspended 1988, Issue Price $10.00, '86

Purchased_____, Price $_____

☐ *Serve With A Smile*, 102458 (Ornament)

🌿	$30.00
🌲	$25.00
⚓	$23.00

Suspended 1988, Issue Price $10.00, '86

Purchased_____, Price $_____

☐ *Reindeer*, 102466 (Ornament)

🌿	$150.00

First ornament in the Birthday Collection. Left off the retailer order form, they were in the stores and gone before the collectors knew about them.

Dated Annual 1986, Issue Price $11.00 '86

Purchased_____, Price $_____

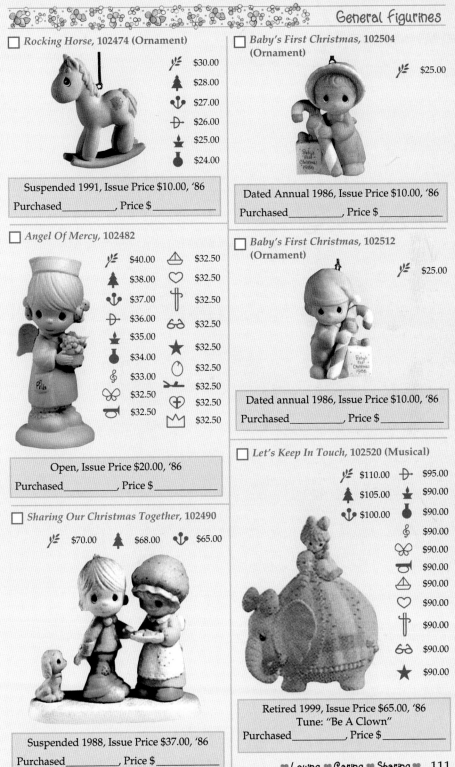

☐ *Rocking Horse*, 102474 (Ornament)

🌿 $30.00
🎄 $28.00
⚓ $27.00
✈ $26.00
🔨 $25.00
🏺 $24.00

Suspended 1991, Issue Price $10.00, '86
Purchased_____, Price $_____

☐ *Angel Of Mercy*, 102482

🌿 $40.00 △ $32.50
🎄 $38.00 ♡ $32.50
⚓ $37.00 ✝ $32.50
✈ $36.00 👓 $32.50
🔨 $35.00 ★ $32.50
🏺 $34.00 ◯ $32.50
𝄞 $33.00 ⚰ $32.50
🦋 $32.50 ⊕ $32.50
📯 $32.50 👑 $32.50

Open, Issue Price $20.00, '86
Purchased_____, Price $_____

☐ *Sharing Our Christmas Together*, 102490

🌿 $70.00 🎄 $68.00 ⚓ $65.00

Suspended 1988, Issue Price $37.00, '86
Purchased_____, Price $_____

☐ *Baby's First Christmas*, 102504 (Ornament)

🌿 $25.00

Dated Annual 1986, Issue Price $10.00, '86
Purchased_____, Price $_____

☐ *Baby's First Christmas*, 102512 (Ornament)

🌿 $25.00

Dated annual 1986, Issue Price $10.00, '86
Purchased_____, Price $_____

☐ *Let's Keep In Touch*, 102520 (Musical)

🌿 $110.00 ✈ $95.00
🎄 $105.00 🔨 $90.00
⚓ $100.00 🏺 $90.00
𝄞 $90.00
🦋 $90.00
📯 $90.00
△ $90.00
♡ $90.00
✝ $90.00
👓 $90.00
★ $90.00

Retired 1999, Issue Price $65.00, '86
Tune: "Be A Clown"
Purchased_____, Price $_____

General Figurines

☐ *We Are All Precious In His Sight*, 102903

🌲 $65.00

Annual 1987, Issue Price $30.00, '87

Purchased_____, Price $_____

☐ *Mom, You're A Sweetheart*, 102913

⊕ $19.99

Open, Issue Price $19.99, '02
Avon Exclusive

Purchased_____, Price $_____

☐ *God Bless America*, 102938

🌿 $60.00

Annual 1986, Reintroduced 2001,
Issue Price $30.00, '86
Series: *America Forever*

Purchased_____, Price $_____

☐ *God Bless America*, 102938R

⊕ $40.00
♛ $40.00

Was reissued
in different
color with stars
on hatband.

Open, Issue Price $40.00, '02
Series: *America Forever*

Purchased_____, Price $_____

☐ *My Peace I Give Unto Thee*, 102954
(Plate)

🌲 $55.00

Dated Annual 1987, Issue Price $45.00, '87
Series: *Christmas Love* — Second Issue

Purchased_____, Price $_____

☐ *It's The Birthday Of A King*, 102962

🌿 $40.00
🌲 $38.00
⚓ $35.00
⌀ $33.00

Suspended 1989, Issue Price $19.00, '86
Nativity Addition

Purchased_____, Price $_____

☐ *I Would Be Sunk Without You*, 102970

🌲 $30.00   ⛵ $20.00
⚓ $28.00   ♡ $20.00
↦ $27.00   ✝ $20.00
🔥 $26.00
🔮 $25.00   👓 $20.00
🎼 $23.00   ⭐ $20.00
∞ $21.00   ◯ $20.00
🎺 $20.00   ⤢ $20.00
            ⊕ $20.00

Retired 2002, Issue Price $15.00, '87

Purchased_____, Price $_____

☐ *We Belong To The Lord*, 103004

◇ $225.00
Without Bible $200.00

The Damien-Dutton Society for Leprosy Aid operates two gift shops and all of the profits go back to this charity. This figurine was a special edition produced for and sold by the Damien-Dutton Society. Comes with a leatherbound Bible.

Special Piece, Issue Price $50.00, '86
Damien-Dutton Piece

Purchased_____, Price $_____

☐ *Living Each Day With Love*, 103175

⊕ $49.95

Limited Ed. 7,500, Issue Price $49.95, '02
Series: *Rose Petal* — Second Issue
Century Circle Exclusive

Purchased_____, Price $_____

☐ *You Are The Rose In My Bouquet*, 103176

⊕ $40.00

Limited Ed. 7,500, Issue Price $40.00, '02
Series: *Rose Petal* — First Issue
CCR Exclusive

Purchased_____, Price $_____

☐ *A Smile Is Cherished In The Heart*, 103177

⊕ $40.00

Open, Issue Price $40.00, '02
Series: *Rose Petal* — Third Issue
CCR Exclusive

Purchased_____, Price $_____

☐ *Hang Onto Your Happiness*, 103178

♙ $16.00

Open, Issue Price $16.00, '03
Japanese Exclusive

Purchased_____, Price $_____

☐ *We Are The Sheep Of His Pasture*, 103180

$16.00

Open, Issue Price $16.00, '03
Japanese Exclusive
Purchased_____, Price $_____

☐ *Life Is No Boar With You*, 103183

$16.00

Open, Issue Price $16.00, '03
Japanese Exclusive
Purchased_____, Price $_____

☐ *The Dawn Of A New Beginning*, 103181

$16.00

Open, Issue Price $16.00, '03
Japanese Exclusive
Purchased_____, Price $_____

☐ *Life's Blessings Are Bountiful*, 103184

$16.00

Open, Issue Price $16.00, '03
Japanese Exclusive
Purchased_____, Price $_____

☐ *Good Fortune Is Just Around The Corner*,
103182

$16.00

Open, Issue Price $16.00, '03
Japanese Exclusive
Purchased_____, Price $_____

☐ *Ringing In A Year Of Good Health*,
103185

$16.00

Open, Issue Price $16.00, '03
Japanese Exclusive
Purchased_____, Price $_____

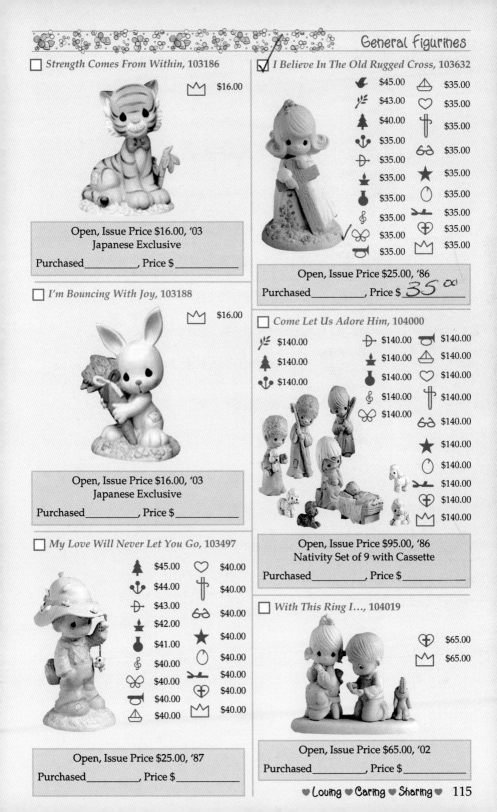

☐ *Strength Comes From Within*, 103186

👑 $16.00

Open, Issue Price $16.00, '03
Japanese Exclusive

Purchased_____, Price $_____

☐ *I'm Bouncing With Joy*, 103188

👑 $16.00

Open, Issue Price $16.00, '03
Japanese Exclusive

Purchased_____, Price $_____

☐ *My Love Will Never Let You Go*, 103497

🌲 $45.00		♡ $40.00
⚓ $44.00		✝ $40.00
$43.00		👓 $40.00
$42.00		★ $40.00
$41.00		○ $40.00
🎼 $40.00		$40.00
🦋 $40.00		✠ $40.00
📯 $40.00		👑 $40.00
△ $40.00		

Open, Issue Price $25.00, '87

Purchased_____, Price $_____

☑ *I Believe In The Old Rugged Cross*, 103632

🌿 $45.00	△ $35.00
🌱 $43.00	♡ $35.00
🌲 $40.00	✝ $35.00
⚓ $35.00	👓 $35.00
$35.00	★ $35.00
$35.00	○ $35.00
$35.00	$35.00
🎼 $35.00	✠ $35.00
🦋 ✓ $35.00	👑 $35.00
📯 $35.00	

Open, Issue Price $25.00, '86

Purchased_____, Price $ 35⁰⁰

☐ *Come Let Us Adore Him*, 104000

🌱 $140.00	👓 $140.00	📯 $140.00
🌲 $140.00	$140.00	△ $140.00
⚓ $140.00	$140.00	♡ $140.00
	🎼 $140.00	✝ $140.00
	🦋 $140.00	👓 $140.00
		★ $140.00
		○ $140.00
		$140.00
		✠ $140.00
		👑 $140.00

Open, Issue Price $95.00, '86
Nativity Set of 9 with Cassette

Purchased_____, Price $_____

☐ *With This Ring I...*, 104019

✠ $65.00
👑 $65.00

Open, Issue Price $65.00, '02

Purchased_____, Price $_____

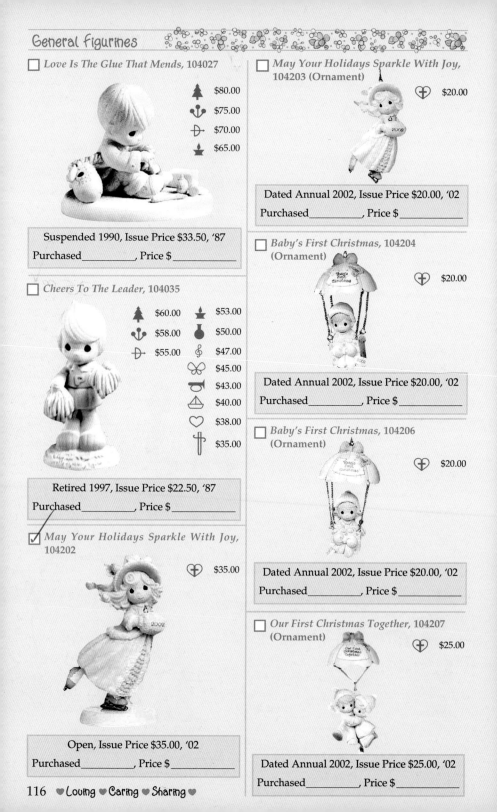

☐ *Love Is The Glue That Mends*, 104027

🌲 $80.00
⚓ $75.00
⯈ $70.00
🕯 $65.00

Suspended 1990, Issue Price $33.50, '87
Purchased_____, Price $_____

☐ *Cheers To The Leader*, 104035

🌲 $60.00   ⬥ $53.00
⚓ $58.00   ⬗ $50.00
⯈ $55.00   § $47.00
              ∞ $45.00
              🎺 $43.00
              ⟁ $40.00
              ♡ $38.00
              ✝ $35.00

Retired 1997, Issue Price $22.50, '87
Purchased_____, Price $_____

☑ *May Your Holidays Sparkle With Joy,*
104202

✚ $35.00

Open, Issue Price $35.00, '02
Purchased_____, Price $_____

☐ *May Your Holidays Sparkle With Joy,*
104203 (Ornament)

✚ $20.00

Dated Annual 2002, Issue Price $20.00, '02
Purchased_____, Price $_____

☐ *Baby's First Christmas*, 104204
(Ornament)

✚ $20.00

Dated Annual 2002, Issue Price $20.00, '02
Purchased_____, Price $_____

☐ *Baby's First Christmas*, 104206
(Ornament)

✚ $20.00

Dated Annual 2002, Issue Price $20.00, '02
Purchased_____, Price $_____

☐ *Our First Christmas Together*, 104207
(Ornament)

✚ $25.00

Dated Annual 2002, Issue Price $25.00, '02
Purchased_____, Price $_____

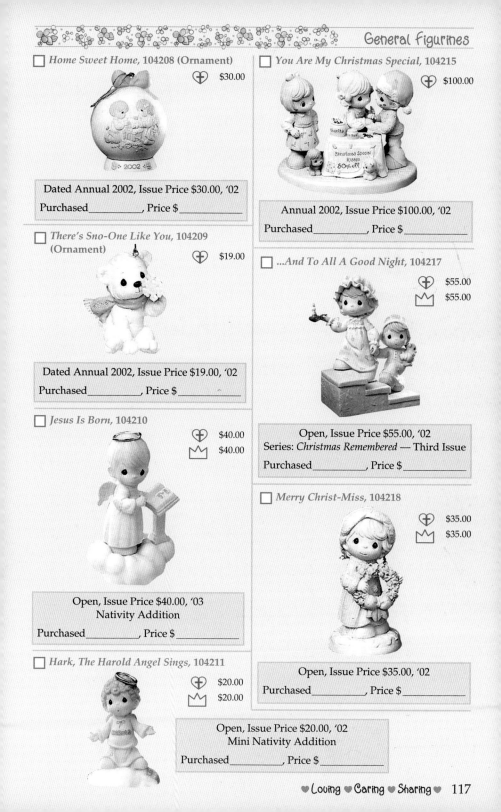

☐ *Home Sweet Home*, 104208 (Ornament)

✝ $30.00

Dated Annual 2002, Issue Price $30.00, '02
Purchased_____, Price $_____

☐ *There's Sno-One Like You*, 104209 (Ornament)

✝ $19.00

Dated Annual 2002, Issue Price $19.00, '02
Purchased_____, Price $_____

☐ *Jesus Is Born*, 104210

✝ $40.00
♛ $40.00

Open, Issue Price $40.00, '03
Nativity Addition
Purchased_____, Price $_____

☐ *Hark, The Harold Angel Sings*, 104211

✝ $20.00
♛ $20.00

Open, Issue Price $20.00, '02
Mini Nativity Addition
Purchased_____, Price $_____

☐ *You Are My Christmas Special*, 104215

✝ $100.00

Annual 2002, Issue Price $100.00, '02
Purchased_____, Price $_____

☐ *...And To All A Good Night*, 104217

✝ $55.00
♛ $55.00

Open, Issue Price $55.00, '02
Series: *Christmas Remembered* — Third Issue
Purchased_____, Price $_____

☐ *Merry Christ-Miss*, 104218

✝ $35.00
♛ $35.00

Open, Issue Price $35.00, '02
Purchased_____, Price $_____

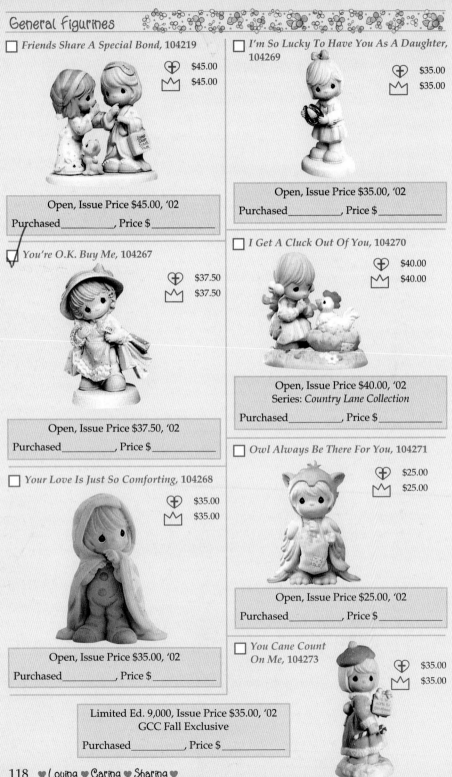

☐ *Friends Share A Special Bond*, **104219**

✝ $45.00
♛ $45.00

Open, Issue Price $45.00, '02
Purchased_____, Price $_____

☐ *You're O.K. Buy Me*, **104267**

✝ $37.50
♛ $37.50

Open, Issue Price $37.50, '02
Purchased_____, Price $_____

☐ *Your Love Is Just So Comforting*, **104268**

✝ $35.00
♛ $35.00

Open, Issue Price $35.00, '02
Purchased_____, Price $_____

☐ *I'm So Lucky To Have You As A Daughter*, **104269**

✝ $35.00
♛ $35.00

Open, Issue Price $35.00, '02
Purchased_____, Price $_____

☐ *I Get A Cluck Out Of You*, **104270**

✝ $40.00
♛ $40.00

Open, Issue Price $40.00, '02
Series: *Country Lane Collection*
Purchased_____, Price $_____

☐ *Owl Always Be There For You*, **104271**

✝ $25.00
♛ $25.00

Open, Issue Price $25.00, '02
Purchased_____, Price $_____

☐ *You Cane Count On Me*, **104273**

✝ $35.00
♛ $35.00

Limited Ed. 9,000, Issue Price $35.00, '02
GCC Fall Exclusive
Purchased_____, Price $_____

☐ *You Cane Count On Me*, 104274
(Ornament)

🕀 $20.00
M $20.00

Limited Ed. 6,000, Issue Price $20.00, '02
GCC Fall Exclusive

Purchased_____, Price $_____

☐ *Life's Ups 'N Downs Are Smoother With
You*, 104275

M $30.00

Comes with tart burner, tea light candle, and Bayberry scented tart.

Open, Issue Price $30.00, '03
Gift To Go

Purchased_____, Price $_____

☐ *Twogether We Can Move Mountains*,
104276

🕀 $80.00

Annual 2002, Issue Price $80.00, '02
Boys & Girls Club Commemorative

Purchased_____, Price $_____

☐ *His Love Is Reflected In You*, 104279

M $85.00

Open, Issue Price $85.00, '03

Purchased_____, Price $_____

☐ *Carry A Song In Your Heart*, 104281

🕀 $35.00

Limited Ed. 8,500, Issue Price $35.00, '02
CCR & DSR Exclusive

Purchased_____, Price $_____

☐ *Hugs Can Tame The Wildest Heart*,
104282

🕀 $35.00

Limited Ed. 8,500, Issue Price $35.00, '02
DSR Exclusive

Purchased_____, Price $_____

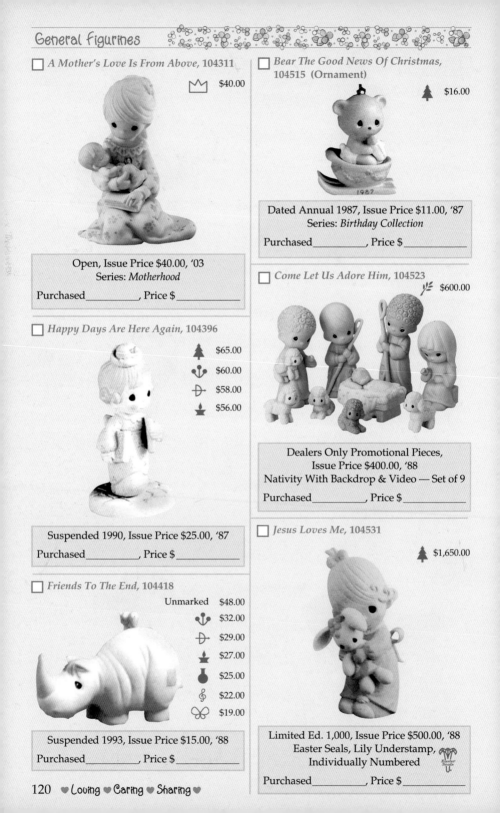

☐ *A Mother's Love Is From Above*, 104311

♔ $40.00

Open, Issue Price $40.00, '03
Series: *Motherhood*

Purchased_____, Price $_____

☐ *Happy Days Are Here Again*, 104396

🌲 $65.00
⚓ $60.00
⊅ $58.00
✦ $56.00

Suspended 1990, Issue Price $25.00, '87

Purchased_____, Price $_____

☐ *Friends To The End*, 104418

Unmarked $48.00
⚓ $32.00
⊅ $29.00
✦ $27.00
🌡 $25.00
𝄞 $22.00
🦋 $19.00

Suspended 1993, Issue Price $15.00, '88

Purchased_____, Price $_____

☐ *Bear The Good News Of Christmas*, 104515 (Ornament)

🌲 $16.00

Dated Annual 1987, Issue Price $11.00, '87
Series: *Birthday Collection*

Purchased_____, Price $_____

☐ *Come Let Us Adore Him*, 104523

🌿 $600.00

Dealers Only Promotional Pieces,
Issue Price $400.00, '88
Nativity With Backdrop & Video — Set of 9

Purchased_____, Price $_____

☐ *Jesus Loves Me*, 104531

🌲 $1,650.00

Limited Ed. 1,000, Issue Price $500.00, '88
Easter Seals, Lily Understamp,
Individually Numbered

Purchased_____, Price $_____

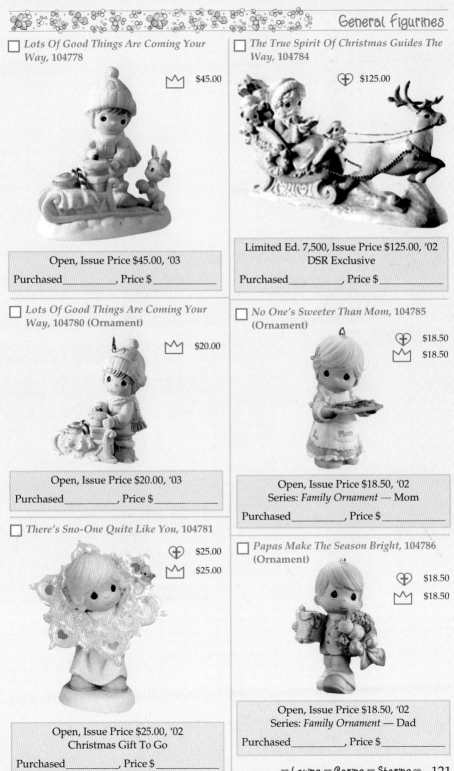

☐ *Lots Of Good Things Are Coming Your Way*, 104778

♔ $45.00

Open, Issue Price $45.00, '03

Purchased_____, Price $_____

☐ *The True Spirit Of Christmas Guides The Way*, 104784

✛ $125.00

Limited Ed. 7,500, Issue Price $125.00, '02
DSR Exclusive

Purchased_____, Price $_____

☐ *Lots Of Good Things Are Coming Your Way*, 104780 (Ornament)

♔ $20.00

Open, Issue Price $20.00, '03

Purchased_____, Price $_____

☐ *No One's Sweeter Than Mom*, 104785 (Ornament)

✛ $18.50
♔ $18.50

Open, Issue Price $18.50, '02
Series: *Family Ornament* — Mom

Purchased_____, Price $_____

☐ *There's Sno-One Quite Like You*, 104781

✛ $25.00
♔ $25.00

Open, Issue Price $25.00, '02
Christmas Gift To Go

Purchased_____, Price $_____

☐ *Papas Make The Season Bright*, 104786 (Ornament)

✛ $18.50
♔ $18.50

Open, Issue Price $18.50, '02
Series: *Family Ornament* — Dad

Purchased_____, Price $_____

General Figurines

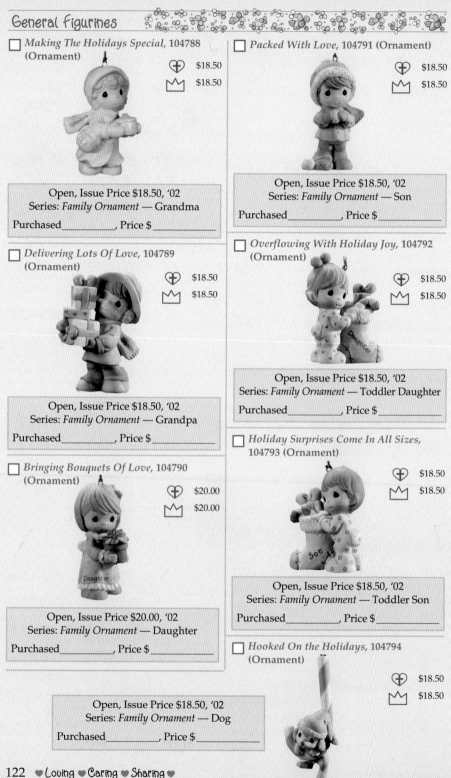

☐ *Making The Holidays Special*, 104788
(Ornament)

✝ $18.50
♛ $18.50

Open, Issue Price $18.50, '02
Series: *Family Ornament* — Grandma
Purchased_____, Price $ _____

☐ *Delivering Lots Of Love*, 104789
(Ornament)

✝ $18.50
♛ $18.50

Open, Issue Price $18.50, '02
Series: *Family Ornament* — Grandpa
Purchased_____, Price $ _____

☐ *Bringing Bouquets Of Love*, 104790
(Ornament)

✝ $20.00
♛ $20.00

Open, Issue Price $20.00, '02
Series: *Family Ornament* — Daughter
Purchased_____, Price $ _____

☐ *Packed With Love*, 104791 (Ornament)

✝ $18.50
♛ $18.50

Open, Issue Price $18.50, '02
Series: *Family Ornament* — Son
Purchased_____, Price $ _____

☐ *Overflowing With Holiday Joy*, 104792
(Ornament)

✝ $18.50
♛ $18.50

Open, Issue Price $18.50, '02
Series: *Family Ornament* — Toddler Daughter
Purchased_____, Price $ _____

☐ *Holiday Surprises Come In All Sizes*,
104793 (Ornament)

✝ $18.50
♛ $18.50

Open, Issue Price $18.50, '02
Series: *Family Ornament* — Toddler Son
Purchased_____, Price $ _____

☐ *Hooked On the Holidays*, 104794
(Ornament)

✝ $18.50
♛ $18.50

Open, Issue Price $18.50, '02
Series: *Family Ornament* — Dog
Purchased_____, Price $ _____

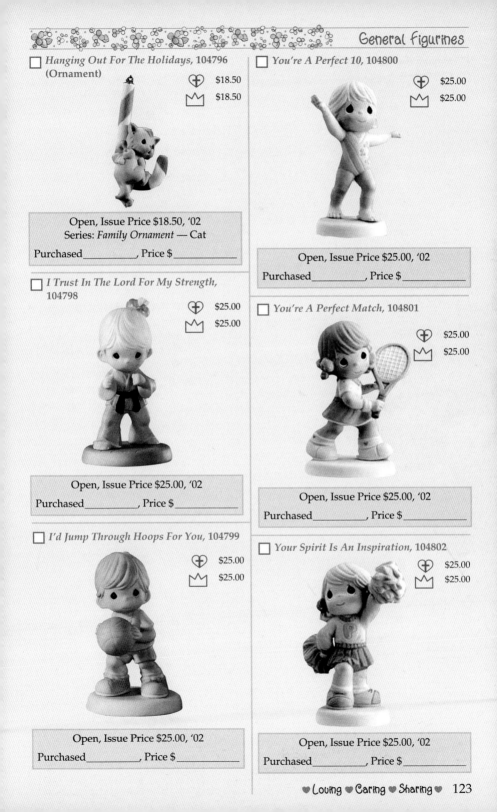

☐ *Hanging Out For The Holidays*, 104796
(Ornament)

✝ $18.50
♛ $18.50

Open, Issue Price $18.50, '02
Series: *Family Ornament* — Cat

Purchased_____, Price $_____

☐ *I Trust In The Lord For My Strength*,
104798

✝ $25.00
♛ $25.00

Open, Issue Price $25.00, '02

Purchased_____, Price $_____

☐ *I'd Jump Through Hoops For You*, 104799

✝ $25.00
♛ $25.00

Open, Issue Price $25.00, '02

Purchased_____, Price $_____

☐ *You're A Perfect 10*, 104800

✝ $25.00
♛ $25.00

Open, Issue Price $25.00, '02

Purchased_____, Price $_____

☐ *You're A Perfect Match*, 104801

✝ $25.00
♛ $25.00

Open, Issue Price $25.00, '02

Purchased_____, Price $_____

☐ *Your Spirit Is An Inspiration*, 104802

✝ $25.00
♛ $25.00

Open, Issue Price $25.00, '02

Purchased_____, Price $_____

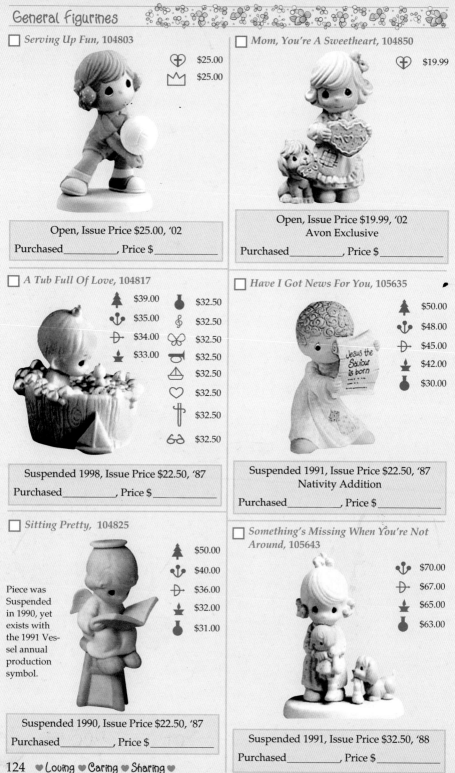

☐ *Serving Up Fun,* 104803

✝ $25.00
♛ $25.00

Open, Issue Price $25.00, '02

Purchased_____, Price $_____

☐ *Mom, You're A Sweetheart,* 104850

✝ $19.99

Open, Issue Price $19.99, '02
Avon Exclusive

Purchased_____, Price $_____

☐ *A Tub Full Of Love,* 104817

🌲 $39.00 $32.50
⚓ $35.00   𝄞 $32.50
𝈔 $34.00   🦋 $32.50
★ $33.00   📯 $32.50
            ⛵ $32.50
            ♡ $32.50
            ✝ $32.50
            👓 $32.50

Suspended 1998, Issue Price $22.50, '87

Purchased_____, Price $_____

☐ *Have I Got News For You,* 105635

🌲 $50.00
⚓ $48.00
𝈔 $45.00
★ $42.00
🌸 $30.00

Suspended 1991, Issue Price $22.50, '87
Nativity Addition

Purchased_____, Price $_____

☐ *Sitting Pretty,* 104825

🌲 $50.00
⚓ $40.00
𝈔 $36.00
★ $32.00
🌸 $31.00

Piece was Suspended in 1990, yet exists with the 1991 Vessel annual production symbol.

Suspended 1990, Issue Price $22.50, '87

Purchased_____, Price $_____

☐ *Something's Missing When You're Not Around,* 105643

⚓ $70.00
𝈔 $67.00
★ $65.00
🌸 $63.00

Suspended 1991, Issue Price $32.50, '88

Purchased_____, Price $_____

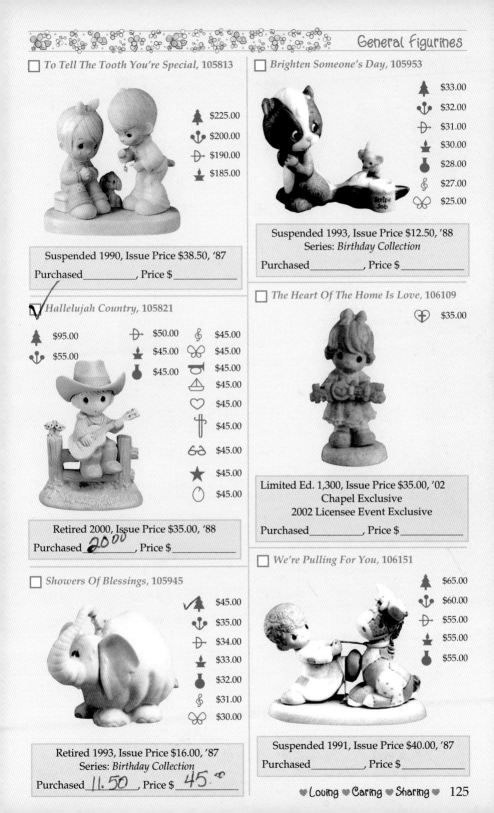

☐ *To Tell The Tooth You're Special*, 105813

🌲 $225.00
⚓ $200.00
🔔 $190.00
✴ $185.00

Suspended 1990, Issue Price $38.50, '87
Purchased_____, Price $_____

✔ *Hallelujah Country*, 105821

🌲 $95.00   🔔 $50.00   🎼 $45.00
⚓ $55.00   ✴ $45.00   🦋 $45.00
                🔴 $45.00   📯 $45.00
                                 ⛵ $45.00
                                 ♡ $45.00
                                 ✝ $45.00
                                 👓 $45.00
                                 ★ $45.00
                                 ◌ $45.00

Retired 2000, Issue Price $35.00, '88
Purchased __2000__, Price $_____

☐ *Showers Of Blessings*, 105945

✔🌲 $45.00
⚓ $35.00
🔔 $34.00
✴ $33.00
🔴 $32.00
🎼 $31.00
🦋 $30.00

Retired 1993, Issue Price $16.00, '87
Series: *Birthday Collection*
Purchased __11.50__, Price $__45.00__

☐ *Brighten Someone's Day*, 105953

🌲 $33.00
⚓ $32.00
🔔 $31.00
✴ $30.00
🔴 $28.00
🎼 $27.00
🦋 $25.00

Suspended 1993, Issue Price $12.50, '88
Series: *Birthday Collection*
Purchased_____, Price $_____

☐ *The Heart Of The Home Is Love*, 106109

🕊 $35.00

Limited Ed. 1,300, Issue Price $35.00, '02
Chapel Exclusive
2002 Licensee Event Exclusive
Purchased_____, Price $_____

☐ *We're Pulling For You*, 106151

🌲 $65.00
⚓ $60.00
🔔 $55.00
✴ $55.00
🔴 $55.00

Suspended 1991, Issue Price $40.00, '87
Purchased_____, Price $_____

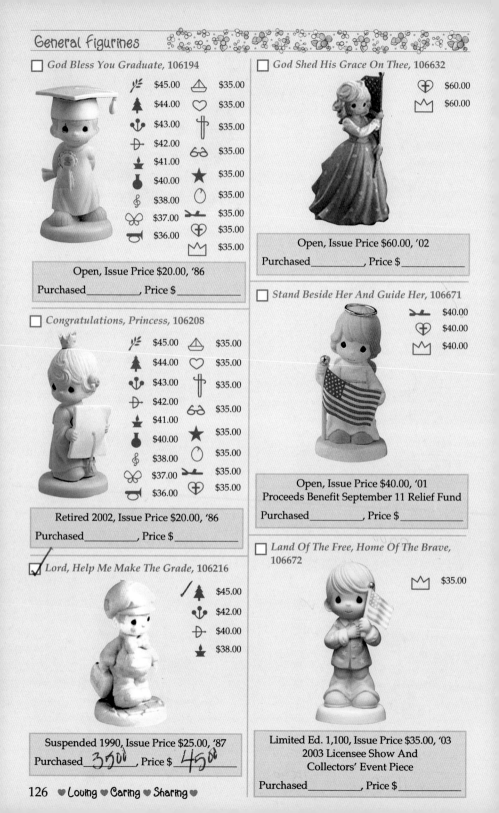

☐ God Bless You Graduate, 106194

🌿	$45.00	⛵	$35.00
🌲	$44.00	♡	$35.00
⚓	$43.00	✝	$35.00
⊅	$42.00	👓	$35.00
🕯	$41.00		
⬥	$40.00	★	$35.00
𝄞	$38.00	○	$35.00
🦋	$37.00	✂	$35.00
⌒	$36.00	⊕	$35.00
		♛	$35.00

Open, Issue Price $20.00, '86

Purchased_____, Price $_____

☐ Congratulations, Princess, 106208

🌿	$45.00	⛵	$35.00
🌲	$44.00	♡	$35.00
⚓	$43.00	✝	$35.00
⊅	$42.00	👓	$35.00
🕯	$41.00		
⬥	$40.00	★	$35.00
𝄞	$38.00	○	$35.00
🦋	$37.00	✂	$35.00
⌒	$36.00	⊕	$35.00

Retired 2002, Issue Price $20.00, '86

Purchased_____, Price $_____

☑ Lord, Help Me Make The Grade, 106216

╱🌲	$45.00
⚓	$42.00
⊅	$40.00
🕯	$38.00

Suspended 1990, Issue Price $25.00, '87

Purchased _3500_, Price $ _450_

☐ God Shed His Grace On Thee, 106632

⊕	$60.00
♛	$60.00

Open, Issue Price $60.00, '02

Purchased_____, Price $_____

☐ Stand Beside Her And Guide Her, 106671

✈	$40.00
⊕	$40.00
♛	$40.00

Open, Issue Price $40.00, '01
Proceeds Benefit September 11 Relief Fund

Purchased_____, Price $_____

☐ Land Of The Free, Home Of The Brave, 106672

♛	$35.00

Limited Ed. 1,100, Issue Price $35.00, '03
2003 Licensee Show And
Collectors' Event Piece

Purchased_____, Price $_____

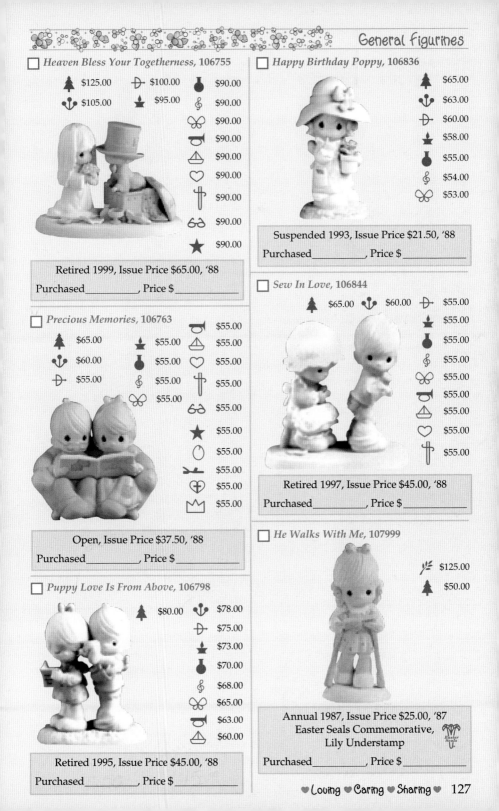

Heaven Bless Your Togetherness, 106755

🌲 $125.00	⚓ $100.00	🏺 $90.00
⚓ $105.00	🔨 $95.00	🔔 $90.00
		♪ $90.00
		🦋 $90.00
		📯 $90.00
		⛵ $90.00
		♡ $90.00
		✝ $90.00
		👓 $90.00
		⭐ $90.00

Retired 1999, Issue Price $65.00, '88

Purchased_____, Price $_____

Precious Memories, 106763

🌲 $65.00	🔨 $55.00	📯 $55.00
⚓ $60.00	🏺 $55.00	⛵ $55.00
⚓ $55.00	♪ $55.00	♡ $55.00
	🦋 $55.00	✝ $55.00
		👓 $55.00
		⭐ $55.00
		◯ $55.00
		➤ $55.00
		✠ $55.00
		👑 $55.00

Open, Issue Price $37.50, '88

Purchased_____, Price $_____

Puppy Love Is From Above, 106798

🌲 $80.00	⚓ $78.00
	⚓ $75.00
	🔨 $73.00
	🏺 $70.00
	♪ $68.00
	🦋 $65.00
	📯 $63.00
	⛵ $60.00

Retired 1995, Issue Price $45.00, '88

Purchased_____, Price $_____

Happy Birthday Poppy, 106836

🌲 $65.00
⚓ $63.00
⚓ $60.00
🔨 $58.00
🏺 $55.00
♪ $54.00
🦋 $53.00

Suspended 1993, Issue Price $21.50, '88

Purchased_____, Price $_____

Sew In Love, 106844

🌲 $65.00	⚓ $60.00	⚓ $55.00
		🔨 $55.00
		🏺 $55.00
		♪ $55.00
		🦋 $55.00
		📯 $55.00
		⛵ $55.00
		♡ $55.00
		✝ $55.00

Retired 1997, Issue Price $45.00, '88

Purchased_____, Price $_____

He Walks With Me, 107999

🌿 $125.00
🌲 $50.00

Annual 1987, Issue Price $25.00, '87
Easter Seals Commemorative,
Lily Understamp

Purchased_____, Price $_____

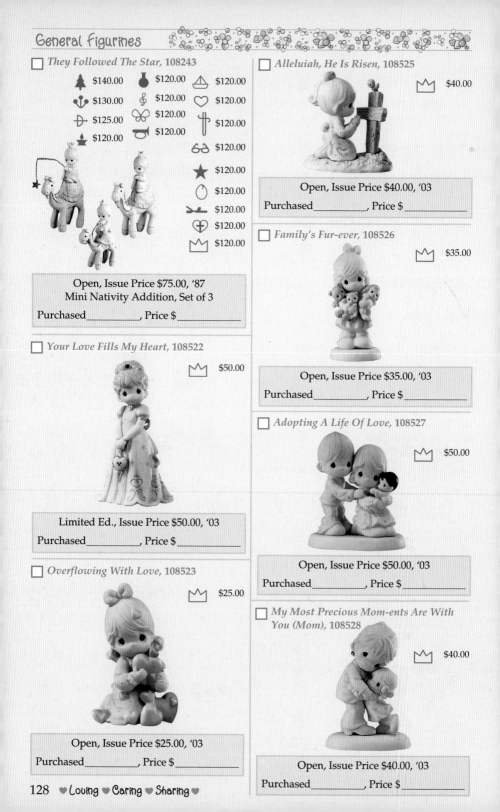

☐ *They Followed The Star*, 108243

🌲 $140.00 🏺 $120.00 🔺 $120.00
⚓ $130.00 🎼 $120.00 ♡ $120.00
➗ $125.00 🦋 $120.00
🔺 $120.00 🎺 $120.00 ✝ $120.00
👓 $120.00
★ $120.00
🥚 $120.00
✂ $120.00
☩ $120.00
👑 $120.00

Open, Issue Price $75.00, '87
Mini Nativity Addition, Set of 3
Purchased_____, Price $_____

☐ *Your Love Fills My Heart*, 108522

👑 $50.00

Limited Ed., Issue Price $50.00, '03
Purchased_____, Price $_____

☐ *Overflowing With Love*, 108523

👑 $25.00

Open, Issue Price $25.00, '03
Purchased_____, Price $_____

☐ *Alleluiah, He Is Risen*, 108525

👑 $40.00

Open, Issue Price $40.00, '03
Purchased_____, Price $_____

☐ *Family's Fur-ever*, 108526

👑 $35.00

Open, Issue Price $35.00, '03
Purchased_____, Price $_____

☐ *Adopting A Life Of Love*, 108527

👑 $50.00

Open, Issue Price $50.00, '03
Purchased_____, Price $_____

☐ *My Most Precious Mom-ents Are With You (Mom)*, 108528

👑 $40.00

Open, Issue Price $40.00, '03
Purchased_____, Price $_____

☐ *Collecting Life's Most Precious Moments,* 108531

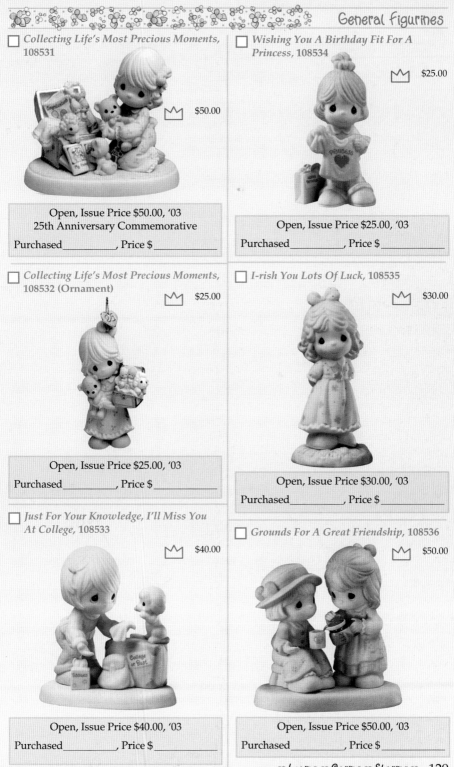

$50.00

Open, Issue Price $50.00, '03
25th Anniversary Commemorative

Purchased_____, Price $_____

☐ *Wishing You A Birthday Fit For A Princess,* 108534

$25.00

Open, Issue Price $25.00, '03

Purchased_____, Price $_____

☐ *Collecting Life's Most Precious Moments,* 108532 (Ornament)

$25.00

Open, Issue Price $25.00, '03

Purchased_____, Price $_____

☐ *I-rish You Lots Of Luck,* 108535

$30.00

Open, Issue Price $30.00, '03

Purchased_____, Price $_____

☐ *Just For Your Knowledge, I'll Miss You At College,* 108533

$40.00

Open, Issue Price $40.00, '03

Purchased_____, Price $_____

☐ *Grounds For A Great Friendship,* 108536

$50.00

Open, Issue Price $50.00, '03

Purchased_____, Price $_____

♥ Loving ♥ Caring ♥ Sharing ♥   129

☐ *Friends Always Deserve Special Treatment*, 108538

👑 $50.00

Open, Issue Price $50.00, '03

Purchased_____, Price $_____

☐ *Forever In Our Hearts*, 108541

👑 $35.00

Open, Issue Price $35.00, '03

Purchased_____, Price $_____

☐ *I'm So Glad I Spotted You As A Friend*, 108539

👑 $25.00

Open, Issue Price $25.00, '03

Purchased_____, Price $_____

☐ *Simple Pleasures Are Life's True Treasures*, 108542

✠ $75.00

👑 $75.00

Open, Issue Price $75.00, '02

Purchased_____, Price $_____

☐ *May Your Faith Grow With Daily Care*, 108540

👑 $40.00

Open, Issue Price $40.00, '03

Purchased_____, Price $_____

☐ *Marching Ahead To Another 25 Years Of Precious Moments*, 108544

👑 $325.00

Open, Issue Price $325.00, '03

Purchased_____, Price $_____

☑ *You Bring Me Out Of My Shell*, 108546

♔ $45.00

Open, Issue Price $45.00, '03
Series: *Sea Of Friendship*
Purchased **22.50** , Price $ **45.00**

☐ *Water I Do Without You?* 108547

♔ $45.00

Open, Issue Price $45.00, '03
Series: *Sea Of Friendship*
Purchased_____ , Price $ _____

☐ *I'm Filled With Love For You*, 108548

♔ $45.00

Open, Issue Price $45.00, '03
Series: *Sea Of Friendship*
Purchased_____ , Price $ _____

☐ *I'd Be Lost Without You*, 108592

♔ $45.00

Limited Ed. 7,500, Issue Price $45.00, '03
Series: *Endangered Species* — Third Issue
Purchased_____ , Price $ _____

☐ *Have You Herd How Much I Love You?*
108593

♔ $45.00

Limited Ed. 7,500, Issue Price $45.00, '03
Series: *Endangered Species* — Sixth Issue
Purchased_____ , Price $ _____

☐ *Stay With Me A Whale*, 108595

♔ $45.00

Limited Ed. 7,500, Issue Price $45.00, '03
Series: *Endangered Species* — First Issue
Purchased_____ , Price $ _____

☐ *Everything's Better When Shared Together,* 108597

♛ $45.00

Limited Ed. 7,500, Issue Price $45.00, '03
Series: *Endangered Species* — Second Issue
Purchased_____, Price $_____

☐ *Head And Shoulders Above The Rest,* 108598

♛ $45.00

Limited Ed. 7,500, Issue Price $45.00, '03
Series: *Endangered Species* — Fourth Issue
Purchased_____, Price $_____

☐ *Together Fur-Ever,* 108600

♛ $45.00

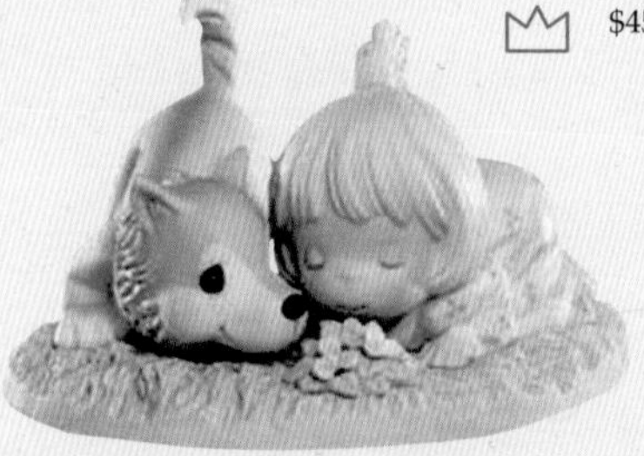

Limited Ed. 7,500, Issue Price $45.00, '03
Series: *Endangered Species* — Fifth Issue
Purchased_____, Price $_____

☐ *Thanks For A Quarter Century Of Loving, Caring, And Sharing,* 108602

♛ $100.00

Open, Issue Price $100.00, '03
Purchased_____, Price $_____

☐ *Love Is The True Reward,* 108603

♛ $37.50

Open, Issue Price $37.50, '03
GCC Exclusive
Purchased_____, Price $_____

☐ *I Love You Knight And Day,* 108604

♛ $25.00

Comes
With
Votive
Holder.

Open, Issue Price $25.00, '03
Purchased_____, Price $_____

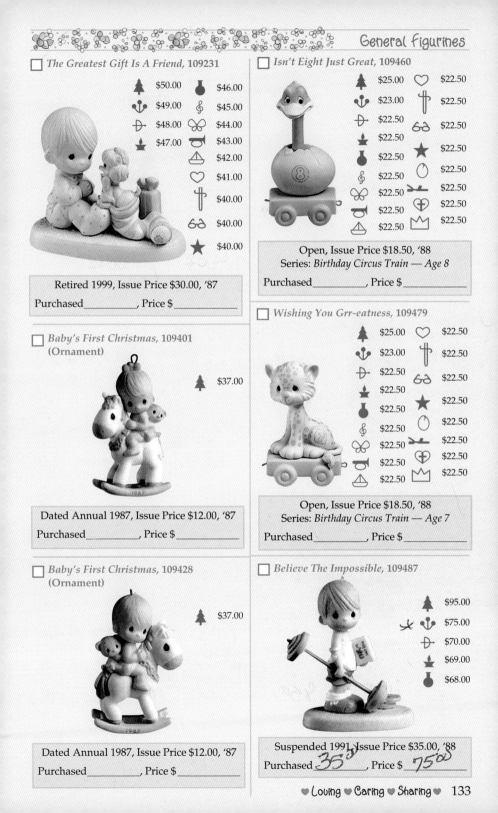

The Greatest Gift Is A Friend, 109231

🎄 $50.00   🏺 $46.00
⚓ $49.00   🎼 $45.00
🜛 $48.00   🦋 $44.00
🕯 $47.00   📯 $43.00
       △ $42.00
       ♡ $41.00
       ✝ $40.00
       👓 $40.00
       ★ $40.00

Retired 1999, Issue Price $30.00, '87
Purchased_____, Price $_____

Baby's First Christmas, 109401
(Ornament)

🎄 $37.00

Dated Annual 1987, Issue Price $12.00, '87
Purchased_____, Price $_____

Baby's First Christmas, 109428
(Ornament)

🎄 $37.00

Dated Annual 1987, Issue Price $12.00, '87
Purchased_____, Price $_____

Isn't Eight Just Great, 109460

🎄 $25.00   ♡ $22.50
⚓ $23.00   ✝ $22.50
🜛 $22.50   👓 $22.50
🕯 $22.50   ★ $22.50
🏺 $22.50   ◯ $22.50
🎼 $22.50   ✂ $22.50
🦋 $22.50   🎁 $22.50
📯 $22.50   👑 $22.50
△ $22.50

Open, Issue Price $18.50, '88
Series: *Birthday Circus Train — Age 8*
Purchased_____, Price $_____

Wishing You Grr-eatness, 109479

🎄 $25.00   ♡ $22.50
⚓ $23.00   ✝ $22.50
🜛 $22.50   👓 $22.50
🕯 $22.50   ★ $22.50
🏺 $22.50   ◯ $22.50
🎼 $22.50   ✂ $22.50
🦋 $22.50   🎁 $22.50
📯 $22.50   👑 $22.50
△ $22.50

Open, Issue Price $18.50, '88
Series: *Birthday Circus Train — Age 7*
Purchased_____, Price $_____

Believe The Impossible, 109487

🎄 $95.00
⚓ $75.00
🜛 $70.00
🕯 $69.00
🏺 $68.00

Suspended 1991, Issue Price $35.00, '88
Purchased _35ʰ_, Price $_75ᵒᵒ_

☐ *Believe The Impossible*, 109487R

◯ $45.00
⤖ $45.00

Limited Ed., Issue Price $45.00, '00
Care-A-Van Exclusive
Purchased_____, Price $_____

☐ *You Are A Real Cool Mommy*, 109495

✛ $20.00

Open, Issue Price $20.00, '02
Purchased_____, Price $_____

☑ *Happiness Divine*, 109584

✓ ⚓ $85.00
Ð $80.00
✦ $75.00
⬥ $70.00
𝄞 $69.00

Retired 1992, Issue Price $25.00, '88
Purchased_40ᵃ_, Price $ 85ᵒᵒ

☐ *Peace On Earth*, 109746 (Musical)

⚓ $150.00
Ð $150.00
✦ $145.00
⬥ $143.00
𝄞 $140.00
∞ $138.00

Suspended 1993, Issue Price $100.00, '88
Tune: "Hark! The Herald Angels Sing"
Purchased_____, Price $_____

☐ *Wishing You A Yummy Christmas*, 109754

🌲 $60.00   Ð $55.00
⚓ $58.00   ✦ $50.00
⬥ $45.00
𝄞 $45.00
∞ $45.00
📯 $45.00

Suspended 1994, Issue Price $35.00, '87
Purchased_____, Price $_____

☐ *We Gather Together To Ask The Lord's Blessing*, 109762

🌲 $325.00   ⛵ $305.00   𝄞 $294.00   ∞ $293.00
⚓ $310.00   ✦ $300.00   📯 $292.00
Ð $305.00   ⬥ $295.00   ⛵ $291.00

Retired 1995, Issue Price $130.00, '87
Family Thanksgiving Set, Set of 6 plus cassette
Purchased_____, Price $_____

There were reports of sets having two fathers or mothers instead of one of each. This does not increase the value.

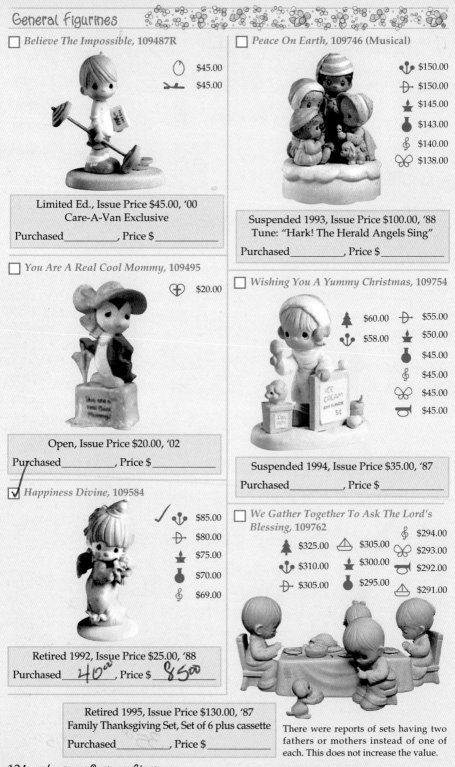

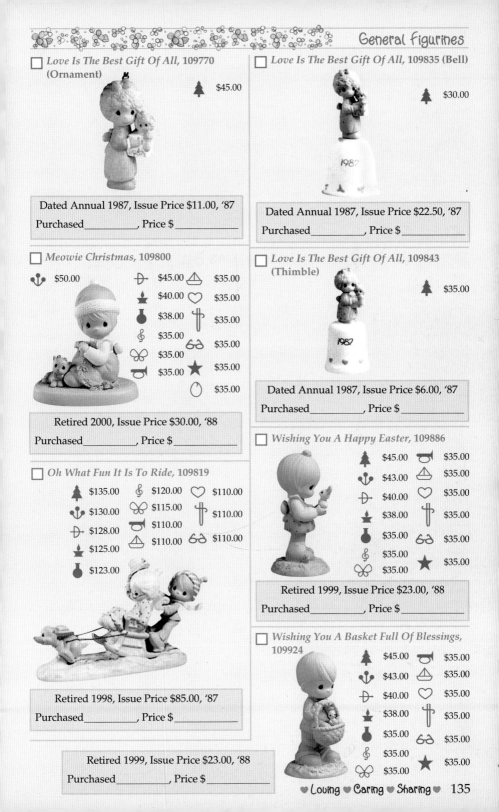

□ *Love Is The Best Gift Of All*, 109770
(Ornament)

🎄 $45.00

Dated Annual 1987, Issue Price $11.00, '87
Purchased_____, Price $_____

□ *Love Is The Best Gift Of All*, 109835 (Bell)

🎄 $30.00

Dated Annual 1987, Issue Price $22.50, '87
Purchased_____, Price $_____

□ *Meowie Christmas*, 109800

⚓ $50.00

⛵ $45.00		⛵ $35.00
🕯 $40.00		♡ $35.00
🏺 $38.00		✝ $35.00
🎵 $35.00		👓 $35.00
🦋 $35.00		
📯 $35.00		★ $35.00
		◯ $35.00

Retired 2000, Issue Price $30.00, '88
Purchased_____, Price $_____

□ *Love Is The Best Gift Of All*, 109843
(Thimble)

🎄 $35.00

Dated Annual 1987, Issue Price $6.00, '87
Purchased_____, Price $_____

□ *Oh What Fun It Is To Ride*, 109819

🎄 $135.00	🎵 $120.00	♡ $110.00
⚓ $130.00	🦋 $115.00	✝ $110.00
🕊 $128.00	📯 $110.00	
🕯 $125.00	⛵ $110.00	👓 $110.00
🏺 $123.00		

Retired 1998, Issue Price $85.00, '87
Purchased_____, Price $_____

□ *Wishing You A Happy Easter*, 109886

🎄 $45.00	📯 $35.00
⚓ $43.00	⛵ $35.00
🕊 $40.00	♡ $35.00
🕯 $38.00	✝ $35.00
🏺 $35.00	👓 $35.00
🎵 $35.00	
🦋 $35.00	★ $35.00

Retired 1999, Issue Price $23.00, '88
Purchased_____, Price $_____

□ *Wishing You A Basket Full Of Blessings*,
109924

🎄 $45.00	📯 $35.00
⚓ $43.00	⛵ $35.00
🕊 $40.00	♡ $35.00
🕯 $38.00	✝ $35.00
🏺 $35.00	👓 $35.00
🎵 $35.00	
🦋 $35.00	★ $35.00

Retired 1999, Issue Price $23.00, '88
Purchased_____, Price $_____

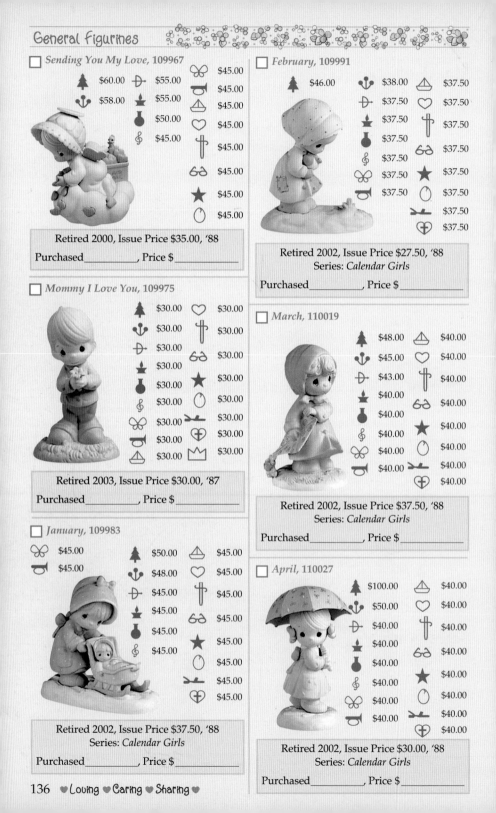

Sending You My Love, 109967

🌲 $60.00	⚓ $55.00	$45.00
⚓ $58.00	✦ $55.00	$45.00
⬤ $50.00	⛵ $45.00	$45.00
♪ $45.00	♡ $45.00	
	✝ $45.00	
	👓 $45.00	
	★ $45.00	
	◯ $45.00	

Retired 2000, Issue Price $35.00, '88

Purchased_____, Price $_____

Mommy I Love You, 109975

✦ $30.00	♡ $30.00	
⚓ $30.00	✝ $30.00	
⚓ $30.00	👓 $30.00	
✦ $30.00	★ $30.00	
⬤ $30.00	◯ $30.00	
♪ $30.00	⤚ $30.00	
🦋 $30.00	✠ $30.00	
📯 $30.00	👑 $30.00	
⛵ $30.00		

Retired 2003, Issue Price $30.00, '87

Purchased_____, Price $_____

January, 109983

🦋 $45.00	🌲 $50.00	⛵ $45.00
📯 $45.00	⚓ $48.00	♡ $45.00
	⚓ $45.00	✝ $45.00
	✦ $45.00	👓 $45.00
	⬤ $45.00	★ $45.00
	♪ $45.00	⤚ $45.00
		✠ $45.00

Retired 2002, Issue Price $37.50, '88
Series: *Calendar Girls*

Purchased_____, Price $_____

February, 109991

🌲 $46.00	⚓ $38.00	⛵ $37.50
	⚓ $37.50	♡ $37.50
	✦ $37.50	✝ $37.50
	⬤ $37.50	👓 $37.50
	♪ $37.50	★ $37.50
	🦋 $37.50	◯ $37.50
	📯 $37.50	⤚ $37.50
		✠ $37.50

Retired 2002, Issue Price $27.50, '88
Series: *Calendar Girls*

Purchased_____, Price $_____

March, 110019

🌲 $48.00	⛵ $40.00	
⚓ $45.00	♡ $40.00	
⚓ $43.00	✝ $40.00	
✦ $40.00	👓 $40.00	
♪ $40.00	★ $40.00	
🦋 $40.00	◯ $40.00	
📯 $40.00	⤚ $40.00	
	✠ $40.00	

Retired 2002, Issue Price $37.50, '88
Series: *Calendar Girls*

Purchased_____, Price $_____

April, 110027

🌲 $100.00	⛵ $40.00	
⚓ $50.00	♡ $40.00	
⚓ $40.00	✝ $40.00	
✦ $40.00	👓 $40.00	
⬤ $40.00	★ $40.00	
♪ $40.00	◯ $40.00	
🦋 $40.00	⤚ $40.00	
📯 $40.00	✠ $40.00	

Retired 2002, Issue Price $30.00, '88
Series: *Calendar Girls*

Purchased_____, Price $_____

☐ *May,* 110035

🌲 $100.00		⛵ $35.00
⚓ $35.00		♡ $35.00
⌀ $35.00		✝ $35.00
🕯 $35.00		👓 $35.00
⚱ $35.00		
♪ $35.00		★ $35.00
🦋 $35.00		◯ $35.00
⚒ $35.00		⤳ $35.00
		✠ $35.00

Retired 2002, Issue Price $25.00, '88
Series: *Calendar Girls*

Purchased_____, Price $_____

☐ *August,* 110078

🦋 $50.00	⚱ $55.00	⛵ $50.00
⚒ $50.00	⚓ $53.00	♡ $50.00
	⌀ $50.00	✝ $50.00
	🕯 $50.00	👓 $50.00
	⚱ $50.00	
	♪ $50.00	★ $50.00
		◯ $50.00
		⤳ $50.00
		✠ $50.00

Retired 2002, Issue Price $40.00, '88
Series: *Calendar Girls*

Purchased_____, Price $_____

☑ *June,* 110043

🦋 $55.00	🌲 $100.00	⛵ $55.00
⚒ $55.00	✓⚓ $55.00	♡ $55.00
	⌀ $55.00	✝ $55.00
	🕯 $55.00	👓 $55.00
	⚱ $55.00	
	♪ $55.00	★ $55.00
		◯ $55.00
		⤳ $55.00
		✠ $55.00

Retired 2002, Issue Price $40.00, '88
Series: *Calendar Girls*

Purchased **24.99**, Price $ **55.00**

☐ *September,* 110086

		⛵ $37.50
⚱ $42.00	🌲	♡ $37.50
⚓ $40.00		✝ $37.50
⌀ $38.00		
🕯 $37.50		👓 $37.50
⚱ $37.50		★ $37.50
♪ $37.50		◯ $37.50
🦋 $37.50		⤳ $37.50
⚒ $37.50		✠ $37.50

Retired 2002, Issue Price $27.50, '88
Series: *Calendar Girls*

Purchased_____, Price $_____

☐ *July,* 110051

⚱ $50.00		⛵ $45.00
⚓ $45.00		♡ $45.00
⌀ $45.00		✝ $45.00
🕯 $45.00		👓 $45.00
⚱ $45.00		
♪ $45.00		★ $45.00
🦋 $45.00		◯ $45.00
⚒ $45.00		⤳ $45.00
		✠ $45.00

Retired 2002, Issue Price $35.00, '88
Series: *Calendar Girls*

Purchased_____, Price $_____

☐ *October,* 110094

		⛵ $45.00
🦋 $45.00	🌲 $54.00	♡ $45.00
⚒ $45.00	⚓ $50.00	✝ $45.00
	⌀ $48.00	
	🕯 $45.00	👓 $45.00
	⚱ $45.00	★ $45.00
	♪ $45.00	◯ $45.00
		⤳ $45.00
		✠ $45.00

Retired 2002, Issue Price $35.00, '88
Series: *Calendar Girls*

Purchased_____, Price $_____

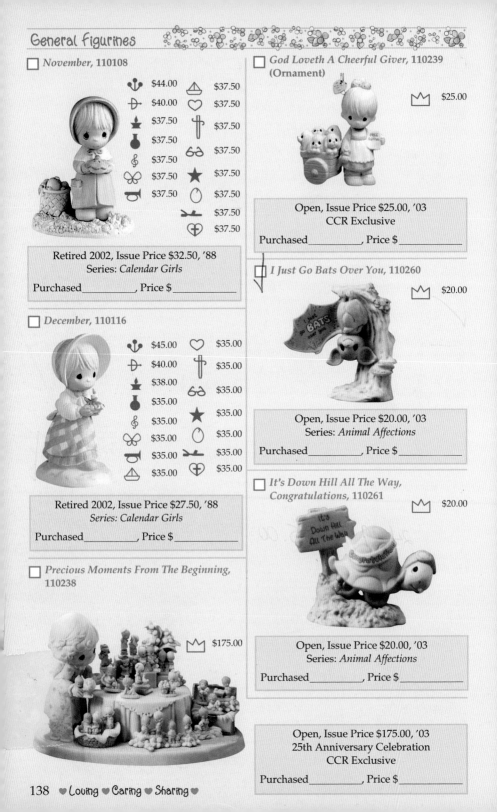

☐ *November*, 110108

⚓	$44.00	⛵	$37.50
⌗	$40.00	♡	$37.50
🕯	$37.50	✝	$37.50
🏺	$37.50	👓	$37.50
🎼	$37.50	★	$37.50
🦋	$37.50	○	$37.50
🎺	$37.50		
		✂	$37.50
		✚	$37.50

Retired 2002, Issue Price $32.50, '88
Series: *Calendar Girls*

Purchased_____, Price $_____

☐ *December*, 110116

⚓	$45.00	♡	$35.00
⌗	$40.00	✝	$35.00
🕯	$38.00	👓	$35.00
🏺	$35.00		
🎼	$35.00	★	$35.00
🦋	$35.00	○	$35.00
🎺	$35.00	✂	$35.00
⛵	$35.00	✚	$35.00

Retired 2002, Issue Price $27.50, '88
Series: *Calendar Girls*

Purchased_____, Price $_____

☐ *Precious Moments From The Beginning*, 110238

♔ $175.00

☐ *God Loveth A Cheerful Giver*, 110239 (Ornament)

♔ $25.00

Open, Issue Price $25.00, '03
CCR Exclusive

Purchased_____, Price $_____

☐ *I Just Go Bats Over You*, 110260

♔ $20.00

Open, Issue Price $20.00, '03
Series: *Animal Affections*

Purchased_____, Price $_____

☐ *It's Down Hill All The Way, Congratulations*, 110261

♔ $20.00

Open, Issue Price $20.00, '03
Series: *Animal Affections*

Purchased_____, Price $_____

Open, Issue Price $175.00, '03
25th Anniversary Celebration
CCR Exclusive

Purchased_____, Price $_____

☐ *Are You Lonesome Tonight?* 110262

👑 $20.00

Open, Issue Price $20.00, '03
Series: *Animal Affections*

Purchased_____, Price $_____

☑ *A Mother's Love Is Beyond Measure,* 110267

👑 $27.50

Open, Issue Price $27.50, '03

Purchased_____, Price $_____

☐ *Remember To Reach For The Stars,* 110263

👑 $20.00

Open, Issue Price $20.00, '03
Series: *Animal Affections*

Purchased_____, Price $_____

☐ *My Heart Belongs To You,* 110268

👑 $125.00

First "Mature" or "Elongated" Figurine to feature both boy and girl.

Open, Issue Price $125.00, '03

Purchased_____, Price $_____

☑ *I Love You A Bushel And A Peck,* 110265

👑 $20.00

Open, Issue Price $20.00, '03
Series: *Animal Affections*

Purchased _10.00_, Price $_20.00_

☐ *Friendship Is Always A Sweet Surprise,* 110269

⊕ $35.00
👑 $35.00

Open, Issue Price $35.00, '02
Carlton Cards Exclusive

Purchased_____, Price $_____

☐ *A Chip Off The Old Block,* 110266

👑 $20.00

Open, Issue Price $20.00, '03
Series: *Animal Affections*

Purchased_____, Price $_____

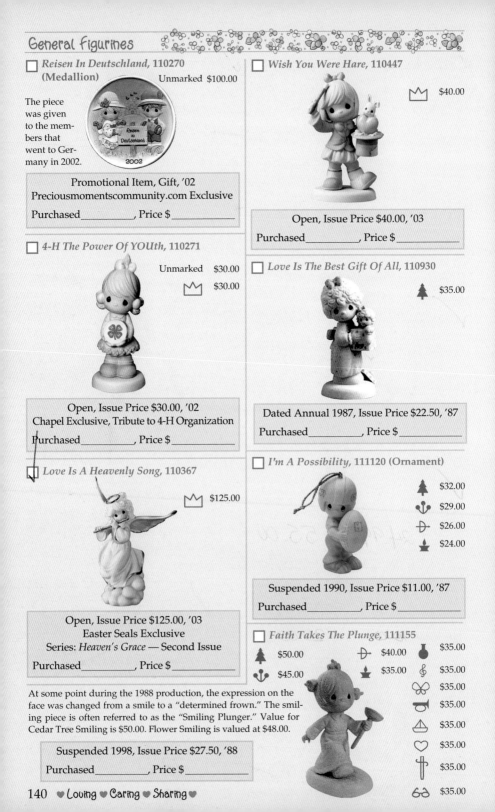

☐ *Reisen In Deutschland*, 110270
(Medallion)
Unmarked $100.00

The piece was given to the members that went to Germany in 2002.

Promotional Item, Gift, '02
Preciousmomentscommunity.com Exclusive

Purchased_____, Price $_____

☐ *4-H The Power Of YOUth*, 110271
Unmarked $30.00
♔ $30.00

Open, Issue Price $30.00, '02
Chapel Exclusive, Tribute to 4-H Organization

Purchased_____, Price $_____

☐ *Love Is A Heavenly Song*, 110367
♔ $125.00

Open, Issue Price $125.00, '03
Easter Seals Exclusive
Series: *Heaven's Grace* — Second Issue

Purchased_____, Price $_____

At some point during the 1988 production, the expression on the face was changed from a smile to a "determined frown." The smiling piece is often referred to as the "Smiling Plunger." Value for Cedar Tree Smiling is $50.00. Flower Smiling is valued at $48.00.

Suspended 1998, Issue Price $27.50, '88

Purchased_____, Price $_____

☐ *Wish You Were Hare*, 110447
♔ $40.00

Open, Issue Price $40.00, '03

Purchased_____, Price $_____

☐ *Love Is The Best Gift Of All*, 110930
🌲 $35.00

Dated Annual 1987, Issue Price $22.50, '87

Purchased_____, Price $_____

☐ *I'm A Possibility*, 111120 (Ornament)
🌲 $32.00
⚓ $29.00
⋺ $26.00
🔥 $24.00

Suspended 1990, Issue Price $11.00, '87

Purchased_____, Price $_____

☐ *Faith Takes The Plunge*, 111155

🌲 $50.00	⋺ $40.00	🍶 $35.00	
⚓ $45.00	🔥 $35.00	💰 $35.00	
		🦋 $35.00	
		🎺 $35.00	
		△ $35.00	
		♡ $35.00	
		✝ $35.00	
		🜨 $35.00	

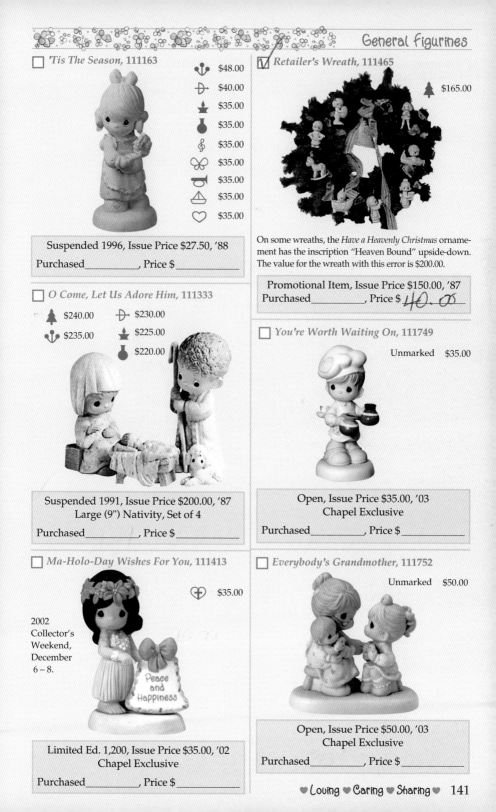

☐ *'Tis The Season*, 111163

- 🌱 $48.00
- ➶ $40.00
- 🗝 $35.00
- 🕯 $35.00
- 𝄞 $35.00
- 🦋 $35.00
- 📯 $35.00
- ⛵ $35.00
- ♡ $35.00

Suspended 1996, Issue Price $27.50, '88

Purchased_____, Price $_____

☐ *O Come, Let Us Adore Him*, 111333

- 🌲 $240.00
- ➶ $230.00
- 🌱 $235.00
- 🕯 $225.00
- 🫗 $220.00

Suspended 1991, Issue Price $200.00, '87
Large (9") Nativity, Set of 4

Purchased_____, Price $_____

☐ *Ma-Holo-Day Wishes For You*, 111413

- ✛ $35.00

2002 Collector's Weekend, December 6 – 8.

Limited Ed. 1,200, Issue Price $35.00, '02
Chapel Exclusive

Purchased_____, Price $_____

☑ *Retailer's Wreath*, 111465

- 🌲 $165.00

On some wreaths, the *Have a Heavenly Christmas* ornament has the inscription "Heaven Bound" upside-down. The value for the wreath with this error is $200.00.

Promotional Item, Issue Price $150.00, '87
Purchased_____, Price $ 40.00

☐ *You're Worth Waiting On*, 111749

Unmarked $35.00

Open, Issue Price $35.00, '03
Chapel Exclusive

Purchased_____, Price $_____

☐ *Everybody's Grandmother*, 111752

Unmarked $50.00

Open, Issue Price $50.00, '03
Chapel Exclusive

Purchased_____, Price $_____

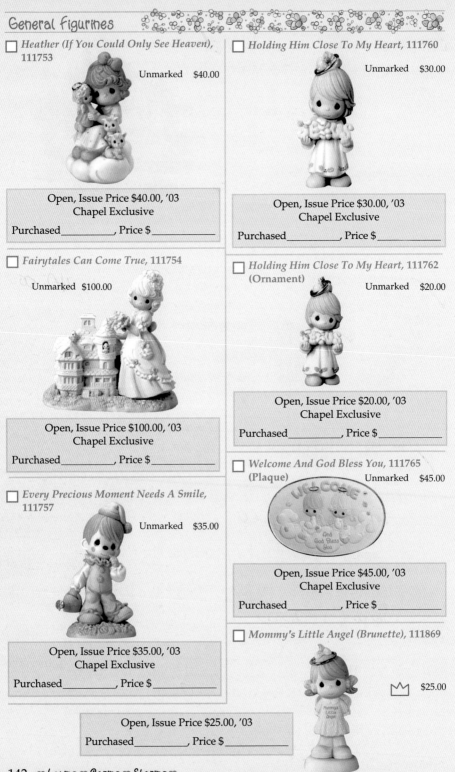

□ *Heather (If You Could Only See Heaven)*, 111753

Unmarked $40.00

Open, Issue Price $40.00, '03
Chapel Exclusive

Purchased_____, Price $_____

□ *Fairytales Can Come True*, 111754

Unmarked $100.00

Open, Issue Price $100.00, '03
Chapel Exclusive

Purchased_____, Price $_____

□ *Every Precious Moment Needs A Smile*, 111757

Unmarked $35.00

Open, Issue Price $35.00, '03
Chapel Exclusive

Purchased_____, Price $_____

□ *Holding Him Close To My Heart*, 111760

Unmarked $30.00

Open, Issue Price $30.00, '03
Chapel Exclusive

Purchased_____, Price $_____

□ *Holding Him Close To My Heart*, 111762
(Ornament)

Unmarked $20.00

Open, Issue Price $20.00, '03
Chapel Exclusive

Purchased_____, Price $_____

□ *Welcome And God Bless You*, 111765
(Plaque)

Unmarked $45.00

Open, Issue Price $45.00, '03
Chapel Exclusive

Purchased_____, Price $_____

□ *Mommy's Little Angel (Brunette)*, 111869

♔ $25.00

Open, Issue Price $25.00, '03

Purchased_____, Price $_____

☐ *Mommy's Little Angel (Blond)*, 111870

♛ $25.00

Open, Issue Price $25.00, '03

Purchased_____, Price $_____

☐ *Simple Pleasures Make Holiday Treasures*, 111898

♛ $125.00

Open, Issue Price $125.00, '03
Set Of 5

Purchased_____, Price $_____

☐ *The Lord Bless You And Keep You*, 111904

♛ $70.00

Open, Issue Price $70.00, '03
Japanese Exclusive

Purchased_____, Price $_____

☐ *Mommy, I Love You*, 112143

🌲 $37.00
⚓ $36.00
Ɖ $35.00
🕯 $34.00
🍶 $33.00
🎼 $32.00
🦋 $31.00

🎺 $30.00   ✝ $30.00   ★ $30.00
△ $30.00
⛵ $30.00   👓 $30.00   ◯ $30.00
♡ $30.00   ✂ $30.00

Retired 2001, Issue Price $22.50, '88
Purchased_____, Price $_____

☐ *A Tub Full Of Love*, 112313

🌲 $36.00   🕯 $33.00   ⛵ $32.50
⚓ $35.00   🍶 $32.50   ♡ $32.50
Ɖ $34.00   🎼 $32.50   ✝ $32.50
                   🦋 $32.50   👓 $32.50
                   🎺 $32.50   ★ $32.50
                                      ◯ $32.50
                                      ✂ $32.50
                                      ⊕ $32.50
                                      ♛ $32.50

Open, Issue Price $22.50, '87

Purchased_____, Price $_____

☐ *Retailer's Wreath Bell*, 112348
(Ornament)

🌲 $60.00

Promotional Item, '87

Purchased_____, Price $_____

☐ *You Have Touched So Many Hearts*, 112356 (Ornament)

🌲 $30.00   🕯 $23.00
⚓ $28.00   🍶 $20.00
Ɖ $25.00   🎼 $18.50
                   🦋 $18.50
                   🎺 $18.50
                   △ $18.50
                   ♡ $18.50

Retired 1997, Issue Price $11.00, '87

Purchased_____, Price $_____

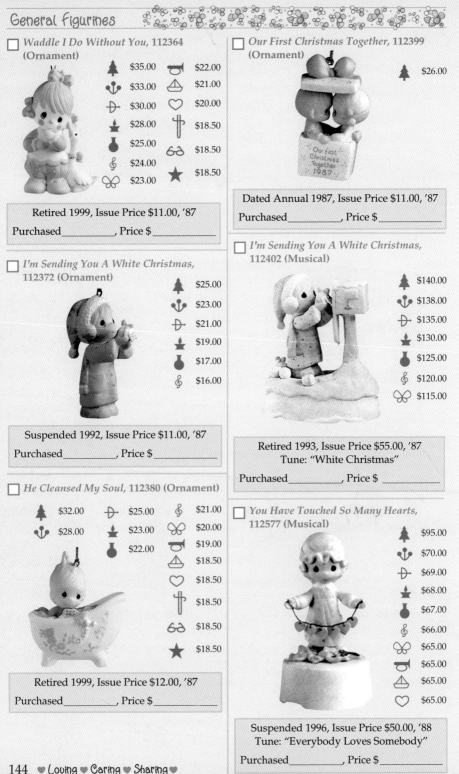

☐ *Waddle I Do Without You*, 112364
(Ornament)

🎄	$35.00	🛷	$22.00
⚓	$33.00	⬖	$21.00
✈	$30.00	♡	$20.00
🕯	$28.00	✝	$18.50
🔔	$25.00	👓	$18.50
🎵	$24.00	⭐	$18.50
🦋	$23.00		

Retired 1999, Issue Price $11.00, '87

Purchased_____, Price $_____

☐ *I'm Sending You A White Christmas*,
112372 (Ornament)

🎄	$25.00
⚓	$23.00
✈	$21.00
🕯	$19.00
🔔	$17.00
🎵	$16.00

Suspended 1992, Issue Price $11.00, '87

Purchased_____, Price $_____

☐ *He Cleansed My Soul*, 112380 (Ornament)

🎄	$32.00	✈	$25.00
⚓	$28.00	🕯	$23.00
		🔔	$22.00

🎵	$21.00
🦋	$20.00
🎺	$19.00
🛷	$18.50
♡	$18.50
✝	$18.50
👓	$18.50
⭐	$18.50

Retired 1999, Issue Price $12.00, '87

Purchased_____, Price $_____

☐ *Our First Christmas Together*, 112399
(Ornament)

🎄	$26.00

Dated Annual 1987, Issue Price $11.00, '87

Purchased_____, Price $_____

☐ *I'm Sending You A White Christmas*,
112402 (Musical)

🎄	$140.00
⚓	$138.00
✈	$135.00
🕯	$130.00
🔔	$125.00
🎵	$120.00
🦋	$115.00

Retired 1993, Issue Price $55.00, '87
Tune: "White Christmas"

Purchased_____, Price $_____

☐ *You Have Touched So Many Hearts*,
112577 (Musical)

🎄	$95.00
⚓	$70.00
✈	$69.00
🕯	$68.00
🔔	$67.00
🎵	$66.00
🦋	$65.00
🎺	$65.00
🛷	$65.00
♡	$65.00

Suspended 1996, Issue Price $50.00, '88
Tune: "Everybody Loves Somebody"

Purchased_____, Price $_____

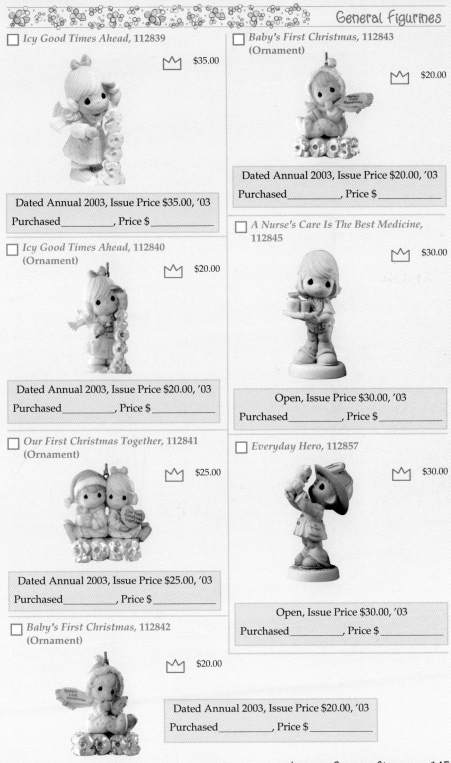

☐ *Icy Good Times Ahead*, 112839

♛ $35.00

Dated Annual 2003, Issue Price $35.00, '03
Purchased_____, Price $ _____

☐ *Icy Good Times Ahead*, 112840
(Ornament)

♛ $20.00

Dated Annual 2003, Issue Price $20.00, '03
Purchased_____, Price $ _____

☐ *Our First Christmas Together*, 112841
(Ornament)

♛ $25.00

Dated Annual 2003, Issue Price $25.00, '03
Purchased_____, Price $ _____

☐ *Baby's First Christmas*, 112842
(Ornament)

♛ $20.00

Dated Annual 2003, Issue Price $20.00, '03
Purchased_____, Price $ _____

☐ *Baby's First Christmas*, 112843
(Ornament)

♛ $20.00

Dated Annual 2003, Issue Price $20.00, '03
Purchased_____, Price $ _____

☐ *A Nurse's Care Is The Best Medicine*,
112845

♛ $30.00

Open, Issue Price $30.00, '03
Purchased_____, Price $ _____

☐ *Everyday Hero*, 112857

♛ $30.00

Open, Issue Price $30.00, '03
Purchased_____, Price $ _____

☐ *Take A Note, You're Great!* 112858

$30.00

Open, Issue Price $30.00, '03
Purchased_____, Price $_____

☐ *Coach, You're A Real Sport,* 112859

$30.00

Open, Issue Price $30.00, '03
Purchased_____, Price $_____

☐ *Teacher, You're A Precious Work Of Art,* 112861

$30.00

Open, Issue Price $30.00, '03
Purchased_____, Price $_____

☐ *It's Only Gauze I Care,* 112862

$30.00

Open, Issue Price $30.00, '03
Purchased_____, Price $_____

☐ *Bearing Gifts Of Great Joy,* 112863

$35.00

Open, Issue Price $35.00, '03
Nativity Addition
Purchased_____, Price $_____

☐ *I Can't Give You Anything But Love,* 112864

$30.00

Open, Issue Price $30.00, '03
Purchased_____, Price $_____

☐ *To A Niece With A Bubbly Personality,* 112870

$25.00

Open, Issue Price $25.00, '03
Purchased_____, Price $_____

☑ *Squashed With Love*, 112874

♔ $45.00

Open, Issue Price $45.00, '03

Purchased_____, Price $_____

☐ *I-cy Potential In You*, 112875 (Ornament)

♔ $30.00

· 2003 ·

Dated Annual 2003, Issue Price $30.00, '03

Purchased_____, Price $_____

☐ *May The Holidays Keep You Bright Eyed And Bushy Tailed*, 112876 (Ornament)

♔ $20.00

Dated Annual 2003, Issue Price $20.00, '03

Purchased_____, Price $_____

☑ *God Rest Ye Merry Gentlemen*, 112878

♔ $55.00

Open, Issue Price $55.00, '03

Purchased_____, Price $_____

☐ *May Your Heart Be Filled With Christmas Joy*, 112880

♔ $50.00

Open, Issue Price $50.00, '03

Purchased_____, Price $_____

☐ *Warmest Wishes For The Holidays*, 112881

♔ $50.00

Open, Issue Price $50.00, '03

Purchased_____, Price $_____

☐ *You're A Gem Of A Friend*, 112882

♔ $37.50

Open, Issue Price $37.50, '03

Purchased_____, Price $_____

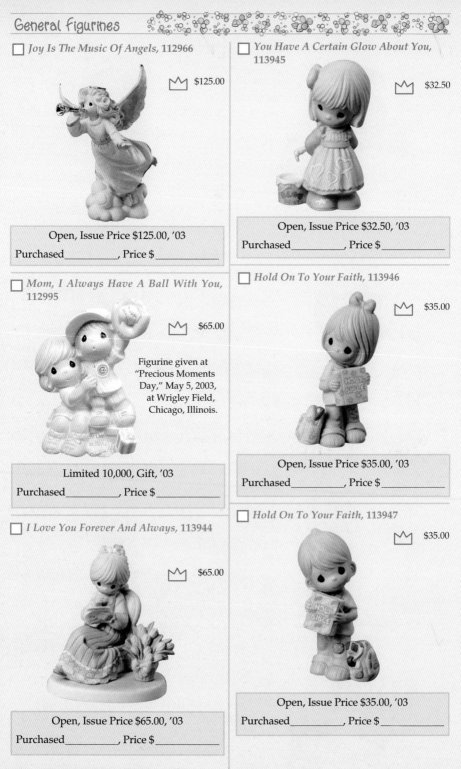

☐ *Joy Is The Music Of Angels*, 112966

♛ $125.00

Open, Issue Price $125.00, '03
Purchased_____, Price $_____

☐ *You Have A Certain Glow About You*, 113945

♛ $32.50

Open, Issue Price $32.50, '03
Purchased_____, Price $_____

☐ *Mom, I Always Have A Ball With You*, 112995

♛ $65.00

Figurine given at "Precious Moments Day," May 5, 2003, at Wrigley Field, Chicago, Illinois.

Limited 10,000, Gift, '03
Purchased_____, Price $_____

☐ *Hold On To Your Faith*, 113946

♛ $35.00

Open, Issue Price $35.00, '03
Purchased_____, Price $_____

☐ *I Love You Forever And Always*, 113944

♛ $65.00

Open, Issue Price $65.00, '03
Purchased_____, Price $_____

☐ *Hold On To Your Faith*, 113947

♛ $35.00

Open, Issue Price $35.00, '03
Purchased_____, Price $_____

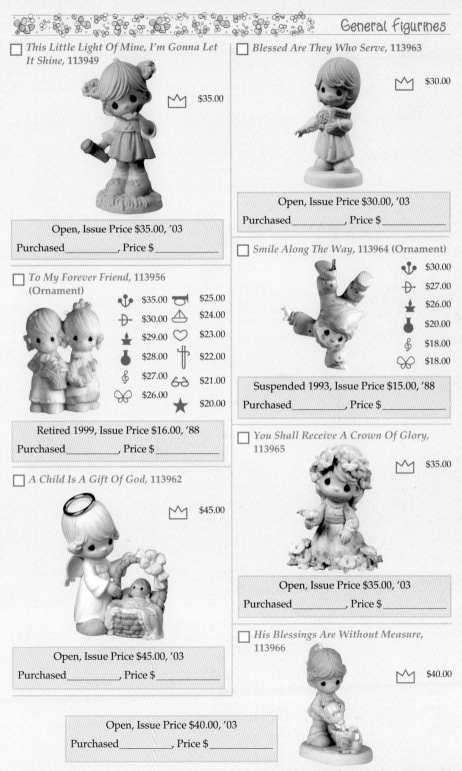

☐ *This Little Light Of Mine, I'm Gonna Let It Shine*, 113949

♔ $35.00

Open, Issue Price $35.00, '03

Purchased_____, Price $_____

☐ *To My Forever Friend*, 113956 (Ornament)

⚓ $35.00   ⌇ $25.00
Ɖ $30.00   ⛵ $24.00
♦ $29.00   ♡ $23.00
⚱ $28.00   † $22.00
𝄞 $27.00   👓 $21.00
∞ $26.00   ★ $20.00

Retired 1999, Issue Price $16.00, '88

Purchased_____, Price $_____

☐ *A Child Is A Gift Of God*, 113962

♔ $45.00

Open, Issue Price $45.00, '03

Purchased_____, Price $_____

☐ *Blessed Are They Who Serve*, 113963

♔ $30.00

Open, Issue Price $30.00, '03

Purchased_____, Price $_____

☐ *Smile Along The Way*, 113964 (Ornament)

⚓ $30.00
Ɖ $27.00
♦ $26.00
⚱ $20.00
𝄞 $18.00
∞ $18.00

Suspended 1993, Issue Price $15.00, '88

Purchased_____, Price $_____

☐ *You Shall Receive A Crown Of Glory*, 113965

♔ $35.00

Open, Issue Price $35.00, '03

Purchased_____, Price $_____

☐ *His Blessings Are Without Measure*, 113966

♔ $40.00

Open, Issue Price $40.00, '03

Purchased_____, Price $_____

General figurines

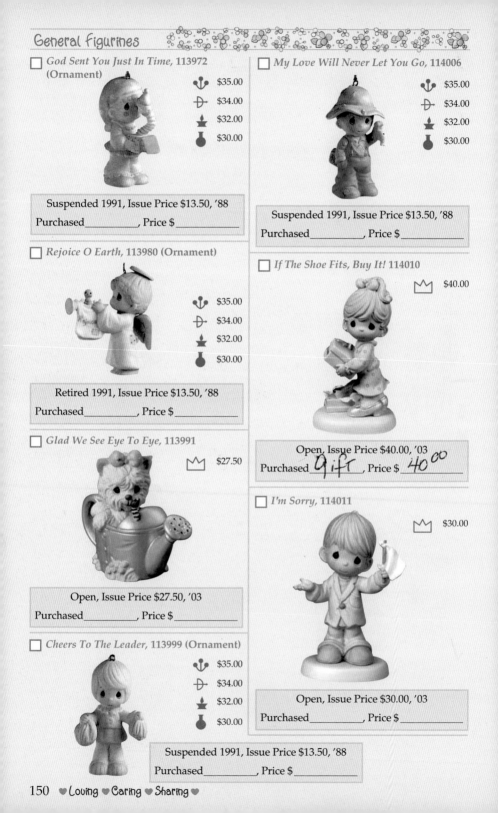

☐ *God Sent You Just In Time*, 113972
(Ornament)

⚓ $35.00
🕊 $34.00
🔥 $32.00
🏺 $30.00

Suspended 1991, Issue Price $13.50, '88
Purchased_____, Price $_____

☐ *Rejoice O Earth*, 113980 (Ornament)

⚓ $35.00
🕊 $34.00
🔥 $32.00
🏺 $30.00

Retired 1991, Issue Price $13.50, '88
Purchased_____, Price $_____

☐ *Glad We See Eye To Eye*, 113991

👑 $27.50

Open, Issue Price $27.50, '03
Purchased_____, Price $_____

☐ *Cheers To The Leader*, 113999 (Ornament)

⚓ $35.00
🕊 $34.00
🔥 $32.00
🏺 $30.00

Suspended 1991, Issue Price $13.50, '88
Purchased_____, Price $_____

☐ *My Love Will Never Let You Go*, 114006

⚓ $35.00
🕊 $34.00
🔥 $32.00
🏺 $30.00

Suspended 1991, Issue Price $13.50, '88
Purchased_____, Price $_____

☐ *If The Shoe Fits, Buy It!* 114010

👑 $40.00

Open, Issue Price $40.00, '03
Purchased _Gift_ , Price $ _40.00_

☐ *I'm Sorry*, 114011

👑 $30.00

Open, Issue Price $30.00, '03
Purchased_____, Price $_____

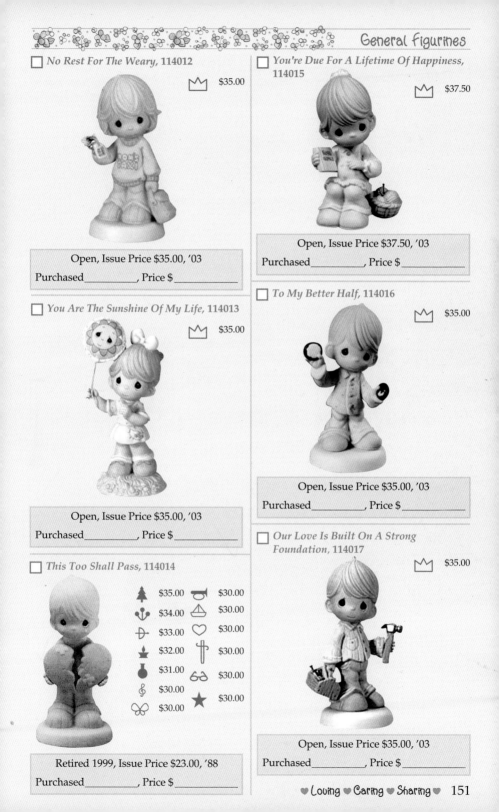

☐ *No Rest For The Weary*, 114012

♔ $35.00

Open, Issue Price $35.00, '03

Purchased_____, Price $_____

☐ *You Are The Sunshine Of My Life*, 114013

♔ $35.00

Open, Issue Price $35.00, '03

Purchased_____, Price $_____

☐ *This Too Shall Pass*, 114014

🌲	$35.00	📯	$30.00
⚓	$34.00	⛵	$30.00
⊶	$33.00	♡	$30.00
★	$32.00	🕈	$30.00
🍶	$31.00	👓	$30.00
𝄞	$30.00	★	$30.00
∞	$30.00		

Retired 1999, Issue Price $23.00, '88

Purchased_____, Price $_____

☐ *You're Due For A Lifetime Of Happiness*, 114015

♔ $37.50

Open, Issue Price $37.50, '03

Purchased_____, Price $_____

☐ *To My Better Half*, 114016

♔ $35.00

Open, Issue Price $35.00, '03

Purchased_____, Price $_____

☐ *Our Love Is Built On A Strong Foundation*, 114017

♔ $35.00

Open, Issue Price $35.00, '03

Purchased_____, Price $_____

♥ Loving ♥ Caring ♥ Sharing ♥   151

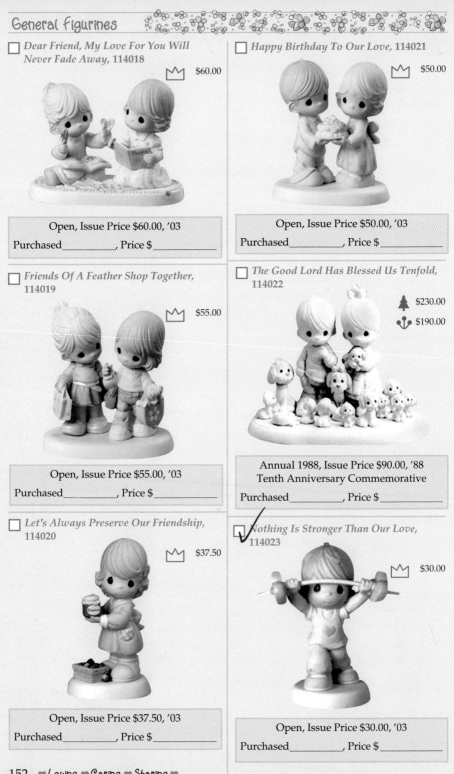

☐ *Dear Friend, My Love For You Will Never Fade Away*, 114018

♛ $60.00

Open, Issue Price $60.00, '03
Purchased_____, Price $_____

☐ *Happy Birthday To Our Love*, 114021

♛ $50.00

Open, Issue Price $50.00, '03
Purchased_____, Price $_____

☐ *Friends Of A Feather Shop Together*, 114019

♛ $55.00

Open, Issue Price $55.00, '03
Purchased_____, Price $_____

☐ *The Good Lord Has Blessed Us Tenfold*, 114022

🎄 $230.00
⚓ $190.00

Annual 1988, Issue Price $90.00, '88
Tenth Anniversary Commemorative
Purchased_____, Price $_____

☐ *Let's Always Preserve Our Friendship*, 114020

♛ $37.50

Open, Issue Price $37.50, '03
Purchased_____, Price $_____

☑ *Nothing Is Stronger Than Our Love*, 114023

♛ $30.00

Open, Issue Price $30.00, '03
Purchased_____, Price $_____

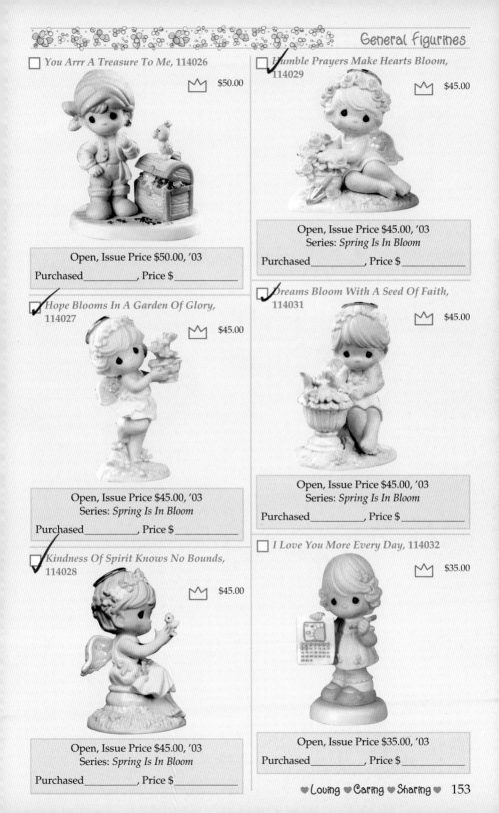

☐ *You Arrr A Treasure To Me*, 114026

♕ $50.00

Open, Issue Price $50.00, '03
Purchased_____, Price $_____

☑ *Hope Blooms In A Garden Of Glory*,
114027

♕ $45.00

Open, Issue Price $45.00, '03
Series: *Spring Is In Bloom*
Purchased_____, Price $_____

☑ *Kindness Of Spirit Knows No Bounds*,
114028

♕ $45.00

Open, Issue Price $45.00, '03
Series: *Spring Is In Bloom*
Purchased_____, Price $_____

☑ *Humble Prayers Make Hearts Bloom*,
114029

♕ $45.00

Open, Issue Price $45.00, '03
Series: *Spring Is In Bloom*
Purchased_____, Price $_____

☑ *Dreams Bloom With A Seed Of Faith*,
114031

♕ $45.00

Open, Issue Price $45.00, '03
Series: *Spring Is In Bloom*
Purchased_____, Price $_____

☐ *I Love You More Every Day*, 114032

♕ $35.00

Open, Issue Price $35.00, '03
Purchased_____, Price $_____

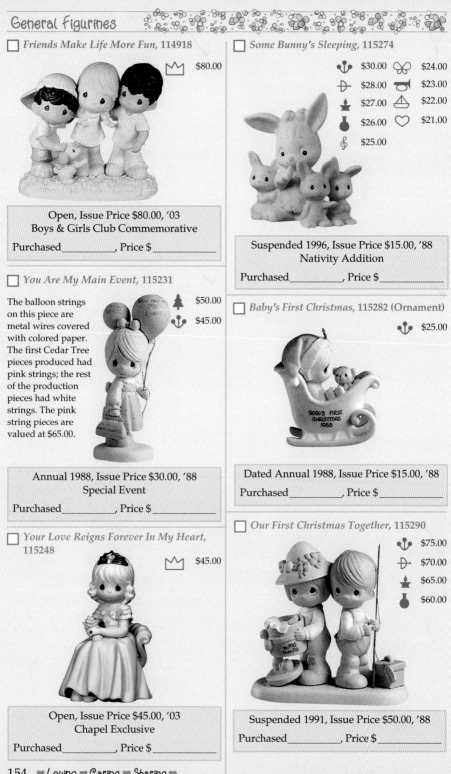

☐ *Friends Make Life More Fun*, 114918

♛ $80.00

Open, Issue Price $80.00, '03
Boys & Girls Club Commemorative

Purchased_____, Price $_____

☐ *You Are My Main Event*, 115231

The balloon strings on this piece are metal wires covered with colored paper. The first Cedar Tree pieces produced had pink strings; the rest of the production pieces had white strings. The pink string pieces are valued at $65.00.

🎄 $50.00
⚓ $45.00

Annual 1988, Issue Price $30.00, '88
Special Event

Purchased_____, Price $_____

☐ *Your Love Reigns Forever In My Heart*, 115248

♛ $45.00

Open, Issue Price $45.00, '03
Chapel Exclusive

Purchased_____, Price $_____

☐ *Some Bunny's Sleeping*, 115274

⚓ $30.00	🦋 $24.00
➴ $28.00	📯 $23.00
★ $27.00	⛵ $22.00
⬛ $26.00	♡ $21.00
𝄞 $25.00	

Suspended 1996, Issue Price $15.00, '88
Nativity Addition

Purchased_____, Price $_____

☐ *Baby's First Christmas*, 115282 (Ornament)

⚓ $25.00

Dated Annual 1988, Issue Price $15.00, '88
Purchased_____, Price $_____

☐ *Our First Christmas Together*, 115290

⚓ $75.00
➴ $70.00
★ $65.00
⬛ $60.00

Suspended 1991, Issue Price $50.00, '88
Purchased_____, Price $_____

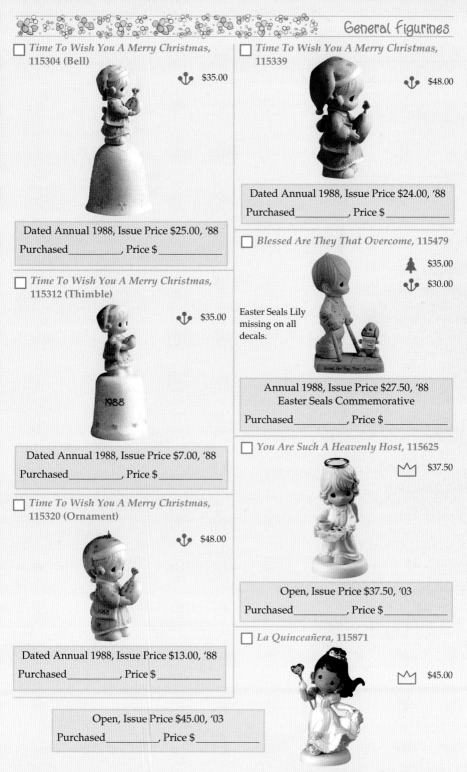

Time To Wish You A Merry Christmas, 115304 (Bell)

$35.00

Dated Annual 1988, Issue Price $25.00, '88

Purchased_____, Price $_____

Time To Wish You A Merry Christmas, 115312 (Thimble)

$35.00

1988

Dated Annual 1988, Issue Price $7.00, '88

Purchased_____, Price $_____

Time To Wish You A Merry Christmas, 115320 (Ornament)

$48.00

Dated Annual 1988, Issue Price $13.00, '88

Purchased_____, Price $_____

Open, Issue Price $45.00, '03

Purchased_____, Price $_____

Time To Wish You A Merry Christmas, 115339

$48.00

Dated Annual 1988, Issue Price $24.00, '88

Purchased_____, Price $_____

Blessed Are They That Overcome, 115479

$35.00

$30.00

Easter Seals Lily missing on all decals.

Annual 1988, Issue Price $27.50, '88
Easter Seals Commemorative

Purchased_____, Price $_____

You Are Such A Heavenly Host, 115625

$37.50

Open, Issue Price $37.50, '03

Purchased_____, Price $_____

La Quinceañera, 115871

$45.00

General Figurines

☐ *Christmas Around The World,* 116710

♔ $35.00

Limited Ed. 1,100, Issue Price $35.00, '03
2003 Christmas Event

Purchased_____, Price $_____

☐ *Age 14 — Walrus,* 116945

♔ $25.00

Open, Issue Price $25.00, '03
Series: *Birthday Train* — Age 14

Purchased_____, Price $_____

☐ *Age 15 — Gorilla,* 116946

♔ $25.00

Open, Issue Price $25.00, '03
Series: *Birthday Train* — Age 15

Purchased_____, Price $_____

☐ *Age 16 — White Tiger,* 116948

♔ $25.00

Open, Issue Price $25.00, '03
Series: *Birthday Train* — Age 16

Purchased_____, Price $_____

☐ *Love Blooms Eternal,* 127019

🎺 $45.00
⛵ $40.00

Dated Annual 1995, Issue Price $35.00, '95
Series: *Dated Cross* — First Issue

Purchased_____, Price $_____

☐ *Congratulations, You Earned Your Stripes,* 127809

⛵ $17.00
♡ $16.00
✝ $15.00
🕯 $15.00
★ $15.00
○ $15.00
✈ $15.00
⚓ $15.00

Retired 2002, Issue Price $15.00, '95
Series: *Two By Two*

Purchased_____, Price $_____

156 ♥ Loving ♥ Caring ♥ Sharing ♥

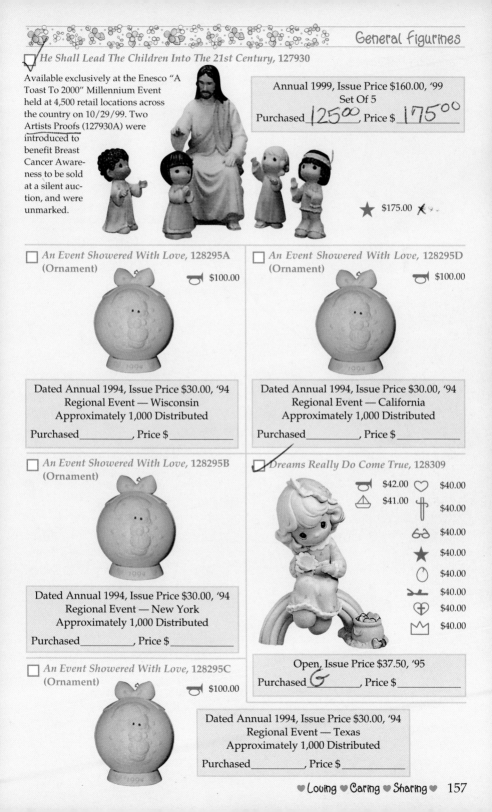

☐ *He Shall Lead The Children Into The 21st Century*, 127930

Available exclusively at the Enesco "A Toast To 2000" Millennium Event held at 4,500 retail locations across the country on 10/29/99. Two Artists Proofs (127930A) were introduced to benefit Breast Cancer Awareness to be sold at a silent auction, and were unmarked.

Annual 1999, Issue Price $160.00, '99
Set Of 5
Purchased **125⁰⁰**, Price $ **175⁰⁰**

★ $175.00

☐ *An Event Showered With Love*, 128295A
(Ornament)

🎺 $100.00

Dated Annual 1994, Issue Price $30.00, '94
Regional Event — Wisconsin
Approximately 1,000 Distributed

Purchased_____, Price $_____

☐ *An Event Showered With Love*, 128295D
(Ornament)

🎺 $100.00

Dated Annual 1994, Issue Price $30.00, '94
Regional Event — California
Approximately 1,000 Distributed

Purchased_____, Price $_____

☐ *An Event Showered With Love*, 128295B
(Ornament)

Dated Annual 1994, Issue Price $30.00, '94
Regional Event — New York
Approximately 1,000 Distributed

Purchased_____, Price $_____

☑ *Dreams Really Do Come True*, 128309

🎺 $42.00   ♡ $40.00
△ $41.00   ⊹ $40.00
           👓 $40.00
           ★ $40.00
           ◯ $40.00
           ⤢ $40.00
           ⊕ $40.00
           👑 $40.00

Open, Issue Price $37.50, '95
Purchased **G**_____, Price $_____

☐ *An Event Showered With Love*, 128295C
(Ornament)

🎺 $100.00

Dated Annual 1994, Issue Price $30.00, '94
Regional Event — Texas
Approximately 1,000 Distributed

Purchased_____, Price $_____

☐ *Another Year And More Grey Hares,* 128686

$20.00 $18.50
$19.00

$18.50
$18.50
$18.50
$18.50
$18.50
$18.50
$18.50
$18.50

Open, Issue Price $17.50, '95

Purchased_____, Price $_____

☐ *Happy Hula Days,* 128694

$35.00
$34.00
$33.00
$32.50
$32.50
$32.50
$32.50
$32.50
$32.50

Open, Issue Price $30.00, '95

Purchased_____, Price $_____

☐ *Owl Be Home For Christmas,* 128708
(Ornament)

$19.00

Dated Annual 1996, Issue Price $18.50, '96
Series: *Birthday Collection*

Purchased_____, Price $_____

☐ *Take Time To Smell The Flowers,* 128899
(Ornament)

Unmarked $10.00

Annual 1995, Issue Price $7.50, '95
Easter Seals Commemorative

Purchased_____, Price $_____

☐ *Love Vows To Always Bloom,* 129097

$72.00
$70.00
$70.00
$70.00
$70.00
$70.00
$70.00
$70.00
$70.00

Open, Issue Price $70.00, '96
Series: *To Have And To Hold*

Purchased_____, Price $_____

☐ *I Give You My Love Forever True,* 129100

$78.00
$70.00
$70.00
$70.00
$70.00
$70.00
$70.00
$70.00
$70.00

Open, Issue Price $70.00, '95

Purchased_____, Price $_____

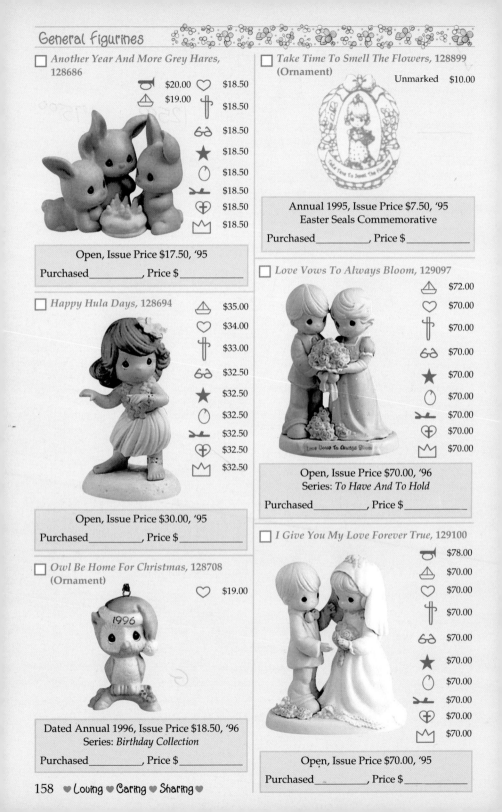

☐ *He Graces The Earth With Abundance,* 129119

⭐ $50.00
🥚 $50.00
✂ $50.00
✝ $50.00
👑 $50.00

Open, Issue Price $50.00, '99
Series: *New Four Seasons — Fall*

Purchased_____, Price $_____

☑ *Beside The Still Waters,* 129127

🥚 $50.00
✂ $50.00
✝ $50.00
👑 $50.00

Open, Issue Price $50.00, '00
Series: *New Four Seasons — Summer*

Purchased _G_____, Price $ 50 00

☑ *He Covers The Earth With His Glory,* 129135

🥚 $50.00
✂ $50.00
✝ $50.00
👑 $50.00

Open, Issue Price $50.00, '00
Series: *New Four Seasons — Winter*

Purchased_____, Price $ 50 00

☐ *The Beauty Of God Blooms Forever,* 129143

🥚 $50.00
✂ $50.00
✝ $50.00
👑 $50.00

Open, Issue Price $50.00, '00
Series: *New Four Seasons — Spring*

Purchased 50 00, Price $ 50 00

☐ *He Hath Made Everything Beautiful In His Time,* 129151 (Plate)

⛵ $50.00

Dated Annual 1995, Issue Price $50.00, '95
Series: *Mother's Day — Second Issue*

Purchased_____, Price $_____

☐ *Grandpa's Island,* 129259

⛵ $135.00
♡ $133.00
✝ $130.00
6∂ $128.00
⭐ $125.00
🥚 $123.00
✂ $120.00
✝ $118.00

Suspended 2002, Issue Price $100.00, '95
Chapel Exclusive

Purchased_____, Price $_____

Lighting The Way To A Happy Holiday, 129267

⛵ $35.00
♥ $33.00

Retired 1998, Issue Price $30.00, '95
Chapel Exclusive

Purchased_____, Price $_____

Lighting The Way To A Happy Holiday, 129275 (Ornament)

⛵ $30.00
♥ $28.00
✝ $25.00

Suspended 1999, Issue Price $20.00, '95
Chapel Exclusive

Purchased_____, Price $_____

Love Letters In The Sand, 129488

♥ $42.00
✝ $38.00
👓 $35.00
★ $35.00
◯ $35.00
✈ $35.00
✚ $35.00

Retired 2002, Issue Price $35.00, '97

Purchased_____, Price $_____

Gone But Never Forgotten, 135976

Unmarked $50.00
✈ $50.00
✚ $50.00
♛ $50.00

Open, Issue Price $50.00, '00
Chapel Exclusive

Purchased_____, Price $_____

He Is My Salvation, 135984

★ $48.00
◯ $45.00

A portion of the proceeds from the sales of this figurine was donated to the Salvation Army.

Annual 2000/2001, Issue Price $45.00, '00

Purchased_____, Price $_____

Heaven Must Have Sent You, 135992

Unmarked $52.00
✝ $48.00

Suspended 2002, Issue Price $45.00, '96
Chapel Exclusive

Purchased_____, Price $_____

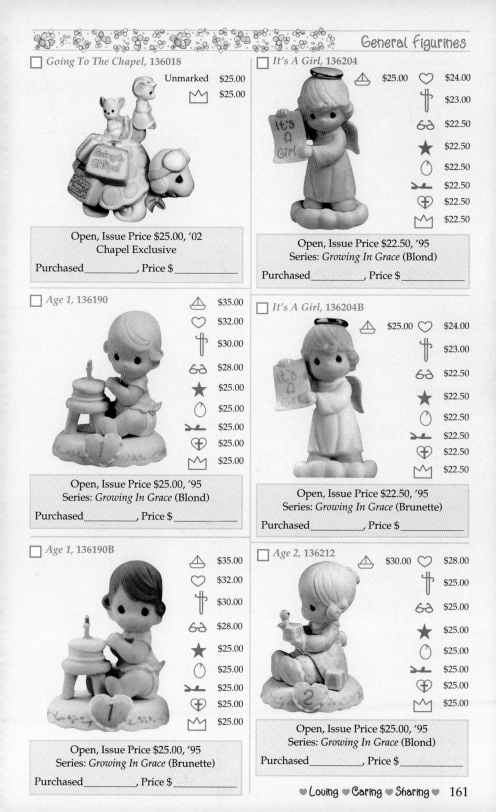

Going To The Chapel, 136018

Unmarked $25.00

♔ $25.00

Open, Issue Price $25.00, '02
Chapel Exclusive

Purchased_____, Price $_____

It's A Girl, 136204

△ $25.00 | ♡ $24.00

✝ $23.00

👓 $22.50

★ $22.50

◯ $22.50

⊱ $22.50

✠ $22.50

♔ $22.50

Open, Issue Price $22.50, '95
Series: *Growing In Grace* (Blond)

Purchased_____, Price $_____

Age 1, 136190

△ $35.00

♡ $32.00

✝ $30.00

👓 $28.00

★ $25.00

◯ $25.00

⊱ $25.00

✠ $25.00

♔ $25.00

Open, Issue Price $25.00, '95
Series: *Growing In Grace* (Blond)

Purchased_____, Price $_____

It's A Girl, 136204B

△ $25.00 | ♡ $24.00

✝ $23.00

👓 $22.50

★ $22.50

◯ $22.50

⊱ $22.50

✠ $22.50

♔ $22.50

Open, Issue Price $22.50, '95
Series: *Growing In Grace* (Brunette)

Purchased_____, Price $_____

Age 1, 136190B

△ $35.00

♡ $32.00

✝ $30.00

👓 $28.00

★ $25.00

◯ $25.00

⊱ $25.00

✠ $25.00

♔ $25.00

Open, Issue Price $25.00, '95
Series: *Growing In Grace* (Brunette)

Purchased_____, Price $_____

Age 2, 136212

△ $30.00 | ♡ $28.00

✝ $25.00

👓 $25.00

★ $25.00

◯ $25.00

⊱ $25.00

✠ $25.00

♔ $25.00

Open, Issue Price $25.00, '95
Series: *Growing In Grace* (Blond)

Purchased_____, Price $_____

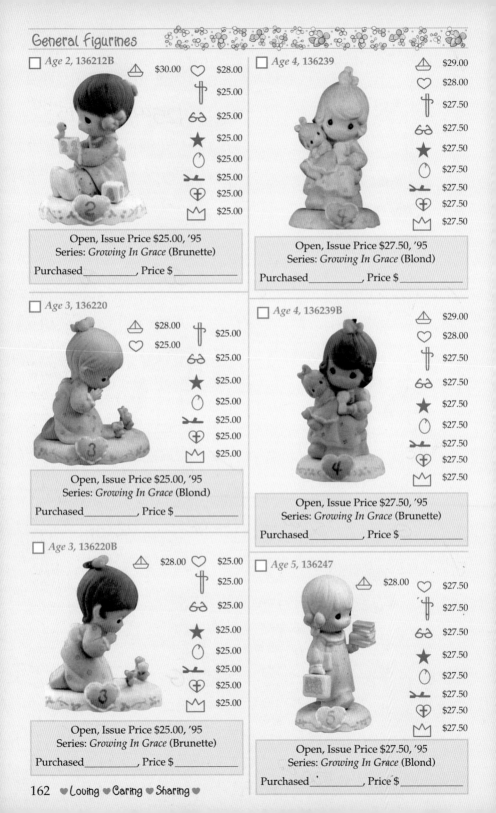

☐ *Age 2*, 136212B

$30.00 $28.00

$25.00

$25.00

$25.00

$25.00

$25.00

$25.00

$25.00

Open, Issue Price $25.00, '95
Series: *Growing In Grace* (Brunette)

Purchased_____, Price $_____

☐ *Age 3*, 136220

$28.00 $25.00

$25.00

$25.00

$25.00

$25.00

$25.00

$25.00

$25.00

Open, Issue Price $25.00, '95
Series: *Growing In Grace* (Blond)

Purchased_____, Price $_____

☐ *Age 3*, 136220B

$28.00 $25.00

$25.00

$25.00

$25.00

$25.00

$25.00

$25.00

$25.00

Open, Issue Price $25.00, '95
Series: *Growing In Grace* (Brunette)

Purchased_____, Price $_____

☐ *Age 4*, 136239

$29.00

$28.00

$27.50

$27.50

$27.50

$27.50

$27.50

$27.50

$27.50

Open, Issue Price $27.50, '95
Series: *Growing In Grace* (Blond)

Purchased_____, Price $_____

☐ *Age 4*, 136239B

$29.00

$28.00

$27.50

$27.50

$27.50

$27.50

$27.50

$27.50

$27.50

Open, Issue Price $27.50, '95
Series: *Growing In Grace* (Brunette)

Purchased_____, Price $_____

☐ *Age 5*, 136247

$28.00 $27.50

$27.50

$27.50

$27.50

$27.50

$27.50

$27.50

$27.50

Open, Issue Price $27.50, '95
Series: *Growing In Grace* (Blond)

Purchased_____, Price $_____

Age 5, 136247B

⛵	$28.00
♡	$27.50
✝	$27.50
👓	$27.50
★	$27.50
⬭	$27.50
✂	$27.50
⚓	$27.50
👑	$27.50

Open, Issue Price $27.50, '95
Series: *Growing In Grace* (Brunette)

Purchased_____, Price $_____

Age 6, 136255

⛵	$33.00
♡	$30.00
✝	$30.00
👓	$30.00
★	$30.00
⬭	$30.00
✂	$30.00
⚓	$30.00
👑	$30.00

Open, Issue Price $30.00, '95
Series: *Growing In Grace* (Blond)

Purchased_____, Price $_____

✓ Age 6, 136255B

Gave to Nicole

⛵	$33.00
♡	$30.00
✝	$30.00
👓	$30.00
★	$30.00
⬭	$30.00
✂	$30.00
⚓	$30.00
👑	$30.00

Open, Issue Price $30.00, '95
Series: *Growing In Grace* (Brunette)

Purchased__15.00__, Price $__30.00__

Sweet Sixteen/Age 16, 136263

⛵	$45.00
♡	$45.00
✝	$45.00
👓	$45.00
★	$45.00
⬭	$45.00
✂	$45.00
⚓	$45.00
👑	$45.00

Open, Issue Price $45.00, '95
Series: *Growing In Grace* (Blond)

Purchased_____, Price $_____

Sweet Sixteen/Age 16, 136263B

⛵	$45.00	♡	$45.00
		✝	$45.00
		👓	$45.00
		★	$45.00
		⬭	$45.00
		✂	$45.00
		⚓	$45.00
		👑	$45.00

Open, Issue Price $45.00, '95
Series: *Growing In Grace* (Brunette)

Purchased_____, Price $_____

You Will Always Be Our Hero, 136271

📯	$50.00
⛵	$45.00

Annual 1995, Issue Price $40.00, '95
Celebrating 50th Anniversary of WWII

Purchased_____, Price $_____

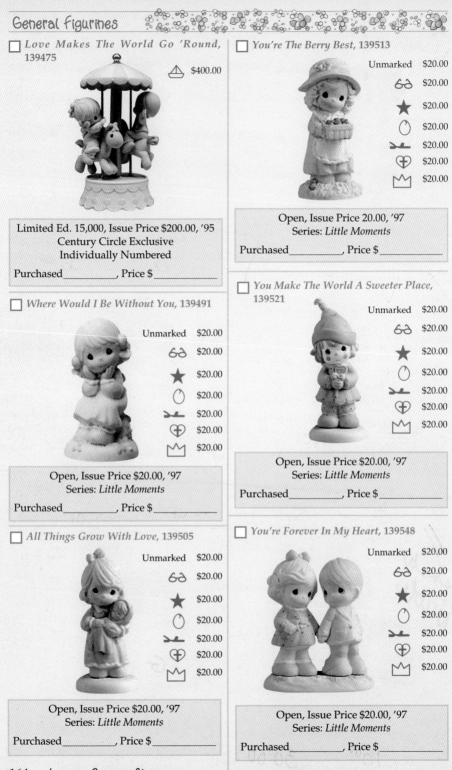

☐ *Love Makes The World Go 'Round,* 139475

△ $400.00

Limited Ed. 15,000, Issue Price $200.00, '95
Century Circle Exclusive
Individually Numbered

Purchased_____, Price $_____

☐ *Where Would I Be Without You,* 139491

Unmarked	$20.00
6∂	$20.00
★	$20.00
◯	$20.00
⊱	$20.00
⊕	$20.00
♛	$20.00

Open, Issue Price $20.00, '97
Series: *Little Moments*

Purchased_____, Price $_____

☐ *All Things Grow With Love,* 139505

Unmarked	$20.00
6∂	$20.00
★	$20.00
◯	$20.00
⊱	$20.00
⊕	$20.00
♛	$20.00

Open, Issue Price $20.00, '97
Series: *Little Moments*

Purchased_____, Price $_____

☐ *You're The Berry Best,* 139513

Unmarked	$20.00
6∂	$20.00
★	$20.00
◯	$20.00
⊱	$20.00
⊕	$20.00
♛	$20.00

Open, Issue Price 20.00, '97
Series: *Little Moments*

Purchased_____, Price $_____

☐ *You Make The World A Sweeter Place,* 139521

Unmarked	$20.00
6∂	$20.00
★	$20.00
◯	$20.00
⊱	$20.00
⊕	$20.00
♛	$20.00

Open, Issue Price $20.00, '97
Series: *Little Moments*

Purchased_____, Price $_____

☐ *You're Forever In My Heart,* 139548

Unmarked	$20.00
6∂	$20.00
★	$20.00
◯	$20.00
⊱	$20.00
⊕	$20.00
♛	$20.00

Open, Issue Price $20.00, '97
Series: *Little Moments*

Purchased_____, Price $_____

☐ *Birthday Wishes With Hugs And Kisses,* 139556

Unmarked	$20.00
6∂	$20.00
★	$20.00
◯	$20.00
⤳	$20.00
✛	$20.00
♕	$20.00

Open, Issue Price $20.00, '97
Series: *Little Moments*

Purchased_____, Price $_____

☐ *You Make My Spirit Soar,* 139564

Unmarked	$20.00
6∂	$20.00
★	$20.00
◯	$20.00
⤳	$20.00
✛	$20.00
♕	$20.00

Open, Issue Price $20.00, '97
Series: *Little Moments*

Purchased_____, Price $_____

☐ *He Covers The Earth With His Beauty,* 142654

△ $38.00

Dated Annual 1995, Issue Price $30.00, '95
Purchased_____, Price $_____

☑ *He Covers The Earth With His Beauty,* 142662 (Ornament)

△ $30.00

Dated Annual 1995, Issue Price $17.00, '95
Purchased *15ºº*, Price $ *30.00*

☐ *He Covers The Earth With His Beauty,* 142670 (Plate)

△ $60.00

Dated Annual 1995, Issue Price $50.00, '95
Series: *Beauty Of Christmas* — Second Issue

Purchased_____, Price $_____

☐ *He Covers The Earth With His Beauty,* 142689 (Ornament)

△ $35.00

Dated Annual 1995, Issue Price $30.00, '95
Purchased_____, Price $_____

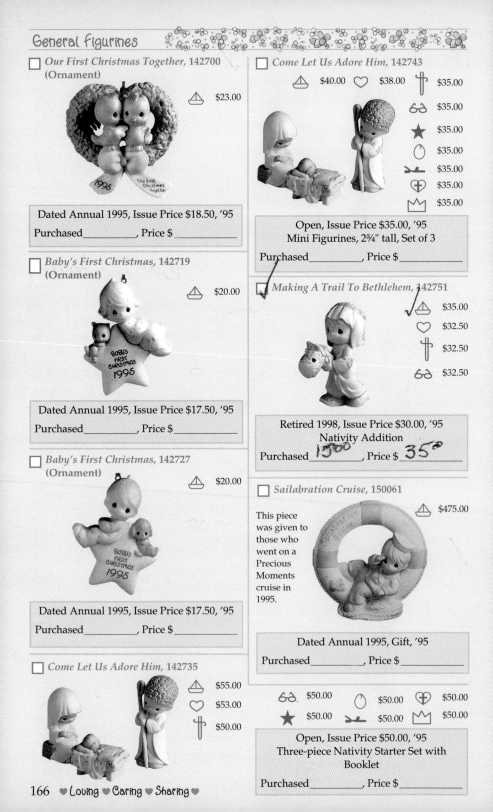

Our First Christmas Together, 142700
(Ornament)

⚓ $23.00

1995

Our First Christmas Together

Dated Annual 1995, Issue Price $18.50, '95

Purchased_____, Price $_____

Baby's First Christmas, 142719
(Ornament)

⚓ $20.00

BABYS FIRST CHRISTMAS 1995

Dated Annual 1995, Issue Price $17.50, '95

Purchased_____, Price $_____

Baby's First Christmas, 142727
(Ornament)

⚓ $20.00

BABYS FIRST CHRISTMAS 1995

Dated Annual 1995, Issue Price $17.50, '95

Purchased_____, Price $_____

Come Let Us Adore Him, 142735

⚓ $55.00

♡ $53.00

✝ $50.00

Come Let Us Adore Him, 142743

⚓ $40.00   ♡ $38.00   ✝ $35.00

👓 $35.00

★ $35.00

◖ $35.00

⤏ $35.00

⚓ $35.00

♔ $35.00

Open, Issue Price $35.00, '95
Mini Figurines, 2¾" tall, Set of 3

Purchased_____, Price $_____

Making A Trail To Bethlehem, 142751

✓⚓ $35.00

♡ $32.50

✝ $32.50

👓 $32.50

Retired 1998, Issue Price $30.00, '95
Nativity Addition

Purchased_1500_, Price $_35⁰⁰_

Sailabration Cruise, 150061

This piece was given to those who went on a Precious Moments cruise in 1995.

⚓ $475.00

Dated Annual 1995, Gift, '95

Purchased_____, Price $_____

👓 $50.00   ◖ $50.00   ⚓ $50.00

★ $50.00   ⤏ $50.00   ♔ $50.00

Open, Issue Price $50.00, '95
Three-piece Nativity Starter Set with Booklet

Purchased_____, Price $_____

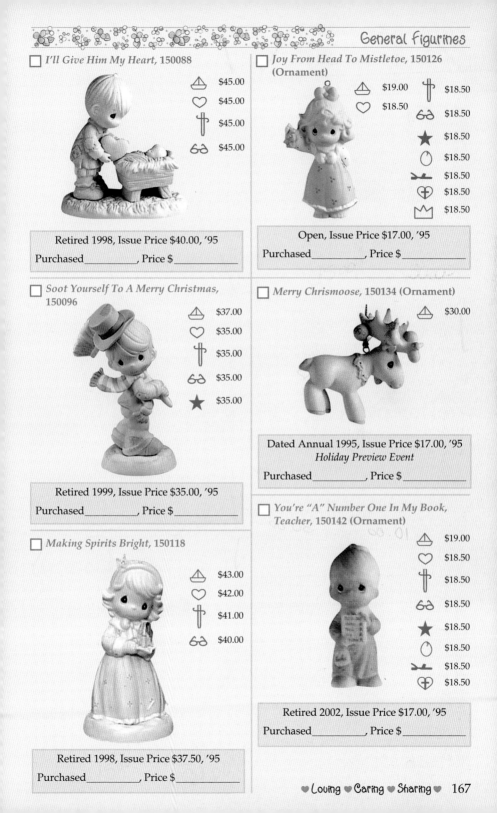

I'll Give Him My Heart, 150088

⛵ $45.00
♡ $45.00
♱ $45.00
👓 $45.00

Retired 1998, Issue Price $40.00, '95
Purchased_____, Price $_____

Soot Yourself To A Merry Christmas, 150096

⛵ $37.00
♡ $35.00
♱ $35.00
👓 $35.00
★ $35.00

Retired 1999, Issue Price $35.00, '95
Purchased_____, Price $_____

Making Spirits Bright, 150118

⛵ $43.00
♡ $42.00
♱ $41.00
👓 $40.00

Retired 1998, Issue Price $37.50, '95
Purchased_____, Price $_____

Joy From Head To Mistletoe, 150126 (Ornament)

⛵ $19.00   ♱ $18.50
♡ $18.50   👓 $18.50
            ★ $18.50
            ○ $18.50
            ⤛ $18.50
            ⊕ $18.50
            ♔ $18.50

Open, Issue Price $17.00, '95
Purchased_____, Price $_____

Merry Chrismoose, 150134 (Ornament)

⛵ $30.00

Dated Annual 1995, Issue Price $17.00, '95
Holiday Preview Event
Purchased_____, Price $_____

You're "A" Number One In My Book, Teacher, 150142 (Ornament)

⛵ $19.00
♡ $18.50
♱ $18.50
👓 $18.50
★ $18.50
○ $18.50
⤛ $18.50
⊕ $18.50

Retired 2002, Issue Price $17.00, '95
Purchased_____, Price $_____

☐ *Train Station*, 150150 (Nightlight)

△ $125.00   ♡ $115.00   ✝ $105.00

Retired 1997, Issue Price $100.00, '95
Series: *Sugar Town*

Purchased_____, Price $_____

☑ *Sam*, 150169

△ $30.00
♡

Annual 1995, Issue Price $20.00, '95
Series: *Sugar Town*

Purchased _10.00_ , Price $ _30.00_

☐ *Railroad Crossing Sign*, 150177

△ $15.00
♡ $13.00
✝ $12.00

Retired 1997, Issue Price $12.00, '95
Series: *Sugar Town*

Purchased_____, Price $_____

☑ *Luggage Cart*, 150185

△ $15.00
♡ $14.00
✝ $13.00

Retired 1997, Issue Price $13.00, '95
Series: *Sugar Town*

Purchased_____, Price $_____

☐ *Train Station Set*, 150193

△ $275.00   ♡ $250.00

Retired 1997, Issue Price $190.00, '95
Series: *Sugar Town*, Set of 6 (Train Station,
Railroad Crossing Sign, Luggage Cart,
Sam, Tammy & Debbie, and Donny)

Purchased_____, Price $_____

☑ *Bus Stop Sign*, 150207

△ $13.00
♡ $12.00
✝ $11.00

Retired 1997, Issue Price $8.50, '95
Series: *Sugar Town*

Purchased_____, Price $_____

☑ *Fire Hydrant*, 150215

△ ✓ $7.00
♡ $6.00
✝ $5.00

Retired 1997, Issue Price $5.00, '95
Series: *Sugar Town*
Purchased __500__, Price $ __7.00__

☑ *Bird Bath*, 150223

△ ✓ $10.00
♡ $9.00
✝ $8.50

Retired 1997, Issue Price $8.50, '95
Series: *Sugar Town*
Purchase __4.25__, Price $ __10.00__

☐ *God Bless Our Home*, 150231
(Ornament)

Note: Never personalized. Samples are selling for $55.00. Issued in Sugar Town boxes.

△ $55.00

Out Of Production, Issue Price $19.95, '95
Purchased _____, Price $ _____

☐ *Even The Heavens Shall Praise Him*, 150312

👓 $135.00

☐ *Joy To The World*, 150320 (Ornament)

△ $25.00
♡ $20.00
✝ $20.00
👓 $20.00
★ $20.00

Retired 1999, Issue Price $20.00, '95
Purchased _____, Price $ _____

☐ *Ssugar Town Enhancement Set*, 152269

△ $60.00
♡ $58.00
✝ $55.00

Retired 1997, Issue Price $45.00, '95
Series: *Sugar Town*, Set of 5
(Fire Hydrant, Bird Bath, Bus Stop Sign,
Bench, and Street Sign)
Purchased _____, Price $ _____

☐ *He Loves Me*, 152277

△ $550.00

Limited Ed. 2,000, Issue Price $500.00, '96
Easter Seals, Lily Understamp
Individually Numbered
Purchased _____, Price $ _____

Limited Ed. 15,000, Issue Price $125.00, '98
Century Circle Exclusive
Purchased _____, Price $ _____

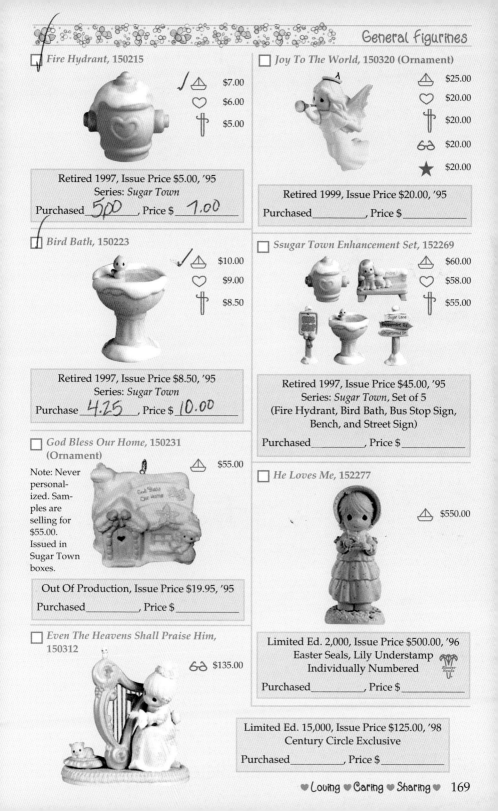

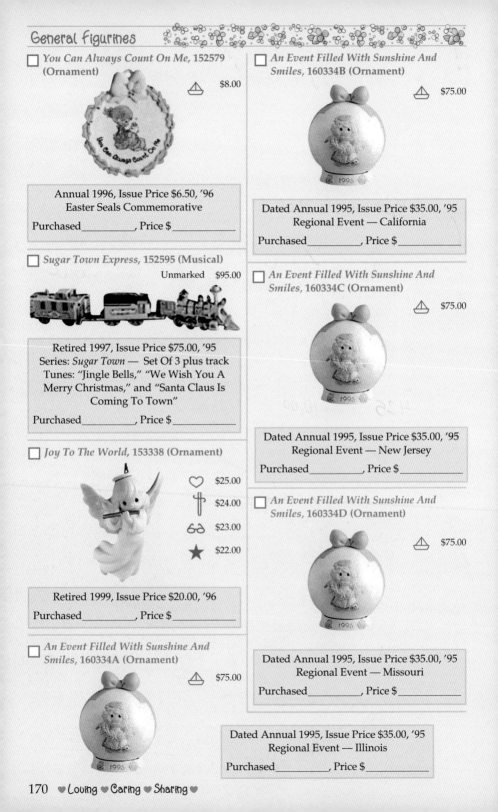

You Can Always Count On Me, 152579
(Ornament)

⛵ $8.00

Annual 1996, Issue Price $6.50, '96
Easter Seals Commemorative

Purchased_____, Price $_____

Sugar Town Express, 152595 (Musical)

Unmarked $95.00

Retired 1997, Issue Price $75.00, '95
Series: *Sugar Town* — Set Of 3 plus track
Tunes: "Jingle Bells," "We Wish You A
Merry Christmas," and "Santa Claus Is
Coming To Town"

Purchased_____, Price $_____

Joy To The World, 153338 (Ornament)

♡ $25.00
✝ $24.00
6∂ $23.00
★ $22.00

Retired 1999, Issue Price $20.00, '96

Purchased_____, Price $_____

**An Event Filled With Sunshine And
Smiles, 160334A (Ornament)**

△ $75.00

**An Event Filled With Sunshine And
Smiles, 160334B (Ornament)**

⛵ $75.00

Dated Annual 1995, Issue Price $35.00, '95
Regional Event — California

Purchased_____, Price $_____

**An Event Filled With Sunshine And
Smiles, 160334C (Ornament)**

△ $75.00

Dated Annual 1995, Issue Price $35.00, '95
Regional Event — New Jersey

Purchased_____, Price $_____

**An Event Filled With Sunshine And
Smiles, 160334D (Ornament)**

△ $75.00

Dated Annual 1995, Issue Price $35.00, '95
Regional Event — Missouri

Purchased_____, Price $_____

Dated Annual 1995, Issue Price $35.00, '95
Regional Event — Illinois

Purchased_____, Price $_____

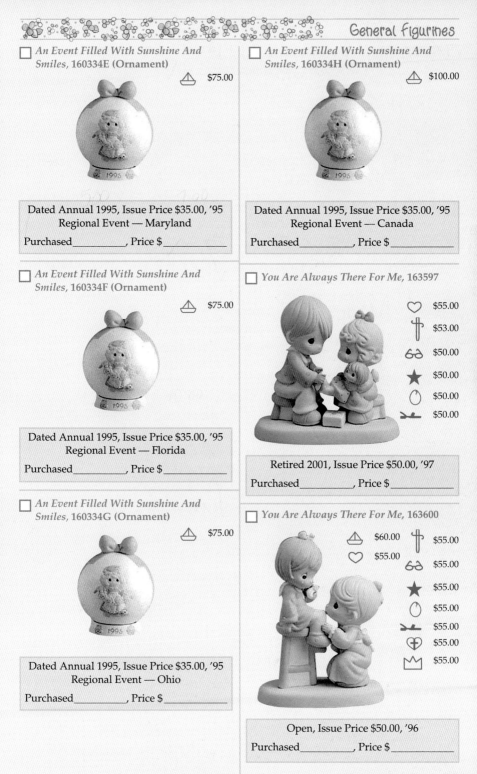

☐ *An Event Filled With Sunshine And Smiles*, 160334E (Ornament)

△ $75.00

Dated Annual 1995, Issue Price $35.00, '95 Regional Event — Maryland

Purchased_____, Price $_____

☐ *An Event Filled With Sunshine And Smiles*, 160334H (Ornament)

△ $100.00

Dated Annual 1995, Issue Price $35.00, '95 Regional Event — Canada

Purchased_____, Price $_____

☐ *An Event Filled With Sunshine And Smiles*, 160334F (Ornament)

△ $75.00

Dated Annual 1995, Issue Price $35.00, '95 Regional Event — Florida

Purchased_____, Price $_____

☐ *You Are Always There For Me*, 163597

♡ $55.00
† $53.00
6ᴕ $50.00
★ $50.00
◯ $50.00
ᗢ $50.00

Retired 2001, Issue Price $50.00, '97

Purchased_____, Price $_____

☐ *An Event Filled With Sunshine And Smiles*, 160334G (Ornament)

△ $75.00

Dated Annual 1995, Issue Price $35.00, '95 Regional Event — Ohio

Purchased_____, Price $_____

☐ *You Are Always There For Me*, 163600

△ $60.00   † $55.00
♡ $55.00   6ᴕ $55.00
            ★ $55.00
            ◯ $55.00
            ᗢ $55.00
            ⊕ $55.00
            ♕ $55.00

Open, Issue Price $50.00, '96

Purchased_____, Price $_____

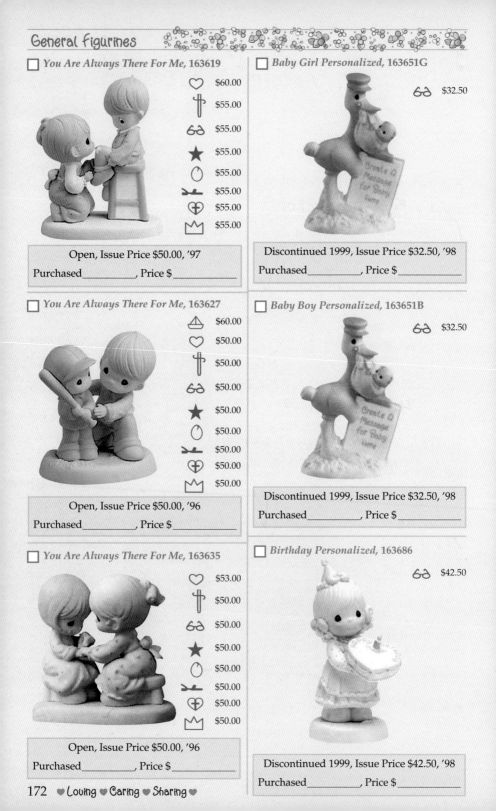

☐ *You Are Always There For Me*, 163619

♡ $60.00
✝ $55.00
6ᴏ $55.00
★ $55.00
◯ $55.00
ᕲ $55.00
⊕ $55.00
ᗢ $55.00

Open, Issue Price $50.00, '97
Purchased_____, Price $_____

☐ *You Are Always There For Me*, 163627

⛵ $60.00
♡ $50.00
✝ $50.00
6ᴏ $50.00
★ $50.00
◯ $50.00
ᕲ $50.00
⊕ $50.00
ᗢ $50.00

Open, Issue Price $50.00, '96
Purchased_____, Price $_____

☐ *You Are Always There For Me*, 163635

♡ $53.00
✝ $50.00
6ᴏ $50.00
★ $50.00
◯ $50.00
ᕲ $50.00
⊕ $50.00
ᗢ $50.00

Open, Issue Price $50.00, '96
Purchased_____, Price $_____

☐ *Baby Girl Personalized*, 163651G

6ᴏ $32.50

Discontinued 1999, Issue Price $32.50, '98
Purchased_____, Price $_____

☐ *Baby Boy Personalized*, 163651B

6ᴏ $32.50

Discontinued 1999, Issue Price $32.50, '98
Purchased_____, Price $_____

☐ *Birthday Personalized*, 163686

6ᴏ $42.50

Discontinued 1999, Issue Price $42.50, '98
Purchased_____, Price $_____

☐ *I'd Goat Anywhere With You,* 163694

△ $12.00
♡ $10.00
✝ $10.00
𝟞𝟛 $10.00
★ $10.00
◯ $10.00
✂ $10.00
✛ $10.00

Retired 2002, Issue Price $10.00, '96
Series: *Two By Two*

Purchased_____, Price $_____

☐ *Blessed Are They With A Caring Heart,* 163724

★ $55.00

Limited Ed. 1999, Issue Price $55.00, '99
Century Circle Exclusive

Purchased_____, Price $_____

☐ *Jennifer,* 163708

△ $25.00
♡ $20.00

Suspended 1996, Issue Price $20.00, '96
Series: *Sammy's Circus,* Set Of 2

Purchased_____, Price $_____

☐ *Standing In The Presence Of The Lord,* 163732

△ $40.00
♡ $38.00

Dated Annual 1996, Issue Price $37.50, '96
Series: *Dated Cross* — Second Issue

Purchased_____, Price $_____

☐ *Of All The Mothers I Have Known, There's None As Precious As My Own,* 163716 (Plate)

♡ $40.00

Dated Annual 1996, Issue Price $37.50, '96
Series: *Mother's Day* — Third Issue

Purchased_____, Price $_____

☐ *Age 7,* 163740

△ $35.00   ✝ $32.50
♡ $33.00   𝟞𝟛 $32.50
           ★ $32.50
           ◯ $32.50
           ✂ $32.50
           ✛ $32.50
           ♛ $32.50

Open, Issue Price $32.50, '96
Series: *Growing In Grace* (Blond)

Purchased_____, Price $_____

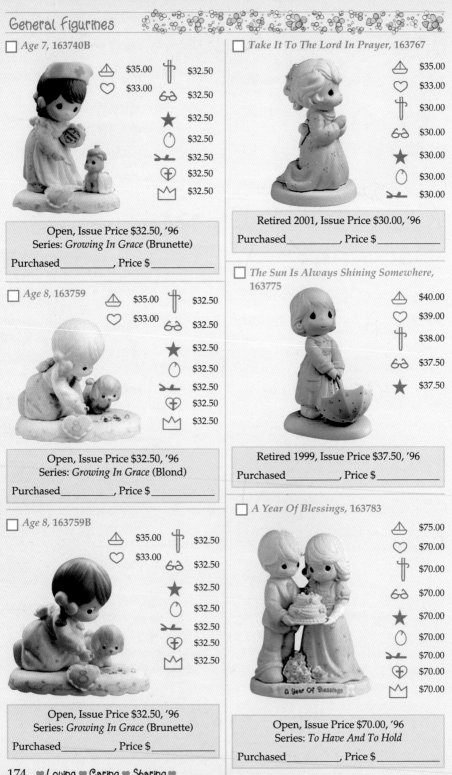

□ *Age 7, 163740B*

⛵	$35.00	✝	$32.50
♡	$33.00	👓	$32.50
		★	$32.50
		◯	$32.50
		⤛	$32.50
		⊕	$32.50
		♔	$32.50

Open, Issue Price $32.50, '96
Series: *Growing In Grace* (Brunette)

Purchased_____, Price $_____

□ *Age 8, 163759*

⛵	$35.00	✝	$32.50
♡	$33.00	👓	$32.50
		★	$32.50
		◯	$32.50
		⤛	$32.50
		⊕	$32.50
		♔	$32.50

Open, Issue Price $32.50, '96
Series: *Growing In Grace* (Blond)

Purchased_____, Price $_____

□ *Age 8, 163759B*

⛵	$35.00	✝	$32.50
♡	$33.00	👓	$32.50
		★	$32.50
		◯	$32.50
		⤛	$32.50
		⊕	$32.50
		♔	$32.50

Open, Issue Price $32.50, '96
Series: *Growing In Grace* (Brunette)

Purchased_____, Price $_____

□ *Take It To The Lord In Prayer, 163767*

⛵	$35.00
♡	$33.00
✝	$30.00
👓	$30.00
★	$30.00
◯	$30.00
⤛	$30.00

Retired 2001, Issue Price $30.00, '96

Purchased_____, Price $_____

□ *The Sun Is Always Shining Somewhere, 163775*

⛵	$40.00
♡	$39.00
✝	$38.00
👓	$37.50
★	$37.50

Retired 1999, Issue Price $37.50, '96

Purchased_____, Price $_____

□ *A Year Of Blessings, 163783*

⛵	$75.00
♡	$70.00
✝	$70.00
👓	$70.00
★	$70.00
◯	$70.00
⤛	$70.00
⊕	$70.00
♔	$70.00

Open, Issue Price $70.00, '96
Series: *To Have And To Hold*

Purchased_____, Price $_____

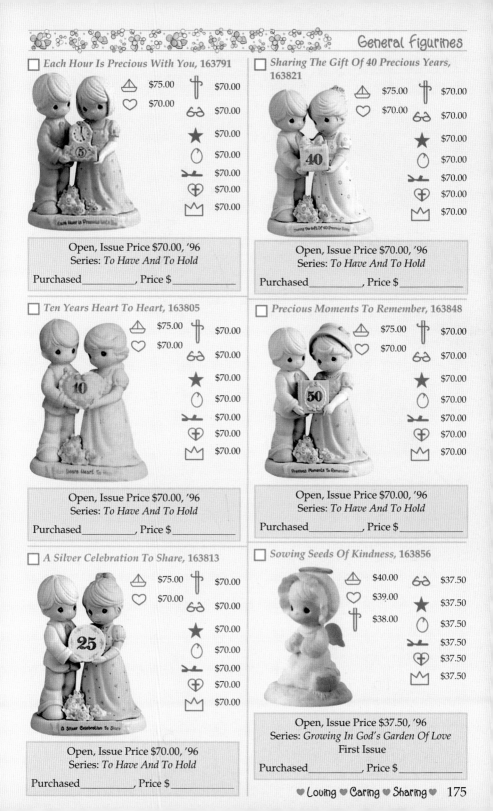

Each Hour Is Precious With You, 163791

△ $75.00 ☦ $70.00
♡ $70.00 👓 $70.00
★ $70.00
○ $70.00
🪓 $70.00
✢ $70.00
👑 $70.00

Open, Issue Price $70.00, '96
Series: *To Have And To Hold*

Purchased_____, Price $_____

Sharing The Gift Of 40 Precious Years, 163821

△ $75.00 ☦ $70.00
♡ $70.00 👓 $70.00
★ $70.00
○ $70.00
🪓 $70.00
✢ $70.00
👑 $70.00

Open, Issue Price $70.00, '96
Series: *To Have And To Hold*

Purchased_____, Price $_____

Ten Years Heart To Heart, 163805

△ $75.00 ☦ $70.00
♡ $70.00 👓 $70.00
★ $70.00
○ $70.00
🪓 $70.00
✢ $70.00
👑 $70.00

Open, Issue Price $70.00, '96
Series: *To Have And To Hold*

Purchased_____, Price $_____

Precious Moments To Remember, 163848

△ $75.00 ☦ $70.00
♡ $70.00 👓 $70.00
★ $70.00
○ $70.00
🪓 $70.00
✢ $70.00
👑 $70.00

Open, Issue Price $70.00, '96
Series: *To Have And To Hold*

Purchased_____, Price $_____

A Silver Celebration To Share, 163813

△ $75.00 ☦ $70.00
♡ $70.00 👓 $70.00
★ $70.00
○ $70.00
🪓 $70.00
✢ $70.00
👑 $70.00

Open, Issue Price $70.00, '96
Series: *To Have And To Hold*

Purchased_____, Price $_____

Sowing Seeds Of Kindness, 163856

△ $40.00 👓 $37.50
♡ $39.00 ★ $37.50
☦ $38.00 ○ $37.50
🪓 $37.50
✢ $37.50
👑 $37.50

Open, Issue Price $37.50, '96
Series: *Growing In God's Garden Of Love*
First Issue

Purchased_____, Price $_____

☐ *Hallelujah Hoedown*, 163864

⛵ $75.00
♡ $50.00

Annual 1996, Issue Price $32.50, '96
Spring Celebration

Purchased_____, Price $_____

☐ *His Presence Is Felt In The Chapel*,
163872

Unmarked $30.00

Retired 1998, Issue Price $25.00, '96
Chapel Exclusive

Purchased_____, Price $_____

☐ *His Presence Is Felt In The Chapel*,
163880 (Ornament)

Unmarked $25.00

Suspended 1997, Issue Price $17.50, '96
Chapel Exclusive

Purchased_____, Price $_____

☐ *It May Be Greener, But It's Just As Hard
To Cut*, 163899

⛵ $40.00
♡ $39.00
✝ $38.00
👓 $37.50
★ $37.50
◯ $37.50
🏹 $37.50

Retired 2001, Issue Price $37.50, '96

Purchased_____, Price $_____

☐ *God's Love Is Reflected In You*, 175277

♡ $225.00

Limited Ed. 15,000, Issue Price $150.00, '96
Century Circle Exclusive,
Individually Numbered

Purchased_____, Price $_____

☐ *Some Plant, Some Water, But God Giveth
The Increase*, 176958

♡ $45.00
✝ $44.00
👓 $43.00
★ $42.00
◯ $40.00
🏹 $40.00
⊕ $40.00
♛ $40.00

Open, Issue Price $37.50, '96
Series: *Growing In God's Garden of Love*
Second Issue

Purchased_____, Price $_____

☐ *A Perfect Display Of 15 Happy Years,* 177083 (Medallion)

⛵ $400.00

This Medallion was given to the attendees of the 1995 Local Club Chapter Convention. This is the fifth in the collection.

Convention Gift, '95

Purchased_____, Price $_____

☐ *Peace On Earth,* 177091 (Ornament)

Unmarked $35.00

Limited Ed. 15,000, Issue Price $25.00, '95
Century Circle Exclusive

Purchased_____, Price $_____

☑ *Peace On Earth... Anyway,* 183342

♡ $35.00

Dated Annual 1996, Issue Price $32.50, '96
Purchased _11.50_, Price $ _35.00_

Retired 2001, Issue Price $40.00, '96
Purchased_____, Price $_____

☐ *Peace On Earth... Anyway,* 183350 (Ornament)

♡ $40.00

Dated Annual 1996, Issue Price $30.00, '96
Purchased_____, Price $_____

☐ *Peace On Earth... Anyway,* 183369 (Ornament)

♡ $22.00

Dated Annual 1996, Issue Price $18.50, '96
Purchased_____, Price $_____

☐ *Peace On Earth... Anyway,* 183377 (Plate)

♡ $55.00

Dated Annual 1996, Issue Price $50.00, '96
Series: *Beauty Of Christmas* — Third Issue
Purchased_____, Price $_____

☐ *Angels On Earth,* 183776

♡ $45.00
♱ $45.00
👓 $45.00
★ $45.00
◐ $45.00
⤴ $45.00

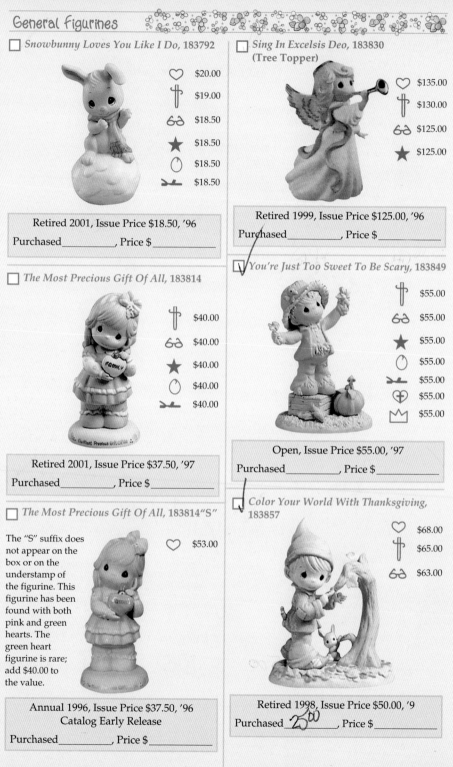

☐ *Snowbunny Loves You Like I Do*, 183792

♡ $20.00
✝ $19.00
6ð $18.50
★ $18.50
◯ $18.50
⊱ $18.50

Retired 2001, Issue Price $18.50, '96
Purchased_____, Price $_____

☐ *The Most Precious Gift Of All*, 183814

✝ $40.00
6ð $40.00
★ $40.00
◯ $40.00
⊱ $40.00

Retired 2001, Issue Price $37.50, '97
Purchased_____, Price $_____

☐ *The Most Precious Gift Of All*, 183814"S"

The "S" suffix does not appear on the box or on the understamp of the figurine. This figurine has been found with both pink and green hearts. The green heart figurine is rare; add $40.00 to the value.

♡ $53.00

Annual 1996, Issue Price $37.50, '96
Catalog Early Release
Purchased_____, Price $_____

☐ *Sing In Excelsis Deo*, 183830
(Tree Topper)

♡ $135.00
✝ $130.00
6ð $125.00
★ $125.00

Retired 1999, Issue Price $125.00, '96
Purchased_____, Price $_____

☐ *You're Just Too Sweet To Be Scary*, 183849

✝ $55.00
6ð $55.00
★ $55.00
◯ $55.00
⊱ $55.00
⊕ $55.00
♕ $55.00

Open, Issue Price $55.00, '97
Purchased_____, Price $_____

☐ *Color Your World With Thanksgiving*, 183857

♡ $68.00
✝ $65.00
6ð $63.00

Retired 1998, Issue Price $50.00, '9
Purchased _25⁰⁰_, Price $_____

☐ *Age 9,* 183865

♡ $30.00
♰ $30.00
👓 $30.00
★ $30.00
◯ $30.00
✂ $30.00
✛ $30.00
♕ $30.00

Open, Issue Price $30.00, '96
Series: *Growing In Grace* (Blond)

Purchased_____, Price $_____

☐ *Age 10,* 183873B

♡ $35.00
♰ $35.00
👓 $35.00
★ $35.00
◯ $35.00
✂ $35.00
✛ $35.00
♕ $35.00

Open, Issue Price $35.00, '96
Series: *Growing In Grace* (Brunette)

Purchased_____, Price $_____

☐ *Age 9,* 183865B

♡ $30.00
♰ $30.00
👓 $30.00
★ $30.00
◯ $30.00
✂ $30.00
✛ $30.00
♕ $30.00

Open, Issue Price $30.00, '96
Series: *Growing In Grace* (Brunette)

Purchased_____, Price $_____

☐ *God's Precious Gift,* 183881 (Ornament)

This
piece is all
white.

♡ $20.00
♰ $20.00
👓 $20.00
★ $20.00
◯ $20.00
✂ $20.00
✛ $20.00
♕ $20.00

Open, Issue Price $20.00, '96

Purchased_____, Price $_____

☐ *Age 10,* 183873

♡ $35.00
♰ $35.00
👓 $35.00
★ $35.00
◯ $35.00
✂ $35.00
✛ $35.00
♕ $35.00

Open, Issue Price $35.00, '96
Series: *Growing In Grace* (Blond)

Purchased_____, Price $_____

☐ *When The Skating's Ruff, Try Prayer,*
183903 (Ornament)

♡ $18.50
♰ $18.50
👓 $18.50
★ $18.50
◯ $18.50
✂ $18.50
✛ $18.50
♕ $18.50

Open, Issue Price $18.50, '96

Purchased_____, Price $_____

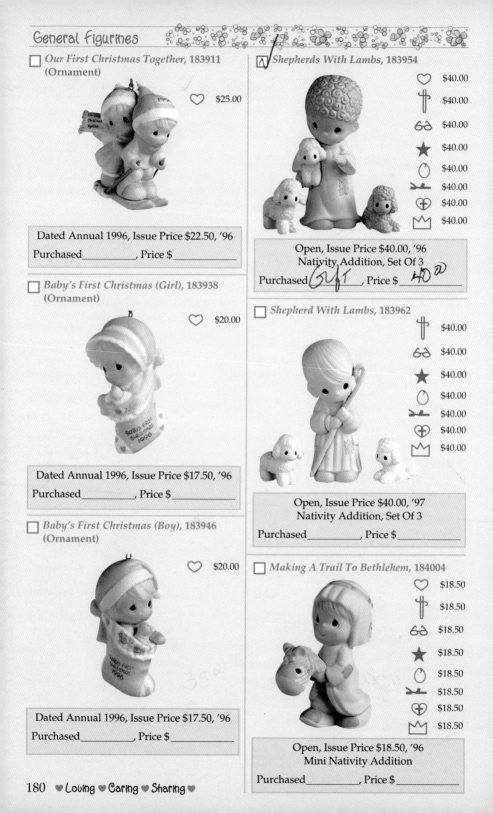

☐ *Our First Christmas Together*, 183911
(Ornament)

♡ $25.00

Dated Annual 1996, Issue Price $22.50, '96

Purchased_____, Price $_____

☐ *Baby's First Christmas (Girl)*, 183938
(Ornament)

♡ $20.00

Dated Annual 1996, Issue Price $17.50, '96

Purchased_____, Price $_____

☐ *Baby's First Christmas (Boy)*, 183946
(Ornament)

♡ $20.00

Dated Annual 1996, Issue Price $17.50, '96

Purchased_____, Price $_____

☑ *Shepherds With Lambs*, 183954

♡ $40.00
† $40.00
∞ $40.00
★ $40.00
◯ $40.00
⤛ $40.00
⊕ $40.00
♔ $40.00

Open, Issue Price $40.00, '96
Nativity Addition, Set Of 3

Purchased *GYT*, Price $ *40 ²⁰*

☐ *Shepherd With Lambs*, 183962

† $40.00
∞ $40.00
★ $40.00
◯ $40.00
⤛ $40.00
⊕ $40.00
♔ $40.00

Open, Issue Price $40.00, '97
Nativity Addition, Set Of 3

Purchased_____, Price $_____

☐ *Making A Trail To Bethlehem*, 184004

♡ $18.50
† $18.50
∞ $18.50
★ $18.50
◯ $18.50
⤛ $18.50
⊕ $18.50
♔ $18.50

Open, Issue Price $18.50, '96
Mini Nativity Addition

Purchased_____, Price $_____

All Sing His Praises, 184012

♡ $32.50
✝ $32.50
👓 $32.50
★ $32.50
◯ $32.50
✂ $32.50
✟ $32.50
♔ $32.50

Open, Issue Price $32.50, '96
Nativity Addition
Purchased_____, Price $_____

Skating Sign, 184020

♡ $25.00

Annual 1996, Issue Price $15.00, '96
Series: *Sugar Town*
Purchased __7.50__, Price $ __25⁰⁰__

Sugar Town Tree, 184039 (Lighted)

♡ $80.00
✝ $70.00

Retired 1997, Issue Price $45.00, '96
Series: *Sugar Town*
Purchased_____, Price $_____

Skating Rink, 184047

♡ $60.00
✝ $55.00

Retired, Issue Price $40.00, '96
Series: *Sugar Town*
Purchased_____, Price $_____

Mazie, 184055

♡ $35.00
✝ $32.00

Retired 1997, Issue Price $18.50, '96
Series: *Sugar Town*
Purchased_____, Price $_____

Cocoa, 184063

♡ $15.00
✝ $12.00

Retired 1997, Issue Price $7.50, '96
Series: *Sugar Town*
Purchased_____, Price $_____

Leroy, 184071

♡ $35.00
✝ $30.00

Retired 1997, Issue Price $18.50, '96
Series: *Sugar Town*
Purchased_____, Price $_____

☑ *Hank And Sharon*, 184098 ✓

♡ $35.00
✝ $33.00

Retired 1997, Issue Price $25.00, '96
Series: *Sugar Town*
Purchased **12.50**, Price $ **35.00**

☐ *Train Station*, 184101 (Ornament)

♡ $25.00

Annual 1996, Issue Price $18.50, '96
Series: *Sugar Town*
Purchased_____, Price $_____

☐ *Skating Rink Set*, 184128

♡ $275.00
✝ $265.00

Retired, Issue Price $184.50, '97
Set of 7 (Warming Hut, Mazie, Hank And
Sharon, Leroy, Cocoa, Skating Sign, And
Skating Pond)
Purchased_____, Price $_____

☑ *Flagpole*, 184136 ✓

♡ $22.00
✝ $20.00

Retired 1997, Issue Price $15.00, '96
Series: *Sugar Town*
Purchased **7.50**, Price $ **22.00**

☐ *Hot Cocoa Stand*, 184144

♡ $22.00
✝ $20.00

Retired 1997, Issue Price $15.00, '96
Series: *Sugar Town*
Purchased_____, Price $_____

☐ *Bonfire*, 184152

♡ $20.00
✝ $17.00

Retired 1997, Issue Price $10.00, '96
Series: *Sugar Town*
Purchased_____, Price $_____

☐ *Sugar Town Enhancement Set*, 184160

♡ $60.00
✝ $60.00

Retired 1997, Issue Price $40.00, '96
Series: *Sugar Town*, Set Of 3 (Hot Cocoa
Stand, Flagpole, and Bonfire)
Purchased_____, Price $_____

☐ *Train Station Set*, 184179

△ $230.00   ♡ $225.00
♰ $215.00

Retired 1997, Issue Price $170.00, '96
Series: *Sugar Town*, Set Of 6 (Train Station,
Donny, Luggage Cart, Tammy and Debbie,
Railroad Crossing Sign, and Sam)

Purchased_____, Price $_____

☑ *Doctor's Office Set*, 184187

△ $250.00   ♡ $245.00
♰ $240.00

Retired 1997, Issue Price $170.00, '96
Series: *Sugar Town*, Set Of 6
(Doctor's Office, Sugar and Her Doghouse,
Jan, Dr. Sam Sugar, Leon and Evelyn Mae,
and Free Christmas Puppies)

Purchased_____, Price $_____

☐ *Sam's House Set*, 184195

△ $250.00   ♡ $245.00
♰ $240.00

Retired 1997, Issue Price $170.00, '96
Series: *Sugar Town*, Set Of 6
(Sam's House, Fence, Sam's Car, Sammy,
Katy Lynne, and Dusty)

Purchased_____, Price $_____

☐ *May The Sun Always Shine On You*,
184217

♡ $55.00

Annual 1996, Issue Price $37.50, '96
Century Circle Event Exclusive

Purchased_____, Price $_____

☐ *Winter Wishes Warm The Heart*, 184241
(Ornament)

◯ $20.00
⤜ $20.00

Annual 2000, Issue Price $20.00, '00
Avon Exclusive

Purchased_____, Price $_____

☐ *A Bouquet From God's Garden Of Love*,
184268

♡ $40.00
♰ $40.00
ᚙ $40.00
★ $40.00
◯ $40.00
⤜ $40.00

Retired 2001, Issue Price $37.50, '97
Series: *Growing In God's Garden Of Love*
Third Issue

Purchased_____, Price $_____

☐ *Love Makes The World Go 'Round*,
184209 (Ornament)

♡ $45.00

Annual 1996, Issue Price $22.50, '96
Century Circle Exclusive

Purchased_____, Price $_____

♥ Loving ♥ Caring ♥ Sharing ♥   183

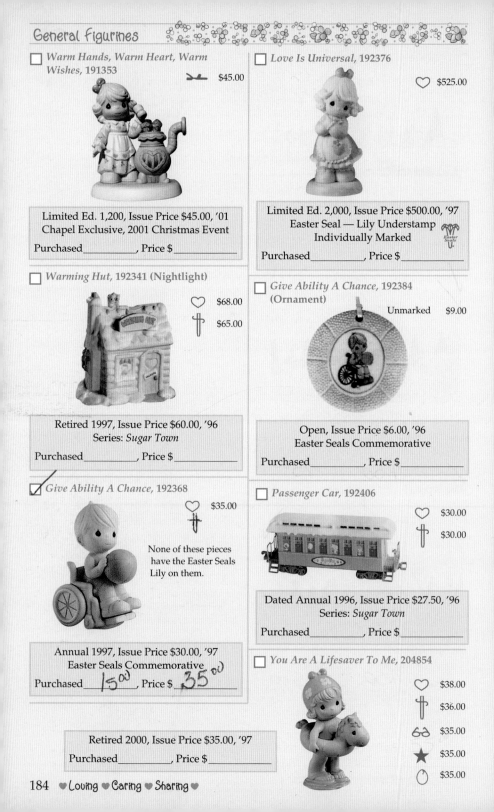

☐ *Warm Hands, Warm Heart, Warm Wishes,* 191353

✂ $45.00

Limited Ed. 1,200, Issue Price $45.00, '01
Chapel Exclusive, 2001 Christmas Event

Purchased_____, Price $_____

☐ *Warming Hut,* 192341 (Nightlight)

♡ $68.00

✝ $65.00

Retired 1997, Issue Price $60.00, '96
Series: *Sugar Town*

Purchased_____, Price $_____

☑ *Give Ability A Chance,* 192368

♡✝ $35.00

None of these pieces
have the Easter Seals
Lily on them.

Annual 1997, Issue Price $30.00, '97
Easter Seals Commemorative

Purchased___*15⁰⁰*___, Price $___*35⁰⁰*___

Retired 2000, Issue Price $35.00, '97

Purchased_____, Price $_____

☐ *Love Is Universal,* 192376

♡ $525.00

Limited Ed. 2,000, Issue Price $500.00, '97
Easter Seal — Lily Understamp
Individually Marked

Purchased_____, Price $_____

☐ *Give Ability A Chance,* 192384
(Ornament)

Unmarked $9.00

Open, Issue Price $6.00, '96
Easter Seals Commemorative

Purchased_____, Price $_____

☐ *Passenger Car,* 192406

♡ $30.00

✝ $30.00

Dated Annual 1996, Issue Price $27.50, '96
Series: *Sugar Town*

Purchased_____, Price $_____

☐ *You Are A Lifesaver To Me,* 204854

♡ $38.00

✝ $36.00

👓 $35.00

★ $35.00

◯ $35.00

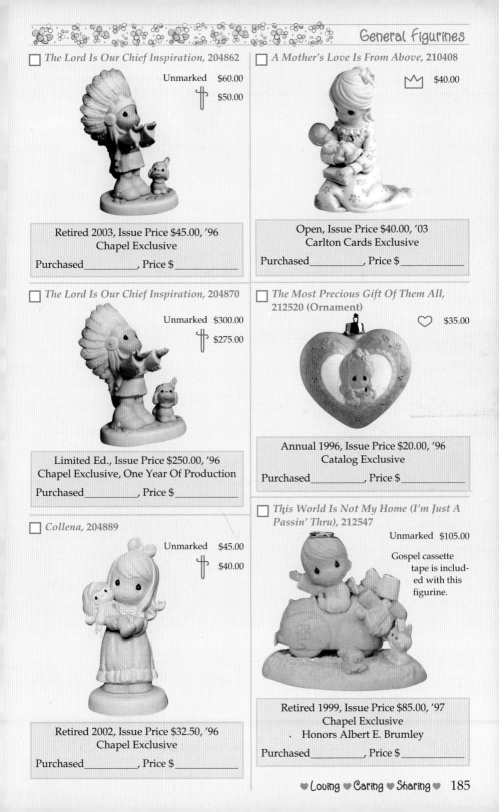

☐ *The Lord Is Our Chief Inspiration*, 204862

Unmarked $60.00

✝ $50.00

Retired 2003, Issue Price $45.00, '96
Chapel Exclusive

Purchased_____, Price $_____

☐ *The Lord Is Our Chief Inspiration*, 204870

Unmarked $300.00

✝ $275.00

Limited Ed., Issue Price $250.00, '96
Chapel Exclusive, One Year Of Production

Purchased_____, Price $_____

☐ *Collena*, 204889

Unmarked $45.00

✝ $40.00

Retired 2002, Issue Price $32.50, '96
Chapel Exclusive

Purchased_____, Price $_____

☐ *A Mother's Love Is From Above*, 210408

♛ $40.00

Open, Issue Price $40.00, '03
Carlton Cards Exclusive

Purchased_____, Price $_____

☐ *The Most Precious Gift Of Them All*,
212520 (Ornament)

♡ $35.00

Annual 1996, Issue Price $20.00, '96
Catalog Exclusive

Purchased_____, Price $_____

☐ *This World Is Not My Home (I'm Just A
Passin' Thru)*, 212547

Unmarked $105.00

Gospel cassette
tape is includ-
ed with this
figurine.

Retired 1999, Issue Price $85.00, '97
Chapel Exclusive
.   Honors Albert E. Brumley

Purchased_____, Price $_____

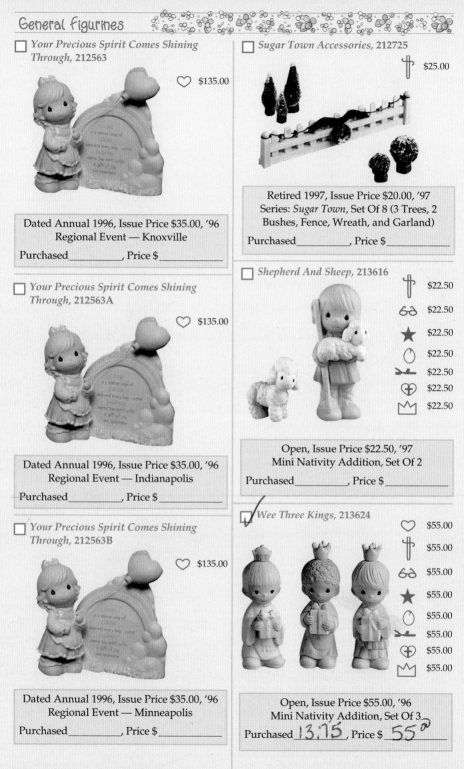

☐ *Your Precious Spirit Comes Shining Through*, 212563

♡ $135.00

Dated Annual 1996, Issue Price $35.00, '96
Regional Event — Knoxville

Purchased_____, Price $_____

☐ *Your Precious Spirit Comes Shining Through*, 212563A

♡ $135.00

Dated Annual 1996, Issue Price $35.00, '96
Regional Event — Indianapolis

Purchased_____, Price $_____

☐ *Your Precious Spirit Comes Shining Through*, 212563B

♡ $135.00

Dated Annual 1996, Issue Price $35.00, '96
Regional Event — Minneapolis

Purchased_____, Price $_____

☐ *Sugar Town Accessories*, 212725

✝ $25.00

Retired 1997, Issue Price $20.00, '97
Series: *Sugar Town*, Set Of 8 (3 Trees, 2
Bushes, Fence, Wreath, and Garland)

Purchased_____, Price $_____

☐ *Shepherd And Sheep*, 213616

✝ $22.50
👓 $22.50
★ $22.50
◯ $22.50
✂ $22.50
✛ $22.50
♔ $22.50

Open, Issue Price $22.50, '97
Mini Nativity Addition, Set Of 2

Purchased_____, Price $_____

☑ *Wee Three Kings*, 213624

♡ $55.00
✝ $55.00
👓 $55.00
★ $55.00
◯ $55.00
✂ $55.00
✛ $55.00
♔ $55.00

Open, Issue Price $55.00, '96
Mini Nativity Addition, Set Of 3

Purchased 13.75, Price $ 55⁰⁰

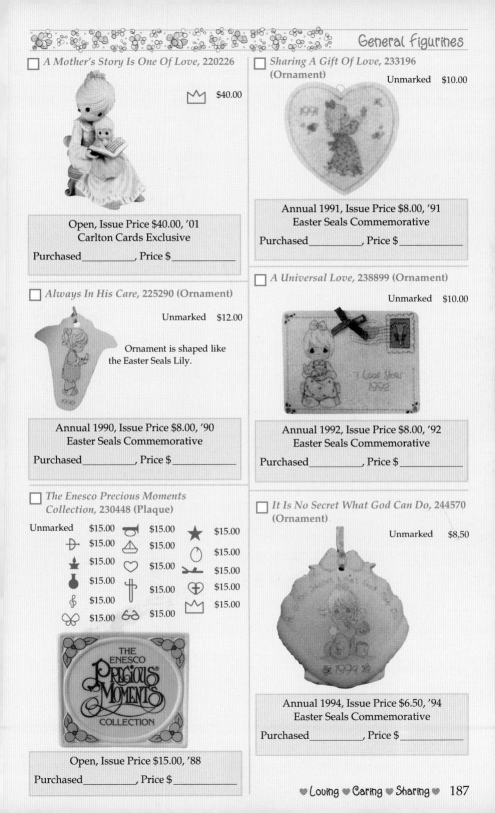

☐ *A Mother's Story Is One Of Love*, 220226

👑 $40.00

Open, Issue Price $40.00, '01
Carlton Cards Exclusive

Purchased_____, Price $ _____

☐ *Always In His Care*, 225290 (Ornament)

Unmarked $12.00

Ornament is shaped like
the Easter Seals Lily.

Annual 1990, Issue Price $8.00, '90
Easter Seals Commemorative

Purchased_____, Price $ _____

☐ *The Enesco Precious Moments
Collection*, 230448 (Plaque)

Unmarked	$15.00	🎺	$15.00	★	$15.00
Ð	$15.00	△	$15.00	◐	$15.00
⚘	$15.00	♡	$15.00	⤙	$15.00
◉	$15.00	✝	$15.00	⊕	$15.00
₰	$15.00			👑	$15.00
✷	$15.00	👓	$15.00		

Open, Issue Price $15.00, '88

Purchased_____, Price $ _____

☐ *Sharing A Gift Of Love*, 233196
(Ornament)

Unmarked $10.00

Annual 1991, Issue Price $8.00, '91
Easter Seals Commemorative

Purchased_____, Price $ _____

☐ *A Universal Love*, 238899 (Ornament)

Unmarked $10.00

Annual 1992, Issue Price $8.00, '92
Easter Seals Commemorative

Purchased_____, Price $ _____

☐ *It Is No Secret What God Can Do*, 244570
(Ornament)

Unmarked $8.50

Annual 1994, Issue Price $6.50, '94
Easter Seals Commemorative

Purchased_____, Price $ _____

General Figurines

☐ *You're My Number One Friend*, 250112
(Ornament)

Unmarked $10.00

Annual 1993, Issue Price $8.00, '93
Easter Seals Commemorative

Purchased_____, Price $_____

☐ *Lead Me To Calvary*, 260916

♡ $40.00

Dated Annual 1997, Issue Price $37.50, '97
Series: *Dated Cross* — Third Issue

Purchased_____, Price $_____

☐ *Age 11*, 260924

♡	$40.00
✝	$39.00
👓	$38.00
★	$37.50
◯	$37.50
✂	$37.50
✠	$37.50
♛	$37.50

Open, Issue Price $37.50, '97
Series: *Growing In Grace* (Blond)

Purchased_____, Price $_____

☐ *Age 11*, 260924B

♡	$40.00
✝	$39.00
👓	$38.00
★	$37.50
◯	$37.50
✂	$37.50
✠	$37.50

Open, Issue Price $37.50, '97
Series: *Growing In Grace* (Brunette)

Purchased_____, Price $_____

☐ *Age 12*, 260932

♡	$40.00
✝	$39.00
👓	$38.00
★	$37.50
◯	$37.50
✂	$37.50
✠	$37.50
♛	$37.50

Open, Issue Price $37.50, '97
Series: *Growing In Grace* (Blond)

Purchased_____, Price $_____

☐ *Age 12*, 260932B

♡	$40.00
✝	$39.00
👓	$38.00
★	$37.50
◯	$37.50
✂	$37.50
✠	$37.50
♛	$37.50

Open, Issue Price $37.50, '97
Series: *Growing In Grace* (Brunette)

Purchased_____, Price $_____

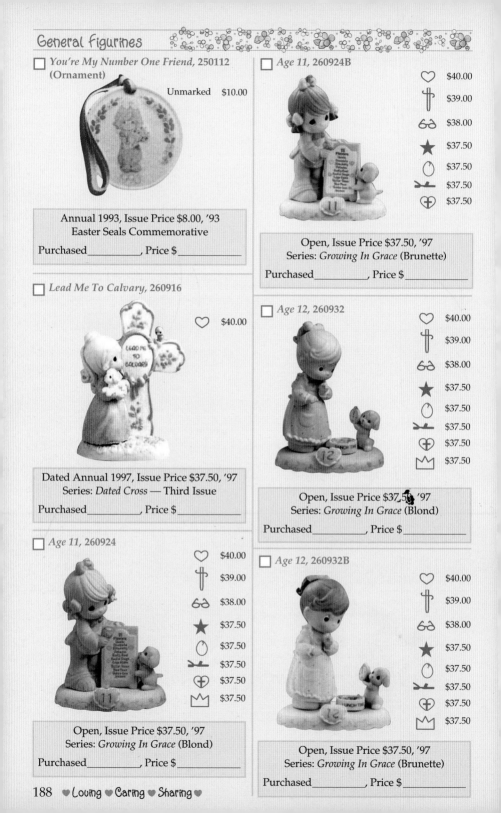

☐ *From The Time I Spotted You I Knew (Know) We'd Be Friends*, 260940

The "Know" error occurred on all Heart Marks and the first production run of the Sword Marks.

♡	$100.00	👓	$20.00
✝	$23.00	★	$20.00
		◯	$20.00

Retired 2000, Issue Price $20.00, '97
Series: *Birthday Collection*

Purchased_____, Price $_____

☐ *You Have Touched So Many Hearts (Brunette)*, 261084B

🜊	$40.00
♛	$40.00

Open, Issue Price $40.00, '02

Purchased_____, Price $_____

☑ *Friends From The Very Beginning*, 261068

Both

♡	$60.00
✝	$55.00
👓	$55.00
★	$55.00
◯	$55.00

Retired 2000, Issue Price $50.00, '97

Purchased **0.00**, Price $_____

☑ *Hogs And Kisses*, 261106

👓	$53.00
★	$50.00
◯	$50.00
✂	$50.00
🜊	$50.00
♛	$50.00

Open, Issue Price $50.00, '99
Series: *Country Lane Collection*

Purchased_____, Price $_____

☐ *You Have Touched So Many Hearts (Blond)*, 261084

♡	$45.00
✝	$43.00
👓	$40.00
★	$40.00
◯	$40.00
✂	$40.00
🜊	$40.00
♛	$40.00

Open, Issue Price $37.50, '97

Purchased_____, Price $_____

Hogs And Kisses, 261106S

Unmarked $125.00

Gift to all attendees of the Fourth Annual Licensee Show and Swap 'N' Sell Weekend at the Chapel on July 31 – August 1, 1998. Special Chapel Understamp.

Limited Ed. 1,500, Gift, '98

Purchased_____, Price $_____

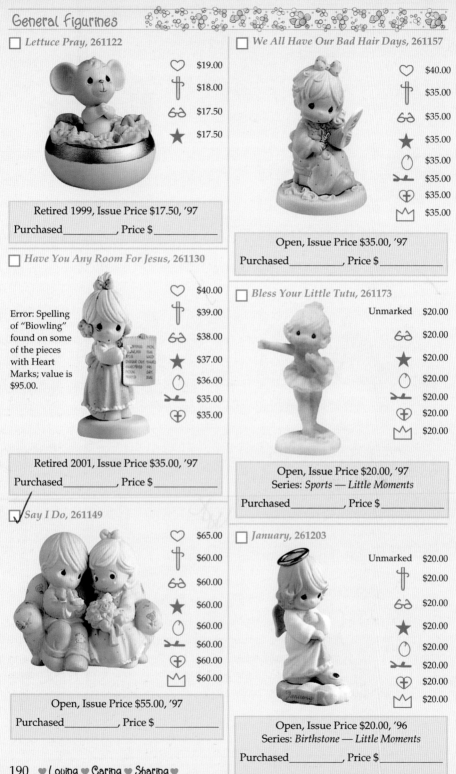

☐ *Lettuce Pray, 261122*

♡	$19.00
✝	$18.00
👓	$17.50
★	$17.50

Retired 1999, Issue Price $17.50, '97

Purchased_____, Price $_____

☐ *Have You Any Room For Jesus, 261130*

Error: Spelling of "Biowling" found on some of the pieces with Heart Marks; value is $95.00.

♡	$40.00
✝	$39.00
👓	$38.00
★	$37.00
◯	$36.00
⤛	$35.00
✚	$35.00

Retired 2001, Issue Price $35.00, '97

Purchased_____, Price $_____

☑ *Say I Do, 261149*

♡	$65.00
✝	$60.00
👓	$60.00
★	$60.00
◯	$60.00
⤛	$60.00
✚	$60.00
♛	$60.00

Open, Issue Price $55.00, '97

Purchased_____, Price $_____

☐ *We All Have Our Bad Hair Days, 261157*

♡	$40.00
✝	$35.00
👓	$35.00
★	$35.00
◯	$35.00
⤛	$35.00
✚	$35.00
♛	$35.00

Open, Issue Price $35.00, '97

Purchased_____, Price $_____

☐ *Bless Your Little Tutu, 261173*

Unmarked	$20.00
👓	$20.00
★	$20.00
◯	$20.00
⤛	$20.00
✚	$20.00
♛	$20.00

Open, Issue Price $20.00, '97
Series: *Sports — Little Moments*

Purchased_____, Price $_____

☐ *January, 261203*

Unmarked	$20.00
✝	$20.00
👓	$20.00
★	$20.00
◯	$20.00
⤛	$20.00
✚	$20.00
♛	$20.00

Open, Issue Price $20.00, '96
Series: *Birthstone — Little Moments*

Purchased_____, Price $_____

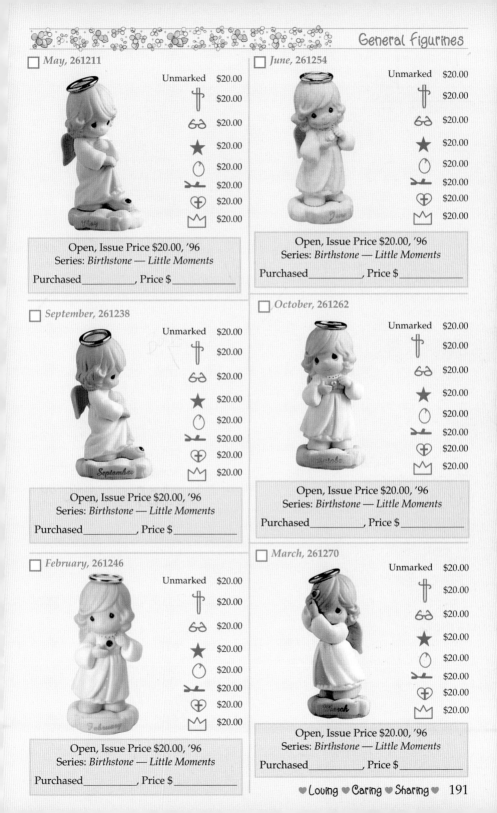

☐ *May*, 261211

Unmarked	$20.00
✝	$20.00
6∂	$20.00
★	$20.00
◯	$20.00
✂	$20.00
⊕	$20.00
♔	$20.00

Open, Issue Price $20.00, '96
Series: *Birthstone — Little Moments*

Purchased_____, Price $_____

☐ *June*, 261254

Unmarked	$20.00
✝	$20.00
6∂	$20.00
★	$20.00
◯	$20.00
✂	$20.00
⊕	$20.00
♔	$20.00

Open, Issue Price $20.00, '96
Series: *Birthstone — Little Moments*

Purchased_____, Price $_____

☐ *September*, 261238

Unmarked	$20.00
✝	$20.00
6∂	$20.00
★	$20.00
◯	$20.00
✂	$20.00
⊕	$20.00
♔	$20.00

Open, Issue Price $20.00, '96
Series: *Birthstone — Little Moments*

Purchased_____, Price $_____

☐ *October*, 261262

Unmarked	$20.00
✝	$20.00
6∂	$20.00
★	$20.00
◯	$20.00
✂	$20.00
⊕	$20.00
♔	$20.00

Open, Issue Price $20.00, '96
Series: *Birthstone — Little Moments*

Purchased_____, Price $_____

☐ *February*, 261246

Unmarked	$20.00
✝	$20.00
6∂	$20.00
★	$20.00
◯	$20.00
✂	$20.00
⊕	$20.00
♔	$20.00

Open, Issue Price $20.00, '96
Series: *Birthstone — Little Moments*

Purchased_____, Price $_____

☐ *March*, 261270

Unmarked	$20.00
✝	$20.00
6∂	$20.00
★	$20.00
◯	$20.00
✂	$20.00
⊕	$20.00
♔	$20.00

Open, Issue Price $20.00, '96
Series: *Birthstone — Little Moments*

Purchased_____, Price $_____

General Figurines

July, 261289

Unmarked	$20.00
✝	$20.00
👓	$20.00
★	$20.00
◯	$20.00
⤙	$20.00
✚	$20.00
♛	$20.00

Open, Issue Price $20.00, '96
Series: *Birthstone — Little Moments*

Purchased_____, Price $_____

August, 261319

Unmarked	$20.00
✝	$20.00
👓	$20.00
★	$20.00
◯	$20.00
⤙	$20.00
✚	$20.00
♛	$20.00

Open, Issue Price $20.00, '96
Series: *Birthstone — Little Moments*

Purchased_____, Price $_____

November, 261297

Unmarked	$20.00
✝	$20.00
👓	$20.00
★	$20.00
◯	$20.00
⤙	$20.00
✚	$20.00
♛	$20.00

Open, Issue Price $20.00, '96
Series: *Birthstone — Little Moments*

Purchased_____, Price $_____

December, 261327

Unmarked	$20.00
✝	$20.00
👓	$20.00
★	$20.00
◯	$20.00
⤙	$20.00
✚	$20.00
♛	$20.00

Open, Issue Price $20.00, '96
Series: *Birthstone — Little Moments*

Purchased_____, Price $_____

April, 261300

Unmarked	$20.00
✝	$20.00
👓	$20.00
★	$20.00
◯	$20.00
⤙	$20.00
✚	$20.00
♛	$20.00

Open, Issue Price $20.00, '96
Series: *Birthstone — Little Moments*

Purchased_____, Price $_____

We're So Hoppy You're Here, 261351

✝	$40.00

Annual 1997, Issue Price $32.50, '97
Spring Celebration Event (April 26, 1997)

Purchased_____, Price $_____

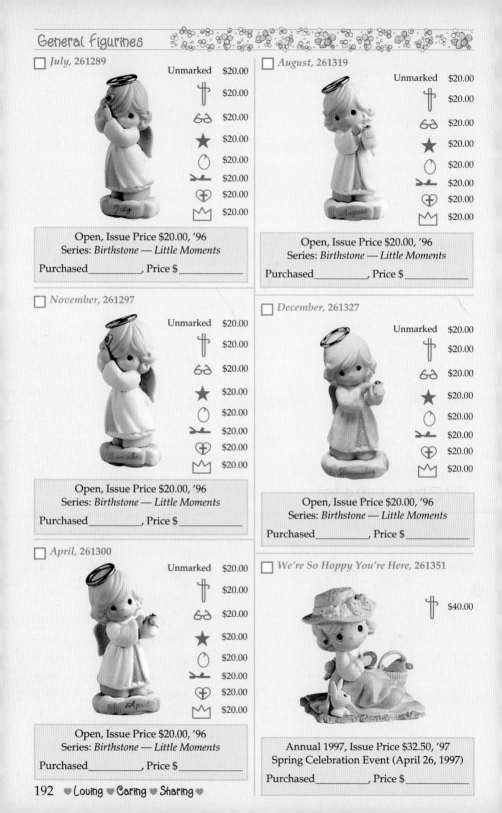

192 ♥ Loving ♥ Caring ♥ Sharing ♥

☐ *Happiness To The Core*, 261378

♡ $39.00

✝ $39.00

Annual 1997, Issue Price $37.50, '97
Catalog Exclusive

Purchased_____, Price $_____

☑ *Blessed Are Thou Amongst Women*, 261556

This piece has been found double marked with both Eyeglasses and Star.

👓 $185.00

✗ ★ $175.00

Annual 1999, Issue Price $175.00, '99
1998 Fall Show Exclusive

Purchased *G-99-00*, Price $ *175.00*

☐ *The Lord Is The Hope Of Our Future*, 261564

♡ $45.00

✝ $43.00

👓 $40.00

★ $40.00

◯ $40.00

✂ $40.00

✛ $40.00

♔ $40.00

Open, Issue Price $40.00, '97

Purchased_____, Price $_____

☐ *The Lord Is The Hope Of Our Future*, 261564B

Comes with a copy of the book "Chicken Soup For The Soul."

◯ $42.00

✂ $42.00

✛ $42.00

♔ $42.00

Open, Issue Price $42.00, '00
Set of 2

Purchased_____, Price $_____

☐ *The Lord Is The Hope Of Our Future*, 261564G

Comes with a copy of the book "Chicken Soup For The Soul."

◯ $42.00

✂ $42.00

✛ $42.00

♔ $42.00

Open, Issue Price $42.00, '00
Set of 2

Purchased_____, Price $_____

☐ *The Lord Is The Hope Of Our Future*, 261564L

◯ $40.00

✂ $40.00

✛ $40.00

♔ $40.00

Open, Issue Price $40.00, '00

Purchased_____, Price $_____

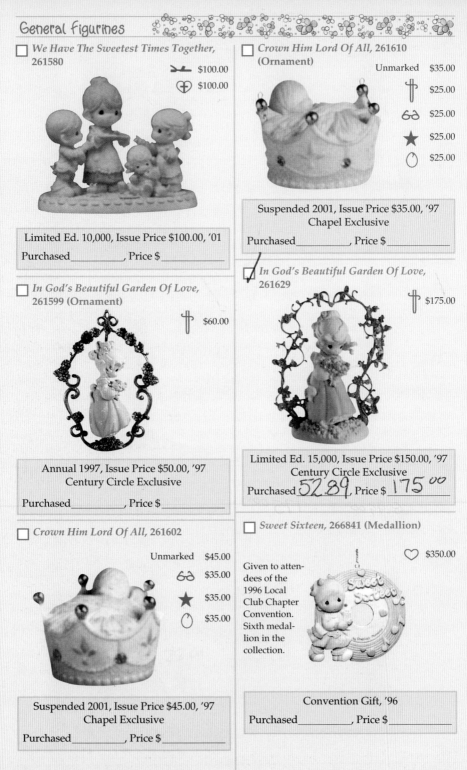

We Have The Sweetest Times Together, 261580

✈ $100.00
✝ $100.00

Limited Ed. 10,000, Issue Price $100.00, '01
Purchased_____, Price $_____

In God's Beautiful Garden Of Love, 261599 (Ornament)

✝ $60.00

Annual 1997, Issue Price $50.00, '97
Century Circle Exclusive
Purchased_____, Price $_____

Crown Him Lord Of All, 261602

Unmarked $45.00
6∂ $35.00
★ $35.00
◯ $35.00

Suspended 2001, Issue Price $45.00, '97
Chapel Exclusive
Purchased_____, Price $_____

Crown Him Lord Of All, 261610 (Ornament)

Unmarked $35.00
✝ $25.00
6∂ $25.00
★ $25.00
◯ $25.00

Suspended 2001, Issue Price $35.00, '97
Chapel Exclusive
Purchased_____, Price $_____

In God's Beautiful Garden Of Love, 261629

✝ $175.00

Limited Ed. 15,000, Issue Price $150.00, '97
Century Circle Exclusive
Purchased 52.89, Price $ 175⁰⁰

Sweet Sixteen, 266841 (Medallion)

♡ $350.00

Given to attendees of the 1996 Local Club Chapter Convention. Sixth medallion in the collection.

Convention Gift, '96
Purchased_____, Price $_____

☐ *A Festival Of Precious Moments*, 270741

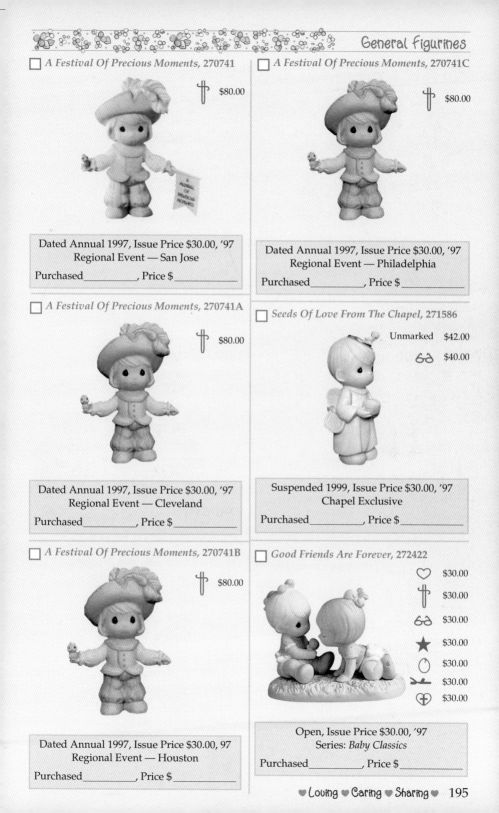

✝ $80.00

Dated Annual 1997, Issue Price $30.00, '97
Regional Event — San Jose

Purchased_____, Price $_____

☐ *A Festival Of Precious Moments*, 270741A

✝ $80.00

Dated Annual 1997, Issue Price $30.00, '97
Regional Event — Cleveland

Purchased_____, Price $_____

☐ *A Festival Of Precious Moments*, 270741B

✝ $80.00

Dated Annual 1997, Issue Price $30.00, 97
Regional Event — Houston

Purchased_____, Price $_____

☐ *A Festival Of Precious Moments*, 270741C

✝ $80.00

Dated Annual 1997, Issue Price $30.00, '97
Regional Event — Philadelphia

Purchased_____, Price $_____

☐ *Seeds Of Love From The Chapel*, 271586

Unmarked $42.00
👓 $40.00

Suspended 1999, Issue Price $30.00, '97
Chapel Exclusive

Purchased_____, Price $_____

☐ *Good Friends Are Forever*, 272422

♡ $30.00
✝ $30.00
👓 $30.00
★ $30.00
○ $30.00
⤚ $30.00
⊕ $30.00

Open, Issue Price $30.00, '97
Series: *Baby Classics*

Purchased_____, Price $_____

♥ Loving ♥ Caring ♥ Sharing ♥ 195

☐ *We Are God's Workmanship*, 272434

♡ $25.00
✝ $25.00
👓 $25.00
★ $25.00
◯ $25.00
⤙ $25.00
✠ $25.00

Open, Issue Price $25.00, '97
Series: *Baby Classics*

Purchased_____, Price $_____

☐ *Make A Joyful Noise*, 272450

♡ $30.00
✝ $30.00
👓 $30.00
★ $30.00
◯ $30.00
⤙ $30.00
✠ $30.00

Open, Issue Price $30.00, '97
Series: *Baby Classics*

Purchased_____, Price $_____

☐ *I Believe In Miracles*, 272469

♡ $28.00
✝ $27.00
👓 $26.00
★ $25.00
◯ $25.00
⤙ $25.00
✠ $25.00

Retired 2002, Issue Price $25.00, '97
Series: *Baby Classics*

Purchased_____, Price $_____

☐ *God Loveth A Cheerful Giver*, 272477

♡ $28.00
✝ $27.00
👓 $26.00

Retired 1998, Issue Price $25.00, '97
Series: *Baby Classics*

Purchased_____, Price $_____

☐ *You Have Touched So Many Hearts*, 272485

♡ $25.00
✝ $25.00
👓 $25.00
★ $25.00
◯ $25.00
⤙ $25.00
✠ $25.00

Open, Issue Price $25.00, '97
Series: *Baby Classics*

Purchased_____ Price $_____

☐ *Love Is Sharing*, 272493

♡ $25.00
✝ $25.00
👓 $25.00
★ $25.00
◯ $25.00
⤙ $25.00
✠ $25.00

Open, Issue Price $25.00, '97
Series: *Baby Classics*

Purchased_____, Price $_____

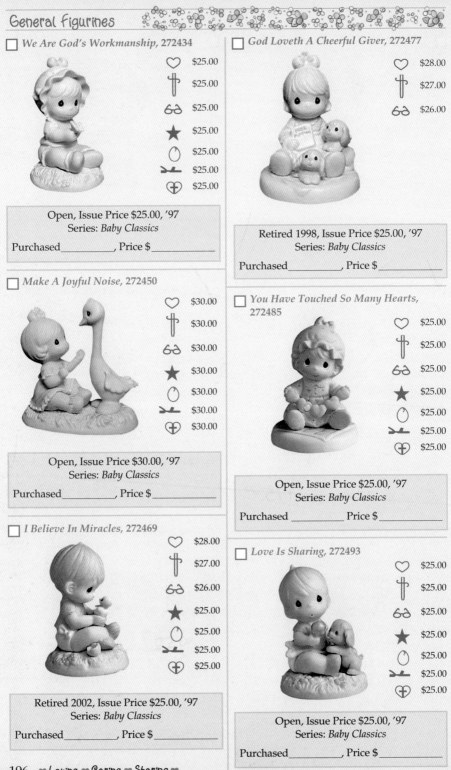

☐ *Love One Another*, 272507

♡ $30.00
✝ $30.00
👓 $30.00
★ $30.00
◯ $30.00
⤳ $30.00
✝ $30.00

Open, Issue Price $30.00, '97
Series: *Baby Classics*

Purchased_____, Price $_____

☐ *Happy Birthday Jesus*, 272523

✝ $35.00
👓 $35.00
★ $35.00
◯ $35.00
⤳ $35.00
✝ $35.00
♕ $35.00

Open, Issue Price $35.00, '97

Purchased_____, Price $_____

☐ *Sharing The Light Of Love*, 272531

✝ $35.00
👓 $35.00
★ $35.00
◯ $35.00
⤳ $35.00
✝ $35.00
♕ $35.00

Open, Issue Price $35.00, '97

Purchased_____, Price $_____

☐ *I Think You're Just Divine*, 272558

✝ $45.00
👓 $43.00
★ $40.00
◯ $40.00
⤳ $40.00

First production pieces have the logo missing from the Understamp. Also known as *Holy Cow*.

Retired 2001, Issue Price $40.00, '97

Purchased_____, Price $_____

☐ *Joy To The World*, 272566 (Ornament)

✝ $25.00
👓 $23.00
★ $20.00

Retired 1999, Issue Price $20.00, '97

Purchased_____, Price $_____

☐ *Palm Trees, Hay Bale And Baby Food*, 272582

✝ $60.00
👓 $60.00
★ $60.00
◯ $60.00
⤳ $60.00
✝ $60.00
♕ $60.00

Open, Issue Price $60.00, '97
Nativity Addition, Set Of 4

Purchased_____, Price $_____

□ *I'm Dreaming Of A White Christmas*, 272590

† $28.00
👓 $27.00
★ $26.00
◯ $25.00
⤚ $25.00
✚ $25.00

Retired 2002, Issue Price $25.00, '97

Purchased_____, Price $_____

□ *You Will Always Be A Winner To Me (Boy)*, 272612

Unmarked $20.00

Open, Issue Price $20.00, '97
Series: *Sports — Little Moments*

Purchased_____, Price $_____

□ *It's Ruff To Always Be Cheery*, 272639

Unmarked $20.00

Open, Issue Price $20.00, '97
Series: *Sports — Little Moments*

Purchased_____, Price $_____

□ *Age 13*, 272647

† $40.00
👓 $40.00
★ $40.00
◯ $40.00
⤚ $40.00
✚ $40.00
♕ $40.00

Open, Issue Price $40.00, '97
Series: *Growing In Grace* (Blond)

Purchased_____, Price $_____

□ *Age 13*, 272647B

† $40.00
👓 $40.00
★ $40.00
◯ $40.00
⤚ $40.00
✚ $40.00
♕ $40.00

Open, Issue Price $40.00, '97
Series: *Growing In Grace* (Brunette)

Purchased_____, Price $_____

□ *Age 14*, 272655

† $35.00
👓 $35.00
★ $35.00
◯ $35.00
⤚ $35.00
✚ $35.00
♕ $35.00

Open, Issue Price $35.00, '97
Series: *Growing In Grace* (Blond)

Purchased_____, Price $_____

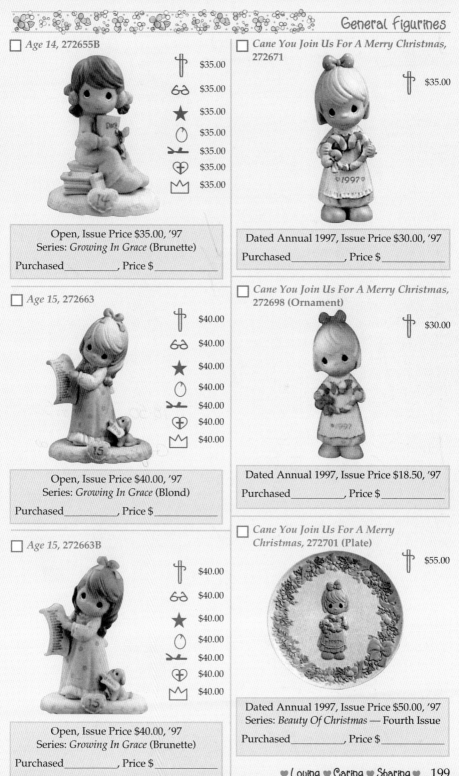

☐ *Age 14*, 272655B

✝ $35.00
👓 $35.00
★ $35.00
◯ $35.00
✂ $35.00
✛ $35.00
♛ $35.00

Open, Issue Price $35.00, '97
Series: *Growing In Grace* (Brunette)

Purchased_____, Price $_____

☐ *Age 15*, 272663

✝ $40.00
👓 $40.00
★ $40.00
◯ $40.00
✂ $40.00
✛ $40.00
♛ $40.00

Open, Issue Price $40.00, '97
Series: *Growing In Grace* (Blond)

Purchased_____, Price $_____

☐ *Age 15*, 272663B

✝ $40.00
👓 $40.00
★ $40.00
◯ $40.00
✂ $40.00
✛ $40.00
♛ $40.00

Open, Issue Price $40.00, '97
Series: *Growing In Grace* (Brunette)

Purchased_____, Price $_____

☐ *Cane You Join Us For A Merry Christmas*,
272671

✝ $35.00

Dated Annual 1997, Issue Price $30.00, '97

Purchased_____, Price $_____

☐ *Cane You Join Us For A Merry Christmas*,
272698 (Ornament)

✝ $30.00

Dated Annual 1997, Issue Price $18.50, '97

Purchased_____, Price $_____

☐ *Cane You Join Us For A Merry
Christmas*, 272701 (Plate)

✝ $55.00

Dated Annual 1997, Issue Price $50.00, '97
Series: *Beauty Of Christmas* — Fourth Issue

Purchased_____, Price $_____

☐ *Cane You Join Us For A Merry Christmas,* 272728 (Ornament)

✝ $35.00

1997

Dated Annual 1997, Issue Price $30.00, '97

Purchased_____, Price $_____

☐ *Slow Down For The Holidays,* 272760 (Ornament)

✝ $25.00

1997

Dated Annual 1997, Issue Price $18.50, '97
Series: *Birthday Collection*

Purchased_____, Price $_____

☐ *Our First Christmas Together,* 272736 (Ornament)

✝ $25.00

1997

Dated Annual 1997, Issue Price $20.00, '97

Purchased_____, Price $_____

☑ *And You Shall See A Star,* 272787

✓ ✝ $35.00

👓 $33.00

★ $32.50

◯ $32.50

✂ $32.50

Follow Me

Retired 2001, Issue Price $32.50, '97
Nativity Addition

Purchased___Gift___, Price $ 35⁰⁰

☐ *Baby's First Christmas (Girl),* 272744 (Ornament)

✝ $22.00

BABY'S FIRST CHRISTMAS 1997

Dated Annual 1997, Issue Price $18.50, '97

Purchased_____, Price $_____

☐ *Schoolhouse,* 272795 (Nightlight)

✝ $90.00

American Flag version. Also came with Canadian flag (same item number).

SCHOOL

Retired 1997, Issue Price $80.00, '97
Series: *Sugar Town*

Purchased_____, Price $_____

☐ *Baby's First Christmas (Boy),* 272752 (Ornament)

✝ $22.00

BABY'S FIRST CHRISTMAS 1997

Dated Annual 1997, Issue Price $18.50, '97

Purchased_____, Price $_____

☑ *Chuck*, 272809

✝ $30.00

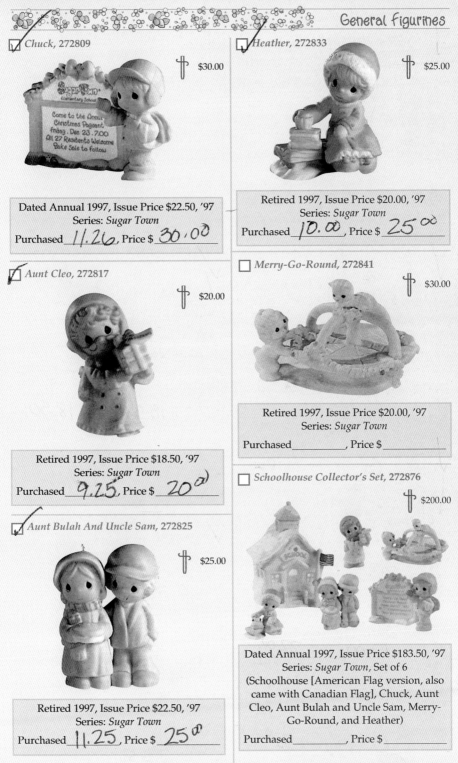

Dated Annual 1997, Issue Price $22.50, '97
Series: *Sugar Town*
Purchased ___11.26___, Price $ ___30.00___

☑ *Heather*, 272833

✝ $25.00

Retired 1997, Issue Price $20.00, '97
Series: *Sugar Town*
Purchased ___10.00___, Price $ ___25 00___

☑ *Aunt Cleo*, 272817

✝ $20.00

Retired 1997, Issue Price $18.50, '97
Series: *Sugar Town*
Purchased ___9.25___, Price $ ___20 00___

☐ *Merry-Go-Round*, 272841

✝ $30.00

Retired 1997, Issue Price $20.00, '97
Series: *Sugar Town*
Purchased _____, Price $ _____

☑ *Aunt Bulah And Uncle Sam*, 272825

✝ $25.00

Retired 1997, Issue Price $22.50, '97
Series: *Sugar Town*
Purchased ___11.25___, Price $ ___25 00___

☐ *Schoolhouse Collector's Set*, 272876

✝ $200.00

Dated Annual 1997, Issue Price $183.50, '97
Series: *Sugar Town*, Set of 6
(Schoolhouse [American Flag version, also
came with Canadian Flag], Chuck, Aunt
Cleo, Aunt Bulah and Uncle Sam, Merry-
Go-Round, and Heather)
Purchased _____, Price $ _____

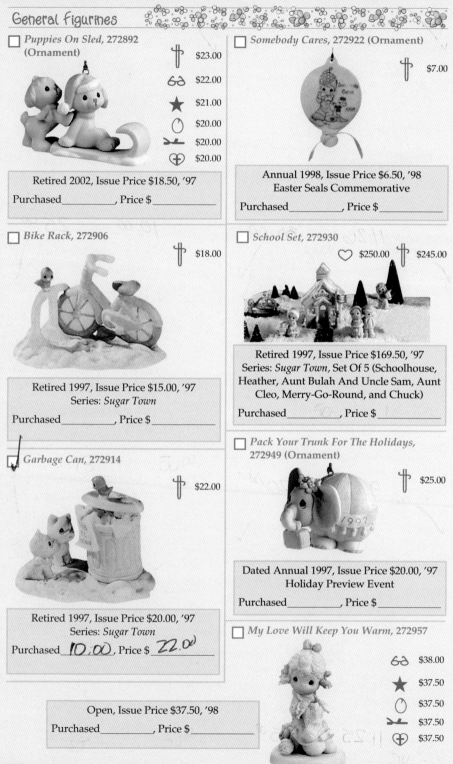

☐ *Puppies On Sled*, 272892 (Ornament)

† $23.00
👓 $22.00
★ $21.00
◯ $20.00
⤙ $20.00
✚ $20.00

Retired 2002, Issue Price $18.50, '97

Purchased_____, Price $_____

☐ *Somebody Cares*, 272922 (Ornament)

† $7.00

Annual 1998, Issue Price $6.50, '98
Easter Seals Commemorative

Purchased_____, Price $_____

☐ *Bike Rack*, 272906

† $18.00

Retired 1997, Issue Price $15.00, '97
Series: *Sugar Town*

Purchased_____, Price $_____

☐ *School Set*, 272930

♡ $250.00   † $245.00

Retired 1997, Issue Price $169.50, '97
Series: *Sugar Town*, Set Of 5 (Schoolhouse,
Heather, Aunt Bulah And Uncle Sam, Aunt
Cleo, Merry-Go-Round, and Chuck)

Purchased_____, Price $_____

☑ *Garbage Can*, 272914

† $22.00

Retired 1997, Issue Price $20.00, '97
Series: *Sugar Town*

Purchased _10.00_, Price $ _22.00_

☐ *Pack Your Trunk For The Holidays*,
272949 (Ornament)

† $25.00

Dated Annual 1997, Issue Price $20.00, '97
Holiday Preview Event

Purchased_____, Price $_____

☐ *My Love Will Keep You Warm*, 272957

👓 $38.00
★ $37.50
◯ $37.50
⤙ $37.50
✚ $37.50

Open, Issue Price $37.50, '98

Purchased_____, Price $_____

☐ *My Love Will Keep You Warm, 272957"S"*

$43.00

The "S" suffix
does not
appear on
the box or
understamp of
the figurine.
Also has no
cat.

Annual 1997, Issue Price $37.50, '97
Catalog Early Release

Purchased_____, Price $_____

☐ *My Love Will Keep You Warm, 272965*
(Ornament)

$25.00

Annual 1997, Issue Price $20.00, '97
Syndicated Catalog Exclusive

Purchased_____, Price $_____

☐ *Love Grows Here, 272981*

$525.00

Limited Ed. 2,000, Issue Price $500.00, '98
Easter Seals Commemorative
Lily Understamp
Individually Numbered

Purchased_____, Price $_____

☐ *Cargo Car, 273007*

$30.00

Dated Annual 1997, Issue Price $27.50, '97
Series: *Sugar Town*

Purchased_____, Price $_____

☐ *Sugar Town Enhancement Set, 273015*

$45.00

Retired 1997, Issue Price $43.50, '97
Series: *Sugar Town*, Set Of 3 (Bike Rack,
Bunnies Caroling, and Garbage Can)

Purchased_____, Price $_____

☐ *Donkey, Camel, And Cow, 279323*

$32.00

$31.00

$30.00

$30.00

$30.00

$30.00

$30.00

Open, Issue Price $30.00, '97
Mini Nativity Addition, Set Of 3

Purchased_____, Price $_____

☐ *Inn*, 283428 (Nightlight)

✝ $100.00
👓 $100.00
★ $100.00
◖ $100.00
✂ $100.00
✛ $100.00
♕ $100.00

Open, Issue Price $100.00, '97
Nativity Addition

Purchased_____, Price $_____

☐ *Nativity Wall*, 283436

✝ $40.00   ★ $40.00
👓 $40.00   ◖ $40.00
✂ $40.00   ✛ $40.00
♕ $40.00

Open, Issue Price $40.00, '97
Mini Nativity Addition

Purchased_____, Price $_____

☐ *For An Angel You're So Down To Earth*,
283444

✝ $18.00   ★ $17.50
👓 $17.50   ◖ $17.50
✂ $17.50   ✛ $17.50
♕ $17.50

Open, Issue Price $17.50, '97
Mini Nativity Addition

Purchased_____, Price $_____

Dated Annual 1998, Issue Price $40.00, '98
Series: *Dated Cross* — Fourth Issue

Purchased_____, Price $_____

☐ *You Will Always Be A Winner To Me
(Girl)*, 283460

Unmarked $20.00

Open, Issue Price $20.00, '97
Series: *Sports — Little Moments*

Purchased_____, Price $_____

☑ *Cats With Kitten*, 291293

✝ $19.00   👓 $18.50
★ $18.50
◖ $18.50
✂ $18.50
✛ $18.50

Open, Issue Price $18.50, '97
Mini Nativity Addition

Purchased 18.50 , Price $ 18.50

☐ *Nativity Well*, 292753

✝ $30.00
👓 $30.00
★ $30.00
◖ $30.00
✂ $30.00

Retired 2001, Issue Price $30.00, '97
Nativity Addition

Purchased_____, Price $_____

☐ *Under His Wings I Am Safely Abiding*,
306835

✝ $40.00
👓 $40.00

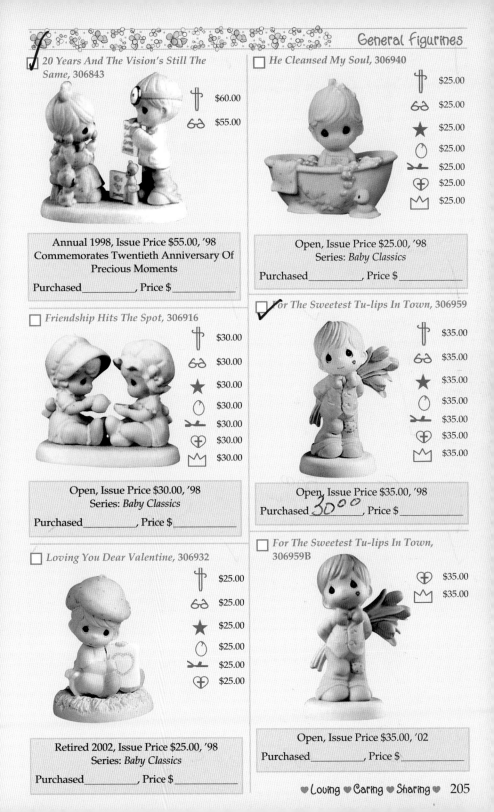

20 Years And The Vision's Still The Same, 306843

✝ $60.00
👓 $55.00

Annual 1998, Issue Price $55.00, '98
Commemorates Twentieth Anniversary Of
Precious Moments

Purchased_____, Price $_____

He Cleansed My Soul, 306940

✝ $25.00
👓 $25.00
★ $25.00
◯ $25.00
✂ $25.00
✚ $25.00
♔ $25.00

Open, Issue Price $25.00, '98
Series: *Baby Classics*

Purchased_____, Price $_____

Friendship Hits The Spot, 306916

✝ $30.00
👓 $30.00
★ $30.00
◯ $30.00
✂ $30.00
✚ $30.00
♔ $30.00

Open, Issue Price $30.00, '98
Series: *Baby Classics*

Purchased_____, Price $_____

For The Sweetest Tu-lips In Town, 306959

✝ $35.00
👓 $35.00
★ $35.00
◯ $35.00
✂ $35.00
✚ $35.00
♔ $35.00

Open, Issue Price $35.00, '98

Purchased _30⁰⁰___, Price $_____

Loving You Dear Valentine, 306932

✝ $25.00
👓 $25.00
★ $25.00
◯ $25.00
✂ $25.00
✚ $25.00

Retired 2002, Issue Price $25.00, '98
Series: *Baby Classics*

Purchased_____, Price $_____

For The Sweetest Tu-lips In Town, 306959B

✚ $35.00
♔ $35.00

Open, Issue Price $35.00, '02

Purchased_____, Price $_____

☐ *You Are Always On My Mind, 306967*

✝	$45.00
👓	$43.00
★	$40.00
○	$40.00
⌇	$40.00

Retired 2000, Issue Price $37.50, '98

Purchased_____, Price $_____

☑ *Missum You, 306991*

✓✝	$50.00
👓	$48.00
★	$45.00
○	$45.00
⌇	$45.00
✛	$45.00

Retired 2000, Issue Price $45.00, '98

Purchased _G_, Price $ 50⁰⁰

☐ *Charity Begins In The Heart, 307009*

✝	$55.00
✓👓	$50.00

Retired 1998, Issue Price $50.00, '98
Series: *Always Victorian* — First Issue

Purchased _G_, Price $ 50ᵈ

☐ *You're Just as Sweet As Pie, 307017*

👓	$48.00
★	$45.00
○	$45.00
⌇	$45.00

Retired 2001, Issue Price $45.00, '98
Series: *Country Lane Collection*

Purchased_____, Price $_____

☑ *Oh Taste And See That The Lord Is Good, 307025*

✓👓	$58.00
★	$55.00
○	$55.00
⌇	$55.00

Retired 2001, Issue Price $55.00, '98
Series: *Country Lane Collection*

Purchased 27.50, Price $ 58.⁰⁰

☑ *Fork Over Those Blessings To Others, 307033*

👓	$50.00
★	$48.00
○	$45.00
⌇	$45.00
✛	$45.00

Open, Issue Price $45.00, '98
Series: *Country Lane Collection*

Purchased 22.50, Price $ 50.⁰⁰

☐ *Nobody Likes To Be Dumped,* 307041

👓 $70.00
⭐ $68.00

Retired 1999, Issue Price $65.00, '98
Series: *Country Lane Collection*
Purchased __65ᵒᵒ__, Price $ __70.00__

☐ *I'll Never Tire Of You,* 307068

👓 $55.00
⭐ $50.00

Retired 1999, Issue Price $50.00, '98
Series: *Country Lane Collection*
Purchased _____, Price $ _____

☑ *Peas Pass The Carrots,* 307076

👓 $38.00
⭐ $35.00
◖ $35.00
✕ $35.00
✛ $35.00

Open, Issue Price $35.00, '98
Series: *Country Lane Collection*
Purchased __17·50__, Price $ __35ᵒᵒ__

☐ *Bringing In The Sheaves,* 307084 (Musical)

✝ $355.00
👓 $225.00
⭐ $200.00

Limited Ed. 12,000, Issue Price $90.00, '98
Series: *Country Lane Collection*
Tune: "Bringing In The Sheaves"
Purchased _____, Price $ _____

☐ *Holiday Wishes, Sweety Pie,* 312444

Unmarked $28.00

Came with
miniature
cinnamon
potpourri pie.

Annual 1997, Issue Price $20.00, '97
Series: *Little Moments,* Set Of 2
Purchased _____, Price $ _____

☐ *You're Just Perfect In My Book,* 320560

Unmarked $25.00

Open, Issue Price $25.00, '98
Series: *Professionals — Little Moments*
Purchased _____, Price $ _____

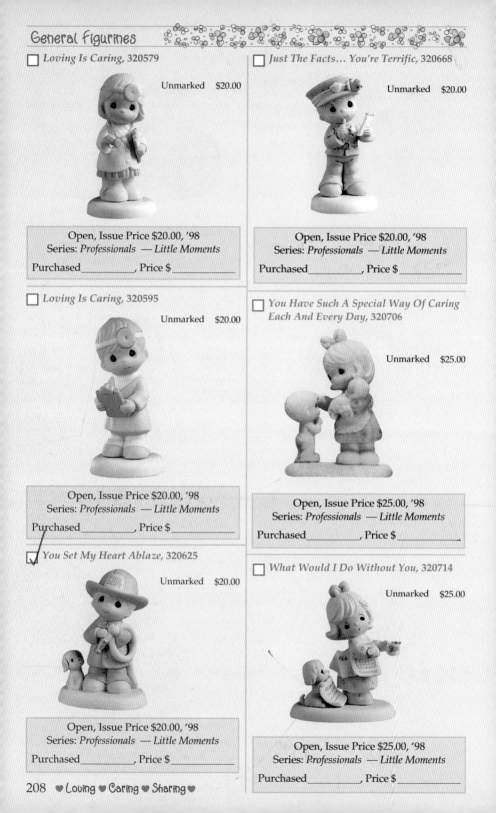

☐ *Loving Is Caring*, 320579

Unmarked $20.00

Open, Issue Price $20.00, '98
Series: *Professionals* — *Little Moments*

Purchased_____, Price $_____

☐ *Just The Facts... You're Terrific*, 320668

Unmarked $20.00

Open, Issue Price $20.00, '98
Series: *Professionals* — *Little Moments*

Purchased_____, Price $_____

☐ *Loving Is Caring*, 320595

Unmarked $20.00

Open, Issue Price $20.00, '98
Series: *Professionals* — *Little Moments*

Purchased_____, Price $_____

☐ *You Have Such A Special Way Of Caring
Each And Every Day*, 320706

Unmarked $25.00

Open, Issue Price $25.00, '98
Series: *Professionals* — *Little Moments*

Purchased_____, Price $_____.

☑ *You Set My Heart Ablaze*, 320625

Unmarked $20.00

Open, Issue Price $20.00, '98
Series: *Professionals* — *Little Moments*

Purchased_____, Price $_____

☐ *What Would I Do Without You*, 320714

Unmarked $25.00

Open, Issue Price $25.00, '98
Series: *Professionals* — *Little Moments*

Purchased_____, Price $_____

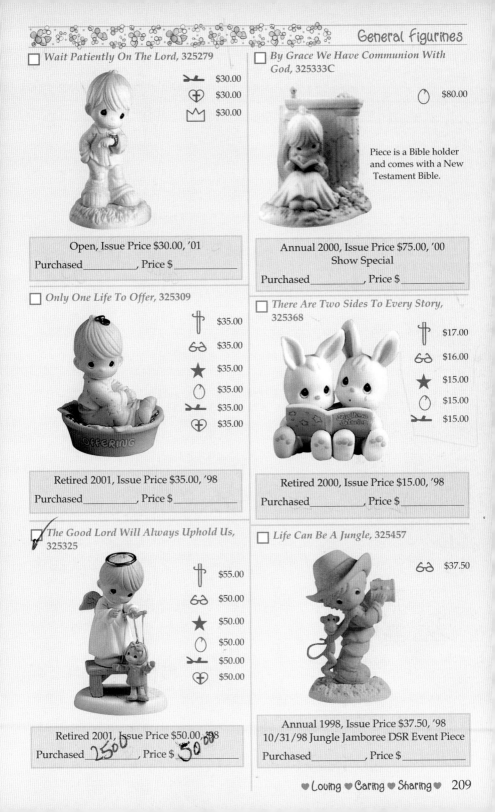

☐ *Wait Patiently On The Lord*, 325279

>— $30.00
✝ $30.00
♔ $30.00

Open, Issue Price $30.00, '01

Purchased_____, Price $_____

☐ *By Grace We Have Communion With God*, 325333C

◯ $80.00

Piece is a Bible holder and comes with a New Testament Bible.

Annual 2000, Issue Price $75.00, '00 Show Special

Purchased_____, Price $_____

☐ *Only One Life To Offer*, 325309

✝ $35.00
👓 $35.00
★ $35.00
◯ $35.00
>— $35.00
✝ $35.00

Retired 2001, Issue Price $35.00, '98

Purchased_____, Price $_____

☐ *There Are Two Sides To Every Story*, 325368

✝ $17.00
👓 $16.00
★ $15.00
◯ $15.00
>— $15.00

Retired 2000, Issue Price $15.00, '98

Purchased_____, Price $_____

☑ *The Good Lord Will Always Uphold Us*, 325325

✝ $55.00
👓 $50.00
★ $50.00
◯ $50.00
>— $50.00
✝ $50.00

Retired 2001, Issue Price $50.00, '98

Purchased _2500_, Price $_50.00_

☐ *Life Can Be A Jungle*, 325457

👓 $37.50

Annual 1998, Issue Price $37.50, '98
10/31/98 Jungle Jamboree DSR Event Piece

Purchased_____, Price $_____

☐ *Mom You Always Make Our House A Home, 325465*

† $45.00

👓 $40.00

Annual 1998, Issue Price $37.50, '98
Catalog Exclusive

Purchased_____, Price $_____

☑ *Mom, You're My Special-Tea, 325473*

✓👓 $25.00

★ $25.00

Early release to retailers attending 1998 Fall Enesco Show. Included a mini *Chicken Soup For The Soul* Book.

Retired 1999, Issue Price $25.00, '99
Mother's Day 1999

Purchased_*12.50*_, Price $_*25.00*_

☐ *Home Is Where The Heart Is, 325481*

† $50.00

👓 $45.00

Annual 1998, Issue Price $37.50, '98
1998 Catalog Exclusive

Purchased_____, Price $_____

☑ *Marvelous Grace, 325503*

✓👓 $55.00

Annual 1998, Issue Price $50.00, '98
Century Circle Exclusive

Purchased_*30.00*_, Price $_*55.00*_

☐ *Our Future Is Looking Much Brighter, 325511*

👓 $450.00

Given to those on the 1998 Precious Moments Cruise.

Dated Annual 1998, Gift, '98
Cruise Piece

Purchased_____, Price $_____

☐ *Well, Blow Me Down It's Yer Birthday, 325538*

† $55.00

👓 $53.00

★ $50.00

◯ $50.00

✂ $50.00

✛ $50.00

Open, Issue Price $50.00, '98

Purchased_____, Price $_____

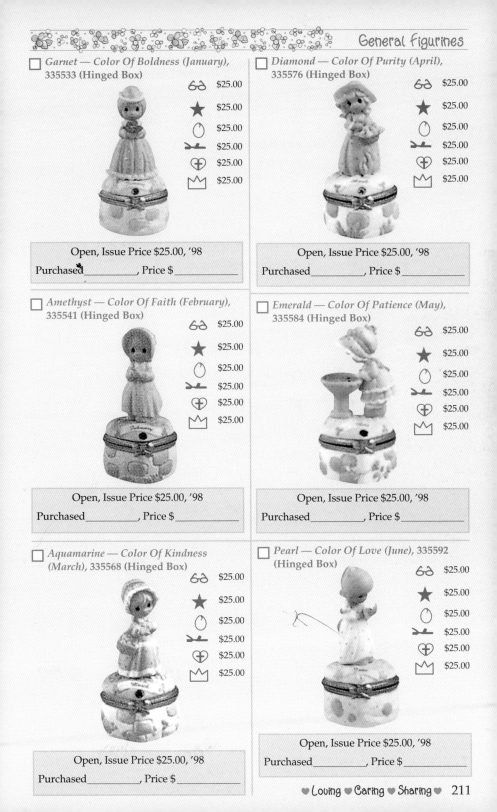

☐ *Garnet — Color Of Boldness (January)*, 335533 (Hinged Box)

👓 $25.00
⭐ $25.00
🥚 $25.00
🎀 $25.00
✝ $25.00
👑 $25.00

Open, Issue Price $25.00, '98
Purchased_____, Price $ _____

☐ *Diamond — Color Of Purity (April)*, 335576 (Hinged Box)

👓 $25.00
⭐ $25.00
🥚 $25.00
🎀 $25.00
✝ $25.00
👑 $25.00

Open, Issue Price $25.00, '98
Purchased_____, Price $ _____

☐ *Amethyst — Color Of Faith (February)*, 335541 (Hinged Box)

👓 $25.00
⭐ $25.00
🥚 $25.00
🎀 $25.00
✝ $25.00
👑 $25.00

Open, Issue Price $25.00, '98
Purchased_____, Price $ _____

☐ *Emerald — Color Of Patience (May)*, 335584 (Hinged Box)

👓 $25.00
⭐ $25.00
🥚 $25.00
🎀 $25.00
✝ $25.00
👑 $25.00

Open, Issue Price $25.00, '98
Purchased_____, Price $ _____

☐ *Aquamarine — Color Of Kindness (March)*, 335568 (Hinged Box)

👓 $25.00
⭐ $25.00
🥚 $25.00
🎀 $25.00
✝ $25.00
👑 $25.00

Open, Issue Price $25.00, '98
Purchased_____, Price $ _____

☐ *Pearl — Color Of Love (June)*, 335592 (Hinged Box)

👓 $25.00
⭐ $25.00
🥚 $25.00
🎀 $25.00
✝ $25.00
👑 $25.00

Open, Issue Price $25.00, '98
Purchased_____, Price $ _____

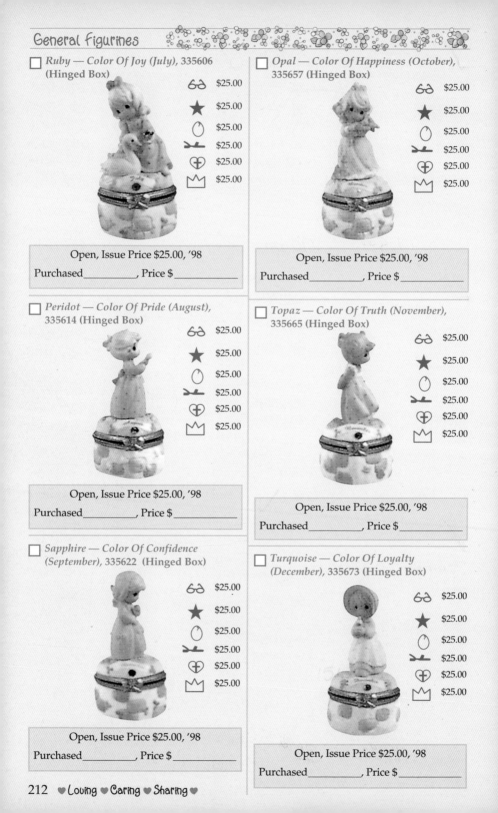

☐ *Ruby — Color Of Joy (July)*, 335606 (Hinged Box)

6ð $25.00
★ $25.00
◯ $25.00
⋊ $25.00
✝ $25.00
♛ $25.00

Open, Issue Price $25.00, '98
Purchased_____, Price $_____

☐ *Opal — Color Of Happiness (October)*, 335657 (Hinged Box)

6ð $25.00
★ $25.00
◯ $25.00
⋊ $25.00
✝ $25.00
♛ $25.00

Open, Issue Price $25.00, '98
Purchased_____, Price $_____

☐ *Peridot — Color Of Pride (August)*, 335614 (Hinged Box)

6ð $25.00
★ $25.00
◯ $25.00
⋊ $25.00
✝ $25.00
♛ $25.00

Open, Issue Price $25.00, '98
Purchased_____, Price $_____

☐ *Topaz — Color Of Truth (November)*, 335665 (Hinged Box)

6ð $25.00
★ $25.00
◯ $25.00
⋊ $25.00
✝ $25.00
♛ $25.00

Open, Issue Price $25.00, '98
Purchased_____, Price $_____

☐ *Sapphire — Color Of Confidence (September)*, 335622 (Hinged Box)

6ð $25.00
★ $25.00
◯ $25.00
⋊ $25.00
✝ $25.00
♛ $25.00

Open, Issue Price $25.00, '98
Purchased_____, Price $_____

☐ *Turquoise — Color Of Loyalty (December)*, 335673 (Hinged Box)

6ð $25.00
★ $25.00
◯ $25.00
⋊ $25.00
✝ $25.00
♛ $25.00

Open, Issue Price $25.00, '98
Purchased_____, Price $_____

☐ *I'm Gonna Let It Shine*, 349852

Unmarked $55.00

Open, Issue Price $50.00, '99
Chapel Exclusive

Purchased_____, Price $_____

☑ *Catch Ya Later*, 358959

$25.00

Open, Issue Price $25.00, '03

Purchased_____, Price $_____

☐ *A Prayer Warrior's Faith Can Move Mountains*, 354406

Unmarked $48.00

Retired 2002, Issue Price $45.00, '98
Chapel Exclusive

Purchased_____, Price $_____

☐ *Thank You For The Time We Share*, 384836

$25.00

Open, Issue Price $22.00, '97
Avon Exclusive

Purchased_____, Price $_____

☐ *A Prayer Warrior's Faith Can Move Mountains*, 354414

Unmarked $260.00

Limited Ed., Issue Price $250.00, '98
Chapel Exclusive, One Year Production

Purchased_____, Price $_____

☐ *Fountain Of Angels*, 384844

Unmarked $45.00

Open, Issue Price $45.00, '98
Chapel Exclusive

Purchased_____, Price $_____

☐ *Many Years Of Blessing You*, 384887

✝ $75.00

👓 $70.00

Sent to 61 retailers from 2/15/98 to 4/1/98. Remainders available to retailers who attended Oct. '98 Enesco Show.

Limited Ed. 1998, Issue Price $60.00, '98 Commemorates Kirlin Hallmark Fiftieth Anniversary

Purchased_____, Price $_____

☐ *Autumn's Praise*, 408751 (Musical)

👑 $225.00

🏺 $225.00

Two Year Collectible, Issue Price $200.00, '90 Series: *The Four Seasons* Tune: "Autumn Leaves"

Purchased _____, Price $_____

☐ *The Voice Of Spring*, 408735 (Musical)

👑 $225.00

🏺 $225.00

Two Year Collectible, Issue Price $200.00, '90 Series: *The Four Seasons*, Tune: "April Love"

Purchased _____, Price $_____

☐ *Winter's Song*, 408778 (Musical)

👑 $225.00

🏺 $225.00

Two Year Collectible, Issue Price $200.00, '90 Series: *The Four Seasons* Tune: "Through The Eyes Of Love"

Purchased_____, Price $_____

☐ *Summer's Joy*, 408743 (Musical)

👑 $225.00

🏺 $225.00

Two Year Collectible, Issue Price $200.00, '90 Series: *The Four Seasons* Tune: "You Are My Sunshine"

Purchased_____, Price $_____

☐ *The Voice Of Spring*, 408786 (Doll)

👑 $175.00

🏺 $175.00

Two Year Collectible, Issue Price $150.00, '90 Series: *The Four Seasons*

Purchased_____, Price $_____

☐ *Summer's Joy*, 408794 (Doll)

♟ $175.00
🍶 $175.00

Two Year Collectible, Issue Price $150.00, '90
Series: *The Four Seasons*

Purchased_____, Price $_____

☐ *May You Have An Old Fashioned Christmas*, 417777 (Musical)

♟ $225.00
🍶 $225.00
🎵 $225.00

Two Year Collectible, Issue Price $200.00, '91
Tune: "Have Yourself A Merry Christmas"

Purchased_____, Price $_____

☐ *Autumn's Praise*, 408808 (Doll)

♟ $175.00
🍶 $175.00

Two Year Collectible, Issue Price $150.00, '90
Series: *The Four Seasons*

Purchased_____, Price $_____

☐ *May You Have An Old Fashioned Christmas*, 417785 (Doll)

♟ $175.00
🍶 $175.00
🎵 $175.00

Two Year Collectible, Issue Price $150.00, '91

Purchased_____, Price $_____

☐ *Winter's Song*, 408816 (Doll)

♟ $175.00
🍶 $175.00

☐ *You Have Touched So Many Hearts*, 422282 (Musical)

♟ $200.00
🍶 $200.00
🎵 $200.00

Two Year Collectible, Issue Price $175.00, '91
Tune: "Everybody Loves Somebody"

Purchased_____, Price $_____

Two Year Collectible, Issue Price $150.00, '90
Series: *The Four Seasons*

Purchased_____, Price $_____

☐ **You Have Touched So Many Hearts,** 422527 (Doll)

✦ $115.00
🔔 $115.00
🎼 $115.00

Two Year Collectible, Issue Price $90.00, '91

Purchased_____, Price $_____

☐ **The Eyes Of The Lord Are Upon You (Boy),** 429570 (Musical)

✦ $75.00
🔔 $73.00
🎼 $70.00
🦋 $68.00
🎺 $65.00

Suspended 1994, Issue Price $65.00, '91
Tune: "Brahms' Lullaby"

Purchased_____, Price $_____

☐ **The Eyes Of The Lord Are Upon You (Girl),** 429589 (Musical)

✦ $75.00
🔔 $73.00
🎼 $70.00
🦋 $68.00
🎺 $65.00

Suspended, 1994, Issue Price $65.00, '91
Tune: "Brahms' Lullaby"

Purchased_____, Price $_____

☐ **20 Years And The Vision's Still The Same,** 451312 (Ornament)

👓 $25.00

Annual 1998, Issue Price $22.50, '98
Commemorates Twentieth Anniversary Of
Precious Moments

Purchased_____, Price $_____

☐ **Feed My Lambs,** 453722

Unmarked $67.50

Open, Issue Price $67.50, '98
Chapel Exclusive
Shepherd Of The Hills Exclusive

Purchased_____, Price $_____

☐ **I'm Sending You A Merry Christmas,** 455601

👓 $33.00

Dated Annual 1998, Issue Price $30.00, '98

Purchased_____, Price $_____

☑ **I'm Sending You A Merry Christmas,** 455628 (Ornament)

?

👓 $18.50

Dated Annual 1998, Issue Price $18.50, '98

Purchased 15.00, Price $ 18.50

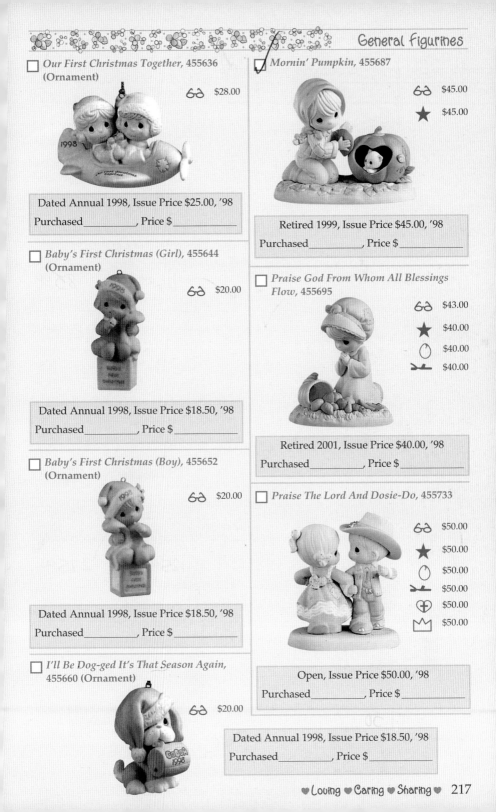

☐ *Our First Christmas Together,* 455636 (Ornament)

👓 $28.00

Dated Annual 1998, Issue Price $25.00, '98
Purchased_____, Price $_____

☐ *Baby's First Christmas (Girl),* 455644 (Ornament)

👓 $20.00

Dated Annual 1998, Issue Price $18.50, '98
Purchased_____, Price $_____

☐ *Baby's First Christmas (Boy),* 455652 (Ornament)

👓 $20.00

Dated Annual 1998, Issue Price $18.50, '98
Purchased_____, Price $_____

☐ *I'll Be Dog-ged It's That Season Again,* 455660 (Ornament)

👓 $20.00

☐ *Mornin' Pumpkin,* 455687

👓 $45.00
★ $45.00

Retired 1999, Issue Price $45.00, '98
Purchased_____, Price $_____

☐ *Praise God From Whom All Blessings Flow,* 455695

👓 $43.00
★ $40.00
◯ $40.00
⤴ $40.00

Retired 2001, Issue Price $40.00, '98
Purchased_____, Price $_____

☐ *Praise The Lord And Dosie-Do,* 455733

👓 $50.00
★ $50.00
◯ $50.00
⤴ $50.00
✛ $50.00
♔ $50.00

Open, Issue Price $50.00, '98
Purchased_____, Price $_____

Dated Annual 1998, Issue Price $18.50, '98
Purchased_____, Price $_____

❤ Loving ❤ Caring ❤ Sharing ❤ 217

☐ Peas On Earth, 455768

👓	$35.00
★	$35.00
◯	$35.00
⊱	$35.00

Retired 2001, Issue Price $32.50, '98

Purchased_____, Price $_____

☐ I'm Just Nutty About The Holidays, 455776 (Ornament)

👓	$19.00
★	$19.00
◯	$18.50
⊱	$18.50
⊕	$18.50

Retired 2002, Issue Price $17.50, '98

Purchased_____, Price $_____

☐ Alaska Once More, How's Yer Christmas? 455784

👓	$38.00
★	$35.00
◯	$35.00
⊱	$35.00
⊕	$35.00
♛	$35.00

Open, Issue Price $35.00, '98

Purchased_____, Price $_____

☑ You Can Always Fudge A Little During The Season, 455792

👓	$38.00
★	$35.00
◯	$35.00
⊱	$35.00
⊕	$35.00
♛	$35.00

Open, Issue Price $35.00, '98

Purchased_____, Price $_____

☐ Things Are Poppin' At Our House This Christmas, 455806

◯	$45.00
⊱	$45.00
⊕	$45.00
♛	$45.00

Open, Issue Price $45.00, '00

Purchased_____, Price $_____

☐ Wishing You A Yummy Christmas, 455814

👓	$35.00
★	$33.00
◯	$30.00
⊱	$30.00

Retired 2002, Issue Price $30.00, '98

Purchased_____, Price $_____

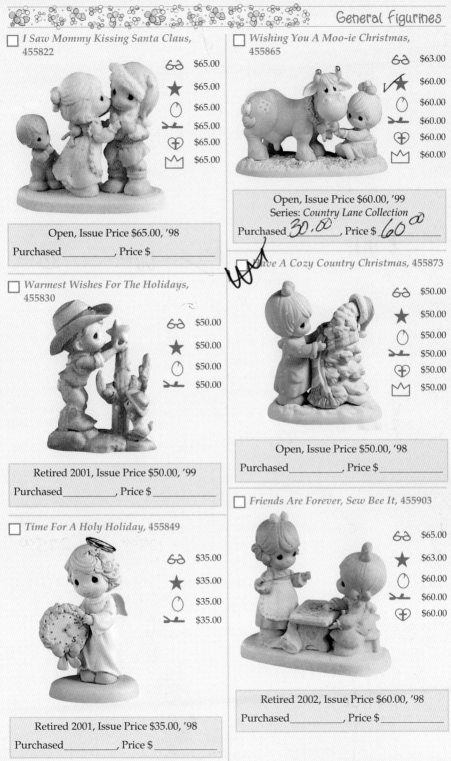

☐ *I Saw Mommy Kissing Santa Claus,* 455822

👓	$65.00
★	$65.00
🥚	$65.00
⌇	$65.00
✝	$65.00
👑	$65.00

Open, Issue Price $65.00, '98

Purchased_____, Price $_____

☐ *Warmest Wishes For The Holidays,* 455830

👓	$50.00
★	$50.00
🥚	$50.00
⌇	$50.00

Retired 2001, Issue Price $50.00, '99

Purchased_____, Price $_____

☐ *Time For A Holy Holiday,* 455849

👓	$35.00
★	$35.00
🥚	$35.00
⌇	$35.00

Retired 2001, Issue Price $35.00, '98

Purchased_____, Price $_____

☐ *Wishing You A Moo-ie Christmas,* 455865

👓	$63.00
✓★	$60.00
🥚	$60.00
⌇	$60.00
✝	$60.00
👑	$60.00

Open, Issue Price $60.00, '99
Series: *Country Lane Collection*
Purchased *30.00*, Price $ *60.00*

☐ *Have A Cozy Country Christmas,* 455873

👓	$50.00
★	$50.00
🥚	$50.00
⌇	$50.00
✝	$50.00
👑	$50.00

Open, Issue Price $50.00, '98

Purchased_____, Price $_____

☐ *Friends Are Forever, Sew Bee It,* 455903

👓	$65.00
★	$63.00
🥚	$60.00
⌇	$60.00
✝	$60.00

Retired 2002, Issue Price $60.00, '98

Purchased_____, Price $_____

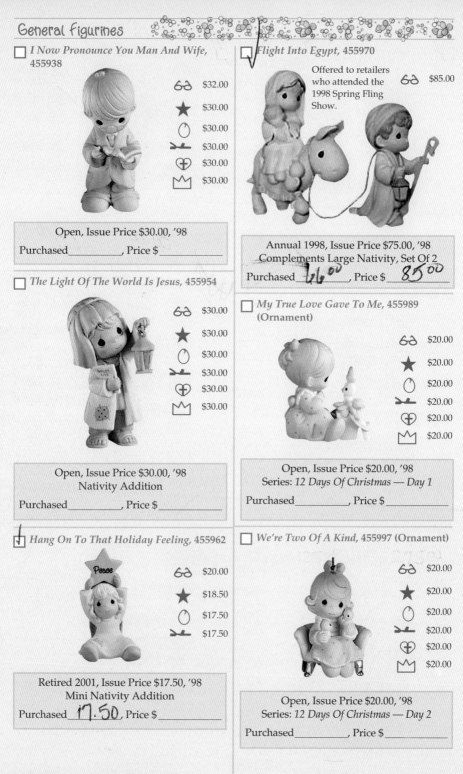

☐ *I Now Pronounce You Man And Wife,* 455938

👓	$32.00
★	$30.00
◯	$30.00
⌇	$30.00
✚	$30.00
♛	$30.00

Open, Issue Price $30.00, '98

Purchased_____, Price $_____

☐ *The Light Of The World Is Jesus,* 455954

👓	$30.00
★	$30.00
◯	$30.00
⌇	$30.00
✚	$30.00
♛	$30.00

Open, Issue Price $30.00, '98
Nativity Addition

Purchased_____, Price $_____

☐ *Hang On To That Holiday Feeling,* 455962

👓	$20.00
★	$18.50
◯	$17.50
⌇	$17.50

Retired 2001, Issue Price $17.50, '98
Mini Nativity Addition

Purchased _17.50_, Price $_____

☐ *Flight Into Egypt,* 455970

Offered to retailers who attended the 1998 Spring Fling Show.

👓 $85.00

Annual 1998, Issue Price $75.00, '98
Complements Large Nativity, Set Of 2

Purchased _66⁰⁰_, Price $ _85⁰⁰_

☐ *My True Love Gave To Me,* 455989
(Ornament)

👓	$20.00
★	$20.00
◯	$20.00
⌇	$20.00
✚	$20.00
♛	$20.00

Open, Issue Price $20.00, '98
Series: *12 Days Of Christmas — Day 1*

Purchased_____, Price $_____

☐ *We're Two Of A Kind,* 455997 (Ornament)

👓	$20.00
★	$20.00
◯	$20.00
⌇	$20.00
✚	$20.00
♛	$20.00

Open, Issue Price $20.00, '98
Series: *12 Days Of Christmas — Day 2*

Purchased_____, Price $_____

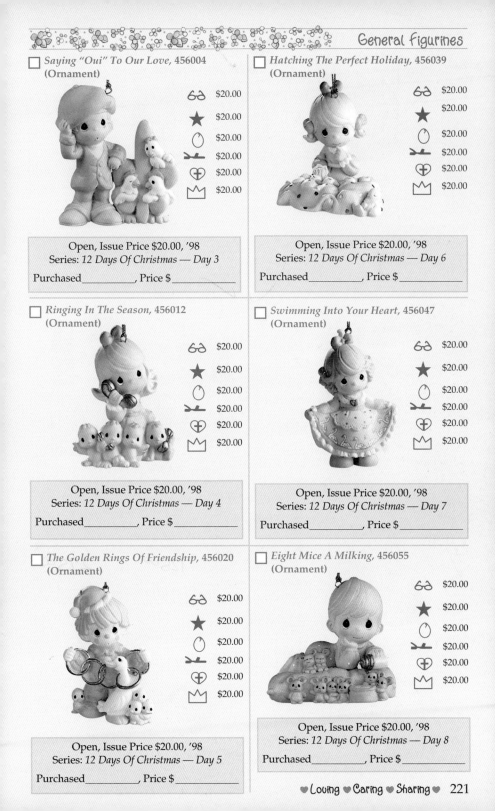

☐ *Saying "Oui" To Our Love*, 456004
(Ornament)

👓 $20.00
⭐ $20.00
🥚 $20.00
✂ $20.00
✝ $20.00
👑 $20.00

Open, Issue Price $20.00, '98
Series: *12 Days Of Christmas — Day 3*

Purchased_____, Price $_____

☐ *Hatching The Perfect Holiday*, 456039
(Ornament)

👓 $20.00
⭐ $20.00
🥚 $20.00
✂ $20.00
✝ $20.00
👑 $20.00

Open, Issue Price $20.00, '98
Series: *12 Days Of Christmas — Day 6*

Purchased_____, Price $_____

☐ *Ringing In The Season*, 456012
(Ornament)

👓 $20.00
⭐ $20.00
🥚 $20.00
✂ $20.00
✝ $20.00
👑 $20.00

Open, Issue Price $20.00, '98
Series: *12 Days Of Christmas — Day 4*

Purchased_____, Price $_____

☐ *Swimming Into Your Heart*, 456047
(Ornament)

👓 $20.00
⭐ $20.00
🥚 $20.00
✂ $20.00
✝ $20.00
👑 $20.00

Open, Issue Price $20.00, '98
Series: *12 Days Of Christmas — Day 7*

Purchased_____, Price $_____

☐ *The Golden Rings Of Friendship*, 456020
(Ornament)

👓 $20.00
⭐ $20.00
🥚 $20.00
✂ $20.00
✝ $20.00
👑 $20.00

Open, Issue Price $20.00, '98
Series: *12 Days Of Christmas — Day 5*

Purchased_____, Price $_____

☐ *Eight Mice A Milking*, 456055
(Ornament)

👓 $20.00
⭐ $20.00
🥚 $20.00
✂ $20.00
✝ $20.00
👑 $20.00

Open, Issue Price $20.00, '98
Series: *12 Days Of Christmas — Day 8*

Purchased_____, Price $_____

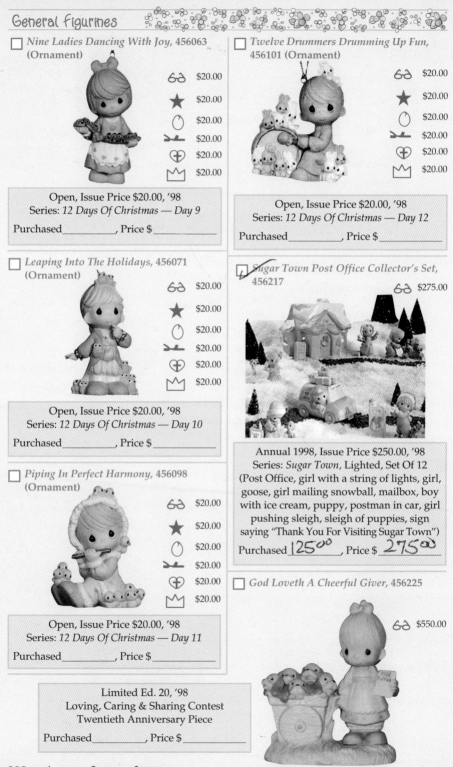

☐ *Nine Ladies Dancing With Joy*, 456063
(Ornament)

👓 $20.00
★ $20.00
◯ $20.00
🥚 $20.00
✚ $20.00
👑 $20.00

Open, Issue Price $20.00, '98
Series: *12 Days Of Christmas — Day 9*

Purchased_____, Price $ _____

☐ *Leaping Into The Holidays*, 456071
(Ornament)

👓 $20.00
★ $20.00
◯ $20.00
🥚 $20.00
✚ $20.00
👑 $20.00

Open, Issue Price $20.00, '98
Series: *12 Days Of Christmas — Day 10*

Purchased_____, Price $ _____

☐ *Piping In Perfect Harmony*, 456098
(Ornament)

👓 $20.00
★ $20.00
◯ $20.00
🥚 $20.00
✚ $20.00
👑 $20.00

Open, Issue Price $20.00, '98
Series: *12 Days Of Christmas — Day 11*

Purchased_____, Price $ _____

Limited Ed. 20, '98
Loving, Caring & Sharing Contest
Twentieth Anniversary Piece

Purchased_____, Price $ _____

☐ *Twelve Drummers Drumming Up Fun*,
456101 (Ornament)

👓 $20.00
★ $20.00
◯ $20.00
🥚 $20.00
✚ $20.00
👑 $20.00

Open, Issue Price $20.00, '98
Series: *12 Days Of Christmas — Day 12*

Purchased_____, Price $ _____

☑ *Sugar Town Post Office Collector's Set*,
456217

👓 $275.00

Annual 1998, Issue Price $250.00, '98
Series: *Sugar Town*, Lighted, Set Of 12
(Post Office, girl with a string of lights, girl,
goose, girl mailing snowball, mailbox, boy
with ice cream, puppy, postman in car, girl
pushing sleigh, sleigh of puppies, sign
saying "Thank You For Visiting Sugar Town")

Purchased 125⁰⁰, Price $ 275⁰⁰

☐ *God Loveth A Cheerful Giver*, 456225

👓 $550.00

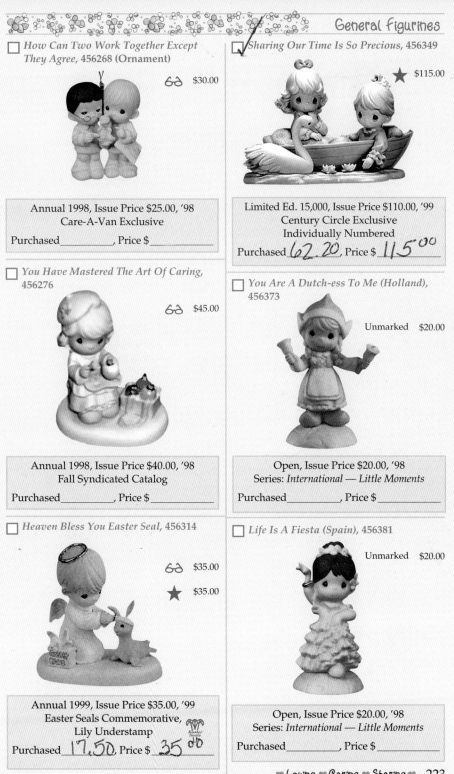

☐ *How Can Two Work Together Except They Agree*, 456268 (Ornament)

6∂ $30.00

Annual 1998, Issue Price $25.00, '98
Care-A-Van Exclusive

Purchased_____, Price $_____

☑ *Sharing Our Time Is So Precious*, 456349

★ $115.00

Limited Ed. 15,000, Issue Price $110.00, '99
Century Circle Exclusive
Individually Numbered

Purchased 62.20, Price $ 115.00

☐ *You Have Mastered The Art Of Caring*, 456276

6∂ $45.00

Annual 1998, Issue Price $40.00, '98
Fall Syndicated Catalog

Purchased_____, Price $_____

☐ *You Are A Dutch-ess To Me (Holland)*, 456373

Unmarked $20.00

Open, Issue Price $20.00, '98
Series: *International — Little Moments*

Purchased_____, Price $_____

☐ *Heaven Bless You Easter Seal*, 456314

6∂ $35.00

★ $35.00

Annual 1999, Issue Price $35.00, '99
Easter Seals Commemorative,
Lily Understamp

Purchased 17.50, Price $ 35.00

☐ *Life Is A Fiesta (Spain)*, 456381

Unmarked $20.00

Open, Issue Price $20.00, '98
Series: *International — Little Moments*

Purchased_____, Price $_____

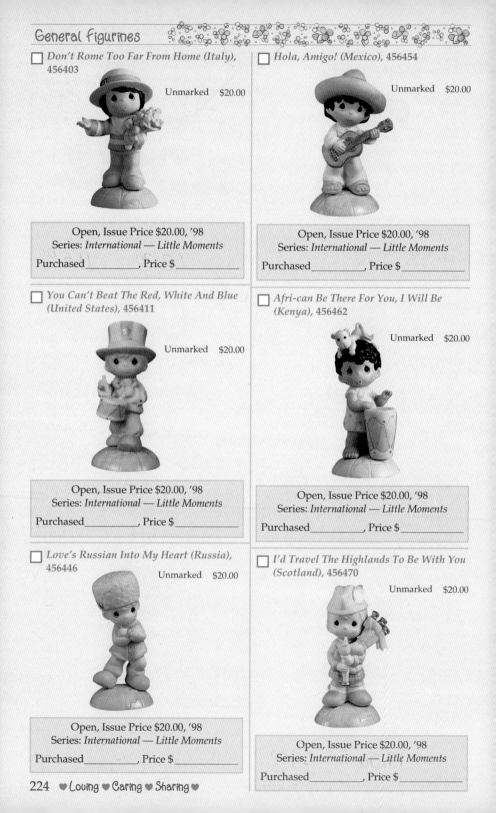

☐ *Don't Rome Too Far From Home (Italy)*, 456403

Unmarked $20.00

Open, Issue Price $20.00, '98
Series: *International — Little Moments*
Purchased_____, Price $_____

☐ *Hola, Amigo! (Mexico)*, 456454

Unmarked $20.00

Open, Issue Price $20.00, '98
Series: *International — Little Moments*
Purchased_____, Price $_____

☐ *You Can't Beat The Red, White And Blue (United States)*, 456411

Unmarked $20.00

Open, Issue Price $20.00, '98
Series: *International — Little Moments*
Purchased_____, Price $_____

☐ *Afri-can Be There For You, I Will Be (Kenya)*, 456462

Unmarked $20.00

Open, Issue Price $20.00, '98
Series: *International — Little Moments*
Purchased_____, Price $_____

☐ *Love's Russian Into My Heart (Russia)*, 456446

Unmarked $20.00

Open, Issue Price $20.00, '98
Series: *International — Little Moments*
Purchased_____, Price $_____

☐ *I'd Travel The Highlands To Be With You (Scotland)*, 456470

Unmarked $20.00

Open, Issue Price $20.00, '98
Series: *International — Little Moments*
Purchased_____, Price $_____

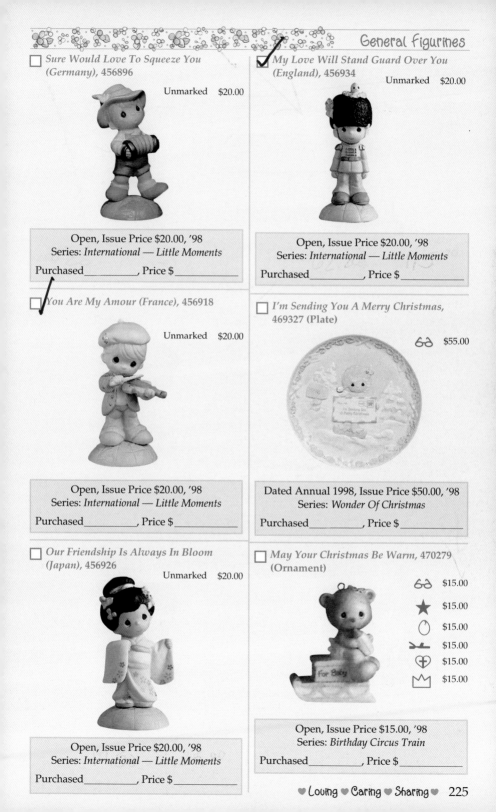

☐ *Sure Would Love To Squeeze You*
(Germany), 456896

Unmarked $20.00

Open, Issue Price $20.00, '98
Series: *International — Little Moments*

Purchased_____, Price $ _____

☑ *My Love Will Stand Guard Over You*
(England), 456934

Unmarked $20.00

Open, Issue Price $20.00, '98
Series: *International — Little Moments*

Purchased_____, Price $ _____

☐ *You Are My Amour (France),* 456918

Unmarked $20.00

Open, Issue Price $20.00, '98
Series: *International — Little Moments*

Purchased_____, Price $ _____

☐ *I'm Sending You A Merry Christmas,*
469327 (Plate)

👓 $55.00

Dated Annual 1998, Issue Price $50.00, '98
Series: *Wonder Of Christmas*

Purchased_____, Price $ _____

☐ *Our Friendship Is Always In Bloom*
(Japan), 456926

Unmarked $20.00

Open, Issue Price $20.00, '98
Series: *International — Little Moments*

Purchased_____, Price $ _____

☐ *May Your Christmas Be Warm,* 470279
(Ornament)

👓 $15.00
★ $15.00
◯ $15.00
⤛ $15.00
✠ $15.00
♕ $15.00

Open, Issue Price $15.00, '98
Series: *Birthday Circus Train*

Purchased_____, Price $ _____

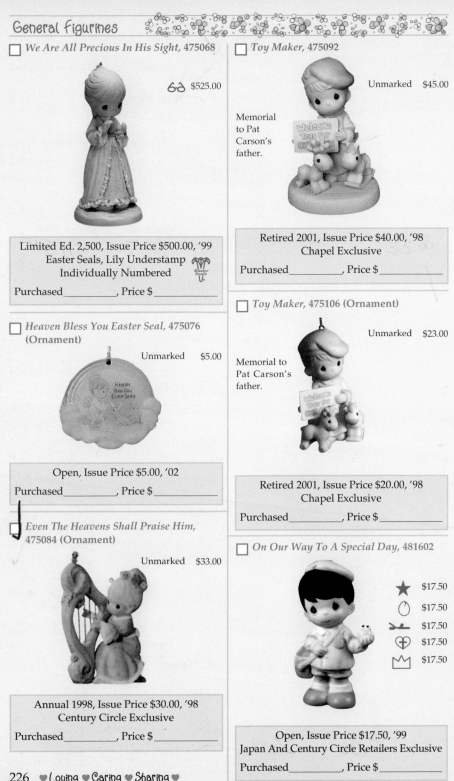

□ *We Are All Precious In His Sight*, 475068

👓 $525.00

Limited Ed. 2,500, Issue Price $500.00, '99
Easter Seals, Lily Understamp
Individually Numbered
Purchased_____, Price $_____

□ *Heaven Bless You Easter Seal*, 475076
(Ornament)

Unmarked $5.00

Open, Issue Price $5.00, '02
Purchased_____, Price $_____

□ *Even The Heavens Shall Praise Him*,
475084 (Ornament)

Unmarked $33.00

Annual 1998, Issue Price $30.00, '98
Century Circle Exclusive
Purchased_____, Price $_____

□ *Toy Maker*, 475092

Unmarked $45.00

Memorial
to Pat
Carson's
father.

Retired 2001, Issue Price $40.00, '98
Chapel Exclusive
Purchased_____, Price $_____

□ *Toy Maker*, 475106 (Ornament)

Unmarked $23.00

Memorial to
Pat Carson's
father.

Retired 2001, Issue Price $20.00, '98
Chapel Exclusive
Purchased_____, Price $_____

□ *On Our Way To A Special Day*, 481602

★ $17.50
◯ $17.50
⤳ $17.50
✝ $17.50
♔ $17.50

Open, Issue Price $17.50, '99
Japan And Century Circle Retailers Exclusive
Purchased_____, Price $_____

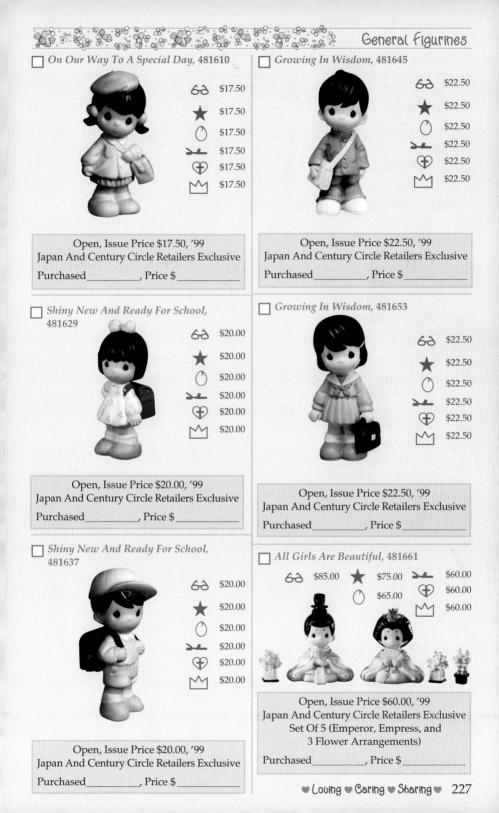

□ *On Our Way To A Special Day*, 481610

👓 $17.50
⭐ $17.50
🥚 $17.50
✂ $17.50
✝ $17.50
👑 $17.50

Open, Issue Price $17.50, '99
Japan And Century Circle Retailers Exclusive
Purchased_____, Price $_____

□ *Shiny New And Ready For School*, 481629

👓 $20.00
⭐ $20.00
🥚 $20.00
✂ $20.00
✝ $20.00
👑 $20.00

Open, Issue Price $20.00, '99
Japan And Century Circle Retailers Exclusive
Purchased_____, Price $_____

□ *Shiny New And Ready For School*, 481637

👓 $20.00
⭐ $20.00
🥚 $20.00
✂ $20.00
✝ $20.00
👑 $20.00

Open, Issue Price $20.00, '99
Japan And Century Circle Retailers Exclusive
Purchased_____, Price $_____

□ *Growing In Wisdom*, 481645

👓 $22.50
⭐ $22.50
🥚 $22.50
✂ $22.50
✝ $22.50
👑 $22.50

Open, Issue Price $22.50, '99
Japan And Century Circle Retailers Exclusive
Purchased_____, Price $_____

□ *Growing In Wisdom*, 481653

👓 $22.50
⭐ $22.50
🥚 $22.50
✂ $22.50
✝ $22.50
👑 $22.50

Open, Issue Price $22.50, '99
Japan And Century Circle Retailers Exclusive
Purchased_____, Price $_____

□ *All Girls Are Beautiful*, 481661

👓 $85.00   ⭐ $75.00   ✂ $60.00
🥚 $65.00   ✝ $60.00
👑 $60.00

Open, Issue Price $60.00, '99
Japan And Century Circle Retailers Exclusive
Set Of 5 (Emperor, Empress, and
3 Flower Arrangements)
Purchased_____, Price $_____

Make Me Strong, 481688

👓 $85.00 ⬭ $65.00 ✝ $60.00

★ $75.00 ✂ $60.00 ♛ $60.00

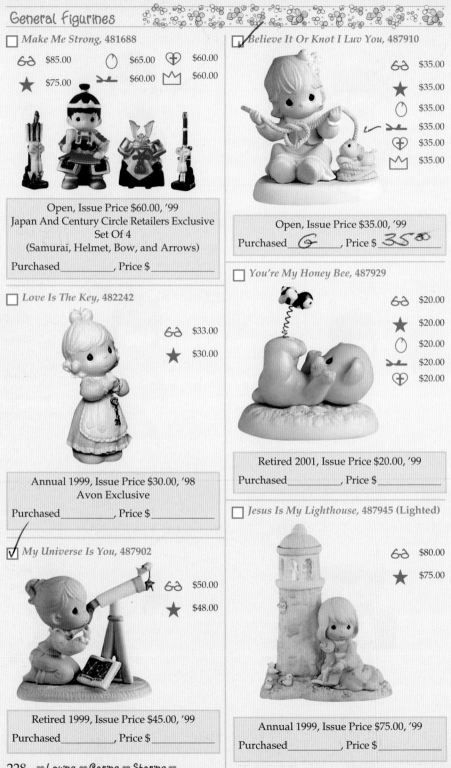

Open, Issue Price $60.00, '99
Japan And Century Circle Retailers Exclusive
Set Of 4
(Samurai, Helmet, Bow, and Arrows)

Purchased_____, Price $_____

Love Is The Key, 482242

👓 $33.00

★ $30.00

Annual 1999, Issue Price $30.00, '98
Avon Exclusive

Purchased_____, Price $_____

☑ My Universe Is You, 487902

👓 $50.00

★ $48.00

Retired 1999, Issue Price $45.00, '99

Purchased_____, Price $_____

Believe It Or Knot I Luv You, 487910

👓 $35.00

★ $35.00

⬭ $35.00

✂ $35.00

✝ $35.00

♛ $35.00

Open, Issue Price $35.00, '99

Purchased___G_____, Price $ 35.⁰⁰

You're My Honey Bee, 487929

👓 $20.00

★ $20.00

⬭ $20.00

✂ $20.00

✝ $20.00

Retired 2001, Issue Price $20.00, '99

Purchased_____, Price $_____

Jesus Is My Lighthouse, 487945 (Lighted)

👓 $80.00

★ $75.00

Annual 1999, Issue Price $75.00, '99

Purchased_____, Price $_____

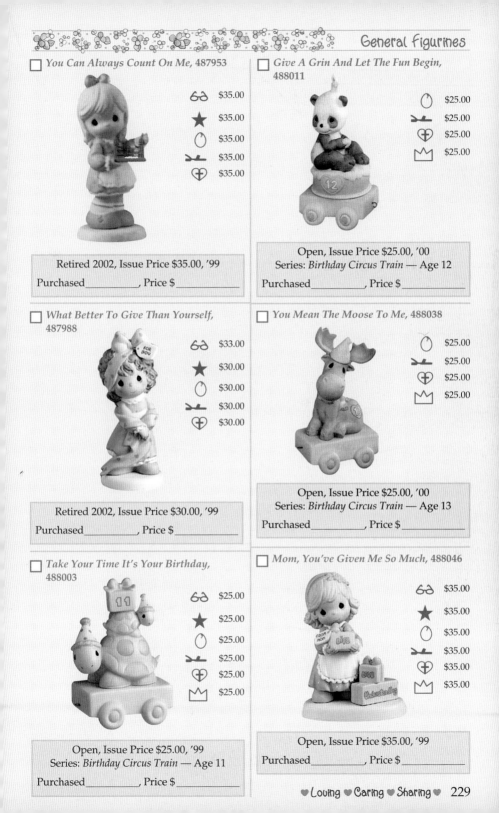

☐ *You Can Always Count On Me, 487953*

👓 $35.00
★ $35.00
🥚 $35.00
⚓ $35.00
✝ $35.00

Retired 2002, Issue Price $35.00, '99

Purchased_____, Price $_____

☐ *What Better To Give Than Yourself, 487988*

👓 $33.00
★ $30.00
🥚 $30.00
⚓ $30.00
✝ $30.00

Retired 2002, Issue Price $30.00, '99

Purchased_____, Price $_____

☐ *Take Your Time It's Your Birthday, 488003*

👓 $25.00
★ $25.00
🥚 $25.00
⚓ $25.00
✝ $25.00
👑 $25.00

Open, Issue Price $25.00, '99
Series: *Birthday Circus Train* — Age 11

Purchased_____, Price $_____

☐ *Give A Grin And Let The Fun Begin, 488011*

🥚 $25.00
⚓ $25.00
✝ $25.00
👑 $25.00

Open, Issue Price $25.00, '00
Series: *Birthday Circus Train* — Age 12

Purchased_____, Price $_____

☐ *You Mean The Moose To Me, 488038*

🥚 $25.00
⚓ $25.00
✝ $25.00
👑 $25.00

Open, Issue Price $25.00, '00
Series: *Birthday Circus Train* — Age 13

Purchased_____, Price $_____

☐ *Mom, You've Given Me So Much, 488046*

👓 $35.00
★ $35.00
🥚 $35.00
⚓ $35.00
✝ $35.00
👑 $35.00

Open, Issue Price $35.00, '99

Purchased_____, Price $_____

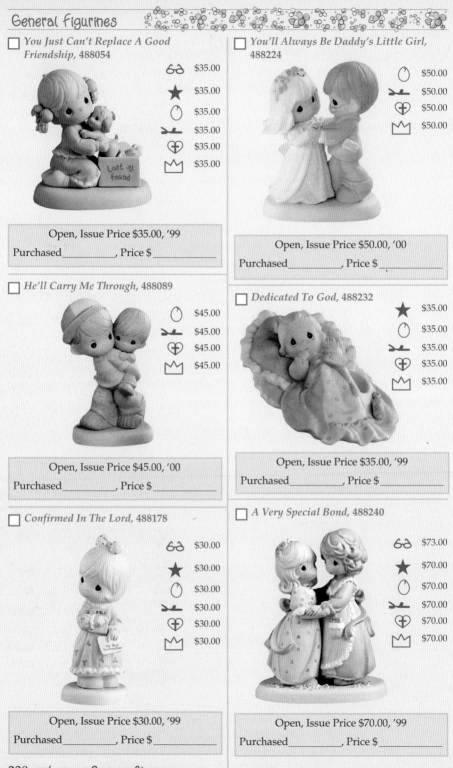

☐ *You Just Can't Replace A Good Friendship, 488054*

👓	$35.00
★	$35.00
◯	$35.00
✂	$35.00
✝	$35.00
👑	$35.00

Open, Issue Price $35.00, '99
Purchased_____, Price $_____

☐ *You'll Always Be Daddy's Little Girl, 488224*

◯	$50.00
✂	$50.00
✝	$50.00
👑	$50.00

Open, Issue Price $50.00, '00
Purchased_____, Price $_____

☐ *He'll Carry Me Through, 488089*

◯	$45.00
✂	$45.00
✝	$45.00
👑	$45.00

Open, Issue Price $45.00, '00
Purchased_____, Price $_____

☐ *Dedicated To God, 488232*

★	$35.00
◯	$35.00
✂	$35.00
✝	$35.00
👑	$35.00

Open, Issue Price $35.00, '99
Purchased_____, Price $_____

☐ *Confirmed In The Lord, 488178*

👓	$30.00
★	$30.00
◯	$30.00
✂	$30.00
✝	$30.00
👑	$30.00

Open, Issue Price $30.00, '99
Purchased_____, Price $_____

☐ *A Very Special Bond, 488240*

👓	$73.00
★	$70.00
◯	$70.00
✂	$70.00
✝	$70.00
👑	$70.00

Open, Issue Price $70.00, '99
Purchased_____, Price $_____

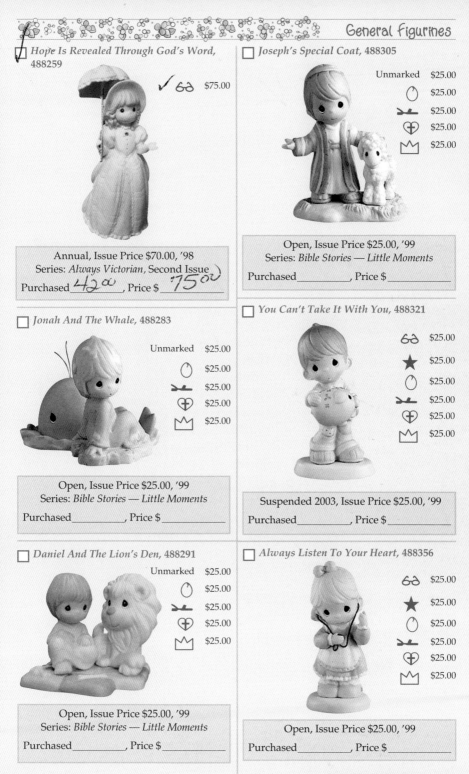

☑ *Hope Is Revealed Through God's Word*, 488259

✓ 👓 $75.00

Annual, Issue Price $70.00, '98
Series: *Always Victorian*, Second Issue
Purchased 42 ∞ , Price $ 75 ∞

☐ *Jonah And The Whale*, 488283

Unmarked		$25.00
🥚		$25.00
✂		$25.00
⊕		$25.00
👑		$25.00

Open, Issue Price $25.00, '99
Series: *Bible Stories — Little Moments*
Purchased_____, Price $ _____

☐ *Daniel And The Lion's Den*, 488291

Unmarked		$25.00
🥚		$25.00
✂		$25.00
⊕		$25.00
👑		$25.00

Open, Issue Price $25.00, '99
Series: *Bible Stories — Little Moments*
Purchased_____, Price $ _____

☐ *Joseph's Special Coat*, 488305

Unmarked		$25.00
🥚		$25.00
✂		$25.00
⊕		$25.00
👑		$25.00

Open, Issue Price $25.00, '99
Series: *Bible Stories — Little Moments*
Purchased_____, Price $ _____

☐ *You Can't Take It With You*, 488321

👓		$25.00
★		$25.00
🥚		$25.00
✂		$25.00
⊕		$25.00
👑		$25.00

Suspended 2003, Issue Price $25.00, '99
Purchased_____, Price $ _____

☐ *Always Listen To Your Heart*, 488356

👓		$25.00
★		$25.00
🥚		$25.00
✂		$25.00
⊕		$25.00
👑		$25.00

Open, Issue Price $25.00, '99
Purchased_____, Price $ _____

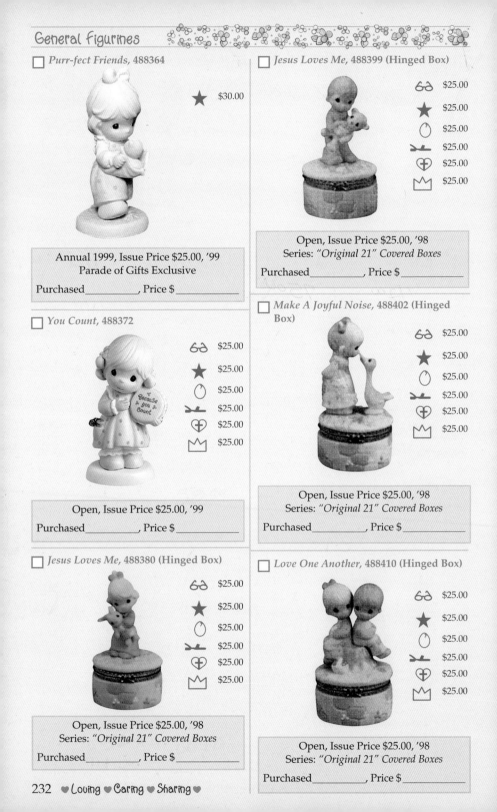

☐ *Purr-fect Friends*, 488364

★ $30.00

Annual 1999, Issue Price $25.00, '99
Parade of Gifts Exclusive

Purchased_____, Price $ _____

☐ *You Count*, 488372

👓 $25.00
★ $25.00
○ $25.00
⤛ $25.00
✝ $25.00
♔ $25.00

Open, Issue Price $25.00, '99

Purchased_____, Price $ _____

☐ *Jesus Loves Me*, 488380 (Hinged Box)

👓 $25.00
★ $25.00
○ $25.00
⤛ $25.00
✝ $25.00
♔ $25.00

Open, Issue Price $25.00, '98
Series: *"Original 21" Covered Boxes*

Purchased_____, Price $ _____

☐ *Jesus Loves Me*, 488399 (Hinged Box)

👓 $25.00
★ $25.00
○ $25.00
⤛ $25.00
✝ $25.00
♔ $25.00

Open, Issue Price $25.00, '98
Series: *"Original 21" Covered Boxes*

Purchased_____, Price $ _____

☐ *Make A Joyful Noise*, 488402 (Hinged Box)

👓 $25.00
★ $25.00
○ $25.00
⤛ $25.00
✝ $25.00
♔ $25.00

Open, Issue Price $25.00, '98
Series: *"Original 21" Covered Boxes*

Purchased_____, Price $ _____

☐ *Love One Another*, 488410 (Hinged Box)

👓 $25.00
★ $25.00
○ $25.00
⤛ $25.00
✝ $25.00
♔ $25.00

Open, Issue Price $25.00, '98
Series: *"Original 21" Covered Boxes*

Purchased_____, Price $ _____

☐ *His Burden Is Light*, 488429 (Hinged Box)

👓	$25.00
★	$25.00
◯	$25.00
⊁	$25.00
⊕	$25.00
♛	$25.00

Open, Issue Price $25.00, '98
Series: *"Original 21" Covered Boxes*

Purchased_____, Price $_____

☐ *Jesus Is The Light*, 488437 (Hinged Box)

👓	$25.00
★	$25.00
◯	$25.00
⊁	$25.00
⊕	$25.00
♛	$25.00

Open, Issue Price $25.00, '98
Series: *"Original 21" Covered Boxes*

Purchased_____, Price $_____

☐ *Give Your Whole Heart*, 490245

★	$33.00
◯	$30.00

Annual 2000, Issue Price $30.00, '00
Easter Seals Commemorative

Purchased_____, Price $_____

☐ *God Knows Our Ups And Downs*, 490318

★	$30.00
◯	$30.00
⊁	$30.00
⊕	$30.00
♛	$30.00

Open, Issue Price $30.00, '99

Purchased_____, Price $_____

☐ *You Oughta Be In Pictures*, 490327

★	$32.50

Annual 1999, Issue Price $32.50, '99
DSR Event Figurine 5/22/99

Purchased_____, Price $_____

☐ *Soap Bubbles, Soap Bubbles, All Is Soap Bubbles*, 490342

Unmarked $20.00

Open, Issue Price $20.00, '99
Series: *Little Moments — Avon Exclusive*

Purchased_____, Price $_____

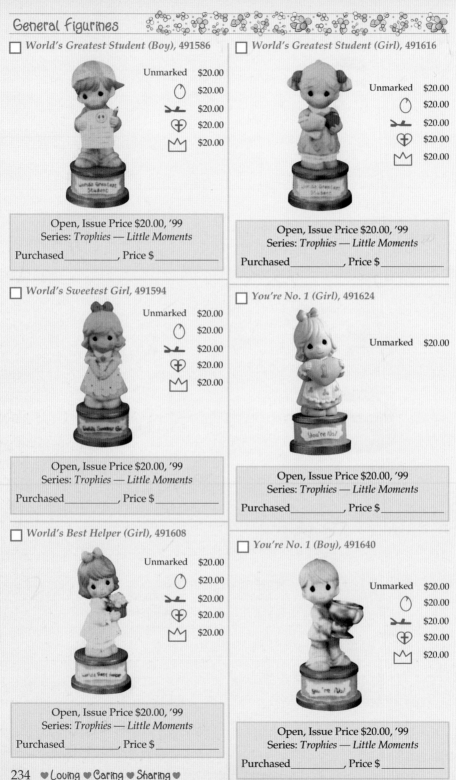

☐ *World's Greatest Student (Boy)*, 491586

Unmarked $20.00
◯ $20.00
✂ $20.00
✝ $20.00
♛ $20.00

Open, Issue Price $20.00, '99
Series: *Trophies — Little Moments*

Purchased_____, Price $_____

☐ *World's Greatest Student (Girl)*, 491616

Unmarked $20.00
◯ $20.00
✂ $20.00
✝ $20.00
♛ $20.00

Open, Issue Price $20.00, '99
Series: *Trophies — Little Moments*

Purchased_____, Price $_____

☐ *World's Sweetest Girl*, 491594

Unmarked $20.00
◯ $20.00
✂ $20.00
✝ $20.00
♛ $20.00

Open, Issue Price $20.00, '99
Series: *Trophies — Little Moments*

Purchased_____, Price $_____

☐ *You're No. 1 (Girl)*, 491624

Unmarked $20.00

Open, Issue Price $20.00, '99
Series: *Trophies — Little Moments*

Purchased_____, Price $_____

☐ *World's Best Helper (Girl)*, 491608

Unmarked $20.00
◯ $20.00
✂ $20.00
✝ $20.00
♛ $20.00

Open, Issue Price $20.00, '99
Series: *Trophies — Little Moments*

Purchased_____, Price $_____

☐ *You're No. 1 (Boy)*, 491640

Unmarked $20.00
◯ $20.00
✂ $20.00
✝ $20.00
♛ $20.00

Open, Issue Price $20.00, '99
Series: *Trophies — Little Moments*

Purchased_____, Price $_____

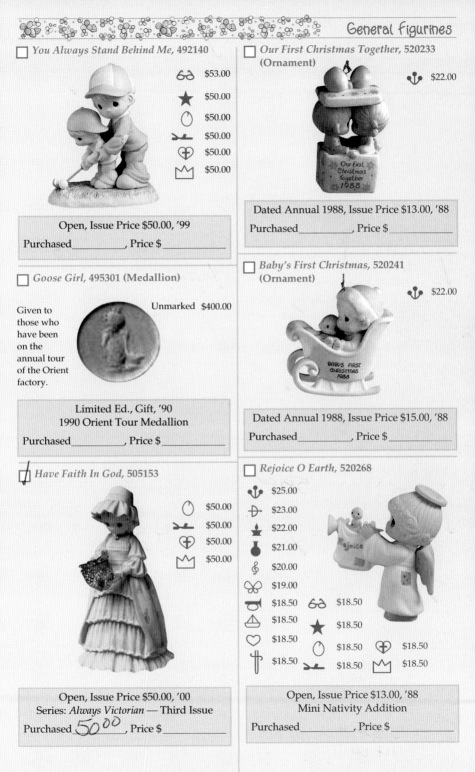

☐ *You Always Stand Behind Me*, **492140**

- 👓 $53.00
- ★ $50.00
- ⬯ $50.00
- ✈ $50.00
- ⊕ $50.00
- ♔ $50.00

Open, Issue Price $50.00, '99
Purchased__________, Price $__________

☐ *Goose Girl*, **495301 (Medallion)**

Given to those who have been on the annual tour of the Orient factory.

Unmarked $400.00

Limited Ed., Gift, '90
1990 Orient Tour Medallion
Purchased__________, Price $__________

☑ *Have Faith In God*, **505153**

- ⬯ $50.00
- ✈ $50.00
- ⊕ $50.00
- ♔ $50.00

Open, Issue Price $50.00, '00
Series: *Always Victorian* — Third Issue
Purchased 50 00, Price $__________

☐ *Our First Christmas Together*, **520233 (Ornament)**

- ⚓ $22.00

Dated Annual 1988, Issue Price $13.00, '88
Purchased__________, Price $__________

☐ *Baby's First Christmas*, **520241 (Ornament)**

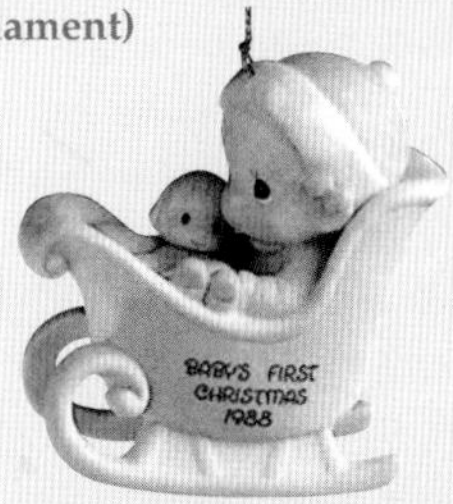

- ⚓ $22.00

Dated Annual 1988, Issue Price $15.00, '88
Purchased__________, Price $__________

☐ *Rejoice O Earth*, **520268**

- ⚓ $25.00
- ➳ $23.00
- 🕯 $22.00
- ⚗ $21.00
- 𝄞 $20.00
- 🦋 $19.00
- 🎺 $18.50
- ⛵ $18.50
- ♡ $18.50
- † $18.50
- 👓 $18.50
- ★ $18.50
- ⬯ $18.50
- ✈ $18.50
- ⊕ $18.50
- ♔ $18.50

Open, Issue Price $13.00, '88
Mini Nativity Addition
Purchased__________, Price $__________

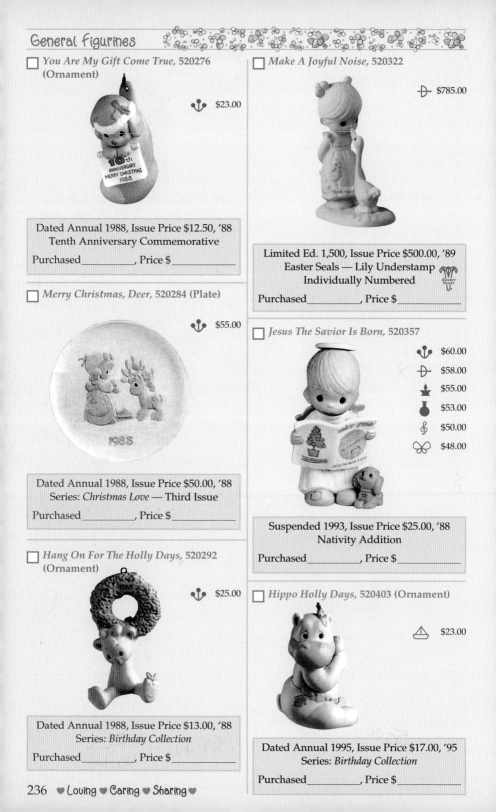

☐ *You Are My Gift Come True*, 520276
(Ornament)

⚓ $23.00

Dated Annual 1988, Issue Price $12.50, '88
Tenth Anniversary Commemorative

Purchased_____, Price $_____

☐ *Merry Christmas, Deer*, 520284 (Plate)

⚓ $55.00

1988

Dated Annual 1988, Issue Price $50.00, '88
Series: *Christmas Love* — Third Issue

Purchased_____, Price $_____

☐ *Hang On For The Holly Days*, 520292
(Ornament)

⚓ $25.00

Dated Annual 1988, Issue Price $13.00, '88
Series: *Birthday Collection*

Purchased_____, Price $_____

☐ *Make A Joyful Noise*, 520322

↦ $785.00

Limited Ed. 1,500, Issue Price $500.00, '89
Easter Seals — Lily Understamp
Individually Numbered

Purchased_____, Price $_____

☐ *Jesus The Savior Is Born*, 520357

⚓ $60.00
↦ $58.00
🕯 $55.00
◖ $53.00
𝄞 $50.00
∞ $48.00

Suspended 1993, Issue Price $25.00, '88
Nativity Addition

Purchased_____, Price $_____

☐ *Hippo Holly Days*, 520403 (Ornament)

△ $23.00

Dated Annual 1995, Issue Price $17.00, '95
Series: *Birthday Collection*

Purchased_____, Price $_____

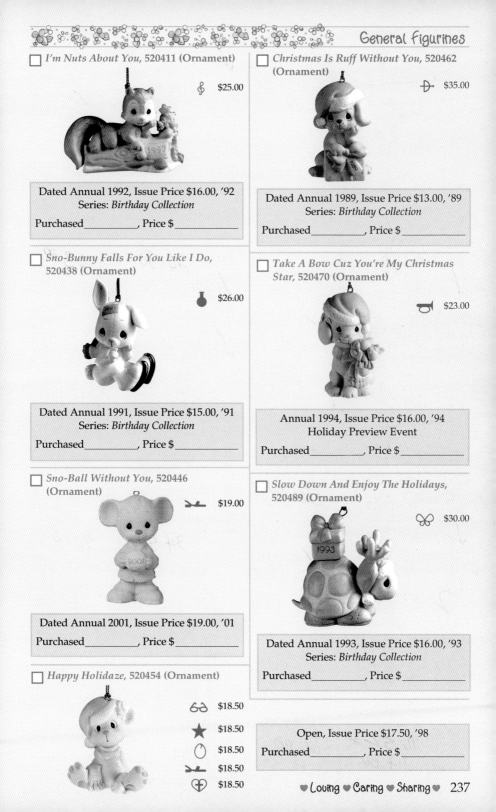

☐ *I'm Nuts About You*, 520411 (Ornament)

🎼 $25.00

Dated Annual 1992, Issue Price $16.00, '92
Series: *Birthday Collection*

Purchased_____, Price $_____

☐ *Sno-Bunny Falls For You Like I Do*, 520438 (Ornament)

🧪 $26.00

Dated Annual 1991, Issue Price $15.00, '91
Series: *Birthday Collection*

Purchased_____, Price $_____

☐ *Sno-Ball Without You*, 520446 (Ornament)

✂ $19.00

Dated Annual 2001, Issue Price $19.00, '01

Purchased_____, Price $_____

☐ *Happy Holidaze*, 520454 (Ornament)

👓 $18.50
★ $18.50
◯ $18.50
✂ $18.50
✝ $18.50

☐ *Christmas Is Ruff Without You*, 520462 (Ornament)

🔪 $35.00

Dated Annual 1989, Issue Price $13.00, '89
Series: *Birthday Collection*

Purchased_____, Price $_____

☐ *Take A Bow Cuz You're My Christmas Star*, 520470 (Ornament)

🎺 $23.00

Annual 1994, Issue Price $16.00, '94
Holiday Preview Event

Purchased_____, Price $_____

☐ *Slow Down And Enjoy The Holidays*, 520489 (Ornament)

🦋 $30.00

Dated Annual 1993, Issue Price $16.00, '93
Series: *Birthday Collection*

Purchased_____, Price $_____

Open, Issue Price $17.50, '98

Purchased_____, Price $_____

☐ *Wishing You A Purr-fect Holiday*, 520497 (Ornament)

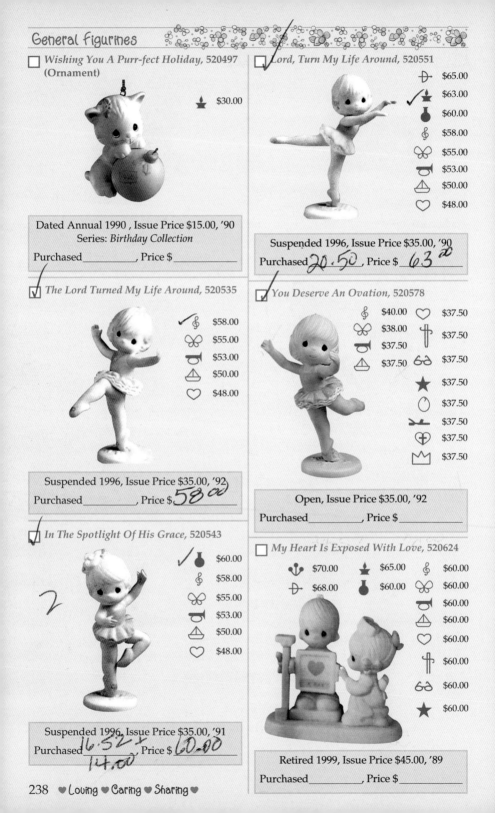

✦ $30.00

Dated Annual 1990 , Issue Price $15.00, '90
Series: *Birthday Collection*

Purchased _____ , Price $ _____

☑ *The Lord Turned My Life Around*, 520535

✓ 𝄞	$58.00
✽	$55.00
◁⊐	$53.00
△	$50.00
♡	$48.00

Suspended 1996, Issue Price $35.00, '92

Purchased _____ , Price $ *58 00*

☑ *In The Spotlight Of His Grace*, 520543

2

✓ ⚗	$60.00
𝄞	$58.00
✽	$55.00
◁⊐	$53.00
△	$50.00
♡	$48.00

Suspended 1996, Issue Price $35.00, '91

Purchased *16:52 ✗* Price $ *60.00*
14.00

✓ ☐ *Lord, Turn My Life Around*, 520551

⊅	$65.00
✓ ⚘	$63.00
●	$60.00
𝄞	$58.00
✽	$55.00
◁⊐	$53.00
△	$50.00
♡	$48.00

Suspended 1996, Issue Price $35.00, '90

Purchased *20.50* , Price $ *63 00*

☑ *You Deserve An Ovation*, 520578

𝄞	$40.00	♡	$37.50
✽	$38.00	✝	$37.50
◁⊐	$37.50		
△	$37.50	6∂	$37.50
★			$37.50
○			$37.50
⊱			$37.50
✝			$37.50
♔			$37.50

Open, Issue Price $35.00, '92

Purchased _____ , Price $ _____

☐ *My Heart Is Exposed With Love*, 520624

⚓	$70.00	✦	$65.00	𝄞	$60.00
⊅	$68.00	●	$60.00	✽	$60.00
				◁⊐	$60.00
				△	$60.00
				♡	$60.00
				✝	$60.00
				6∂	$60.00
				★	$60.00

Retired 1999, Issue Price $45.00, '89

Purchased _____ , Price $ _____

A Friend Is Someone Who Cares, 520632

✗ ⚓	$95.00
⌿	$90.00
☀	$87.00
⬤	$85.00
♪	$80.00
✿	$77.00
◁	$75.00
△	$73.00

Retired 1995, Issue Price $30.00, '89

Purchased _28 00_, Price $ _95 00_

I'm So Glad You Fluttered Into My Life, 520640

⚓	$295.00
⌿	$235.00
☀	$225.00
⬤	$215.00

Retired 1991, Issue Price $40.00, '89

Purchased_____, Price $_____

Wishing You A Happy Bear Hug, 520659

◁	$35.00
△	$33.00
♡	$30.00

Suspended 1996, Issue Price $27.50, '95
Series: *Birthday Collection*

Purchased_____, Price $_____

Egg-specially For You, 520667

⚓	$65.00	♪	$55.00
⌿	$63.00	✿	$53.00
☀	$60.00	◁	$50.00
⬤	$58.00	△	$50.00
		♡	$50.00
		✝	$50.00
		👓	$50.00
		★	$50.00

Retired 1999, Issue Price $45.00, '89

Purchased_____, Price $_____

Your Love Is So Uplifting, 520675

⚓	$90.00	⬤	$80.00
⌿	$85.00	♪	$78.00
☀	$83.00	✿	$75.00
		◁	$75.00
		△	$75.00
		♡	$75.00
		✝	$75.00
		👓	$75.00

Retired 1998, Issue Price $60.00, '89

Purchased_____, Price $_____

Sending You Showers Of Blessings, 520683

⚓	$85.00
⌿	$80.00
☀	$78.00
⬤	$75.00
♪	$73.00

Retired 1992, Issue Price $32.50, '89

Purchased_____, Price $_____

☐ *Lord, Keep My Life In Balance*, 520691 (Musical)

🕯 $85.00
🎵 $80.00
🦋 $78.00

Suspended 1993, Issue Price $60.00, '91
Tune: "Music Box Dancer"

Purchased_____, Price $_____

☐ *Baby's First Pet*, 520705

⚓ $85.00
🕊 $80.00
🕯 $78.00
🫙 $75.00
🎵 $73.00
🦋 $70.00
🎺 $68.00

Suspended 1994, Issue Price $45.00, '89
Series: *Baby's First* — Fifth Issue

Purchased_____, Price $_____

☐ *Just A Line To Wish You A Happy Day*, 520721

⚓ $93.00   🕯 $88.00
🕊 $90.00   🫙 $85.00
🎵 $83.00
🦋 $80.00
🎺 $75.00
🔺 $75.00
♡ $75.00

Suspended 1996, Issue Price $65.00, '89

Purchased_____, Price $_____

☐ *Friendship Hits The Spot*, 520748

⚓ $78.00   🕯 $70.00   🦋 $70.00
🕊 $75.00   🫙 $70.00   🎺 $70.00
　　　　 🎵 $70.00   🛥 $70.00
　　　　 　　　　 ♡ $70.00
　　　　 　　　　 ✝ $70.00
　　　　 　　　　 👓 $70.00
　　　　 　　　　 ★ $70.00
　　　　 　　　　 🥚 $70.00

Errors: Misspelled "Friendship" on boxes and figurines in Trumpet and Ship marks. Several have been found with tables missing.

Retired 2000, Issue Price $55.00, '89

Purchased_____, Price $_____

☐ *Jesus Is The Only Way*, 520756

X ⚓ $70.00
🕊 $68.00
🕯 $65.00
🫙 $63.00
🎵 $60.00
🦋 $58.00

Suspended 1993, Issue Price $40.00, '89
Purchased 34.57, Price $ 20 00

☐ *Puppy Love*, 520764

⚓ $25.00   🦋 $17.50
🕊 $20.00   🎺 $17.50
🕯 $19.00   🔺 $17.50
🫙 $18.50   ♡ $17.50
🎵 $18.00   ✝ $17.50
　　　　 👓 $17.50
　　　　 ★ $17.50

Retired 2/14/99, Issue Price $12.50, '89
Purchased_____, Price $_____

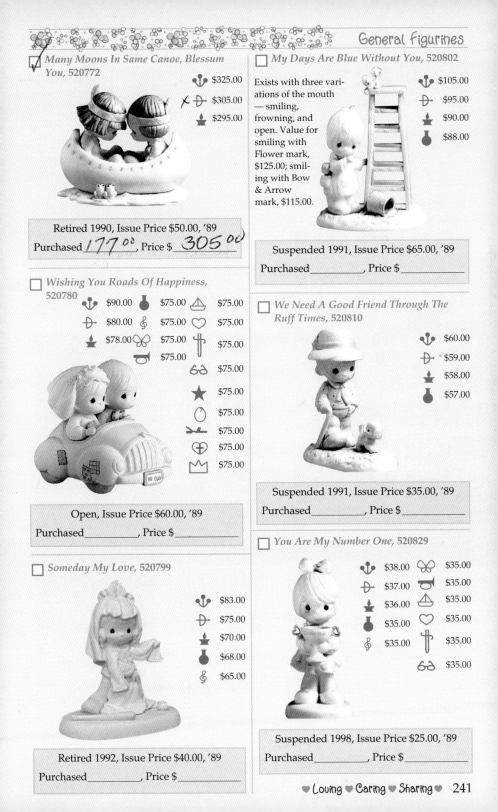

☑ *Many Moons In Same Canoe, Blessum You*, 520772

⚓ $325.00
✗ ⅁ $305.00
⚒ $295.00

Retired 1990, Issue Price $50.00, '89
Purchased *177⁰⁰*, Price $ *305⁰⁰*

☐ *Wishing You Roads Of Happiness*, 520780

⚓ $90.00   ⚒ $75.00   ⛵ $75.00
⅁ $80.00   ♪ $75.00   ♡ $75.00
⚒ $78.00   ⋈ $75.00   ✝ $75.00
📯 $75.00
          👓 $75.00
          ★ $75.00
          ◯ $75.00
          ⋊ $75.00
          ⊕ $75.00
          ♛ $75.00

Open, Issue Price $60.00, '89
Purchased_____, Price $_____

☐ *Someday My Love*, 520799

⚓ $83.00
⅁ $75.00
⚒ $70.00
♀ $68.00
♪ $65.00

Retired 1992, Issue Price $40.00, '89
Purchased_____, Price $_____

☐ *My Days Are Blue Without You*, 520802

Exists with three variations of the mouth — smiling, frowning, and open. Value for smiling with Flower mark, $125.00; smiling with Bow & Arrow mark, $115.00.

⚓ $105.00
⅁ $95.00
⚒ $90.00
♀ $88.00

Suspended 1991, Issue Price $65.00, '89
Purchased_____, Price $_____

☐ *We Need A Good Friend Through The Ruff Times*, 520810

⚓ $60.00
⅁ $59.00
⚒ $58.00
♀ $57.00

Suspended 1991, Issue Price $35.00, '89
Purchased_____, Price $_____

☐ *You Are My Number One*, 520829

⚓ $38.00   ⋈ $35.00
⅁ $37.00   📯 $35.00
⚒ $36.00   △ $35.00
♀ $35.00   ♡ $35.00
♪ $35.00   ✝ $35.00
          👓 $35.00

Suspended 1998, Issue Price $25.00, '89
Purchased_____, Price $_____

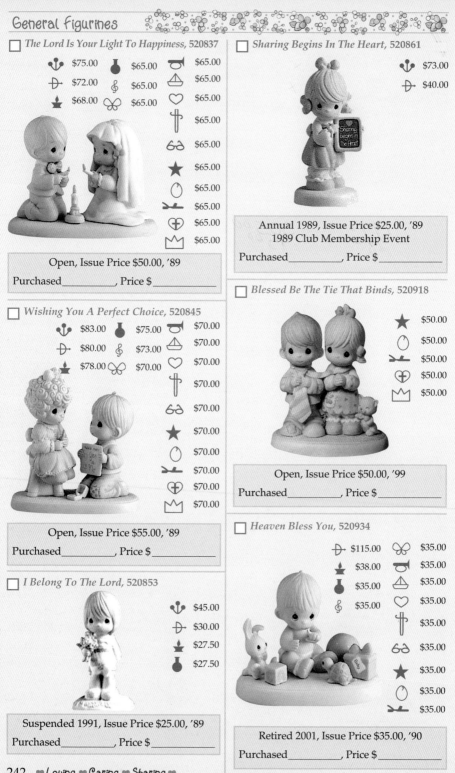

☐ *The Lord Is Your Light To Happiness*, 520837

⚓	$75.00	🏺	$65.00	🎺	$65.00	
⌐	$72.00	𝄞	$65.00	⛵	$65.00	
🕯	$68.00	🦋	$65.00	♡	$65.00	
				✝	$65.00	
				👓	$65.00	
				★	$65.00	
				◯	$65.00	
				⊱	$65.00	
				✛	$65.00	
				♕	$65.00	

Open, Issue Price $50.00, '89

Purchased_____, Price $_____

☐ *Wishing You A Perfect Choice*, 520845

⚓	$83.00	🏺	$75.00	🎺	$70.00	
⌐	$80.00	𝄞	$73.00	⛵	$70.00	
🕯	$78.00	🦋	$70.00	♡	$70.00	
				✝	$70.00	
				👓	$70.00	
				★	$70.00	
				◯	$70.00	
				⊱	$70.00	
				✛	$70.00	
				♕	$70.00	

Open, Issue Price $55.00, '89

Purchased_____, Price $_____

☐ *I Belong To The Lord*, 520853

⚓	$45.00
⌐	$30.00
🕯	$27.50
🏺	$27.50

Suspended 1991, Issue Price $25.00, '89

Purchased_____, Price $_____

☐ *Sharing Begins In The Heart*, 520861

⚓	$73.00
⌐	$40.00

Annual 1989, Issue Price $25.00, '89
1989 Club Membership Event

Purchased_____, Price $_____

☐ *Blessed Be The Tie That Binds*, 520918

★	$50.00
◯	$50.00
⊱	$50.00
✛	$50.00
♕	$50.00

Open, Issue Price $50.00, '99

Purchased_____, Price $_____

☐ *Heaven Bless You*, 520934

⌐	$115.00	🦋	$35.00
🕯	$38.00	🎺	$35.00
🏺	$35.00	⛵	$35.00
𝄞	$35.00	♡	$35.00
		✝	$35.00
		👓	$35.00
		★	$35.00
		◯	$35.00
		⊱	$35.00

Retired 2001, Issue Price $35.00, '90

Purchased_____, Price $_____

☐ *There Is No Greater Treasure Than To Have A Friend Like You, 521000*

🎼 $35.00
🦋 $32.00
〽 $30.00
△ $30.00
♡ $30.00
✝ $30.00
👓 $30.00

Retired 1998, Issue Price $30.00, '93

Purchased_____, Price $_____

☐ *To My Favorite Fan, 521043*

⅁ $30.00
🕯 $28.00
🍶 $25.00
🎼 $23.00
🦋 $22.00

Suspended 1993, Issue Price $16.00, '90

Purchased_____, Price $_____

☐ *Merry Christmas, Little Lamb, 521078*
(Ornament)

👓 $15.00
★ $15.00
◯ $15.00
✂ $15.00
✛ $15.00

Suspended 2003, Issue Price $15.00, '98
Series: *Birthday Circus Train* — Age 1

Purchased_____, Price $_____

☐ *Heaven Bless Your Special Christmas, 521086* (Ornament)

👓 $15.00
★ $15.00
◯ $15.00
✂ $15.00
✛ $15.00

Suspended 2003, Issue Price $15.00, '98
Series: *Birthday Circus Train* — Age 3

Purchased_____, Price $_____

☐ *God Bless You This Christmas, 521094* (Ornament)

👓 $15.00
★ $15.00
◯ $15.00
✂ $15.00
✛ $15.00

Suspended 2003, Issue Price $15.00, '98
Series: *Birthday Circus Train* — Age 2

Purchased_____, Price $_____

☐ *May Your Christmas Be Gigantic, 521108* (Ornament)

👓 $15.00
★ $15.00
◯ $15.00
✂ $15.00
✛ $15.00

Suspended 2003, Issue Price $15.00, '98
Series: *Birthday Circus Train* — Age 4

Purchased_____, Price $_____

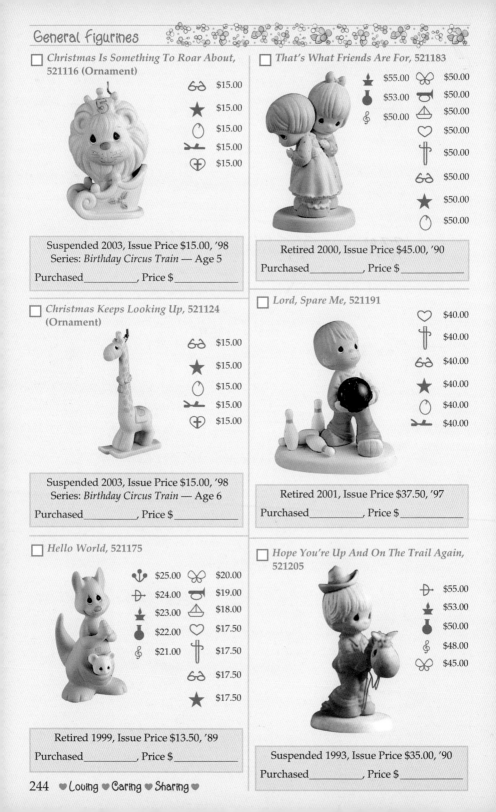

Christmas Is Something To Roar About, 521116 (Ornament)

- 6∂ $15.00
- ★ $15.00
- ◯ $15.00
- ⤛ $15.00
- ⊕ $15.00

Suspended 2003, Issue Price $15.00, '98
Series: *Birthday Circus Train* — Age 5

Purchased_____, Price $_____

Christmas Keeps Looking Up, 521124 (Ornament)

- 6∂ $15.00
- ★ $15.00
- ◯ $15.00
- ⤛ $15.00
- ⊕ $15.00

Suspended 2003, Issue Price $15.00, '98
Series: *Birthday Circus Train* — Age 6

Purchased_____, Price $_____

Hello World, 521175

- ⚓ $25.00
- ⌿ $24.00
- ⚖ $23.00
- ⬮ $22.00
- 𝄞 $21.00

- ✿ $20.00
- ⌒ $19.00
- △ $18.00
- ♡ $17.50
- ✝ $17.50
- 6∂ $17.50
- ★ $17.50

Retired 1999, Issue Price $13.50, '89

Purchased_____, Price $_____

That's What Friends Are For, 521183

- ▲ $55.00
- ⬮ $53.00
- 𝄞 $50.00

- ✿ $50.00
- ⌒ $50.00
- △ $50.00
- ♡ $50.00
- ✝ $50.00
- 6∂ $50.00
- ★ $50.00
- ◯ $50.00

Retired 2000, Issue Price $45.00, '90

Purchased_____, Price $_____

Lord, Spare Me, 521191

- ♡ $40.00
- ✝ $40.00
- 6∂ $40.00
- ★ $40.00
- ◯ $40.00
- ⤛ $40.00

Retired 2001, Issue Price $37.50, '97

Purchased_____, Price $_____

Hope You're Up And On The Trail Again, 521205

- ⌿ $55.00
- ⚖ $53.00
- ⬮ $50.00
- 𝄞 $48.00
- ✿ $45.00

Suspended 1993, Issue Price $35.00, '90

Purchased_____, Price $_____

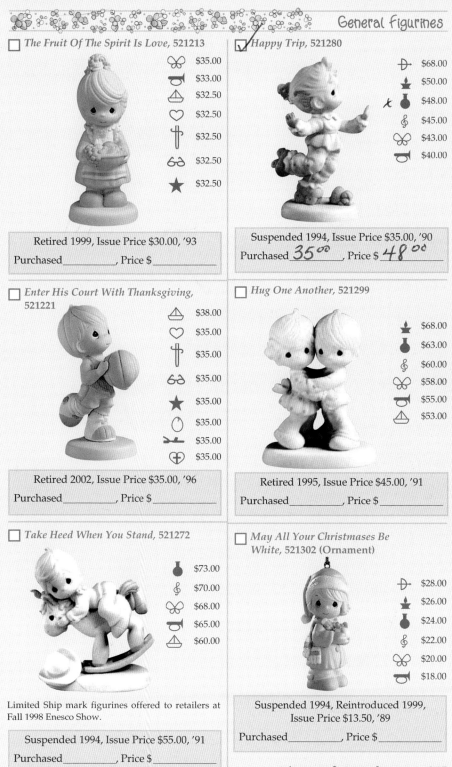

☐ *The Fruit Of The Spirit Is Love*, 521213

⬠	$35.00
◁	$33.00
△	$32.50
♡	$32.50
✝	$32.50
👓	$32.50
★	$32.50

Retired 1999, Issue Price $30.00, '93

Purchased_____, Price $_____

☑ *Happy Trip*, 521280

⅁	$68.00
⚱	$50.00
x 🍶	$48.00
𝄞	$45.00
⬠	$43.00
◁	$40.00

Suspended 1994, Issue Price $35.00, '90

Purchased *35 00*, Price $ *48 00*

☐ *Enter His Court With Thanksgiving*, 521221

△	$38.00
♡	$35.00
✝	$35.00
👓	$35.00
★	$35.00
◯	$35.00
⤛	$35.00
✛	$35.00

Retired 2002, Issue Price $35.00, '96

Purchased_____, Price $_____

☐ *Hug One Another*, 521299

⚱	$68.00
🍶	$63.00
𝄞	$60.00
⬠	$58.00
◁	$55.00
△	$53.00

Retired 1995, Issue Price $45.00, '91

Purchased_____, Price $_____

☐ *Take Heed When You Stand*, 521272

🍶	$73.00
𝄞	$70.00
⬠	$68.00
◁	$65.00
△	$60.00

Limited Ship mark figurines offered to retailers at Fall 1998 Enesco Show.

Suspended 1994, Issue Price $55.00, '91

Purchased_____, Price $_____

☐ *May All Your Christmases Be White*, 521302 (Ornament)

⅁	$28.00
⚱	$26.00
🍶	$24.00
𝄞	$22.00
⬠	$20.00
◁	$18.00

Suspended 1994, Reintroduced 1999, Issue Price $13.50, '89

Purchased_____, Price $_____

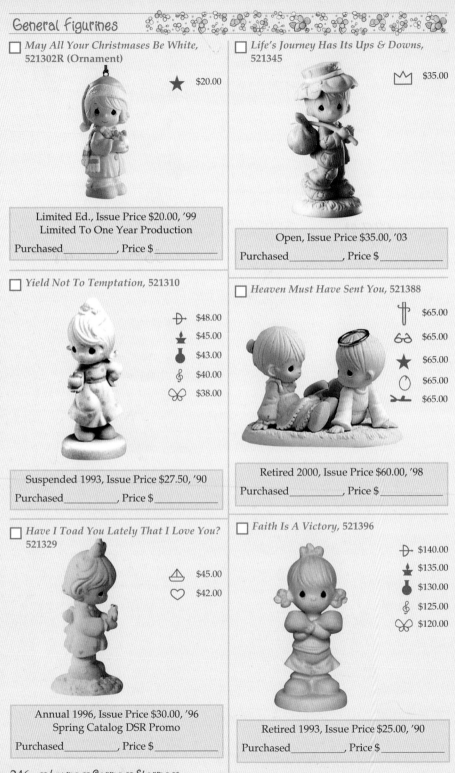

**May All Your Christmases Be White,
521302R (Ornament)**

★ $20.00

Limited Ed., Issue Price $20.00, '99
Limited To One Year Production

Purchased_____, Price $_____

**Life's Journey Has Its Ups & Downs,
521345**

♛ $35.00

Open, Issue Price $35.00, '03

Purchased_____, Price $_____

Yield Not To Temptation, 521310

⅁ $48.00
✦ $45.00
⬤ $43.00
ƒ $40.00
∞ $38.00

Suspended 1993, Issue Price $27.50, '90

Purchased_____, Price $_____

Heaven Must Have Sent You, 521388

✝ $65.00
👓 $65.00
★ $65.00
◯ $65.00
⤜ $65.00

Retired 2000, Issue Price $60.00, '98

Purchased_____, Price $_____

**Have I Toad You Lately That I Love You?
521329**

△ $45.00
♡ $42.00

Annual 1996, Issue Price $30.00, '96
Spring Catalog DSR Promo

Purchased_____, Price $_____

Faith Is A Victory, 521396

⅁ $140.00
✦ $135.00
⬤ $130.00
ƒ $125.00
∞ $120.00

Retired 1993, Issue Price $25.00, '90

Purchased_____, Price $_____

I'll Never Stop Loving You, 521418 ✓

⊅	$58.00
✓ ★	$50.00
🔴	$48.00
🎼	$45.00
🦋	$43.00
◁∂	$40.00
△	$40.00
♡	$40.00

Retired 1996, Issue Price $37.50, '90
Purchased _G_ , Price $ _50 ∞_

I'll Weight For You, 521469

◯	$30.00

Annual 2000, Issue Price $30.00, '00
Spring Catalog Syndicated Exclusive
Purchased_____, Price $_____

To A Very Special Mom And Dad, 521434

🔴	$40.00
🎼	$38.00
🦋	$35.00

Suspended 1993, Issue Price $35.00, '91
Purchased_____, Price $_____

Tell It To Jesus, 521477

⊅	$53.00	△	$40.00
★	$50.00	♡	$40.00
🔴	$47.00	✝	$40.00
🎼	$43.00		
🦋	$40.00	👓	$40.00
◁∂	$40.00	★	$40.00
		◯	$40.00
		✂	$40.00
		⊕	$40.00
		♙	$40.00

Open, Issue Price $35.00, '89
Purchased_____, Price $_____

Lord, Help Me Stick To My Job, 521450

⊅	$60.00
★	$58.00
🔴	$55.00
🎼	$54.00
🦋	$53.00
◁∂	$53.00
△	$53.00
♡	$52.00
✝	$50.00

Retired 1997, Issue Price $30.00, '90
Purchased_____, Price $_____

There's A Light At The End Of The Tunnel, 521485

🔴	$80.00
🎼	$78.00
🦋	$75.00
◁∂	$72.00
△	$68.00
♡	$65.00

Suspended 1996, Issue Price $55.00, '91
Purchased_____, Price $_____

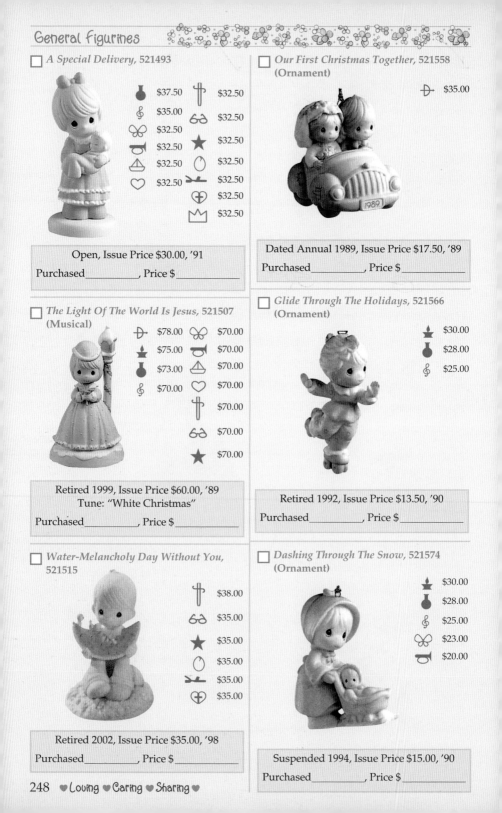

☐ *A Special Delivery*, 521493

🌡	$37.50	✝	$32.50
ℰ	$35.00	👓	$32.50
🦋	$32.50	★	$32.50
🎺	$32.50		
⛵	$32.50	○	$32.50
♡	$32.50	⤚	$32.50
		🜲	$32.50
		👑	$32.50

Open, Issue Price $30.00, '91

Purchased_____, Price $_____

☐ *The Light Of The World Is Jesus*, 521507
(Musical)

⸕	$78.00	🦋	$70.00
🌡	$75.00	🎺	$70.00
🌡	$73.00	⛵	$70.00
ℰ	$70.00	♡	$70.00
		✝	$70.00
		👓	$70.00
		★	$70.00

Retired 1999, Issue Price $60.00, '89
Tune: "White Christmas"

Purchased_____, Price $_____

☐ *Water-Melancholy Day Without You*,
521515

✝	$38.00
👓	$35.00
★	$35.00
○	$35.00
⤚	$35.00
🜲	$35.00

Retired 2002, Issue Price $35.00, '98

Purchased_____, Price $_____

☐ *Our First Christmas Together*, 521558
(Ornament)

⸕ $35.00

Dated Annual 1989, Issue Price $17.50, '89

Purchased_____, Price $_____

☐ *Glide Through The Holidays*, 521566
(Ornament)

🌡	$30.00
🌡	$28.00
ℰ	$25.00

Retired 1992, Issue Price $13.50, '90

Purchased_____, Price $_____

☐ *Dashing Through The Snow*, 521574
(Ornament)

🌡	$30.00
🌡	$28.00
ℰ	$25.00
🦋	$23.00
🎺	$20.00

Suspended 1994, Issue Price $15.00, '90

Purchased_____, Price $_____

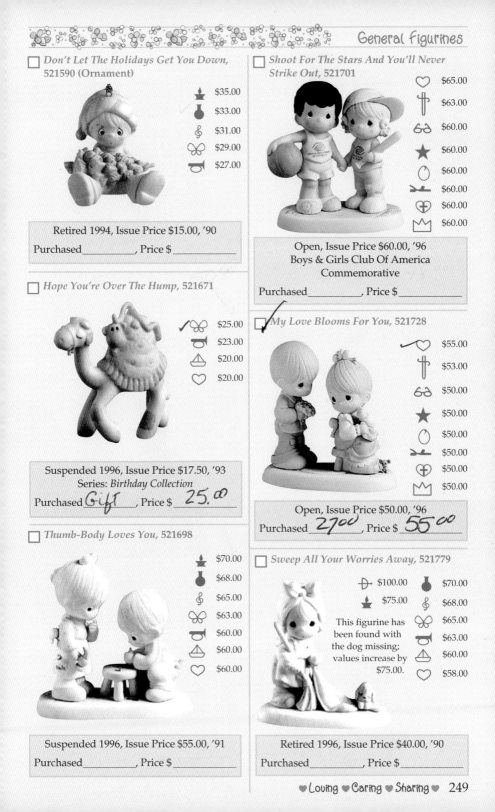

Don't Let The Holidays Get You Down,
521590 (Ornament)

🕯 $35.00
🫗 $33.00
𝄞 $31.00
🦋 $29.00
◖ $27.00

Retired 1994, Issue Price $15.00, '90

Purchased_____, Price $_____

Hope You're Over The Hump, 521671

✓🦋 $25.00
◖ $23.00
⛵ $20.00
♡ $20.00

Suspended 1996, Issue Price $17.50, '93
Series: *Birthday Collection*

Purchased *Gift*, Price $ *25.00*

Thumb-Body Loves You, 521698

🕯 $70.00
🫗 $68.00
𝄞 $65.00
🦋 $63.00
◖ $60.00
⛵ $60.00
♡ $60.00

Suspended 1996, Issue Price $55.00, '91

Purchased_____, Price $_____

Shoot For The Stars And You'll Never
Strike Out, 521701

♡ $65.00
✝ $63.00
👓 $60.00
★ $60.00
◯ $60.00
⤝ $60.00
✛ $60.00
♔ $60.00

Open, Issue Price $60.00, '96
Boys & Girls Club Of America
Commemorative

Purchased_____, Price $_____

My Love Blooms For You, 521728

◝♡ $55.00
✝ $53.00
👓 $50.00
★ $50.00
◯ $50.00
⤝ $50.00
✛ $50.00
♔ $50.00

Open, Issue Price $50.00, '96

Purchased *2700*, Price $ *55.00*

Sweep All Your Worries Away, 521779

⌿ $100.00   🫗 $70.00
🕯 $75.00   𝄞 $68.00

This figurine has   🦋 $65.00
been found with   ◖ $63.00
the dog missing;   ⛵ $60.00
values increase by   ♡ $58.00
$75.00.

Retired 1996, Issue Price $40.00, '90

Purchased_____, Price $_____

☐ *Good Friends Are Forever*, 521817

⌓	$70.00	♪	$55.00	⟁	$55.00	
★	$65.00	✇	$55.00	♡	$55.00	
◊	$60.00	⊐	$55.00			

✝	$55.00
👓	$55.00
★	$55.00
◯	$55.00
⤚	$55.00
⊕	$55.00
♛	$55.00

Open, Issue Price $50.00, '90

Purchased_____, Price $_____

☐ *May Your Birthday Be Mammoth*, 521825

♪	$28.00	♡	$25.00
✇	$25.00	✝	$25.00
⊐	$25.00		
⟁	$25.00	👓	$25.00

★	$25.00
◯	$25.00
⤚	$25.00
⊕	$25.00
♛	$25.00

Open, Issue Price $25.00, '92
Series: *Birthday Circus Train* — Age 10

Purchased_____, Price $_____

☐ *Being Nine Is Just Divine*, 521833

♪	$28.00	👓	$25.00
✇	$25.00	★	$25.00
⊐	$25.00	◯	$25.00
⟁	$25.00	⤚	$25.00
♡	$25.00	⊕	$25.00
✝	$25.00	♛	$25.00

Open, Issue Price $25.00, '92
Series: *Birthday Circus Train* — Age 9

Purchased_____, Price $_____

☐ *Love Is From Above*, 521841

⌓	$60.00
★	$55.00
◊	$50.00
♪	$50.00
✇	$50.00
⊐	$50.00
⟁	$50.00
♡	$50.00

Suspended 1996, Issue Price $45.00, '90

Purchased_____, Price $_____

☐ *The Greatest Of These Is Love*, 521868

⌓	$45.00
★	$38.00
◊	$35.00

Suspended 1991, Issue Price $27.50, '89

Purchased_____, Price $_____

☐ *Pizza On Earth*, 521884

✝	$55.00
👓	$55.00
★	$55.00
◯	$55.00
⤚	$55.00
⊕	$55.00

Retired 2001, Issue Price $55.00, '97

Purchased_____, Price $_____

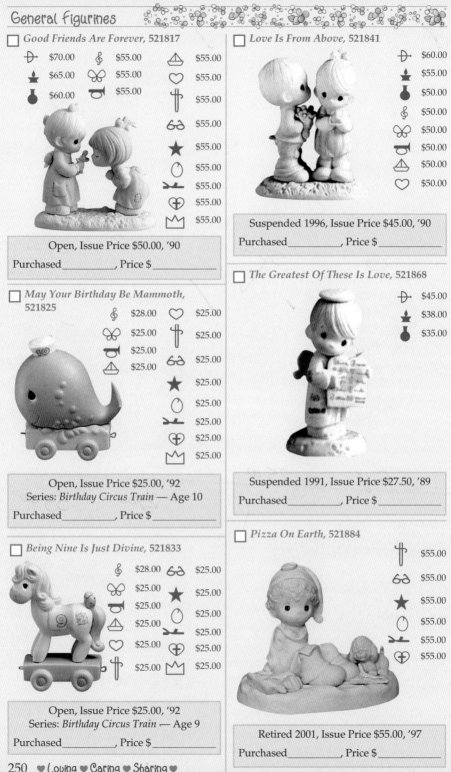

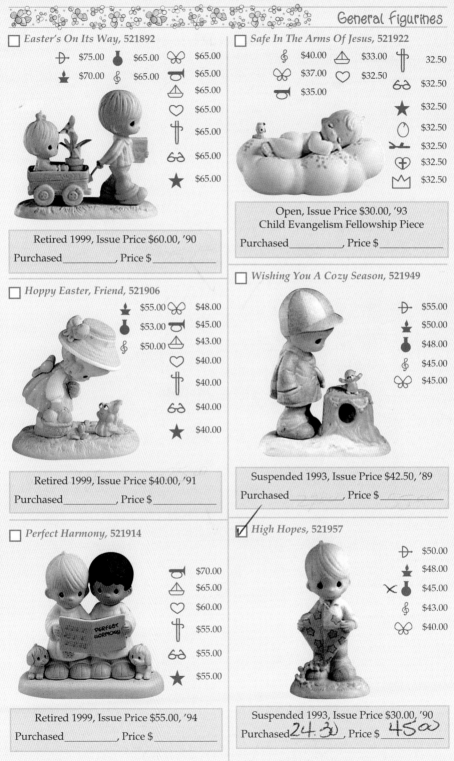

☐ *Easter's On Its Way, 521892*

⅁	$75.00	🕯	$65.00	✂	$65.00
★	$70.00	♪	$65.00	◹	$65.00
				△	$65.00
				♡	$65.00
				✟	$65.00
				6ð	$65.00
				★	$65.00

Retired 1999, Issue Price $60.00, '90

Purchased_____, Price $_____

☐ *Hoppy Easter, Friend, 521906*

🕯	$55.00	✂	$48.00
◖	$53.00	◹	$45.00
♪	$50.00	△	$43.00
		♡	$40.00
		✟	$40.00
		6ð	$40.00
		★	$40.00

Retired 1999, Issue Price $40.00, '91

Purchased_____, Price $_____

☐ *Perfect Harmony, 521914*

◹	$70.00
△	$65.00
♡	$60.00
✟	$55.00
6ð	$55.00
★	$55.00

Retired 1999, Issue Price $55.00, '94

Purchased_____, Price $_____

☐ *Safe In The Arms Of Jesus, 521922*

♪	$40.00	△	$33.00	✟	32.50
✂	$37.00	♡	$32.50		
◹	$35.00			6ð	$32.50
				★	$32.50
				○	$32.50
				⪤	$32.50
				✛	$32.50
				♕	$32.50

Open, Issue Price $30.00, '93
Child Evangelism Fellowship Piece

Purchased_____, Price $_____

☐ *Wishing You A Cozy Season, 521949*

⅁	$55.00
🕯	$50.00
◖	$48.00
♪	$45.00
✂	$45.00

Suspended 1993, Issue Price $42.50, '89

Purchased_____, Price $_____

☑ *High Hopes, 521957*

⅁	$50.00
🕯	$48.00
✗ ◖	$45.00
♪	$43.00
✂	$40.00

Suspended 1993, Issue Price $30.00, '90

Purchased 24.30, Price $ 45.00

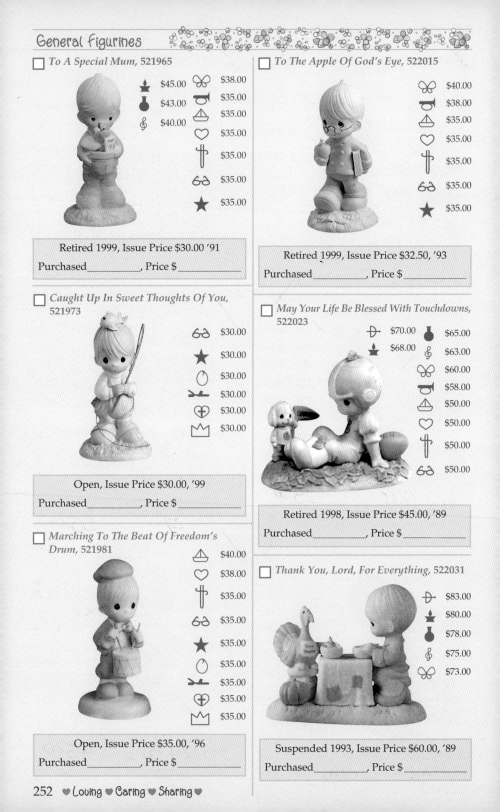

☐ *To A Special Mum, 521965*

☥	$45.00	🦋	$38.00
🌡	$43.00	🎺	$35.00
𝄞	$40.00	⛵	$35.00
		♡	$35.00
		✝	$35.00
		👓	$35.00
		★	$35.00

Retired 1999, Issue Price $30.00 '91

Purchased_____, Price $_____

☐ *Caught Up In Sweet Thoughts Of You,*
521973

👓	$30.00
★	$30.00
◯	$30.00
🔗	$30.00
⊕	$30.00
👑	$30.00

Open, Issue Price $30.00, '99

Purchased_____, Price $_____

☐ *Marching To The Beat Of Freedom's*
Drum, 521981

⛵	$40.00
♡	$38.00
✝	$35.00
👓	$35.00
★	$35.00
◯	$35.00
🔗	$35.00
⊕	$35.00
👑	$35.00

Open, Issue Price $35.00, '96

Purchased_____, Price $_____

☐ *To The Apple Of God's Eye, 522015*

🦋	$40.00
🎺	$38.00
⛵	$35.00
♡	$35.00
✝	$35.00
👓	$35.00
★	$35.00

Retired 1999, Issue Price $32.50, '93

Purchased_____, Price $_____

☐ *May Your Life Be Blessed With Touchdowns,*
522023

⌂	$70.00	🌡	$65.00
☥	$68.00	𝄞	$63.00
		🦋	$60.00
		🎺	$58.00
		⛵	$50.00
		♡	$50.00
		✝	$50.00
		👓	$50.00

Retired 1998, Issue Price $45.00, '89

Purchased_____, Price $_____

☐ *Thank You, Lord, For Everything, 522031*

⌂	$83.00
☥	$80.00
🌡	$78.00
𝄞	$75.00
🦋	$73.00

Suspended 1993, Issue Price $60.00, '89

Purchased_____, Price $_____

☑ *Now I Lay Me Down To Sleep*, 522058 ✓

⊐⊐ $45.00
△ $43.00 ✓
♡ $40.00
† $38.00

Retired 1997, Issue Price $30.00, '94
Purchased 8.12 , Price $ 43 00

☐ *It's No Yolk When I Say I Love You*, 522104

♠ $100.00
§ $95.00
∞ $90.00
⊐ $85.00

Suspended 1994, Issue Price $60.00, '92
Purchased_____, Price $_____

☐ *May Your World Be Trimmed With Joy*, 522082

♠ $65.00
§ $63.00
∞ $60.00
⊐ $58.00
△ $55.00
♡ $55.00

Suspended 1996, Issue Price $55.00, '91
Purchased_____, Price $_____

☑ *Don't Let The Holidays Get You Down*, 522112

Ð $110.00
✦ $105.00
✗♠ $100.00
§ $95.00
∞ $90.00

Retired 1993, Issue Price $42.50, '89
Purchased 28.50 Price $ 100 00

☐ *There Shall Be Showers Of Blessings*, 522090

Ð $80.00   § $73.00
✦ $78.00   ∞ $70.00
♠ $75.00   ⊐ $70.00
            △ $70.00
            ♡ $70.00
            † $70.00
            ᑫᕉ $70.00
            ★ $70.00

Retired 1999, Issue Price $60.00, '90
Purchased_____, Price $_____

☐ *Wishing You A Very Successful Season*, 522120

Ð $95.00   ♠ $90.00
✦ $93.00   § $88.00
            ∞ $85.00
            ⊐ $83.00
            △ $80.00
            ♡ $78.00
            † $75.00
            ᑫᕉ $73.00
            ★ $70.00

Retired 1999, Issue Price $60.00, '89
Purchased_____, Price $_____

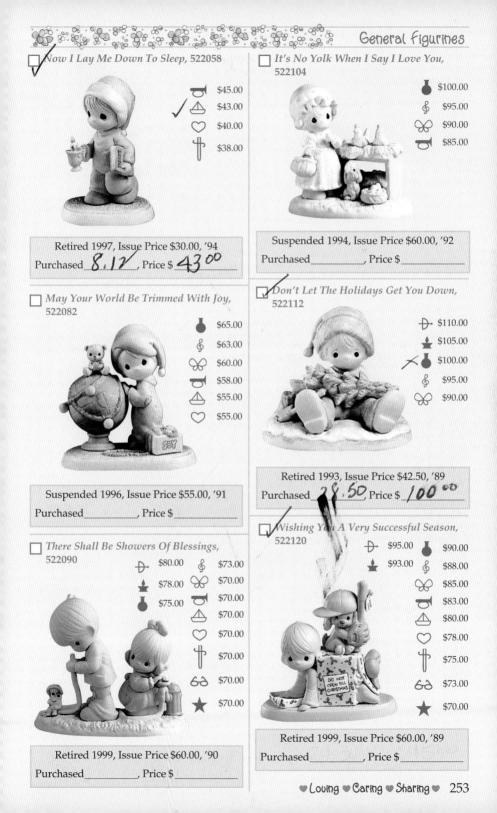

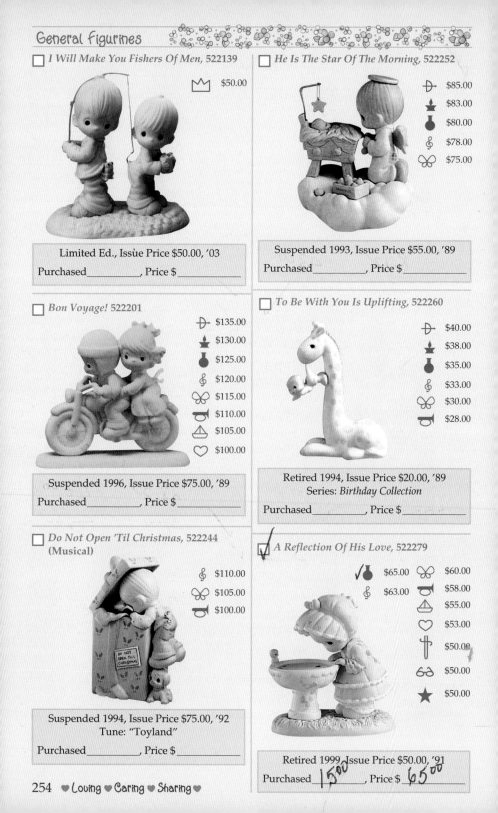

☐ *I Will Make You Fishers Of Men, 522139*

♛ $50.00

Limited Ed., Issue Price $50.00, '03

Purchased_____, Price $_____

☐ *He Is The Star Of The Morning, 522252*

⌐ $85.00
★ $83.00
◗ $80.00
♪ $78.00
🦋 $75.00

Suspended 1993, Issue Price $55.00, '89

Purchased_____, Price $_____

☐ *Bon Voyage! 522201*

⌐ $135.00
★ $130.00
◗ $125.00
♪ $120.00
🦋 $115.00
📯 $110.00
△ $105.00
♡ $100.00

Suspended 1996, Issue Price $75.00, '89

Purchased_____, Price $_____

☐ *To Be With You Is Uplifting, 522260*

⌐ $40.00
★ $38.00
◗ $35.00
♪ $33.00
🦋 $30.00
📯 $28.00

Retired 1994, Issue Price $20.00, '89
Series: *Birthday Collection*

Purchased_____, Price $_____

☐ *Do Not Open 'Til Christmas, 522244*
(Musical)

♪ $110.00
🦋 $105.00
📯 $100.00

Suspended 1994, Issue Price $75.00, '92
Tune: "Toyland"

Purchased_____, Price $_____

☑ *A Reflection Of His Love, 522279*

✔◗ $65.00   🦋 $60.00
♪ $63.00   📯 $58.00
              △ $55.00
              ♡ $53.00
              ✝ $50.00
              👓 $50.00
              ★ $50.00

Retired 1999, Issue Price $50.00, '91

Purchased __1500__, Price $ __65⁰⁰__

☐ *Thinking Of You Is What I Really Like To Do, 522287*

⊅	$45.00
♣	$43.00
🏺	$40.00
𝄞	$38.00
✎ (butterfly)	$35.00
◁ (trumpet)	$33.00
△	$33.00
♡	$33.00

Suspended 1996, Issue Price $30.00, '90

Purchased_____, Price $_____

☐ *Sweeter As The Years Go By, 522333*

♡	$65.00
✝	$63.00
👓	$60.00

Retired 1998, Issue Price $60.00, '96

Purchased_____, Price $_____

☐ *Merry Christmas Deer, 522317*

⊅	$105.00	🏺	$98.00
♣	$100.00	𝄞	$95.00
		✎	$93.00
		◁	$90.00
		△	$87.00
		♡	$85.00
		✝	$83.00

Retired 1997, Issue Price $50.00, '89

Purchased_____, Price $_____

☐ *His Love Will Shine On You, 522376*

⚜	$55.00
⊅	$53.00

Annual 1989, Issue Price $30.00, '89
Easter Seals Commemorative,
Lily Understamp

Purchased_____, Price $_____

☑ *Somebody Cares, 522325*

✝	$45.00

bd-

Annual 1998, Issue Price $40.00, '98
Easter Seals Commemorative,
Lily Understamp

Purchased 10⁰⁰, Price $ 45⁰⁰

☐ *Oh Holy Night, 522546*

⊅	$40.00

Dated Annual 1989, Issue Price $25.00, '89

Purchased_____, Price $_____

☐ *Oh Holy Night*, 522554 (Thimble)

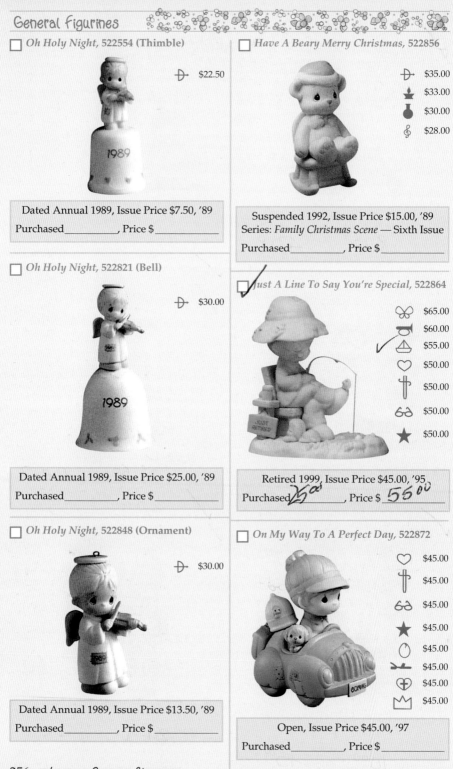

〄 $22.50

Dated Annual 1989, Issue Price $7.50, '89
Purchased_____, Price $ _____

☐ *Oh Holy Night*, 522821 (Bell)

〄 $30.00

Dated Annual 1989, Issue Price $25.00, '89
Purchased_____, Price $ _____

☐ *Oh Holy Night*, 522848 (Ornament)

〄 $30.00

Dated Annual 1989, Issue Price $13.50, '89
Purchased_____, Price $ _____

☐ *Have A Beary Merry Christmas*, 522856

〄 $35.00
♣ $33.00
♠ $30.00
𝄞 $28.00

Suspended 1992, Issue Price $15.00, '89
Series: *Family Christmas Scene* — Sixth Issue
Purchased_____, Price $ _____

☑ *Just A Line To Say You're Special*, 522864

∝ $65.00
📯 $60.00
△ $55.00
♡ $50.00
✝ $50.00
6∂ $50.00
★ $50.00

Retired 1999, Issue Price $45.00, '95
Purchased__*5 a*____, Price $ *55 00*

☐ *On My Way To A Perfect Day*, 522872

♡ $45.00
✝ $45.00
6∂ $45.00
★ $45.00
◯ $45.00
⤛ $45.00
⊕ $45.00
♕ $45.00

Open, Issue Price $45.00, '97
Purchased_____, Price $ _____

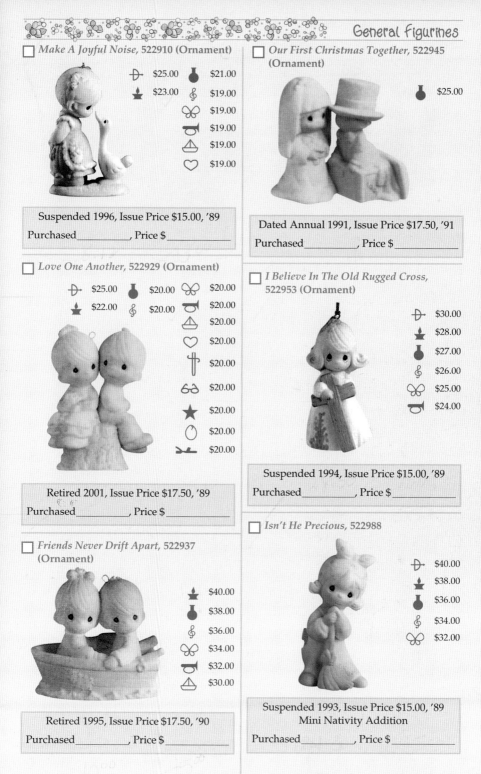

☐ *Make A Joyful Noise*, 522910 (Ornament)

    ☐⟍ $25.00   🕯 $21.00

    🕯 $23.00   🎼 $19.00

                🦋 $19.00

                ◁ $19.00

                △ $19.00

                ♡ $19.00

Suspended 1996, Issue Price $15.00, '89

Purchased_____, Price $_____

☐ *Love One Another*, 522929 (Ornament)

  ☐⟍ $25.00 🏺 $20.00 🦋 $20.00

  🕯 $22.00 🎼 $20.00 ◁ $20.00

                          △ $20.00

                          ♡ $20.00

                          ✝ $20.00

                          👓 $20.00

                          ★ $20.00

                          ◯ $20.00

                          ⤛ $20.00

Retired 2001, Issue Price $17.50, '89

Purchased_____, Price $_____

☐ *Friends Never Drift Apart*, 522937 (Ornament)

    🕯 $40.00

    🏺 $38.00

    🎼 $36.00

    🦋 $34.00

    ◁ $32.00

    △ $30.00

Retired 1995, Issue Price $17.50, '90

Purchased_____, Price $_____

☐ *Our First Christmas Together*, 522945 (Ornament)

    🏺 $25.00

Dated Annual 1991, Issue Price $17.50, '91

Purchased_____, Price $_____

☐ *I Believe In The Old Rugged Cross*, 522953 (Ornament)

    ☐⟍ $30.00

    🕯 $28.00

    🏺 $27.00

    🎼 $26.00

    🦋 $25.00

    ◁ $24.00

Suspended 1994, Issue Price $15.00, '89

Purchased_____, Price $_____

☐ *Isn't He Precious*, 522988

    ☐⟍ $40.00

    🕯 $38.00

    🏺 $36.00

    🎼 $34.00

    🦋 $32.00

Suspended 1993, Issue Price $15.00, '89
Mini Nativity Addition

Purchased_____, Price $_____

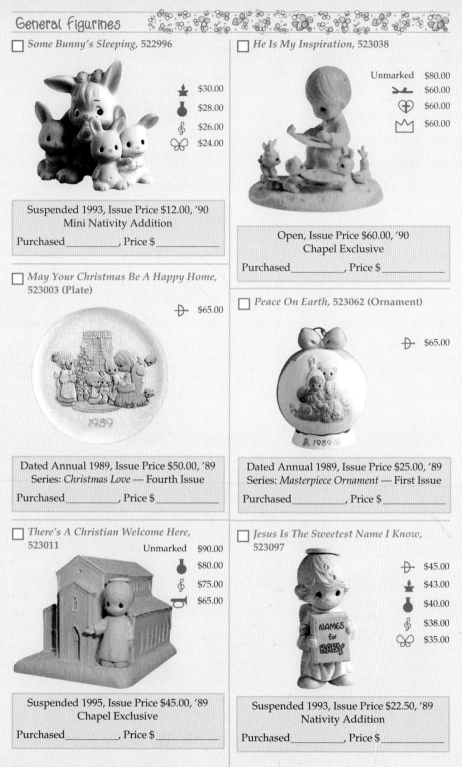

☐ *Some Bunny's Sleeping*, 522996

🔆 $30.00
🏺 $28.00
𝄞 $26.00
🦋 $24.00

Suspended 1993, Issue Price $12.00, '90
Mini Nativity Addition

Purchased_____, Price $_____

☐ *May Your Christmas Be A Happy Home*, 523003 (Plate)

⟊ $65.00

Dated Annual 1989, Issue Price $50.00, '89
Series: *Christmas Love* — Fourth Issue

Purchased_____, Price $_____

☐ *There's A Christian Welcome Here*, 523011

Unmarked $90.00
🏺 $80.00
𝄞 $75.00
📯 $65.00

Suspended 1995, Issue Price $45.00, '89
Chapel Exclusive

Purchased_____, Price $_____

☐ *He Is My Inspiration*, 523038

Unmarked $80.00
➤ $60.00
✛ $60.00
👑 $60.00

Open, Issue Price $60.00, '90
Chapel Exclusive

Purchased_____, Price $_____

☐ *Peace On Earth*, 523062 (Ornament)

⟊ $65.00

Dated Annual 1989, Issue Price $25.00, '89
Series: *Masterpiece Ornament* — First Issue

Purchased_____, Price $_____

☐ *Jesus Is The Sweetest Name I Know*, 523097

⟊ $45.00
🔆 $43.00
🏺 $40.00
𝄞 $38.00
🦋 $35.00

Suspended 1993, Issue Price $22.50, '89
Nativity Addition

Purchased_____, Price $_____

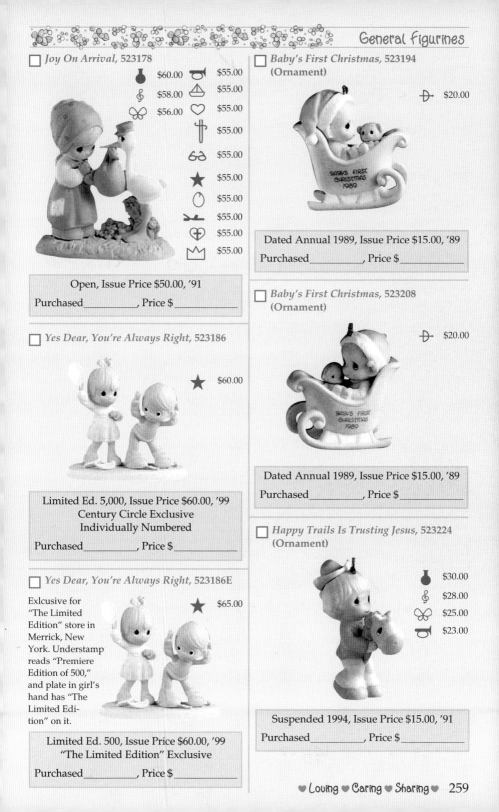

☐ *Joy On Arrival*, 523178

🎺 $60.00   🎺 $55.00
🎼 $58.00   ⛵ $55.00
🎶 $56.00   ♡ $55.00
             ✝ $55.00
             👓 $55.00
             ★ $55.00
             ○ $55.00
             ⊱ $55.00
             ✠ $55.00
             👑 $55.00

Open, Issue Price $50.00, '91

Purchased_____, Price $_____

☐ *Yes Dear, You're Always Right*, 523186

★ $60.00

Limited Ed. 5,000, Issue Price $60.00, '99
Century Circle Exclusive
Individually Numbered

Purchased_____, Price $_____

☐ *Yes Dear, You're Always Right*, 523186E

Exlcusive for
"The Limited
Edition" store in
Merrick, New
York. Understamp
reads "Premiere
Edition of 500,"
and plate in girl's
hand has "The
Limited Edi-
tion" on it.

★ $65.00

Limited Ed. 500, Issue Price $60.00, '99
"The Limited Edition" Exclusive

Purchased_____, Price $_____

☐ *Baby's First Christmas*, 523194
(Ornament)

⊕ $20.00

Dated Annual 1989, Issue Price $15.00, '89

Purchased_____, Price $_____

☐ *Baby's First Christmas*, 523208
(Ornament)

⊕ $20.00

Dated Annual 1989, Issue Price $15.00, '89

Purchased_____, Price $_____

☐ *Happy Trails Is Trusting Jesus*, 523224
(Ornament)

🎺 $30.00
🎼 $28.00
🎶 $25.00
⊱ $23.00

Suspended 1994, Issue Price $15.00, '91

Purchased_____, Price $_____

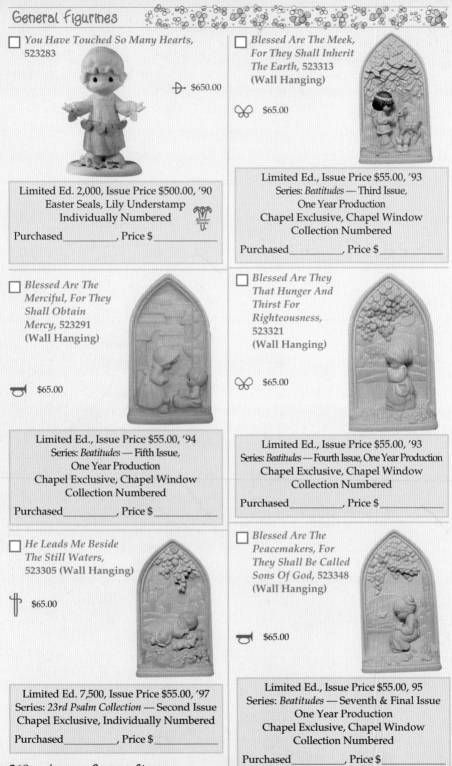

☐ *You Have Touched So Many Hearts,* 523283

⊕ $650.00

Limited Ed. 2,000, Issue Price $500.00, '90
Easter Seals, Lily Understamp
Individually Numbered

Purchased_____, Price $_____

☐ *Blessed Are The Meek,*
For They Shall Inherit
The Earth, 523313
(Wall Hanging)

✿ $65.00

Limited Ed., Issue Price $55.00, '93
Series: *Beatitudes* — Third Issue,
One Year Production
Chapel Exclusive, Chapel Window
Collection Numbered

Purchased_____, Price $_____

☐ *Blessed Are The*
Merciful, For They
Shall Obtain
Mercy, 523291
(Wall Hanging)

🎺 $65.00

Limited Ed., Issue Price $55.00, '94
Series: *Beatitudes* — Fifth Issue,
One Year Production
Chapel Exclusive, Chapel Window
Collection Numbered

Purchased_____, Price $_____

☐ *Blessed Are They*
That Hunger And
Thirst For
Righteousness,
523321
(Wall Hanging)

✿ $65.00

Limited Ed., Issue Price $55.00, '93
Series: *Beatitudes* — Fourth Issue, One Year Production
Chapel Exclusive, Chapel Window
Collection Numbered

Purchased_____, Price $_____

☐ *He Leads Me Beside*
The Still Waters,
523305 (Wall Hanging)

✝ $65.00

Limited Ed. 7,500, Issue Price $55.00, '97
Series: *23rd Psalm Collection* — Second Issue
Chapel Exclusive, Individually Numbered

Purchased_____, Price $_____

☐ *Blessed Are The*
Peacemakers, For
They Shall Be Called
Sons Of God, 523348
(Wall Hanging)

🎺 $65.00

Limited Ed., Issue Price $55.00, 95
Series: *Beatitudes* — Seventh & Final Issue
One Year Production
Chapel Exclusive, Chapel Window
Collection Numbered

Purchased_____, Price $_____

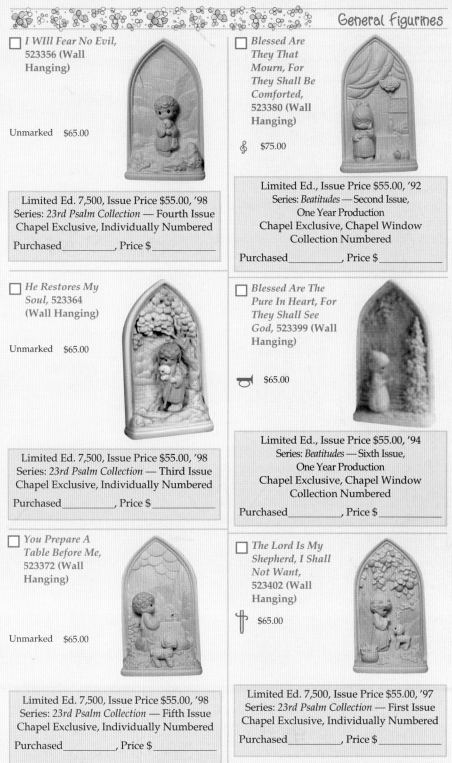

I WIll Fear No Evil, 523356 (Wall Hanging)

Unmarked $65.00

Limited Ed. 7,500, Issue Price $55.00, '98
Series: *23rd Psalm Collection* — Fourth Issue
Chapel Exclusive, Individually Numbered
Purchased_____, Price $_____

Blessed Are They That Mourn, For They Shall Be Comforted, 523380 (Wall Hanging)

♪ $75.00

Limited Ed., Issue Price $55.00, '92
Series: *Beatitudes* — Second Issue,
One Year Production
Chapel Exclusive, Chapel Window
Collection Numbered
Purchased_____, Price $_____

He Restores My Soul, 523364 (Wall Hanging)

Unmarked $65.00

Limited Ed. 7,500, Issue Price $55.00, '98
Series: *23rd Psalm Collection* — Third Issue
Chapel Exclusive, Individually Numbered
Purchased_____, Price $_____

Blessed Are The Pure In Heart, For They Shall See God, 523399 (Wall Hanging)

🎺 $65.00

Limited Ed., Issue Price $55.00, '94
Series: *Beatitudes* — Sixth Issue,
One Year Production
Chapel Exclusive, Chapel Window
Collection Numbered
Purchased_____, Price $_____

You Prepare A Table Before Me, 523372 (Wall Hanging)

Unmarked $65.00

Limited Ed. 7,500, Issue Price $55.00, '98
Series: *23rd Psalm Collection* — Fifth Issue
Chapel Exclusive, Individually Numbered
Purchased_____, Price $_____

The Lord Is My Shepherd, I Shall Not Want, 523402 (Wall Hanging)

† $65.00

Limited Ed. 7,500, Issue Price $55.00, '97
Series: *23rd Psalm Collection* — First Issue
Chapel Exclusive, Individually Numbered
Purchased_____, Price $_____

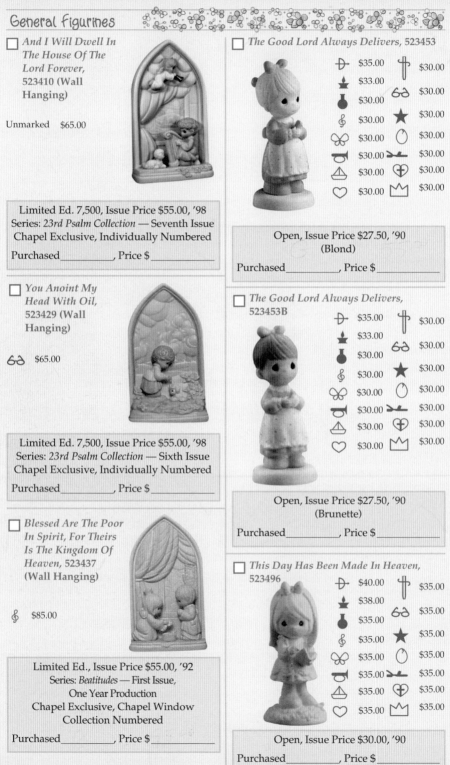

☐ *And I Will Dwell In The House Of The Lord Forever,* 523410 (Wall Hanging)

Unmarked $65.00

Limited Ed. 7,500, Issue Price $55.00, '98
Series: *23rd Psalm Collection* — Seventh Issue
Chapel Exclusive, Individually Numbered

Purchased_____, Price $_____

☐ *You Anoint My Head With Oil,* 523429 (Wall Hanging)

👓 $65.00

Limited Ed. 7,500, Issue Price $55.00, '98
Series: *23rd Psalm Collection* — Sixth Issue
Chapel Exclusive, Individually Numbered

Purchased_____, Price $_____

☐ *Blessed Are The Poor In Spirit, For Theirs Is The Kingdom Of Heaven,* 523437 (Wall Hanging)

🎵 $85.00

Limited Ed., Issue Price $55.00, '92
Series: *Beatitudes* — First Issue,
One Year Production
Chapel Exclusive, Chapel Window
Collection Numbered

Purchased_____, Price $_____

☐ *The Good Lord Always Delivers,* 523453

⌐ $35.00		✝ $30.00	
✦ $33.00		👓 $30.00	
🏺 $30.00			
🎵 $30.00		★ $30.00	
∞ $30.00		◯ $30.00	
⊲ $30.00		⊁ $30.00	
△ $30.00		✛ $30.00	
♡ $30.00		♔ $30.00	

Open, Issue Price $27.50, '90
(Blond)

Purchased_____, Price $_____

☐ *The Good Lord Always Delivers,* 523453B

⌐ $35.00		✝ $30.00	
✦ $33.00		👓 $30.00	
🏺 $30.00			
🎵 $30.00		★ $30.00	
∞ $30.00		◯ $30.00	
⊲ $30.00		⊁ $30.00	
△ $30.00		✛ $30.00	
♡ $30.00		♔ $30.00	

Open, Issue Price $27.50, '90
(Brunette)

Purchased_____, Price $_____

☐ *This Day Has Been Made In Heaven,* 523496

⌐ $40.00		✝ $35.00	
✦ $38.00		👓 $35.00	
🏺 $35.00			
🎵 $35.00		★ $35.00	
∞ $35.00		◯ $35.00	
⊲ $35.00		⊁ $35.00	
△ $35.00		✛ $35.00	
♡ $35.00		♔ $35.00	

Open, Issue Price $30.00, '90

Purchased_____, Price $_____

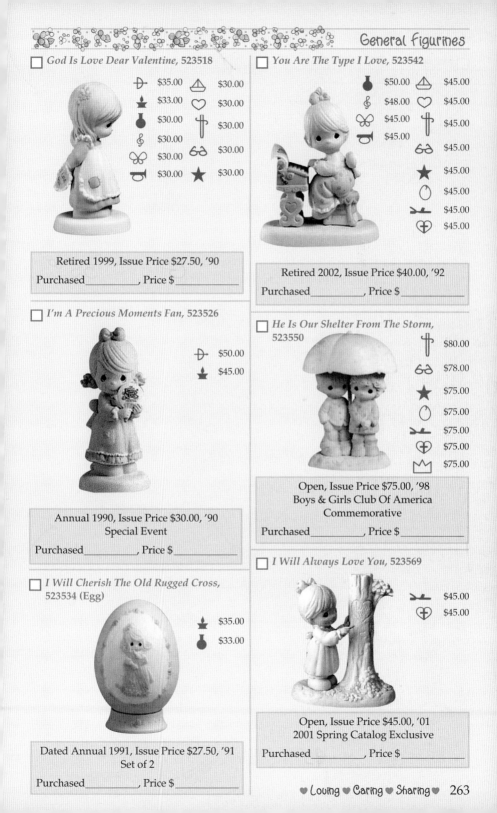

☐ *God Is Love Dear Valentine*, 523518

⅁	$35.00	△	$30.00
☀	$33.00	♡	$30.00
⬤	$30.00	✝	$30.00
♪	$30.00		
⚭	$30.00	👓	$30.00
⊐	$30.00	★	$30.00

Retired 1999, Issue Price $27.50, '90

Purchased_____, Price $_____

☐ *I'm A Precious Moments Fan*, 523526

⅁	$50.00
☀	$45.00

Annual 1990, Issue Price $30.00, '90
Special Event

Purchased_____, Price $_____

☐ *I Will Cherish The Old Rugged Cross*,
523534 (Egg)

☀	$35.00
⬤	$33.00

Dated Annual 1991, Issue Price $27.50, '91
Set of 2

Purchased_____, Price $_____

☐ *You Are The Type I Love*, 523542

⬤	$50.00	△	$45.00
♪	$48.00	♡	$45.00
⚭	$45.00	✝	$45.00
⊐	$45.00		
		👓	$45.00
		★	$45.00
		◯	$45.00
		⤛	$45.00
		⨁	$45.00

Retired 2002, Issue Price $40.00, '92

Purchased_____, Price $_____

☐ *He Is Our Shelter From The Storm*,
523550

✝	$80.00
👓	$78.00
★	$75.00
◯	$75.00
⤛	$75.00
⨁	$75.00
♛	$75.00

Open, Issue Price $75.00, '98
Boys & Girls Club Of America
Commemorative

Purchased_____, Price $_____

☐ *I Will Always Love You*, 523569

⤛	$45.00
⨁	$45.00

Open, Issue Price $45.00, '01
2001 Spring Catalog Exclusive

Purchased_____, Price $_____

☐ *The Lord Will Provide, 523593*

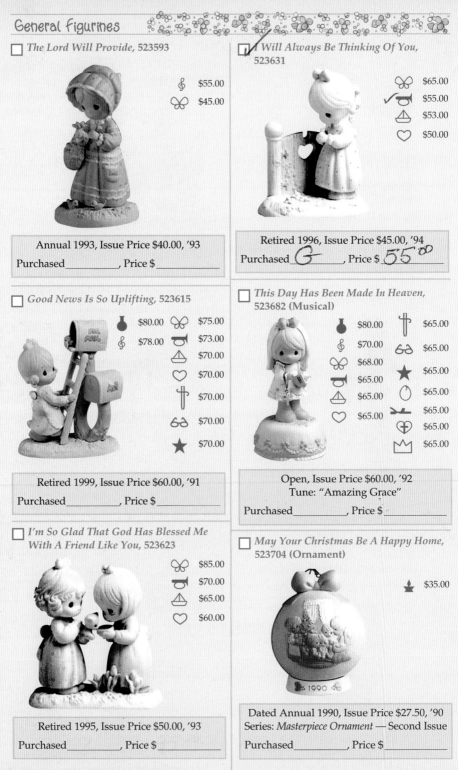

🔔 $55.00
🦋 $45.00

Annual 1993, Issue Price $40.00, '93
Purchased_____, Price $_____

☑ *I Will Always Be Thinking Of You, 523631*

🦋 $65.00
✓📯 $55.00
⛵ $53.00
♡ $50.00

Retired 1996, Issue Price $45.00, '94
Purchased _G_, Price $ _55⁰⁰_

☐ *Good News Is So Uplifting, 523615*

🏺 $80.00   🦋 $75.00
🎼 $78.00   📯 $73.00
⛵ $70.00
♡ $70.00
✝ $70.00
👓 $70.00
★ $70.00

Retired 1999, Issue Price $60.00, '91
Purchased_____, Price $_____

☐ *This Day Has Been Made In Heaven, 523682 (Musical)*

🏺 $80.00   ✝ $65.00
🎼 $70.00   👓 $65.00
🦋 $68.00   ★ $65.00
📯 $65.00   ◯ $65.00
⛵ $65.00   ⤳ $65.00
♡ $65.00   ⊕ $65.00
             ♛ $65.00

Open, Issue Price $60.00, '92
Tune: "Amazing Grace"
Purchased_____, Price $_____

☐ *I'm So Glad That God Has Blessed Me With A Friend Like You, 523623*

🦋 $85.00
📯 $70.00
⛵ $65.00
♡ $60.00

Retired 1995, Issue Price $50.00, '93
Purchased_____, Price $_____

☐ *May Your Christmas Be A Happy Home, 523704 (Ornament)*

🕯 $35.00

Dated Annual 1990, Issue Price $27.50, '90
Series: *Masterpiece Ornament* — Second Issue
Purchased_____, Price $_____

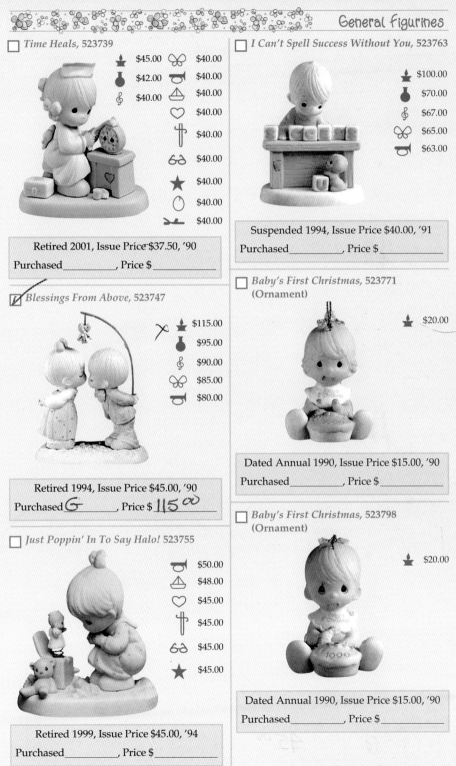

☐ *Time Heals, 523739*

✦	$45.00	✦	$40.00
●	$42.00	◯	$40.00
♪	$40.00	△	$40.00
		♡	$40.00
		✝	$40.00
		👓	$40.00
		★	$40.00
		◯	$40.00
		➤	$40.00

Retired 2001, Issue Price $37.50, '90

Purchased_____, Price $_____

✓ *Blessings From Above, 523747*

✦	$115.00
●	$95.00
♪	$90.00
◯	$85.00
◯	$80.00

Retired 1994, Issue Price $45.00, '90

Purchased G_____, Price $ 115 00

☐ *Just Poppin' In To Say Halo! 523755*

◯	$50.00
△	$48.00
♡	$45.00
✝	$45.00
👓	$45.00
★	$45.00

Retired 1999, Issue Price $45.00, '94

Purchased_____, Price $_____

☐ *I Can't Spell Success Without You, 523763*

✦	$100.00
●	$70.00
♪	$67.00
◯	$65.00
◯	$63.00

Suspended 1994, Issue Price $40.00, '91

Purchased_____, Price $_____

☐ *Baby's First Christmas, 523771*
(Ornament)

✦	$20.00

Dated Annual 1990, Issue Price $15.00, '90

Purchased_____, Price $_____

☐ *Baby's First Christmas, 523798*
(Ornament)

✦	$20.00

Dated Annual 1990, Issue Price $15.00, '90

Purchased_____, Price $_____

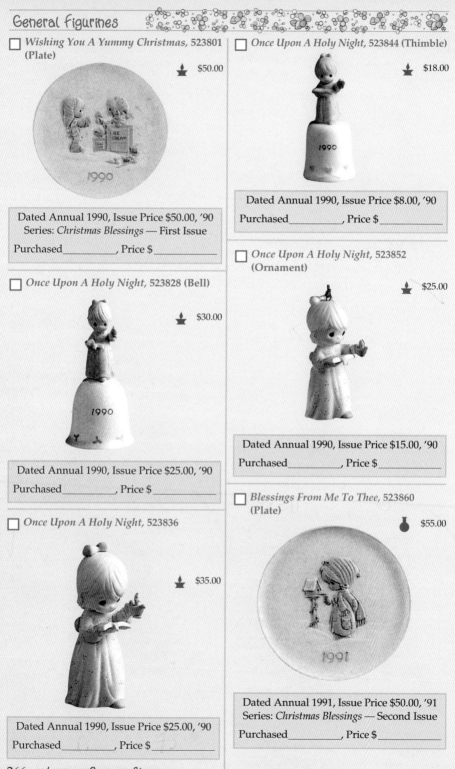

☐ *Wishing You A Yummy Christmas*, 523801
(Plate)

🕯 $50.00

Dated Annual 1990, Issue Price $50.00, '90
Series: *Christmas Blessings* — First Issue

Purchased_____, Price $_____

☐ *Once Upon A Holy Night*, 523828 (Bell)

🕯 $30.00

Dated Annual 1990, Issue Price $25.00, '90

Purchased_____, Price $_____

☐ *Once Upon A Holy Night*, 523836

🕯 $35.00

Dated Annual 1990, Issue Price $25.00, '90

Purchased_____, Price $_____

☐ *Once Upon A Holy Night*, 523844 (Thimble)

🕯 $18.00

Dated Annual 1990, Issue Price $8.00, '90

Purchased_____, Price $_____

☐ *Once Upon A Holy Night*, 523852
(Ornament)

🕯 $25.00

Dated Annual 1990, Issue Price $15.00, '90

Purchased_____, Price $_____

☐ *Blessings From Me To Thee*, 523860
(Plate)

🏺 $55.00

Dated Annual 1991, Issue Price $50.00, '91
Series: *Christmas Blessings* — Second Issue

Purchased_____, Price $_____

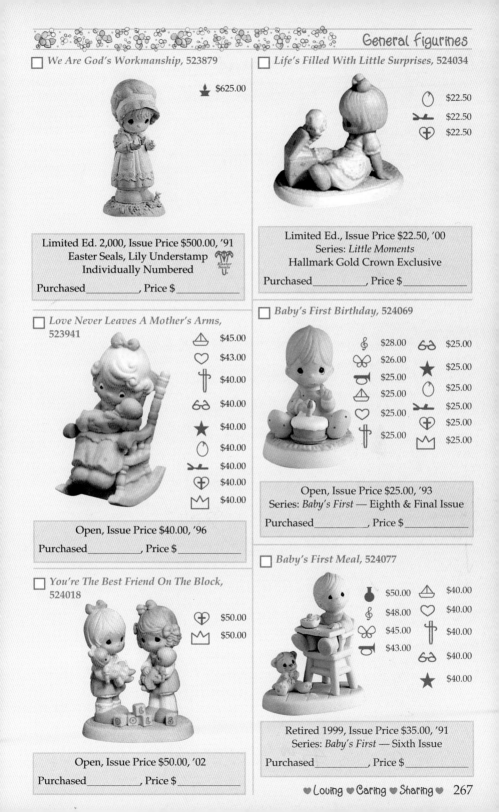

☐ *We Are God's Workmanship*, 523879

★ $625.00

Limited Ed. 2,000, Issue Price $500.00, '91
Easter Seals, Lily Understamp
Individually Numbered

Purchased_____, Price $_____

☐ *Love Never Leaves A Mother's Arms*, 523941

△ $45.00
♡ $43.00
♱ $40.00
6ᴎ $40.00
★ $40.00
◯ $40.00
ᗩ $40.00
⊕ $40.00
ᗰ $40.00

Open, Issue Price $40.00, '96

Purchased_____, Price $_____

☐ *You're The Best Friend On The Block*, 524018

⊕ $50.00
ᗰ $50.00

Open, Issue Price $50.00, '02

Purchased_____, Price $_____

☐ *Life's Filled With Little Surprises*, 524034

◯ $22.50
ᗩ $22.50
⊕ $22.50

Limited Ed., Issue Price $22.50, '00
Series: *Little Moments*
Hallmark Gold Crown Exclusive

Purchased_____, Price $_____

☐ *Baby's First Birthday*, 524069

♪ $28.00   6ᴎ $25.00
❀ $26.00   ★ $25.00
♩ $25.00   ◯ $25.00
△ $25.00   ᗩ $25.00
♡ $25.00   ⊕ $25.00
♱ $25.00   ᗰ $25.00

Open, Issue Price $25.00, '93
Series: *Baby's First* — Eighth & Final Issue

Purchased_____, Price $_____

☐ *Baby's First Meal*, 524077

♨ $50.00   △ $40.00
♪ $48.00   ♡ $40.00
❀ $45.00   ♱ $40.00
♩ $43.00   6ᴎ $40.00
             ★ $40.00

Retired 1999, Issue Price $35.00, '91
Series: *Baby's First* — Sixth Issue

Purchased_____, Price $_____

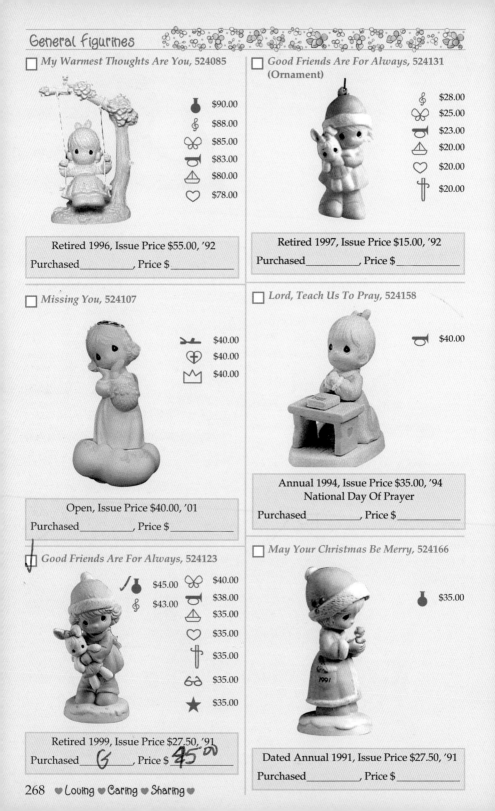

☐ *My Warmest Thoughts Are You*, 524085

🏺 $90.00
🎼 $88.00
🦋 $85.00
📯 $83.00
⛵ $80.00
♡ $78.00

Retired 1996, Issue Price $55.00, '92
Purchased_____, Price $_____

☐ *Good Friends Are For Always*, 524131
(Ornament)

🎼 $28.00
🦋 $25.00
📯 $23.00
⛵ $20.00
♡ $20.00
☦ $20.00

Retired 1997, Issue Price $15.00, '92
Purchased_____, Price $_____

☐ *Missing You*, 524107

✂ $40.00
⊕ $40.00
♔ $40.00

Open, Issue Price $40.00, '01
Purchased_____, Price $_____

☐ *Lord, Teach Us To Pray*, 524158

📯 $40.00

Annual 1994, Issue Price $35.00, '94
National Day Of Prayer
Purchased_____, Price $_____

☐ *Good Friends Are For Always*, 524123

🧪 $45.00   🦋 $40.00
🎼 $43.00   📯 $38.00
⛵ $35.00
♡ $35.00
☦ $35.00
👓 $35.00
★ $35.00

Retired 1999, Issue Price $27.50, '91
Purchased___G___, Price $ 45.00

☐ *May Your Christmas Be Merry*, 524166

🏺 $35.00

Dated Annual 1991, Issue Price $27.50, '91
Purchased_____, Price $_____

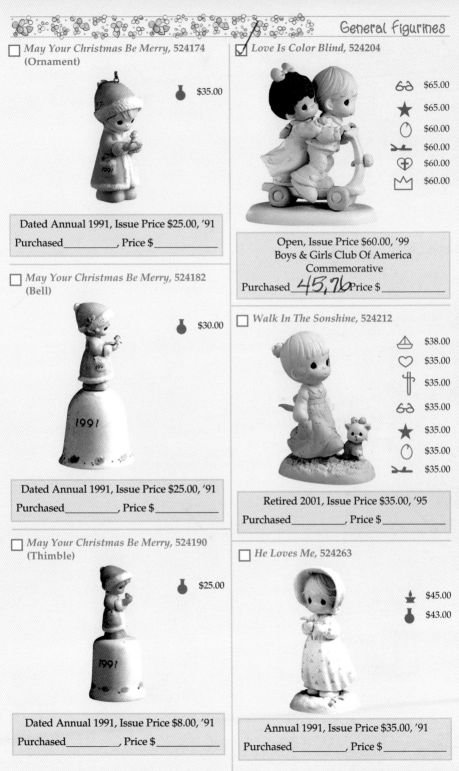

☐ *May Your Christmas Be Merry*, 524174
(Ornament)

🍶 $35.00

Dated Annual 1991, Issue Price $25.00, '91
Purchased_____, Price $_____

☐ *May Your Christmas Be Merry*, 524182
(Bell)

🍶 $30.00

Dated Annual 1991, Issue Price $25.00, '91
Purchased_____, Price $_____

☐ *May Your Christmas Be Merry*, 524190
(Thimble)

🍶 $25.00

Dated Annual 1991, Issue Price $8.00, '91
Purchased_____, Price $_____

☑ *Love Is Color Blind*, 524204

6∂ $65.00
★ $65.00
◯ $60.00
⋈ $60.00
⊕ $60.00
♛ $60.00

Open, Issue Price $60.00, '99
Boys & Girls Club Of America
Commemorative
Purchased _45.76_ Price $_____

☐ *Walk In The Sonshine*, 524212

△ $38.00
♡ $35.00
✝ $35.00
6∂ $35.00
★ $35.00
◯ $35.00
⋈ $35.00

Retired 2001, Issue Price $35.00, '95
Purchased_____, Price $_____

☐ *He Loves Me*, 524263

✦ $45.00
🍶 $43.00

Annual 1991, Issue Price $35.00, '91
Purchased_____, Price $_____

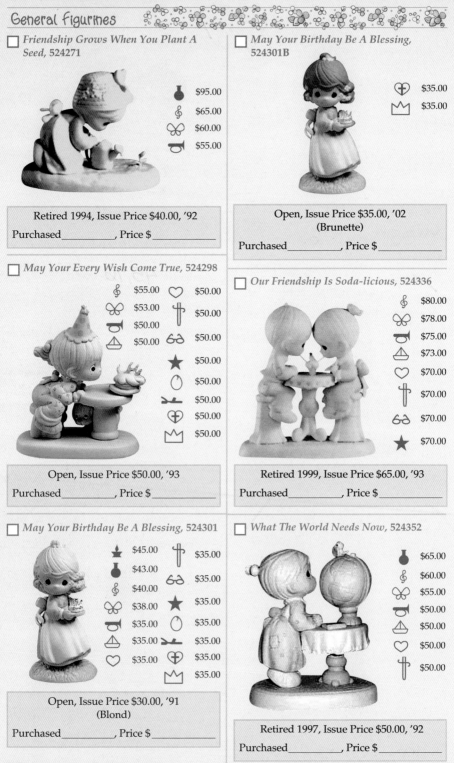

☐ *Friendship Grows When You Plant A Seed, 524271*

🏺 $95.00
🎼 $65.00
🦋 $60.00
📯 $55.00

Retired 1994, Issue Price $40.00, '92

Purchased_____, Price $_____

☐ *May Your Birthday Be A Blessing, 524301B*

🕈 $35.00
👑 $35.00

Open, Issue Price $35.00, '02
(Brunette)

Purchased_____, Price $_____

☐ *May Your Every Wish Come True, 524298*

🎼 $55.00 ♡ $50.00
🦋 $53.00 ✝ $50.00
📯 $50.00
⛵ $50.00 👓 $50.00
         ★ $50.00
         ◯ $50.00
         ⤙ $50.00
         🕈 $50.00
         👑 $50.00

Open, Issue Price $50.00, '93

Purchased_____, Price $_____

☐ *Our Friendship Is Soda-licious, 524336*

🎼 $80.00
🦋 $78.00
📯 $75.00
⛵ $73.00
♡ $70.00
✝ $70.00
👓 $70.00
★ $70.00

Retired 1999, Issue Price $65.00, '93

Purchased_____, Price $_____

☐ *May Your Birthday Be A Blessing, 524301*

⚘ $45.00   ✝ $35.00
🏺 $43.00   👓 $35.00
🎼 $40.00
🦋 $38.00   ★ $35.00
📯 $35.00   ◯ $35.00
⛵ $35.00   ⤙ $35.00
♡ $35.00   🕈 $35.00
           👑 $35.00

Open, Issue Price $30.00, '91
(Blond)

Purchased_____, Price $_____

☐ *What The World Needs Now, 524352*

🏺 $65.00
🎼 $60.00
🦋 $55.00
📯 $50.00
⛵ $50.00
♡ $50.00
✝ $50.00

Retired 1997, Issue Price $50.00, '92

Purchased_____, Price $_____

Something Precious From Above, 524360

Symbol	Price
♡	$55.00
✝	$55.00
👓	$55.00
★	$55.00
◖	$55.00
✕	$55.00
⊕	$55.00
♕	$55.00

Open, Issue Price $50.00, '97

Purchased_____, Price $_____

You Are Such A Purr-fect Friend, 524395

Symbol	Price	Symbol	Price
𝄞	$45.00	✝	$35.00
✾	$43.00	👓	$35.00
☭	$40.00	★	$35.00
△	$38.00	◖	$35.00
♡	$35.00	✕	$35.00
		⊕	$35.00
		♕	$35.00

Open, Issue Price $35.00, '93

Purchased_____, Price $_____

So Glad I Picked You As A Friend, 524379

Symbol	Price
✾	$45.00
☭	$45.00

Annual 1994, Issue Price $40.00, '94
DSR Spring Catalog Exclusive

Purchased_____, Price $_____

Be Fruitful And Multiply, 524409

Symbol	Price
★	$50.00
◖	$50.00
✕	$50.00
⊕	$50.00
♕	$50.00

Open, Issue Price $50.00, '99

Purchased_____, Price $_____

Take Time To Smell The Flowers, 524387

Symbol	Price
☭	$40.00
△	$40.00

Annual 1995, Issue Price $30.00, '95
Easter Seals Commemorative,
Lily Understamp

Purchased_____, Price $_____

May Only Good Things Come Your Way, 524425

Symbol	Price	Symbol	Price
♟	$50.00	✾	$43.00
♟	$48.00	☭	$40.00
𝄞	$45.00	△	$40.00
		♡	$40.00
		✝	$40.00
		👓	$40.00

Retired 1998, Issue Price $30.00, '91

Purchased_____, Price $_____

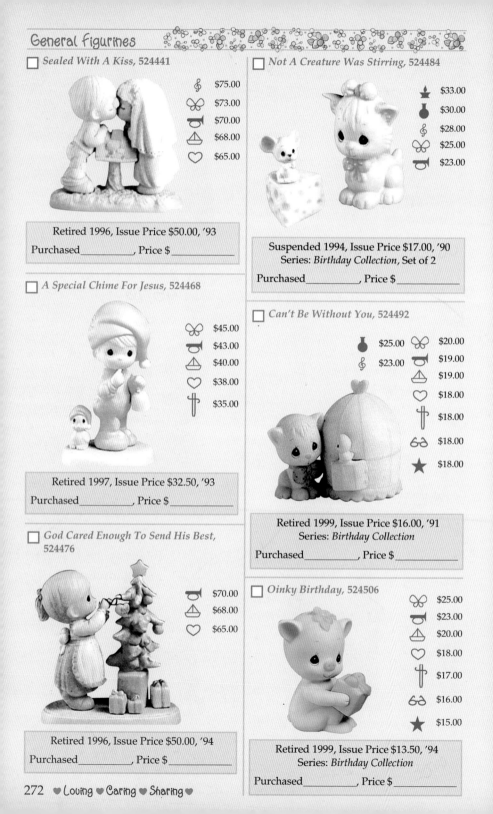

☐ *Sealed With A Kiss, 524441*

𝄞	$75.00
✖	$73.00
◁|	$70.00
△	$68.00
♡	$65.00

Retired 1996, Issue Price $50.00, '93

Purchased_____, Price $_____

☐ *A Special Chime For Jesus, 524468*

✖	$45.00
◁|	$43.00
△	$40.00
♡	$38.00
†	$35.00

Retired 1997, Issue Price $32.50, '93

Purchased_____, Price $_____

☐ *God Cared Enough To Send His Best, 524476*

◁|	$70.00
△	$68.00
♡	$65.00

Retired 1996, Issue Price $50.00, '94

Purchased_____, Price $_____

☐ *Not A Creature Was Stirring, 524484*

⚲	$33.00
◉	$30.00
𝄞	$28.00
✖	$25.00
◁|	$23.00

Suspended 1994, Issue Price $17.00, '90
Series: *Birthday Collection*, Set of 2

Purchased_____, Price $_____

☐ *Can't Be Without You, 524492*

◉	$25.00	✖	$20.00
𝄞	$23.00	◁|	$19.00
		△	$19.00
		♡	$18.00
		†	$18.00
		👓	$18.00
		★	$18.00

Retired 1999, Issue Price $16.00, '91
Series: *Birthday Collection*

Purchased_____, Price $_____

☐ *Oinky Birthday, 524506*

✖	$25.00
◁|	$23.00
△	$20.00
♡	$18.00
†	$17.00
👓	$16.00
★	$15.00

Retired 1999, Issue Price $13.50, '94
Series: *Birthday Collection*

Purchased_____, Price $_____

☑ *Always In His Care*, 524522

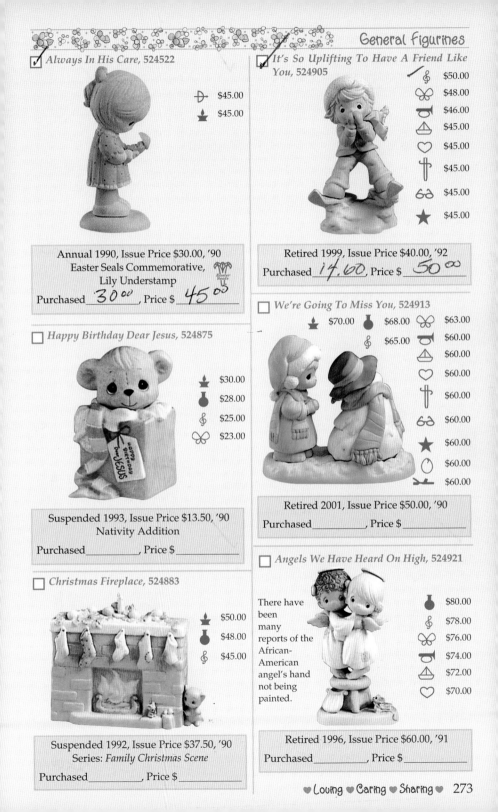

⊅ $45.00
🕯 $45.00

Annual 1990, Issue Price $30.00, '90
Easter Seals Commemorative,
Lily Understamp
Purchased __30⁰⁰__, Price $ __45⁰⁰__

☐ *Happy Birthday Dear Jesus*, 524875

🕯 $30.00
🍶 $28.00
𝄞 $25.00
🦋 $23.00

Suspended 1993, Issue Price $13.50, '90
Nativity Addition
Purchased _____, Price $ _____

☐ *Christmas Fireplace*, 524883

🕯 $50.00
🍶 $48.00
𝄞 $45.00

Suspended 1992, Issue Price $37.50, '90
Series: *Family Christmas Scene*
Purchased _____, Price $ _____

☑ *It's So Uplifting To Have A Friend Like You*, 524905

𝄞 $50.00
🦋 $48.00
🗝 $46.00
△ $45.00
♡ $45.00
✝ $45.00
🔗 $45.00
★ $45.00

Retired 1999, Issue Price $40.00, '92
Purchased __14.60__, Price $ __50⁰⁰__

☐ *We're Going To Miss You*, 524913

★ $70.00   🍶 $68.00   🦋 $63.00
          𝄞 $65.00   🗝 $60.00
          △ $60.00
          ♡ $60.00
          ✝ $60.00
          🔗 $60.00
          ★ $60.00
          ○ $60.00
          ⚓ $60.00

Retired 2001, Issue Price $50.00, '90
Purchased _____, Price $ _____

☐ *Angels We Have Heard On High*, 524921

There have been many reports of the African-American angel's hand not being painted.

🍶 $80.00
𝄞 $78.00
🦋 $76.00
🗝 $74.00
△ $72.00
♡ $70.00

Retired 1996, Issue Price $60.00, '91
Purchased _____, Price $ _____

Good Friends Are Forever, 525049

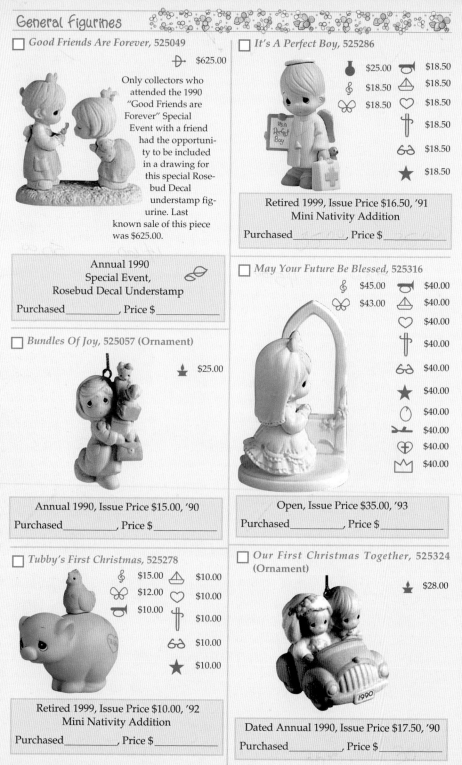

⌐ $625.00

Only collectors who attended the 1990 "Good Friends are Forever" Special Event with a friend had the opportunity to be included in a drawing for this special Rosebud Decal understamp figurine. Last known sale of this piece was $625.00.

Annual 1990 Special Event, Rosebud Decal Understamp
Purchased_____, Price $_____

Bundles Of Joy, 525057 (Ornament)

🕯 $25.00

Annual 1990, Issue Price $15.00, '90
Purchased_____, Price $_____

Tubby's First Christmas, 525278

𝄞 $15.00	△ $10.00
✻ $12.00	♡ $10.00
◡ $10.00	✝ $10.00
	👓 $10.00
	★ $10.00

Retired 1999, Issue Price $10.00, '92 Mini Nativity Addition
Purchased_____, Price $_____

It's A Perfect Boy, 525286

🏺 $25.00	📯 $18.50
𝄞 $18.50	△ $18.50
✻ $18.50	♡ $18.50
	✝ $18.50
	👓 $18.50
	★ $18.50

Retired 1999, Issue Price $16.50, '91 Mini Nativity Addition
Purchased_____, Price $_____

May Your Future Be Blessed, 525316

𝄞 $45.00	📯 $40.00
✻ $43.00	△ $40.00
	♡ $40.00
	✝ $40.00
	👓 $40.00
	★ $40.00
	◐ $40.00
	⤫ $40.00
	⊕ $40.00
	♔ $40.00

Open, Issue Price $35.00, '93
Purchased_____, Price $_____

Our First Christmas Together, 525324 (Ornament)

🕯 $28.00

Dated Annual 1990, Issue Price $17.50, '90
Purchased_____, Price $_____

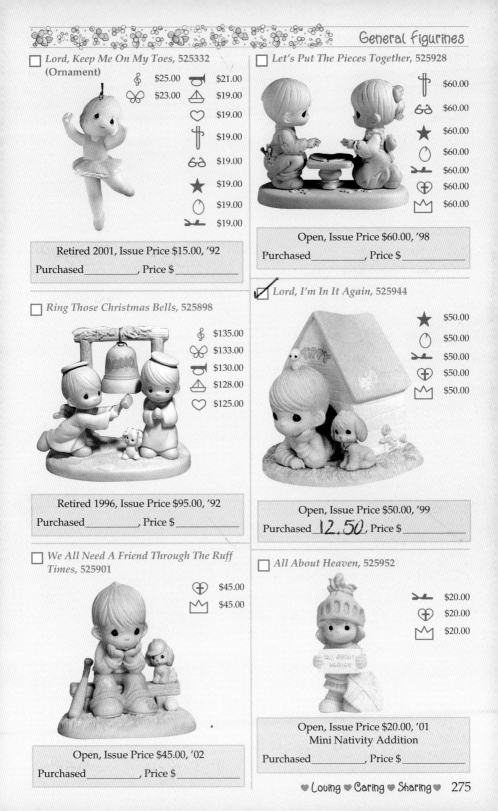

☐ *Lord, Keep Me On My Toes, 525332*
(Ornament)

🎷	$25.00	🎺	$21.00
🦋	$23.00	⛵	$19.00
		♡	$19.00
		✝	$19.00
		👓	$19.00
		★	$19.00
		◯	$19.00
		⤳	$19.00

Retired 2001, Issue Price $15.00, '92
Purchased_____, Price $_____

☐ *Ring Those Christmas Bells, 525898*

🎷	$135.00
🦋	$133.00
🎺	$130.00
⛵	$128.00
♡	$125.00

Retired 1996, Issue Price $95.00, '92
Purchased_____, Price $_____

☐ *We All Need A Friend Through The Ruff Times, 525901*

✠	$45.00
👑	$45.00

Open, Issue Price $45.00, '02
Purchased_____, Price $_____

☐ *Let's Put The Pieces Together, 525928*

✝	$60.00
👓	$60.00
★	$60.00
◯	$60.00
⤳	$60.00
✠	$60.00
👑	$60.00

Open, Issue Price $60.00, '98
Purchased_____, Price $_____

☑ *Lord, I'm In It Again, 525944*

★	$50.00
◯	$50.00
⤳	$50.00
✠	$50.00
👑	$50.00

Open, Issue Price $50.00, '99
Purchased _12.50_, Price $_____

☐ *All About Heaven, 525952*

⤳	$20.00
✠	$20.00
👑	$20.00

Open, Issue Price $20.00, '01
Mini Nativity Addition
Purchased_____, Price $_____

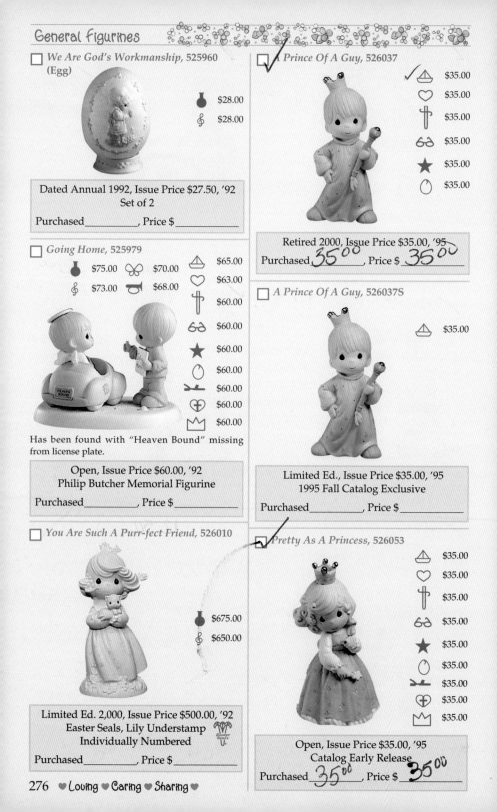

We Are God's Workmanship, 525960
(Egg)

🏺 $28.00

🎼 $28.00

Dated Annual 1992, Issue Price $27.50, '92
Set of 2
Purchased_____, Price $_____

Going Home, 525979

🏺 $75.00   🦋 $70.00   ⛵ $65.00
🎼 $73.00   🎺 $68.00   ♡ $63.00
                          ✝ $60.00
                          👓 $60.00
                          ★ $60.00
                          ◯ $60.00
                          ⟖ $60.00
                          ⊕ $60.00
                          ♛ $60.00

Has been found with "Heaven Bound" missing
from license plate.

Open, Issue Price $60.00, '92
Philip Butcher Memorial Figurine
Purchased_____, Price $_____

You Are Such A Purr-fect Friend, 526010

🏺 $675.00
🎼 $650.00

Limited Ed. 2,000, Issue Price $500.00, '92
Easter Seals, Lily Understamp
Individually Numbered
Purchased_____, Price $_____

A Prince Of A Guy, 526037

✓⛵ $35.00
♡ $35.00
✝ $35.00
👓 $35.00
★ $35.00
◯ $35.00

Retired 2000, Issue Price $35.00, '95
Purchased 35⁰⁰, Price $ 35⁰⁰

A Prince Of A Guy, 526037S

⛵ $35.00

Limited Ed., Issue Price $35.00, '95
1995 Fall Catalog Exclusive
Purchased_____, Price $_____

Pretty As A Princess, 526053

⛵ $35.00
♡ $35.00
✝ $35.00
👓 $35.00
★ $35.00
◯ $35.00
⟖ $35.00
⊕ $35.00
♛ $35.00

Open, Issue Price $35.00, '95
Catalog Early Release
Purchased 35⁰⁰, Price $ 35⁰⁰

☐ *The Pearl Of Great Price*, 526061

✝ $63.00

Annual 1997, Issue Price $50.00, '97
Century Circle Event Exclusive

Purchased_____, Price $_____

☑ *I'm Completely Suspended With Love*, 526096

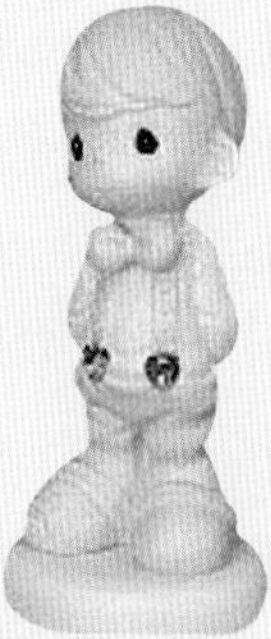

✓ 🪰 $23.00

Annual 2001, Issue Price $23.00, '01
Purchased *G*, Price $ *23 ⁰⁰*

☐ *I'm Completely Suspended With Love*, 526096S

🪰 $28.50

Comes with crystal heart-shaped box.

Annual 2001, Issue Price $28.50, '01
Purchased●_____, Price $_____

☐ *I Would Be Lost Without You*, 526142

🏺 $30.00		🦋 $30.00
𝄞 $30.00		◁	$30.00
		◁ $30.00
		♡ $30.00
		✝ $30.00
		👓 $30.00
		★ $30.00

Retired 1999, Issue Price $27.50, '92

Purchased_____, Price $_____

☐ *Friends To The Very End*, 526150

🦋	$68.00
◁|	$65.00
◁	$63.00
♡	$60.00
✝	$58.00

Retired 1997, Issue Price $40.00, '94

Purchased_____, Price $_____

☐ *You Are My Happiness*, 526185

🏺	$70.00
𝄞	$68.00

Annual 1992, Issue Price $37.50, '92

Purchased_____, Price $_____

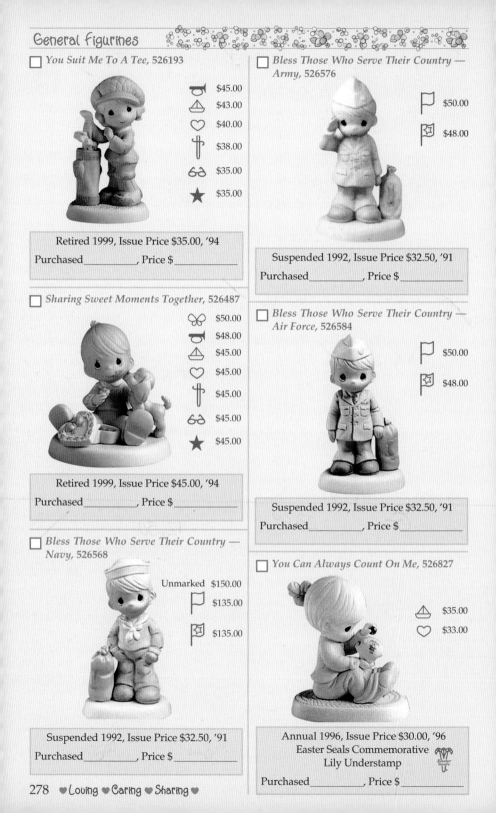

☐ *You Suit Me To A Tee*, 526193

𝄞	$45.00
△	$43.00
♡	$40.00
†	$38.00
👓	$35.00
★	$35.00

Retired 1999, Issue Price $35.00, '94

Purchased_____, Price $_____

☐ *Sharing Sweet Moments Together*, 526487

✿	$50.00
𝄞	$48.00
△	$45.00
♡	$45.00
†	$45.00
👓	$45.00
★	$45.00

Retired 1999, Issue Price $45.00, '94

Purchased_____, Price $_____

☐ *Bless Those Who Serve Their Country — Navy*, 526568

Unmarked	$150.00
⚑	$135.00
⚐	$135.00

Suspended 1992, Issue Price $32.50, '91

Purchased_____, Price $_____

☐ *Bless Those Who Serve Their Country — Army*, 526576

⚑	$50.00
⚐	$48.00

Suspended 1992, Issue Price $32.50, '91

Purchased_____, Price $_____

☐ *Bless Those Who Serve Their Country — Air Force*, 526584

⚑	$50.00
⚐	$48.00

Suspended 1992, Issue Price $32.50, '91

Purchased_____, Price $_____

☐ *You Can Always Count On Me*, 526827

△	$35.00
♡	$33.00

Annual 1996, Issue Price $30.00, '96
Easter Seals Commemorative
Lily Understamp

Purchased_____, Price $_____

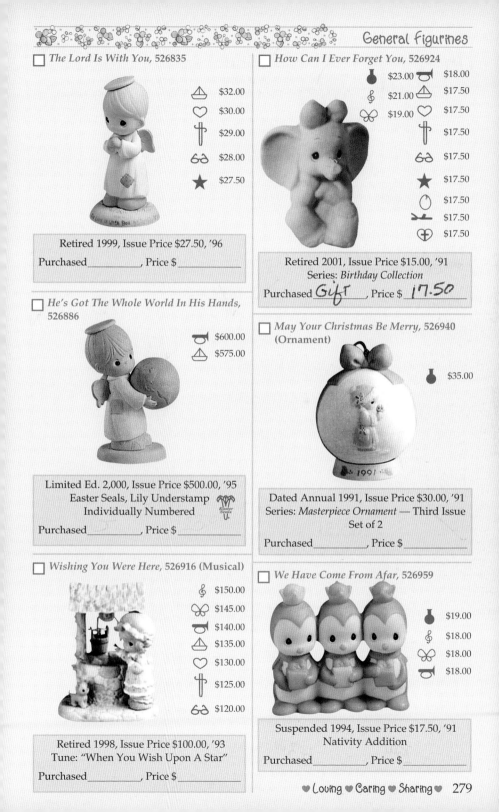

☐ *The Lord Is With You, 526835*

⛵ $32.00
♡ $30.00
✝ $29.00
👓 $28.00
★ $27.50

Retired 1999, Issue Price $27.50, '96

Purchased_____, Price $_____

☐ *He's Got The Whole World In His Hands,*
526886

📯 $600.00
⛵ $575.00

Limited Ed. 2,000, Issue Price $500.00, '95
Easter Seals, Lily Understamp
Individually Numbered

Purchased_____, Price $_____

☐ *Wishing You Were Here, 526916* (Musical)

𝄞 $150.00
🦋 $145.00
📯 $140.00
⛵ $135.00
♡ $130.00
✝ $125.00
👓 $120.00

Retired 1998, Issue Price $100.00, '93
Tune: "When You Wish Upon A Star"

Purchased_____, Price $_____

☐ *How Can I Ever Forget You, 526924*

🔔 $23.00   📯 $18.00
𝄞 $21.00   ⛵ $17.50
🦋 $19.00   ♡ $17.50
✝ $17.50
👓 $17.50
★ $17.50
🥚 $17.50
✂ $17.50
✝ $17.50

Retired 2001, Issue Price $15.00, '91
Series: *Birthday Collection*

Purchased Gift , Price $ 17.50

☐ *May Your Christmas Be Merry, 526940*
(Ornament)

🔔 $35.00

Dated Annual 1991, Issue Price $30.00, '91
Series: *Masterpiece Ornament* — Third Issue
Set of 2

Purchased_____, Price $_____

☐ *We Have Come From Afar, 526959*

🔔 $19.00
𝄞 $18.00
🦋 $18.00
📯 $18.00

Suspended 1994, Issue Price $17.50, '91
Nativity Addition

Purchased_____, Price $_____

♥ Loving ♥ Caring ♥ Sharing ♥   279

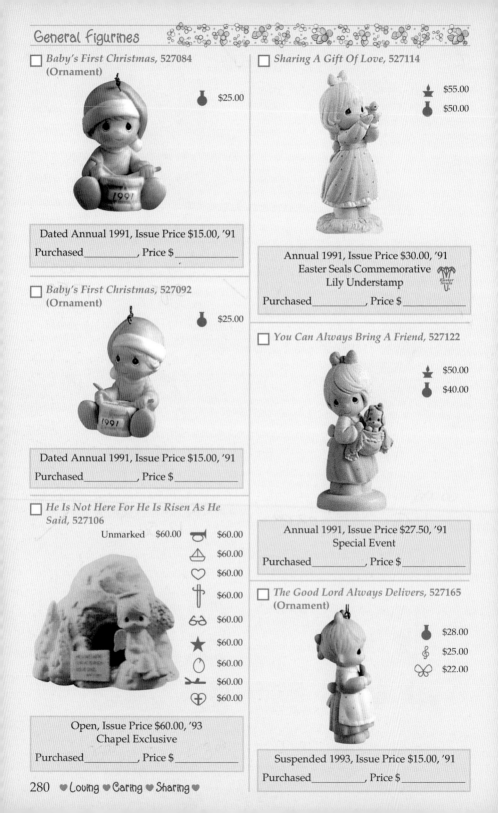

☐ *Baby's First Christmas*, 527084
(Ornament)

🏺 $25.00

Dated Annual 1991, Issue Price $15.00, '91

Purchased_____, Price $_____

☐ *Baby's First Christmas*, 527092
(Ornament)

🏺 $25.00

Dated Annual 1991, Issue Price $15.00, '91

Purchased_____, Price $_____

☐ *He Is Not Here For He Is Risen As He Said*, 527106

Unmarked $60.00

🎺 $60.00
⛵ $60.00
♡ $60.00
✝ $60.00
👓 $60.00
★ $60.00
◯ $60.00
⤸ $60.00
✛ $60.00

Open, Issue Price $60.00, '93
Chapel Exclusive

Purchased_____, Price $_____

280   ♥ Loving ♥ Caring ♥ Sharing ♥

☐ *Sharing A Gift Of Love*, 527114

🏵 $55.00
🏺 $50.00

Annual 1991, Issue Price $30.00, '91
Easter Seals Commemorative
Lily Understamp

Purchased_____, Price $_____

☐ *You Can Always Bring A Friend*, 527122

🏵 $50.00
🏺 $40.00

Annual 1991, Issue Price $27.50, '91
Special Event

Purchased_____, Price $_____

☐ *The Good Lord Always Delivers*, 527165
(Ornament)

🏺 $28.00
🎵 $25.00
🦋 $22.00

Suspended 1993, Issue Price $15.00, '91

Purchased_____, Price $_____

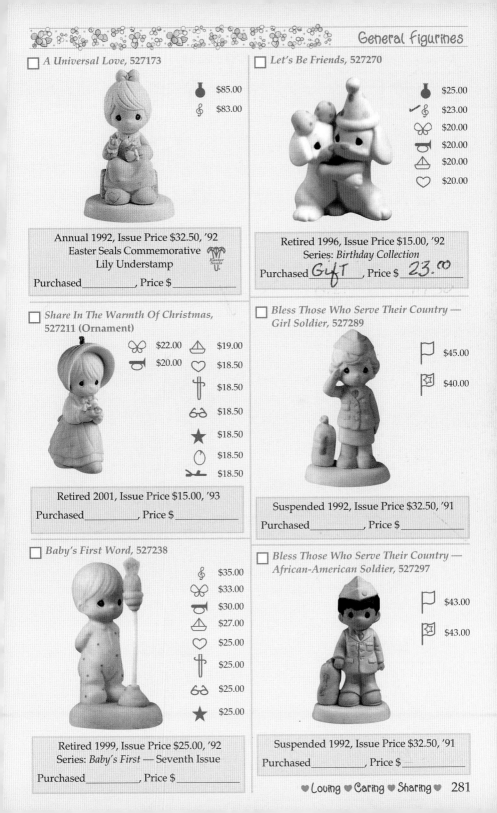

A Universal Love, 527173

🏺 $85.00
🎼 $83.00

Annual 1992, Issue Price $32.50, '92
Easter Seals Commemorative
Lily Understamp
Purchased_____, Price $ _____

Let's Be Friends, 527270

🏺 $25.00
✔🎼 $23.00
🦋 $20.00
🎺 $20.00
⛵ $20.00
♡ $20.00

Retired 1996, Issue Price $15.00, '92
Series: *Birthday Collection*
Purchased *Gift*, Price $ *23.00*

Share In The Warmth Of Christmas, 527211 (Ornament)

🦋 $22.00   ⛵ $19.00
🎺 $20.00   ♡ $18.50
           ✝ $18.50
           👓 $18.50
           ★ $18.50
           ○ $18.50
           ⤜ $18.50

Retired 2001, Issue Price $15.00, '93
Purchased_____, Price $ _____

Bless Those Who Serve Their Country — Girl Soldier, 527289

🚩 $45.00
🏴 $40.00

Suspended 1992, Issue Price $32.50, '91
Purchased_____, Price $ _____

Baby's First Word, 527238

🎼 $35.00
🦋 $33.00
🎺 $30.00
⛵ $27.00
♡ $25.00
✝ $25.00
👓 $25.00
★ $25.00

Retired 1999, Issue Price $25.00, '92
Series: *Baby's First* — Seventh Issue
Purchased_____, Price $ _____

Bless Those Who Serve Their Country — African-American Soldier, 527297

🚩 $43.00
🏴 $43.00

Suspended 1992, Issue Price $32.50, '91
Purchased_____, Price $ _____

☐ *An Event Worth Wading For*, 527319

🏺 $45.00
🎵 $43.00

Annual 1992, Issue Price $32.50, '92
Special Event

Purchased_____, Price $_____

☐ *Onward Christmas Soldiers*, 527327
(Ornament)

📯 $22.00   ♡ $19.00
⚖ $20.00   ✝ $18.50
　　　　　　👓 $18.50
　　　　　　★ $18.50
　　　　　　◯ $18.50
　　　　　　⤸ $18.50

Retired 2001, Issue Price $16.00, '94

Purchased_____, Price $_____

☑ *Bless-um You*, 527335

🎵 $45.00
✗ 🦋 $43.00
⚖ $40.00
⛵ $37.00
♡ $35.00
✝ $35.00
👓 $35.00

Retired 1998, Issue Price $35.00, '93

Purchased *25⁰⁰*, Price $ *43⁰⁰*

☐ *Happy Birdie*, 527343

🎵 $25.00
🦋 $22.00
📯 $20.00
⛵ $18.00
♡ $17.50

Suspended 1996, Issue Price $16.00, '92
Series: *Birthday Collection*

Purchased_____, Price $_____

☐ *You Are My Favorite Star*, 527378

🎵 $85.00
🦋 $83.00
📯 $80.00
⛵ $78.00
♡ $75.00
✝ $73.00

Retired 1997, Issue Price $60.00, '92

Purchased_____, Price $_____

☐ *Baby's First Christmas (Girl)*, 527475
(Ornament)

🎵 $25.00

Dated Annual 1992, Issue Price $15.00, '92

Purchased_____, Price $_____

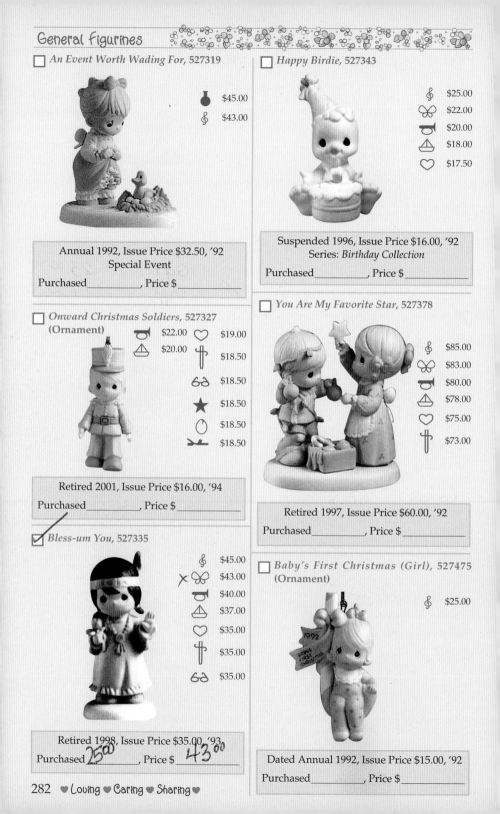

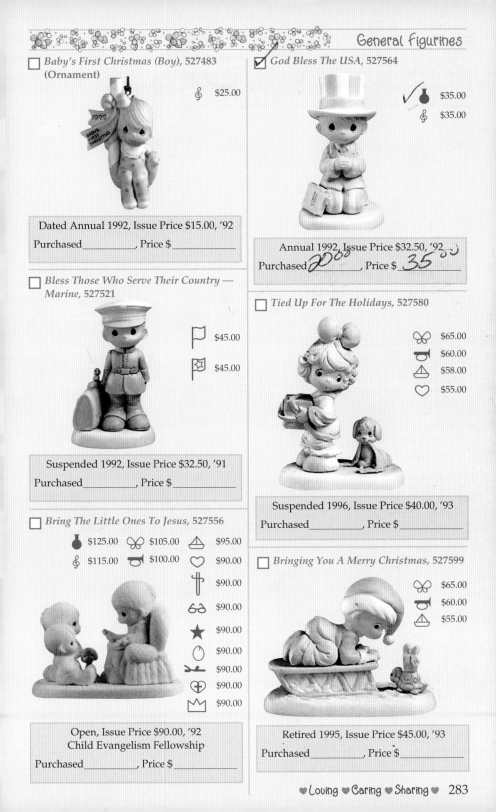

☐ *Baby's First Christmas (Boy)*, 527483
(Ornament)

🎼 $25.00

Dated Annual 1992, Issue Price $15.00, '92

Purchased_____, Price $_____

☐ *Bless Those Who Serve Their Country —*
Marine, 527521

⚑ $45.00

⚑ $45.00

Suspended 1992, Issue Price $32.50, '91

Purchased_____, Price $_____

☐ *Bring The Little Ones To Jesus*, 527556

🍼 $125.00 🦋 $105.00 ⛵ $95.00
🎼 $115.00 🐚 $100.00 ♡ $90.00
                              ✝ $90.00
                          👓 $90.00
                           ★ $90.00
                           🥚 $90.00
                          ⌇ $90.00
                          ⊕ $90.00
                          👑 $90.00

Open, Issue Price $90.00, '92
Child Evangelism Fellowship

Purchased_____, Price $_____

☑ *God Bless The USA*, 527564

✓ 🍼 $35.00

🎼 $35.00

Annual 1992, Issue Price $32.50, '92

Purchased *2008*, Price $ *35⁰⁰*

☐ *Tied Up For The Holidays*, 527580

🦋 $65.00
🐚 $60.00
⛵ $58.00
♡ $55.00

Suspended 1996, Issue Price $40.00, '93

Purchased_____, Price $_____

☐ *Bringing You A Merry Christmas*, 527599

🦋 $65.00
🐚 $60.00
⛵ $55.00

Retired 1995, Issue Price $45.00, '93

Purchased_____, Price $_____

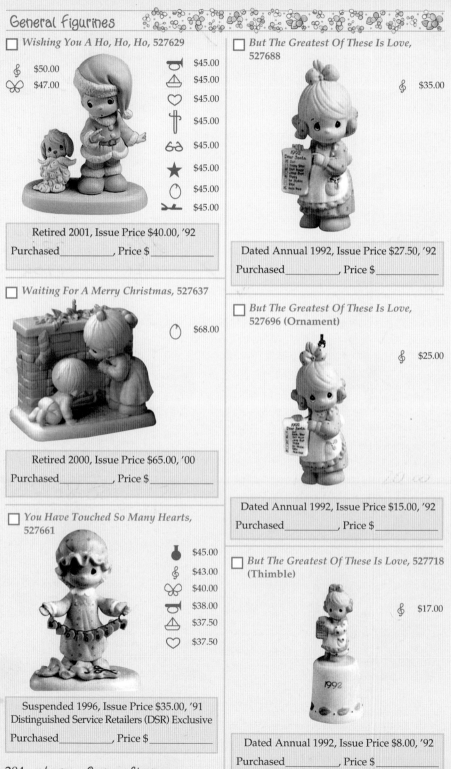

☐ *Wishing You A Ho, Ho, Ho, 527629*

℘ $50.00
⊗ $47.00

🎺 $45.00
△ $45.00
♡ $45.00
✝ $45.00
6∂ $45.00
★ $45.00
◯ $45.00
⤙ $45.00

Retired 2001, Issue Price $40.00, '92

Purchased_____, Price $_____

☐ *Waiting For A Merry Christmas, 527637*

◯ $68.00

Retired 2000, Issue Price $65.00, '00

Purchased_____, Price $_____

☐ *You Have Touched So Many Hearts,*
527661

🔔 $45.00
℘ $43.00
⊗ $40.00
🎺 $38.00
△ $37.50
♡ $37.50

Suspended 1996, Issue Price $35.00, '91
Distinguished Service Retailers (DSR) Exclusive

Purchased_____, Price $_____

☐ *But The Greatest Of These Is Love,*
527688

℘ $35.00

Dated Annual 1992, Issue Price $27.50, '92

Purchased_____, Price $_____

☐ *But The Greatest Of These Is Love,*
527696 (Ornament)

℘ $25.00

Dated Annual 1992, Issue Price $15.00, '92

Purchased_____, Price $_____

☐ *But The Greatest Of These Is Love, 527718*
(Thimble)

℘ $17.00

Dated Annual 1992, Issue Price $8.00, '92

Purchased_____, Price $_____

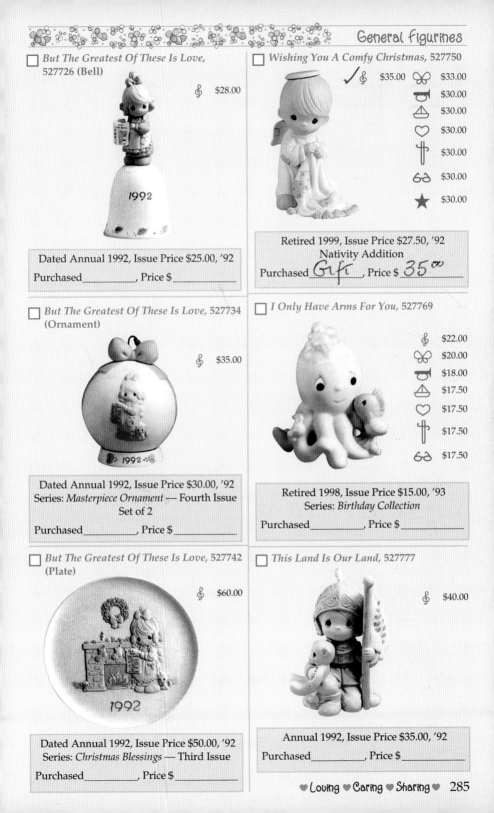

☐ *But The Greatest Of These Is Love,* 527726 (Bell)

🎵 $28.00

1992

Dated Annual 1992, Issue Price $25.00, '92

Purchased_____, Price $_____

☐ *Wishing You A Comfy Christmas,* 527750

✓ 🎵 $35.00 ✖ $33.00
🎺 $30.00
△ $30.00
♡ $30.00
✝ $30.00
👓 $30.00
★ $30.00

Retired 1999, Issue Price $27.50, '92
Nativity Addition

Purchased _Gift_ , Price $ _35.00_

☐ *But The Greatest Of These Is Love,* 527734 (Ornament)

🎵 $35.00

1992

Dated Annual 1992, Issue Price $30.00, '92
Series: *Masterpiece Ornament* — Fourth Issue
Set of 2

Purchased_____, Price $_____

☐ *I Only Have Arms For You,* 527769

🎵 $22.00
✖ $20.00
🎺 $18.00
△ $17.50
♡ $17.50
✝ $17.50
👓 $17.50

Retired 1998, Issue Price $15.00, '93
Series: *Birthday Collection*

Purchased_____, Price $_____

☐ *But The Greatest Of These Is Love,* 527742 (Plate)

🎵 $60.00

1992

Dated Annual 1992, Issue Price $50.00, '92
Series: *Christmas Blessings* — Third Issue

Purchased_____, Price $_____

☐ *This Land Is Our Land,* 527777

🎵 $40.00

Annual 1992, Issue Price $35.00, '92

Purchased_____, Price $_____

☐ *There's A Christian Welcome Here,* 528021 (Ornament)

Unmarked	$28.00
✗	$25.00
♡	$22.50
✝	$22.50

Suspended 1997, Issue Price $22.50, '92
Chapel Exclusive

Purchased_____, Price $_____

☐ *Free Christmas Puppies,* 528064

◁	$35.00
△	$32.00
♡	$30.00
✝	$28.00

Retired 1997, Issue Price $12.50, '94
Series: *Sugar Town*

Purchased_____, Price $_____

☐ *Nativity Cart,* 528072

◁	$20.00
△	$20.00
♡	$18.50
✝	$18.50
6∂	$18.50
★	$18.50
◯	$18.50
≻	$18.50

Retired 2001, Issue Price $18.50, '94
Nativity Addition

Purchased_____, Price $_____

☐ *Follow Your Heart,* 528080

◁	$38.00
△	$30.00

There have been reports of the decal being on backwards.

Annual 1995, Issue Price $30.00, '95
Spring Celebration Event

Purchased_____, Price $_____

☑ *Markie,* 528099

✗	$22.00
✓ ◁	$20.00

Suspended 1996, Issue Price $18.50, '94
Series: *Sammy's Circus*

Purchased 18.50, Price $ 20.00

☐ *He Came As The Gift Of God's Love,* 528129

★	$30.00	≻	$30.00
◯	$30.00	⊕	$30.00
		♛	$30.00

Open, Issue Price $30.00, '99
Nativity, Set Of 4

Purchased_____, Price $_____

☐ *Have I Got News For You*, 528137

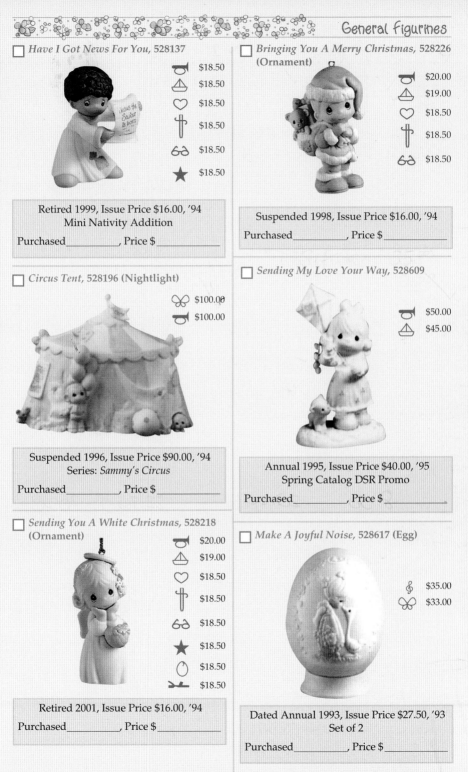

🎺 $18.50
⛵ $18.50
♡ $18.50
✝ $18.50
👓 $18.50
★ $18.50

Retired 1999, Issue Price $16.00, '94
Mini Nativity Addition

Purchased_____, Price $_____

☐ *Bringing You A Merry Christmas*, 528226
(Ornament)

🎺 $20.00
⛵ $19.00
♡ $18.50
✝ $18.50
👓 $18.50

Suspended 1998, Issue Price $16.00, '94

Purchased_____, Price $_____

☐ *Circus Tent*, 528196 (Nightlight)

🦋 $100.00
🎺 $100.00

Suspended 1996, Issue Price $90.00, '94
Series: *Sammy's Circus*

Purchased_____, Price $_____

☐ *Sending My Love Your Way*, 528609

🎺 $50.00
⛵ $45.00

Annual 1995, Issue Price $40.00, '95
Spring Catalog DSR Promo

Purchased_____, Price $_____

☐ *Sending You A White Christmas*, 528218
(Ornament)

🎺 $20.00
⛵ $19.00
♡ $18.50
✝ $18.50
👓 $18.50
★ $18.50
○ $18.50
⊱ $18.50

Retired 2001, Issue Price $16.00, '94

Purchased_____, Price $_____

☐ *Make A Joyful Noise*, 528617 (Egg)

𝄞 $35.00
🦋 $33.00

Dated Annual 1993, Issue Price $27.50, '93
Set of 2

Purchased_____, Price $_____

☐ *To A Very Special Sister, 528633*

🎺 $65.00   ♡ $65.00

⛵ $65.00   ♱ $65.00

      👓 $65.00

      ★ $65.00

      ◐ $65.00

      ⤢ $65.00

      ⊕ $65.00

      ♛ $65.00

Open, Issue Price $60.00, '94

Purchased_____, Price $_____

☑ *Sammy, 528668*

🦋 $25.00

🎺 $22.00

⛵ $20.00

♡ $18.00

♱ $17.00

Retired 1997, Issue Price $17.00, '93
Series: *Sugar Town*

Purchased *8.50*, Price $ *20.00*

☐ *Evergreen Tree, 528684*

🎼 $30.00

🦋 $28.00

🎺 $25.00

Retired 1994, Issue Price $15.00, '92
Series: *Sugar Town*

Purchased_____, Price $_____

☐ *It's So Uplifting To Have A Friend Like You, 528846 (Ornament)*

🦋 $22.00

🎺 $20.00

⛵ $19.00

♡ $18.50

♱ $18.50

👓 $18.50

★ $18.50

Retired 1999, Issue Price $16.00, '93

Purchased_____, Price $_____

☐ *America, You're Beautiful, 528862*

🎼 $55.00

🦋 $45.00

Annual 1993, Issue Price $35.00, '93
National Day Of Prayer

Purchased_____, Price $_____

☐ *America, You're Beautiful, 528862R*

⤢ $35.00

⊕ $35.00

♛ $35.00

A portion of the proceeds from the sales of this figurine will benefit the September 11th Relief Fund.

Open, Issue Price $35.00, '01

Purchased_____, Price $_____

☐ *Our First Christmas Together*, 528870 (Ornament)

🎼 $22.00

Dated Annual 1992, Issue Price $17.50, '92
Purchased_____, Price $_____

☐ *A Reflection Of His Love*, 529095 (Egg)

🦋 $29.00
♪ $28.00

Dated Annual 1994, Issue Price $27.50, '94
Series: *Annual Eggs* — Fourth & Final Issue
Purchased_____, Price $_____

☐ *Friends Never Drift Apart*, 529079 (Medallion)

🦋 $700.00

Dated Annual 1993, Gift, '93
Fifteenth Anniversary Cruise Piece
Purchased_____, Price $_____

☐ *Jordan*, 529168

⛵ $25.00

Suspended 1996, Issue Price $20.00, '95
Series: *Sammy's Circus*, Set Of 2
Purchased_____, Price $_____

☐ *15 Years, Tweet Music Together*, 529087 (Medallion)

🦋 $75.00

Dated Annual 1993, Gift, '93
Fifteenth Anniversary Convention
Purchased_____, Price $_____

☐ *Dusty*, 529176

🦋 $25.00
♪ $25.00

Suspended 1996, Issue Price $22.50, '94
Series: *Sammy's Circus*
Purchased_____, Price $_____

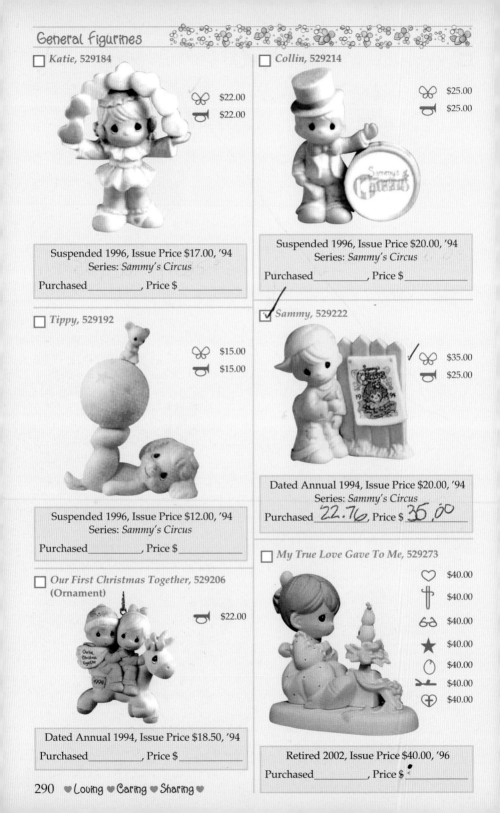

☐ *Katie*, 529184

$22.00
$22.00

Suspended 1996, Issue Price $17.00, '94
Series: *Sammy's Circus*

Purchased_____, Price $_____

☐ *Collin*, 529214

$25.00
$25.00

Suspended 1996, Issue Price $20.00, '94
Series: *Sammy's Circus*

Purchased_____, Price $_____

☐ *Tippy*, 529192

$15.00
$15.00

Suspended 1996, Issue Price $12.00, '94
Series: *Sammy's Circus*

Purchased_____, Price $_____

☑ *Sammy*, 529222

$35.00
$25.00

Dated Annual 1994, Issue Price $20.00, '94
Series: *Sammy's Circus*

Purchased 22.76, Price $ 35.00

☐ *Our First Christmas Together*, 529206
(Ornament)

$22.00

Dated Annual 1994, Issue Price $18.50, '94

Purchased_____, Price $_____

☐ *My True Love Gave To Me*, 529273

♡ $40.00
✝ $40.00
6♂ $40.00
★ $40.00
○ $40.00
⊁ $40.00
⊕ $40.00

Retired 2002, Issue Price $40.00, '96

Purchased_____, Price $_____

☑ Doctor's Office Set, 529281

✿ $225.00   ♡ $225.00

✓ ☐ $225.00   ✝ $225.00

Retired 1997, Issue Price $150.00, '94
Series: *Sugar Town*, Set of 7 (Doctor's
Office, Dr. Sam Sugar, Jan, Stork with Baby
Sam, Free Christmas Puppies, Leon and
Evelyn Mae, and Sugar And Her Doghouse)

Purchased **111.50**, Price $ **225.00**

☐ Dusty, 529435

✿ $33.00

△ $25.00

⊿ $23.00

♡ $20.00

✝ $17.00

Retired 1997, Issue Price $17.00, '93
Series: *Sugar Town*

Purchased_____, Price $_____

☑ Sam's Car, 529443

✓ ✿ $45.00

⊿ $40.00

△ $35.00

♡ $30.00

✝ $25.00

Retired 1997, Issue Price $22.50, '93
Series: *Sugar Town*

Purchased **25.51**, Price $ **45.00**

☐ Aunt Ruth & Aunt Dorothy, 529486

𝄞 $45.00

✿ $43.00

⊿ $40.00

Retired 1994, Issue Price $20.00, '92
Series: *Sugar Town*

Purchased_____, Price $_____

☐ Philip, 529494

𝄞 $35.00

✿ $32.00

⊿ $30.00

Retired 1994, Issue Price $17.00, '92
Series: *Sugar Town*

Purchased_____, Price $_____

☐ Nativity, 529508

𝄞 $60.00

✿ $55.00

⊿ $50.00

Retired 1994, Issue Price $20.00, '92
Series: *Sugar Town*

Purchased_____, Price $_____

☑ *Grandfather*, 529516

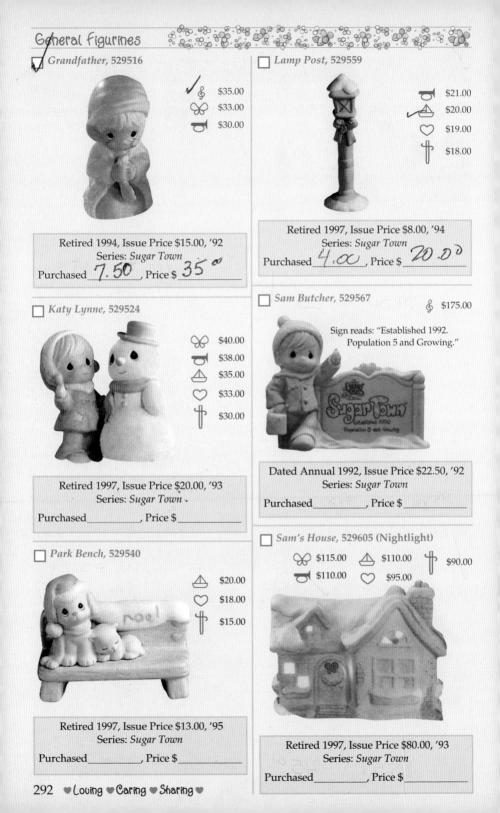

✓ 🎼 $35.00
🦋 $33.00
♩ $30.00

Retired 1994, Issue Price $15.00, '92
Series: *Sugar Town*
Purchased **7.50**, Price $ **35 ⁰⁰**

☐ *Katy Lynne*, 529524

🦋 $40.00
♩ $38.00
⛵ $35.00
♡ $33.00
✝ $30.00

Retired 1997, Issue Price $20.00, '93
Series: *Sugar Town* •
Purchased_____, Price $_____

☐ *Park Bench*, 529540

⛵ $20.00
♡ $18.00
✝ $15.00

Retired 1997, Issue Price $13.00, '95
Series: *Sugar Town*
Purchased_____, Price $_____

☐ *Lamp Post*, 529559

📯 $21.00
⛵ $20.00
♡ $19.00
✝ $18.00

Retired 1997, Issue Price $8.00, '94
Series: *Sugar Town*
Purchased **4.00**, Price $ **20.00**

☐ *Sam Butcher*, 529567

🎼 $175.00

Sign reads: "Established 1992.
Population 5 and Growing."

Dated Annual 1992, Issue Price $22.50, '92
Series: *Sugar Town*
Purchased_____, Price $_____

☐ *Sam's House*, 529605 (Nightlight)

🦋 $115.00   ⛵ $110.00   ✝ $90.00
📯 $110.00   ♡ $95.00

Retired 1997, Issue Price $80.00, '93
Series: *Sugar Town*
Purchased_____, Price $_____

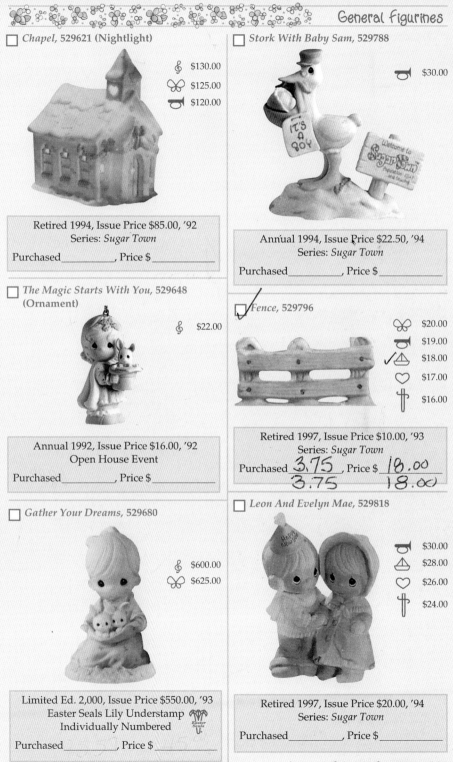

☐ *Chapel*, 529621 (Nightlight)

♪ $130.00
🦋 $125.00
📯 $120.00

Retired 1994, Issue Price $85.00, '92
Series: *Sugar Town*

Purchased_____, Price $_____

☐ *The Magic Starts With You*, 529648
(Ornament)

♪ $22.00

Annual 1992, Issue Price $16.00, '92
Open House Event

Purchased_____, Price $_____

☐ *Gather Your Dreams*, 529680

♪ $600.00
🦋 $625.00

Limited Ed. 2,000, Issue Price $550.00, '93
Easter Seals Lily Understamp
Individually Numbered

Purchased_____, Price $_____

☐ *Stork With Baby Sam*, 529788

📯 $30.00

Annual 1994, Issue Price $22.50, '94
Series: *Sugar Town*

Purchased_____, Price $_____

☑ *Fence*, 529796

🦋 $20.00
📯 $19.00
✓△ $18.00
♡ $17.00
✝ $16.00

Retired 1997, Issue Price $10.00, '93
Series: *Sugar Town*

Purchased 3.75 , Price $ 18.00
3.75   18.00

☐ *Leon And Evelyn Mae*, 529818

📯 $30.00
△ $28.00
♡ $26.00
✝ $24.00

Retired 1997, Issue Price $20.00, '94
Series: *Sugar Town*

Purchased_____, Price $_____

☐ *Jan*, 529826

⌐∂ $25.00
△ $22.00
♡ $20.00
♰ $18.00

Retired 1997, Issue Price $17.00, '94
Series: *Sugar Town*

Purchased_____, Price $_____

☐ **Sam Butcher With Sugar Town Population Sign, 529842**

∝ $60.00

Annual 1993, Issue Price $22.50, '93
Series: *Sugar Town*

Purchased_____, Price $_____

☐ *Dr. Sam Sugar*, 529850

⌐∂ $33.00
△ $25.00
♡ $23.00
♰ $20.00

Retired 1997, Issue Price $17.00, '94
Series: *Sugar Town*

Purchased_____, Price $_____

☐ *Doctor's Office* , 529869 (Nightlight)

⌐∂ $115.00
△ $105.00
♡ $98.00
♰ $95.00

Retired 1997, Issue Price $80.00, '94
Series: *Sugar Town*

Purchased_____, Price $_____

☐ *Happiness Is At Our Fingertips, 529931*

♪ $70.00
✝ ∝ $68.00

Annual 1993, Issue Price $35.00, '93
Catalog Exclusive

Purchased _35°°_ , Price $ _68°°_

☐ *Ring Out The Good News, 529966*

♪ $65.00
∝ $50.00
⌐∂ $45.00

Retired 1997, Issue Price $27.50, '93
Nativity Addition

Purchased_____, Price $_____

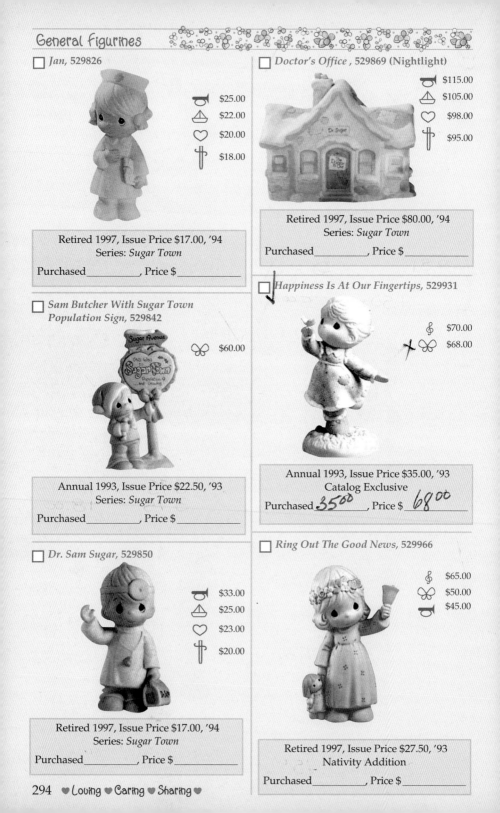

☐ *An Event For All Seasons, 529974*
(Ornament)

🦋 $20.00

Annual 1993, Issue Price $15.00, '93
Open House Event

Purchased_____, Price $_____

☐ *Memories Are Made Of This, 529982*

🦋 $45.00
📯 $40.00

Annual 1994, Issue Price $30.00, '94
Special Event

Purchased_____, Price $_____

☑ *Wishes For The World, 530018*

⭐ $38.00

Annual 1999, Issue Price $35.00, '99
Millennium Event Exclusive

Purchased_____, Price $ *38⁰⁰*

☐ *You're My Number One Friend, 530026*

🔔 $45.00
🦋 $43.00
📯 $40.00

Annual 1993, Issue Price $30.00, '93
Easter Seals Commemorative
Lily Understamp

Purchased_____, Price $_____

☐ *Noah's Ark, 530042*
(Nightlight)

📯 $130.00	♡ $125.00
🦋 $135.00	⛵ $125.00	✝ $125.00
	👓 $125.00
	⭐ $125.00
	◯ $125.00
	✂ $125.00
	⊕ $125.00

Retired 2002, Issue Price $125.00, '93
Series: *Two By Two*, Set Of 3

Purchased_____, Price $_____

☐ *Sheep, 530077*

	♡ $10.00
🦋 $12.00	✝ $10.00
📯 $10.00	👓 $10.00
⛵ $10.00	⭐ $10.00
	◯ $10.00
	✂ $10.00
	⊕ $10.00

Retired 2002, Issue Price $10.00, '93
Series: *Two By Two*

Purchased *G*, Price $ *10.00*

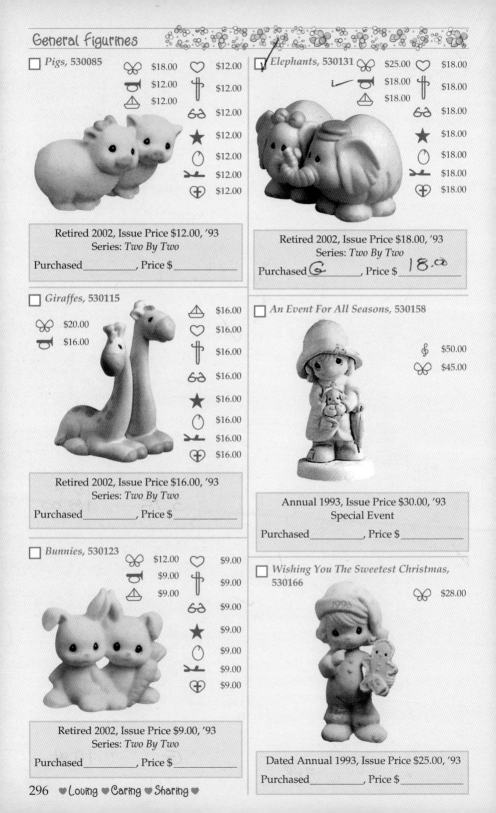

☐ *Pigs, 530085*

✄	$18.00	♡	$12.00
	$12.00	✝	$12.00
△	$12.00		
		6∂	$12.00
		★	$12.00
		◯	$12.00
		✄	$12.00
		⊕	$12.00

Retired 2002, Issue Price $12.00, '93
Series: *Two By Two*

Purchased_____, Price $_____

☐ *Giraffes, 530115*

✄	$20.00	△	$16.00
	$16.00	♡	$16.00
		✝	$16.00
		6∂	$16.00
		★	$16.00
		◯	$16.00
		✄	$16.00
		⊕	$16.00

Retired 2002, Issue Price $16.00, '93
Series: *Two By Two*

Purchased_____, Price $_____

☐ *Bunnies, 530123*

✄	$12.00	♡	$9.00
	$9.00	✝	$9.00
△	$9.00		
		6∂	$9.00
		★	$9.00
		◯	$9.00
		✄	$9.00
		⊕	$9.00

Retired 2002, Issue Price $9.00, '93
Series: *Two By Two*

Purchased_____, Price $_____

☐ *Elephants, 530131*

✄	$25.00	♡	$18.00
	$18.00	✝	$18.00
△	$18.00		
		6∂	$18.00
		★	$18.00
		◯	$18.00
		✄	$18.00
		⊕	$18.00

Retired 2002, Issue Price $18.00, '93
Series: *Two By Two*

Purchased G_____, Price $ 18.00

☐ *An Event For All Seasons, 530158*

⚶	$50.00
✄	$45.00

Annual 1993, Issue Price $30.00, '93
Special Event

Purchased_____, Price $_____

☐ *Wishing You The Sweetest Christmas,*
530166

✄	$28.00

Dated Annual 1993, Issue Price $25.00, '93

Purchased_____, Price $_____

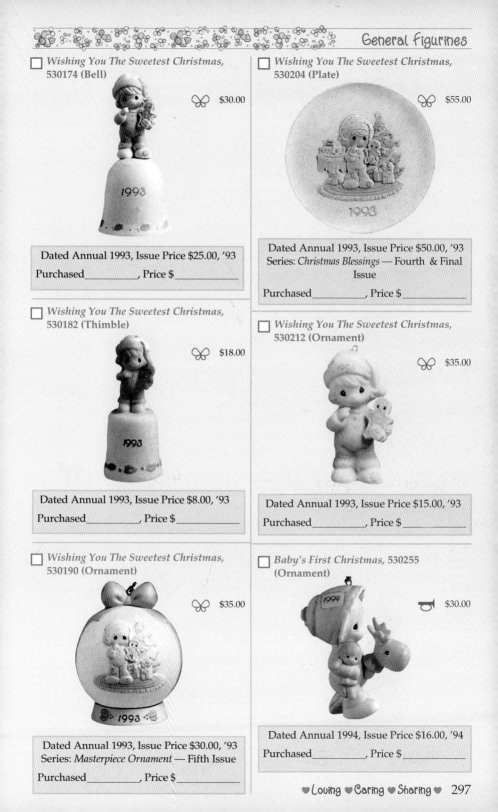

☐ *Wishing You The Sweetest Christmas,*
530174 (Bell)

✂ $30.00

1993

Dated Annual 1993, Issue Price $25.00, '93

Purchased_____, Price $_____

☐ *Wishing You The Sweetest Christmas,*
530182 (Thimble)

✂ $18.00

1993

Dated Annual 1993, Issue Price $8.00, '93

Purchased_____, Price $_____

☐ *Wishing You The Sweetest Christmas,*
530190 (Ornament)

✂ $35.00

1993

Dated Annual 1993, Issue Price $30.00, '93
Series: *Masterpiece Ornament* — Fifth Issue

Purchased_____, Price $_____

☐ *Wishing You The Sweetest Christmas,*
530204 (Plate)

✂ $55.00

1993

Dated Annual 1993, Issue Price $50.00, '93
Series: *Christmas Blessings* — Fourth & Final
Issue

Purchased_____, Price $_____

☐ *Wishing You The Sweetest Christmas,*
530212 (Ornament)

✂ $35.00

Dated Annual 1993, Issue Price $15.00, '93

Purchased_____, Price $_____

☐ *Baby's First Christmas,* 530255
(Ornament)

1994

🎺 $30.00

Dated Annual 1994, Issue Price $16.00, '94

Purchased_____, Price $_____

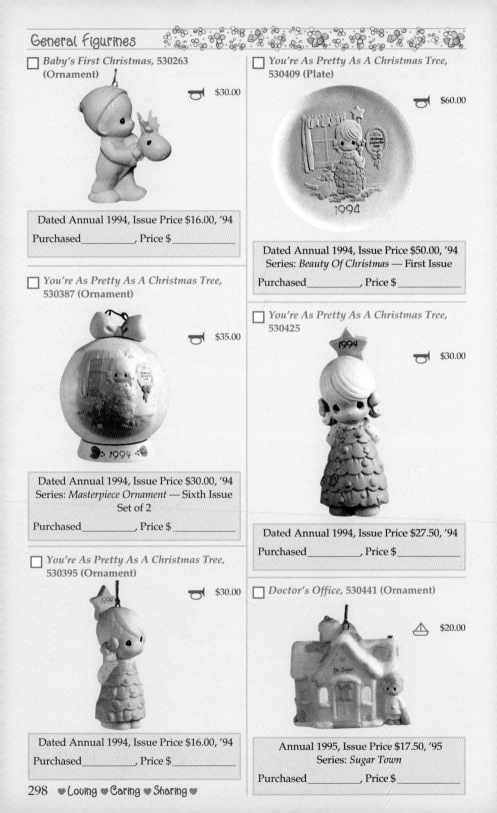

☐ *Baby's First Christmas*, 530263
(Ornament)

$30.00

Dated Annual 1994, Issue Price $16.00, '94

Purchased_____, Price $_____

☐ *You're As Pretty As A Christmas Tree*,
530387 (Ornament)

$35.00

Dated Annual 1994, Issue Price $30.00, '94
Series: *Masterpiece Ornament* — Sixth Issue
Set of 2

Purchased_____, Price $_____

☐ *You're As Pretty As A Christmas Tree*,
530395 (Ornament)

$30.00

Dated Annual 1994, Issue Price $16.00, '94

Purchased_____, Price $_____

☐ *You're As Pretty As A Christmas Tree*,
530409 (Plate)

$60.00

1994

Dated Annual 1994, Issue Price $50.00, '94
Series: *Beauty Of Christmas* — First Issue

Purchased_____, Price $_____

☐ *You're As Pretty As A Christmas Tree*,
530425

$30.00

Dated Annual 1994, Issue Price $27.50, '94

Purchased_____, Price $_____

☐ *Doctor's Office*, 530441 (Ornament)

$20.00

Annual 1995, Issue Price $17.50, '95
Series: *Sugar Town*

Purchased_____, Price $_____

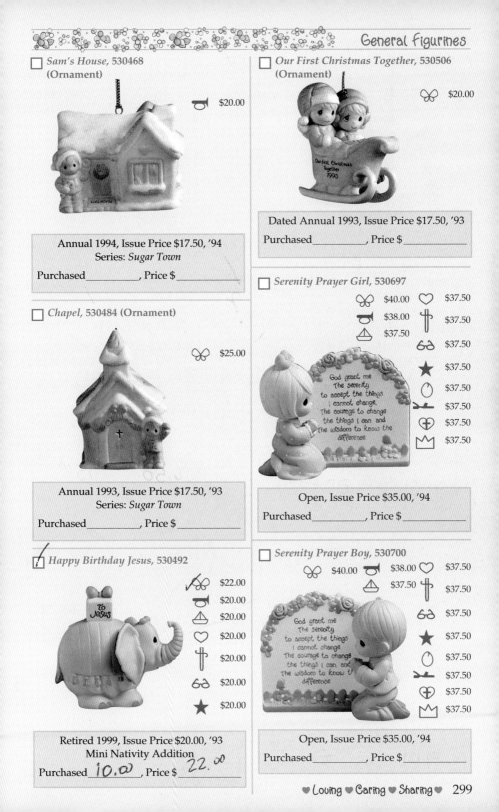

☐ *Sam's House*, 530468 (Ornament)

◁ $20.00

Annual 1994, Issue Price $17.50, '94
Series: *Sugar Town*

Purchased_____, Price $_____

☐ *Chapel*, 530484 (Ornament)

∞ $25.00

Annual 1993, Issue Price $17.50, '93
Series: *Sugar Town*

Purchased_____, Price $_____

☐ *Happy Birthday Jesus*, 530492

✗∞	$22.00
◁	$20.00
△	$20.00
♡	$20.00
✝	$20.00
6∂	$20.00
★	$20.00

Retired 1999, Issue Price $20.00, '93
Mini Nativity Addition

Purchased _10.00_, Price $_22.00_

☐ *Our First Christmas Together*, 530506 (Ornament)

∞ $20.00

Dated Annual 1993, Issue Price $17.50, '93

Purchased_____, Price $_____

☐ *Serenity Prayer Girl*, 530697

∞	$40.00	♡	$37.50
◁	$38.00	✝	$37.50
△	$37.50		
		6∂	$37.50
		★	$37.50
		◔	$37.50
		✕	$37.50
		⊕	$37.50
		♛	$37.50

Open, Issue Price $35.00, '94

Purchased_____, Price $_____

☐ *Serenity Prayer Boy*, 530700

∞	$40.00	◁	$38.00	♡	$37.50
		△	$37.50	✝	$37.50
				6∂	$37.50
				★	$37.50
				◔	$37.50
				✕	$37.50
				⊕	$37.50
				♛	$37.50

Open, Issue Price $35.00, '94

Purchased_____, Price $_____

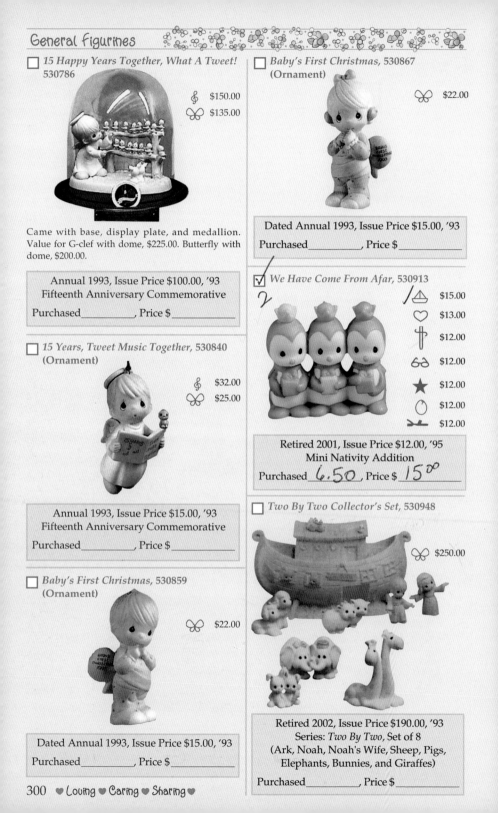

□ *15 Happy Years Together, What A Tweet!* 530786

♪ $150.00
🦋 $135.00

Came with base, display plate, and medallion. Value for G-clef with dome, $225.00. Butterfly with dome, $200.00.

Annual 1993, Issue Price $100.00, '93
Fifteenth Anniversary Commemorative

Purchased_____ , Price $ _____

□ *15 Years, Tweet Music Together*, 530840 (Ornament)

♪ $32.00
🦋 $25.00

Annual 1993, Issue Price $15.00, '93
Fifteenth Anniversary Commemorative

Purchased_____ , Price $ _____

□ *Baby's First Christmas*, 530859 (Ornament)

🦋 $22.00

Dated Annual 1993, Issue Price $15.00, '93

Purchased_____ , Price $ _____

□ *Baby's First Christmas*, 530867 (Ornament)

🦋 $22.00

Dated Annual 1993, Issue Price $15.00, '93

Purchased_____ , Price $ _____

☑ *We Have Come From Afar*, 530913

2

△ $15.00
♡ $13.00
✝ $12.00
🔯 $12.00
★ $12.00
○ $12.00
⤚ $12.00

Retired 2001, Issue Price $12.00, '95
Mini Nativity Addition

Purchased **6.50** , Price $ **15 00**

□ *Two By Two Collector's Set*, 530948

🦋 $250.00

Retired 2002, Issue Price $190.00, '93
Series: *Two By Two*, Set of 8
(Ark, Noah, Noah's Wife, Sheep, Pigs, Elephants, Bunnies, and Giraffes)

Purchased_____ , Price $ _____

☐ *I Only Have Ice For You, 530956*

⛵ $60.00
♡ $58.00
✝ $55.00
👓 $55.00
★ $55.00

Retired 1999, Issue Price $55.00, '95

Purchased_____, Price $_____

☐ *Sometimes You're Next To Impossible,*
530964

♡ $55.00
✝ $52.00
👓 $50.00
★ $50.00
◯ $50.00
⊱ $50.00
⊕ $50.00
♛ $50.00

Open, Issue Price $50.00, '97

Purchased_____, Price $_____

☐ *You Are Always In My Heart, 530972*
(Ornament)

✏ $20.00

Dated Annual 1994, Issue Price $16.00, '94
Series: *Birthday Collection*

Purchased_____, Price $_____

☐ *I Still Do, 530999*

🦋 $55.00   ♡ $30.00
✏ $35.00   ✝ $30.00
⛵ $30.00
👓 $30.00
★ $30.00
◯ $30.00
⊱ $30.00
⊕ $30.00
♛ $30.00

Open, Issue Price $30.00, '94

Purchased_____, Price $_____

☐ *I Still Do, 531006*

🦋 $55.00   ⛵ $30.00
✏ $35.00   ♡ $30.00
✝ $30.00
👓 $30.00
★ $30.00
◯ $30.00
⊱ $30.00
⊕ $30.00
♛ $30.00

Open, Issue Price $30.00, '94

Purchased_____, Price $_____

☐ *My World's Upside Down Without You,*
531014

✝ $20.00
👓 $18.00
★ $15.00
◯ $15.00
⊱ $15.00
⊕ $15.00
♛ $15.00

Open, Issue Price $15.00, '98

Purchased_____, Price $_____

☐ *Potty Time*, 531022

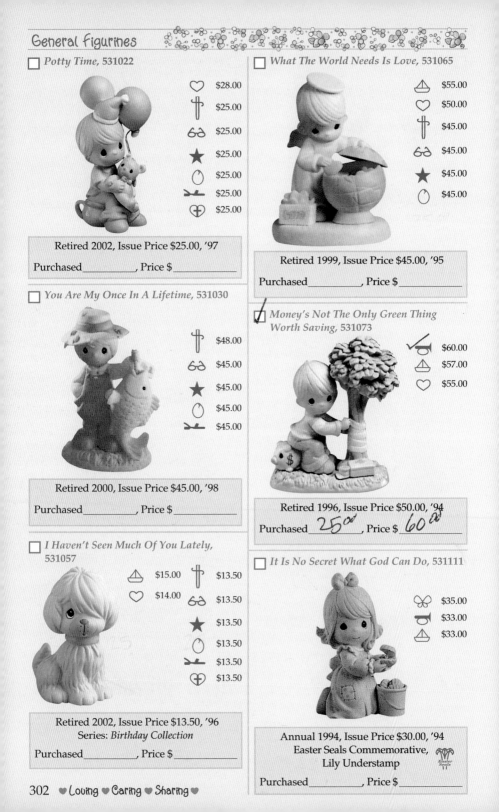

♡ $28.00
† $25.00
👓 $25.00
★ $25.00
◐ $25.00
⤝ $25.00
⊕ $25.00

Retired 2002, Issue Price $25.00, '97

Purchased_____, Price $_____

☐ *You Are My Once In A Lifetime*, 531030

† $48.00
👓 $45.00
★ $45.00
◐ $45.00
⤝ $45.00

Retired 2000, Issue Price $45.00, '98

Purchased_____, Price $_____

☐ *I Haven't Seen Much Of You Lately,*
531057

△ $15.00   † $13.50
♡ $14.00   👓 $13.50
             ★ $13.50
             ◐ $13.50
             ⤝ $13.50
             ⊕ $13.50

Retired 2002, Issue Price $13.50, '96
Series: *Birthday Collection*

Purchased_____, Price $_____

☐ *What The World Needs Is Love*, 531065

△ $55.00
♡ $50.00
† $45.00
👓 $45.00
★ $45.00
◐ $45.00

Retired 1999, Issue Price $45.00, '95

Purchased_____, Price $_____

☑ *Money's Not The Only Green Thing
Worth Saving*, 531073

✓ 📯 $60.00
△ $57.00
♡ $55.00

Retired 1996, Issue Price $50.00, '94

Purchased _25⁰⁰_, Price $ _60⁰⁰_

☐ *It Is No Secret What God Can Do*, 531111

🦋 $35.00
📯 $33.00
△ $33.00

Annual 1994, Issue Price $30.00, '94
Easter Seals Commemorative,
Lily Understamp

Purchased_____, Price $_____

☐ *What A Difference You've Made In My Life*, 531138

△	$55.00
♡	$50.00
⊤	$50.00
6ᴈ	$50.00
★	$50.00
◔	$50.00
⤙	$50.00
⊕	$50.00

Retired 2001, Issue Price $50.00, '96

Purchased_____, Price $_____

☑ *Vaya Con Dios (To Go With God)*, 531146

⊤	$38.00	♡	$35.00
△	$35.00	⊤	$35.00
		6ᴈ	$35.00
		★	$35.00
		◔	$35.00
		⤙	$35.00
		⊕	$35.00
		♔	$35.00

Open, Issue Price $32.50, '95

Purchased_____, Price $_____

☐ *Bless Your Soul*, 531162

⊤	$28.00	♡	$27.50
△	$28.00	⊤	$27.50
		6ᴈ	$27.50
		★	$27.50
		◔	$27.50
		⤙	$27.50
		⊕	$27.50
		♔	$27.50

Open, Issue Price $25.00, '95

Purchased_____, Price $_____

☐ *Wishing You A Bear-ie Merry Christmas*, 531200 (Ornament)

♡	$20.00

Dated Annual 1996, Issue Price $17.50, '96 Holiday Preview Event

Purchased_____, Price $_____

☐ *You Are The Rose Of His Creation*, 531243

⋈	$575.00
⊤	$550.00

Limited Ed. 2,000, Issue Price $500.00, '94
Easter Seals Commemorative,
Lily Understamp
Individually Numbered

Purchased_____, Price $_____

☐ *Bring The Little Ones To Jesus*, 531359 (Plate)

⋈	$60.00
⊤	$55.00

Dated Annual 1994, Issue Price $50.00, '94
Child Evangelism Fellowship

Purchased_____, Price $_____

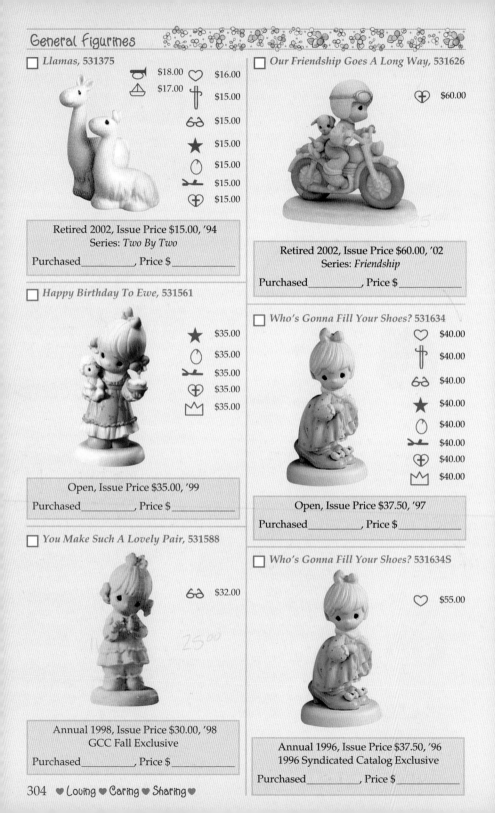

☐ *Llamas*, 531375

⛄ $18.00	♡ $16.00
⛵ $17.00	♱ $15.00
	👓 $15.00
	★ $15.00
	◯ $15.00
	⤙ $15.00
	✛ $15.00

Retired 2002, Issue Price $15.00, '94
Series: *Two By Two*

Purchased_____, Price $_____

☐ *Happy Birthday To Ewe*, 531561

★	$35.00
◯	$35.00
⤙	$35.00
✛	$35.00
👑	$35.00

Open, Issue Price $35.00, '99

Purchased_____, Price $_____

☐ *You Make Such A Lovely Pair*, 531588

👓	$32.00

25.00

Annual 1998, Issue Price $30.00, '98
GCC Fall Exclusive

Purchased_____, Price $_____

☐ *Our Friendship Goes A Long Way*, 531626

✛	$60.00

Retired 2002, Issue Price $60.00, '02
Series: *Friendship*

Purchased_____, Price $_____

☐ *Who's Gonna Fill Your Shoes?* 531634

♡ $40.00	♱ $40.00
	👓 $40.00
	★ $40.00
	◯ $40.00
	⤙ $40.00
	✛ $40.00
	👑 $40.00

Open, Issue Price $37.50, '97

Purchased_____, Price $_____

☐ *Who's Gonna Fill Your Shoes?* 531634S

♡	$55.00

Annual 1996, Issue Price $37.50, '96
1996 Syndicated Catalog Exclusive

Purchased_____, Price $_____

Surrounded With Joy, 531677

Unmarked	$35.00	♡	$30.00
⊲	$33.00	†	$30.00
△	$30.00	6∂	$30.00
		★	$30.00
		◐	$30.00
		✂	$30.00
		⊕	$30.00
		♕	$30.00

Suspended 2001, Issue Price $30.00, '93
Chapel Exclusive

Purchased_____, Price $_____

Surrounded With Joy, 531685 (Ornament)

Unmarked	$17.50	†	$17.50
⊲	$17.50	†	$17.50
△	$17.50	6∂	$17.50
♡	$17.50	★	$17.50
		◐	$17.50
		✂	$17.50
		⊕	$17.50
		♕	$17.50

Suspended 2002, Issue Price $17.50, '93
Chapel Exclusive

Purchased_____, Price $_____

You Deserve A Halo – Thank You, 531693

△	$60.00
♡	$58.00
†	$56.00
6∂	$55.00

Retired 1998, Issue Price $55.00, '96

Purchased_____, Price $_____

The Lord Is Counting On You, 531707

		♡	$35.00
⊲	$35.00	†	$35.00
△	$35.00	6∂	$35.00
		★	$35.00
		◐	$35.00
		✂	$35.00
		⊕	$35.00

Retired 2002, Issue Price $32.50, '94

Purchased_____, Price $_____

Thinking Of You Is What I Really Like To Do, 531766 (Plate)

✾	$55.00
⊲	$55.00

Dated Annual 1994, Issue Price $50.00, '94
Series: *Mother's Day* — First Issue

Purchased_____, Price $_____

Chapel Set, 531773

✾	$325.00
⊲	$325.00

Retired 1994, Issue Price $189.00, '93
Series: *Sugar Town*, Set Of 7
(Chapel, Sam Butcher, Evergreen Tree,
Aunt Ruth & Aunt Dorothy, Philip,
Grandfather, and Nativity)

Purchased _____, Price $_____

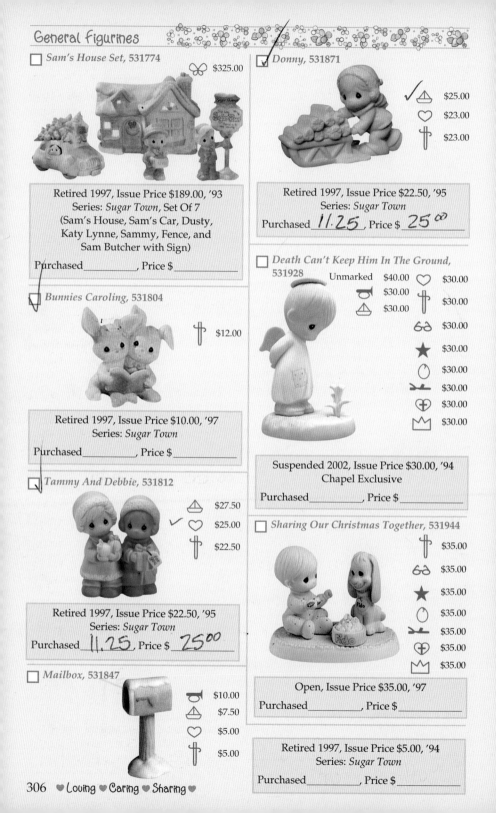

☐ **Sam's House Set**, 531774

$325.00

Retired 1997, Issue Price $189.00, '93
Series: *Sugar Town*, Set Of 7
(Sam's House, Sam's Car, Dusty,
Katy Lynne, Sammy, Fence, and
Sam Butcher with Sign)

Purchased_____, Price $_____

☐ **Bunnies Caroling**, 531804

☦ $12.00

Retired 1997, Issue Price $10.00, '97
Series: *Sugar Town*

Purchased_____, Price $_____

☐ **Tammy And Debbie**, 531812

△ $27.50
♡ $25.00
☦ $22.50

Retired 1997, Issue Price $22.50, '95
Series: *Sugar Town*

Purchased _11.25_, Price $ _25 00_

☐ **Mailbox**, 531847

◁ $10.00
△ $7.50
♡ $5.00
☦ $5.00

☑ **Donny**, 531871

△ ✓ $25.00
♡ $23.00
☦ $23.00

Retired 1997, Issue Price $22.50, '95
Series: *Sugar Town*

Purchased _11.25_, Price $ _25 00_

☐ **Death Can't Keep Him In The Ground**, 531928

Unmarked	$40.00	♡	$30.00
◁	$30.00	☦	$30.00
△	$30.00		
		6∂	$30.00
		★	$30.00
		○	$30.00
		⤛	$30.00
		⊕	$30.00
		♔	$30.00

Suspended 2002, Issue Price $30.00, '94
Chapel Exclusive

Purchased_____, Price $_____

☐ **Sharing Our Christmas Together**, 531944

☦ $35.00
6∂ $35.00
★ $35.00
○ $35.00
⤛ $35.00
⊕ $35.00
♔ $35.00

Open, Issue Price $35.00, '97

Purchased_____, Price $_____

Retired 1997, Issue Price $5.00, '94
Series: *Sugar Town*

Purchased_____, Price $_____

☑ *Dropping In For The Holidays*, 531952

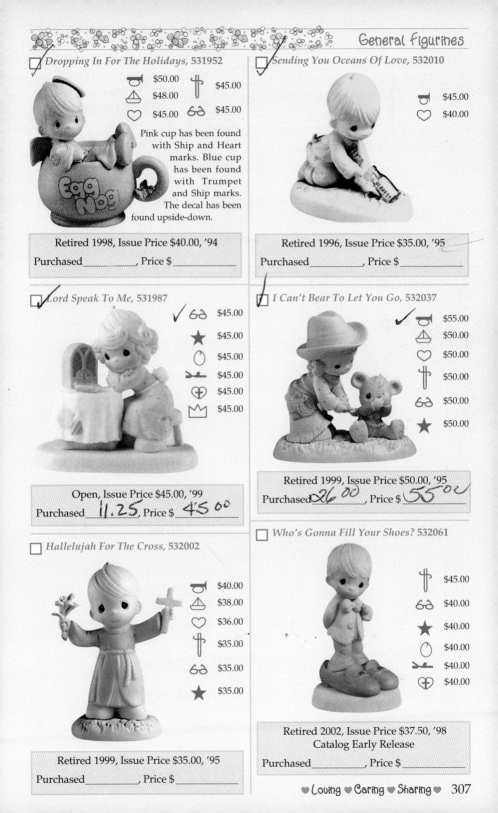

🎺 $50.00 ✝ $45.00
⛵ $48.00
♡ $45.00 👓 $45.00

Pink cup has been found with Ship and Heart marks. Blue cup has been found with Trumpet and Ship marks. The decal has been found upside-down.

Retired 1998, Issue Price $40.00, '94

Purchased_____, Price $_____

☑ *Lord Speak To Me*, 531987

✓ 👓 $45.00
★ $45.00
○ $45.00
⤳ $45.00
✝ $45.00
♕ $45.00

Open, Issue Price $45.00, '99
Purchased **11.25**, Price $ **45 00**

☐ *Hallelujah For The Cross*, 532002

🎺 $40.00
⛵ $38.00
♡ $36.00
✝ $35.00
👓 $35.00
★ $35.00

Retired 1999, Issue Price $35.00, '95
Purchased_____, Price $_____

☑ *Sending You Oceans Of Love*, 532010

🎺 $45.00
♡ $40.00

Retired 1996, Issue Price $35.00, '95
Purchased_____, Price $_____

☑ *I Can't Bear To Let You Go*, 532037

🎺 $55.00
⛵ $50.00
♡ $50.00
✝ $50.00
👓 $50.00
★ $50.00

Retired 1999, Issue Price $50.00, '95
Purchased **26 00**, Price $ **55 00**

☐ *Who's Gonna Fill Your Shoes?* 532061

✝ $45.00
👓 $40.00
★ $40.00
○ $40.00
⤳ $40.00
⊕ $40.00

Retired 2002, Issue Price $37.50, '98
Catalog Early Release
Purchased_____, Price $_____

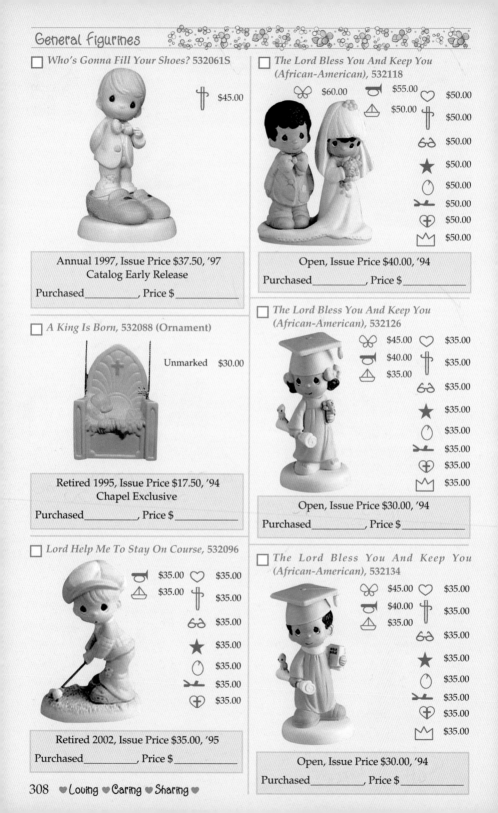

☐ *Who's Gonna Fill Your Shoes?* 532061S

✝ $45.00

Annual 1997, Issue Price $37.50, '97
Catalog Early Release
Purchased_____, Price $_____

☐ *A King Is Born*, 532088 (Ornament)

Unmarked $30.00

Retired 1995, Issue Price $17.50, '94
Chapel Exclusive
Purchased_____, Price $_____

☐ *Lord Help Me To Stay On Course*, 532096

🎺 $35.00		♡ $35.00
⊿ $35.00		✝ $35.00
		👓 $35.00
		★ $35.00
		◯ $35.00
		⤞ $35.00
		⊕ $35.00

Retired 2002, Issue Price $35.00, '95
Purchased_____, Price $_____

☐ *The Lord Bless You And Keep You*
(African-American), 532118

🦋 $60.00	🎺 $55.00	♡ $50.00
	⊿ $50.00	✝ $50.00
		👓 $50.00
		★ $50.00
		◯ $50.00
		⤞ $50.00
		⊕ $50.00
		♛ $50.00

Open, Issue Price $40.00, '94
Purchased_____, Price $_____

☐ *The Lord Bless You And Keep You*
(African-American), 532126

🦋 $45.00		♡ $35.00
🎺 $40.00		✝ $35.00
⊿ $35.00		
		👓 $35.00
		★ $35.00
		◯ $35.00
		⤞ $35.00
		⊕ $35.00
		♛ $35.00

Open, Issue Price $30.00, '94
Purchased_____, Price $_____

☐ *The Lord Bless You And Keep You*
(African-American), 532134

🦋 $45.00		♡ $35.00
🎺 $40.00		✝ $35.00
⊿ $35.00		
		👓 $35.00
		★ $35.00
		◯ $35.00
		⤞ $35.00
		⊕ $35.00
		♛ $35.00

Open, Issue Price $30.00, '94
Purchased_____, Price $_____

☐ *Street Sign*, 532185

⛵ $15.00
♡ $13.00
✝ $10.00

Retired 1997, Issue Price $10.00, '95
Series: *Sugar Town*

Purchased_____, Price $_____

☐ *Merry Giftness*, 532223 (Ornament)

★ $20.00

Annual 1999, Issue Price $20.00, '99
DSR Exclusive

Purchased_____, Price $_____

☐ *Town Square Clock*, 532908

📯 $115.00
⛵ $105.00
♡ $100.00
✝ $90.00

Retired 1997, Issue Price $80.00, '94
Series: *Sugar Town*

Purchased_____, Price $_____

Retired 1997, Issue Price $10.00, '94
Series: *Sugar Town*

Purchased_____, Price $_____

☐ *Luke 2:10 – 11*, 532916

📯 $40.00
⛵ $38.00
♡ $37.50
✝ $37.50
👓 $37.50
★ $37.50

Retired 1999, Issue Price $35.00, '94

Purchased_____, Price $_____

☐ *It's Almost Time For Santa*, 532932

✂ $75.00

Annual 2001, Issue Price $75.00, '01

Purchased_____, Price $_____

☐ *Curved Sidewalk*, 533149

👓 $22.00
⛵ $20.00
♡ $18.00
✝ $13.00

Retired 1997, Issue Price $10.00, '94
Series: *Sugar Town*

Purchased_____, Price $_____

☐ *Straight Sidewalk*, 533157

📯 $22.00   ♡ $18.00
⛵ $20.00   ✝ $13.00

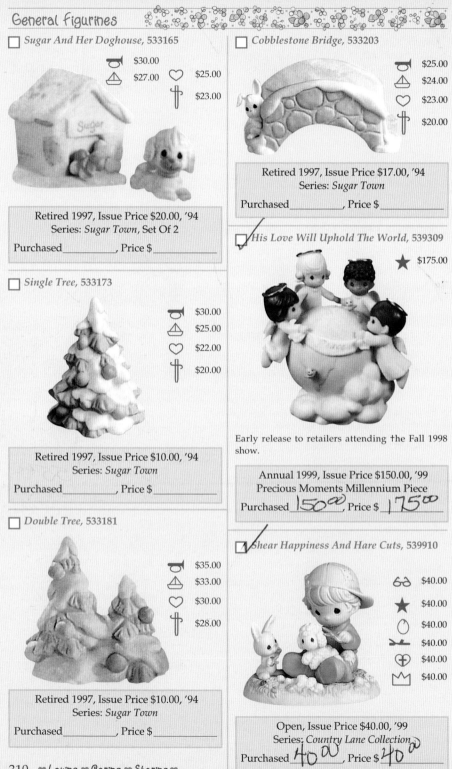

☐ *Sugar And Her Doghouse*, 533165

📯 $30.00
⛵ $27.00
♡ $25.00
✝ $23.00

Retired 1997, Issue Price $20.00, '94
Series: *Sugar Town*, Set Of 2
Purchased_____, Price $_____

☐ *Single Tree*, 533173

📯 $30.00
⛵ $25.00
♡ $22.00
✝ $20.00

Retired 1997, Issue Price $10.00, '94
Series: *Sugar Town*
Purchased_____, Price $_____

☐ *Double Tree*, 533181

📯 $35.00
⛵ $33.00
♡ $30.00
✝ $28.00

Retired 1997, Issue Price $10.00, '94
Series: *Sugar Town*
Purchased_____, Price $_____

☐ *Cobblestone Bridge*, 533203

📯 $25.00
⛵ $24.00
♡ $23.00
✝ $20.00

Retired 1997, Issue Price $17.00, '94
Series: *Sugar Town*
Purchased_____, Price $_____

☑ *His Love Will Uphold The World*, 539309

★ $175.00

Early release to retailers attending the Fall 1998 show.

Annual 1999, Issue Price $150.00, '99
Precious Moments Millennium Piece
Purchased 150⁰⁰, Price $ 175⁰⁰

☑ *Shear Happiness And Hare Cuts*, 539910

👓 $40.00
★ $40.00
◯ $40.00
⚔ $40.00
⊕ $40.00
♔ $40.00

Open, Issue Price $40.00, '99
Series: *Country Lane Collection*
Purchased 40 ⁰⁰, Price $ 40 ⁰⁰

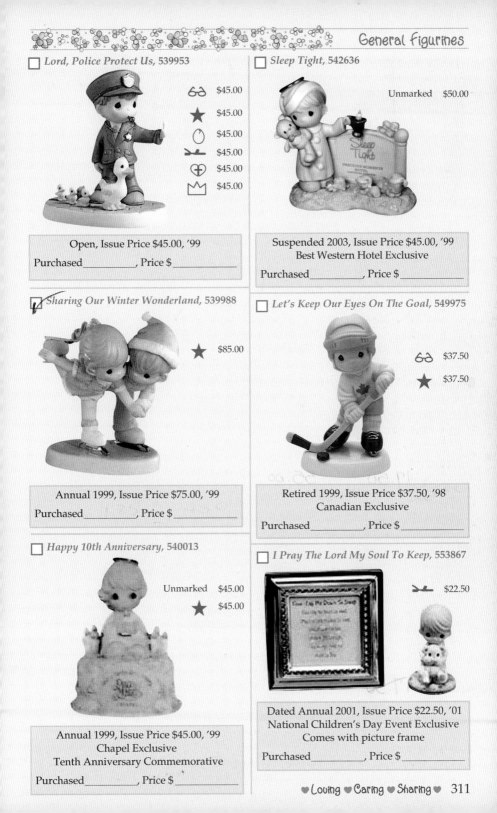

☐ *Lord, Police Protect Us*, 539953

👓	$45.00
★	$45.00
◐	$45.00
✂	$45.00
✚	$45.00
♛	$45.00

Open, Issue Price $45.00, '99
Purchased_____, Price $_____

☑ *Sharing Our Winter Wonderland*, 539988

★ $85.00

Annual 1999, Issue Price $75.00, '99
Purchased_____, Price $_____

☐ *Happy 10th Anniversary*, 540013

Unmarked $45.00
★ $45.00

Annual 1999, Issue Price $45.00, '99
Chapel Exclusive
Tenth Anniversary Commemorative
Purchased_____, Price $_____

☐ *Sleep Tight*, 542636

Unmarked $50.00

Suspended 2003, Issue Price $45.00, '99
Best Western Hotel Exclusive
Purchased_____, Price $_____

☐ *Let's Keep Our Eyes On The Goal*, 549975

👓 $37.50
★ $37.50

Retired 1999, Issue Price $37.50, '98
Canadian Exclusive
Purchased_____, Price $_____

☐ *I Pray The Lord My Soul To Keep*, 553867

✈ $22.50

Dated Annual 2001, Issue Price $22.50, '01
National Children's Day Event Exclusive
Comes with picture frame
Purchased_____, Price $_____

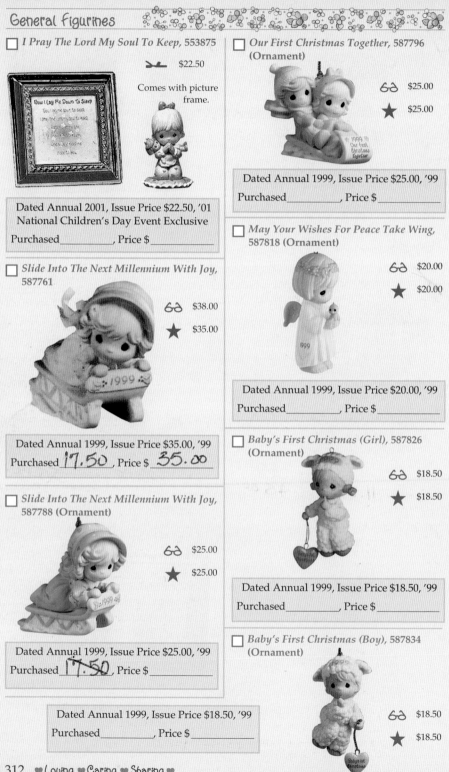

☐ *I Pray The Lord My Soul To Keep*, 553875

✈ $22.50

Comes with picture frame.

Dated Annual 2001, Issue Price $22.50, '01
National Children's Day Event Exclusive

Purchased_____, Price $_____

☐ *Slide Into The Next Millennium With Joy*,
587761

◌◌ $38.00

★ $35.00

Dated Annual 1999, Issue Price $35.00, '99

Purchased **17.50**, Price $ **35.00**

☐ *Slide Into The Next Millennium With Joy*,
587788 (Ornament)

◌◌ $25.00

★ $25.00

Dated Annual 1999, Issue Price $25.00, '99

Purchased **17.50**, Price $_____

☐ *Our First Christmas Together*, 587796
(Ornament)

◌◌ $25.00

★ $25.00

Dated Annual 1999, Issue Price $25.00, '99

Purchased_____, Price $_____

☐ *May Your Wishes For Peace Take Wing*,
587818 (Ornament)

◌◌ $20.00

★ $20.00

Dated Annual 1999, Issue Price $20.00, '99

Purchased_____, Price $_____

☐ *Baby's First Christmas (Girl)*, 587826
(Ornament)

◌◌ $18.50

★ $18.50

Dated Annual 1999, Issue Price $18.50, '99

Purchased_____, Price $_____

☐ *Baby's First Christmas (Boy)*, 587834
(Ornament)

◌◌ $18.50

★ $18.50

Dated Annual 1999, Issue Price $18.50, '99

Purchased_____, Price $_____

☐ *Eat Ham*, 587842

6∂ $25.00
★ $25.00
◯ $25.00
⤳ $25.00
✝ $25.00
♕ $25.00

Open, Issue Price $25.00, '99
Series: *Country Lane Collection*
Purchased_____, Price $_____

☑ *You Brighten My Field Of Dreams*, 587850

6∂ $55.00
★ $55.00
◯ $55.00
⤳ $55.00
✝ $55.00

Retired 2002, Issue Price $55.00, '99
Series: *Country Lane Collection*
Purchased_____, Price $_____

☑ *Witch Way Do You Spell Love?* 587869

6∂ $25.00
★ $25.00
◯ $25.00
⤳ $25.00
✝ $25.00

Retired 2002, Issue Price $25.00, '99
Purchased_____, Price $_____

☐ *Snow Man Like My Man*, 587877

6∂ $55.00
★ $55.00
◯ $55.00
⤳ $55.00
✝ $55.00
♕ $55.00

Open, Issue Price $55.00, '99
Purchased_____, Price $_____

☐ *May Your Season Be Jelly And Bright*, 587885

6∂ $37.50
★ $37.50
◯ $37.50
⤳ $37.50
✝ $37.50
♕ $37.50

Open, Issue Price $37.50, '99
Purchased_____, Price $_____

☐ *God Loves A Happy Camper*, 587893

★ $37.50
◯ $37.50
⤳ $37.50
✝ $37.50
♕ $37.50

Open, Issue Price $37.50, '99
Purchased_____, Price $_____

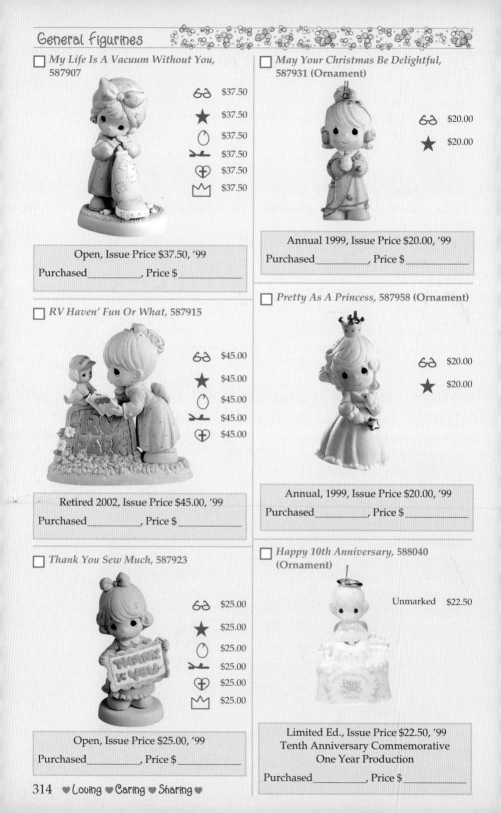

☐ *My Life Is A Vacuum Without You,* 587907

👓	$37.50
★	$37.50
◯	$37.50
⊱	$37.50
✞	$37.50
👑	$37.50

Open, Issue Price $37.50, '99

Purchased_____, Price $_____

☐ *RV Haven' Fun Or What,* 587915

👓	$45.00
★	$45.00
◯	$45.00
⊱	$45.00
✞	$45.00

Retired 2002, Issue Price $45.00, '99

Purchased_____, Price $_____

☐ *Thank You Sew Much,* 587923

👓	$25.00
★	$25.00
◯	$25.00
⊱	$25.00
✞	$25.00
👑	$25.00

Open, Issue Price $25.00, '99

Purchased_____, Price $_____

☐ *May Your Christmas Be Delightful,* 587931 (Ornament)

👓	$20.00
★	$20.00

Annual 1999, Issue Price $20.00, '99

Purchased_____, Price $_____

☐ *Pretty As A Princess,* 587958 (Ornament)

👓	$20.00
★	$20.00

Annual, 1999, Issue Price $20.00, '99

Purchased_____, Price $_____

☐ *Happy 10th Anniversary,* 588040 (Ornament)

Unmarked $22.50

Limited Ed., Issue Price $22.50, '99
Tenth Anniversary Commemorative
One Year Production

Purchased_____, Price $_____

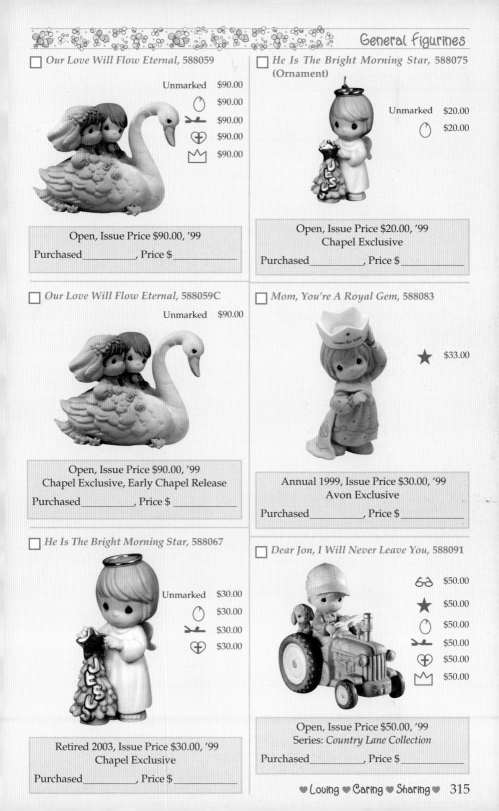

☐ *Our Love Will Flow Eternal*, 588059

Unmarked	$90.00
⬭	$90.00
⤛	$90.00
✛	$90.00
♛	$90.00

Open, Issue Price $90.00, '99
Purchased_____, Price $_____

☐ *He Is The Bright Morning Star*, 588075
(Ornament)

Unmarked	$20.00
⬭	$20.00

Open, Issue Price $20.00, '99
Chapel Exclusive
Purchased_____, Price $_____

☐ *Our Love Will Flow Eternal*, 588059C

Unmarked	$90.00

Open, Issue Price $90.00, '99
Chapel Exclusive, Early Chapel Release
Purchased_____, Price $_____

☐ *Mom, You're A Royal Gem*, 588083

★	$33.00

Annual 1999, Issue Price $30.00, '99
Avon Exclusive
Purchased_____, Price $_____

☐ *He Is The Bright Morning Star*, 588067

Unmarked	$30.00
⬭	$30.00
⤛	$30.00
✛	$30.00

Retired 2003, Issue Price $30.00, '99
Chapel Exclusive
Purchased_____, Price $_____

☐ *Dear Jon, I Will Never Leave You*, 588091

👓	$50.00
★	$50.00
⬭	$50.00
⤛	$50.00
✛	$50.00
♛	$50.00

Open, Issue Price $50.00, '99
Series: *Country Lane Collection*
Purchased_____, Price $_____

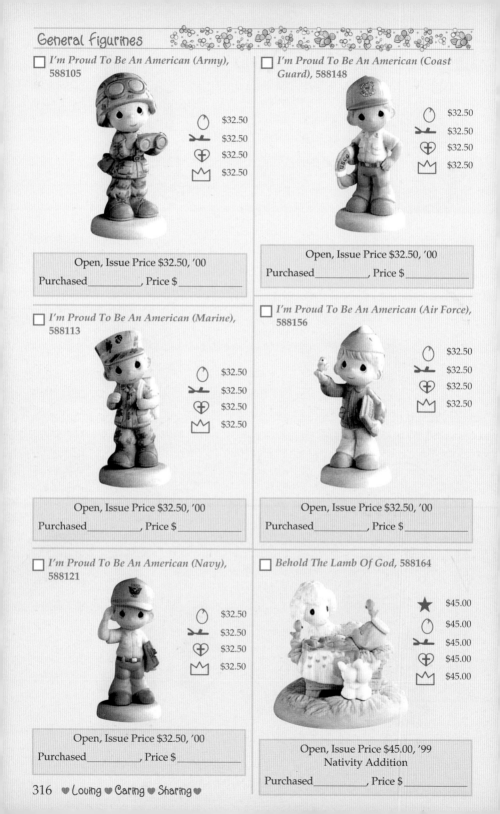

☐ *I'm Proud To Be An American (Army),* 588105

○ $32.50
✈ $32.50
✛ $32.50
♕ $32.50

Open, Issue Price $32.50, '00
Purchased_____, Price $_____

☐ *I'm Proud To Be An American (Coast Guard),* 588148

○ $32.50
✈ $32.50
✛ $32.50
♕ $32.50

Open, Issue Price $32.50, '00
Purchased_____, Price $_____

☐ *I'm Proud To Be An American (Marine),* 588113

○ $32.50
✈ $32.50
✛ $32.50
♕ $32.50

Open, Issue Price $32.50, '00
Purchased_____, Price $_____

☐ *I'm Proud To Be An American (Air Force),* 588156

○ $32.50
✈ $32.50
✛ $32.50
♕ $32.50

Open, Issue Price $32.50, '00
Purchased_____, Price $_____

☐ *I'm Proud To Be An American (Navy),* 588121

○ $32.50
✈ $32.50
✛ $32.50
♕ $32.50

Open, Issue Price $32.50, '00
Purchased_____, Price $_____

☐ *Behold The Lamb Of God,* 588164

★ $45.00
○ $45.00
✈ $45.00
✛ $45.00
♕ $45.00

Open, Issue Price $45.00, '99
Nativity Addition
Purchased_____, Price $_____

☐ *Bisque Ornament Holder*, 603171

🎺 $30.00   ♡ $30.00
△ $30.00   ✝ $30.00
👓 $30.00
★ $30.00
◯ $30.00
⤚ $30.00
✝ $30.00
♛ $30.00

Open, Issue Price $30.00, '94

Purchased_____, Price $_____

☐ *On A Hill Overlooking A Quiet Blue Stream*, 603503

Unmarked $65.00
♡ $50.00

Unmarked version has 3 verses of poem; Heart version has 4 verses.

Retired 1997, Issue Price $45.00, '94
Chapel Exclusive

Purchased_____, Price $_____

☐ *Nothing Can Dampen The Spirit Of Caring*, 603864

🦋 $35.00   △ $35.00
🎺 $35.00   ♡ $35.00
✝ $35.00
👓 $35.00
★ $35.00
◯ $35.00
⤚ $35.00
✝ $35.00

Retired 2002, Issue Price $35.00, '94
Series: *Good Samaritan* — First Issue

Purchased_____, Price $_____

☐ *Sammy's Circus Set*, 604070

🦋 $350.00
🎺 $350.00

Retired 1994, Issue Price $200.00, '94
Series: *Sammy's Circus*, Set Of 8
(Circus Tent, Markie, Dusty,
Sammy, Tippy, Katie, & Collin)

Purchased_____, Price $_____

☐ *May Your Christmas Be Delightful*, 604135

✝ $45.00
👓 $40.00
★ $40.00
◯ $40.00
⤚ $40.00
✝ $40.00
♛ $40.00

Open, Issue Price $40.00, '97

Purchased_____, Price $_____

☑ *A King Is Born*, 604151

Unmarked $85.00

Retired 1995, Issue Price $25.00, '94
Chapel Exclusive

Purchased_____, Price $ 25.00

☐ *A Poppy For You, 604208*

🎺 $35.00
⛵ $35.00
♡ $35.00
✝ $35.00
👓 $35.00

Suspended 1998, Issue Price $35.00, '94
Purchased_____, Price $_____

☐ *You're As Pretty As A Christmas Tree,*
604216 (Bell)

1994

🎺 $35.00

Dated Annual 1994, Issue Price $27.50, '94
Purchased_____, Price $_____

☐ *Rejoice, O Earth, 617334* (Musical Tree
Topper)

🕯 $175.00

Annual 1990, Issue Price $125.00, '90
Tune: "Hark! The Herald Angels Sing!"
Purchased_____, Price $_____

☐ *I Pray The Lord My Soul To Keep, 632341*

♛ $20.00

Open, Issue Price $20.00, '03
Series: *Little Moments*
Purchased_____, Price $_____

☐ *I Pray The Lord My Soul To Keep, 632430*

♛ $20.00

Open, Issue Price $20.00, '03
Series: *Little Moments*
Purchased_____, Price $_____

☐ *Jesus Loves Me, 634735*

★ $525.00

Limited Ed. 1,500, Issue Price $500.00, '00
Easter Seals,
Lily Understamp
Individually Numbered
Purchased_____, Price $_____

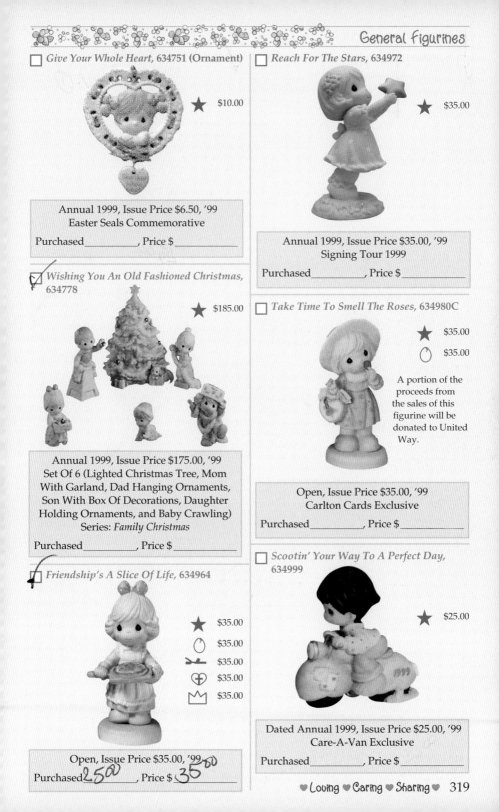

☐ *Give Your Whole Heart*, 634751 (Ornament)

★ $10.00

Annual 1999, Issue Price $6.50, '99
Easter Seals Commemorative

Purchased_____, Price $_____

☑ *Wishing You An Old Fashioned Christmas*, 634778

★ $185.00

Annual 1999, Issue Price $175.00, '99
Set Of 6 (Lighted Christmas Tree, Mom
With Garland, Dad Hanging Ornaments,
Son With Box Of Decorations, Daughter
Holding Ornaments, and Baby Crawling)
Series: *Family Christmas*

Purchased_____, Price $_____

☐ *Friendship's A Slice Of Life*, 634964

★ $35.00
○ $35.00
✂ $35.00
⊕ $35.00
♔ $35.00

Open, Issue Price $35.00, '99
Purchased 25⁰⁰, Price $ 35⁰⁰

☐ *Reach For The Stars*, 634972

★ $35.00

Annual 1999, Issue Price $35.00, '99
Signing Tour 1999

Purchased_____, Price $_____

☐ *Take Time To Smell The Roses*, 634980C

★ $35.00
○ $35.00

A portion of the
proceeds from
the sales of this
figurine will be
donated to United
Way.

Open, Issue Price $35.00, '99
Carlton Cards Exclusive

Purchased_____, Price $_____

☐ *Scootin' Your Way To A Perfect Day*, 634999

★ $25.00

Dated Annual 1999, Issue Price $25.00, '99
Care-A-Van Exclusive

Purchased_____, Price $_____

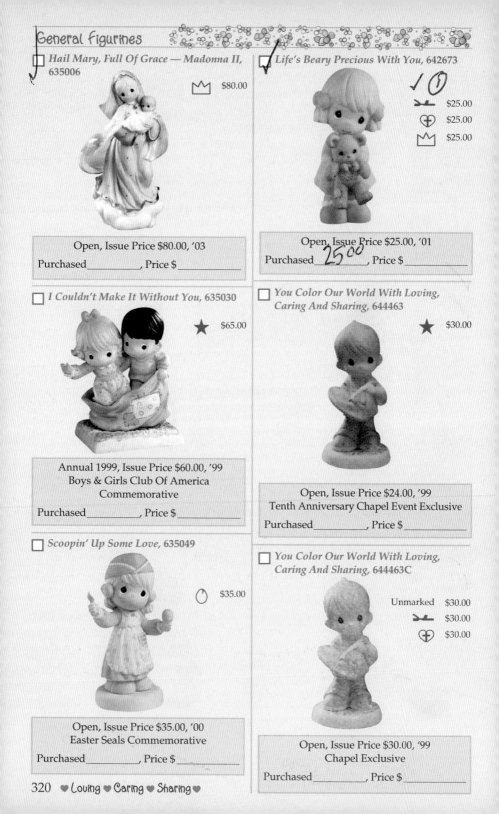

☐ *Hail Mary, Full Of Grace — Madonna II,*
635006

♛ $80.00

Open, Issue Price $80.00, '03
Purchased_____, Price $_____

☐ *Life's Beary Precious With You, 642673*

✓ ①
✂ $25.00
⊕ $25.00
♛ $25.00

Open, Issue Price $25.00, '01
Purchased _2500_, Price $_____

☐ *I Couldn't Make It Without You, 635030*

★ $65.00

Annual 1999, Issue Price $60.00, '99
Boys & Girls Club Of America
Commemorative
Purchased_____, Price $_____

☐ *You Color Our World With Loving,
Caring And Sharing, 644463*

★ $30.00

Open, Issue Price $24.00, '99
Tenth Anniversary Chapel Event Exclusive
Purchased_____, Price $_____

☐ *Scoopin' Up Some Love, 635049*

◯ $35.00

Open, Issue Price $35.00, '00
Easter Seals Commemorative
Purchased_____, Price $_____

☐ *You Color Our World With Loving,
Caring And Sharing, 644463C*

Unmarked $30.00
✂ $30.00
⊕ $30.00

Open, Issue Price $30.00, '99
Chapel Exclusive
Purchased_____, Price $_____

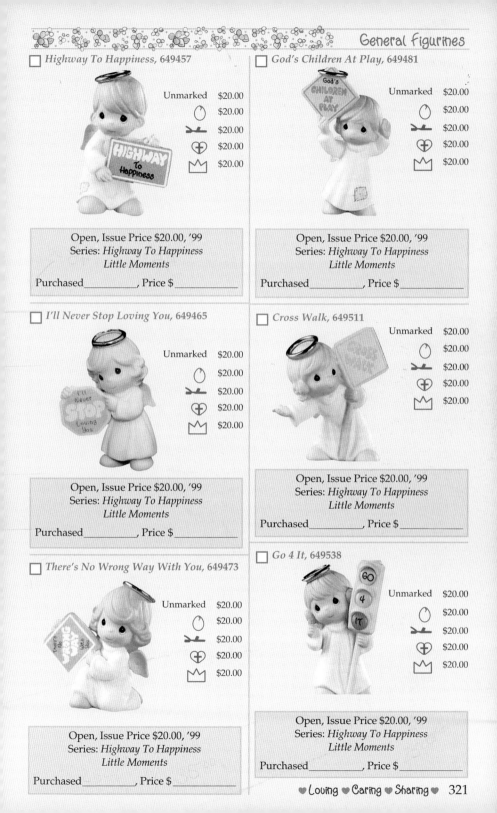

☐ *Highway To Happiness*, 649457

Unmarked	$20.00
◯	$20.00
✕	$20.00
✛	$20.00
♔	$20.00

Open, Issue Price $20.00, '99
Series: *Highway To Happiness*
Little Moments

Purchased_____, Price $_____

☐ *God's Children At Play*, 649481

Unmarked	$20.00
◯	$20.00
✕	$20.00
✛	$20.00
♔	$20.00

Open, Issue Price $20.00, '99
Series: *Highway To Happiness*
Little Moments

Purchased_____, Price $_____

☐ *I'll Never Stop Loving You*, 649465

Unmarked	$20.00
◯	$20.00
✕	$20.00
✛	$20.00
♔	$20.00

Open, Issue Price $20.00, '99
Series: *Highway To Happiness*
Little Moments

Purchased_____, Price $_____

☐ *Cross Walk*, 649511

Unmarked	$20.00
◯	$20.00
✕	$20.00
✛	$20.00
♔	$20.00

Open, Issue Price $20.00, '99
Series: *Highway To Happiness*
Little Moments

Purchased_____, Price $_____

☐ *There's No Wrong Way With You*, 649473

Unmarked	$20.00
◯	$20.00
✕	$20.00
✛	$20.00
♔	$20.00

Open, Issue Price $20.00, '99
Series: *Highway To Happiness*
Little Moments

Purchased_____, Price $_____

☐ *Go 4 It*, 649538

Unmarked	$20.00
◯	$20.00
✕	$20.00
✛	$20.00
♔	$20.00

Open, Issue Price $20.00, '99
Series: *Highway To Happiness*
Little Moments

Purchased_____, Price $_____

☐ *Yield To Him*, 649546

>≺— $20.00
✛ $20.00
♕ $20.00

Open, Issue Price $20.00, '01
Series: *Highway To Happiness*
Little Moments

Purchased_____, Price $_____

☐ *Let Him Enter Your Heart*, 649554

>≺— $20.00
✛ $20.00
♕ $20.00

Open, Issue Price $20.00, '01
Series: *Highway To Happiness*
Little Moments

Purchased_____, Price $_____

☐ *Give'em A Brake For Jesus*, 649562

>≺— $20.00
✛ $20.00
♕ $20.00

Open, Issue Price $20.00, '01
Series: *Highway To Happiness*
Little Moments

Purchased_____, Price $_____

☑ *Hay Good Lookin'*, 649732

★ $45.00
◯ $45.00
>≺— $45.00
✛ $45.00
♕ $45.00

Open, Issue Price $45.00, '99
Series: *Country Lane Collection*

Purchased___45⁰⁰___, Price $___45⁰⁰___

☐ *Peace In The Valley*, 649929

★ $125.00
◯ $125.00

Limited Ed. 12,500, Issue Price $125.00, '99
1999 Enesco Fall Show Exclusive

Purchased_____, Price $_____

☐ *Ice See In You A Champion*, 649937

This figurine
was also
produced
for the Spring
Dating Pro-
gram in a Lim-
ited Edition
run of 4,800 in
1999 (649937S).

★ $37.50

Open, Issue Price $37.50, '00
Canadian Exclusive

Purchased_____, Price $_____

☑ *Baby Moses*, 649953

Unmarked $25.00

Annual 1999, Issue Price $25.00, '99
Series: *Bible Stories — Little Moments*
Purchased_____, Price $_____

☐ *The Great Pearl*, 649996

★ $25.00
◐ $25.00
⤛ $25.00
✚ $25.00
♛ $25.00

Open, Issue Price $25.00, '99
Series: *Bible Stories — Little Moments*
Purchased_____, Price $_____

☐ *Ruth & Naomi*, 649961

⤛ $25.00
✚ $25.00
♛ $25.00

Open, Issue Price $25.00, '01
Series: *Bible Stories — Little Moments*
Purchased_____, Price $_____

☐ *The Sower And The Seed*, 650005

⤛ $20.00
✚ $20.00
♛ $20.00

Open, Issue Price $20.00, '01
Series: *Bible Stories — Little Moments*
Purchased_____, Price $_____

☐ *The Good Samaritan*, 649988

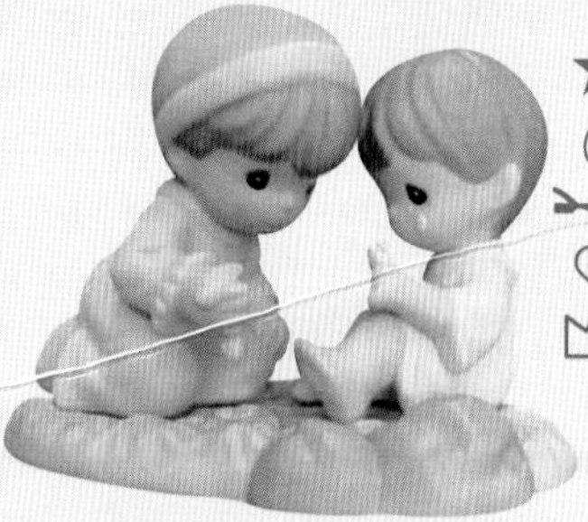

★ $25.00
◐ $25.00
⤛ $25.00
✚ $25.00
♛ $25.00

Open, Issue Price $25.00, '99
Series: *Bible Stories — Little Moments*
Purchased_____, Price $_____

☐ *Giving My Heart Freely*, 650013

⤛ $40.00
✚ $40.00
♛ $40.00

Open, Issue Price $40.00, '01
Purchased_____, Price $_____

♥ Loving ♥ Caring ♥ Sharing ♥   323

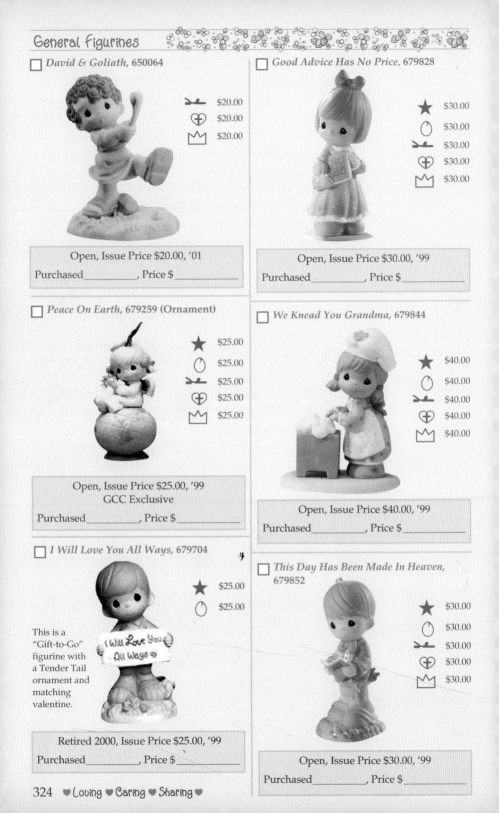

☐ *David & Goliath*, 650064

✂ $20.00
✝ $20.00
♛ $20.00

Open, Issue Price $20.00, '01

Purchased_____, Price $_____

☐ *Good Advice Has No Price*, 679828

★ $30.00
○ $30.00
✂ $30.00
✝ $30.00
♛ $30.00

Open, Issue Price $30.00, '99

Purchased_____, Price $_____

☐ *Peace On Earth*, 679259 (Ornament)

★ $25.00
○ $25.00
✂ $25.00
✝ $25.00
♛ $25.00

Open, Issue Price $25.00, '99
GCC Exclusive

Purchased_____, Price $_____

☐ *We Knead You Grandma*, 679844

★ $40.00
○ $40.00
✂ $40.00
✝ $40.00
♛ $40.00

Open, Issue Price $40.00, '99

Purchased_____, Price $_____

☐ *I Will Love You All Ways*, 679704

★ $25.00
○ $25.00

This is a "Gift-to-Go" figurine with a Tender Tail ornament and matching valentine.

Retired 2000, Issue Price $25.00, '99

Purchased_____, Price $_____

☐ *This Day Has Been Made In Heaven*, 679852

★ $30.00
○ $30.00
✂ $30.00
✝ $30.00
♛ $30.00

Open, Issue Price $30.00, '99

Purchased_____, Price $_____

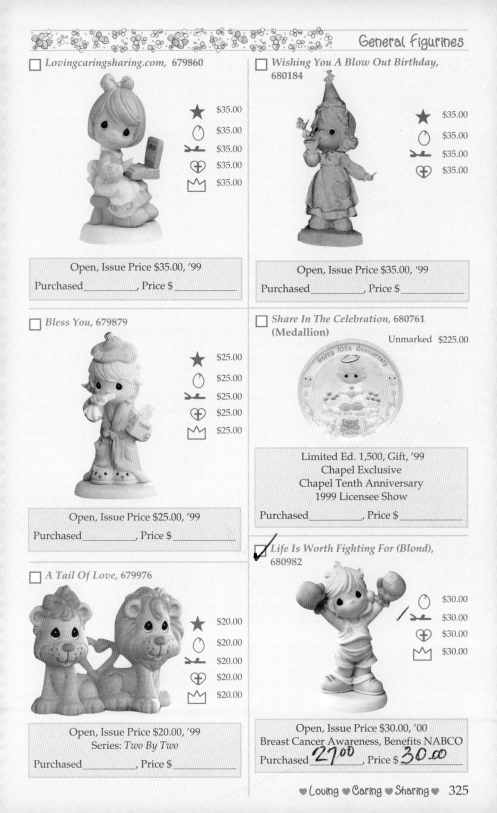

☐ *Lovingcaringsharing.com,* 679860

★ $35.00
◖ $35.00
⊱ $35.00
✣ $35.00
♕ $35.00

Open, Issue Price $35.00, '99
Purchased_____, Price $_____

☐ *Wishing You A Blow Out Birthday,* 680184

★ $35.00
◖ $35.00
⊱ $35.00
✣ $35.00

Open, Issue Price $35.00, '99
Purchased_____, Price $_____

☐ *Bless You,* 679879

★ $25.00
◖ $25.00
⊱ $25.00
✣ $25.00
♕ $25.00

Open, Issue Price $25.00, '99
Purchased_____, Price $_____

☐ *Share In The Celebration,* 680761 **(Medallion)**

Unmarked $225.00

Limited Ed. 1,500, Gift, '99
Chapel Exclusive
Chapel Tenth Anniversary
1999 Licensee Show
Purchased_____, Price $_____

☑ *Life Is Worth Fighting For (Blond),* 680982

◖ $30.00
⊱ $30.00
✣ $30.00
♕ $30.00

Open, Issue Price $30.00, '00
Breast Cancer Awareness, Benefits NABCO
Purchased *27.00*, Price $ *30.00*

☐ *A Tail Of Love,* 679976

★ $20.00
◖ $20.00
⊱ $20.00
✣ $20.00
♕ $20.00

Open, Issue Price $20.00, '99
Series: *Two By Two*
Purchased_____, Price $_____

☐ *Life Is Worth Fighting For (Brunette),* 680982B

◯ $30.00
≻⊱ $30.00
✚ $30.00
♛ $30.00

Open, Issue Price $30.00, '00
Breast Cancer Awareness, Benefits NABCO
Purchased_____, Price $_____

☐ *His Name Is Jesus,* 681032

Unmarked $65.00

Limited Ed. 1,500, Issue Price $40.00, '99
1999 Collector's Christmas Weekend
Purchased_____, Price $_____

☐ *God Gives Us Memories So That We Might Have Roses In December,* 680990

◯ $45.00
≻⊱ $45.00
✚ $45.00
♛ $45.00

Open, Issue Price $45.00, '00
Benefits Compassionate Friends
Purchased_____, Price $_____

☐ *Let Freedom Ring,* 681059

★ $45.00
◯ $45.00
≻⊱ $45.00
✚ $45.00
♛ $45.00

Open, Issue Price $45.00, '99
Purchased_____, Price $_____

☐ *Precious Moments Will Last Forever,* 681008

★ $35.00
◯ $35.00

Annual 1999, Issue Price $35.00, '99
Purchased_____, Price $_____

☐ *Let Freedom Ring,* 681059E

★ $45.00
◯ $45.00

Only attendees of the Enesco Summer Shows were able to offer this piece with a special understamp.

Open, Issue Price $45.00, '99
Purchased_____, Price $_____

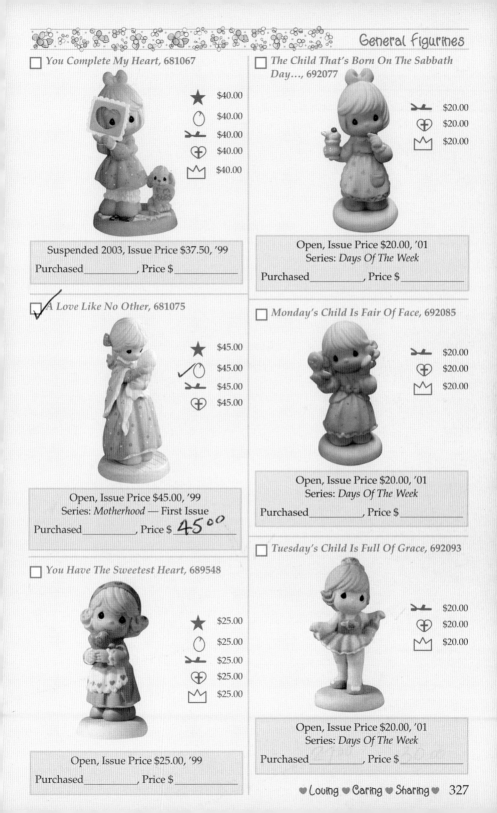

☐ *You Complete My Heart*, 681067

★ $40.00
⬯ $40.00
✂ $40.00
✝ $40.00
♔ $40.00

Suspended 2003, Issue Price $37.50, '99
Purchased_____, Price $_____

☑ *A Love Like No Other*, 681075

★ $45.00
✓⬯ $45.00
✂ $45.00
✝ $45.00

Open, Issue Price $45.00, '99
Series: *Motherhood* — First Issue
Purchased_____, Price $ *45⁰⁰*

☐ *You Have The Sweetest Heart*, 689548

★ $25.00
⬯ $25.00
✂ $25.00
✝ $25.00
♔ $25.00

Open, Issue Price $25.00, '99
Purchased_____, Price $_____

☐ *The Child That's Born On The Sabbath Day...*, 692077

✂ $20.00
✝ $20.00
♔ $20.00

Open, Issue Price $20.00, '01
Series: *Days Of The Week*
Purchased_____, Price $_____

☐ *Monday's Child Is Fair Of Face*, 692085

✂ $20.00
✝ $20.00
♔ $20.00

Open, Issue Price $20.00, '01
Series: *Days Of The Week*
Purchased_____, Price $_____

☐ *Tuesday's Child Is Full Of Grace*, 692093

✂ $20.00
✝ $20.00
♔ $20.00

Open, Issue Price $20.00, '01
Series: *Days Of The Week*
Purchased_____, Price $_____

☐ *Wednesday's Child Is Full Of Woe,* 692107

>⤚ $20.00
✛ $20.00
♛ $20.00

Open, Issue Price $20.00, '01
Series: *Days Of The Week*

Purchased_____, Price $_____

☐ *Saturday's Child Works Hard For A Living,* 692131

>⤚ $20.00
✛ $20.00
♛ $20.00

Open, Issue Price $20.00, '01
Series: *Days Of The Week*

Purchased_____, Price $_____

☐ *Thursday's Child Has Far To Go,* 692115

>⤚ $20.00
✛ $20.00
♛ $20.00

Open, Issue Price $20.00, '01
Series: *Days Of The Week*

Purchased_____, Price $_____

☐ *Alleluia, He Is Risen,* 692409

★ $30.00
○ $30.00
>⤚ $30.00
✛ $30.00
♛ $30.00

Open, Issue Price $30.00, '99

Purchased_____, Price $_____

☐ *Friday's Child Is Loving And Giving,* 692123

>⤚ $20.00
✛ $20.00
♛ $20.00

Open, Issue Price $20.00, '01
Series: *Days Of The Week*

Purchased_____, Price $_____

☐ *Repunt Or Else,* 729620

○ $30.00
>⤚ $30.00

Open, Issue Price $30.00, '00

Purchased_____, Price $_____

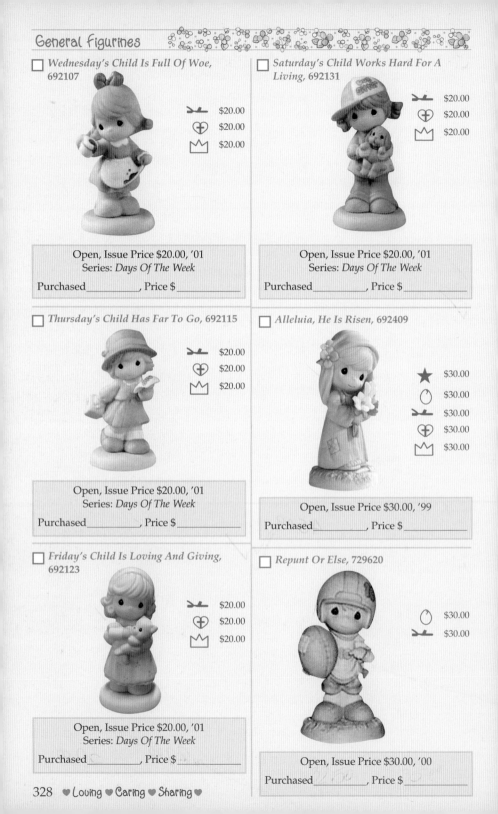

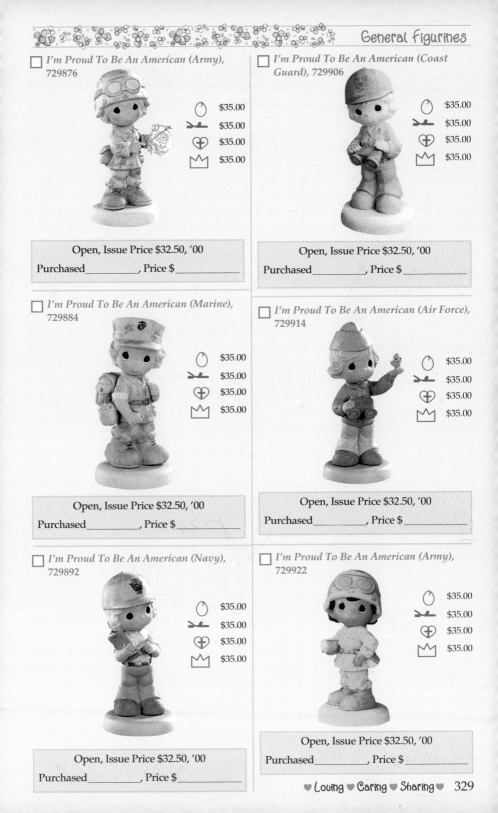

☐ *I'm Proud To Be An American (Army),* 729876

◯ $35.00
⤙ $35.00
✝ $35.00
♕ $35.00

Open, Issue Price $32.50, '00

Purchased_____, Price $_____

☐ *I'm Proud To Be An American (Coast Guard),* 729906

◯ $35.00
⤙ $35.00
✝ $35.00
♕ $35.00

Open, Issue Price $32.50, '00

Purchased_____, Price $_____

☐ *I'm Proud To Be An American (Marine),* 729884

◯ $35.00
⤙ $35.00
✝ $35.00
♕ $35.00

Open, Issue Price $32.50, '00

Purchased_____, Price $_____

☐ *I'm Proud To Be An American (Air Force),* 729914

◯ $35.00
⤙ $35.00
✝ $35.00
♕ $35.00

Open, Issue Price $32.50, '00

Purchased_____, Price $_____

☐ *I'm Proud To Be An American (Navy),* 729892

◯ $35.00
⤙ $35.00
✝ $35.00
♕ $35.00

Open, Issue Price $32.50, '00

Purchased_____, Price $_____

☐ *I'm Proud To Be An American (Army),* 729922

◯ $35.00
⤙ $35.00
✝ $35.00
♕ $35.00

Open, Issue Price $32.50, '00

Purchased_____, Price $_____

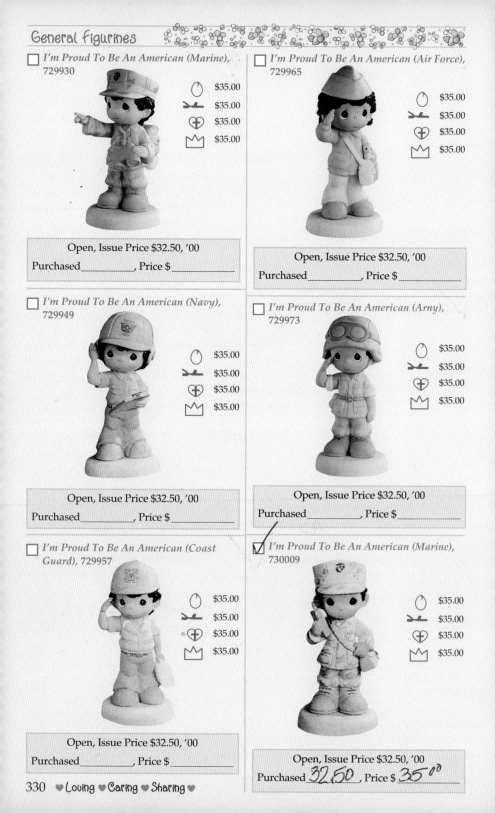

☐ *I'm Proud To Be An American (Marine),* 729930

- ⬭ $35.00
- ⤙ $35.00
- ✠ $35.00
- ♕ $35.00

Open, Issue Price $32.50, '00
Purchased_____, Price $_____

☐ *I'm Proud To Be An American (Air Force),* 729965

- ⬭ $35.00
- ⤙ $35.00
- ✠ $35.00
- ♕ $35.00

Open, Issue Price $32.50, '00
Purchased_____, Price $_____

☐ *I'm Proud To Be An American (Navy),* 729949

- ⬭ $35.00
- ⤙ $35.00
- ✠ $35.00
- ♕ $35.00

Open, Issue Price $32.50, '00
Purchased_____, Price $_____

☐ *I'm Proud To Be An American (Arny),* 729973

- ⬭ $35.00
- ⤙ $35.00
- ✠ $35.00
- ♕ $35.00

Open, Issue Price $32.50, '00
Purchased_____, Price $_____

☐ *I'm Proud To Be An American (Coast Guard),* 729957

- ⬭ $35.00
- ⤙ $35.00
- ✠ $35.00
- ♕ $35.00

Open, Issue Price $32.50, '00
Purchased_____, Price $_____

☑ *I'm Proud To Be An American (Marine),* 730009

- ⬭ $35.00
- ⤙ $35.00
- ✠ $35.00
- ♕ $35.00

Open, Issue Price $32.50, '00
Purchased _32.50_, Price $ _35⁰⁰_

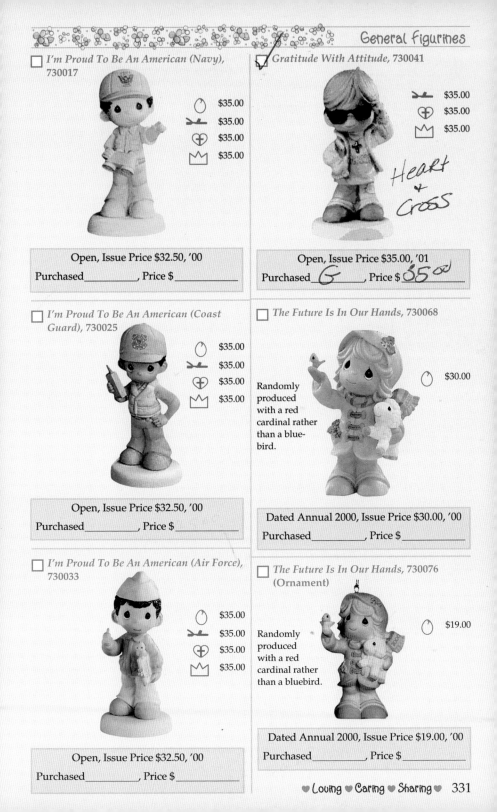

☐ *I'm Proud To Be An American (Navy),* 730017

🥚 $35.00
🐟 $35.00
✝ $35.00
👑 $35.00

Open, Issue Price $32.50, '00

Purchased_____, Price $_____

☑ *Gratitude With Attitude,* 730041

🐟 $35.00
✝ $35.00
👑 $35.00

Heart + Cross

Open, Issue Price $35.00, '01

Purchased__G_____, Price $ 35⁰⁰

☐ *I'm Proud To Be An American (Coast Guard),* 730025

🥚 $35.00
🐟 $35.00
✝ $35.00
👑 $35.00

Open, Issue Price $32.50, '00

Purchased_____, Price $_____

☐ *The Future Is In Our Hands,* 730068

Randomly produced with a red cardinal rather than a blue-bird.

🥚 $30.00

Dated Annual 2000, Issue Price $30.00, '00

Purchased_____, Price $_____

☐ *I'm Proud To Be An American (Air Force),* 730033

🥚 $35.00
🐟 $35.00
✝ $35.00
👑 $35.00

Open, Issue Price $32.50, '00

Purchased_____, Price $_____

☐ *The Future Is In Our Hands,* 730076 (Ornament)

Randomly produced with a red cardinal rather than a bluebird.

🥚 $19.00

Dated Annual 2000, Issue Price $19.00, '00

Purchased_____, Price $_____

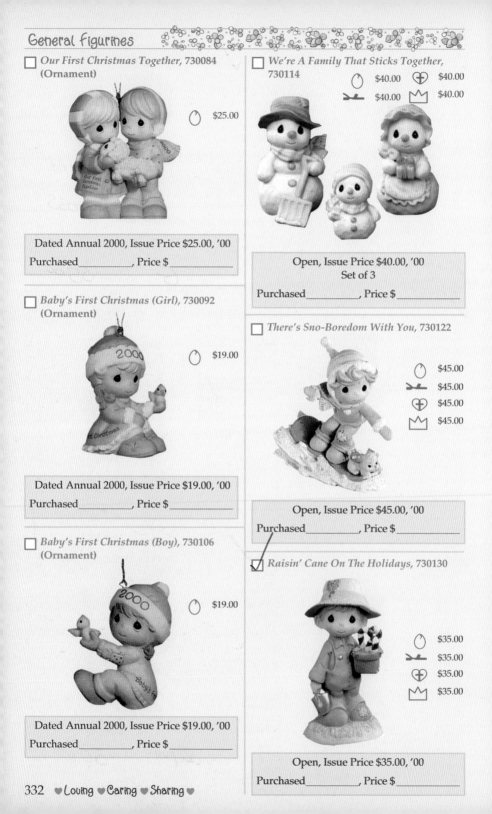

☐ *Our First Christmas Together*, 730084
(Ornament)

🥚 $25.00

Dated Annual 2000, Issue Price $25.00, '00

Purchased_____, Price $_____

☐ *Baby's First Christmas (Girl)*, 730092
(Ornament)

🥚 $19.00

Dated Annual 2000, Issue Price $19.00, '00

Purchased_____, Price $_____

☐ *Baby's First Christmas (Boy)*, 730106
(Ornament)

🥚 $19.00

Dated Annual 2000, Issue Price $19.00, '00

Purchased_____, Price $_____

☐ *We're A Family That Sticks Together*,
730114

🥚 $40.00   ✛ $40.00

✂ $40.00   👑 $40.00

Open, Issue Price $40.00, '00
Set of 3

Purchased_____, Price $_____

☐ *There's Sno-Boredom With You*, 730122

🥚 $45.00
✂ $45.00
✛ $45.00
👑 $45.00

Open, Issue Price $45.00, '00

Purchased_____, Price $_____

☑ *Raisin' Cane On The Holidays*, 730130

🥚 $35.00
✂ $35.00
✛ $35.00
👑 $35.00

Open, Issue Price $35.00, '00

Purchased_____, Price $_____

☐ *Everything Is Beautiful In Its Own Way,* 730149

◯ $25.00
〜 $25.00
✠ $25.00
♛ $25.00

Open, Issue Price $25.00, '00

Purchased_____, Price $_____

☑ *I'll Never Let You Down,* 730165

◯✓
〜 $45.00
✠ $45.00
♛ $45.00

Open, Issue Price $45.00, '01

Purchased 45⁰⁰, Price $_____

☐ *The Peace That Passes Understanding,* 730173

◯ $100.00
〜 $100.00
✠ $100.00

Limited Ed. 10,000, Issue Price $100.00, '00
CCR And DSR Exclusive
Set of 7

Purchased_____, Price $_____

☐ *Home-Made Of Love,* 730211

◯ $45.00
〜 $45.00
✠ $45.00
♛ $45.00

Open, Issue Price $45.00, '00

Purchased_____, Price $_____

☐ *I'm A Reflection Of Your Love,* 730238

Unmarked $21.00

Open, Issue Price $14.99, '00
Avon Exclusive

Purchased_____, Price $_____

☐ *You Have The Beary Best Heart,* 730254

〜 $35.00

Limited Ed., Issue Price $35.00, '01
Authorized Retailer 3/10/01 Event

Purchased_____, Price $_____

The Fun Is Being Together, 730262

○ $200.00
⊁ $200.00
⊕ $200.00

Limited Ed. 10,000, Issue Price $200.00, '00
CCR Exclusive, Individually Numbered

Purchased_____, Price $_____

Squeaky Clean, 731048

○ $45.00

Annual 2000, Issue Price $45.00, '00
CCR Event Exclusive

Purchased_____, Price $_____

Take Thyme For Yourself, 731064

⊁ $35.00
⊕ $35.00
♔ $35.00

Open, Issue Price $35.00, '01

Purchased_____, Price $_____

A Collection Of Precious Moments, 731129

○ $25.00
⊁ $25.00
⊕ $25.00
♔ $25.00

Open, Issue Price $25.00, '00

Purchased_____, Price $_____

Sharing Sweet Moments Together, 731579

○ $20.00

Limited Ed., Issue Price $20.00, '00
Series: *Little Moments*
2000 Sweetest Day Promo

Purchased_____, Price $_____

Grandma, I'll Never Outgrow You! 731587

○ $25.00
⊁ $25.00
⊕ $25.00
♔ $25.00

Open, Issue Price $25.00, '00
Grandparents' Day Promo

Purchased_____, Price $_____

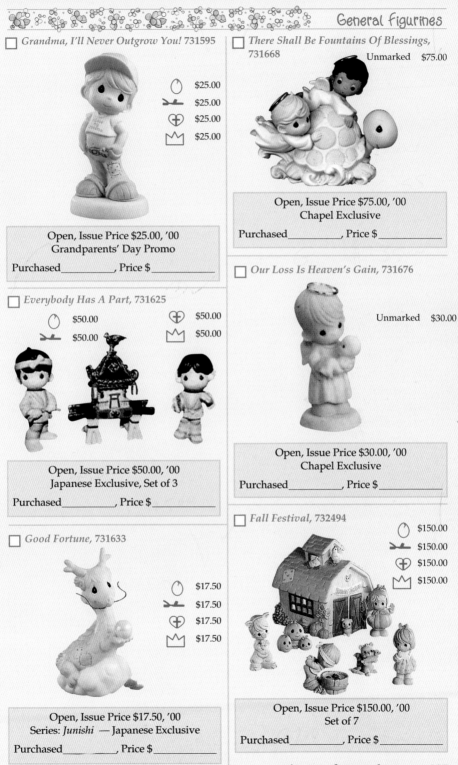

☐ *Grandma, I'll Never Outgrow You!* 731595

○ $25.00
⤳ $25.00
✛ $25.00
♛ $25.00

Open, Issue Price $25.00, '00
Grandparents' Day Promo

Purchased_____, Price $ _____

☐ *Everybody Has A Part,* 731625

○ $50.00   ✛ $50.00
⤳ $50.00   ♛ $50.00

Open, Issue Price $50.00, '00
Japanese Exclusive, Set of 3

Purchased_____, Price $ _____

☐ *Good Fortune,* 731633

○ $17.50
⤳ $17.50
✛ $17.50
♛ $17.50

Open, Issue Price $17.50, '00
Series: *Junishi* — Japanese Exclusive

Purchased_____, Price $ _____

☐ *There Shall Be Fountains Of Blessings,* 731668

Unmarked $75.00

Open, Issue Price $75.00, '00
Chapel Exclusive

Purchased_____, Price $ _____

☐ *Our Loss Is Heaven's Gain,* 731676

Unmarked $30.00

Open, Issue Price $30.00, '00
Chapel Exclusive

Purchased_____, Price $ _____

☐ *Fall Festival,* 732494

○ $150.00
⤳ $150.00
✛ $150.00
♛ $150.00

Open, Issue Price $150.00, '00
Set of 7

Purchased_____, Price $ _____

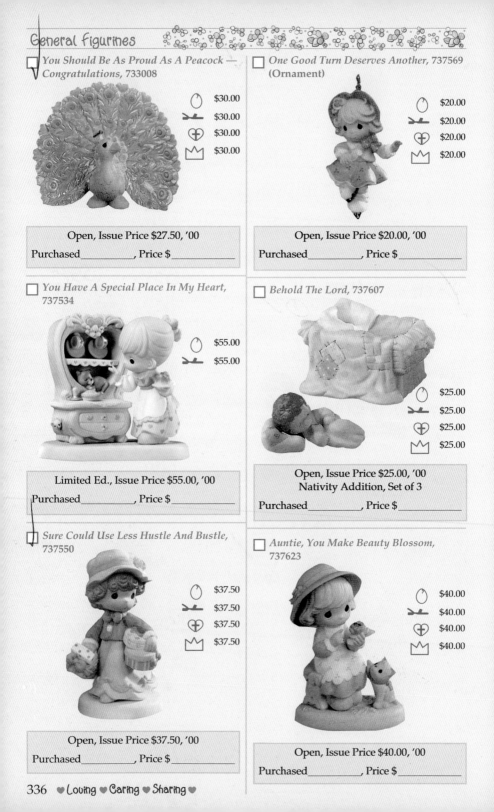

☐ *You Should Be As Proud As A Peacock — Congratulations*, 733008

◯ $30.00
✄ $30.00
✝ $30.00
♔ $30.00

Open, Issue Price $27.50, '00
Purchased_____, Price $_____

☐ *One Good Turn Deserves Another*, 737569 (Ornament)

◯ $20.00
✄ $20.00
✝ $20.00
♔ $20.00

Open, Issue Price $20.00, '00
Purchased_____, Price $_____

☐ *You Have A Special Place In My Heart*, 737534

◯ $55.00
✄ $55.00

Limited Ed., Issue Price $55.00, '00
Purchased_____, Price $_____

☐ *Behold The Lord*, 737607

◯ $25.00
✄ $25.00
✝ $25.00
♔ $25.00

Open, Issue Price $25.00, '00
Nativity Addition, Set of 3
Purchased_____, Price $_____

☐ *Sure Could Use Less Hustle And Bustle*, 737550

◯ $37.50
✄ $37.50
✝ $37.50
♔ $37.50

Open, Issue Price $37.50, '00
Purchased_____, Price $_____

☐ *Auntie, You Make Beauty Blossom*, 737623

◯ $40.00
✄ $40.00
✝ $40.00
♔ $40.00

Open, Issue Price $40.00, '00
Purchased_____, Price $_____

☐ *You're A Real Barbe-cutie*, 742872

⊕ $35.00

♔ $35.00

Open, Issue Price $35.00, '02
Series: *Special Wishes*

Purchased_____, Price $_____

☐ *To The Sweetest Girl In The Cast*, 742880

⤛ $35.00

⊕ $35.00

♔ $35.00

Open, Issue Price $35.00, '01

Purchased_____, Price $_____

☐ *You Add Sparkle To My Life*, 745413

⤛ $25.00

Open, Issue Price $25.00, '01
Series: *Heavenly Daze* – First Issue
Care-A-Van Exclusive

Purchased_____, Price $_____

☐ *A Collection Of Precious Moments*, 745510

★ $30.00

◯ $30.00

Comes with a
copy of the
book *Chicken
Soup For The Soul*.

Retired 2000, Issue Price $27.00, '99
Set Of 2

Purchased_____, Price $_____

☐ *Let Earth Receive Her King*, 748382

Unmarked $32.50

⤛ $32.50

Open, Issue Price $32.50, '00
Chapel Exclusive

Purchased_____, Price $_____

☐ *Let Earth Receive Her King*, 748390
(Ornament)

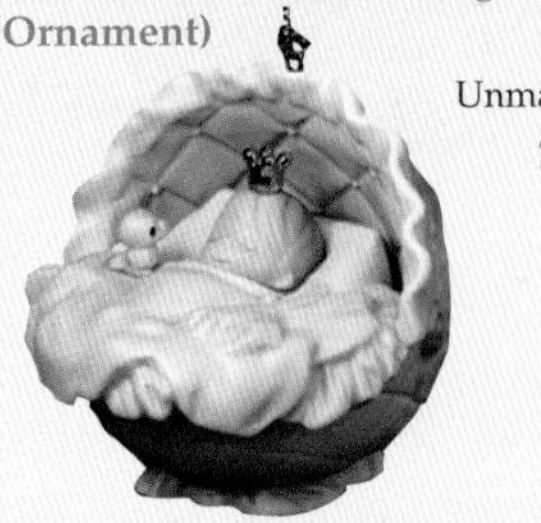

Unmarked $25.00

⤛ $25.00

Open, Issue Price $25.00, '00
Chapel Exclusive

Purchased_____, Price $_____

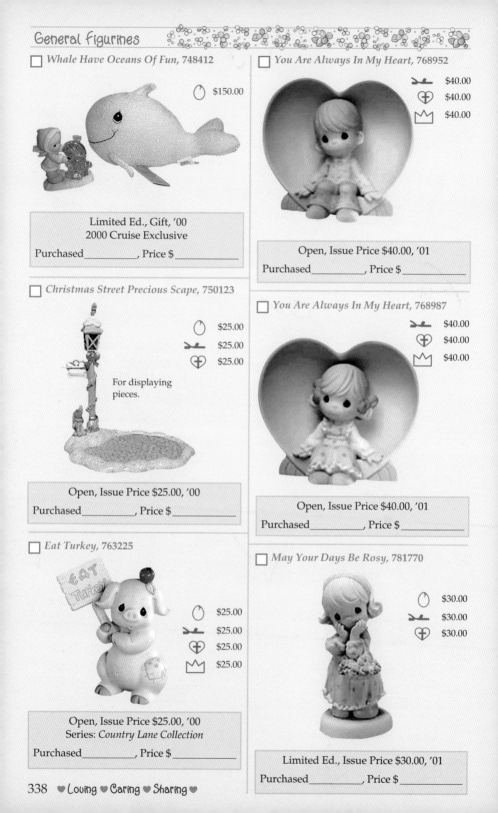

☐ *Whale Have Oceans Of Fun*, 748412

◯ $150.00

Limited Ed., Gift, '00
2000 Cruise Exclusive

Purchased_____, Price $_____

☐ *Christmas Street Precious Scape*, 750123

◯ $25.00
🛬 $25.00
🕀 $25.00

For displaying
pieces.

Open, Issue Price $25.00, '00

Purchased_____, Price $_____

☐ *Eat Turkey*, 763225

◯ $25.00
🛬 $25.00
🕀 $25.00
♛ $25.00

Open, Issue Price $25.00, '00
Series: *Country Lane Collection*

Purchased_____, Price $_____

☐ *You Are Always In My Heart*, 768952

🛬 $40.00
🕀 $40.00
♛ $40.00

Open, Issue Price $40.00, '01

Purchased_____, Price $_____

☐ *You Are Always In My Heart*, 768987

🛬 $40.00
🕀 $40.00
♛ $40.00

Open, Issue Price $40.00, '01

Purchased_____, Price $_____

☐ *May Your Days Be Rosy*, 781770

◯ $30.00
🛬 $30.00
🕀 $30.00

Limited Ed., Issue Price $30.00, '01

Purchased_____, Price $_____

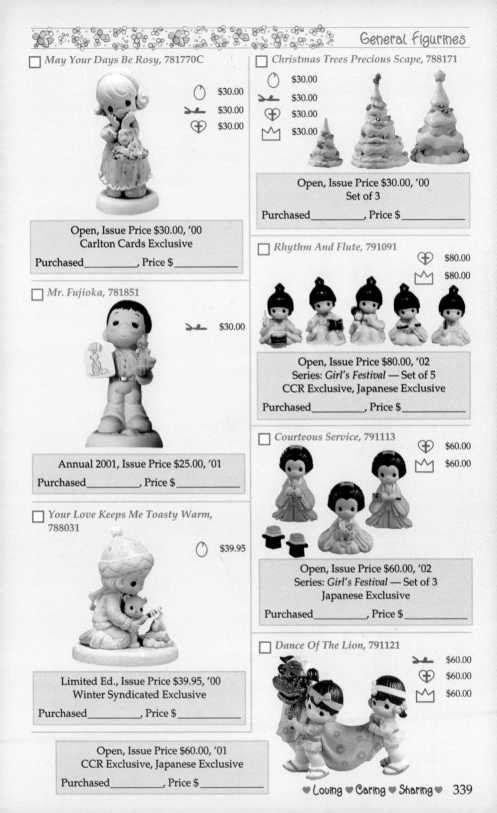

□ *May Your Days Be Rosy, 781770C*

○ $30.00
✂ $30.00
✝ $30.00

Open, Issue Price $30.00, '00
Carlton Cards Exclusive

Purchased_____, Price $_____

□ *Mr. Fujioka, 781851*

✂ $30.00

Annual 2001, Issue Price $25.00, '01

Purchased_____, Price $_____

□ *Your Love Keeps Me Toasty Warm,*
781031

○ $39.95

Limited Ed., Issue Price $39.95, '00
Winter Syndicated Exclusive

Purchased_____, Price $_____

□ *Christmas Trees Precious Scape, 788171*

○ $30.00
✂ $30.00
✝ $30.00
♔ $30.00

Open, Issue Price $30.00, '00
Set of 3

Purchased_____, Price $_____

□ *Rhythm And Flute, 791091*

✝ $80.00
♔ $80.00

Open, Issue Price $80.00, '02
Series: *Girl's Festival* — Set of 5
CCR Exclusive, Japanese Exclusive

Purchased_____, Price $_____

□ *Courteous Service, 791113*

✝ $60.00
♔ $60.00

Open, Issue Price $60.00, '02
Series: *Girl's Festival* — Set of 3
Japanese Exclusive

Purchased_____, Price $_____

□ *Dance Of The Lion, 791121*

✂ $60.00
✝ $60.00
♔ $60.00

Open, Issue Price $60.00, '01
CCR Exclusive, Japanese Exclusive

Purchased_____, Price $_____

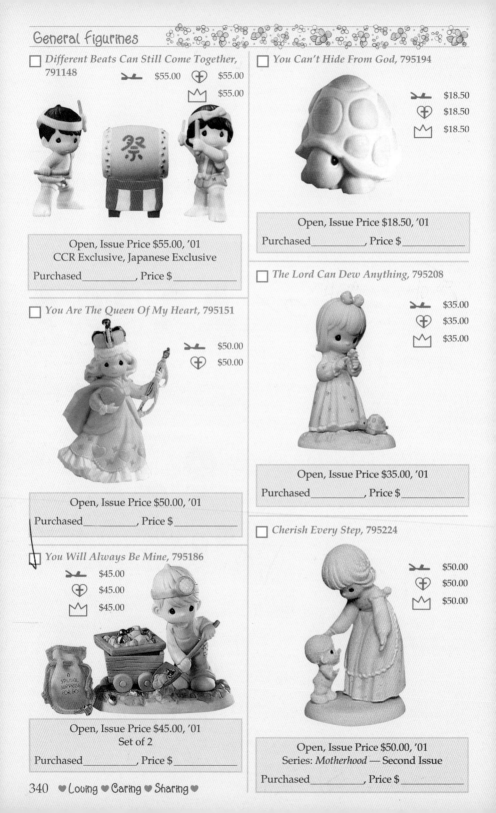

☐ *Different Beats Can Still Come Together,* 791148

$55.00 $55.00

$55.00

Open, Issue Price $55.00, '01
CCR Exclusive, Japanese Exclusive
Purchased_____, Price $_____

☐ *You Are The Queen Of My Heart,* 795151

$50.00

$50.00

Open, Issue Price $50.00, '01
Purchased_____, Price $_____

☐ *You Will Always Be Mine,* 795186

$45.00

$45.00

$45.00

Open, Issue Price $45.00, '01
Set of 2
Purchased_____, Price $_____

☐ *You Can't Hide From God,* 795194

$18.50

$18.50

$18.50

Open, Issue Price $18.50, '01
Purchased_____, Price $_____

☐ *The Lord Can Dew Anything,* 795208

$35.00

$35.00

$35.00

Open, Issue Price $35.00, '01
Purchased_____, Price $_____

☐ *Cherish Every Step,* 795224

$50.00

$50.00

$50.00

Open, Issue Price $50.00, '01
Series: *Motherhood* — Second Issue
Purchased_____, Price $_____

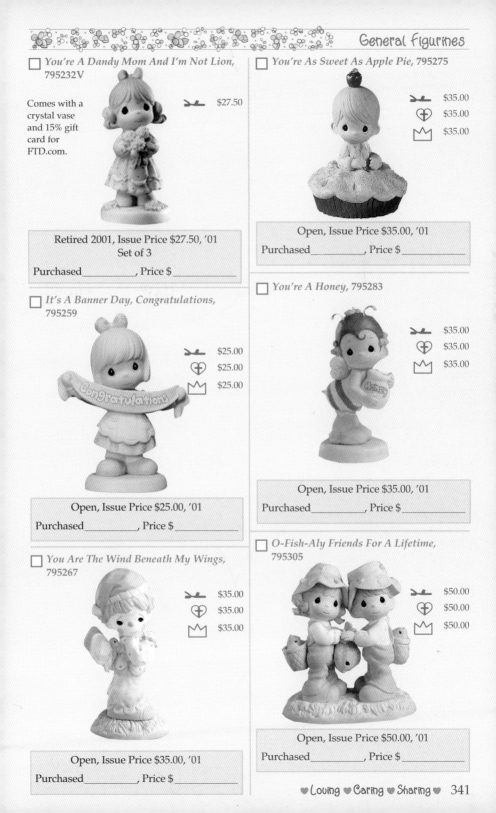

☐ *You're A Dandy Mom And I'm Not Lion,* 795232V

Comes with a crystal vase and 15% gift card for FTD.com.

$27.50

Retired 2001, Issue Price $27.50, '01
Set of 3

Purchased_____, Price $_____

☐ *It's A Banner Day, Congratulations,* 795259

$25.00
$25.00
$25.00

Open, Issue Price $25.00, '01

Purchased_____, Price $_____

☐ *You Are The Wind Beneath My Wings,* 795267

$35.00
$35.00
$35.00

Open, Issue Price $35.00, '01

Purchased_____, Price $_____

☐ *You're As Sweet As Apple Pie,* 795275

$35.00
$35.00
$35.00

Open, Issue Price $35.00, '01

Purchased_____, Price $_____

☐ *You're A Honey,* 795283

$35.00
$35.00
$35.00

Open, Issue Price $35.00, '01

Purchased_____, Price $_____

☐ *O-Fish-Aly Friends For A Lifetime,* 795305

$50.00
$50.00
$50.00

Open, Issue Price $50.00, '01

Purchased_____, Price $_____

☐ *Wishing You A Birthday Full Of Surprises*, 795313

$40.00
$40.00
$40.00

Open, Issue Price $40.00, '01

Purchased_____, Price $_____

☐ *No Bones About It — You're Grrreat*, 795321

$40.00
$40.00

Open, Issue Price $40.00, '02
Series: *Special Wishes*

Purchased_____, Price $_____

☐ *Blessed With A Loving Godmother*, 795348

$40.00
$40.00
$40.00

Open, Issue Price $40.00, '01

Purchased_____, Price $_____

☐ *Life Would Be The Pits Without Friends*, 795356

$40.00
$40.00
$40.00

Open, Issue Price $40.00, '01
Series: *Country Lane Collection*

Purchased____40.00____, Price $____40.00____

☐ *Bride (African-American)*, 795364

$30.00
$30.00
$30.00

Open, Issue Price $30.00, '01

Purchased_____, Price $_____

☐ *Groom (African-American)*, 795372

$30.00
$30.00
$30.00

Open, Issue Price $30.00, '01

Purchased_____, Price $_____

☐ *Bride (Hispanic)*, 795380

✄ $30.00
✝ $30.00
♛ $30.00

Open, Issue Price $30.00, '01
Purchased_____, Price $_____

☐ *Groom (Hispanic)*, 795399

✄ $30.00
✝ $30.00
♛ $30.00

Open, Issue Price $30.00, '01
Purchased_____, Price $_____

☐ *Bride (Asian)*, 795402

✄ $30.00
✝ $30.00
♛ $30.00

Open, Issue Price $30.00, '01
Purchased_____, Price $_____

☐ *Groom (Asian)*, 795410

✄ $30.00
✝ $30.00
♛ $30.00

Open, Issue Price $30.00, '01
Purchased_____, Price $_____

☐ *Friendship Grows From The Heart*, 795496

✄ $35.00

Limited Ed. 1,500, Issue Price $35.00, '01
2001 Licensee Event Exclusive
Purchased_____, Price $_____

☐ *On Our Way To The Chapel*, 795518

Unmarked $32.50

Open, Issue Price $32.50, '00
Chapel Exclusive
Purchased_____, Price $_____

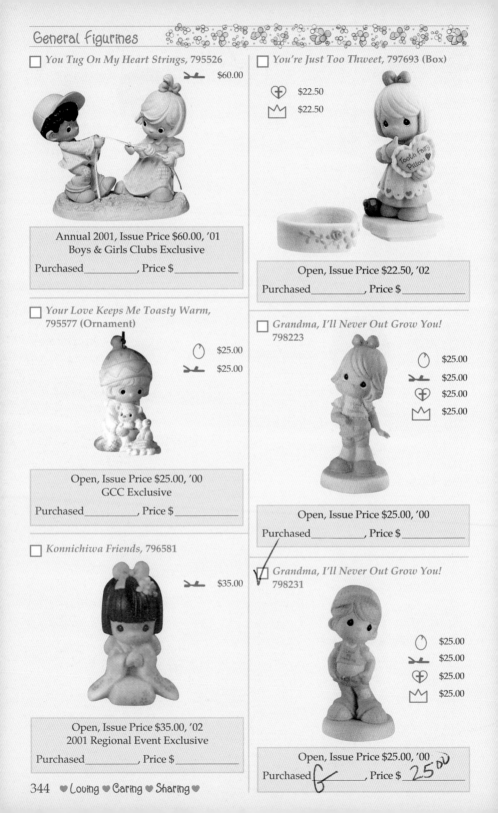

☐ *You Tug On My Heart Strings*, 795526

✂ $60.00

Annual 2001, Issue Price $60.00, '01
Boys & Girls Clubs Exclusive

Purchased_____, Price $_____

☐ *Your Love Keeps Me Toasty Warm*, 795577 (Ornament)

◯ $25.00
✂ $25.00

Open, Issue Price $25.00, '00
GCC Exclusive

Purchased_____, Price $_____

☐ *Konnichiwa Friends*, 796581

✂ $35.00

Open, Issue Price $35.00, '02
2001 Regional Event Exclusive

Purchased_____, Price $_____

☐ *You're Just Too Thweet*, 797693 (Box)

✟ $22.50
♔ $22.50

Open, Issue Price $22.50, '02

Purchased_____, Price $_____

☐ *Grandma, I'll Never Out Grow You!* 798223

◯ $25.00
✂ $25.00
✟ $25.00
♔ $25.00

Open, Issue Price $25.00, '00

Purchased_____, Price $_____

☑ *Grandma, I'll Never Out Grow You!* 798231

◯ $25.00
✂ $25.00
✟ $25.00
♔ $25.00

Open, Issue Price $25.00, '00

Purchased ✓_____, Price $ 25.00

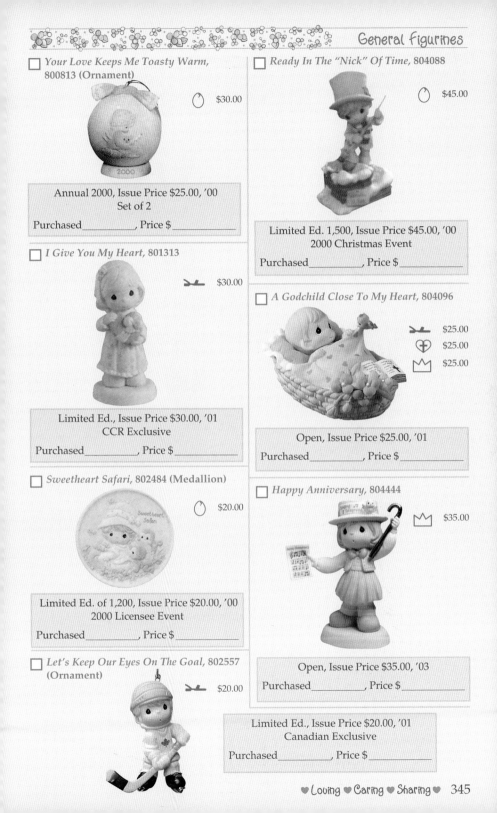

□ *Your Love Keeps Me Toasty Warm,*
800813 (Ornament)

⬭ $30.00

Annual 2000, Issue Price $25.00, '00
Set of 2

Purchased_____, Price $_____

□ *I Give You My Heart,* 801313

✂ $30.00

Limited Ed., Issue Price $30.00, '01
CCR Exclusive

Purchased_____, Price $_____

□ *Sweetheart Safari,* 802484 (Medallion)

⬭ $20.00

Limited Ed. of 1,200, Issue Price $20.00, '00
2000 Licensee Event

Purchased_____, Price $_____

□ *Let's Keep Our Eyes On The Goal,* 802557
(Ornament)

✂ $20.00

□ *Ready In The "Nick" Of Time,* 804088

⬭ $45.00

Limited Ed. 1,500, Issue Price $45.00, '00
2000 Christmas Event

Purchased_____, Price $_____

□ *A Godchild Close To My Heart,* 804096

✂ $25.00
♱ $25.00
♕ $25.00

Open, Issue Price $25.00, '01

Purchased_____, Price $_____

□ *Happy Anniversary,* 804444

♕ $35.00

Open, Issue Price $35.00, '03

Purchased_____, Price $_____

Limited Ed., Issue Price $20.00, '01
Canadian Exclusive

Purchased_____, Price $_____

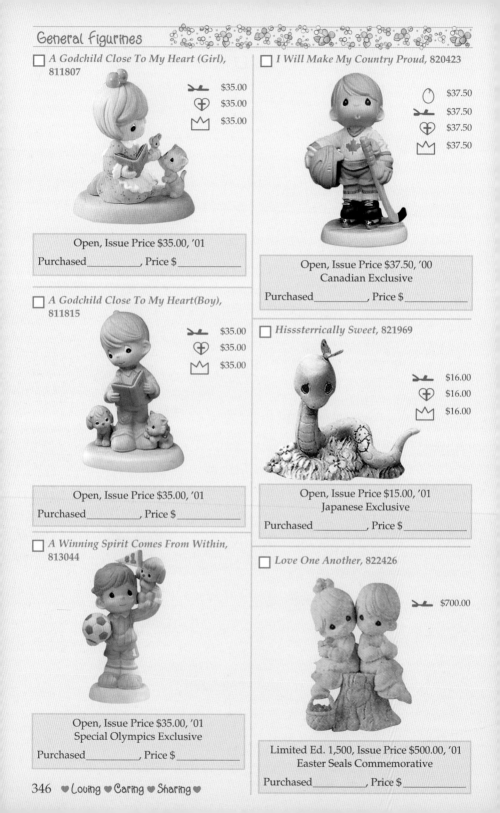

☐ *A Godchild Close To My Heart (Girl),* 811807

✂ $35.00
✚ $35.00
♔ $35.00

Open, Issue Price $35.00, '01

Purchased_____, Price $_____

☐ *A Godchild Close To My Heart(Boy),* 811815

✂ $35.00
✚ $35.00
♔ $35.00

Open, Issue Price $35.00, '01

Purchased_____, Price $_____

☐ *A Winning Spirit Comes From Within,* 813044

Open, Issue Price $35.00, '01
Special Olympics Exclusive

Purchased_____, Price $_____

☐ *I Will Make My Country Proud,* 820423

◐ $37.50
✂ $37.50
✚ $37.50
♔ $37.50

Open, Issue Price $37.50, '00
Canadian Exclusive

Purchased_____, Price $_____

☐ *Hisssterrically Sweet,* 821969

✂ $16.00
✚ $16.00
♔ $16.00

Open, Issue Price $15.00, '01
Japanese Exclusive

Purchased_____, Price $_____

☐ *Love One Another,* 822426

✂ $700.00

Limited Ed. 1,500, Issue Price $500.00, '01
Easter Seals Commemorative

Purchased_____, Price $_____

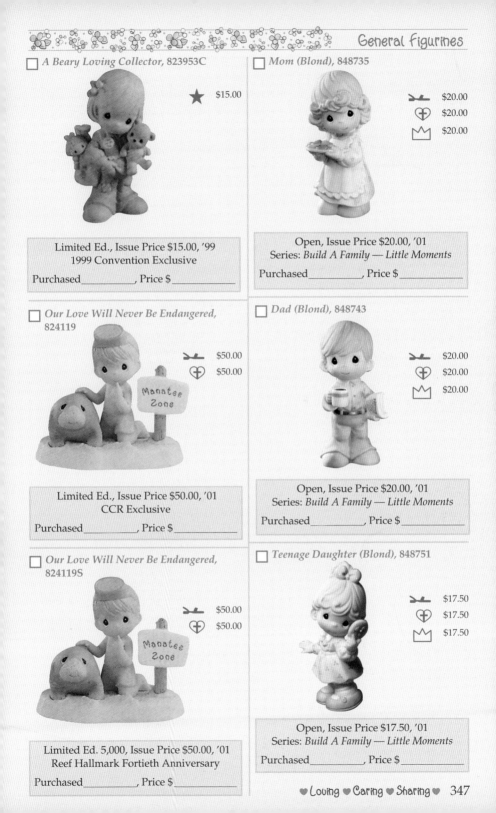

☐ *A Beary Loving Collector*, 823953C

★ $15.00

Limited Ed., Issue Price $15.00, '99
1999 Convention Exclusive

Purchased_____, Price $_____

☐ *Our Love Will Never Be Endangered*,
824119

$50.00
$50.00

Limited Ed., Issue Price $50.00, '01
CCR Exclusive

Purchased_____, Price $_____

☐ *Our Love Will Never Be Endangered*,
824119S

$50.00
$50.00

Limited Ed. 5,000, Issue Price $50.00, '01
Reef Hallmark Fortieth Anniversary

Purchased_____, Price $_____

☐ *Mom (Blond)*, 848735

$20.00
$20.00
$20.00

Open, Issue Price $20.00, '01
Series: *Build A Family — Little Moments*

Purchased_____, Price $_____

☐ *Dad (Blond)*, 848743

$20.00
$20.00
$20.00

Open, Issue Price $20.00, '01
Series: *Build A Family — Little Moments*

Purchased_____, Price $_____

☐ *Teenage Daughter (Blond)*, 848751

$17.50
$17.50
$17.50

Open, Issue Price $17.50, '01
Series: *Build A Family — Little Moments*

Purchased_____, Price $_____

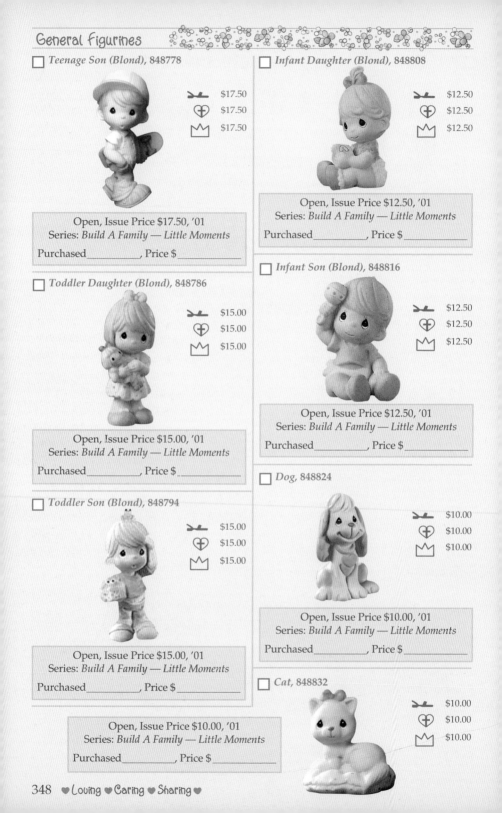

☐ *Teenage Son (Blond)*, 848778

✂ $17.50
⊕ $17.50
♛ $17.50

Open, Issue Price $17.50, '01
Series: *Build A Family — Little Moments*

Purchased_____, Price $_____

☐ *Toddler Daughter (Blond)*, 848786

✂ $15.00
⊕ $15.00
♛ $15.00

Open, Issue Price $15.00, '01
Series: *Build A Family — Little Moments*

Purchased_____, Price $_____

☐ *Toddler Son (Blond)*, 848794

✂ $15.00
⊕ $15.00
♛ $15.00

Open, Issue Price $15.00, '01
Series: *Build A Family — Little Moments*

Purchased_____, Price $_____

☐ *Infant Daughter (Blond)*, 848808

✂ $12.50
⊕ $12.50
♛ $12.50

Open, Issue Price $12.50, '01
Series: *Build A Family — Little Moments*

Purchased_____, Price $_____

☐ *Infant Son (Blond)*, 848816

✂ $12.50
⊕ $12.50
♛ $12.50

Open, Issue Price $12.50, '01
Series: *Build A Family — Little Moments*

Purchased_____, Price $_____

☐ *Dog*, 848824

✂ $10.00
⊕ $10.00
♛ $10.00

Open, Issue Price $10.00, '01
Series: *Build A Family — Little Moments*

Purchased_____, Price $_____

☐ *Cat*, 848832

✂ $10.00
⊕ $10.00
♛ $10.00

Open, Issue Price $10.00, '01
Series: *Build A Family — Little Moments*

Purchased_____, Price $_____

☐ *Bride And Groom Picture Frame*, 848840

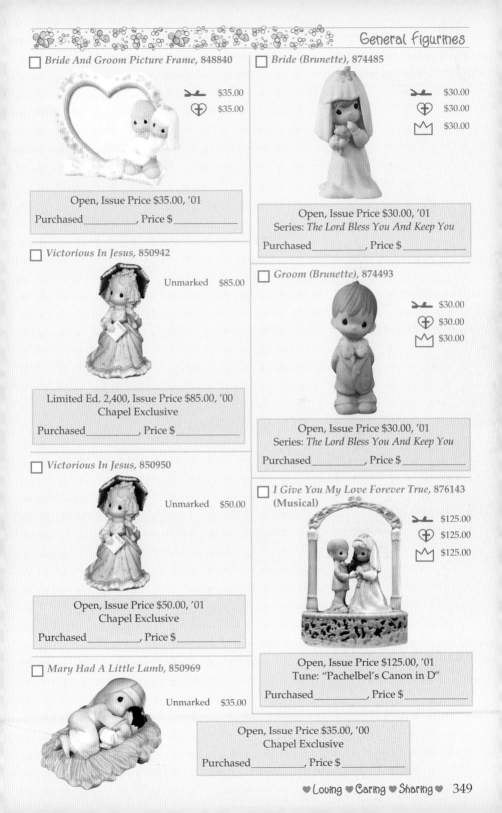

✈ $35.00
✝ $35.00

Open, Issue Price $35.00, '01

Purchased_____, Price $_____

☐ *Victorious In Jesus*, 850942

Unmarked $85.00

Limited Ed. 2,400, Issue Price $85.00, '00
Chapel Exclusive

Purchased_____, Price $_____

☐ *Victorious In Jesus*, 850950

Unmarked $50.00

Open, Issue Price $50.00, '01
Chapel Exclusive

Purchased_____, Price $_____

☐ *Mary Had A Little Lamb*, 850969

Unmarked $35.00

Open, Issue Price $35.00, '00
Chapel Exclusive

Purchased_____, Price $_____

☐ *Bride (Brunette)*, 874485

✈ $30.00
✝ $30.00
♛ $30.00

Open, Issue Price $30.00, '01
Series: *The Lord Bless You And Keep You*

Purchased_____, Price $_____

☐ *Groom (Brunette)*, 874493

✈ $30.00
✝ $30.00
♛ $30.00

Open, Issue Price $30.00, '01
Series: *The Lord Bless You And Keep You*

Purchased_____, Price $_____

☐ *I Give You My Love Forever True*, 876143
(Musical)

✈ $125.00
✝ $125.00
♛ $125.00

Open, Issue Price $125.00, '01
Tune: "Pachelbel's Canon in D"

Purchased_____, Price $_____

☐ *Bridal Arch, 876151 (Musical)*

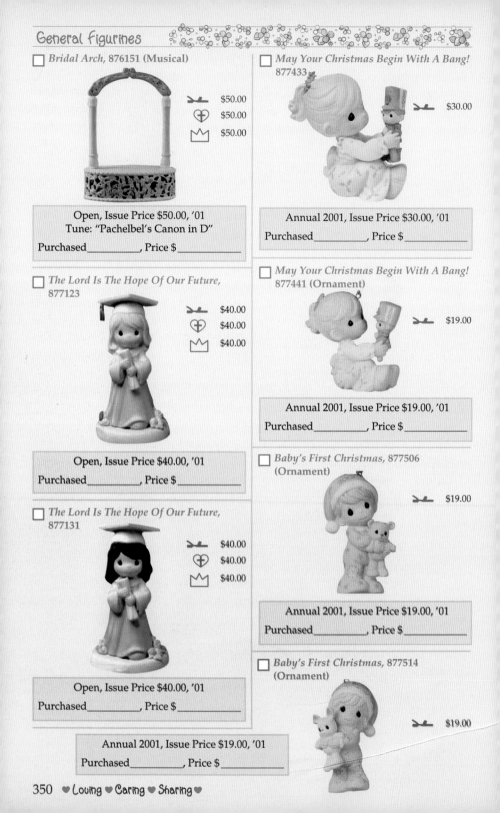

➤ $50.00
⊕ $50.00
♕ $50.00

Open, Issue Price $50.00, '01
Tune: "Pachelbel's Canon in D"

Purchased_____, Price $_____

☐ *The Lord Is The Hope Of Our Future, 877123*

➤ $40.00
⊕ $40.00
♕ $40.00

Open, Issue Price $40.00, '01

Purchased_____, Price $_____

☐ *The Lord Is The Hope Of Our Future, 877131*

➤ $40.00
⊕ $40.00
♕ $40.00

Open, Issue Price $40.00, '01

Purchased_____, Price $_____

☐ *May Your Christmas Begin With A Bang! 877433*

➤ $30.00

Annual 2001, Issue Price $30.00, '01

Purchased_____, Price $_____

☐ *May Your Christmas Begin With A Bang! 877441 (Ornament)*

➤ $19.00

Annual 2001, Issue Price $19.00, '01

Purchased_____, Price $_____

☐ *Baby's First Christmas, 877506 (Ornament)*

➤ $19.00

Annual 2001, Issue Price $19.00, '01

Purchased_____, Price $_____

☐ *Baby's First Christmas, 877514 (Ornament)*

➤ $19.00

Annual 2001, Issue Price $19.00, '01

Purchased_____, Price $_____

☐ *Our First Christmas Together, 878855*
(Ornament)

$25.00

Annual 2001, Issue Price $25.00, '01
Purchased_____, Price $_____

☐ *May Your Days Be Merry And Bright,*
878901

$45.00
$45.00
$45.00

Open, Issue Price $45.00, '01
Series: *Christmas Remembered*
Purchased_____, Price $_____

☐ *On A Scale From 1 To 10 You Are The*
Deerest, 878944

$30.00
$30.00

Retired 2002, Issue Price $30.00, '01
Purchased_____, Price $_____

☐ *Celebrating His Arrival, 878952*

$40.00
$40.00
$40.00

Open, Issue Price $40.00, '01
Purchased_____, Price $_____

☑ *The Royal Budge Is Good For The Soul,*
878987

$45.00 ✓
$45.00
$45.00

Open, Issue Price $45.00, '01
Nativity Addition
Purchased _45⁰⁰_, Price $ _45⁰⁰_

☑ *Life Is So Uplifting, 878995*

✓ $35.00
$35.00
$35.00

Open, Issue Price $35.00, '01
Purchased_____, Price $ _35⁰⁰_

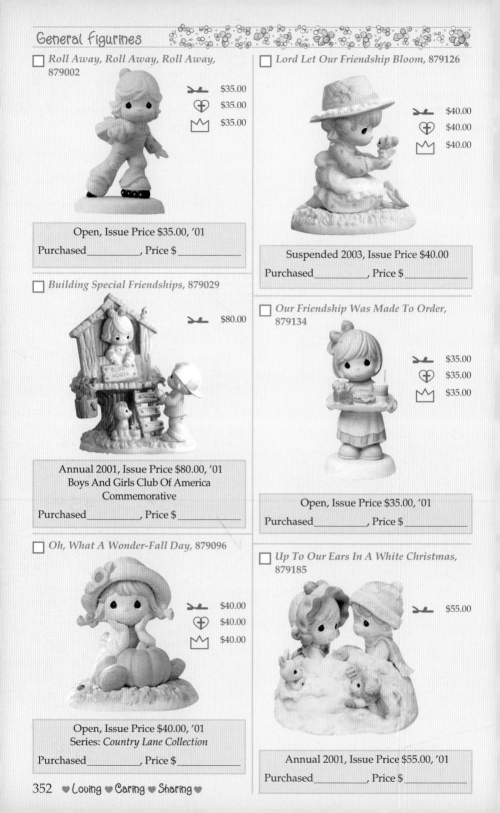

☐ *Roll Away, Roll Away, Roll Away,* 879002

✂ $35.00
✝ $35.00
♛ $35.00

Open, Issue Price $35.00, '01

Purchased_____, Price $_____

☐ *Building Special Friendships*, 879029

✂ $80.00

Annual 2001, Issue Price $80.00, '01
Boys And Girls Club Of America
Commemorative

Purchased_____, Price $_____

☐ *Oh, What A Wonder-Fall Day*, 879096

✂ $40.00
✝ $40.00
♛ $40.00

Open, Issue Price $40.00, '01
Series: *Country Lane Collection*

Purchased_____, Price $_____

☐ *Lord Let Our Friendship Bloom*, 879126

✂ $40.00
✝ $40.00
♛ $40.00

Suspended 2003, Issue Price $40.00

Purchased_____, Price $_____

☐ *Our Friendship Was Made To Order,* 879134

✂ $35.00
✝ $35.00
♛ $35.00

Open, Issue Price $35.00, '01

Purchased_____, Price $_____

☐ *Up To Our Ears In A White Christmas,* 879185

✂ $55.00

Annual 2001, Issue Price $55.00, '01

Purchased_____, Price $_____

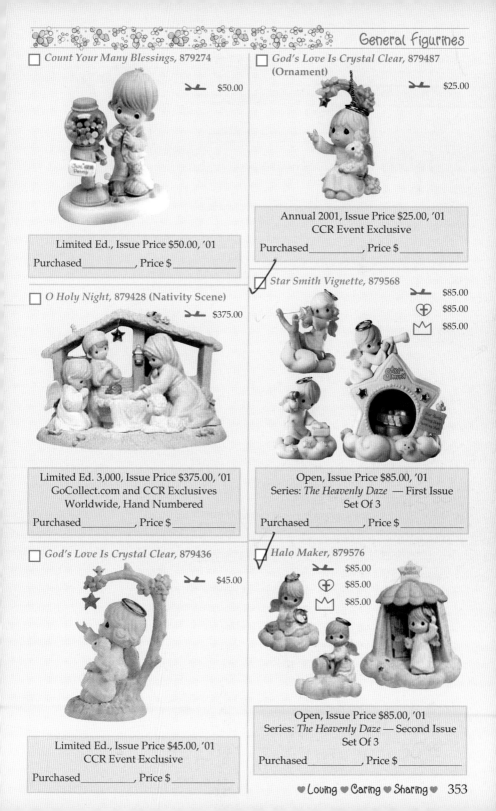

☐ *Count Your Many Blessings*, 879274

$50.00

Limited Ed., Issue Price $50.00, '01

Purchased_____, Price $_____

☐ *O Holy Night*, 879428 (Nativity Scene)

$375.00

Limited Ed. 3,000, Issue Price $375.00, '01
GoCollect.com and CCR Exclusives
Worldwide, Hand Numbered

Purchased_____, Price $_____

☐ *God's Love Is Crystal Clear*, 879436

$45.00

Limited Ed., Issue Price $45.00, '01
CCR Event Exclusive

Purchased_____, Price $_____

☐ *God's Love Is Crystal Clear*, 879487
(Ornament)

$25.00

Annual 2001, Issue Price $25.00, '01
CCR Event Exclusive

Purchased_____, Price $_____

☑ *Star Smith Vignette*, 879568

$85.00
$85.00
$85.00

Open, Issue Price $85.00, '01
Series: *The Heavenly Daze* — First Issue
Set Of 3

Purchased_____, Price $_____

☑ *Halo Maker*, 879576

$85.00
$85.00
$85.00

Open, Issue Price $85.00, '01
Series: *The Heavenly Daze* — Second Issue
Set Of 3

Purchased_____, Price $_____

☑ *The Golden Gown Seamstress*, 879606

✝ $85.00

♔ $85.00

Open, Issue Price $85.00, '02
Series: *The Heavenly Daze* — Third Issue
Set Of 3

Purchased_____, Price $_____

☐ *House Of Bells Vignette*, 879614

✝ $85.00

♔ $85.00

Open, Issue Price $85.00, '02
Series: *The Heavenly Daze* — Fourth Issue
Set Of 3

Purchased_____, Price $_____

☐ *The Good Book Library*, 879622

✝ $85.00

♔ $85.00

Open, Issue Price $85.00, '02
Series: *The Heavenly Daze* — Fifth Issue
Set Of 3

Purchased_____, Price $_____

☐ *Dream Makers*, 879630

♔ $85.00

Open, Issue Price $85.00, '03
Series: *The Heavenly Daze* — Sixth Issue
Set Of 3

Purchased_____, Price $_____

☐ *We Would See Jesus*, 879681

Unmarked $300.00

Limited Ed. 1,500, Issue Price $300.00, '01
Chapel Exclusive

Purchased_____, Price $_____

☐ *He Is The Rose Of Sharon*, 879703

Unmarked $30.00

✝ $30.00

♔ $30.00

Open, Issue Price $30.00, '01
Chapel Exclusive

Purchased_____, Price $_____

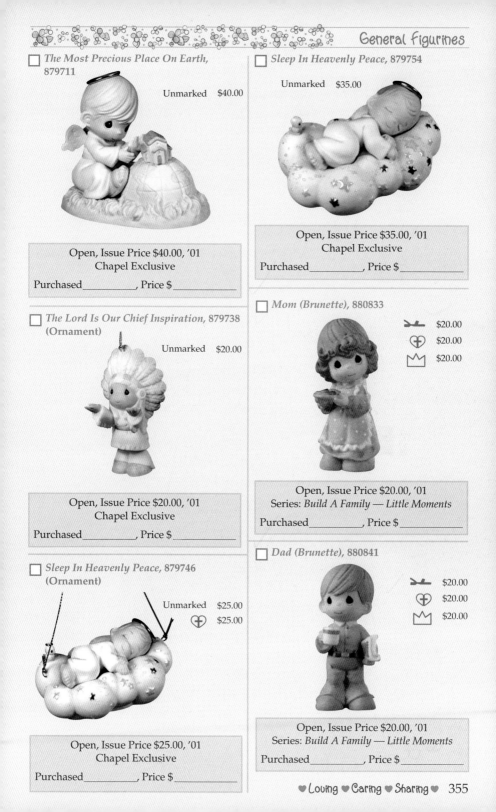

☐ *The Most Precious Place On Earth,* 879711

Unmarked $40.00

Open, Issue Price $40.00, '01
Chapel Exclusive

Purchased_____, Price $_____

☐ *The Lord Is Our Chief Inspiration,* 879738 (Ornament)

Unmarked $20.00

Open, Issue Price $20.00, '01
Chapel Exclusive

Purchased_____, Price $_____

☐ *Sleep In Heavenly Peace,* 879746 (Ornament)

Unmarked $25.00
          $25.00

Open, Issue Price $25.00, '01
Chapel Exclusive

Purchased_____, Price $_____

☐ *Sleep In Heavenly Peace,* 879754

Unmarked $35.00

Open, Issue Price $35.00, '01
Chapel Exclusive

Purchased_____, Price $_____

☐ *Mom (Brunette),* 880833

$20.00
$20.00
$20.00

Open, Issue Price $20.00, '01
Series: *Build A Family — Little Moments*

Purchased_____, Price $_____

☐ *Dad (Brunette),* 880841

$20.00
$20.00
$20.00

Open, Issue Price $20.00, '01
Series: *Build A Family — Little Moments*

Purchased_____, Price $_____

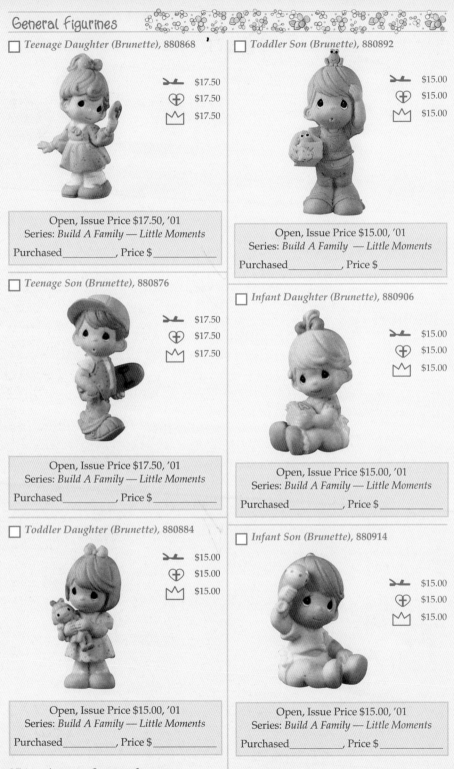

☐ *Teenage Daughter (Brunette)*, 880868

$17.50
$17.50
$17.50

Open, Issue Price $17.50, '01
Series: *Build A Family — Little Moments*
Purchased_____, Price $_____

☐ *Teenage Son (Brunette)*, 880876

$17.50
$17.50
$17.50

Open, Issue Price $17.50, '01
Series: *Build A Family — Little Moments*
Purchased_____, Price $_____

☐ *Toddler Daughter (Brunette)*, 880884

$15.00
$15.00
$15.00

Open, Issue Price $15.00, '01
Series: *Build A Family — Little Moments*
Purchased_____, Price $_____

☐ *Toddler Son (Brunette)*, 880892

$15.00
$15.00
$15.00

Open, Issue Price $15.00, '01
Series: *Build A Family — Little Moments*
Purchased_____, Price $_____

☐ *Infant Daughter (Brunette)*, 880906

$15.00
$15.00
$15.00

Open, Issue Price $15.00, '01
Series: *Build A Family — Little Moments*
Purchased_____, Price $_____

☐ *Infant Son (Brunette)*, 880914

$15.00
$15.00
$15.00

Open, Issue Price $15.00, '01
Series: *Build A Family — Little Moments*
Purchased_____, Price $_____

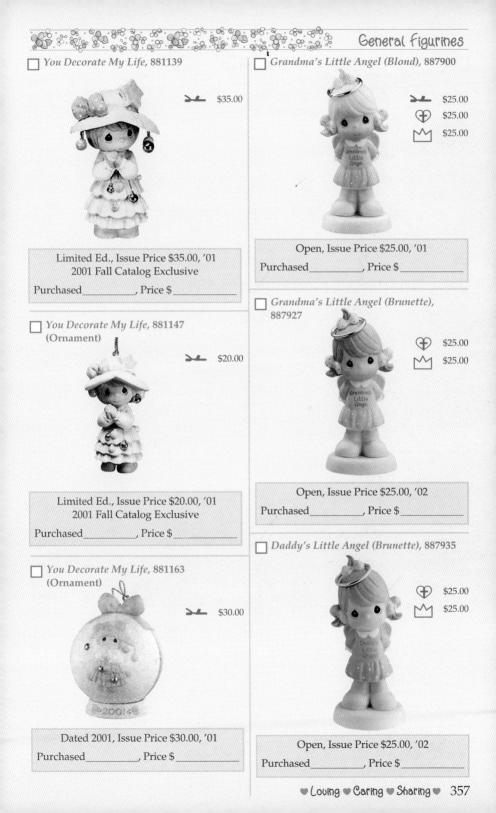

☐ *You Decorate My Life*, 881139

✈ $35.00

Limited Ed., Issue Price $35.00, '01
2001 Fall Catalog Exclusive
Purchased_____, Price $_____

☐ *You Decorate My Life*, 881147
(Ornament)

✈ $20.00

Limited Ed., Issue Price $20.00, '01
2001 Fall Catalog Exclusive
Purchased_____, Price $_____

☐ *You Decorate My Life*, 881163
(Ornament)

✈ $30.00

Dated 2001, Issue Price $30.00, '01
Purchased_____, Price $_____

☐ *Grandma's Little Angel (Blond)*, 887900

✈ $25.00
✞ $25.00
♔ $25.00

Open, Issue Price $25.00, '01
Purchased_____, Price $_____

☐ *Grandma's Little Angel (Brunette)*,
887927

✞ $25.00
♔ $25.00

Open, Issue Price $25.00, '02
Purchased_____, Price $_____

☐ *Daddy's Little Angel (Brunette)*, 887935

✞ $25.00
♔ $25.00

Open, Issue Price $25.00, '02
Purchased_____, Price $_____

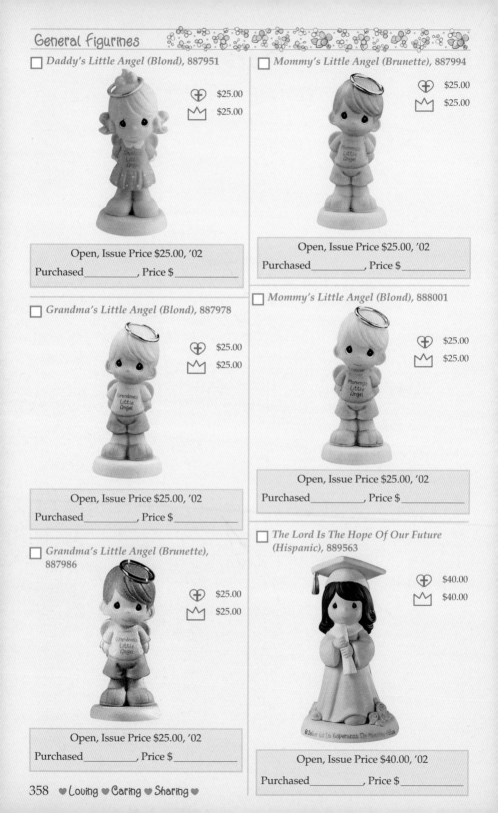

☐ *Daddy's Little Angel (Blond)*, 887951

✝ $25.00
♔ $25.00

Open, Issue Price $25.00, '02
Purchased_____, Price $_____

☐ *Mommy's Little Angel (Brunette)*, 887994

✝ $25.00
♔ $25.00

Open, Issue Price $25.00, '02
Purchased_____, Price $_____

☐ *Grandma's Little Angel (Blond)*, 887978

✝ $25.00
♔ $25.00

Open, Issue Price $25.00, '02
Purchased_____, Price $_____

☐ *Mommy's Little Angel (Blond)*, 888001

✝ $25.00
♔ $25.00

Open, Issue Price $25.00, '02
Purchased_____, Price $_____

☐ *Grandma's Little Angel (Brunette)*, 887986

✝ $25.00
♔ $25.00

Open, Issue Price $25.00, '02
Purchased_____, Price $_____

☐ *The Lord Is The Hope Of Our Future (Hispanic)*, 889563

✝ $40.00
♔ $40.00

Open, Issue Price $40.00, '02
Purchased_____, Price $_____

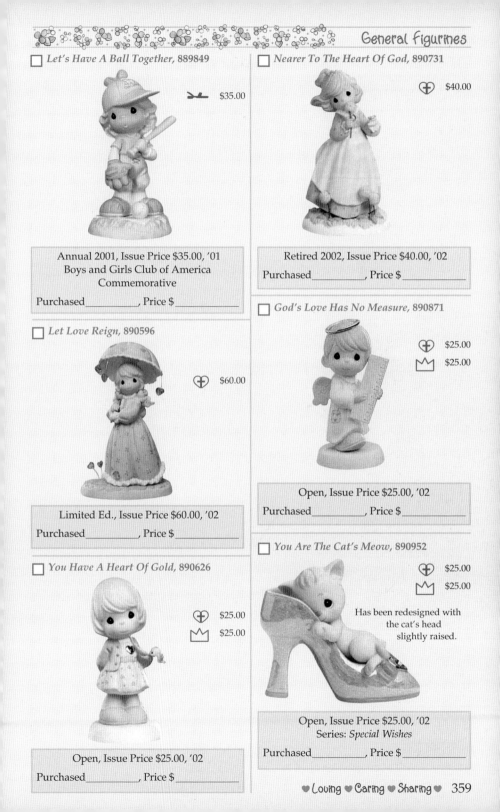

☐ *Let's Have A Ball Together, 889849*

>— $35.00

Annual 2001, Issue Price $35.00, '01
Boys and Girls Club of America
Commemorative

Purchased_____, Price $_____

☐ *Let Love Reign, 890596*

✝ $60.00

Limited Ed., Issue Price $60.00, '02

Purchased_____, Price $_____

☐ *You Have A Heart Of Gold, 890626*

✝ $25.00
♛ $25.00

Open, Issue Price $25.00, '02

Purchased_____, Price $_____

☐ *Nearer To The Heart Of God, 890731*

✝ $40.00

Retired 2002, Issue Price $40.00, '02

Purchased_____, Price $_____

☐ *God's Love Has No Measure, 890871*

✝ $25.00
♛ $25.00

Open, Issue Price $25.00, '02

Purchased_____, Price $_____

☐ *You Are The Cat's Meow, 890952*

✝ $25.00
♛ $25.00

Has been redesigned with
the cat's head
slightly raised.

Open, Issue Price $25.00, '02
Series: *Special Wishes*

Purchased_____, Price $_____

♥ Loving ♥ Caring ♥ Sharing ♥ 359

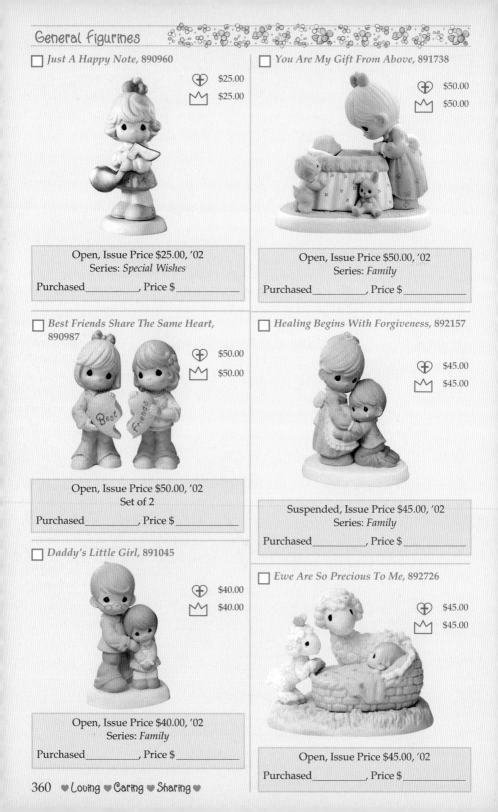

☐ *Just A Happy Note*, 890960

✝ $25.00
♔ $25.00

Open, Issue Price $25.00, '02
Series: *Special Wishes*

Purchased_____, Price $_____

☐ *You Are My Gift From Above*, 891738

✝ $50.00
♔ $50.00

Open, Issue Price $50.00, '02
Series: *Family*

Purchased_____, Price $_____

☐ *Best Friends Share The Same Heart*,
890987

✝ $50.00
♔ $50.00

Open, Issue Price $50.00, '02
Set of 2

Purchased_____, Price $_____

☐ *Healing Begins With Forgiveness*, 892157

✝ $45.00
♔ $45.00

Suspended, Issue Price $45.00, '02
Series: *Family*

Purchased_____, Price $_____

☐ *Daddy's Little Girl*, 891045

✝ $40.00
♔ $40.00

Open, Issue Price $40.00, '02
Series: *Family*

Purchased_____, Price $_____

☐ *Ewe Are So Precious To Me*, 892726

✝ $45.00
♔ $45.00

Open, Issue Price $45.00, '02

Purchased_____, Price $_____

☐ *Overalls, I Think You're Special*, 898147

🕀 $45.00
👑 $45.00

Open, Issue Price $45.00, '02
Series: *Country Lane Collection*

Purchased_____, Price $_____

☐ *How Can I Says Thanks*, 898309

Unmarked $35.00

Open, Issue Price $35.00, '01
Chapel Exclusive

Purchased_____, Price $_____

☐ *How Can I Says Thanks*, 898317
(Ornament)

Unmarked $20.00

Open, Issue Price $20.00, '01
Chapel Exclusive

Purchased_____, Price $_____

☐ *Loving, Caring And Shearing*, 898414

✈ $60.00
🕀 $60.00

Limited Ed. 10,000, Issue Price $60.00, '01

Purchased_____, Price $_____

☐ *You Are My Favorite Dish*, 898457

🕀 $25.00
👑 $25.00

Retired 2002, Issue Price $25.00, '02

Purchased_____, Price $_____

☐ *You Are My Favorite Dish*, 898457S

🕀 $25.00

Comes with a
cookie cutter.

Retired 2002, Issue Price $25.00, '02

Purchased_____, Price $_____

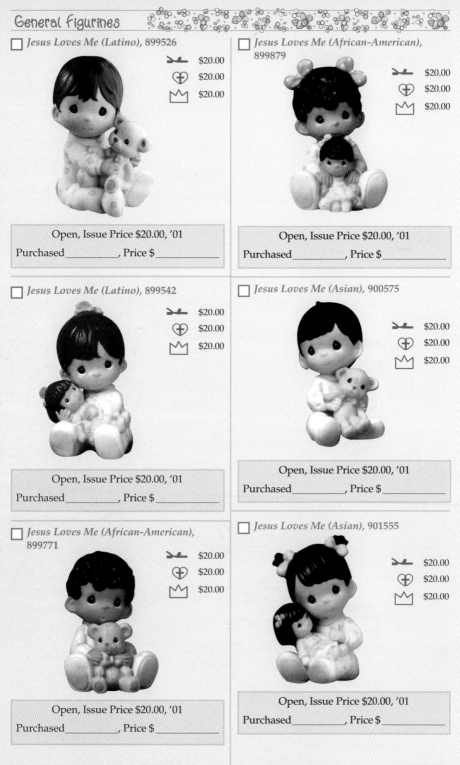

☐ *Jesus Loves Me (Latino)*, 899526

✈ $20.00
✝ $20.00
♔ $20.00

Open, Issue Price $20.00, '01
Purchased_____, Price $_____

☐ *Jesus Loves Me (African-American)*, 899879

✈ $20.00
✝ $20.00
♔ $20.00

Open, Issue Price $20.00, '01
Purchased_____, Price $_____

☐ *Jesus Loves Me (Latino)*, 899542

✈ $20.00
✝ $20.00
♔ $20.00

Open, Issue Price $20.00, '01
Purchased_____, Price $_____

☐ *Jesus Loves Me (Asian)*, 900575

✈ $20.00
✝ $20.00
♔ $20.00

Open, Issue Price $20.00, '01
Purchased_____, Price $_____

☐ *Jesus Loves Me (African-American)*, 899771

✈ $20.00
✝ $20.00
♔ $20.00

Open, Issue Price $20.00, '01
Purchased_____, Price $_____

☐ *Jesus Loves Me (Asian)*, 901555

✈ $20.00
✝ $20.00
♔ $20.00

Open, Issue Price $20.00, '01
Purchased_____, Price $_____

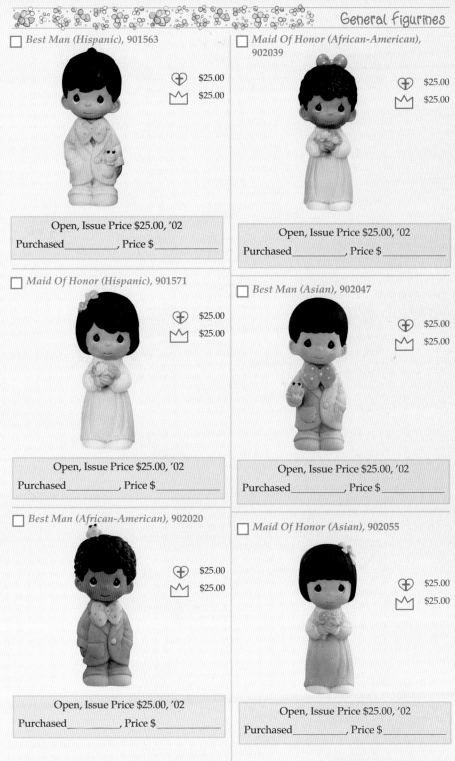

☐ *Best Man (Hispanic)*, 901563

✝ $25.00
♕ $25.00

Open, Issue Price $25.00, '02
Purchased_____, Price $_____

☐ *Maid Of Honor (African-American)*, 902039

✝ $25.00
♕ $25.00

Open, Issue Price $25.00, '02
Purchased_____, Price $_____

☐ *Maid Of Honor (Hispanic)*, 901571

✝ $25.00
♕ $25.00

Open, Issue Price $25.00, '02
Purchased_____, Price $_____

☐ *Best Man (Asian)*, 902047

✝ $25.00
♕ $25.00

Open, Issue Price $25.00, '02
Purchased_____, Price $_____

☐ *Best Man (African-American)*, 902020

✝ $25.00
♕ $25.00

Open, Issue Price $25.00, '02
Purchased_____, Price $_____

☐ *Maid Of Honor (Asian)*, 902055

✝ $25.00
♕ $25.00

Open, Issue Price $25.00, '02
Purchased_____, Price $_____

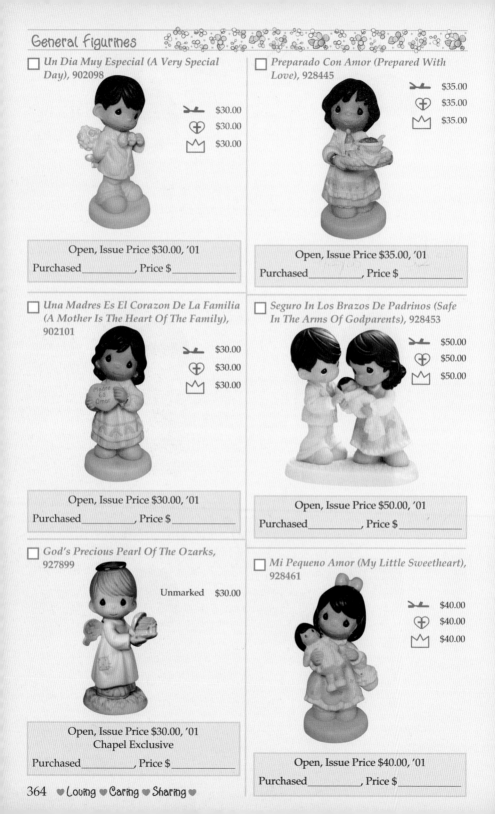

□ **Un Dia Muy Especial (A Very Special Day)**, 902098

✈ $30.00
✝ $30.00
♛ $30.00

Open, Issue Price $30.00, '01
Purchased_____, Price $_____

□ **Una Madres Es El Corazon De La Familia (A Mother Is The Heart Of The Family)**, 902101

✈ $30.00
✝ $30.00
♛ $30.00

Open, Issue Price $30.00, '01
Purchased_____, Price $_____

□ **God's Precious Pearl Of The Ozarks**, 927899

Unmarked $30.00

Open, Issue Price $30.00, '01
Chapel Exclusive
Purchased_____, Price $_____

□ **Preparado Con Amor (Prepared With Love)**, 928445

✈ $35.00
✝ $35.00
♛ $35.00

Open, Issue Price $35.00, '01
Purchased_____, Price $_____

□ **Seguro In Los Brazos De Padrinos (Safe In The Arms Of Godparents)**, 928453

✈ $50.00
✝ $50.00
♛ $50.00

Open, Issue Price $50.00, '01
Purchased_____, Price $_____

□ **Mi Pequeno Amor (My Little Sweetheart)**, 928461

✈ $40.00
✝ $40.00
♛ $40.00

Open, Issue Price $40.00, '01
Purchased_____, Price $_____

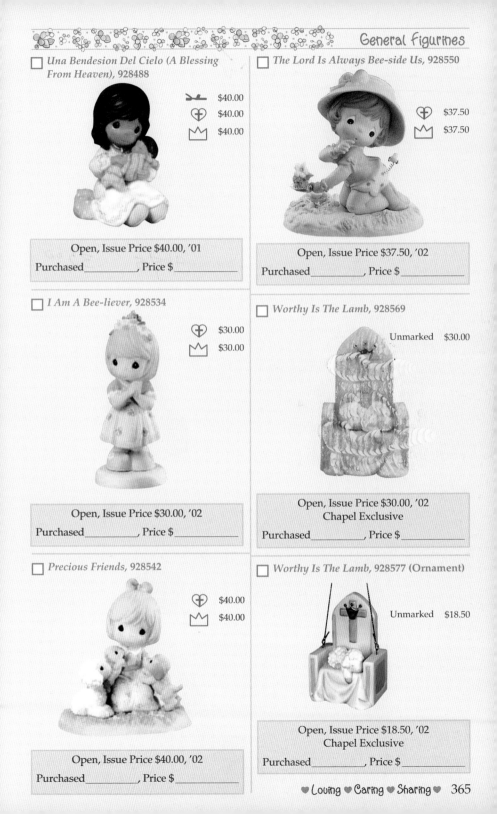

☐ *Una Bendesion Del Cielo (A Blessing From Heaven)*, 928488

✈ $40.00
✝ $40.00
♛ $40.00

Open, Issue Price $40.00, '01
Purchased_____, Price $_____

☐ *I Am A Bee-liever*, 928534

✝ $30.00
♛ $30.00

Open, Issue Price $30.00, '02
Purchased_____, Price $_____

☐ *Precious Friends*, 928542

✝ $40.00
♛ $40.00

Open, Issue Price $40.00, '02
Purchased_____, Price $_____

☐ *The Lord Is Always Bee-side Us*, 928550

✝ $37.50
♛ $37.50

Open, Issue Price $37.50, '02
Purchased_____, Price $_____

☐ *Worthy Is The Lamb*, 928569

Unmarked $30.00

Open, Issue Price $30.00, '02
Chapel Exclusive
Purchased_____, Price $_____

☐ *Worthy Is The Lamb*, 928577 (Ornament)

Unmarked $18.50

Open, Issue Price $18.50, '02
Chapel Exclusive
Purchased_____, Price $_____

General Figurines

☐ *It Came Upon A Midnight Clear, 928585*
(Tree Topper)

Unmarked $125.00

Limited Ed. 2,500, Issue Price $125.00, '02
Chapel Exclusive

Purchased_____ , Price $_____

☐ *My Teacher, My Friend, 928607*

Unmarked $70.00

Open, Issue Price $70.00, '02
Chapel Exclusive

Purchased_____ , Price $_____

☐ *Ice See In You A Champion, 934852*
(Ornament)

✝ $25.00

Limited Ed., Issue Price $25.00, '02
Canadian Exclusive

Purchased_____ , Price $_____

☑ *We've Got The Right Plan, 937282*

✝ $80.00

♛ $80.00

Open, Issue Price $80.00, '02
Purchased 4/25/05, Price $ 32⁰⁰

☐ *Our Heroes In The Sky, 958832*

✝ $35.00

♛ $35.00

Open, Issue Price $35.00, '02
Purchased_____ , Price $_____

☐ *Our Heroes In The Sky, 958840*

✝ $35.00

♛ $35.00

Open, Issue Price $35.00, '02
Purchased_____ , Price $_____

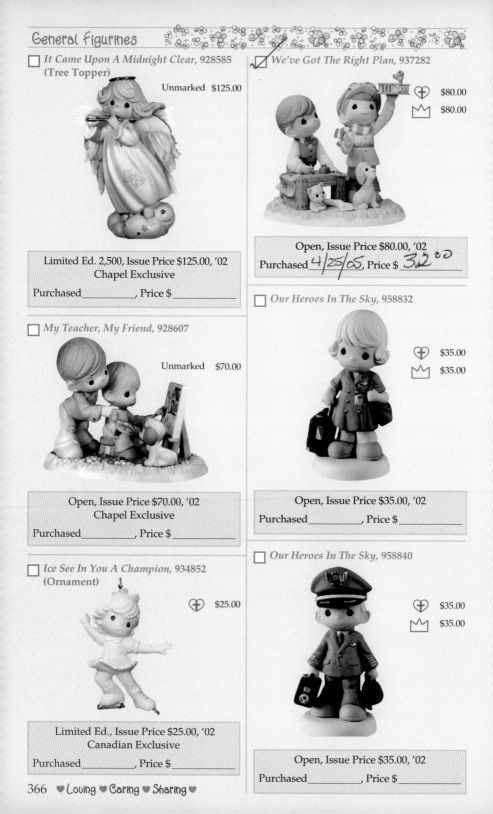

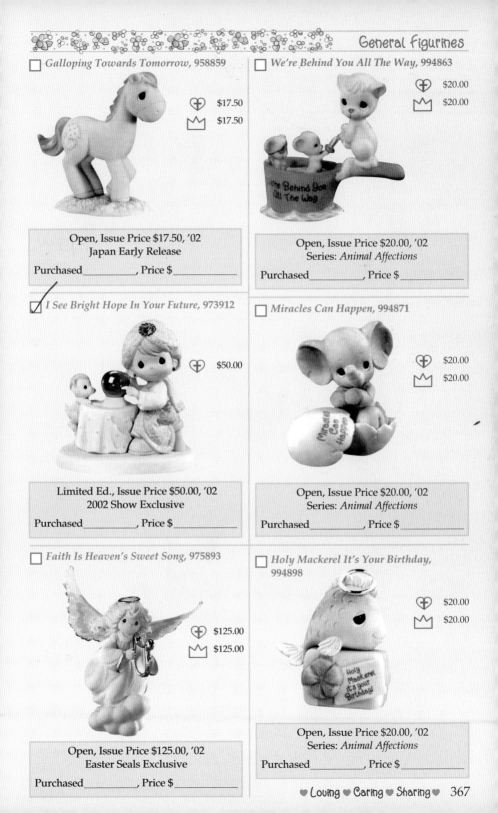

☐ *Galloping Towards Tomorrow*, 958859

✝ $17.50
♛ $17.50

Open, Issue Price $17.50, '02
Japan Early Release
Purchased_____, Price $_____

☐ *We're Behind You All The Way*, 994863

✝ $20.00
♛ $20.00

Open, Issue Price $20.00, '02
Series: *Animal Affections*
Purchased_____, Price $_____

☑ *I See Bright Hope In Your Future*, 973912

✝ $50.00

Limited Ed., Issue Price $50.00, '02
2002 Show Exclusive
Purchased_____, Price $_____

☐ *Miracles Can Happen*, 994871

✝ $20.00
♛ $20.00

Open, Issue Price $20.00, '02
Series: *Animal Affections*
Purchased_____, Price $_____

☐ *Faith Is Heaven's Sweet Song*, 975893

✝ $125.00
♛ $125.00

Open, Issue Price $125.00, '02
Easter Seals Exclusive
Purchased_____, Price $_____

☐ *Holy Mackerel It's Your Birthday*, 994898

✝ $20.00
♛ $20.00

Open, Issue Price $20.00, '02
Series: *Animal Affections*
Purchased_____, Price $_____

Collectors' Club

☐ *I Will Make You Fishers Of Men (Lithograph)*

Unmarked $25.00

Club members entitled to this exclusive lithograph free with purchase of $25.00 on January 25, 2002.

Members Only, Gift, '02

Purchased_____, Price $_____

☐ *God Bless Our Years Together*, 12440

There have been reports of this piece being completely unpainted.

🌿 $255.00

Members Only, Issue Price $175.00, '85
Fifth Anniversary Club Commemorative

Purchased_____, Price $_____

☐ *Bubble Your Troubles Away*, 101730

✚ $45.00

Members Only, Issue Price $45.00, '02

Purchased_____, Price $_____

☐ *A Portrait Of Loving, Caring And Sharing*, 108543

👑 $375.00

Available for preorder from January 25 through February 19, 2003.

Members Only, Issue Price $375.00, '03
Limited Ed.

Purchased_____, Price $_____

☐ *The Sweetest Treat Is Friendship*, 110855

👑 $55.00

Members Only, Issue Price $55.00, '03

Purchased_____, Price $_____

☐ *A Perfect Display Of 15 Happy Years*, 127817

△ $125.00

Club's Fifteenth Anniversary Commemorative figurine.

Members Only, Issue Price $100.00, '95

Purchased_____, Price $_____

Collectors' Club

Teach Us To Love One Another, 211672 — $25.00

Members Only, Issue Price $7.00, '96
Purchased_____, Price $ _____

Celebrating A Decade Of Loving, Caring And Sharing, 227986 (Ornament) — Unmarked $15.00

Members Only, Issue Price $7.00, '89
Purchased_____, Price $ _____

Sweet Sixteen, 266841 (Ornament) — Unmarked $200.00

Members Only, Gift, '96 Convention Ornament
Purchased_____, Price $ _____

Rejoice In The Victory, 283541 — $55.00
Precious Rewards Frequent Buyer Program, Level 1: 300 points.

Members Only, Issue Price $30.00, '97
Purchased_____, Price $ _____

God Bless You With Bouquets Of Victory, 283584 — $50.00
Precious Rewards Frequent Buyer Program, Level 2: 500 points.

Members Only, Issue Price $50.00, '97
Purchased_____, Price $ _____

Faith Is The Victory, 283592 — $135.00
Precious Rewards Frequent Buyer Program, Level 3: 1,000 points.

Members Only, Issue Price $75.00, '97
Purchased_____, Price $ _____

Put On A Happy Face, 440906 (Mask) — Unmarked $395.00
Given to attendess of the 1997 Local Club Chapter Convention.

Convention Gift, '97
Purchased_____, Price $ _____

♥ Loving ♥ Caring ♥ Sharing ♥ 369

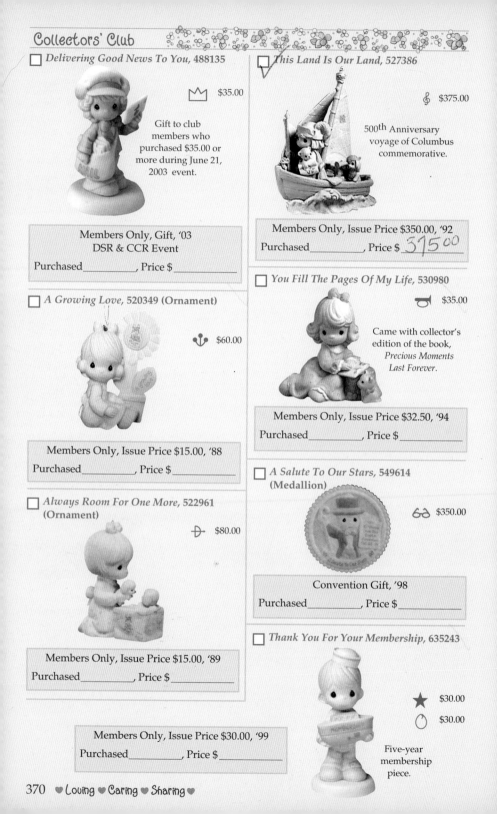

☐ *Delivering Good News To You*, 488135

♔ $35.00

Gift to club members who purchased $35.00 or more during June 21, 2003 event.

Members Only, Gift, '03
DSR & CCR Event
Purchased_____ , Price $_____

☐ *A Growing Love*, 520349 (Ornament)

⚓ $60.00

Members Only, Issue Price $15.00, '88
Purchased_____ , Price $_____

☐ *Always Room For One More*, 522961 (Ornament)

đ $80.00

Members Only, Issue Price $15.00, '89
Purchased_____ , Price $_____

Members Only, Issue Price $30.00, '99
Purchased_____ , Price $_____

✓ *This Land Is Our Land*, 527386

𝄞 $375.00

500th Anniversary voyage of Columbus commemorative.

Members Only, Issue Price $350.00, '92
Purchased_____ , Price $ *375.00*

☐ *You Fill The Pages Of My Life*, 530980

🎺 $35.00

Came with collector's edition of the book, *Precious Moments Last Forever.*

Members Only, Issue Price $32.50, '94
Purchased_____ , Price $_____

☐ *A Salute To Our Stars*, 549614 (Medallion)

👓 $350.00

Convention Gift, '98
Purchased_____ , Price $_____

☐ *Thank You For Your Membership*, 635243

★ $30.00

○ $30.00

Five-year membership piece.

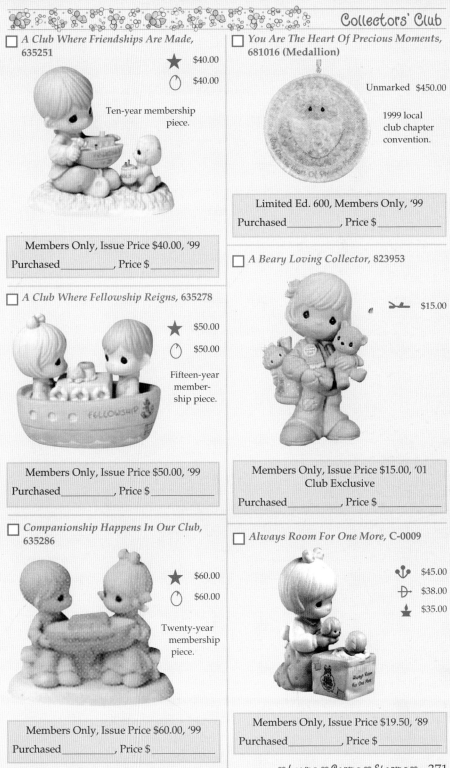

☐ *A Club Where Friendships Are Made,* 635251

★ $40.00

◔ $40.00

Ten-year membership piece.

Members Only, Issue Price $40.00, '99
Purchased_____, Price $_____

☐ *You Are The Heart Of Precious Moments,* 681016 (Medallion)

Unmarked $450.00

1999 local club chapter convention.

Limited Ed. 600, Members Only, '99
Purchased_____, Price $_____

☐ *A Club Where Fellowship Reigns,* 635278

★ $50.00

◔ $50.00

Fifteen-year member-ship piece.

Members Only, Issue Price $50.00, '99
Purchased_____, Price $_____

☐ *A Beary Loving Collector,* 823953

$15.00

Members Only, Issue Price $15.00, '01
Club Exclusive
Purchased_____, Price $_____

☐ *Companionship Happens In Our Club,* 635286

★ $60.00

◔ $60.00

Twenty-year membership piece.

Members Only, Issue Price $60.00, '99
Purchased_____, Price $_____

☐ *Always Room For One More,* C-0009

♈ $45.00

Ɖ $38.00

★ $35.00

Members Only, Issue Price $19.50, '89
Purchased_____, Price $_____

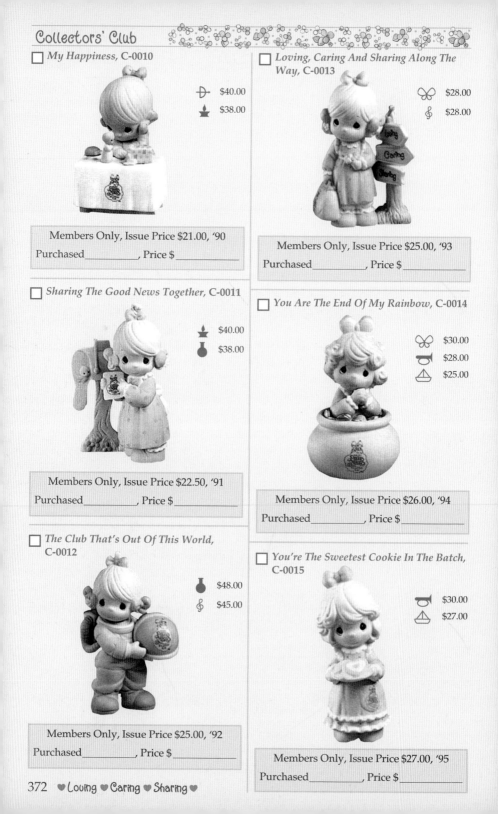

☐ *My Happiness*, C-0010

⊅ $40.00
⚖ $38.00

Members Only, Issue Price $21.00, '90
Purchased_____, Price $_____

☐ *Sharing The Good News Together*, C-0011

⚓ $40.00
⚗ $38.00

Members Only, Issue Price $22.50, '91
Purchased_____, Price $_____

☐ *The Club That's Out Of This World*, C-0012

⚗ $48.00
𝄞 $45.00

Members Only, Issue Price $25.00, '92
Purchased_____, Price $_____

☐ *Loving, Caring And Sharing Along The Way*, C-0013

🦋 $28.00
𝄞 $28.00

Members Only, Issue Price $25.00, '93
Purchased_____, Price $_____

☐ *You Are The End Of My Rainbow*, C-0014

🦋 $30.00
📯 $28.00
⛵ $25.00

Members Only, Issue Price $26.00, '94
Purchased_____, Price $_____

☐ *You're The Sweetest Cookie In The Batch*, C-0015

📯 $30.00
⛵ $27.00

Members Only, Issue Price $27.00, '95
Purchased_____, Price $_____

☐ *You're As Pretty As A Picture*, C-0016

△ $30.00
♡ $28.00

Members Only, Issue Price $25.00, '96
Purchased_____, Price $_____

☐ *A Special Toast To Precious Moments*, C-0017

♡ $28.00
✝ $28.00

Members Only, Issue Price $25.00, '97
Purchased_____, Price $_____

☑ *Focusing In On Those Precious Moments*, C-0018

✝ $30.00
👓 $30.00

Members Only, Issue Price $28.00, '98
Purchased_____, Price $_____

☐ *Wishing You A World Of Peace*, C-0019

👓 $30.00
★ $28.00

Members Only, Issue Price $25.00, '99
Purchased_____, Price $_____

☑ *Thanks A Bunch*, C-0020

★ $33.00
○ $30.00

Members Only, Issue Price $28.50, '00
Purchased_____, Price $_____

☐ *Friends Write From The Start*, C-0021

○ $28.50
⤢ $28.50

Members Only, Issue Price $28.50, '01
Purchased_____, Price $_____

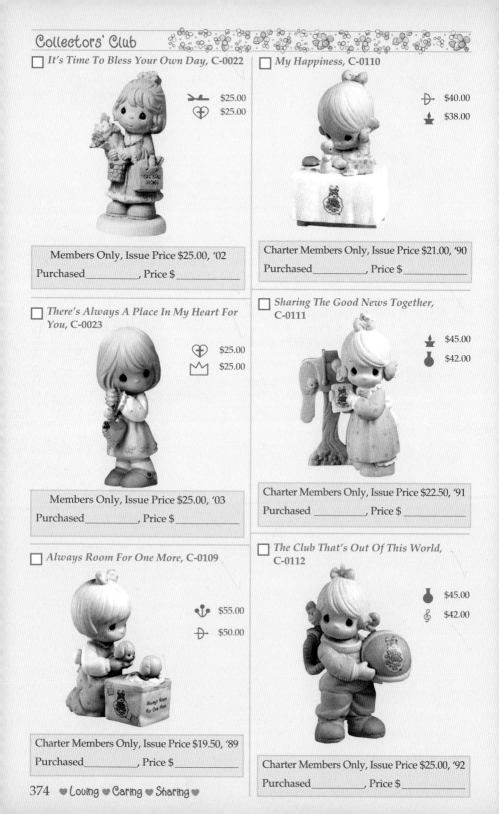

☐ *It's Time To Bless Your Own Day,* **C-0022**

$25.00
$25.00

Members Only, Issue Price $25.00, '02
Purchased_____, Price $_____

☐ *There's Always A Place In My Heart For You,* **C-0023**

$25.00
$25.00

Members Only, Issue Price $25.00, '03
Purchased_____, Price $_____

☐ *Always Room For One More,* **C-0109**

$55.00
$50.00

Charter Members Only, Issue Price $19.50, '89
Purchased_____, Price $_____

☐ *My Happiness,* **C-0110**

$40.00
$38.00

Charter Members Only, Issue Price $21.00, '90
Purchased_____, Price $_____

☐ *Sharing The Good News Together,* **C-0111**

$45.00
$42.00

Charter Members Only, Issue Price $22.50, '91
Purchased _____, Price $_____

☐ *The Club That's Out Of This World,* **C-0112**

$45.00
$42.00

Charter Members Only, Issue Price $25.00, '92
Purchased_____, Price $_____

☐ *Loving, Caring, And Sharing Along The Way*, C-0113

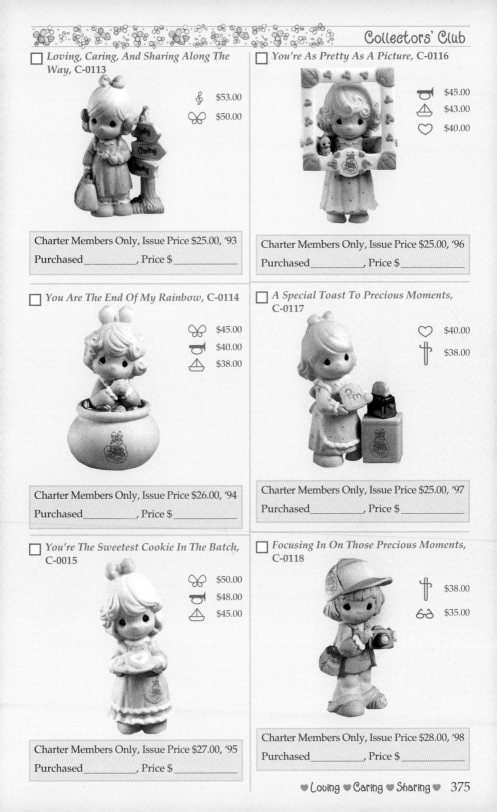

🕯 $53.00

🦋 $50.00

Charter Members Only, Issue Price $25.00, '93
Purchased_____, Price $_____

☐ *You Are The End Of My Rainbow*, C-0114

🦋 $45.00

🎺 $40.00

⛵ $38.00

Charter Members Only, Issue Price $26.00, '94
Purchased_____, Price $_____

☐ *You're The Sweetest Cookie In The Batch*, C-0015

🦋 $50.00

🎺 $48.00

⛵ $45.00

Charter Members Only, Issue Price $27.00, '95
Purchased_____, Price $_____

☐ *You're As Pretty As A Picture*, C-0116

🎺 $45.00

⛵ $43.00

♡ $40.00

Charter Members Only, Issue Price $25.00, '96
Purchased_____, Price $_____

☐ *A Special Toast To Precious Moments*, C-0117

♡ $40.00

✝ $38.00

Charter Members Only, Issue Price $25.00, '97
Purchased_____, Price $_____

☐ *Focusing In On Those Precious Moments*, C-0118

✝ $38.00

👓 $35.00

Charter Members Only, Issue Price $28.00, '98
Purchased_____, Price $_____

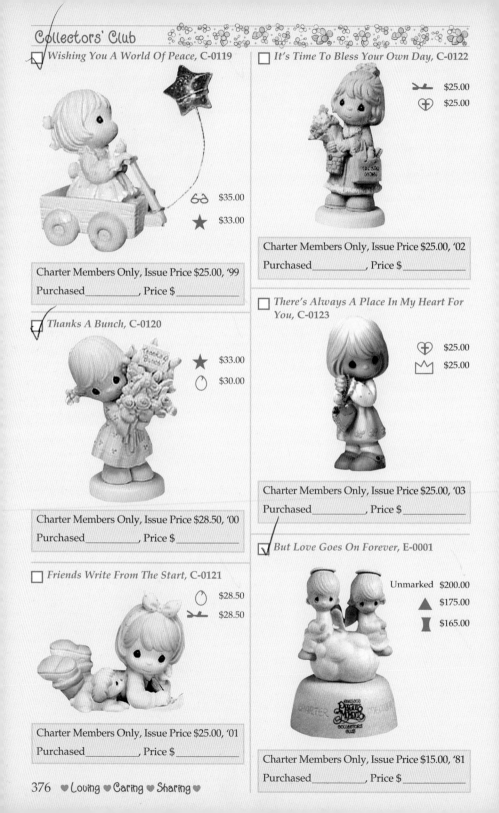

Wishing You A World Of Peace, C-0119

👓 $35.00

⭐ $33.00

Charter Members Only, Issue Price $25.00, '99
Purchased_____, Price $_____

Thanks A Bunch, C-0120

⭐ $33.00

🥚 $30.00

Charter Members Only, Issue Price $28.50, '00
Purchased_____, Price $_____

Friends Write From The Start, C-0121

🥚 $28.50

$28.50

Charter Members Only, Issue Price $25.00, '01
Purchased_____, Price $_____

It's Time To Bless Your Own Day, C-0122

$25.00

$25.00

Charter Members Only, Issue Price $25.00, '02
Purchased_____, Price $_____

There's Always A Place In My Heart For You, C-0123

$25.00

$25.00

Charter Members Only, Issue Price $25.00, '03
Purchased_____, Price $_____

But Love Goes On Forever, E-0001

Unmarked $200.00

▲ $175.00

▮ $165.00

Charter Members Only, Issue Price $15.00, '81
Purchased_____, Price $_____

☐ *Seek And Ye Shall Find*, E-0005

✝ $35.00
⚓ $30.00

Members Only, Issue Price $17.50, '85
Purchased_____, Price $_____

☐ *Birds Of A Feather Collect Together*,
E-0006

🕊 $30.00
🌿 $28.00

Members Only, Issue Price $17.50, '86
Purchased_____, Price $_____

☐ *Sharing Is Universal*, E-0007

🌿 $38.00
🌲 $35.00

Members Only, Issue Price $17.50, '87
Purchased_____, Price $_____

☐ *A Growing Love*, E-0008

🌲 $35.00
⚓ $30.00

Members Only, Issue Price $18.50, '88
Purchased_____, Price $_____

☐ *But Love Goes On Forever*, E-0102
(Plaque)

Unmarked $150.00
▲ $90.00
𝕀 $80.00

Charter Members Only, Issue Price $15.00, '82
Purchased_____, Price $_____

☐ *Let Us Call The Club To Order*, E-0103

𝕀 $65.00
🐟 $60.00

Charter Members Only, Issue Price $15.00 '83
Purchased_____, Price $_____

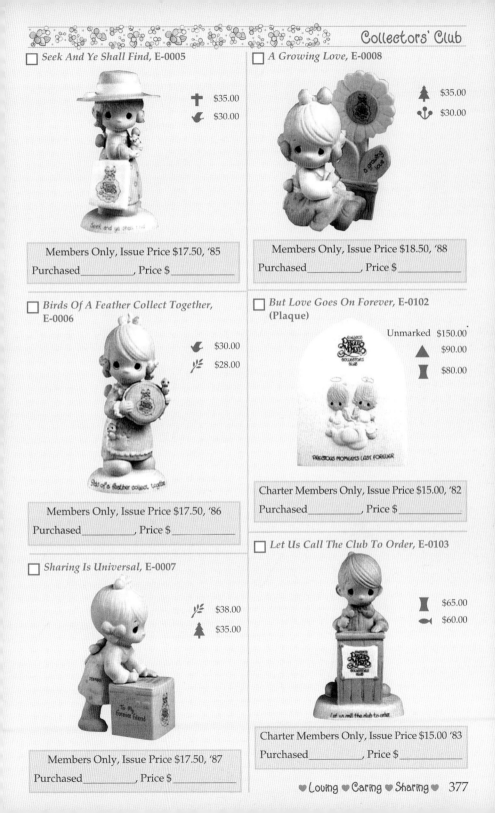

☐ *Join In On The Blessings*, E-0104

🐟 $55.00
✝ $53.00

Charter Members Only, Issue Price $17.50, '84
Purchased_____, Price $_____

☐ *Seek And Ye Shall Find*, E-0105

✝ $50.00
🕊 $45.00

Charter Members Only, Issue Price $17.50, '85
Purchased_____, Price $_____

☐ *Birds Of A Feather Collect Together*, E-0106

🕊 $45.00
🌿 $43.00

Charter Members Only, Issue Price $17.50, '86
Purchased_____, Price $_____

☐ *Sharing Is Universal*, E-0107

🌿 $43.00
🌲 $38.00

Charter Members Only, Issue Price $17.50, '87
Purchased_____, Price $_____

☐ *A Growing Love*, E-0108

🌲 $38.00
⚓ $35.00

Charter Members Only, Issue Price $18.50, '88
Purchased_____, Price $_____

☐ *But Love Goes On Forever*, E-0202 (Plaque)

Unmarked $130.00

Precious Moments Last Forever inscription on front confused many because the title of this piece is *But Love Goes On Forever*. Termed the "Canadian Plaque Error," approximately 750 pieces of this 1982 symbol of membership were produced in 1985 and shipped to Canada. These pieces are stamped TAIWAN and have a Dove annual production symbol. Value for the "Canadian Plaque Error" is $125.00.

▲ $75.00
Ɪ $65.00

Members Only, Issue Price $15.00, '82
Purchased_____, Price $_____

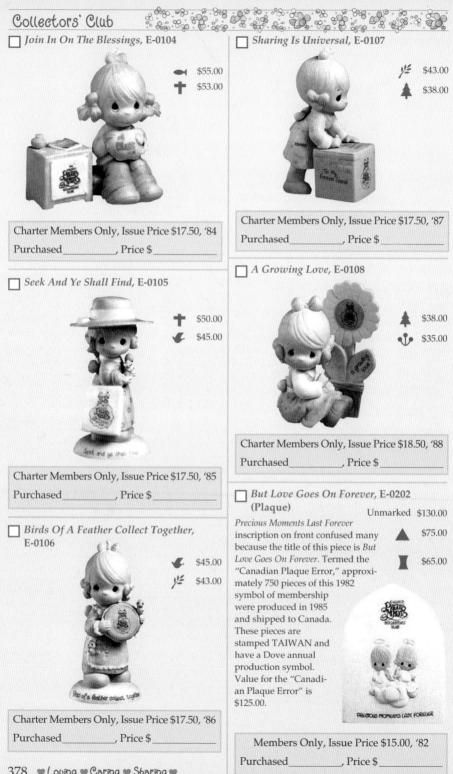

☐ *Let Us Call The Club To Order*, E-0303

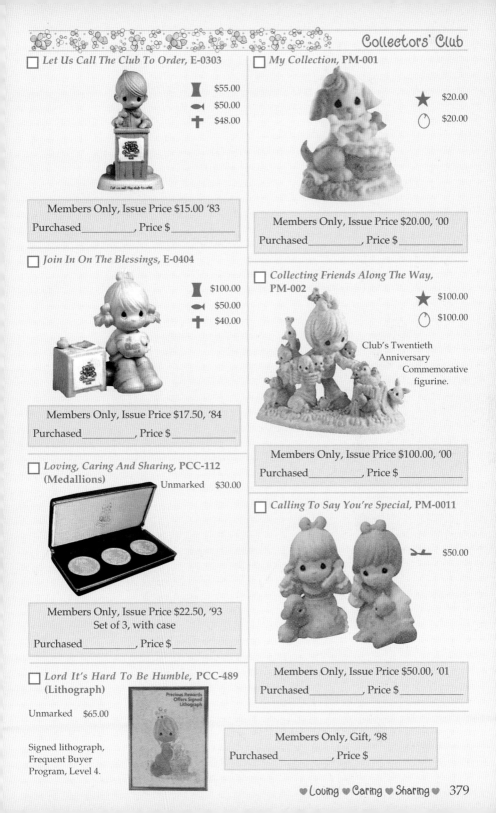

⬛ $55.00
🐟 $50.00
✝ $48.00

Members Only, Issue Price $15.00 '83

Purchased_____, Price $_____

☐ *Join In On The Blessings*, E-0404

⬛ $100.00
🐟 $50.00
✝ $40.00

Members Only, Issue Price $17.50, '84

Purchased_____, Price $_____

☐ *Loving, Caring And Sharing*, PCC-112 (Medallions)

Unmarked $30.00

Members Only, Issue Price $22.50, '93
Set of 3, with case

Purchased_____, Price $_____

☐ *Lord It's Hard To Be Humble*, PCC-489 (Lithograph)

Unmarked $65.00

Signed lithograph, Frequent Buyer Program, Level 4.

☐ *My Collection*, PM-001

★ $20.00
◯ $20.00

Members Only, Issue Price $20.00, '00

Purchased_____, Price $_____

☐ *Collecting Friends Along The Way*, PM-002

★ $100.00
◯ $100.00

Club's Twentieth Anniversary Commemorative figurine.

Members Only, Issue Price $100.00, '00

Purchased_____, Price $_____

☐ *Calling To Say You're Special*, PM-0011

✂ $50.00

Members Only, Issue Price $50.00, '01

Purchased_____, Price $_____

Members Only, Gift, '98

Purchased_____, Price $_____

☐ *You're A Computie Cutie*, PM-0012

$35.00

Members Only, Issue Price $35.00, '01
Purchased_____, Price $_____

☐ *You Are My In-Spa-ration*, PM-0021

$45.00

Members Only, Issue Price $45.00, '02
Purchased_____, Price $_____

☐ *You Are My Favorite Pastime*, PM-0022

$40.00

Members Only, Issue Price $40.00, '02
Purchased_____, Price $_____

☐ *Blessed With Small Miracles*, PM-0031A

$40.00

Members Only, Issue Price $40.00, '03
Purchased_____, Price $_____

☐ *Safe In The Hands Of Love*, PM-0032

$55.00

Members Only, Issue Price $55.00, '03
Purchased_____, Price $_____

☐ *Mug*, PM-032

Unmarked $7.00

Members Only, Issue Price $7.00, '90
Purchased_____, Price $_____

☐ *Desk Flag*, PM-034

Unmarked $4.00

Members Only, Issue Price $4.00, '90
Purchased_____, Price $_____

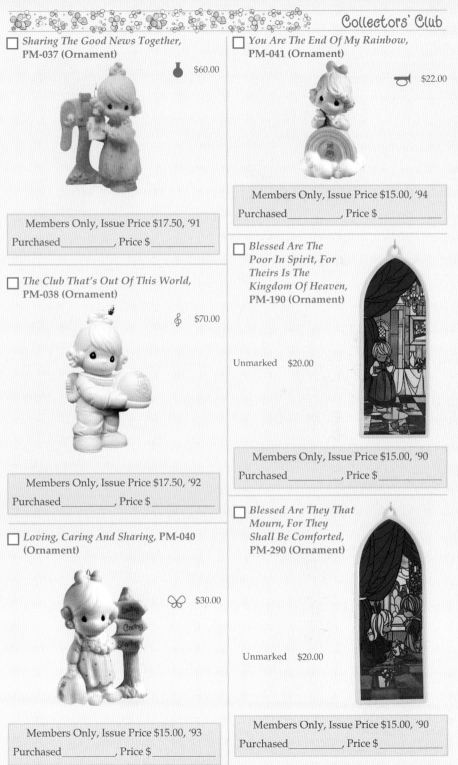

Sharing The Good News Together,
PM-037 (Ornament)

$60.00

Members Only, Issue Price $17.50, '91

Purchased_____, Price $_____

The Club That's Out Of This World,
PM-038 (Ornament)

$70.00

Members Only, Issue Price $17.50, '92

Purchased_____, Price $_____

Loving, Caring And Sharing, **PM-040**
(Ornament)

$30.00

Members Only, Issue Price $15.00, '93

Purchased_____, Price $_____

You Are The End Of My Rainbow,
PM-041 (Ornament)

$22.00

Members Only, Issue Price $15.00, '94

Purchased_____, Price $_____

Blessed Are The Poor In Spirit, For Theirs Is The Kingdom Of Heaven, **PM-190 (Ornament)**

Unmarked $20.00

Members Only, Issue Price $15.00, '90

Purchased_____, Price $_____

Blessed Are They That Mourn, For They Shall Be Comforted, **PM-290 (Ornament)**

Unmarked $20.00

Members Only, Issue Price $15.00, '90

Purchased_____, Price $_____

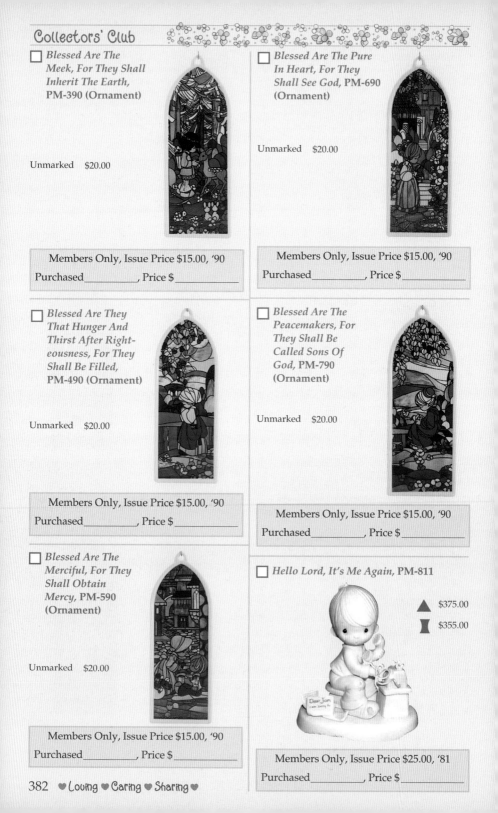

☐ *Blessed Are The Meek, For They Shall Inherit The Earth, PM-390 (Ornament)*

Unmarked $20.00

Members Only, Issue Price $15.00, '90
Purchased_____, Price $_____

☐ *Blessed Are The Pure In Heart, For They Shall See God, PM-690 (Ornament)*

Unmarked $20.00

Members Only, Issue Price $15.00, '90
Purchased_____, Price $_____

☐ *Blessed Are They That Hunger And Thirst After Right- eousness, For They Shall Be Filled, PM-490 (Ornament)*

Unmarked $20.00

Members Only, Issue Price $15.00, '90
Purchased_____, Price $_____

☐ *Blessed Are The Peacemakers, For They Shall Be Called Sons Of God, PM-790 (Ornament)*

Unmarked $20.00

Members Only, Issue Price $15.00, '90
Purchased_____, Price $_____

☐ *Blessed Are The Merciful, For They Shall Obtain Mercy, PM-590 (Ornament)*

Unmarked $20.00

Members Only, Issue Price $15.00, '90
Purchased_____, Price $_____

☐ *Hello Lord, It's Me Again, PM-811*

▲ $375.00

❚ $355.00

Members Only, Issue Price $25.00, '81
Purchased_____, Price $_____

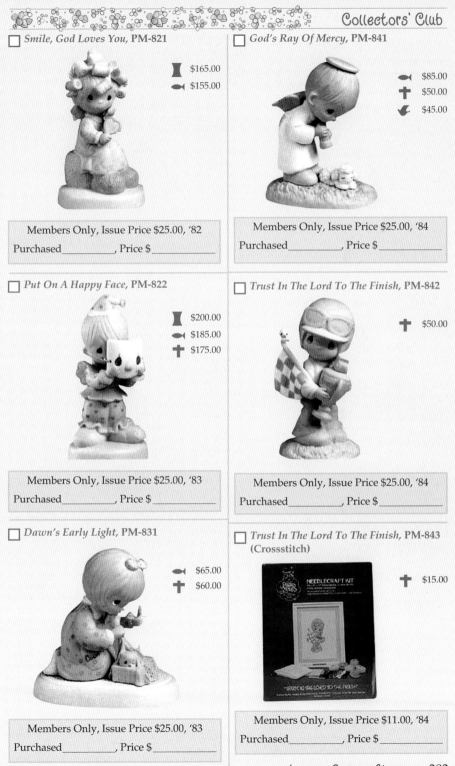

☐ *Smile, God Loves You*, PM-821

  ▮ $165.00
  ☞ $155.00

Members Only, Issue Price $25.00, '82
Purchased_____, Price $_____

☐ *Put On A Happy Face*, PM-822

  ▮ $200.00
  ☞ $185.00
  ✝ $175.00

Members Only, Issue Price $25.00, '83
Purchased_____, Price $_____

☐ *Dawn's Early Light*, PM-831

  ☞ $65.00
  ✝ $60.00

Members Only, Issue Price $25.00, '83
Purchased_____, Price $_____

☐ *God's Ray Of Mercy*, PM-841

  ☞ $85.00
  ✝ $50.00
  ☞ $45.00

Members Only, Issue Price $25.00, '84
Purchased_____, Price $_____

☐ *Trust In The Lord To The Finish*, PM-842

  ✝ $50.00

Members Only, Issue Price $25.00, '84
Purchased_____, Price $_____

☐ *Trust In The Lord To The Finish*, PM-843
(Crossstitch)

  ✝ $15.00

Members Only, Issue Price $11.00, '84
Purchased_____, Price $_____

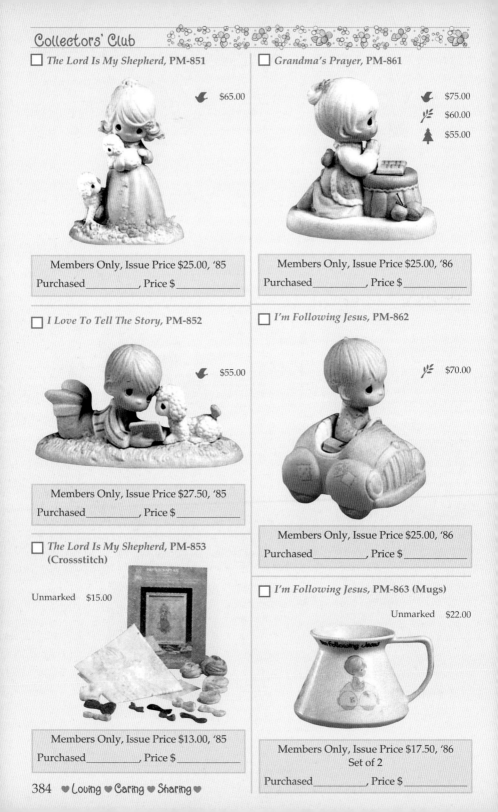

☐ *The Lord Is My Shepherd*, PM-851

🕊 $65.00

Members Only, Issue Price $25.00, '85
Purchased_____, Price $ _____

☐ *I Love To Tell The Story*, PM-852

🕊 $55.00

Members Only, Issue Price $27.50, '85
Purchased_____, Price $ _____

☐ *The Lord Is My Shepherd*, PM-853
(Crossstitch)

Unmarked $15.00

Members Only, Issue Price $13.00, '85
Purchased_____, Price $ _____

☐ *Grandma's Prayer*, PM-861

🕊 $75.00
🌿 $60.00
🌲 $55.00

Members Only, Issue Price $25.00, '86
Purchased_____, Price $ _____

☐ *I'm Following Jesus*, PM-862

🌿 $70.00

Members Only, Issue Price $25.00, '86
Purchased_____, Price $ _____

☐ *I'm Following Jesus*, PM-863 (Mugs)

Unmarked $22.00

Members Only, Issue Price $17.50, '86
Set of 2
Purchased_____, Price $ _____

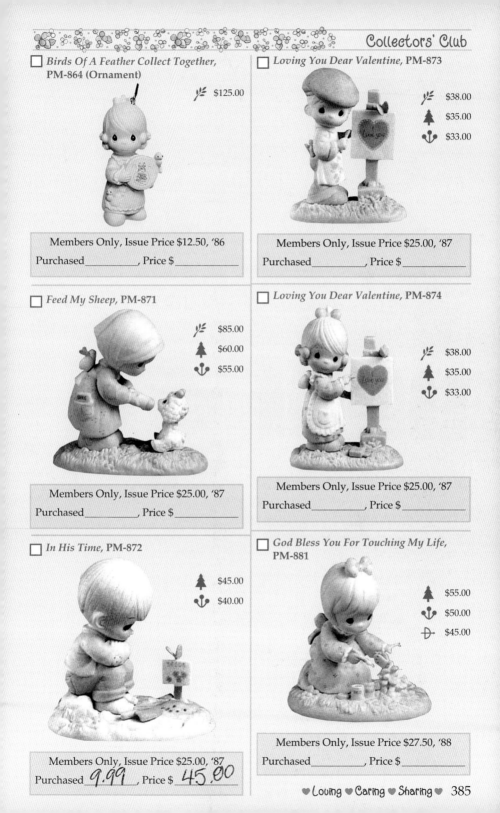

☐ *Birds Of A Feather Collect Together,* **PM-864 (Ornament)**

✿ $125.00

Members Only, Issue Price $12.50, '86
Purchased_____, Price $_____

☐ *Loving You Dear Valentine,* **PM-873**

✿ $38.00
🌲 $35.00
⚓ $33.00

Members Only, Issue Price $25.00, '87
Purchased_____, Price $_____

☐ *Feed My Sheep,* **PM-871**

✿ $85.00
🌲 $60.00
⚓ $55.00

Members Only, Issue Price $25.00, '87
Purchased_____, Price $_____

☐ *Loving You Dear Valentine,* **PM-874**

✿ $38.00
🌲 $35.00
⚓ $33.00

Members Only, Issue Price $25.00, '87
Purchased_____, Price $_____

☐ *In His Time,* **PM-872**

🌲 $45.00
⚓ $40.00

Members Only, Issue Price $25.00, '87
Purchased _9.99_, Price $ _45.00_

☐ *God Bless You For Touching My Life,* **PM-881**

🌲 $55.00
⚓ $50.00
♐ $45.00

Members Only, Issue Price $27.50, '88
Purchased_____, Price $_____

☐ *You Just Cannot Chuck A Good Friendship*, PM-882

⚓ $45.00

⚕ $40.00

Members Only, Issue Price $27.50, '88

Purchased_____, Price $_____

☐ *Mow Power To Ya*, PM-892

⚕ $40.00

★ $38.00

Members Only, Issue Price $27.50, '89

Purchased_____, Price $_____

☐ *Beatitudes Ornament Series*, PM-890 (Ornaments)

Unmarked $115.00

Members Only, Issue Price $105.00, '90
Set of 7, Individually Numbered PM-190
through PM-790

Purchased_____, Price $_____

☐ *Ten Years And Still Going Strong*, PM-901

★ $40.00

🏺 $38.00

Members Only, Issue Price $30.00, '90

Purchased_____, Price $_____

☐ *You Will Always Be My Choice*, PM-891

⚕ $40.00

★ $38.00

Members Only, Issue Price $27.50, '89

Purchased_____, Price $_____

☐ *You Are A Blessing To Me*, PM-902

★ $45.00

🏺 $42.00

Members Only, Issue Price $27.50, '90

Purchased_____, Price $_____

☐ *You Are A Blessing To Me*, PM-903
(Needlepoint Pillow)

Unmarked $8.50

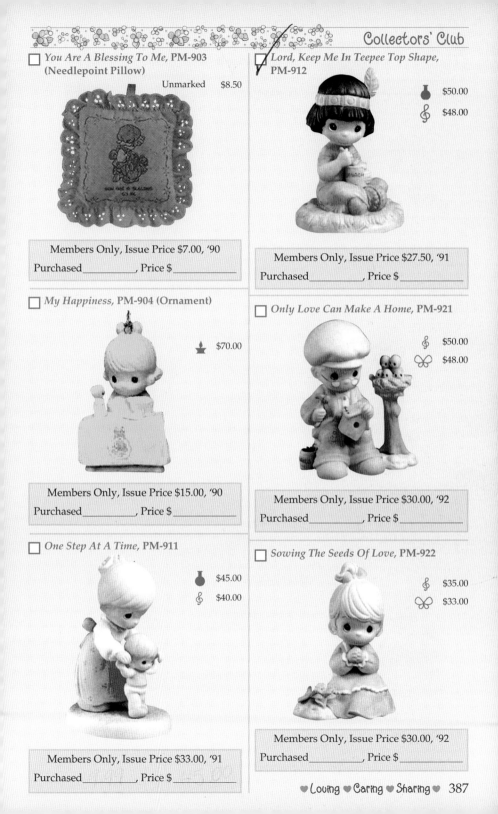

Members Only, Issue Price $7.00, '90
Purchased_____, Price $_____

☑ *Lord, Keep Me In Teepee Top Shape*,
PM-912

🏺 $50.00
🎼 $48.00

Members Only, Issue Price $27.50, '91
Purchased_____, Price $_____

☐ *My Happiness*, PM-904 (Ornament)

🔥 $70.00

Members Only, Issue Price $15.00, '90
Purchased_____, Price $_____

☐ *Only Love Can Make A Home*, PM-921

🎼 $50.00
🦋 $48.00

Members Only, Issue Price $30.00, '92
Purchased_____, Price $_____

☐ *One Step At A Time*, PM-911

🏺 $45.00
🎼 $40.00

Members Only, Issue Price $33.00, '91
Purchased_____, Price $_____

☐ *Sowing The Seeds Of Love*, PM-922

🎼 $35.00
🦋 $33.00

Members Only, Issue Price $30.00, '92
Purchased_____, Price $_____

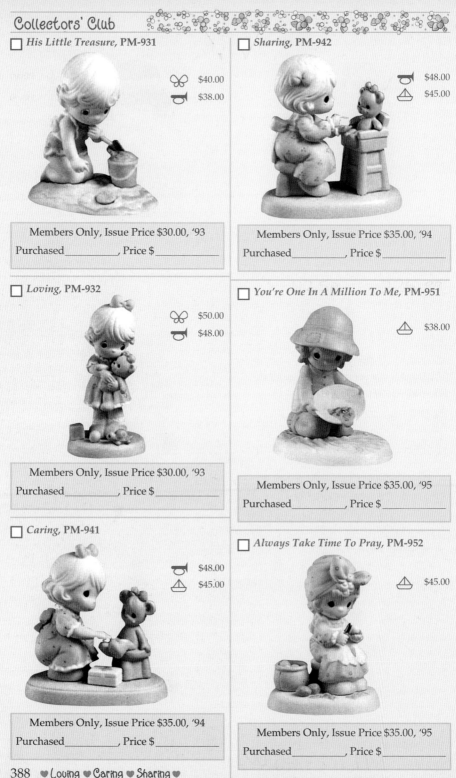

□ *His Little Treasure*, PM-931

$40.00
$38.00

Members Only, Issue Price $30.00, '93
Purchased_____, Price $_____

□ *Sharing*, PM-942

$48.00
$45.00

Members Only, Issue Price $35.00, '94
Purchased_____, Price $_____

□ *Loving*, PM-932

$50.00
$48.00

Members Only, Issue Price $30.00, '93
Purchased_____, Price $_____

□ *You're One In A Million To Me*, PM-951

$38.00

Members Only, Issue Price $35.00, '95
Purchased_____, Price $_____

□ *Caring*, PM-941

$48.00
$45.00

Members Only, Issue Price $35.00, '94
Purchased_____, Price $_____

□ *Always Take Time To Pray*, PM-952

$45.00

Members Only, Issue Price $35.00, '95
Purchased_____, Price $_____

☐ *Teach Us To Love One Another, PM-961*

△ $48.00

♡ $45.00

Sam Butcher honors Aunt Cleo.

Members Only, Issue Price $40.00, '96

Purchased_____, Price $_____

☐ *Our Club Is Soda-licious, PM-962*

♡ $50.00

Members Only, Issue Price $35.00, '96

Purchased_____, Price $_____

☐ *You Will Always Be A Treasure To Me, PM-971*

♡ $55.00

† $50.00

Members Only, Issue Price $50.00, '97

Purchased_____, Price $_____

☐ *Blessed Are The Merciful, PM-972*

♡ $45.00

† $42.00

Members Only, Issue Price $40.00, '97

Purchased_____, Price $_____

☐ *Happy Trails, PM-981*

† $55.00

👓 $50.00

★ $50.00

Members Only, Issue Price $50.00, '98

Purchased_____, Price $_____

☐ *Lord Please Don't Put Me On Hold, PM-982*

† $40.00

👓 $40.00

★ $40.00

Members Only, Issue Price $40.00, '98

Purchased_____, Price $_____

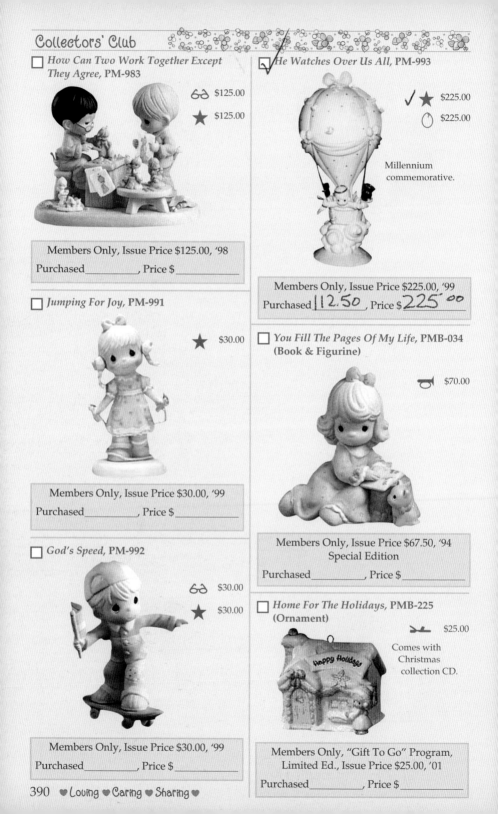

☐ *How Can Two Work Together Except They Agree*, PM-983

👓 $125.00
★ $125.00

Members Only, Issue Price $125.00, '98
Purchased_____, Price $_____

☐ *Jumping For Joy*, PM-991

★ $30.00

Members Only, Issue Price $30.00, '99
Purchased_____, Price $_____

☐ *God's Speed*, PM-992

👓 $30.00
★ $30.00

Members Only, Issue Price $30.00, '99
Purchased_____, Price $_____

☑ *He Watches Over Us All*, PM-993

✓★ $225.00
◯ $225.00

Millennium commemorative.

Members Only, Issue Price $225.00, '99
Purchased 112.50, Price $ 225 00

☐ *You Fill The Pages Of My Life*, PMB-034
(Book & Figurine)

$70.00

Members Only, Issue Price $67.50, '94
Special Edition
Purchased_____, Price $_____

☐ *Home For The Holidays*, PMB-225
(Ornament)

$25.00

Comes with Christmas collection CD.

Members Only, "Gift To Go" Program,
Limited Ed., Issue Price $25.00, '01
Purchased_____, Price $_____

Birthday Club

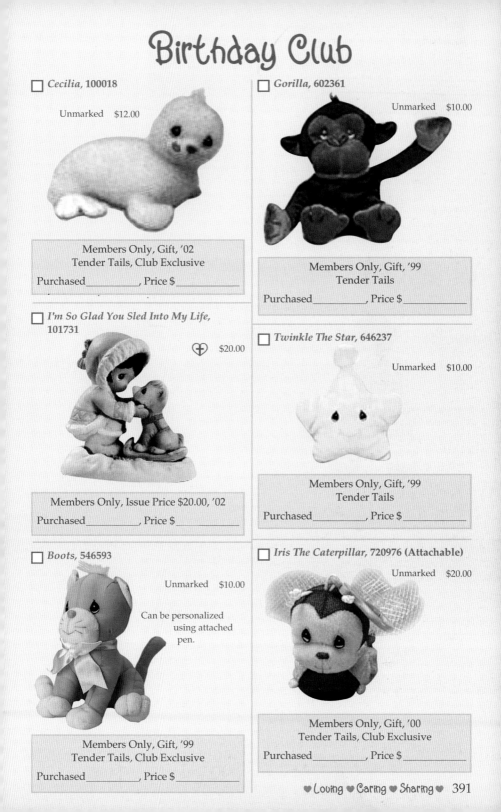

☐ *Cecilia*, **100018**

Unmarked $12.00

Members Only, Gift, '02
Tender Tails, Club Exclusive
Purchased_____, Price $_____

☐ *I'm So Glad You Sled Into My Life*,
101731

✝ $20.00

Members Only, Issue Price $20.00, '02
Purchased_____, Price $_____

☐ *Boots*, **546593**

Unmarked $10.00

Can be personalized
using attached
pen.

Members Only, Gift, '99
Tender Tails, Club Exclusive
Purchased_____, Price $_____

☐ *Gorilla*, **602361**

Unmarked $10.00

Members Only, Gift, '99
Tender Tails
Purchased_____, Price $_____

☐ *Twinkle The Star*, **646237**

Unmarked $10.00

Members Only, Gift, '99
Tender Tails
Purchased_____, Price $_____

☐ *Iris The Caterpillar*, **720976 (Attachable)**

Unmarked $20.00

Members Only, Gift, '00
Tender Tails, Club Exclusive
Purchased_____, Price $_____

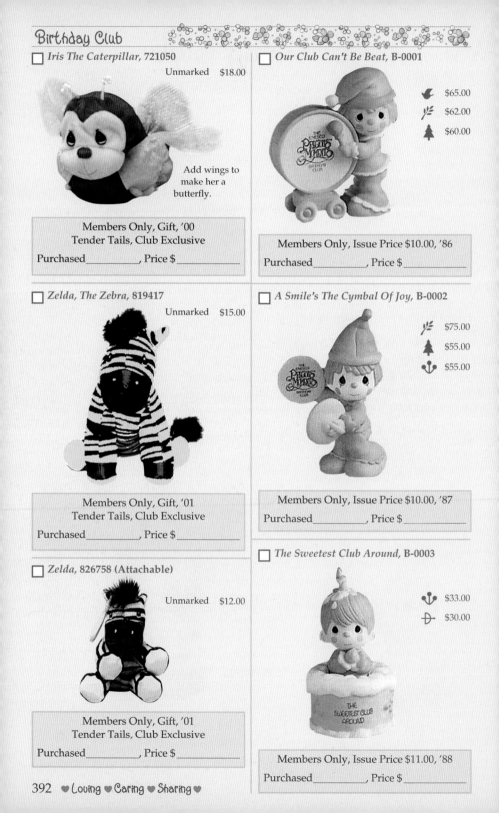

☐ *Iris The Caterpillar, 721050*

Unmarked $18.00

Add wings to make her a butterfly.

Members Only, Gift, '00
Tender Tails, Club Exclusive

Purchased_____, Price $_____

☐ *Zelda, The Zebra, 819417*

Unmarked $15.00

Members Only, Gift, '01
Tender Tails, Club Exclusive

Purchased_____, Price $_____

☐ *Zelda, 826758 (Attachable)*

Unmarked $12.00

Members Only, Gift, '01
Tender Tails, Club Exclusive

Purchased_____, Price $_____

☐ *Our Club Can't Be Beat, B-0001*

$65.00
$62.00
$60.00

Members Only, Issue Price $10.00, '86

Purchased_____, Price $_____

☐ *A Smile's The Cymbal Of Joy, B-0002*

$75.00
$55.00
$55.00

Members Only, Issue Price $10.00, '87

Purchased_____, Price $_____

☐ *The Sweetest Club Around, B-0003*

$33.00
$30.00

Members Only, Issue Price $11.00, '88

Purchased_____, Price $_____

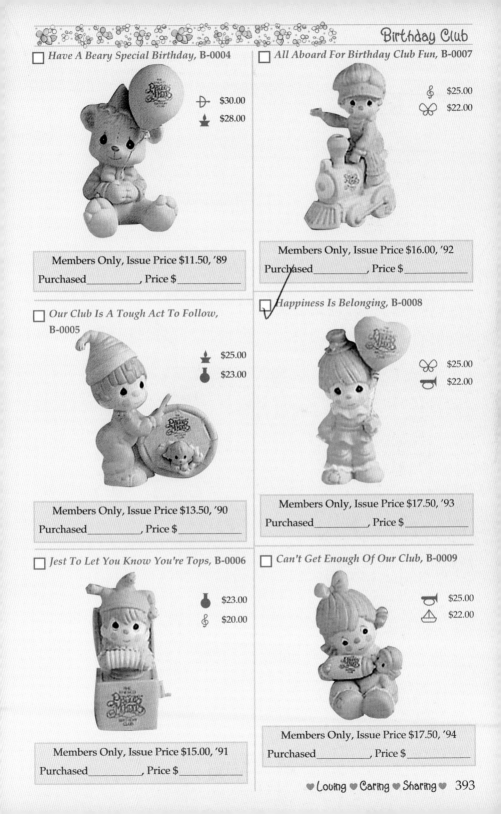

☐ *Have A Beary Special Birthday, B-0004*

⊅ $30.00

♠ $28.00

Members Only, Issue Price $11.50, '89

Purchased_____, Price $ _____

☐ *Our Club Is A Tough Act To Follow,*
B-0005

♠ $25.00

♦ $23.00

Members Only, Issue Price $13.50, '90

Purchased_____, Price $ _____

☐ *Jest To Let You Know You're Tops, B-0006*

♦ $23.00

♪ $20.00

Members Only, Issue Price $15.00, '91

Purchased_____, Price $ _____

☐ *All Aboard For Birthday Club Fun, B-0007*

♪ $25.00

∞ $22.00

Members Only, Issue Price $16.00, '92

Purchased_____, Price $ _____

☐ *Happiness Is Belonging, B-0008*

∞ $25.00

⌐ $22.00

Members Only, Issue Price $17.50, '93

Purchased_____, Price $ _____

☐ *Can't Get Enough Of Our Club, B-0009*

⊿ $25.00

△ $22.00

Members Only, Issue Price $17.50, '94

Purchased_____, Price $ _____

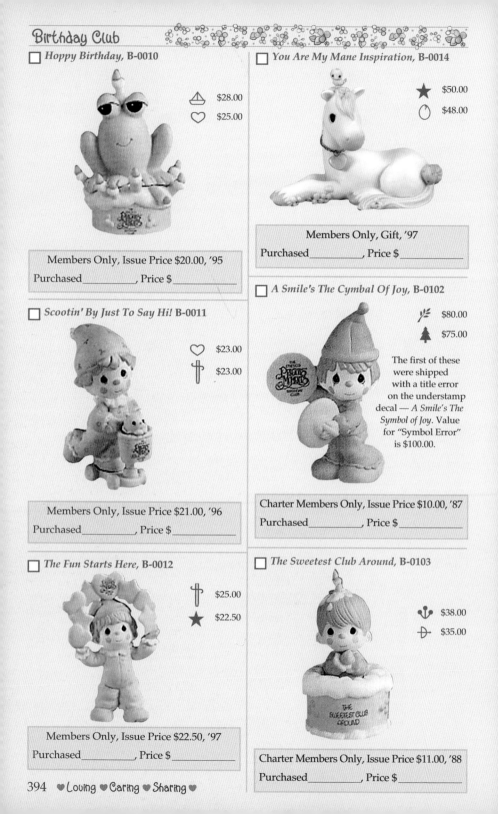

☐ *Hoppy Birthday*, B-0010

△ $28.00

♡ $25.00

Members Only, Issue Price $20.00, '95

Purchased_____, Price $_____

☐ *Scootin' By Just To Say Hi!* B-0011

♡ $23.00

✝ $23.00

Members Only, Issue Price $21.00, '96

Purchased_____, Price $_____

☐ *The Fun Starts Here*, B-0012

✝ $25.00

★ $22.50

Members Only, Issue Price $22.50, '97

Purchased_____, Price $_____

☐ *You Are My Mane Inspiration*, B-0014

★ $50.00

◐ $48.00

Members Only, Gift, '97

Purchased_____, Price $_____

☐ *A Smile's The Cymbal Of Joy*, B-0102

≈ $80.00

🌲 $75.00

The first of these
were shipped
with a title error
on the understamp
decal — *A Smile's The
Symbol of Joy*. Value
for "Symbol Error"
is $100.00.

Charter Members Only, Issue Price $10.00, '87

Purchased_____, Price $_____

☐ *The Sweetest Club Around*, B-0103

♧ $38.00

⊣ $35.00

Charter Members Only, Issue Price $11.00, '88

Purchased_____, Price $_____

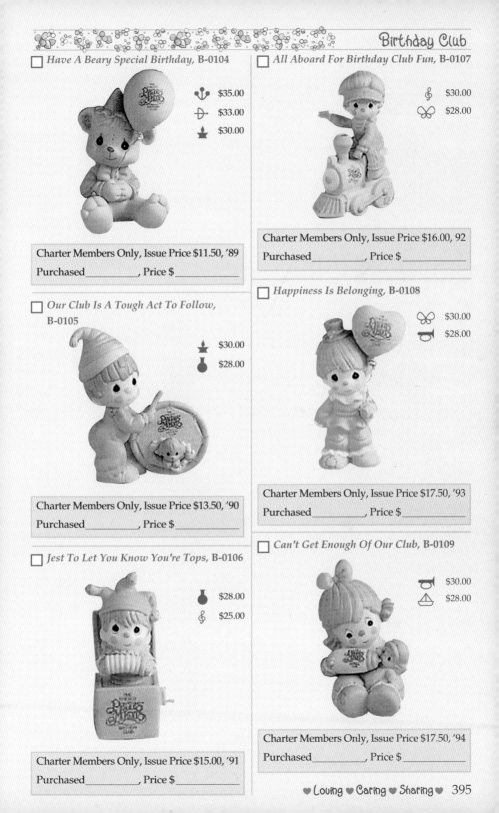

☐ *Have A Beary Special Birthday*, B-0104

⚓ $35.00

⊹ $33.00

⚖ $30.00

Charter Members Only, Issue Price $11.50, '89

Purchased_____, Price $_____

☐ *Our Club Is A Tough Act To Follow*, B-0105

⚖ $30.00

⚱ $28.00

Charter Members Only, Issue Price $13.50, '90

Purchased_____, Price $_____

☐ *Jest To Let You Know You're Tops*, B-0106

⚱ $28.00

𝄞 $25.00

Charter Members Only, Issue Price $15.00, '91

Purchased_____, Price $_____

☐ *All Aboard For Birthday Club Fun*, B-0107

𝄞 $30.00

🦋 $28.00

Charter Members Only, Issue Price $16.00, 92

Purchased_____, Price $_____

☐ *Happiness Is Belonging*, B-0108

🦋 $30.00

♥ $28.00

Charter Members Only, Issue Price $17.50, '93

Purchased_____, Price $_____

☐ *Can't Get Enough Of Our Club*, B-0109

♥ $30.00

△ $28.00

Charter Members Only, Issue Price $17.50, '94

Purchased_____, Price $_____

☐ *Hoppy Birthday*, B-0110

△ $28.00
♡ $25.00

Charter Members Only, Issue Price $20.00, '95
Purchased_____, Price $_____

☐ *Scootin' By Just To Say Hi!* B-0111

♡ $25.00
† $22.00

Charter Members Only, Issue Price $21.00, '96
Purchased_____, Price $_____

☐ *The Fun Starts Here*, B-0112

† $25.00

Charter Members Only, Issue Price $22.50, '97
Purchased_____, Price $_____

☐ *You Are My Mane Inspiration*, B-0114

★ $50.00
◐ $48.00

Charter Members Only, Gift, '99
Purchased_____, Price $_____

☐ *Fishing For Friends*, BC-861

⚘ $125.00
🌲 $105.00

Members Only, Issue Price $10.00, '86
Purchased_____, Price $_____

☐ *Hi Sugar*, BC-871

🌲 $100.00
⚓ $95.00
Ð $90.00

Members Only, Issue Price $11.00, '87
Purchased_____, Price $_____

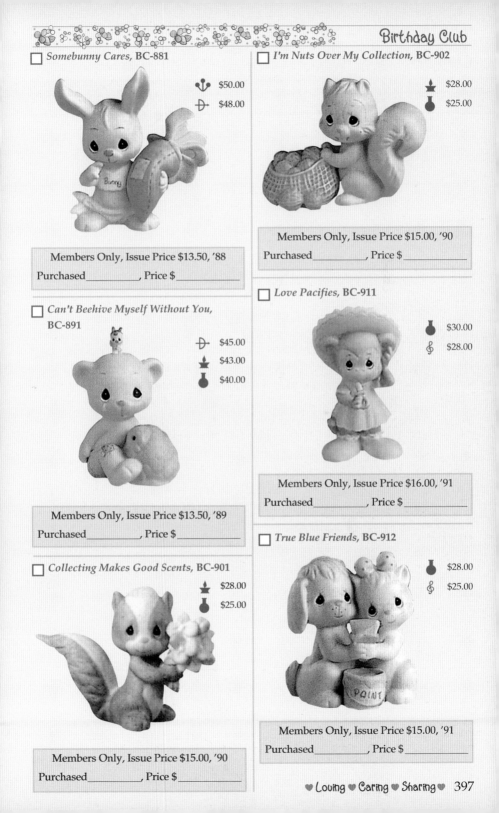

□ *Somebunny Cares*, BC-881

⚓ $50.00
〒 $48.00

Members Only, Issue Price $13.50, '88
Purchased_____, Price $_____

□ *Can't Beehive Myself Without You,*
  BC-891

〒 $45.00
⚒ $43.00
⬥ $40.00

Members Only, Issue Price $13.50, '89
Purchased_____, Price $_____

□ *Collecting Makes Good Scents*, BC-901

⚒ $28.00
⬥ $25.00

Members Only, Issue Price $15.00, '90
Purchased_____, Price $_____

□ *I'm Nuts Over My Collection*, BC-902

⚒ $28.00
⬥ $25.00

Members Only, Issue Price $15.00, '90
Purchased_____, Price $_____

□ *Love Pacifies*, BC-911

⬥ $30.00
𝄞 $28.00

Members Only, Issue Price $16.00, '91
Purchased_____, Price $_____

□ *True Blue Friends*, BC-912

⬥ $28.00
𝄞 $25.00

Members Only, Issue Price $15.00, '91
Purchased_____, Price $_____

☐ *Every Man's House Is His Castle*, BC-921

🎵 $30.00
🦋 $27.00
🎺 $25.00

Members Only, Issue Price $16.50, '92
Purchased_____, Price $_____

☐ *I Got You Under My Skin*, BC-922

🎵 $25.00
🦋 $23.00

Members Only, Issue Price $16.00, '92
Purchased_____, Price $_____

☐ *Put A Little Punch In Your Birthday*,
BC-931

🦋 $23.00
🎺 $21.00

Members Only, Issue Price $15.00, '93
Purchased_____, Price $_____

☐ *Owl Always Be Your Friend*, BC-932

🦋 $23.00
🎺 $21.00

Members Only, Issue Price $16.00, '93
Purchased_____, Price $_____

☐ *God Bless Our Home*, BC-941

🎺 $23.00
⛵ $20.00

Members Only, Issue Price $16.00, '94
Purchased_____, Price $_____

☐ *Yer A Pel-I-Can Count On*, BC-942

🎺 $23.00
⛵ $20.00

Members Only, Issue Price $16.00, '94
Purchased_____, Price $_____

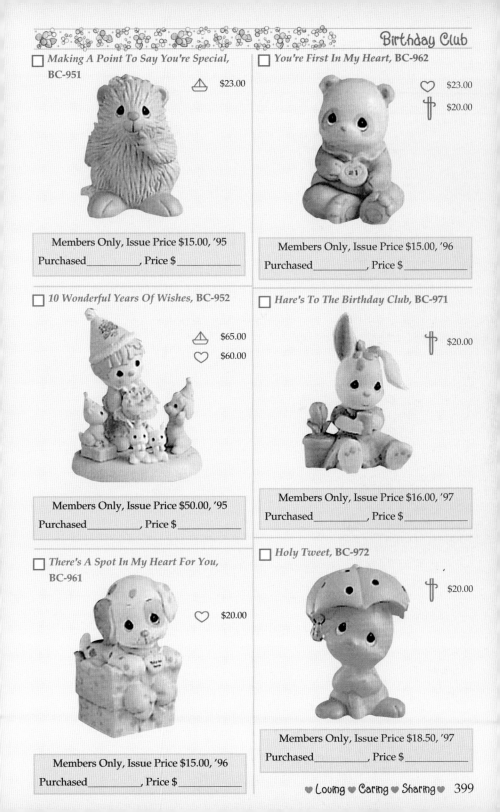

☐ *Making A Point To Say You're Special,*
BC-951

$23.00

Members Only, Issue Price $15.00, '95
Purchased_____, Price $_____

☐ *10 Wonderful Years Of Wishes, BC-952*

$65.00
$60.00

Members Only, Issue Price $50.00, '95
Purchased_____, Price $_____

☐ *There's A Spot In My Heart For You,*
BC-961

$20.00

Members Only, Issue Price $15.00, '96
Purchased_____, Price $_____

☐ *You're First In My Heart, BC-962*

$23.00
$20.00

Members Only, Issue Price $15.00, '96
Purchased_____, Price $_____

☐ *Hare's To The Birthday Club, BC-971*

$20.00

Members Only, Issue Price $16.00, '97
Purchased_____, Price $_____

☐ *Holy Tweet, BC-972*

$20.00

Members Only, Issue Price $18.50, '97
Purchased_____, Price $_____

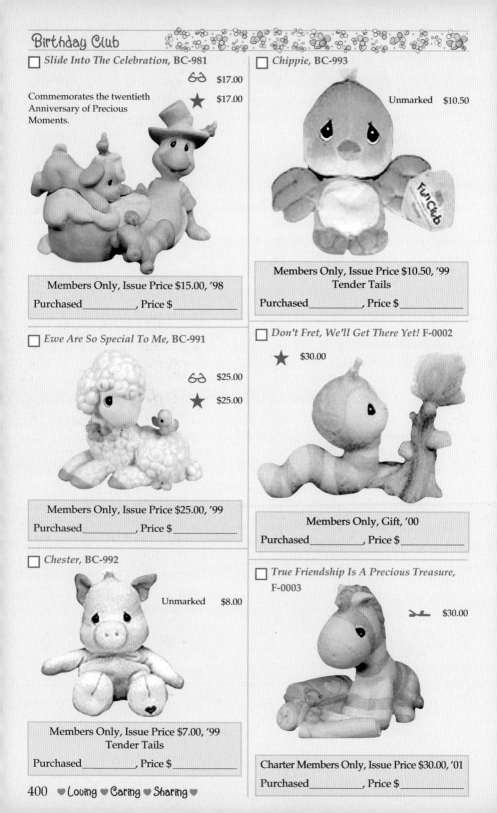

Birthday Club

☐ *Slide Into The Celebration*, BC-981

                👓 $17.00

Commemorates the twentieth   ⭐ $17.00
Anniversary of Precious
Moments.

Members Only, Issue Price $15.00, '98

Purchased_____, Price $_____

☐ *Ewe Are So Special To Me*, BC-991

                👓 $25.00

                ⭐ $25.00

Members Only, Issue Price $25.00, '99

Purchased_____, Price $_____

☐ *Chester*, BC-992

Unmarked $8.00

Members Only, Issue Price $7.00, '99
Tender Tails

Purchased_____, Price $_____

☐ *Chippie*, BC-993

Unmarked $10.50

Members Only, Issue Price $10.50, '99
Tender Tails

Purchased_____, Price $_____

☐ *Don't Fret, We'll Get There Yet!* F-0002

    ⭐ $30.00

Members Only, Gift, '00

Purchased_____, Price $_____

☐ *True Friendship Is A Precious Treasure*,
   F-0003

        ✈ $30.00

Charter Members Only, Issue Price $30.00, '01

Purchased_____, Price $_____

400 💜 Loving 💜 Caring 💜 Sharing 💜

☐ *Seal-ed With A Kiss, F-0004*

☐ $25.00

Members Only, Gift, '02
Purchased_____, Price $ _____

☐ *I'm All Ears For You, F-0005*

♔ $25.00

Members Only, Gift, '03
Purchased_____, Price $ _____

☐ *Don't Fret, We'll Get There Yet, F-0102*

★ $30.00
◔ $30.00

Charter Members Only, Gift, '00
Purchased_____, Price $ _____

☐ *True Friendship Is A Precious Treasure, F-0103*

✈ $30.00

Charter Members Only , Issue Price $30.00, '01
Purchased_____, Price $ _____

☐ **Seal-ed With A Kiss, F-0104**

☐ $25.00

Charter Members Only, Gift, '02
Purchased_____, Price $ _____

☐ **I'm All Ears For You, F-0105**

♔ $25.00

Charter Members Only, Gift, '03
Purchased_____, Price $ _____

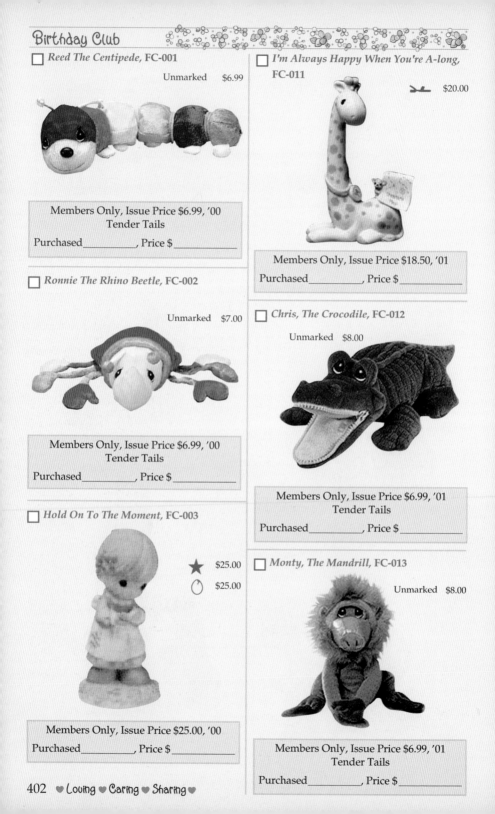

☐ *Reed The Centipede, FC-001*

Unmarked $6.99

Members Only, Issue Price $6.99, '00
Tender Tails

Purchased_____, Price $_____

☐ *Ronnie The Rhino Beetle, FC-002*

Unmarked $7.00

Members Only, Issue Price $6.99, '00
Tender Tails

Purchased_____, Price $_____

☐ *Hold On To The Moment, FC-003*

★ $25.00
◯ $25.00

Members Only, Issue Price $25.00, '00

Purchased_____, Price $_____

☐ *I'm Always Happy When You're A-long, FC-011*

✂ $20.00

Members Only, Issue Price $18.50, '01

Purchased_____, Price $_____

☐ *Chris, The Crocodile, FC-012*

Unmarked $8.00

Members Only, Issue Price $6.99, '01
Tender Tails

Purchased_____, Price $_____

☐ *Monty, The Mandrill, FC-013*

Unmarked $8.00

Members Only, Issue Price $6.99, '01
Tender Tails

Purchased_____, Price $_____

☐ *Wade, The Waterbuffalo*, FC-014

Unmarked $8.00

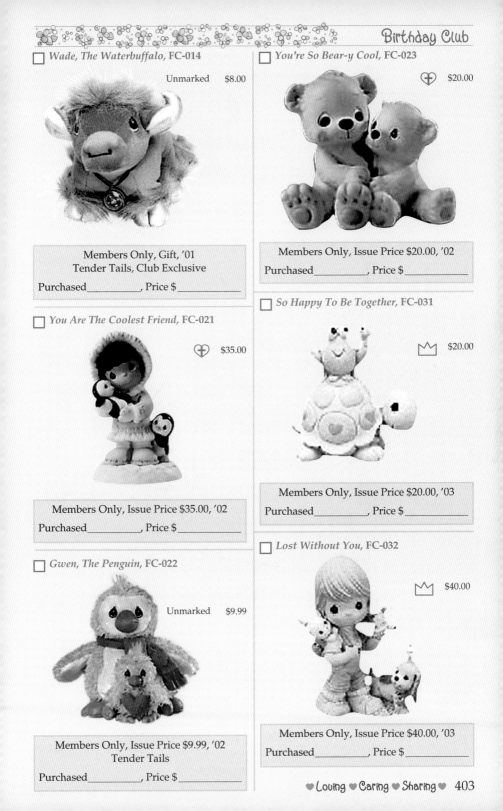

Members Only, Gift, '01
Tender Tails, Club Exclusive

Purchased_____, Price $ _____

☐ *You Are The Coolest Friend*, FC-021

☩ $35.00

Members Only, Issue Price $35.00, '02

Purchased_____, Price $ _____

☐ *Gwen, The Penguin*, FC-022

Unmarked $9.99

Members Only, Issue Price $9.99, '02
Tender Tails

Purchased_____, Price $ _____

☐ *You're So Bear-y Cool*, FC-023

☩ $20.00

Members Only, Issue Price $20.00, '02

Purchased_____, Price $ _____

☐ *So Happy To Be Together*, FC-031

♛ $20.00

Members Only, Issue Price $20.00, '03

Purchased_____, Price $ _____

☐ *Lost Without You*, FC-032

♛ $40.00

Members Only, Issue Price $40.00, '03

Purchased_____, Price $ _____

☐ *Sam, FC-033*

Unmarked $9.99

☐ *Shelly, The Turtle, FC-034*

Unmarked $9.99

Shell opens.
Comes with frog
figurine.

Members Only, Issue Price $9.99, '03
Tender Tails

Purchased_____, Price $_____

Members Only, Issue Price $9.99, '03
Tender Tails

Purchased_____, Price $_____

Precious Moments Websites

Precious Moments Chapel And Store   www.preciousmoments.com
Precious Moments Community   www.preciousmomentscommunity.com
Enesco Corporation   www.enesco.com
Gocollect Collector's site   www.gocollect.com
Precious Moments Company Dolls   www.pmcdolls.com
Limited Of Michigan   www.limitedweb.com/index.vml
eBay online auction site   www.ebay.com
Precious Memory   www.preciousmemory.com
Collector Books   www.collectorbooks.com

Glossary

Annual (Non-Dated): Pieces sold once a year or introduced only once a year.

Care-A-Van Exclusive: Piece that is only sold when the Precious Moments Van travels to different cities.

Carlton Card Exclusive: Special pieces made just for the Carlton Card Company.

CCR: Century Circle Retailer Exclusive.

Chapel Exclusive: Special pieces made just for the Precious Moments Chapel in Carthage, Missouri.

Dated Annual: A piece with a date on that bottom that was released for only one year.

Discontinued: Pieces not being made presently.

DSR: Distinguished Service Retailer, a recognition given by Enesco for a retailer's high level of goods and services.

Easter Seals Commemorative: Limited edition pieces made to benefit the National Easter Seals Society.

GCC: Gift Creation Concept; retailer receives special Limited Edition pieces made exclusively for their stores.

Limited Ed.: Pieces of which only certain amounts were produced.

Limited To One Day Only: A collector is given a specific date to order a piece. Only that one-day order is manufactured.

Open: A piece that is still in production that can be purchased on the open market.

Original "21": Designates the first 21 pieces manufactured in 1979.

Regional Event: Special pieces made just for events held in certain parts of the country.

Re-Introduced: A Suspended piece that has been changed and brought back to the open market. These pieces can vary from a color change to a sculptor change.

Retired: A mold of a bisque piece that has been destroyed and permanently removed from production.

Suspended: A bisque piece that has been removed from production for an undetermined period of time.

Unmarked: A piece that has no Annual Production mark on the bottom of the base.

Variation: Certain pieces that have different coloring or were fired differently. These variations can be caused by human error or be deliberate production changes made by the company.

Numerical Index

Numerical Index

General Index

Precious Notes

Title of piece _Here's My Heart_   Item # _0000974_

☑ Figurine ☐ Ornament ☐ Plate ☐ Bell ☐ Thimble ☐ Other

☑ Open ☐ Retired ☐ Suspended ☐ Limited Ed. ☐ Exclusive

Issue Price $_____ Issue Date _____ Series _____

Date Purchased _2/7/05_ Value _40 00_ Purchase Price $ _40 00_

Title of piece _MAP A Route Toward loving Caring + Sharing_ Item # _C0025_

☐ Figurine ☐ Ornament ☐ Plate ☐ Bell ☐ Thimble ☐ Other

☐ Open ☐ Retired ☐ Suspended ☐ Limited Ed. ☑ Exclusive

Issue Price $_____ Issue Date _2005_ Series _____

Date Purchased _____ Value _____ Purchase Price $ _____

Title of piece _You Bet Your Boots I Love You_ Item # _____

☑ Figurine ☐ Ornament ☐ Plate ☐ Bell ☐ Thimble ☐ Other

☐ Open ☐ Retired ☐ Suspended ☐ Limited Ed. ☐ Exclusive

Issue Price $ _30 00_ Issue Date _____ Series _2 pieces_

Date Purchased _____ Value _____ Purchase Price $ _15 00_

Title of piece _Grandma + Me   2_   Item # _115903_

☑ Figurine ☐ Ornament ☐ Plate ☐ Bell ☐ Thimble ☐ Other

☐ Open ☐ Retired ☐ Suspended ☐ Limited Ed. ☐ Exclusive

Issue Price $ _25 00_ Issue Date _____ Series _80 both_

Date Purchased _2005 + 2006_ Value _____ Purchase Price $ _Gifts_

Title of piece _I Love You This Much_ Item # 4001668

☑ Figurine ☐ Ornament ☐ Plate ☐ Bell ☐ Thimble ☐ Other

☐ Open ☐ Retired ☐ Suspended ☐ Limited Ed. ☐ Exclusive

Issue Price $ 30⁰⁰ Issue Date _____ Series _____

Date Purchased 2006 Value 30⁰⁰ Purchase Price $ Gift

Title of piece _____ Item # _____

☐ Figurine ☐ Ornament ☐ Plate ☐ Bell ☐ Thimble ☐ Other

☐ Open ☐ Retired ☐ Suspended ☐ Limited Ed. ☐ Exclusive

Issue Price $ _____ Issue Date _____ Series _____

Date Purchased _____ Value _____ Purchase Price $ _____

Title of piece _____ Item # _____

☐ Figurine ☐ Ornament ☐ Plate ☐ Bell ☐ Thimble ☐ Other

☐ Open ☐ Retired ☐ Suspended ☐ Limited Ed. ☐ Exclusive

Issue Price $ _____ Issue Date _____ Series _____

Date Purchased _____ Value _____ Purchase Price $ _____

Title of piece _____ Item # _____

☐ Figurine ☐ Ornament ☐ Plate ☐ Bell ☐ Thimble ☐ Other

☐ Open ☐ Retired ☐ Suspended ☐ Limited Ed. ☐ Exclusive

Issue Price $ _____ Issue Date _____ Series _____

Date Purchased _____ Value _____ Purchase Price $ _____

Title of piece _____ Item #_____

☐ Figurine ☐ Ornament ☐ Plate ☐ Bell ☐ Thimble ☐ Other

☐ Open ☐ Retired ☐ Suspended ☐ Limited Ed. ☐ Exclusive

Issue Price $_____ Issue Date _____ Series _____

Date Purchased_____ Value _____ Purchase Price $ _____

Title of piece _____ Item #_____

☐ Figurine ☐ Ornament ☐ Plate ☐ Bell ☐ Thimble ☐ Other

☐ Open ☐ Retired ☐ Suspended ☐ Limited Ed. ☐ Exclusive

Issue Price $_____ Issue Date _____ Series _____

Date Purchased_____ Value _____ Purchase Price $ _____

Title of piece _____ Item #_____

☐ Figurine ☐ Ornament ☐ Plate ☐ Bell ☐ Thimble ☐ Other

☐ Open ☐ Retired ☐ Suspended ☐ Limited Ed. ☐ Exclusive

Issue Price $_____ Issue Date _____ Series _____

Date Purchased_____ Value _____ Purchase Price $ _____

Title of piece _____ Item #_____

☐ Figurine ☐ Ornament ☐ Plate ☐ Bell ☐ Thimble ☐ Other

☐ Open ☐ Retired ☐ Suspended ☐ Limited Ed. ☐ Exclusive

Issue Price $_____ Issue Date _____ Series _____

Date Purchased_____ Value _____ Purchase Price $ _____